Approaching China's Pharmaceutical Market

Ming Q. Lu
Editor

Approaching China's Pharmaceutical Market

A Fundamental Guide to Clinical Drug Development

Springer

Editor
Ming Q. Lu
Helsinn Therapeutics Inc.
Bridgewater
New Jersey
USA

This authoritative volume examines the major laws, regulations and guidelines related to pharmaceutical product development in China. With a focus on patent, clinical and registration strategies, the book helps Western companies introduce their clinical drugs to the Chinese market, determine a strategic path and bridge the gap for regulatory and legal differences between China and the Western world. For a better understanding of the drug registration process, it explores the differences between the China Food and Drug Administration (CFDA)—including its regulations and registration procedures—and those of the Western world. The volume discusses disparities between China's application requirements compared to Western standards to make it easier for companies to prepare their application packages. It also provides detailed commentary on CFDA guidelines in reference to clinical trial (IND) and market application (NDA) requirements. Overall, this book offers guidance for Western companies aspiring to expand into China's pharmaceutical market in hopes that they may gain a fundamental understanding of its rules and complexities in order to ensure a smooth transition and prevent future issues.

ISBN 978-3-319-15575-3 ISBN 978-3-319-15576-0 (eBook)
DOI 10.1007/978-3-319-15576-0

Library of Congress Control Number: 2015943073

Springer Cham Heidelberg New York Dordrecht London

Printed on acid-free paper

Springer International Publishing AG Switzerland is part of Science+Business Media
(www.springer.com)

Preface

Since its opening in the early 1980's, China's pharmaceutical market has been burgeoning at a breathtaking rate. According to the China Pharmaceutical Market Report (2012), it has been and continues to undergo rapid expansion and intense market competition. An aging population contributes to the increase in the potential demand for drugs. This, coupled with an elevated level of purchasing power brought by economic development, is the driving force of pharmaceutical market expansion. Between 2005 and 2010, the integrated Chinese pharmaceutical market annual growth rate went over 20 %. In 2012, the market scale reached 926.1 billion RMB (~$ 150 billion). Looking ahead to 2020, the market will continue its rapid expansion with an average rate of 12 %. In 2013 Chinese pharmaceutical market size exceeded 1 trillion RMB (~$ 161 billion). In 2019, Chinese pharmaceutical market size is predicted to exceed 2 trillion RMB (~$ 322 billion). In 2020, the scale will reach 2.3 trillion RMB (~$ 483 billion). Unsurprisingly over the years, then, more and more foreign companies have entered China's market. Met with this and the increased demand for drugs, domestic Chinese pharmaceutical companies have synchronized their expansion. The result has been a trend towards foreign-funded enterprises in the pharmaceutical market. According to the marketing sharing and sales data of 2011, the top five companies in China are all foreign pharmaceutical enterprises.

However, while Chinese pharmaceutical regulations are indeed growing more mature with the market, there are still myriad differences between China's drug management law, regulations, and procedure and those of the Western world. To bridge these differences, many private consulting companies have been established, but with varied levels of success, and all bearing varied and faulty interpretations of the same regulations. To solve these issues, these consulting companies usually overemphasize their public relations, personal connections, and their strategies that limit equal opportunity in the market and in fact contradict Western common practice and basic law, such as the Sunshine Act. Ultimately, language barriers, misinterpretation of guidelines, and a lack of systematic educational materials have hindered many endeavors to effectively engage in and introduce new and needed drugs to the Chinese pharmaceutical market.

To elucidate these misunderstandings, the authors, together with the industry and government experts who have worked many years in the field of medicinal product development, have put together this guide to approaching and engaging with the Chinese market. As explained in the US FDA or other regulatory agencies' websites, all text and graphics regarding regulations are in the public domain—not copyrighted—and can be used freely. In contrast, there are different translated Chinese regulations and guidelines from various sources due to unknown reasons. Unfortunately, none of them are free of mistakes. The authors made corrections and modifications, and added some interpretations in reference to those publications in public domains, but strongly suggest that the readers check the original Chinese FDA's documents through the provided link if an uncertainty arises. The authors also cannot guarantee that the content and the opinions are totally error-free and accepted by all parties. Thus, in case of disagreement, the official adopted text in Chinese will always be the most authoritative source. This book aims to clarify the distinctions between Western and Chinese markets, taking the reader step-by-step through new drug development for Western companies hoping to expand into the Chinese market, running the gamut from the initial preparation phase to marketing approval abroad. The authors hope this book can help bridge the gap between languages and cultures, tackle unmet medical needs, and achieve a win-win outcome for not only pharmaceutical companies, but also patients and a larger society.

Ming Q. Lu, MD. Ph. D

Acknowledgments

The authors wish to thank our colleagues and friends, such as Drs. Ying Shao and Medea Meng for their continual encouragement in the making of this book and for their aspirations to globalize medicine and improve quality of life across the world. We are also indebted to Lillian Lu for her extensive editorial work on the book from its advent to its first completed drafts. The editor would like to thank all of the authors who have contributed their experiences and knowledge to this work—and finally, he would like to thank his wife, Yen, for her unconditional support.

Contents

1 **Law, Regulation and Guidance** 1
Xianchao Qiao, Yuyuan Tan, Sandy Bai and Yanbin Xie

2 **Pharmaceutical Intellectual Property Rights in China** 221
Ming Q. Lu, Sandy Bai, Yuyuan Tan and Cheng Xu

3 **The China Food and Drug Administration (CFDA)** 239
Yuyuan Tan, Yanbin Xie, Xianchao Qiao and Sandy Bai

4 **Registration** 285
Ming Q. Lu, Yanbin Xie and Sandy Bai

5 **Guidance for Application Materials/Booklets (Chemical)** 329
Ming Q. Lu, Yuan Qiao, Edbert D. Lu and Yuyuan Tan

6 **New Investivational Drug Application** 435
Yanbin Xie, Sandy Bai and Ming Q. Lu

7 **Clinical Development of Investigational New Drug** 467
Qinping Liao, Tao Lv, Yuan Qiao and Jianpeng Wang

8 **Strategic Drug Development in China and Surrounding Countries** ... 507
Ming Q. Lu, Yanbin Xie, Qinping Liao and Yuyuan Tan

9 **Drug Safety Monitoring and Reporting Systems in China** 533
Ming Q. Lu, Qinping Liao, Jianpeng Wang and Tao Lv

10 **In Vitro Diagnostic Product Development** 579
Cheng Xu, Edbert D. Lu and Jianpeng Wang

Index 645

Contributors

Sandy Bai Group Investment Company Beijing of China, Beijing, P. R. China

Qinping Liao Division of Gynecology/Obstetrics and Pediatrics, Beijing Tsinghua Chang Gung Hospital, Beijing, P. R. China

Edbert D. Lu Molecular and Cellular Biology, University of California, Berkeley, CA, USA

Ming Q. Lu Helsinn Therapeutics (U.S.), Inc., Bridgewater, NJ, USA

Tao Lv Division of Gynecology/Obstetrics and Pediatrics, Beijing Tsinghua Chang Gung Hospital, Beijing, P. R. China

Xianchao Qiao Konney Science and Technology Co., Ltd., Qingdao, P. R. China

Yuan Qiao Neurophysiology and Orthopedics, School of Medicine, Shandong University, Shandong, P. R. China

Yuyuan Tan Beijing PRI BioScience Development Co, Ltd., Beijing, P. R. China

Jianpeng Wang Echocardiography, Cardiovascular Institute and Fuwai Hospital, Chinese Academy of Medical Sciences, Beijing, P. R. China

Yanbin Xie China ICON PLC., Beijing, P. R. China

Cheng Xu Shanghai Zhangjiang Center for Translational Medicine, Shanghai Biotecan Co., Ltd., Shanghai, P. R. China

About the Editor

Ming Q. Lu received his M.D in P.R. China and his Ph. D. from the University of Connecticut, and completed a fellowship at Johns Hopkins Medical Schools under academician Peter Agre, M.D, who in 2003 received the Nobel Prize. Dr. Lu has expansive experience in both academia and the pharmaceutical industry, particularly in research and development of new medications.

Since 1998, he has been heavily involved in the conduct and management of various aspects of clinical drug research and development, running the gamut from project initiation, to drug candidate discovery, and from pre-clinical pharmacology to all the clinical phases in both the US and overseas, especially in mainland China. He has also chaired the regulatory filing and defense processes with China Food and Drug Administration (CFDA), leading to the success of marketing approval in both China and Hong Kong. His work has led to many scientific publications.

He was appointed to the Editorial Board of the Journal of China Pharmaceutical University, and later received the honor of Adjunct Research Professor at Peking University First Hospital in China. He is currently Executive Director of Clinical, and Senior Medical Director in Helsinn Therapeutics (U.S.), Inc.

His experiences in management of drug research and development with China regulatory agencies and documentations in the FDA served as his impetus to write this book and share it with pharmaceutical peers.

List of Abbreviations and Definitions of Terms

ACTD	ASEAN Common Technical Dossier
ADR	Adverse drug reaction
API	Active pharmaceutical ingredients
ASEAN	The Association of Southeast Asian Nations
CBER	Center for Biologics Evaluation and Research
CDE	The Center for Drug Evaluation
CDER	Center for Drug Evaluation and Research
CFDA	China Food and Drug Administration
CFR	Code of Federal Regulations
CH-CTD	ICH-Common Technical Document
ChPC	China Pharmacopoeia Commission
CMC	Chemistry, manufacturing and control
CMDE	Center for Medical Device Evaluation
CPP	Certificate of Pharmaceutical Product
CRO	Contract research organization
CTA	Clinical trial authorization (application)
CTD	Common Technical Document
CTW	Clinical trial waiver
DMF	Drug Master file
EC	Ethics Committee
EMA	The European Medicines Agency
FDA	Food and Drug Administration
FSC	Free sale certificate
GCP	Good clinical practice
GLP	Good laboratory practice
GMP	Good manufacturing practice
GSP	Good supply practice
ICF	Informed consent form
ICH	International Conference on Harmonization
IDL	Imported drugs license
IEC	Independent Ethics Committee
IMCT	International multi-country (multi-center) Clinical Trial

IND	Investigational new drug (Application)
IPR	Intellectual property right
IRB	Institutional Review Board
IVD	In vitro diagnostic (diagnosis)
MOH	Ministry of Health
MRCT	Multi-Regional Clinical Trial
NDA	New drug applications
NICPBP	National Institute of Control Pharmaceutical and Biological products
NIDFC	National Institute of Drug and Food Control
PI	Principle investigator
PMC	Packaging materials and containers
RA	Regulatory affairs
RMCT	Regional multi-center clinical trial
SAE	Serious adverse event
SDA	The State Drug Administration
SFDA	The State Food and Drug Administration
SOP	Standard Operating Procedure
SUSAR	Suspected Unexpected Serious Adverse Reaction
TCM	Traditional Chinese medicine
WHO	World Health Organization

Chapter 1
Law, Regulation and Guidance

Xianchao Qiao, Yuyuan Tan, Sandy Bai and Yanbin Xie

1.1 A Brief Outline

Due to differences in Chinese legal tradition, medical care system, and other factors, its pharmaceutical legislation bears many differences to that of western countries.

However, since the late 1970s, China has adopted a new market policy and China's pharmaceutical market began to open to western countries. Currently, overseas pharmaceutical companies share a quarter of China's pharmaceutical market. With China's accession to the World Trade Organization (WTO), as well as economic integration and globalization of the pharmaceutical market, more and more overseas pharmaceutical companies have engaged with China's pharmaceutical market. China's pharmaceutical legislation has developed rather rapidly since its beginnings, then (Table 1.1). In this book, we will discuss the multifarious similarities between Chinese and the western regulatory affairs, as well as the various differences between. The legal norms in China can still be placed in the following three categories (Huang 2010; Zhang et al. 2007), all of which we will delineate and discuss in further detail: (1) Laws and regulations, which are legally binding; (2) Guidance (See Table 1.2), which is not legally binding, but serves as an interpretation of the

X. Qiao (✉)
Konney Science and Technology Co., Ltd., 14 Songshan Road, Shandong,
266021 Qingdao, P. R. China
e-mail: konneyqxc@163.com

Y. Tan
Beijing PRI BioScience Development Co, Ltd., C-505 Building 102, ZhuJiang Di Jing No. 28, Guangqu Road, Chao Yang District, 100022 Beijing, P. R. China

S. Bai
Group Investment Company Beijing of China, 138 Building B-538, Zhang Hua Road, Hai Dian District, 100036 Beijing, P. R. China

Y. Xie
China ICON PLC., Room 1502–1506, Tower B Global Trade Center, No.36, North Ring East Road, Dongcheng District, 100013 Beijing, P. R. China

M. Q. Lu (ed.), *Approaching China's Pharmaceutical Market*,
DOI 10.1007/978-3-319-15576-0_1

Table 1.1 Major law and regulation comparison

USA	The US has two established legal system: The Code of Federal Regulations (CFR) and The United States Code (USC). The law and regulations related to drug administrations are included in the CFR and USC (Part I). CFR is the codification of the general and permanent rules published in the Federal Register by the executive departments and agencies of the Federal Government. USC is the official compilation and http://en.wikipedia.org/wiki/Codification_(law) codification by subject matter of the general and permanent laws of the United States. They are different, as they deal with two separate areas (one administrative rules/regulations, and one laws/codes) and should be discussed separately
	The main laws:
	Federal Food, Drug and Cosmetic Act;
	1997 Modernization Act; Best Pharmaceuticals for Children Act;
	Bioterrorism Act of 2002;
	Controlled Substances Act;
	Dietary Supplement Health and Education Act of 1994;
	Fair Packaging and Labeling Act;
	Miscellaneous Provisions Relating to Orphan Drugs;
	Prescription Drug User Fee Act;
	Public Health Service Act;
	The Model State Pharmacy Act and Model Regulation of the National Association of Boards
Europe	European union's pharmaceutical laws and regulations are comparatively more complicated. They are mainly divided into:
	1) Legally binding rules:
	Regulations
	Directives
	Decisions
	2) None legally binding notices:
	Recommendations and opinions
	In Eudralex including:
	Directives: 2001/83/EC, 91/256/EEC, 89/105/EEC
	Regulations: (EEC) N02309/93, (EC)N0297/95, (EC) N0540/95, (EC) N0541/95, (EC) N0542/95
	Country Based Law and Regulation:
	UK—The Medicines Act
	Germany—Medicinal Product Act
China	China currently has the following major drug laws and regulations:
	Law
	Pharmaceutical Administration Law of the People's Republic of China
	Regulations for Implementation of the Drug Administration Law of the People's Republic of China
	Regulations
	Regulations related to Registration:
	Provisions for drug registration
	Administrative measures for the import of drugs

Table 1.1 (continued)

	Special review and approval procedure for drug registration of the State Food and Drug Administration
	Administrative regulations for technology transfer registration of drugs
	Regulations of special examination and approval in new drug registration
	Provisions for Drug Insert Sheets and Labels
	Application dossier writing requirements in CTD format for Chemical drugs
	Regulations related to quality management, GLP, GMP, GCP certification:
	Good manufacturing practice for pharmaceutical products
	Good laboratory practice for non-clinical laboratory studies或non-clinical good laboratory practice (GLP)
	Good clinical practice of pharmaceutical products
	Examination and approval for import of packaging materials and containers in direct contact with drugs
	Regulations related to inspection:
	Regulations requirements for on-site verification for drug registration
	The on-site inspection and sampling procedure and requirements for drug registration (Trial)
	Notice on the related convergence problems to the implementation of on-site verification of drug registration regulations
	Guidance
	Introduction (all guidance will be discussed with corresponding booklets)

law and regulation, and can be used as a reference; and (3) Technical standards and specifications, which bear no direct legal effect, yet play a considerable, indirect role.

Currently, it is generally accepted that America's pharmaceutical regulatory system is the world's most complete and most scientifically sound. America's leading drug administration FDA is well known for its strict and scientific management and has become the model that many other regulatory agencies reference and follow.

The U.S. pharmaceutical legislation can be dated back to 1820 in the United States Pharmacopoeia. Yet, this publication, though it speaks of the technical standard, does not capture the legal aspects of drug management. Thereafter, the U.S. pharmaceutical regulations have three major milestones, namely the 1906 Food and Drug Act; the 1938 Federal Food, Drug, and Cosmetic Act; and the 1962 Kefauver-Harris amendment. These legislations placed the US far ahead of other western countries: these regulations were the first expounded pharmacy management systems drug bill, the first proposed concept of adulterated drugs and counterfeit medicines, the first time drugs were made to undergo security review, the first requirement for effective drugs to be listed of the review, and also the first adverse drug reaction (ADR) reporting system (Table 1.1).

Table 1.2 Guidance of drug research technology

Guidance of drug research technology	
Chemical drugs	Technical guideline for making post approval changes to chemical drug
	Guidance for drug genotoxicity research
	Guidance for pharmaceutical research of synthetic polypeptide drugs
	Guidance for pharmaceutical research of oral sustained release preparation of chemical drugs
	Guidance for quality control research of the inhalation preparation
	Guidance for non-clinical drug dependence research
	Guidance for non-clinical pharmacodynamic research of anti-HIV drugs
	Guidance for quality control research of chiral drugs
	Guidance for reproductive toxicity research of drugs
	Guidance for non-clinical research of cytotoxic anticancer drugs
	Guidance for writing format and content of chemical drug review—Summary and evaluation of the main research results.
	Guidance for writing format and content of chemical drug review—Project target indication and rationale
	Guidance for writing format and content of chemical drug review—Review of pharmaceutical research
	Guidance for writing format and content of of chemical drug application mateirials—Review of pharmacology and toxicology research
	Guidance for writing format and content of chemical drug application materials—Review of clinical trial data review
	Guidance for chemical drug research with established national standards
	Guidance for long-term toxicity study of chemical drugs
	Guidance for quality control analytical method validation of chemical drug
	Guidance for the normalization process of quality standard establishment of chemical drug
	Guidance for basic technologies of chemical drug preparation
	Guidance for research of chemical drug impurities
	Guidance for structure and content of clinical study report of chemical drugs
	Guidance for clinical pharmacokinetics of chemical drugs
	Guidance for irritation, allergic and haemolytic research of chemical drugs
	Guidance for human bioavailability and bioequivalence research of chemical pharmaceutical preparations
	Guidance for API preparation and structure confirmation research of chemical drugs
	Guidance for general pharmacological research of chemical drugs
Biological products	Guidance for grading standards of clinical trial adverse reactions of preventive vaccine
	Guidance for preclinical research of preventive vaccine
	Guidance for management of the changes of the production process of biological products

Table 1.2 (continued)

Guidance of drug research technology	
	Guidance for preclinical and clinical research of combined vaccine
	Guidance for quality control and clinical research of conjugated vaccine
	Guidance for clinical studies of vaccines
	Guidance for the production and quality control of polypeptide vaccine
	Guidance for preclinical research of preventive vaccine
	Guidance for preventive live vaccine preparation using virus as a vector
	Guidance for the quality control of recombinant DNA products for human use
	Guidance for the production and quality control of bovine serum for cell culture use
	Guidance for the quality control of monoclonal antibodies for human use
	Guidance for human somatic cell therapy research and quality control of the preparation
	Guidance for human gene therapy research and quality control of the preparation
	Guidance for quality control of allergen product
	Guidance for AIDS vaccine clinical research
	Guidance for the method and verification of blood product removal/inactivation of virus technology
	Guidance for the clinical research of in vitro diagnostic reagent
	Guidance for instruction writing of in vitro diagnostic reagent
	General principles for technical evaluation of the quality control of mammalian cells for the production of recombinant products
	General principles for technical review of preclinical safety evaluation of preventive biological products
	General principles for technical review of cell matrix for the production of vaccines
	General principles for review of the viral safety evaluation technologies of biological tissue extract and eukaryotic expression products
	General principles for review of the quality control and analytical method validation of biological products
Imported drugs	A comprehensive guidance of imported drug registration
	A guidance of registration application for imported chemical drugs
	A guidance of registration application for imported biological products

In contrast, China's first pharmaceutical regulation was the 1984 Drug Administration Law. This law has played a positive role in enhancing drug administration, quality insurance, protection of consumers' legal interest, and the legal concept of society as a whole. In 2001, the newly revised Drug Administration Law set up the regulation for the pharmaceutical industry to strengthen their legal responsibility regarding illegal drugs, as well as legally establish a drug classification system, safety monitoring system, and drug certification system (Table 1.1).

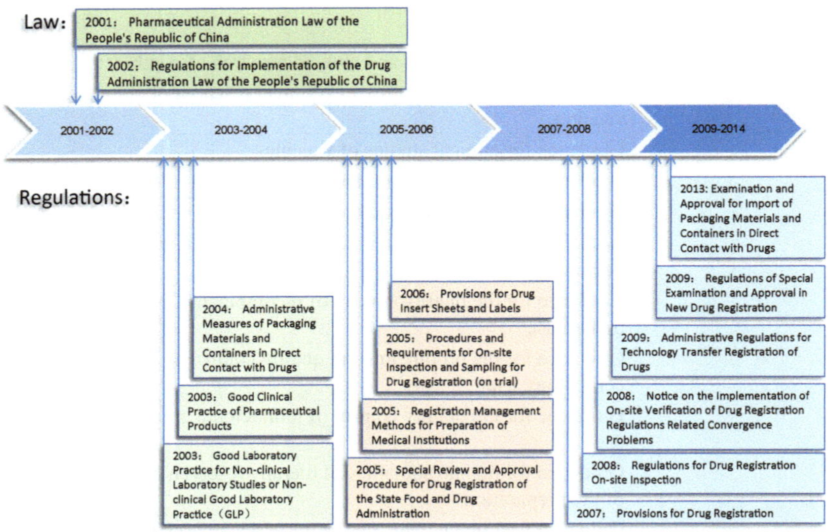

Fig. 1.1 The major CFDA regulation development in China

Among the current pharmaceutical legislations enacted in China, the following legal norms are the comparatively important ones for the foreign pharmaceutical companies that wish to enter the Chinese market: "Pharmaceutical Administration Law of the People's Republic of China"; "Drug Administration Law Implementation Regulations of People's Republic of China"; "Provisions for Drug Registration"; "Medical Toxicity Drug Administration"; "The Administrative Measures on Narcotic Drugs"; "Measures for the Administration of Psychotropic Drugs"; "Good Manufacturing Practice"; "Non-clinical pharmaceutical research and quality management practices"; "Good Clinical Practice"; "Drug quality management specifications"; "Drug Registration"; "Drug production supervision and management measures"; "Drug supervision and management measures in circulation"; "Adverse drug reaction monitoring management approach"; and "Drug packaging, labels and instructions regulations (provisional)," etc. In addition, "People's Republic of China Pharmacopoeia" and other technical standards are considered crucial (Fig. 1.1).

1.2 Pharmaceutical Administration Law

Introduction

The core contents of Drug Administration Law of People's Republic of China (National People's Congress 2001) issued by Standing Committee of the National People's Congress, effective date on Dec. 28, 2001, focus on drug supervision and management. In this law, the following main topics are discussed in detail:

1. The drug review and quality inspection,
2. Supervision and management of medical devices,
3. Pharmaceutical production and management,
4. Drug use and safety monitoring and management,
5. Standardized management of hospital pharmacy, pharmaceutical inspection and management,
6. Centralized drug bidding, procurement management and other topics.

A new, revised version of the Drug Administration Law was issued on December 28, 2013. On the basis of the current law, Article 13 was modified and the rest of the articles remain the same. The new version intends to solve the issue of concealed adverse reactions. In this chapter based on previous questions and answers of Chinese National People's Congress for the Drug Administration Law, and its interpretations (Bian et al 2002), the authors added a brief explanation under each article that may be related to multinational pharmaceutical companies. We hope these explanatory notes will make it easier to read and understand the corresponding articles.

Drug management refers to the exercise of state authority for implementation of their supervision and management in drug research and development, production, operation, and drug use. Drug Administration Law is the basic law. It established the basic legal norms for Drug Administration and is the legal basis for the implementation of drug administration. In this law, the country's top legislature established the conduct code of drug administration in the following aspects:

- How to implement the power of drug supervision and management by state agencies;
- How the drug management system is structured, which national institutions implement administration
- Confirmation of the purpose of Drug Administration
- Pharmaceutical production and operating rules, including the qualifications and specifications
- Standardized conduction for the relevant requirements of the Drug Administration;
- In the management of prohibited drugs, especially to prohibit the production and sale of counterfeit or substandard drugs act;
- How to manage drug packaging, drug prices, drug ads must comply with the rules;
- Follow the rules about how to supervise and inspect drug production, its management and use;
- The liabilities for violation of the Drug Administration law, and what kind of punishment should apply.

Drug Administration Law is the legal basis for drug administration and lays the legal foundation for the drug management. It requires the management teams from both government and pharmaceutical companies to correctly understand, interpret, and strictly adhere to the law. The law is serious and the content of the law is expressed by the articles. The intention is to prevent any misleading or contrary interpretations.

1.2.1 *Pharmaceutical Administration Law of the People's Republic of China*

Issued by Standing Committee of the National People's Congress, effective date on December 28, 2001; Additional brief explanations (Bian et al 2002) are added to the articles that are most relevant to overseas pharmaceutical companies

Contents

Chapter I General Provisions
Chapter II Administration of Pharmaceutical Producing Enterprises
Chapter III Administration of Pharmaceutical Trading Enterprises
Chapter IV Administration of Pharmaceuticals at Medical Organizations
Chapter V Pharmaceutical Administration
Chapter VI Administration of the Packaging of Pharmaceuticals
Chapter VII Administration of the Prices and Advertising of Pharmaceuticals
Chapter VIII Supervision over Pharmaceuticals
Chapter IX Legal Responsibility
Chapter X Supplementary Provisions

Chapter I General Provisions

Article 1 This law is formulated to enhance the supervision and control of pharmaceuticals, ensure their quality, guarantee safety in medication, and safeguard the health and legal rights and interests of the people.

Interpretation:

This article is about the legislative purpose of the law. The legislative purpose of this law is to strengthen the supervision and management of pharmaceuticals. In order to guarantee the people's safety, effectiveness of drugs, and a reasonable price, it is necessary for the state government to provide control, supervision, and management of the drugs. For drug supervision and management, a comprehensive use of legal, economic and necessary administrative means is mandatory. The Pharmaceutical Administration Law sets the basis and is the rule to follow. The fundamental purpose is to ensure drug quality, safety for human beings, and the health of the people. The law provides the base to directly safeguard the legitimate rights and interests of users of drugs.

The law is formulated to strengthen the supervision and management of drug quality. It clarifies the responsibilities of pharmaceutical producing enterprises, pharmaceutical trading enterprises and medical institutions in drug quality assurance and human drug safety. In addition, the law sets the rules to guarantee the companies' legal duties and responsibilities; strengthen the supervision and management of drug price; establish reasonable pharmaceuticals price formation mechanism, so that the drug prices remain at a reasonable level; standardize drug advertising procedures; prevent misleading users; severely punish the production and sales of counterfeit drug behavior,; and protect the legitimate rights and interests of drug users.

Article 2 The law shall be applicable to any units or individuals engaged in research, production, trade, use, supervision and management of pharmaceuticals within the territory of the People's Republic of China.

Interpretation:

This article clarifies the scope of the law application, which includes the legal effect of time and deadlines; the legal effect of the space, namely the geographical scope of application of the law; and the validity of the law, the people to whom the law applies in various ways (including natural or legal person or any other organization applies). Article 116 describes the geographical and subject scope.

The geographical scope (scope of validity or space), is the People's Republic of China, and all the regions within the People's Republic of China. The scope of validity of law's general principles of space is applicable to all areas to establish its authority under the jurisdiction. Of course, in accordance with the provisions of the basic law of the Hongkong and Macao Special Administrative Regions, only the basic laws in Annex 3 can be used in the two special administrative regions. Drug Administration Law does not include the two basic laws in Annex 3; therefore, the Drug Administration Law does not apply in Hongkong and Macao, as they are special administrative regions.

The law covers any entity or individuals engaged in drug development, production, management, including relevant scientific research institutions, as well as various enterprises and medical institutions. The drug "used" mainly refers to the medical use of drugs for clinical treatment, and does not include various ways in which patients could use them (i.e. recreational use). The direct-use behavior of patients does not belong to the scope of this law. If the drug regulatory agency of the government and other relevant departments in the implementation of the drug development, production, management and the relevant administrative law enforcement departments do not perform or neglect their duties, play favoritism, commit irregularities, or commit a breach of privilege, this law makes clear a regulation to investigate its legal liability.

Article 3 The State shall develop both modern and traditional medicines encourage their role in the prevention and treatment of diseases and in health care. The State shall protect the resources of wild medicinal resources and encourage the domestic cultivation of Chinese traditional medicinal crops.

Interpretation:

This article clarifies the basic principles of national development of modern medicine and traditional medicine. Basically, the state encourages the development of modern medicine and traditional medicine. They vigorously promote the level of medical science and technology. On the other hand, they also encourage the use of Chinese medicine under the guide of traditional medicine theory, to make full use of Chinese national medicine, and to ensure the role of traditional medicine in prevention, medical treatment, and health care.

Article 4 The State shall encourage the research and production of new medicine and protect the legal rights and interests of its citizens, natural persons and other organizations in the research and development of new medicine.

Interpretation:

This article clarifies the principle that the State shall encourage the research and production of new medicine.

New drugs in accordance with the provisions of the drug regulatory agency refer to those drug that have, to date, never been produced in China. The narrow sense of "new drug" refers to the new or innovative drug in China, not including the drugs that have been developed or manufactured overseas.

The consistent policy of the state is to encourage research and development of new drugs, and to meet the people's needs for preventing and curing diseases. The state employs various ways to support the activities from the aspects of financial assistance, price, tax, intellectual property protection, and to support new drug research, development and production. In order to fully mobilize the enthusiasm of new drug research and development, the patent law of China was revised in 1993. The State Drug Administration has also developed a new drug protection and technology transfer regulation, named administrative protection to protect the drugs without patent given.

Article 5 The pharmaceuticals supervisory and administrative departments under the State Council shall be responsible for the supervision and control of pharmaceuticals throughout the country. Other relevant departments under the State Council shall be responsible for the supervision and control of pharmaceuticals related to the scope of their functions.

The pharmaceutical supervisory and administrative departments of the provinces, autonomous regions and municipalities directly under the central government shall be responsible for the supervision and control of pharmaceuticals within their administrative regions. Other relevant departments of the provinces, autonomous regions and municipalities directly under the central government shall be responsible for the supervision and control of pharmaceuticals related to the scope of their functions.

The pharmaceutical supervisory and administrative departments under the State Council shall cooperate with the general administrative department of the economy under the State Council to carry out pharmaceutical development plans and industrial policies formulated by the State.

Interpretation:

This article clarifies the drug supervision and management system.

The first paragraph of this article "the drug regulatory agency of the State Council," refers to the State Drug administration (SDA, later changed to SFDA, now named CFDA). The series of reforms aims to strengthen the supervision and management of drugs, improve administrative efficiency, reduce the burden of enterprises, and ensure drug quality.

The second paragraph of this article indicates that the pharmaceutical supervisory and administrative departments of the provinces, autonomous regions, and municipalities are directly responsible for the supervision and control of pharmaceuticals within the administrative region. In June 2000, SDA approved the reform of the management system of drug supervision, set on the drug supervision and management mechanism of local government and its responsibilities stipulated.

In accordance with this Law and the relevant provisions of the State Council, the main responsibility of the pharmaceutical supervisory and administrative department is the supervision and management of drugs including: pre-approval of pharmaceutical production enterprises, pharmaceutical trading enterprises, issue "drug production license" and "drug business license"; develop "drug production quality management standards", "drug quality management standards", supervise the implementation; approval of new drugs and generic drugs, issue new drug certificate, drug production approval number; approval of imported drugs, issue the Drug Import Registration Certificate that meets the requirements for import; review and approve the qualified medicine preparation room; medical preparations; implementation of the supervision and management of packaging materials that have direct contact with drugs; approval of drug advertising, drug advertisement approval number; the quality of drug supervision and inspection, issue inspection results; investigation of violations of the law, the possible harm to human health and drug in the statutory scope to take administrative compulsory measures. Those in violation of this act and of the relevant provisions of this act shall receive administrative punishment.

Article 6 The pharmaceutical inspection institutions established or approved by the pharmaceutical supervisory and administrative departments shall be charged with the work of pharmaceutical examination and approval, as well as quality inspection, in accordance with laws and regulations.

Interpretation:

This article is relevant to the drug inspection institutions bearing the statutory inspection work.

The drug inspection in accordance with the validity of the test and inspection results can be divided into two categories.

The first category of drug testing includes that drug producers, operators, and medical institutions need inspection to their own drug. For such drug inspection, the law is not mandatory. The drug producers or medical institutes can do by themselves if they have the capability, or can use other social or government agencies to do such inspection. The test results can be used for their own reference without the legal effect. The secondary category of drug testing for drug supervision and management departments is to fulfill the pharmaceutical supervisory and administrative functions according to law for inspection, including inspection related to approval of new drugs and generic drugs, approval of imported drugs, and the implementation of drug quality supervision and inspection, etc. This category of drug inspection belongs to the mandatory and statutory action. The test result is the technical basis of administrative law enforcement of drug supervision and management departments. For this type of inspection, the implementation of the pharmaceutical inspection institutions shall be prescribed by law.

In accordance with the provisions of this article, the implementation of the statutory inspection can be undertaken by the pharmaceutical inspection institutions established by the pharmaceutical supervisory and administrative departments or other institutions determined by the departments.

In accordance with article 67, pharmaceutical inspection institutions of the pharmaceutical supervisory and administrative departments may determine the inspection result acceptability. The drug companies may apply to the pharmaceutical supervisory and administrative department at a higher level for re-inspection to confirm the test results and provide conclusion.

Chapter II Administration of Pharmaceutical Producing Enterprises
Article 7 The establishment of a pharmaceutical producing enterprise must be approved by and issued a Pharmaceutical Production License by the pharmaceutical supervisory and administrative department of the province, autonomous region, or municipality directly under the Central government in which the enterprise is located.

The establishment shall be registered at the industry and commerce administrative department based on the Pharmaceutical Production License, without which no pharmaceuticals shall be produced.

The Pharmaceutical Production License shall bear the scope of production and a period of validity, and upon expiration a new license shall be issued after examination for its renewal.

The approval of the establishment of pharmaceutical producing enterprises by the pharmaceutical supervisory and administrative departments shall be in conformity with Article 8 of this law, as well as the pharmaceutical development plan and the industrial policies formulated by the State to avoid the instance of a repeat establishment.

Article 8 To establish a pharmaceutical producing enterprise, the following requirements must be met:

1. It shall be staffed with legally certified pharmaceutical technical personnel, engineering technical personnel, as well as corresponding skilled workers.
2. It shall have factory premises, facilities and a sanitary environment suitable for the medicines produced.
3. It shall have a unit or competent personnel capable of inspecting the quality of the medicines produced, as well as necessary instruments and equipment.
4. It shall have rules and regulations to ensure the quality of medicines.

Article 9 Pharmaceutical producing enterprises must organize production in accordance with the "Standards for Quality Control of Pharmaceutical Production" formulated by the pharmaceutical supervisory and administrative departments under the State Council on the basis of this Law. Pharmaceutical supervisory and administrative departments shall confirm whether the pharmaceutical producing enterprises have met the requirements of the "Standards," and shall issue certificates to those qualified ones.

The detailed implementation measures and implementation process of the "Standards for Quality Control of Pharmaceutical Production" shall be formulated by the pharmaceutical supervisory and administrative department under the State Council.

Article 10 Except in the preparation of traditional Chinese medicines into ready-to-use forms, pharmaceuticals must be produced in accordance with the national pharmaceutical standard and the technological procedures approved by the supervisory and administrative departments of pharmaceuticals under the State Council, and the record of production must be complete and accurate. The changes of technological procedure made by the pharmaceutical producing enterprises which affect the quality of the pharmaceuticals shall be examined and approved by the original approval authorities.

The process for preparing traditional Chinese medicines into ready-to-use forms must conform to the national pharmaceutical standards, and in the absence of such standards, the process must conform to the processing standards stipulated by the supervisory and administrative departments of pharmaceuticals of the provinces, autonomous regions, or municipalities directly under the central government. The processing standards stipulated by the supervisory and administrative departments of pharmaceuticals of the provinces, autonomous regions, or municipalities directly under the central governments shall be placed on record at the pharmaceutical supervisory and administrative department under the State Council.

Article 11 The raw and supplementary materials used for the production of pharmaceuticals must conform to the requirements for medicinal use.

Article 12 The pharmaceutical producing enterprises must conduct quality inspections on the pharmaceuticals they produce; products which do not meet national pharmaceutical standards or are not prepared in conformity with the processing standards stipulated by the pharmaceutical supervisory and administrative departments of the provinces, autonomous regions, or municipalities directly under the central government shall not leave the factory.

Article 13 Pharmaceutical producing enterprises can accept the authorization to produce pharmaceuticals after they obtain approval from the pharmaceutical supervisory and administrative department under the State Council or the pharmaceutical supervisory and administrative departments of the provinces, autonomous regions, or municipalities directly under the central government authorized by the supervisory and administrative department of pharmaceuticals under the State Council.

Interpretation:

This article refers to drug production enterprises in accordance with contract production of drugs.

Commissioned production of pharmaceuticals refers to the enterprises with legally obtained national drug approval number entrusts other pharmaceutical production enterprises to manufacture the drug varieties. Commissioned production of the drug approval number is still owned by the commissioning party. Commissioned production of pharmaceutical companies are only responsible for the commissioning party in accordance with the requirements of the production of pharmaceuticals. The relevant foreign pharmaceutical production involving drug approval number should be the original owner's responsibility. Generally speaking, the client is responsible for selling commissioned production of drugs.

Drug manufacturers can accept the commission for the production of drugs. This model has been widely recognized and adopted internationally. For commissioned enterprises for pharmaceutical production, the enterprises can make full use of the production potential for entrusted production and create more economic benefits. For the commissioning party, it can be organized under approval number, does not lose ownership of varieties of pharmaceutical drug manufacturing premise, can reduce their additional funds needed for investment in productive capacity without affecting the production of pharmaceuticals by commission sales to obtain economic benefits.

Chapter III Administration of Pharmaceutical Trading Enterprises

Article 14 The establishment of pharmaceutical wholesale enterprises must be sanctioned by the competent local authorities of the production and trade of pharmaceuticals of the provinces, autonomous regions or municipalities directly under the central government, which will issue a Pharmaceutical Trade License. The establishment of pharmaceutical retail enterprises must be sanctioned by local authorities for the supervision and control of pharmaceuticals at or above the county level, which will issue a Pharmaceutical Trade License, on the basis of which registration at the industry and commerce administrative departments shall be conducted. Without the Pharmaceutical Trade License, any enterprises shall not engage in the trade of pharmaceuticals.

A Pharmaceutical Trade License shall bear a scope of trade and a period of validity, and upon expiration a new license shall be issued after examination for its renewal.

The approval of the establishment of pharmaceutical trading enterprises by the pharmaceutical supervisory and administrative departments shall adhere to the principle of reasonable positioning and convenience for buying of pharmaceuticals, and in addition must conform to Article 15 of this Law.

Article 15 To establish a pharmaceutical trading enterprise, the following requirements must be met

1. It shall be staffed with legally certified pharmaceutical technical personnel.
2. It shall have business premises, equipment, storage facilities and a sanitary environment suitable for the pharmaceuticals in which it trades.
3. It shall have a quality control organ or personnel suitable for the pharmaceuticals in which it trades.
4. It shall have rules and regulations to ensure the quality of the pharmaceuticals in which it trades.

Article 16 Pharmaceutical producing enterprises must trade in pharmaceuticals in accordance with the "Standards for Quality Control of Pharmaceutical Trading" stipulated by the pharmaceutical supervisory and administrative departments under the State Council on the basis of this Law. Pharmaceutical supervisory and administrative departments shall certify whether pharmaceutical trading enterprises meet the requirements of the "Standards for Quality Control of Pharmaceutical Trading" in accordance with relevant regulations, and issue certifications to qualified enterprises.

Detailed implementation measures and procedures for the "Standards for Quality Control of Pharmaceutical Trading" shall be stipulated by the pharmaceutical supervisory and administrative departments under the State Council.

Article 17 Pharmaceutical trading enterprises must formulate and implement check and approval rules for the purchase of pharmaceuticals, and check pharmaceutical certifications and other marks while purchasing pharmaceuticals. Pharmaceuticals that do not meet the required standards must not be purchased.

Article 18 Pharmaceutical trading enterprises shall keep accurate and complete records of purchased pharmaceuticals. Purchasing records must bear information on the pharmaceutical product's generic names, types, specifications, batches, valid periods, producing enterprises, purchasing (selling) units, purchasing (selling) quantity, purchasing and selling price, purchasing (selling) date and other contents required by the pharmaceutical supervisory and administrative department under the State Council.

Article 19 It is imperative for pharmaceutical trading enterprises, in the sale of pharmaceuticals, to be accurate and free of mistakes, and to provide correct directions for use, dosage and precautions. Prescriptions being dispensed must be checked. Pharmaceutical products listed in the prescription must not be presumptuously changed or substituted. Prescriptions containing incompatible substances or excessive dosages shall be rejected by the dispensary. If necessary, such prescriptions can be dispensed after they have been corrected or re-signed by the doctors who wrote them.

When traditional Chinese medicinal materials are offered for sale by pharmaceutical trading enterprises, their origin must be indicated.

Article 20 Rules for storage of pharmaceuticals shall be formulated and implemented by pharmaceutical trading enterprises, which must adopt necessary measures to facilitate cold storage and protection against freezing, moisture, insects and rodents to ensure pharmaceutical quality.

An inspection system shall be carried out for pharmaceuticals entering or leaving a warehouse

Article 21 Unless otherwise stipulated by the State, traditional Chinese medicinal materials may be marketed at urban or rural fairs.

Pharmaceuticals other than traditional Chinese medicinal materials may not be sold at urban or rural fairs, but those retail enterprises which have the Pharmaceutical Trade License may set up stalls at urban or rural fairs to sell pharmaceuticals other than traditional Chinese medicinal materials within prescribed areas. Detailed measures shall be stipulated by the State Council.

Chapter IV Administration of Pharmaceuticals at Medical Organizations

Article 22 Medical organizations must be staffed with legally certified pharmaceutical technical personnel. Non-pharmaceutical technical personnel may not be directly engaged in the technical work of the pharmacy.

Article 23 To make medicinal preparations, a medical organization must be examined and approved by the administrative departments of health of the provinces, autonomous regions, or municipalities directly under the central government where the organization is located, and approved and issued a Dispensing Permit for Medical Organizations by the pharmaceutical supervisory and administrative departments of the provinces, autonomous regions or municipalities directly under the central government. No medicinal preparations shall be made without a Dispensing Permit for Medical Organizations.

The Dispensing Permit for Medical Organizations shall bear a period of validity, and upon expiration a new license shall be issued after examination for its renewal.

Article 24 Medical organizations that make medicinal preparations must have facilities, a managerial system, inspection instruments, and a sanitary environment to ensure quality.

Article 25 The medicinal preparations made by medical organizations shall be of the kinds that supply the clinical needs of the units themselves but have not been supplied on the market, and must not be made until the approval of the pharmaceutical supervisory and administrative departments of the provinces, autonomous regions and municipalities directly under the central government where the units are located. The quality of the medicinal preparations made by medical organizations must be inspected in accordance with relevant regulations. Those preparations conforming to standard can be used as the doctor prescribes. Under special circumstances, with approval from the pharmaceutical supervisory and administrative departments of the central government or of the provinces, autonomous regions and municipalities directly under the central government, the medicinal preparations made by medical organizations can be shared among appointed medical organizations.

Medicinal preparations made by medical organizations may not be sold on the market.

Article 26 When purchasing pharmaceuticals, medical organizations must formulate and implement a system of quality inspection and check the certificates and other marks of pharmaceuticals. Those pharmaceuticals that do not meet the requirements of relevant regulations shall not be purchased and used.

Article 27 Prescriptions being dispensed by the dispensers of medical organizations must be checked. Pharmaceuticals listed in prescriptions must not be presumptuously changed or substituted. Prescriptions containing incompatible substances or excessive dosages shall be rejected by the dispensary. If necessary, such prescriptions can be dispensed after they have been corrected or re-signed by the doctors who wrote them.

Article 28 Rules for storage of pharmaceuticals shall be formulated and implemented by medical organizations, which must adopt necessary measures to facilitate cold storage and protection against cold, moisture, insects and rodents to ensure the quality of pharmaceuticals.

Chapter V Pharmaceutical Administration

Article 29 When producing a new medicine, it is necessary to submit information about the methods of production, quality indices, pharmacological and toxicological testing results, and other related materials and sales as required by the pharmaceutical supervisory and administrative department of the State Council, toxicological testing results, and other related materials and sales as required by the pharmaceutical supervisory and administrative department of the State Council, only after whose approval can clinical tests be carried out. Certifying measures for clinical test units shall be jointly formulated by the pharmaceutical supervisory and administrative department under the State Council and the administrative department of health under the State Council.

A new medicine which has completed its clinical tests and been approved after appraisal shall be issued a certificate of new medicine by the pharmaceutical supervisory and administrative department under the State Council.

Interpretation:

In accordance with this article, a new drug certificate shall be issued if all the clinical trials have been completed, and have met the regulatory requirements. Based on current regulations, clinical trials are divided into phases I, II, III, and IV. The specific requirements for phase I, II, III, and IV clinical and bioequivalence trials on all categories of new drugs have been specified. At the completion of clinical trials, if the new drug meets all the requirements, a new drug certificate shall be issued by the regulatory agency. It should be noted that a new drug certificate only makes relevant rights and interests with the drug statutory qualifications (i.e. it does not mean that the sponsor can carry out the drug manufacturing, but drug manufacturing also has to have the corresponding manufacturing technologies.). Therefore, the sponsor should apply for the drug manufacturing license in order to manufacture the new drug in accordance with the provisions of this Law in article 31. Briefly, a new drug certificate can be used to apply for manufacturing or technology transfer. To ensure the scientific nature of drug clinical trials, and to ensure that clinical sites can really play a role in the inspection of drug safety and effectiveness, medical institutions including medical centers or hospitals, are usually used as the clinical sites. As a qualified clinical trial sites, they have to obtain a certificate from the regulatory agencies.

Article 30 The pharmaceutical non-clinical safety appraisal and research units and the clinical test units must respectively carry out the quality control standard for pharmaceutical non-clinical research and the quality control standard for pharmaceutical clinical test. The quality control standard for pharmaceutical non-clinical research and the quality control standard for pharmaceutical clinical test shall be formulated by the department appointed by the State Council.

Interpretation: This article describes that safety evaluation and research institutions for non-clinical studies and clinical sites for clinical trials must execute the provisions on administrative norms. In accordance with this article, GLP and GCP criteria are determined by the State Council department. To conduct non-clinical safety evaluation and clinical trials of new drugs, GLP and GCP are mandatory.

Article 31 A new medicine or medicine standardized by the State can be put into production only after the pharmaceutical supervisory and administrative department under the State Council has approved it and issued a registered document of approval. However, this does not apply to the production of traditional Chinese medicinal herbs and traditional Chinese medicine prepared in ready-to-use forms that are not controlled under a registered document of approval. For those traditional Chinese medicinal herbs and traditional Chinese medicines prepared in ready-to-use forms that are controlled with registered document of approval, the pharmaceutical supervisory and administrative department under the State Council and the administrative department of traditional Chinese medicines under the State Council shall jointly formulate their type catalogue.

Pharmaceutical producing enterprises can produce medicine only after obtaining the registered document of approval.

Interpretation:

For production of a new drug or production of drugs that have already met national standards, the enterprises should submit an application to the drug regulatory department. After regulatory examination and approval, a drug approval number shall be issued. The State Drug Administration has issued the corresponding provisions and regulations for the approval of new drugs and generic drugs, which include the detailed descriptions.

According to this article, the drug production approval number is a necessary document that made the drug production legally qualified. The drug production enterprise can produce the corresponding medicine only if they have obtained a drug approval number.

Article 32 Pharmaceuticals must meet the pharmaceutical standards of the State. Article 10 (2) of this Law shall be applied to traditional Chinese medicines prepared in ready-to-use forms. The "Pharmacopoeia of the People's Republic of China" and the pharmaceutical standards promulgated by the pharmaceutical supervisory and administrative department under the State Council shall be the State pharmaceutical standards.

The Pharmacopoeia Committee organized by the pharmaceutical supervisory and administrative department under the State Council shall be responsible for the formulation and revision of the State pharmaceutical standards. The pharmaceutical inspection institutions of the pharmaceutical supervisory and administrative department under the State Council shall be responsible for the designation of State standard and contrastive pharmaceuticals.

Interpretation:

Drug standards are technical provisions of the State of drug quality specifications and test methods. It serves the legal basis for drug production, supply, use, inspection and management departments to follow.

In accordance with the provisions of this paragraph, the national drug standards are the standards listed in the "People's Republic of China Pharmacopoeia" and the standard promulgated by the drug regulatory department under the State Council. At present, the State Drug Administration has issued a 2000 edition of the "People's Republic of China Pharmacopoeia," which contains a total of nearly 2700 kinds of Chinese and western medicine standards.

Article 33 The pharmaceutical supervisory and administrative department under the State Council may organize pharmaceutical, medicinal and other technological personnel to carry out examination and evaluation of new medicines, and to reevaluate medicines already placed into production.
Interpretation:

This article is about technical review of the new drugs and re-evaluation of drugs that have already been approved for production. In this article, the so-called "pharmacy, medicine and other technical personnel" includes the experts in the list of regulatory agencies' expert pool and the professional and technical personnel for Drug Evaluation departments of the State Council.

In accordance with this Article, the drug regulatory department of the State Council shall organize relevant experts and technical staff to conduct technical review of new drugs and re-evaluation of the marketed drugs to ensure safety and effectiveness.

Article 34 Pharmaceutical producing enterprises, pharmaceutical trading enterprises and medical organizations must purchase pharmaceuticals from the qualified enterprises with the certificates for production and trade of pharmaceuticals. However, this does not apply to the purchase of the traditional Chinese medicinal herbs which are not controlled under the registered document of approval.

Interpretation:

This article is about the pharmaceutical producing enterprises, trading enterprises and medical institutions drug purchase management. In accordance with this article, only qualified pharmaceutical production enterprises and trading enterprises with a "drug production license" or "drug license" can engage in drug production and drug business activities.

Article 35 For narcotics, psychotropic substances, toxic drugs for medicinal use, and radioactive drugs, the State Council shall formulate administrative measures to carry out special control.

Interpretation:

This article is about the provisions of the four special classes of drugs' special management system, including narcotic drugs, psychotropic drugs, toxic drugs for medical use and radioactive pharmaceuticals.

"Narcotic drugs" refers to the drugs with continuous use that are easy to produce physical dependence, or addiction. Narcotic drugs include opiates, cocaine, cannabis, synthetic narcotic class, other addictive drugs, medicinal plants and their preparations that may cause addiction.

"Psychotropic drugs" refers to the drugs that have direct effect on the central nervous system, so that the continuous use can lead to dependency of drugs.

"Toxic drugs for medical use" refers to the drugs with severe toxicity. Their therapeutic dose and toxic dose are similar; therefore, improper use of those drugs will be poisonous or cause death.

The State Council in December 1988 issued the "management measures" for psychotropic drugs and "toxic drugs for medical use management approach", in January 1989 issued the "measures for the control of radioactive drugs". All parties must be in accordance with the laws and regulations of the state Council referring to the aforementioned four categories of drugs. For details, please also see the appendix 1—MEASURES FOR THE CONTROL OF PSYCHOTROPIC DRUGS.

"Radioactive drugs" refers to the radionuclide preparations for clinical diagnosis or treatment or the marker of drug. In view of the special nature of these four kinds of drugs, their production, sale, import and export or use should be under more strict supervision and management. For details, please also see the appendix 2—MEASURES FOR THE CONTROL OF NARCOTIC DRUGS

Article 36 The State Council shall formulate detailed measures to carry out a protection system for the categorization of traditional Chinese medicines.

Article 37 The State Council shall formulate detailed measures to carry out a classified control system for prescription pharmaceuticals and non-prescription pharmaceuticals.

Article 38 Import of medicines whose curative effects are uncertain or poor, or which produce adverse reactions or have other harmful effects on people's health shall be prohibited.

Interpretation:

This article is about the ban on the import of hazardous drugs.

The implementation of this provision is aimed to prevent the drugs with uncertain curative effects, serious adverse reaction, or other harmful factors to human health to enter China. Therefore, it is required that:

1. The drug supervision and management departments must be in accordance with the article 9, and strictly perform the drug import approval management duty. Imported drugs only after examination to comply with the quality standards, safe and effectiveness requirements can be approved for its import license.
2. The departments responsible for the inspection of imported drugs must conscientiously perform supervision and inspections duties in accordance with this article. The inspection agency shall report to the drug regulatory authority with the provision, prohibiting their import.
3. The drug regulatory department under the State Council shall, according to Article 42, organize the inspection for the drugs with import drug registration certificate. If they find that the drug has uncertain effect, more adverse reactions or other harmful effects on human health medicines, they shall revoke the import drug registration certificate, prohibit re-importation.

4. Imported drug manufacturers must fulfill the provisions of the law for importing drug, and follow the drug application and approval procedures. They have to accomplish that which is required in China for further regulatory review and assessment. After the approval, they must note that the collection of adverse reactions and the timely reporting to the drug supervision and management departments are needed. In addition, for the approved import drugs, any of the changes relating to prescription, quality standards, package insert, validity and other matters must be reported to the drug regulatory department for approval.

Article 39 The import of medicines must go through examinations organized by the pharmaceutical supervisory and administrative department under the State Council. Those confirmed to conform to quality standards to be safe and effective can be approved to be imported and shall be issued a registered certificate for import.

Medicines to be imported in small quantities for urgent clinical needs by medical organizations or for personal use shall go through import formalities according to relevant regulations of the State.

Interpretation:

This article is about the review system of imported drugs registration.

In regards to the first paragraph, China implements the review and approval system prior to awarding the certificates for imported drugs. This system aims to ensure that the drugs are in compliance with the relevant quality standards, and are safe and effective before they make the decision whether to approve its import. Under the existing provisions of the management of imported drugs, the application of imported drugs must be clinically necessary, safe and effective, and controllable for its quality. Specifically, imported drugs shall meet the following requirements:

1. Achieve the national drug registration approval of the competent authorities of the manufacturing country and the marketing authorization;
2. Conforms to the standard for quality control of pharmaceutical production and GMP in the original country and China;
3. The relevant materials were submitted to the drug regulatory department including the quality standard and inspection method of imported drugs, prescription, manufacturing technology, pharmacology, toxicology and clinical research, technical information as required by the drug regulatory agency of the State Council;
4. After completion of the drug quality and its clinical trials, the State Drug Administration departments will confirm the drug's compliance with the relevant standards of quality, safety and effectiveness of the drug before they make the decision to approve the import and issued a certificate of registration of imported drugs. Imported Drug Registration Certificate is a legal document for foreign drug to enter the Chinese market for sales.

In some special cases, such as urgent clinical need of foreign drugs, it is often too late to apply for approval of imported drug registration in accordance with the provisions of paragraph 1; therefore, it is reasonably necessary to import a small amount of an individual's use of drugs and, in such a case, it doesn't have to follow the provisions of the first paragraph for imported drug registration approval.

Article 40 Pharmaceuticals must be imported through the ports which allow the import of pharmaceuticals, and the pharmaceutical import enterprise shall submit a report to the pharmaceutical supervisory and administrative department of the place where the port is located. Customs shall rely on the Import Pharmaceuticals Customs Form issued by the pharmaceutical supervisory and administrative department to proceed. Those without the Import Pharmaceuticals Customs Form shall not be permitted to pass through customs.

The pharmaceutical supervisory and administrative department of the place where the port is located shall notify the pharmaceutical inspection institution to carry out selective examinations and inspections on the imported pharmaceuticals according to the regulations stipulated by the pharmaceutical supervisory and administrative department under the State Council, and to collect inspection fees according to Article 41(2) of this Law.

The nomination of the ports allowable for import of pharmaceuticals shall be jointly conducted by the pharmaceutical supervisory and administrative department under the State Council and the Customs Headquarters, and be reported to the State Council for approval.

Interpretation:

This article relates to pharmaceutical import ports, customs clearance regulations, and random inspection of imported.

Drug regulatory department at the port location should review the record, to confirm if the imported drug registration certificate is legally obtained, meets the laws and administrative regulations, or other regulations on imported medicines. If the imported drug registration is in line with the state regulations, the drug regulatory department shall issue a "Drug Import Note." The customs shall release the drugs on the basis of the Drug Import Note issued by the said departments, and may not release those drugs for which no Drug Import Note is issued.

To ensure the quality of imported drugs meet the required standards, safety and effectiveness, port and drug administration departments shall notify the drug testing agency in accordance with the provisions of the random inspection of imported medicines. If the tests confirm that the imported medicines do not meet the grant criteria, the drug regulatory departments shall not permit the drug to be sold in China.

Article 41 The pharmaceutical supervisory and administrative department under the State Council shall appoint inspection institutions to carry out inspections before the sale and import of the following pharmaceuticals. Those having not passed the inspection shall not be allowed to be sold or imported.

1. Bio-products prescribed by the pharmaceutical supervisory and administrative department of the State Council.
2. Pharmaceuticals to be sold for the first time in China.
3. Other pharmaceuticals prescribed by the State Council.

The inspection fee and charge standards for the above-mentioned pharmaceuticals shall be jointly checked, ratified and promulgated by the financial department under the State Council and the competent authority of price control under the State

Council. The measures for the collection of inspection fees shall be jointly formulated by the financial department under the State Council and the pharmaceutical supervisory and administrative department under the State Council.

Interpretation:

This article relates to the madatory testing for specific drugs conducted at the time of pre-sold or imported stages by drug regulatory departments.

The provisions of this article set a specific supervision and inspection for the drugs that may have a significant impact on the safety, or need to strengthen the supervision and management.

According to this article, three categories of drugs at or before the time of import must accept supervision and inspection including:

1. It includes the defined biological products by drug regulatory department under the State Council.
2. Whether the drug is manufactured within China or imported from overseas, the drug must pass inspection within China if it is its first introduction to the market.
3. The state council may call in manufacturers for inspection if they deem it necessary.

Article 42 The pharmaceutical supervisory and administrative department under the State Council shall organize investigations on medicines which have been approved for production or import. It shall revoke the registered documents of approval or the registered certificate of import if it discovers that the curative effects of the medicines are uncertain or poor, that they produce serious adverse reactions, or that for other reasons they are harmful to people's health.

The medicines whose registered documents of approval or registered certificate of import have been revoked shall not be allowed to be produced, imported, sold or used. Those which have already been produced or imported shall be destroyed or disposed of under the supervision of the local pharmaceutical supervisory and administrative departments.

Article 43 A pharmaceutical reserve system shall be carried out by the State.

In case of serious disasters, plagues and other sudden emergencies, the department prescribed by the State Council can requisite the pharmaceuticals of enterprises to deal with such emergencies.

Article 44 The State Council shall have the power to restrict or prohibit the export of the pharmaceuticals which are in short supply in the domestic market.

Article 45 Import or export licenses issued by the pharmaceutical supervisory and administrative department under the State Council are required for the import or export of narcotics and psychotropic substances falling within the restricted scope prescribed by the State.

Interpretation:

This article relates to the regulations for import and export of narcotic drugs and psychotropic substances within the scope prescribed by the State. For details, please see Appendix 1 MEASURES FOR THE CONTROL OF PSYCHOTROPIC

DRUGS, and Appendix 2—MEASURES FOR THE CONTROL OF NARCOTIC DRUGS.

Article 46 Newly discovered domestic medicinal plants or medicinal plants introduced from abroad may be sold only after they have been examined and approved by the pharmaceutical supervisory and administrative department under the State Council.'

Article 47 Measures for controlling medicinal materials traditionally used by local people in certain regions shall be jointly formulated by the pharmaceutical supervisory and administrative department under the State Council and the administrative department of traditional Chinese medicines under the State Council.

Article 48 The production (including preparation, which also applies to the following) and sale of fake medicines are prohibited. A fake medicine has any one of the following characteristics:

1. Its components are different from those prescribed by state pharmaceutical standards.
2. A non-medical substance is passed off as a medicine, or one medicine is passed off as another.

A medicine shall be handled as fake medicine in any of the following cases:

1. Where the use of the medicine has been prohibited by the pharmaceutical supervisory and administrative department under the State Council;
2. Where the medicine is produced and imported without an approval dictated according to this Law, or the medicine is sold without being inspected as dictated according to this Law;
3. Where the medicine has deteriorated; or
4. Where the medicine has been contaminated;
5. Where the medicine has been produced with pharmaceutical materials without obtaining the dictated registration document of approval for the materials.
6. Where the indications or the functions marked on the labels of the pharmaceuticals do not fall within the prescribed scope.

Article 49 It is prohibited to produce and sell medicines of inferior quality, referring to the medicines whose components do not conform in quantity to that required by State pharmaceutical standards. A medicine shall be handled as medicine of inferior quality in any of the following cases:

1. An expiry date is not indicated or is altered; or
2. A registration number is not indicated or is altered; or
3. The medicine has passed its expiration date; or
4. The packages and containers which have direct contact with pharmaceuticals have not obtained approval; or
5. The medicine has been added presumptuously with color or preservative additives, spice, disguising odor or supplementary materials; or
6. The medicine fails to meet the prescribed standards in other respects.

Article 50 The names of the pharmaceuticals listed in the State pharmaceutical standards are the generic names of the pharmaceuticals. Those names that have become the generic names of pharmaceuticals shall not be used as trademarks of pharmaceuticals.

Article 51 Personnel in pharmaceutical producing or trading enterprises and in medical organizations who have direct contact with medicines must undergo an annual medical examination. Persons who have contracted contagious diseases or any other disease which may contaminate the medicine shall not be allowed to engage in any work which has direct contact with pharmaceuticals.

Chapter VI Administration on Pharmaceutical Packaging

Article 52 The pharmaceutical packaging materials and containers which have direct contact with pharmaceuticals must meet the requirements of medicinal use, conform with the standards of protecting people's health and safety, and obtain the approval of the pharmaceutical supervisory and administrative departments at the same time as the approval of the pharmaceutical product.

Pharmaceutical producing enterprises shall use the packaging materials and containers which have direct contact with the pharmaceuticals only after they have obtained approval for them.

The pharmaceutical supervisory and administrative departments shall stop the use of those unqualified packaging materials and containers which have direct contact with the pharmaceuticals.

Interpretation:

This article is about the direct contact with the drug packaging materials and container management system. See "Examination and approval for import of packaging materials and containers in direct contact with drugs" for more details.

Article 53 Packaging must meet the specific quality requirements of the pharmaceuticals and facilitate their storage, transportation and medical use.

Traditional Chinese medicinal materials must be packaged before transportation. There must appear on the package the name of the medicine, place of production, date, name of the consignor, and an indication showing that the quality of the medicine meets standards.

Article 54 Packages of pharmaceuticals must be labeled and include directions for use in accordance with the regulations.

The label or directions must indicate the generic name of the medicine, components, specifications, the producer, registration number, batch number of the product, production date, expiry date, indications or major functions, directions for use, dosage, restrictions, adverse reactions and precautions.

Special indications must be printed as required on the labels of narcotics, psychotropic substances, toxic drugs for medical use, radioactive drugs, medicines for external use and non-prescriptive pharmaceuticals.

Chapter VII Administration of the Prices and Advertising of Pharmaceuticals

Article 55 For pharmaceuticals controlled by the fixed and directive pricing system of the government, the competent authority of pricing of the government shall fix and adjust the price with reason in conformity with the principles for fixing prices as prescribed by the Price Law of the PRC and according to the considerations of societal average costs, market supply and demand, and the level of societal tolerance to achieve accord between quality and price, to avoid excessive prices, and to safeguard the due interests of the users of the pharmaceuticals.

Pharmaceutical producing enterprises, trading enterprises and medical organizations must carry out the fixed price and directive price system of the government, and shall not presumptuously raise prices in any form.

Pharmaceutical producing enterprises shall provide the competent authority of pricing of the government with the producing and trading costs of pharmaceuticals and shall not refuse to report, make a false report or withhold the truth in such a report.

Article 56 For the pharmaceuticals whose prices are to be adjusted by the market, the pharmaceutical producing enterprises, trading enterprises, and medical organizations shall fix the price in conformity with the principles of fairness, rationality, honesty, good faith and accord between quality and price to provide the users of the pharmaceuticals with reasonable prices.

Pharmaceutical producing enterprises, trading enterprises and medical organizations shall abide by the regulations concerning the control on prices of pharmaceuticals prescribed by the competent authority of pricing under the State Council, shall fix and mark the retail prices of pharmaceuticals, and shall avoid sudden excessive profits and deceptive acts on pricing which will harm the interests of the users of the pharmaceuticals.

Article 57 Pharmaceutical producing enterprises, trading enterprises and medical organizations shall, in accordance with this Law, provide the competent authority of pricing of the government with information such as the actual purchasing and selling prices and quantities of the pharmaceuticals.

Article 58 Medical organizations shall provide the patient with the price list of the pharmaceuticals used. Medical organizations appointed by medical insurance shall faithfully promulgate the prices of frequently used pharmaceuticals according to prescribed measures to enhance the reasonable use of pharmaceuticals.

Article 59 Pharmaceutical producing enterprises, trading enterprises and medical organizations are prohibited to give or receive secret commissions and other benefits during the purchasing and selling of pharmaceuticals.

Pharmaceutical producing enterprises, trading enterprises or their representatives are prohibited to give any property or other benefits under any name to the principals, buyers of pharmaceuticals, physicians and other relevant persons in the medical organizations where their pharmaceuticals are used. The principals, buyers of pharmaceuticals, physicians and other relevant persons are prohibited from receiving any property or other benefits under any name from pharmaceutical producing enterprises, trading enterprises or their agents.

Article 60 Advertisements of pharmaceuticals must be approved and issued a registration number of advertisement by the pharmaceutical supervisory and administrative departments of the provinces, autonomous regions, or municipalities directly under the central government of the place where the enterprises are located.

In the absence of such registration numbers, advertisements for any medicines may not be placed. Prescription pharmaceuticals may be introduced in medicinal and pharmaceutical magazines jointly appointed by the administrative department of health under the

State Council and the pharmaceutical supervisory and administrative department under the State Council, but shall not be advertised through mass media or publicized in any other form to the public.

Article 61 The contents of pharmaceutical advertisement must be true, legitimate, and be based on the directions for use approved by the pharmaceutical supervisory and administrative department under the State Council, and be also free of falsehood.

Advertisements of pharmaceuticals shall not contain any unscientific assertion or guarantee on effects, and shall not be endorsed using the names and images of government bodies, pharmaceutical scientific research units, academic organizations, experts, scholars, physicians and sufferers.

The advertisements of non-pharmaceuticals shall not be involved in the publicizing of pharmaceuticals.

Article 62 The pharmaceutical supervisory and administrative departments of the provinces, autonomous regions and municipalities directly under the central government shall inspect on the pharmaceutical advertisements they approve, and shall notify and advise the administrative departments of advertising if the government shall inspect on the pharmaceutical advertisements they approve, and shall notify and advise the administrative departments of advertising if the advertisements is not in conformity with this Law and the Advertisement Law of the PRC. The administrative departments of advertising shall deal with such advertisements according to relevant regulations.

Article 63 In the absence of regulations as provided in this Law, the Price Law of the PRC and the Advertisement Law of the PRC shall be applied to the control of pharmaceutical prices and advertisements.

Chapter VIII Supervision over Pharmaceuticals

Article 64 Pharmaceutical supervisory and administrative departments are authorized to conduct, in accordance with laws and administrative regulations, supervision and inspection over the research, development, production and trade of pharmaceuticals which they have approved, as well as the medical organizations' use of pharmaceuticals. The units and individuals concerned shall not refuse to comply.

Pharmaceutical supervisory and administrative departments shall present certificate documents while conducting supervision and inspection, and shall not divulge technological and business secrets gained during the process of supervision and inspection.

Article 65 According to the needs of supervision and inspection, pharmaceutical supervisory and administrative departments may conduct sampling examinations on the quality of pharmaceuticals. The sampling examinations shall be conducted according to relevant regulations and shall not be charged a fee. The expenses incurred shall be dispensed with in conformity with the regulations prescribed by the State Council.

Pharmaceutical supervisory and administrative departments may take administrative coercive measures including sequestration and banning against pharmaceuticals and other relevant materials which have been proven to be of possible harm to people's health; administrative measures must be taken within 7 days. For pharmaceuticals which need to be inspected, decisions regarding administrative handling must be made within 15 days from the date of issue of the inspection reports.

Article 66 The pharmaceutical supervisory and administrative departments under the State Council and of the provinces, autonomous regions and municipalities directly under the central government shall regularly promulgate the results of sampling examinations and inspections on the quality of pharmaceuticals, and shall, in the case of improperly published statements, amend such statements in the original published documents.

Article 67 If a party concerned disagrees with the inspection decision made by the inspection institutions, it may apply for re-inspection to the original inspection institutions or ones established or appointed by the pharmaceutical supervisory and administrative departments of superior levels within 7 days from the date of receiving the pharmaceutical inspection decision, and may directly apply for re-inspection to the inspection institutions established or appointed by the pharmaceutical supervisory and administrative department under the State Council. The inspection institutions which have accepted the re-inspections shall conclude the re-inspections within the time limit prescribed by the pharmaceutical supervisory and administrative department under the State Council.

Article 68 Pharmaceutical supervisory and administrative departments shall follow up on the inspections of the pharmaceutical producing enterprises or pharmaceutical trading enterprises which they have certified in conformity with the "Quality Control Standard of Pharmaceutical Production" and the "Quality Control Standard of Pharmaceutical Trade."

Article 69 The local people's governments and pharmaceutical supervisory and administrative departments shall not restrict or exclude the entrance of pharmaceuticals produced according to this Law by pharmaceutical producing enterprises in other regions of the country through the excuse of conducting inspection, examination and approval of the pharmaceuticals.

Article 70 Pharmaceutical supervisory and administrative departments and the pharmaceutical inspection institutions they have established, as well as the institutions exclusively engaged in pharmaceutical inspection they have appointed, shall not participate in pharmaceutical production and trade, and shall not endorse or supervise the production and sale of pharmaceuticals in their own names.

The functionaries of pharmaceutical supervisory and administrative departments, of the pharmaceutical inspection institutions they established, and of the institutions exclusively engaged in the inspection of pharmaceuticals they appointed, shall not participate in pharmaceutical production and trade.

Article 71 A reporting system over any adverse reactions of pharmaceuticals shall be practiced by state. pharmaceutical producing enterprises, pharmaceutical trading enterprises, and medical institutions shall conduct regular surveys on the quality, curative effects and adverse reactions of the pharmaceuticals they have produced, traded or used. When serious adverse reactions possibly related to the use of the pharmaceuticals are discovered, they must be promptly reported to the pharmaceutical supervisory and administrative departments and the administrative departments of health of the provinces, autonomous regions and municipalities directly under the central government. Detailed measures shall be formulated jointly by the pharmaceutical supervisory and administrative department under the State Council and the administrative department of health under the State Council.

Regarding the pharmaceuticals which have been confirmed to cause serious adverse reactions, the pharmaceutical supervisory and administrative department under the State Council and of the provinces, autonomous regions and municipalities directly under the central government, shall take urgent control measures including the cessation of the production, sale, and use of the pharmaceuticals, shall organize appraisals within 5 days, and shall make decisions on their administrative handling within 15 days from the conclusion date of the appraisals.

Interpretation:

This article is about adverse drug reaction monitoring and reporting system and procedures.

The first paragraph specifies the national adverse drug reaction (ADR) monitoring and reporting system. ADR are classified as type A (Quantitative exceptions), or type B (quality). Type A is caused by pharmacological enhancement, and it can be predicted. It has high incidence in the population but its mortality is low. Type B is independent of the normal pharmacological effects and difficult to predict. It has low incidence in the population but its mortality is high. ADRs mainly include:

1. side effects: harmful on the human body. These are the effects with therapeutic dose, which are unrelated to the targeted indication, e.g., atropine is often used to relieve gastrointestinal spasm, but may cause dry mouth, etc.
2. toxicity: common clinical toxicities include central nervous system reactions, (headache, dizziness); hematopoietic system response (aplastic anemia; liver and kidney damage); cardiovascular reactions (hypotension, tachycardia) etc.
3. allergic reactions including systemic reactions and local reactions, e.g. allergic shock or local skin reactions;

4. drug addiction: commonly seen in the long-term use of narcotic drugs.
5. the mutagenic, teratogenic, carcinogenic effect: mainly caused by the use of the drugs with mutagenic, teratogenic, and carcinogenic effects.
6. other adverse reactions, such as superinfection, etc.

Adverse drug reaction reporting system is one of the international science and normative system. ADR monitoring report system is a legal system and all parties concerned should conscientiously implement. Based on the ADRs and the drug safety profile, regulatory agencies will monitor and re-evaluate the drug safety. If the drug is found unsafe, the regulatory agencies may provide suggestions or cancel the drug license.

In accordance with the provisions of this article, when the pharmaceutical producing enterprises, pharmaceutical enterprises or medical institutions found that certain drug may have serious adverse reactions associated with its use. In this case, the enterprise in question must report to the local province, autonomous region, or municipality directly under the central government and drug supervision and management departments and the public health administrative department in a timely manner. The "serious adverse reaction" mainly includes:

1. death caused by taking the drug;
2. cancer or birth defects caused by taking the drug;
3. damage to vital organs, life threatening or loss of normal life ability caused by taking the drug;
4. physical damage while the resulting in hospitalization caused by taking the drug;
5. prolongs the time of hospitalization due to adverse drug reaction.

Regarding the specific measures for the adverse drug reaction reporting system, this act authorized that the drug regulatory department under the State Council jointly with the administrative department of health under the State Council shall formulate it.

The second paragraph of the article confirmed the handling procedure for drug serious adverse reactions.

The drug regulatory department under the State Council or of the provinces, autonomous regions, municipalities directly under the Central People's government could take the action to stop drug production, sale, or use in emergency control measures. They may use the emergency control measures once the ADRs are confirmed based on the integrated information of ADRs in domestic and overseas regions.

In this way, it can effectively prevent the expanding of the damages to the crowd; while at the same time during this period; regulatory agencies may organize relevant experts to further evaluate the drug for the final decisions.

In addition to stopping the production, sale, use of emergency control measures for the serious adverse reactions, the organization, i.e. the drug regulatory department under the State Council or of the provinces, autonomous regions, municipalities directly under the central government, should organize the authentication within 5 days, provide the technical basis for the administrative process.

Relevant administrative supervision departments shall make administrative decisions within 15 days after the authentication conclusion is drawn. The administrative decisions generally include two types:

1. The first is through the identification process if the continued use of the drug can not be guaranteed for its safety, or the drug can be substituted by other drugs in accordance with the provisions of this Law in article 42, the drug approval number or the drug import registration certificate is revoked by the drug regulatory department under the State Council has production. For the imported or already manufactured drug, it should be destroyed under the supervision of the local drug regulatory department.
2. The second is to continue the use of the drug under controlled conditions with the maximum possible guarantee of the drug safety as the prerequisite. In such condition, the emergency control measures on the drug can be canceled since the continued use of the drug is in a controlled environment through amending the specification, adjusting the dosage, heightening attention, and giving special warning measures.

Article 72 The organs or personnel in charge of pharmaceutical inspection in pharmaceutical producing enterprises, pharmaceutical trading enterprises and medical organizations shall receive operational guidance from the pharmaceutical inspection institutions established by local pharmaceutical supervisory and administrative departments.

Chapter IX Legal Responsibility

Article 73 Those who produce or trade in medicines without obtaining a Pharmaceutical Production License, Pharmaceutical Trade License, or Dispensing Permit of Medical Organizations, shall be placed under ban, have the unlawfully produced and sold medicines and any unlawful income confiscated, and may concurrently be fined a sum of money more than two but less than five times the value of the medicines unlawfully made or sold (including both sold and unsold pharmaceuticals, which also applies below). Those whose acts constitute a crime shall be investigated for criminal liabilities.

Article 74 Those who produce and sell fake medicines shall have his unlawfully produced or sold medicines and any unlawful income confiscated, and concurrently be fined a sum of money more than two but less than five times the value of the medicines unlawfully produced and sold. Those who have an approval certificate of pharmaceuticals shall have the certificate revoked, and be ordered to suspend production or business operations pending rectification; if the circumstances are serious, the party shall have Pharmaceutical Production License, or Pharmaceutical Trade License or Dispensing Permit of Medical Organizations revoked. Those whose acts constitute a crime shall be investigated for criminal liabilities.

Article 75 Those who produce and sell medicines of inferior quality shall have his unlawfully made and sold medicines and any unlawful income confiscated, and be concurrently fined the sum of money more than two but less than three times the value of the medicines unlawfully made or sold; if the circumstances are serious, the party shall be ordered to suspend production or business pending rectification, or have the pharmaceutical approval certificate revoked and his Pharmaceutical Production License, or Pharmaceutical Trade License or Dispensing Permit of Medical Organizations revoked. Those whose acts constitute a crime will be investigated for criminal liabilities.

Article 76 The person-in-charge or personnel directly liable in the enterprise or other unit which produces and sells fake medicines or produces and sells pharmaceuticals of inferior quality shall not be permitted to engage in the production and trade of pharmaceuticals for 10 years, if the circumstances are serious.

The producers' supplementary materials, packaging materials and production equipment which are used exclusively for producing fake medicines and medicines of inferior quality shall be confiscated.

Article 77 Those who provide facilities including transportation, preservation and storage that have been or should have been aware of the fakery or inferior quality of the pharmaceuticals, shall have the entirety of his income from such transportation, preservation and storage confiscated, and concurrently be fined a sum of money more than 50% but less than three times the value of the unlawful income. Those whose acts constitute a crime shall be investigated for criminal liabilities.

Article 78 The notice of penalties on fake medicines and medicines of inferior quality shall indicate the inspection results of the inspection institution. However, this does not apply to the circumstances prescribed by Article 48(3)(a)(b)(e)(f) and Article 49 (3) of this Law.

Article 79 Pharmaceutical producing enterprises, trading enterprises, pharmaceutical non-clinical safety appraisal research institution, and pharmaceutical clinical testing institutions, shall be served a warning and be ordered to amend themselves within a prescribed time limit if they do not carry out the stipulations of the "Quality Control Standard of Pharmaceutical Production," the "Quality Control Standard of Pharmaceutical Trade," the quality control standard of pharmaceutical non-clinical research, and the quality control standard of pharmaceutical clinical testing. Those who do not rectify their mistakes within the prescribed time limit shall be ordered to suspend production and business operations pending rectification, and be concurrently fined more than 5000 but less than 20,000 RMB. If the circumstances are serious, they shall have their Pharmaceutical Production License, Pharmaceutical Trading License or Dispensing Permit of Medical Organizations revoked.

Article 80 If any pharmaceutical producing enterprises, pharmaceutical trading enterprises or medical organizations violate Article 34 of this Law and purchase medicines from enterprises without the Pharmaceutical Production License or Pharmaceutical Trade License, they shall be ordered to amend themselves, have their unlawfully purchased medicines confiscated, and be concurrently fined the sum of money more than two but less than five times the value of the unlawfully purchased medicines. If they have obtained any unlawful income, the unlawful income shall be confiscated; if the circumstances are serious, their Pharmaceutical Production License, Pharmaceutical Trading License or Practicing Permit of Medical Organizations shall be revoked.

Article 81 Those who import pharmaceuticals with a pharmaceutical import registration document and fail to register according to this Law at the pharmaceutical supervisory and administrative department at the location of the port allowed for pharmaceutical import, shall be served a warning and be ordered to correct its mistakes within a prescribed time limit. Those who have not corrected its mistakes within the prescribed time limit shall have their registration document to import pharmaceuticals revoked.

Article 82 Those who forge, alter, trade, lease or lend licenses or pharmaceutical approval certificates, shall have their unlawful income confiscated and be concurrently fined the sum of money more than two but less than three times the amount of the unlawful income. If the party has not obtained unlawful income yet, it will be fined more than 20,000 but less than 100,000 RMB; if the circumstances are serious, the Pharmaceutical Production License, Pharmaceutical trading License or Dispensing Permit of Medical Organizations of the seller, lessor or lender shall be revoked, or the pharmaceutical approval certificate shall be recalled. Those whose acts constitute a crime shall be investigated for criminal liabilities.

Article 83 Those who violate this Law by providing false certificates or samples of documents, or obtaining the Pharmaceutical Production License, the Pharmaceutical Trading License, the Dispensing Permit of Medical Organizations or pharmaceutical approval certificates through cheating, shall have their Pharmaceutical Production License, Pharmaceutical Trade License, or Dispensing Permit of Medical Organizations revoked, have their pharmaceutical approval certificates revoked, have their application rejected for 5 years, and have a concurrent fine of more than 10,000 but less than 30,000 RMB be imposed upon them.

Article 84 If a medical organization sells its preparations on the market, it shall be ordered to correct its mistakes, have its unlawfully sold preparations confiscated and concurrently be fined a sum of money more than two but less than three times the value of the unlawfully sold preparations. If it has obtained any unlawful income, the unlawful income shall be confiscated.

Article 85 If a pharmaceutical trading enterprise violates Article 18 and Article 19 of this law, it shall be ordered to amend itself and be served a warning. If the circumstances are serious, its Pharmaceutical Trading License shall be revoked.

Article 86 A medicine whose mark is not in conformity with Article 54 of this Law shall be handled as fake medicine or medicine of inferior quality. In addition, a correction shall be made and a warning shall be served. If the circumstances are serious, the approval certificate of this medicine shall be revoked.

Article 87 A pharmaceutical inspection institution which produces false inspection reports, where the circumstances are so serious as to constitute a crime, shall be investigated for criminal liabilities; if a crime is not constituted, it shall be ordered to amend and be served a warning. The institution shall be concurrently imposed a fine of more than 30,000 but less than 50,000 RMB, and the person-in-charge and other personnel directly liable shall be demoted, dismissed from their posts, or expelled according to law, and shall be concurrently be fined less than 30,000 RMB. If any unlawful income has been obtained, the unlawful income shall

be confiscated. If the circumstances are serious, the inspection qualification certificate shall be revoked. If an inspection institution produces false inspection reports and causes serious consequences, it shall bear corresponding liabilities for compensation.

Article 88 The decision to impose administrative sanctions stipulated from Article 73 to Article 87 by this Law shall be made by the pharmaceutical supervisory and administrative departments at or above the county level in conformity with the division of functions prescribed by the pharmaceutical supervisory and administrative department under the State Council. The original issue and approval departments shall decide regarding the revocation of the Pharmaceutical Production License, the Pharmaceutical Trading License, the Dispensing Permit of Medical Organizations, the practicing permit of medical organizations, and the pharmaceutical approval certificates.

Article 89 Violations of Article 55, 56, 57 of this Law concerning the price control of pharmaceuticals shall be punished according to the Price Law of the People's Republic of China.

Article 90 If pharmaceutical producing enterprises, trading enterprises and medical organizations give or receive commissions or other interests in secret during the purchase or sale of pharmaceuticals; and if pharmaceutical producing enterprises, trading enterprises or their agents give any property or other interests to the directors, buyers, physicians and other relevant persons in the medical organizations where their medicines are used, a fine of more than 10,000 but less than 200,000 RMB shall be imposed and the unlawful income shall be confiscated by the government body of industry and commerce administration who, if the circumstances are serious, shall revoke the business licenses of the pharmaceutical producing enterprises and pharmaceutical trading enterprises, and shall notify the pharmaceutical supervisory and administrative departments which shall revoke the Pharmaceutical Production License and Pharmaceutical Trading License. If a crime is constituted, an investigation shall be made for criminal liabilities.

Article 91 If directors or buyers of pharmaceutical producing enterprises or trading enterprises receive any property or other interests from other producing enterprises, trading enterprises or their agents during the purchase or sale of medicines, they shall be punished according to relevant regulations and shall have their unlawful income confiscated. If a crime is constituted, an investigation shall be made for criminal liabilities.

If the directors, buyers, physicians or other relevant persons in medical organizations receive any property or other interests from pharmaceutical producing enterprises, pharmaceutical trading enterprises or their agents, they shall be punished by the administrative departments of health or the work units where they work, and have their unlawful income confiscated. If practicing physicians seriously violate the law, his practice certificate shall be revoked by the administrative departments of health. If a crime is constituted, an investigation shall be made for criminal liabilities in conformity with relevant laws and regulations.

Article 92 Those who act against the administrative regulations concerning pharmaceutical advertisement as provided in this Law shall be sanctioned in conformity with the Advertisement Law of the PRC, have its advertisement registration number revoked by the pharmaceutical supervisory and administrative departments from which the registration number has been issued, and its application for the approval of the advertisement regarding this variety of medicines shall not be accepted for 1 year. If a crime is constituted, an investigation of criminal liabilities shall be made in conformity with relevant laws and regulations.

If a pharmaceutical supervisory or administrative department does not perform its duty of inspection on pharmaceutical advertisements which results in the publishing of advertisements containing falsehoods or other content against laws and administrative regulations, the directly liable person in charge and other responsible personnel shall be subject to administrative sanction. If their acts constitute a crime, they shall be investigated for criminal liabilities in conformity with relevant regulations.

Article 93 If pharmaceutical producing enterprises, trading enterprises or medical organizations act against this law which results in damages to the users of pharmaceuticals, they shall bear liabilities of compensation in conformity with relevant regulations.

Article 94 If a pharmaceutical supervisory and administrative department violates this law with one of the following acts, a competent authority of a higher level or a supervisory organization shall order it to withdraw the unlawfully issued certificates, revoke the pharmaceutical approval certificates, and render administrative sanctions against the directly liable person in charge and other responsible personnel. If their acts constitute a crime, they shall be investigated for criminal liabilities.

1. Issue a certificate of qualification to an enterprise which does not meet the requirements of the "Quality Control Standard of Pharmaceutical Production" and the "Quality Control Standard of Pharmaceutical Trading," fail to conduct inspections according to relevant regulations on the enterprises which have already obtained certificates, or fail to order the unqualified enterprises to amend themselves or revoke their certificates according to relevant regulations; or (2) issue a Pharmaceutical Production License, a Pharmaceutical Trading License or a Dispensing Permit of Medical Organizations to a unit which does not meet legal requirements;

2. Issue a registration certificate of import to a medicine which does not meet the requirements for import; or
3. Approve a clinic test when the requirements for clinic tests are not met, or issue certificates of new medicines and pharmaceutical approval document numbers when requirements for production are not met.

Article 95 If a pharmaceutical supervisory and administrative department, or an inspection institution it has established, or an organization exclusively engaged in pharmaceutical inspection it has appointed, participates in the production and trade of pharmaceuticals, the responsible authority of a higher level or a supervisory organization shall order it to amend itself and have its unlawful income confiscated. If the circumstances are serious, the directly liable person in charge and other responsible personnel shall be subject to administrative sanctions.

If a staff member in a pharmaceutical supervisory and administrative department, or in an inspection institution it has established, or in an organization exclusively engaged in pharmaceutical inspection it has appointed, participates in the production and trade of pharmaceuticals, he or she shall be subject to administrative sanction.

Article 96 If a pharmaceutical supervisory and administrative department or a pharmaceutical inspection institution it has established or appointed unlawfully collects inspection fees during a pharmaceutical supervision and inspection, it shall be ordered by the government bodies concerned to make reimbursements, and the directly liable person and other responsible personnel shall be subject to administrative sanctions. If the circumstances are serious, the certificate of qualification of the inspection institution which has unlawfully collected inspection fees shall be revoked.

Article 97 A pharmaceutical supervisory and administrative department shall perform its duty of supervision and inspection according to laws and regulations, and shall supervise the production and trade of the enterprises which have obtained a Pharmaceutical Production License or a Pharmaceutical Trade License according to the regulations of this Law.

If an enterprise which has obtained a Pharmaceutical Production License or a Pharmaceutical Trade License produces and sells fake medicines and medicines of inferior quality, the enterprise shall be investigated for legal liabilities according to laws and regulations. In addition, the directly liable person in charge and other responsible personnel in the pharmaceutical supervisory and administrative department who have neglected or have been derelict in their duty shall be subject to administrative sanction. If a crime is constituted, the party shall be investigated for criminal liabilities according to laws and regulations.

Article 98 A pharmaceutical supervisory and administrative department shall, within a prescribed time limit, order a pharmaceutical supervisory and administrative department of a lower level to correct an administrative act which is not in conformity with this Law. If the administrative act is not corrected within the prescribed time limit, the department shall have the power to change or repeal it.

Article 99 If the personnel of the pharmaceutical supervision and administration misuse their authority, engage in irregular practices due to favoritism, or neglect their duties to such an extent that a crime is constituted, they shall be investigated for criminal liabilities. If their acts have not constituted a crime, they shall be subject to administrative sanctions.

Article 100 If a Pharmaceutical Production License or a Pharmaceutical Trade License is revoked according to this Law, the pharmaceutical supervisory and administrative department shall notify the industry and commerce administrative department to alter or annul the registration.

Article 101 The value of goods as prescribed in this chapter is designated according to the marked price of the unlawfully made or sold medicines. In the absence of a marked price, the value of goods shall be designated according to the market price of pharmaceuticals of the same kind.

Chapter X Supplementary Provisions

Article 102 For the purpose of this Law, the following definitions are offered:

"Pharmaceuticals" means the articles intended for use in the prevention, treatment or diagnosis of human diseases, or intended to effect the purposive regulation of human physiological functions, for which indications or major functions, usage and dosage are prescribed. They include raw traditional Chinese medicinal materials, traditional medicines prepared in ready-to-use forms, and other prepared Chinese medicines, medicinal chemicals and their preparations, antibiotics, biochemical medicines, radioactive drugs, serums, vaccines, blood products, diagnostic aids, etc.

"Supplementary materials" means the excipients and additives used for the production and dispensing of pharmaceuticals.

"Pharmaceutical producing enterprise" means an enterprise exclusively or partly engaged in the production of pharmaceuticals.

"Pharmaceutical trading enterprise" means an enterprise exclusively or partly engaged in the trade of pharmaceuticals.

Article 103 Measures for the control of cultivation, collection and breeding of all categories of medicinal materials used in traditional Chinese medicine shall be separately formulated by the State Council.

Article 104 The State Council shall formulate detailed measures to carry out special control on the circulation of preventive bio-products.

Article 105 Detailed measures for the implementation of this law by the Chinese People's Army shall be formulated by the State Council and the Central Military Committee of the State on the basis of this Law.

Article 106 This Law shall enter into force as of December 1, 2001.

Appendix 1
MEASURES FOR THE CONTROL OF PSYCHOTROPIC DRUGS

(Approved by the 25th Executive Meeting of the State Council on November 15, 1988 and promulgated by Decree No. 24 of the State Council of the People's Republic of China on December 27, 1988 and effective as of the date of promulgation)

Chapter I General Provisions
Article 1 These Measures are formulated in accordance with the Medicine Administration Law of the People's Republic of China in order to further control psychotropic drugs.

Article 2 Psychotropic drugs refer to those drugs that produce direct effect on the central nerve system so as to excite or sooth the sense and may result in drug dependence through constant use.

Article 3 According to the extent of drug dependence and hazards to health, psychotropic drugs are classified into category I and category II. The classification shall be done by the Ministry of Public Health.

Chapter II The Production of Psychotropic Drugs
Article 4 Psychotropic drugs shall be produced according to the plan by the production units appointed by the State. No other unit or individual shall be allowed to engage in the production of psychotropic drugs. The units that may produce raw materials of psychotropic drugs and psychotropic drugs of category I shall be appointed jointly by the Ministry of Public Health and the State Administration for Medicine. The units that may produce psychotropic drugs of category II shall be appointed jointly by the health administration department at the provincial, autonomous regional or municipal (directly under the Central Government) level and the administrative department for medicine at the corresponding level.

Article 5 The annual production plan for raw materials of psychotropic drugs and for the psychotropic drugs of category I shall be made jointly by the Ministry of Public Health and the State Administration for Medicine. The annual production plan for the psychotropic drugs of category II shall be made jointly by the health administration department at the provincial, autonomous regional or municipal (directly under the Central Government) level and the administrative department for medicine at the corresponding level. Without authorization, no production unit shall be allowed to change the production plan of psychotropic drugs.

Article 6 Raw materials of psychotropic drugs and psychotropic drugs shall be allotted by the State according to plan. No production unit shall be allowed to sell them without authorization.

Article 7 The units that produce raw materials of psychotropic drugs and the units that produce psychotropic drugs must establish a strict control system. The raw materials and the drugs must be kept in separate storage under the charge of person(s) specially appointed for the purpose. They must make regular reports about the fulfillment of the seasonal production plan to the health administration department at the provincial, autonomous regional or municipal (directly under the Central Government) level and the administration department for medicine at the corresponding level and send copies of the reports to the Ministry of Public Health and the State Administration for Medicine for the record. Waste materials discharged during the production of psychotropic drugs must be treated properly so as not to pollute the environment.

Chapter III The Supply of Psychotropic Drugs
Article 8 Raw materials of psychotropic drugs and psychotropic drugs of category I shall be allotted or purchased by the drug dealer units appointed jointly by the Ministry of Public Health and the State Administration for Medicine. Psychotropic drugs of category II shall be handled by the drug dealer units appointed jointly by the health administrative department at or above the county level and the administrative department for medicine at the corresponding level. No other unit or individual shall be allowed to engage in the trading of psychotropic drugs.

Article 9 The plan for the supply of raw materials of psychotropic drugs and for the supply of psychotropic drugs of category I shall be made jointly by the Ministry of Public Health and the State Administration for Medicine after balancing the plans made by the administration department for medicine of each province, autonomous region or municipality directly under the Central Government and shall be assigned together with the production plan by the Ministry of Public Health and the State Administration for Medicine. The plan for the supply of psychotropic drugs of category II shall be assigned jointly by the health administrative department of each province, autonomous region or municipality directly under the Central Government and the administration department for medicine at the corresponding level.

Article 10 The psychotropic drugs of category I are available only to those medical treatment units appointed by the health administrative department at or above the county level. No retail sale of these drugs shall be allowed at any drug stores. The psychotropic drugs of category II are available to all medical treatment units. Drug stores may sell such drugs by retail on the strength of a doctor's prescription with an official seal of a medical treatment unit stamped on. The prescriptions must be kept for 2 years for reference. Any medical unit in need of psychotropic drugs of category I must purchase them at a designated drugstore with a Purchasing Card for Psychotropic Drugs issued by the health administrative department at or above the county level. The Purchasing Card for Psychotropic Drugs shall be made solely by the Ministry of Public Health.

Article 11 The psychotropic drugs needed in scientific research or teaching shall be provided by the appointed drug dealers with an approval by the health administrative department at or above the county level.

Chapter IV Transportation of Psychotropic Drugs
Article 12 When consigning psycho-pharmaceuticals, the production unit or the supply unit must fill out the full name of the drug on the parcel form, and stamp, in the space for the consigner, a special Seal for Psychotropic drugs.

Article 13 The transportation units must strengthen administration work to ensure prompt shipment of psychotropic drugs by shortening its storage time at the station, on the dock or at the airport. They must not be transported in open wagons on railways and, if by ship, no top loading is allowed; if by truck, they must be securely fastened up and safely protected.

Article 14 In the event that any of the psychotropic drugs is found missing in the course of transportation, the freighter-unit must report the case promptly to the local public security organ and the health administrative department for investigation.

Chapter V The Use of Psychotropic Drugs

Article 15 Doctors must prescribe psychotropic drugs on the basis of the actual need in treatment. Abuse of such drugs is strictly forbidden. Normally, a prescription for the psychotropic drugs of category I shall not exceed the therapeutic dosage for 3 days. A prescription for the psychotropic drugs of category II shall not exceed the therapeutic dosage for 7 days. The prescriptions must be kept for 2 years for reference.

Article 16 On a prescription of psychotropic drugs, the name, age, sex of the user, the name of the drug, dosage and administration must be written down clearly. The drug dealer unit and the medical treatment unit are not allowed to alter the purchasing certificates and the prescriptions for psychotropic drugs.

Article 17 The drug dealer unit and the medical treatment unit are required to keep a balance account book of psychotropic drugs. An inventory of the drugs must be made every 3 months to ensure the stock conforms to the account book. Should anything suspicious is found, a report must be made promptly to the local health administrative department and the latter must make immediate investigation in the matter. Psychotropic drugs purchased by the medical treatment unit can only be used in their unit. No resale of the drugs shall be allowed.

Chapter VI The Import and Export of Psychotropic Drugs

Article 18 The import and export of psychotropic drugs shall be handled by the units appointed by the Ministry of Foreign Economic Relations and Trade in accordance with the State provisions governing foreign trade. The annual plan for the import or export of psychotropic drugs must be submitted to the Ministry of Public Health for examination and approval.

Article 19 Medical treatment units, medical colleges or medical science research institutions that are in need of imported psychotropic drugs must submit an application to the Ministry of Public Health for examination and approval. Only after a License for the Import of Psychotropic Drugs is issued to them can they go through import formalities.

Article 20 The units that export psychotropic drugs are required to submit an application to the Ministry of Public Health, together with an import license issued by the competent government department of the importing country, for examination and approval. Only after a License for the Export of Psychotropic Drugs is issued to them can they go through export formalities.

Article 21 The License for the Import of Psychotropic Drugs and the License for the Export of Psychotropic Drugs shall be exclusively printed by the Ministry of Public health.

Chapter VII Penalty Provisions

Article 22 Any violator of these Measures for any one of the following acts shall be punished by the local health administrative department. The penalty shall cover confiscation of all the psychotropic drugs and the illegal gains, a fine 5–10 times the illegal gains according to the seriousness of the case, suspension of business operations for rectification or revocation of the License for Pharmaceutical Production Enterprise, License for Pharmaceutical Business Enterprise or License for Medicaments:

1. those who produce psychotropic drugs or change the production plan or produce additional kinds of psychotropic drugs without authorization;
2. those who are engaged in the trading of psychotropic drugs without authorization;
3. those who prepare and sell any form of psychotropic drugs without authorization;
4. those who use veterinary psychotropic drugs on the human beings;
5. those who import or export psychotropic drugs without authorization.

Article 23 Those who take advantage of their professional work by prescribing psychotropic drugs to other persons without complying with the rules or by prescribing the psychotropic drugs for themselves, and those who are directly responsible for cheating to gain or abusing the drugs shall be given disciplinary sanctions by the authorities of the unit they are in.

Article 24 Those who violate these rules by producing, shipping or trading psychotropic drugs illegally, if the circumstances are serious enough to constitute a crime, shall be prosecuted for criminal responsibility to be investigated by the judicial organs according to law.

Article 25 A party who is dissatisfied with the decision on an administrative sanction may, within 15 days of receiving the notification on the sanction, make a request for reconsideration to the authorities at the next higher level who shall make a reply within 15 days after it receives the appeal. If he is dissatisfied with the decision of reconsideration, he may, within 15 days of receiving reconsideration decision, bring a suit before a people's court. if, upon the expiration of this period, the party has neither complied with the sanction nor has brought a suit before a people's court, the authorities that impose the sanction shall request the people's court to issue an injunction for compulsory enforcement.

Chapter VIII Supplementary Provisions

Article 26 Specific measures for the control of veterinary psychotropic drugs shall be formulated jointly by the Ministry of Agriculture and the Ministry of Public Health in accordance with these Measures.

Article 27 The right to interpret these Measures resides in the Ministry of Public Health.

Article 28 These Measures shall go into effect as of the date of promulgation.

Appendix 2
MEASURES FOR THE CONTROL OF NARCOTIC DRUGS

(Promulgated by the State Council of the People's Republic of China on November 28, 1987)

Chapter I General Provisions

Article 1 These Measures are formulated in accordance with the Medicine Administration Law of the People's Republic of China, for the purpose of tightening control over narcotic drugs so as to ensure their safe use in medical treatment units, medical colleges and medical research institutions.

Article 2 Narcotic drugs refer to those drugs that may cause dependence and addiction after continuous administration.

Article 3 Narcotic drugs include opium, cocaine, marijuana, synthetic anesthetic drugs and those defined by the Ministry of Public Health as addict-forming drugs, anesthetic raw herbs and the products made from them.

Article 4 The State shall strictly supervise and control the cultivation of the mother plants of narcotics and the production, supply, export and import of narcotic drugs. Narcotic drugs shall not be used except for the purpose of medical treatment, teaching and research when necessary.

Chapter II The Cultivation of Mother Plants of Narcotics and the Production of Narcotic Drugs

Article 5 The units that cultivate mother plants of narcotics must be examined and approved jointly by the Ministry of Public Health, the Ministry of Agriculture, Animal Husbandry and Fishery and the State Administration for Medicine. A copy of the report shall be sent to the Ministry of Public Security. The units that produce narcotic drugs must be examined and approved jointly by the Ministry of Public Health and the State Administration for Medicine. Without approval, no unit or individual shall be allowed to produce narcotic drugs.

Article 6 The annual cultivation plan for mother plants of narcotics shall be examined and approved jointly by the Ministry of Public Health and the Ministry of Agriculture, Animal Husbandry and Fishery. The annual production plan of narcotic drugs shall be examined and approved jointly by the Ministry of Public Health and the State Administration for Medicine. The cultivation units and the production units shall not change the plans without authorization. The cultivation unit and the production unit must assign a person or persons with the special responsibility for the storage of the finished products, semi-finished products, poppy capsules and poppy seeds. Sale or use of these things without authorization shall be strictly prohibited.

Article 7 Narcotic drugs must be brought under strict quality control. The quality of the products must meet the standards set for medicines by the State.

Article 8 Before the development of any new kind of narcotic drugs, the research unit must first of all draw up a plan and submit it to the Ministry of Public Health for examination and approval. After the new drug is developed, the research and trial production units must go through the formalities for the approval of such new drugs. The storage and use of the trial products must follow strict procedures so as to prevent their loss.

Chapter III The Supply of Narcotic Drugs

Article 9 Narcotic drugs shall be provided in a planned way according to the demand of medical treatment units, medical colleges and scientific research institutions. A national supply plan of narcotic drugs shall be drawn by a department appointed by the State

Administration for Medicine and submitted to the Ministry of Public Health and the State Administration for Medicine for examination and approval before it is issued for implementation.

Article 10 The plan for the setting up of a trading unit of narcotic drugs shall be put forward jointly by the administrative department of health and medicine administrative department in each province, autonomous region, or municipality directly under the Central Government and shall be examined and approved by the Ministry of Public Health and the State Administration for Medicine. The trading units shall provide narcotic drugs only to those consumer units approved by the administrative department of health and within the prescribed quota. No supply for any other unit or person is permitted.

Article 11 Poppy capsules used for medical purposes shall be supplied by the trading units appointed by the State Administration for Medicine and medicine department in each province, autonomous region, or municipality directly under the Central Government. No other unit shall be allowed to engage in such business. Poppy capsules must be allotted to the consumer units in accordance with the plan examined and approved jointly by the Ministry of Public Health and the State Administration for Medicine. Poppy capsules shall be supplied to the medical treatment units for clinical use and to the trading units designated by the administrative departments of health at or above the county level for clinical application endorsed with an office seal of their respective medical treatment units. No retail sale of poppy capsules is allowed. The pharmaceutical factories that need poppy capsules in the production of ready made Chinese medicine must submit plans to the medicine administrative department in their province, autonomous region, or municipality directly under the Central Government for examination and then to the administrative department of health for approval before production.

Article 12 A trading unit of narcotic drugs must have a special storehouse or counter(s) with good storage conditions and assign a person or persons with special responsibility for the storage, transportation and supply of narcotic drugs.

Chapter IV Transportation of Narcotic Drugs

Article 13 A permit for domestic consignment issued by the Ministry of Public Health is needed when going through shipment formalities for transporting medicinal opium. Shipment of medicinal opium from the cultivation unit to the storehouse of the State Administration for Medicine shall be escorted by the people sent by the consignor unit. Shipment of medicinal opium from the storehouse to the production enterprises shall be escorted by the people sent by consignee unit. The number of escorts shall be decided in accordance with the regulations of the transportation department. Permit for domestic transportation of such drugs shall be printed solely by the Ministry of Public Health.

Article 14 When consigning narcotic drugs or poppy capsules (not including medicinal opium), the production unit or the supply unit must put down clearly the words of Narcotic Drug in the blank for the name of goods on the shipping document and a seal for consignment of Narcotic Drug must be stamped in the space left for the consignor.

Article 15 The freighter unit must tighten control over the shipment of narcotic drugs and poppy capsules by dispatching the consignment promptly and shortening its storage time at the station, on the dock or at the airport. They must not be transported in open wagons on railways and, if by ship, no loading on hold surface is allowed and, if by truck, they must be securely fastened up and safely protected.

Article 16 In the event that any of the narcotic drugs or poppy capsules are found missing in the course of transportation, the freighter-unit must report the case promptly to the local public security organ and the administrative department of health for investigation.

Chapter V Import and Export of Narcotic Drugs

Article 17 The import and export of narcotic drugs shall be handled by the units appointed by the Ministry of Foreign Economic Relations and Trade in accordance with State regulations concerning foreign trade. No other units shall be allowed to engage in the business. The annual plan for import and export of narcotic drugs shall be subject to examination and approval by the Ministry of Public Health.

Article 18 The import of narcotic drugs needed in medical treatment units, medical colleges of or medical science research institutions must be verified and approved by the Ministry of Public Health. Only after an Import License for Narcotic Drugs is granted can these units apply to go through import formalities.

Article 19 The export of narcotic drugs must be verified and approved by the Ministry of Public Health. An application and an import license which is a prerequisite to going through import formalities for narcotic drugs issued by the competent government department of the importing country must be presented before the Ministry of Public Health issues an Export License for Narcotic Drugs.

Article 20 Import and export licenses for narcotic drugs shall be printed exclusively by the Ministry of Public Health.

Chapter VI The Use of Narcotic Drugs

Article 21 Narcotic drugs shall only be used for medical treatment, in teaching at medical colleges and in medical science research. Any medical treatment unit with medical wards and with surgical or other necessary medical treatment facilities may file an application to the local administrative department of health. Upon approval by the administrative department of health at a higher level, and after the level of supply is verified, a Purchase Card for Narcotic Drugs shall be issued. The aforesaid unit may purchase the needed narcotic drugs from the designated trading units according to the fixed quota. When the medical colleges or scientific research institutions are in need of narcotic drugs, they shall file an application to the administrative department of health at a higher level and, upon approval, may purchase these drugs from the trading units of narcotic drugs. The Ministry of Public Health is the authority to make out the grading standard of rations.

Article 22 Narcotic consuming unit must fill out an application form for when purchasing, narcotic drugs and the supplying unit must check the various seals and the number of seals stamped on the form before supplying them with the kind of drugs on quarterly ration as stipulated in the regulations set by the Ministry of Public Health.

Article 23 The unit in need of narcotic drugs can either purchase them directly from the trading units or by mail order. In the latter case, however, the shipping documents and certificates must be sent out by registered mail. When sending the narcotic drugs by post, the sender-trading unit is required to stamp a Seal for Narcotic Drugs on the parcel form and to present to the post office the invoice with a Seal for Narcotic Drugs stamped on.

Article 24 Preparations that fall under the category of narcotic drugs must be purchased from the trading units of narcotic drugs. In case that they are not available or special preparations are needed by the medical treatment units, the authorized consuming medical units may prepare them by themselves with approval by the administrative department of health at or above the county level. No other unit shall be allowed to prepare any form of anesthetics.

Article 25 The medical worker who prescribes any anesthetics for the patient must be a qualified physician or a surgeon, who is tested to have been able to use such drugs properly. The surgeon at the induced abortion ward who is tested to have been able to use such drugs properly may have the right to prescribe anesthetics for the person to be operated on.

Article 26 Dosage for injection in each prescription must not exceed 2 days of daily dose, as for the tablet, tincture, syrup, the dosage must not exceed 3 days of daily dose. Administration of narcotic must not exceed a period of 7 days running. Prescription of narcotic drugs must be fully and clearly stated with signature of the physician or surgeon on. When preparing a narcotic drug, the pharmacist and the checker are required to sign their names and keep the prescription of the narcotic drug on file. No medical worker is allowed to prescribe any narcotic drug for him/herself.

Article 27 In the case of a patient in serious conditions who is diagnosed by a hospital at or above county level to be in need of narcotic drugs as a pain killer, the hospital appointed by the administrative department of health at or above the county level may issue the patient with a Special Purchasing Card for Narcotic on the basis of the Prescription and by checking his permanent residence booklet, and the patient may take this to the appointed medical treatment unit to have the drug prepared. If the patient holding a Special Purchasing Card for Narcotic is in need of a larger dose and the seasonal ration of the medical treatment unit fails to meet the demand, additional amount of narcotic shall be made available only with the approval by the administrative department of health at a higher level.

Article 28 Medical treatment units are required to tighten control over narcotic drugs. Any illegal use, storage, transfer or borrowing of narcotic drugs is prohibited. Narcotic drugs must be put under the charge of a person specially appointed for the purpose and kept in a separate place under lock. The distribution and prescriptions of narcotic drugs must be kept in record separately from those of other medicine. The prescriptions must be kept on file for a period of 3 years. The medical treatment unit shall have the right to refuse dispensing of drugs to those who abuse them in violation of relevant rules and regulations and shall report the case to the local administrative department of health promptly.

Article 29 In the event of an emergency case which is in need of narcotic drugs, the medical treatment unit so involved and the trading unit of narcotic drugs are required to supply a dose of narcotic promptly for the case only, and the necessary formalities shall be done after the event.

Chapter VII Penalty Provisions

Article 30 Any violation of these Measures shall be subject to penalty by the local administrative department of health according to the seriousness of the case. The penalty shall cover confiscation of all the narcotic drugs and the illegal earnings, a fine ranging from 5 to 10 times the illegal profits, closing down of the business or revocation of "License for Pharmaceutical Production Enterprise", "License for Pharmaceutical Business Enterprise" or "License for Medicaments"

1. those who, without authorization, are engaged in the production of narcotic drugs or have changed the production plan and made additional kinds of narcotic drugs;
2. those who are engaged in unauthorized trading business of narcotic drugs and poppy capsules;
3. those who supply or oversupply narcotics to any unit or person that has not been granted the permission to use the stuff;
4. those who prepare and sell any form of narcotic drugs without authorization;
5. those who are engaged in unauthorized import or export of narcotic Drugs;
6. those who apply any new kind of narcotic drugs to patients clinically or have produced any new kind of narcotic drugs without authorization.

Article 31 Those who have taken advantage of their professional work by prescribing narcotics to other persons without complying with the rules or by prescribing narcotics for themselves, and those who are directly responsible for cheating to obtain or abusing the stuff, shall be given disciplinary sanctions by the authorities of their units.

Article 32 Those who, in violation of these Measures, cultivate poppy without authorization or take in narcotic drugs illegally shall be punished by a public security organ in accordance with the Regulations on Administrative Penalties for Public Security or other related rules.

Article 33 With respect to any one who produces, transports or sells narcotics or poppy capsules, if the circumstances are serious enough to constitute a crime, he shall be prosecuted for criminal liability by the judicial organs according to law.

Article 34 A party, who is dissatisfied with the decision on an administrative sanction may, within 15 days of receiving the notification on the sanction, make a request for reconsideration to the authorities at the level next higher, which shall make a reply within 10 days of receipt of the appeal. If he is dissatisfied with the decision on reconsideration, he may, within 15 days of receiving the reconsideration decision, bring a suit before a people's court. If, upon the expiration of this period, the party has neither complied with the sanction nor has brought a suit before a people's court, the authorities that impose the sanction shall apply to the people's court for compulsory enforcement.

Chapter VIII Supplementary Provisions

Article 35 The specific administration rules for the supply and use of narcotic drugs in the health and medical treatment units of the Chinese People's Liberation Army and the Chinese People's Armed Police Force shall be formulated jointly by the Ministry of Public Health, the General Logistics Department of the Chinese People's Liberation Army and the Logistics Department of the Chinese People's Armed Police Force in accordance with these Measures.

Article 36 The specific administration rules for the supply and use of veterinary narcotic drugs shall be formulated jointly by the Ministry of Public Health and the Ministry of Agriculture, Animal Husbandry and Fishery in accordance with these Measures.

Article 37 The rules for the implementation of these Measures shall be formulated by the Ministry of Public Health.

Article 38 These Measures shall go into effect as of the date of promulgation. The Provisions for the Administration of Narcotic Drugs, promulgated by the State Council of the People's Republic of China on September 13, 1978, shall become null and void on the same day.

1.2.2 Regulations for Implementation of the Drug Administration Law of the People's Republic of China

Table of Content

Preface
Chapter I General Provisions
Chapter II Control over Drug Manufacturers
Chapter III Control over Drug Distributors
Chapter IV Control over Pharmaceuticals in Medical Institutions
Chapter V Control over Drugs
Chapter VI Control over Drug Packaging
Chapter VII Control over Drug Pricing and Advertising
Chapter VIII Inspection of Drugs
Chapter IX Legal Liabilities
Chapter X Supplementary Provisions

Decree of the State Council of the People's Republic of China, No. 360
The Regulations for Implementation of the Drug Administration Law of the People's Republic of China are hereby promulgated and shall go into effect as of September 15, 2002 (SFDA 2002).

Chapter I General Provisions
Article 1 The Regulations are formulated in accordance with the Drug Administration Law of the People's Republic of China (hereinafter referred to as the Drug Administration law).

Article 2 The drug regulatory department under the State Council shall establish a national drug testing institute.

The drug regulatory department of the people's government of the province, autonomous region or municipality directly under the Central Government may establish drug testing institutes within its respective administrative area. The plan for the establishment of local drug testing institutes shall be proposed by the drug regulatory department of the people's government of the province, autonomous region and municipality directly under the Central Government and submitted to the people's government of the province, autonomous region and municipality directly under the Central Government for approval.

The drug regulatory department under the State Council and the drug regulatory department of the people's government of the province, autonomous region or municipality directly under the Central Government may, when necessary, designate any testing institute fulfilling the requirements for drug testing to undertake drug testing.

Chapter II Control over Drug Manufacturers
Article 3 A Drug Manufacturing Certificate shall be acquired for establishment of a drug manufacturer according to the following procedures:

1. The applicant shall submit an application to the drug regulatory department of the people's government of the province, autonomous region or municipality directly under the Central Government, where the manufacturing site is to be located. The drug regulatory department of the people's government of the province, autonomous region or municipality directly under the Central Government shall, within 30 working days from the date it receives the application, make a review according to the pharmaceutical industry development programs and policies issued by the State and make a decision on approval or disapproval.
2. After completion of establishment of the planned manufacturer, the applicant shall apply to the original approving department for acceptance inspection. The original approving department shall, within 30 working days from the date it receives the application, arrange an acceptance inspection according to the requirements for the establishment of such manufacturers set forth in Article 8 of the Drug Administration Law; a Drug Manufacturing Certificate shall be issued to the applicant if the inspection is passed. The applicant shall, by holding the Drug Manufacturing Certificate, register with the administrative department for industry and commerce in accordance with law.

Article 4 Any drug manufacturer that intends to alter the approved items in the Drug Manufacturing Certificate shall, 30 days prior to alteration of any approved items, apply to the original certificate-issuing authority for registration of alteration; no approved items may be altered without approval. The original certificate-issuing authority shall make a decision within 15 working days from the date it receives the application. The application shall, by holding the Drug Manufacturing Certificate with altered items, register the alteration with the administrative department for industry and commerce in accordance with law.

Article 5 The drug regulatory department of the people's government at or above the provincial level shall organize inspections of drug manufacturers in accordance with the Good Manufacturing Practice for Pharmaceutical Products (GMP) and the measures and schedule for implementing the GMP formulated by the drug regulatory department under the State Council, and issue a certificate to the manufacturer that complies with the GMP. For the manufacturer producing injections or radioactive pharmaceuticals and for that producing biological products specified by the drug regulatory department under the State Council, the inspection of which shall be conducted by the drug regulatory department under the State Council. The format of GMP certificate shall be uniformly provided for by the drug regulatory department under the State Council.

Article 6 Any newly-established drug manufacturer or manufacturer with newly-built drug manufacturing workshops or newly-added dosage forms for production shall, within 30 days from the date it obtains the approval documents for manufacturing drug or from the date its formal production is approved, apply to the drug regulatory department for GMP certification as required. The drug regulatory department accepting the application shall, within 6 months from the date it receives the application, organize inspections as to the compliance with the GMP requirements by the applying manufacturer. A certificate shall be issued to the manufacturer if the inspection is passed.

Article 7 The drug regulatory department under the State Council shall set up a database of GMP inspectors. A GMP inspector shall be qualified as required by the drug regulatory department under the State Council. A GMP inspection shall be conducted by a team of inspectors randomly selected from the database of GMP inspectors according to the provisions of the drug regulatory department under the State Council.

Article 8 The valid term of a Drug Manufacturing Certificate is 5 years. To continue its drug production, the Certificate holder shall, 6 months prior to the expiry date of the Certificate, apply for the renewal of the Drug Manufacturing Certificate according to the provisions of the drug regulatory department under the State Council.

Where a drug manufacturer terminates its drug production or is closed down, its Drug Manufacturing Certificate shall be withdrawn by the original certificate-issuing authority.

Article 9 Any drug substance used by a drug manufacturer to produce drug products shall have a drug approval number or an import drug license or a pharmaceutical product license issued by the drug regulatory department under the State Council upon examination, with the exception of Chinese crude drugs and the prepared slices of Chinese crude drugs over which no control by approval number is exercised.

Article 10 In accordance with the provisions in Article 13 of the Drug Administration Law, any drug manufacturer being entrusted with contract production of the drug shall have a GMP certificate corresponding to the contracted drug.

No vaccines, blood products or other drugs specified by the drug regulatory department under the State Council may be contracted for production.

Chapter III Control over Drug Distributors

Article 11 For establishment of a drug wholesaler, the applicant shall submit an application to the drug regulatory department of the people's government of the province, autonomous region or municipality directly under the Central Government, where the planned drug wholesaler is to be located. The drug regulatory department of the people's government of the province, autonomous region or municipality directly under the Central Government shall, within 30 working days from the date it receives the application, make a decision on approval or disapproval according to the standards for establishment set forth by the drug regulatory department under the State Council. After completion of establishment of the planned wholesaler, the applicant shall apply to the original approving department for acceptance inspection. The original approving department shall, within 30 working days from the date it receives the application, organize an acceptance inspection according to the requirements for establishment of drug distributors set forth in Article 15 or the Drug Administration Law and issue the Drug Supply Certificate to the applicant if the inspection is passed. The applicant shall, with the Certificate, register with the administrative department for industry and commerce in accordance with law.

Article 12 For establishment of a drug retailer, the applicant shall submit an application to the drug regulatory institution of the municipality divided into districts, or to the drug regulatory institution at the county level which is directly set up by the drug regulatory department of the people's government of the province, autonomous region or municipality directly under the Central Government, where the planned retailer is to be located. The drug regulatory institution accepting the application shall, within 30 working days from the date it receives the application, make a decision on approval or disapproval after the review according to the provisions of the drug regulatory department under the State Council, taking into consideration the number of permanent residents, territory, transportation and practical needs in the place. After completion of establishment of the planned retailer, the applicant shall apply to the original approving department for acceptance inspections. The original approving department shall, within 15 working days from the date it receives the application, organize acceptance inspections according to the requirements for establishment of drug distributors set forth in Article 15 of the Drug Administration Law and issue a Drug Supply Certificate if inspections are passed. The applicant shall, with the Certificate, register with the administrative department for industry and commerce in accordance with law.

Article 13 The drug regulatory department of the people's government of the province, autonomous region or municipality directly under the Central Government shall be responsible for the certification of drug distributors. A drug distributor shall, according to the implementing measures and schedule formulated by the drug regulatory department under the State Council, undergo the Good Supply Practice for Pharmaceutical Products (GSP) inspections organized by the local drug regulatory department of the people's government of the province, autonomous region or municipality directly under the Central Government and obtain a GSP certificate. The format of GSP certificate shall be uniformly provided for by the drug regulatory department under the State Council.

Any newly-established drug wholesaler or retailer shall, within 30 days from the date it obtains the Drug Supply Certificate, apply for the GSP certification to the drug regulatory department or institution which has issued it the Drug Supply Certificate. The drug regulatory institution accepting the drug retailer's application for certification shall, within 7 working days from the date it receives the application, transfer the application to the drug regulatory department of the people's government of the province, autonomous region or municipality directly under the Central Government, which is responsible for organizing inspections of drug distributors. The drug regulatory department of the people's government of the province, autonomous region or municipality directly under the Central government shall, within 3 months from the date it receives the application, organize inspections of the drug wholesaler or retailer as to its compliance with the GSP according to the provisions of the drug regulatory department under the State Council and issue a GSP certificate to the drug wholesaler or retailer passing the inspections.

Article 14 A database of GSP inspectors shall be set up by the drug regulatory department of the people's government of the province, autonomous region or municipality directly under the Central Government. A GSP inspector shall be qualified as required by the drug regulatory department under the State Council. A GSP inspection shall be conducted by a team of inspectors randomly selected from the said database according to the provisions of the drug regulatory department under the State Council.

Article 15 The State adopts a classification system for prescription drugs and non-prescription drugs. The State subdivides non-prescription drugs into Class A drugs and Class B drugs according to the level of safety.

Any drug retailer distributing prescription drugs or Class A non-prescription drugs shall have licensed pharmacists or other pharmaceutical technicians whose qualifications are legally recognized. Any retailer distributing Class B non-prescription drugs shall have pharmacy staff members who have passed the examination organized by the local drug regulatory institution of the municipality divided into districts or by the local drug regulatory institution at the county level which is directly set up by the drug regulatory department of the people's government of the province, autonomous region or municipality directly under the Central Government.

Article 16 Any drug distributor that intends to alter the approved items in the Drug Supply Certificate shall, 30 days prior to the alteration of any approved items, apply to the original certificate-issuing authority for registration of alteration; no approved items may be altered without approval. The original certificate-issuing authority shall make a decision within 15 working days from the date it receives the application. The application shall, by holding the Drug Supply Certificate with the altered items, register the alteration with the administrative department for industry and commerce in accordance with law.

Article 17 The valid term of a Drug Supply Certificate is 5 years. To continue its drug distribution, the Certificate holder shall, 6 months prior to the expiry date of the Certificate, apply for the renewal of the Drug Supply Certificate according to the provisions of the drug regulatory department under the State Council.

Where a drug distributor terminates its drug distribution or is closed down, its Drug Supply Certificate shall be withdrawn by the original certificate-issuing authority.

Article 18 Where there is no drug retailers at town or country fairs in remote areas with poor communications, the local drug retailers may, after obtaining approval from the local drug regulatory institution of the county (municipality) and being registered with the administrative department for industry and commerce, set up stores at the fairs to sell non-prescription drugs within the approved scope for drug distribution.

Article 19

Drug manufacturers, drug distributors and medical institutions engaged in on-line drug transactions through Internet and the drugs so transacted shall be in conformity with the provisions in the Drug Administration Law and in the Regulations. The measures for administration of on-line drug distribution services shall be formulated by the drug regulatory department under the State Council jointly with the other relevant departments under the State Council.

Chapter IV Control over Pharmaceuticals in Medical Institutions

Article 20 To establish a pharmaceutical preparation unit in a medical institution, an application shall be submitted to the local health administrative department of the people's government of the province, autonomous region or municipality directly under the Central Government, and, after being consented upon examination, be presented to the drug regulatory department of the people's government at the same level for review and approval. Approval shall be given to the medical institution if it passes the review by the said drug regulatory department and a Pharmaceutical Preparation Certificate for Medical Institution shall be issued to it.

The health administrative department and the drug regulatory department of the people's government of the province, autonomous region or municipality directly under the Central Government shall, within 30 working days from the dates they receive the application respectively, make their own decisions whether or not to consent or approve the application accordingly.

Article 21 Any medical institution that intends to alter the approved items in the Pharmaceutical Preparation Certificate for Medical Institution shall, 30 days prior to the alteration of any approved items, apply to the original examining and approving departments for registration of alteration according to the provisions in Article 20 of the Regulations; no approved items may be altered without approval. The original examining and approving departments shall make their own decisions within 15 working days from the dates they receive the application respectively.

Any medical institution which intends to add new dosage forms or change dispensing sites shall, after passing the acceptance inspection by the local drug regulatory department of the people's government of the province, autonomous region or municipality directly under the Central Government, go through the registration of alteration of the Pharmaceutical Preparation Certificate for Medical Institution according to the provisions in the preceding paragraph.

Article 22 The valid term of a Pharmaceutical Preparation Certificate for Medical institution is 5 years. To continue dispensing a pharmaceutical preparation, the medical institution shall, 6 month prior to the expiry date of the Certificate, apply for the renewal of the Pharmaceutical Preparation Certificate for Medical Institution according to the provisions of the drug regulatory department under the State Council.

Where a medical institution terminates dispensing Pharmaceutical Preparations or is closed down, its Pharmaceutical Preparation Certificate for Medical Institution shall be withdrawn by the original certificate-issuing authority.

Article 23 To dispense a pharmaceutical preparation, the medical institution shall submit the dossier and samples according to the provisions of the drug regulatory department under the State Council, and the pharmaceutical preparation may only be dispensed after being approved by the local drug regulatory department of the people's government of the province, autonomous region or municipality directly under the Central Government and being issued a pharmaceutical preparation approval number.

Article 24 No pharmaceutical preparations dispensed by medical institutions may be marketed or marketed in disguised forms, nor may any advertisement of such pharmaceutical preparations be released.

When a major disaster, epidemic situation or any other emergency occurs, or there is an urgent need clinically but no supply of the needed drug in market, the pharmaceutical preparations dispensed by a medical institution may be subject to transfer allocation and use by other designated medical institutions within a specified time limit, upon approval by the drug regulatory department under the State Council or by the drug regulatory department of the people's government of a province, autonomous region or municipality directly under the Central Government.

Transfer allocation and use of special pharmaceutical preparations regulated by the drug regulatory department under the State Council, and the transfer allocation and use of pharmaceutical preparations dispensed by medical institutions among provinces, autonomous regions, or municipalities directly under the Central Government shall be subject to the approval by the drug regulatory department under the State Council.

Article 25 Pharmacy personnel of medical institutions who check and dispense prescriptions shall be the pharmaceutical technicians whose qualifications are legally recognized.

Article 26 When purchasing drugs, medical institutions shall keep the authentic and complete records. In purchase records shall be indicted the adopted name of the drug in China, dosage form, strength, batch number, date of expiry, manufacturer, supplier, purchase volume, purchase price, date of purchase and other items specified by the drug regulatory department under the State Council.

Article 27 Drugs provided to patients by medical institutions shall be within the scope of diagnoses and treatments and dispensed according to the prescriptions of licensed doctors or licensed assistant doctors.

The scope of drugs purchased and provided to patients by family planning technical service institutions shall be in conformity with the scope of services approved and the drugs shall be dispensed according to the prescriptions of licensed doctors or licensed assistant doctors.

Out-patient departments, clinics and any other medical institutions, which are set up by individuals, may not purchase or provide drugs other than those commonly used and those for emergency treatment. The range and category of the drugs commonly used and those for emergency treatment shall be determined by the local health administrative department of the people's government of the province, autonomous region, or municipality directly under the Central Government jointly with the drug regulatory department at the same level.

Chapter V Control over Drugs

Article 28 Institutions for non-clinical safety evaluation and study of drugs shall implement the Good Laboratory Practice for Non-Clinical Laboratory Studies (GLP) and institutions for drug clinical trial shall implement the Good Clinical Practice (GCP). The GLP and GCP shall be formulated by the drug regulatory department under the State Council through respective consultation with the science and technology administrative department under the State Council and the health administrative department under the State Council.

Article 29 Clinical trials, manufacturing or importation of drugs shall be in conformity with the provisions in the Drug Administration Law and in the Regulations, and shall be reviewed and approved by the drug regulatory department under the State Council. The drug regulatory department under the State Council may authorize the drug regulatory department of the people's government of the province, autonomous region or municipality directly under the Central Government to conduct site inspection of research and development conditions of the drugs being applied, to conduct preliminary review of the submitted dossier, and to test the pilot samples. The specific measures therefore shall be formulated by the drug regulatory department under the State Council.

Article 30 Any clinical trial to be conducted for research and development of a new drug shall be subject to the approval by the drug regulatory department under the State Council in accordance with the provisions in Article 29 of the Drug Administration Law.

When an application for conducting clinical trials is approved by the drug regulatory department under the State Council, the applicant shall select institutions for clinical trials from the lawfully certified ones to conduct the trials, and make a report thereof to the drug regulatory department and health administrative department under the State Council for the record.

Prior to the drug clinical trial, the institution for drug clinical trial shall provide the subjects or their guardians with the truthful information on the trial, and obtain a written informed consent

Article 31 For production of a drug admitted by national drug standards, an application shall, in accordance with the provisions of the drug regulatory department under the State Council, be submitted to the drug regulatory department of the people's government of the province, autonomous region or municipality directly under the Central Government or to the drug regulatory department under the State Council, and the relevant technical data and supporting documents shall be provided. The drug regulatory department of the people's government of the province, autonomous region or municipality directly under the Central Government shall, within 30 working days from the date it receives the application, review and make comments, and report the matter to the drug regulatory department under the State Council for review while notifying the applicant of its comments. If all the requirements are fulfilled upon review, a drug approval number shall be issued by the drug regulatory department under the State Council.

Article 32 Where a drug is produced according to an interim standard, an application shall be submitted for formalization of the standard 3 months prior to the expiry date of the interim standard according to the provisions of the drug regulatory department under the State Council; the drug regulatory department under the State Council shall, within 12 months from the expiry date of the interim standard, review and approve the interim standard as formal one if it fulfills the requirements for the formalization set forth by the drug regulatory department under the State Council. Where an applicant does not make such an application or the original interim standard fails to fulfill the requirements for the formalization, the drug regulatory department under the State Council shall withdraw the interim standard and the approval number for drug production issued on the basis of the said interim standard.

Article 33 For alteration of any items indicated in the approval documents and their attachments for new drug research and development, production or importation of a drug, a supplementary application shall be submitted to the drug regulatory department under the State Council; if all the requirements are fulfilled upon review, an approval shall be given by the drug regulatory department under the State Council.

Article 34 The drug regulatory department under the State Council may, based on the needs for protection of public health, set an observation period of not more than 5 years for a new drug produced by a drug manufacturer; and no approval shall be given to any other manufacturer to produce or import the said drug during the observations period.

Article 35 The State protects undisclosed data of drug study and others which are independently acquired and submitted by drug manufacturers or sellers to obtain production or marketing approval of the drugs in question which contain new chemical entities. No one may make unfair commercial use of the said data.

Within 6 years from the date a drug manufacturer or seller obtains the approval documents for producing or marketing a drug containing new chemical entities, if any other applicant uses the data mentioned in the preceding paragraph to apply for approval for production or marketing of the drug in question without permission of the original applicant who has obtained the approval, no approval may be given to any other applicant by the drug regulatory department except that the data submitted are acquired independently.

No drug regulatory department may disclose the data set forth in the first paragraph of this Article except

1. for the need of public interests; or
2. where steps are taken to ensure that the data are protected against unfair commercial use.

Article 36 Any drug applied to be imported shall be the one obtained marketing authorization in the country or region of manufacturing. A drug without such an authorization may be approved of its importation in accordance with the provisions in the Drug Administration Law and in the Regulations, provided that its safety, efficacy and clinical needs have been confirmed by the drug regulatory department under the State Council.

For importation of a drug, an application for registration shall be made according to provisions of the drug regulatory department under the State Council. A drug may only be imported after an Import Drug License is given if it is produced by a foreign manufacturer, or a Pharmaceutical Product License is given if it is produced by a manufacturer in Hong Kong, Macao or Taiwan of China.

Article 37 Any medical institution that urgently needs to import a small amount of drugs shall, with a Practicing License of Medical Institution, submit an application to the drug regulatory department under the State Council, and the drugs in question may only be imported upon approval. Such import drugs shall only be used in the designated medical institution for specified purpose.

Article 38 After import drugs arrive at the port, the drug importer shall file a record with the local drug regulatory department in the place where the port is located with the Import Drug License or Pharmaceutical Product License, the original copy of the certificate or origin, duplicate copy of the purchase contract, packing list, bill of freight, shipping invoice, certificate of analysis for the release of drugs by the manufacturer, inset sheet and other documents. The said drug regulatory department shall review the documents submitted and issued a Drug Import Note if they comply with the requirements. The drug importer shall, with the Drug Import Note, complete the formalities for customs declaration and clearance with the Customs.

The drug regulatory department in the place where the port is located shall notify the drug testing institution to conduct sampling and testing of the import drugs on each batch basis with the exception of the circumstances set forth in Article 41 of the Drug Administration Law.

Article 39 Vaccines, blood products, diagnostic reagents in vitro for blood donor screening and other biological products regulated by the drug regulatory department under the State Council shall be subject to testing or review for approval according to the provisions of the drug regulatory department under the State Council before being marketed or imported; any product that fails in testing or has not been approved shall not be marketed or imported.

Article 40 The State encourages cultivation of Chinese crude drugs. Control through approval number shall be exercised over the Chinese crude drugs that can be cultivated or raised on a large scale and in an intensified way and whose quality can be controlled and fulfills the requirements laid down by the drug regulatory department under the State Council.

Article 41 The drug regulatory department under the State Council shall re-evaluate the drugs approved for production and marketing and, on the basis of the re-evaluation results, may take measures to order the revision of insert sheet or suspension of production, marketing or use of a drug, or withdraw the approval documents of drugs with serious adverse reaction or harmful to human health due to other reasons.

Article 42 The valid term of a drug approval number, Import Drug License and Pharmaceutical Product License issued by the drug regulatory department under the State Council is 5 years. To continue its drug production or importation, the applicant shall submit a re-registration application 6 months prior to the expiry date. When making re-registration of a drug, the applicant shall submit the relevant data according to the provisions of the drug regulatory department under the State Council. If no application for the re-registration of a drug is made upon expiration of the valid term, or the application fails to comply with the provisions on re-registration of the drug regulatory department under the State Council upon review, the drug approval number, Import Drug License or Pharmaceutical Product License shall be withdrawn.

Article 43 No contents involving prevention, treatment or diagnosis of human diseases shall be included in the package, label or insert sheet and the related promotional materials for promoting a non-drug product, except as otherwise provided by laws or administrative regulations.

Chapter VI Control over Drug Packaging

Article 44 Immediate packaging materials and containers used by drug manufacturers shall fulfill the requirements for medicinal use and the standards for ensuring human health and safety, and be subject to registration upon approval by the drug regulatory department under the State Council.

The drug regulatory department under the State Council shall be responsible for working out and issuing the measures for control over immediate packaging materials and containers, the product directories and the requirements and standards for medicinal use.

Article 45 Packaging materials and containers selected for production of prepared slices of a Chinese crude drug shall accommodate to drug properties. No prepared slices of a Chinese crude drug may be marketed whose package fails to conform to regulations. A label shall be printed on or attached to the package of prepared slices of a Chinese crude drug.

On the label of prepared slices of a Chinese crude drug shall be indicated the name of the drug, specifications, origin or production, manufacturer, product batch number and production date; if the said drug is controlled by approval number, the drug approval number shall also be indicated.

Article 46 The package, label and insert sheet of a drug shall be printed in accordance with the provisions in Article 54 of the Drug Administration Law and those formulated by the drug regulatory department under the State Council.
The trade name of a drug shall conform to the provisions of the drug regulatory department under the State Council.

Article 47 The immediate packaging materials and containers, used by medical institutions for dispensing pharmaceutical preparations, as well as the labels and insert sheets thereof, shall conform to the provisions in Chapter VI of the Drug Administration Law and the relevant provisions in the Regulations, and be subject to approval by the drug regulatory department of the people's government of the province, autonomous region or municipality directly under the Central Government.

Chapter VII Control over Drug Pricing and Advertising

Article 48 For drug pricing, the State exercises a system under which the prices are fixed or guided by the government or regulated by the market.

For drugs listed in the directory of drugs for national basic medical insurance and drugs not listed in the directory but monopolistically manufactured and distributed, their prices shall be fixed or guided by the government; the prices of other drugs shall be regulated by the market.

Article 49 For a drug whose price is fixed or guided by the government according to law, the competent pricing department of the government shall fix and adjust its sale prices in accordance with the principle set forth in Article 55 of the Drug Administration Law; and, in fixing and adjusting its sale price, control over the average social rate of drug sales cost, drug sales profit margin, and the differential rate in drug circulation shall be manifested. The specific pricing measures shall be formulated by the competent pricing department under the State Council in accordance with the relevant provisions in the Pricing Law of the People's Republic of China (hereinafter referred to as the Pricing Law).

Article 50 For a drug whose price shall be fixed or guided by the government and is so established, the competent pricing department shall publish the said price and specify the date for going into effect in designated publications in accordance with the provisions in article 24 of the Pricing Law.

Article 51 For a drug whose price is fixed or guided by the government, the competent pricing department shall, in fixing or adjusting the price, organize experts in pharmaceutical, medical, economic and other fields to conduct assessment; and, if necessary, it shall solicit comments from drug manufacturers, drug distributors, medical institutions, citizens and other relevant units and persons.

Article 52 The competent pricing department of the government may, in practicing drug price monitoring according to the provisions in Article 28 of the Pricing Law, appoint certain drug manufactures, drug distributors and medical institutions as drug price monitoring units for the purpose of understanding and analyzing the changes and trends of drug prices; the appointed units shall provide cooperation, support and truthful information.

Article 53 For publishing a drug advertisement, the relevant materials shall be submitted to the local drug regulatory department of the people's government of the province, autonomous region or municipality directly under the Central Government where the drug manufacturer is located. The drug regulatory department of the people's government of the province, autonomous region or municipality directly under the Central Government shall, within 10 working days after it receives the relevant materials, make a decision upon review on whether to issue the approval number for drug advertisement. Where the approval number for drug advertisement is issued upon review, a record shall be filed with the drug regulatory department under the State Council concurrently. The specific measures for drug advertisement shall be formulated by the drug regulatory department under the State Council.

For publishing an advertisement for an import drug, an application for approval number for drug advertisement shall be submitted to the local drug regulatory department of the people's government of the province, autonomous region or municipality directly under the Central Government where the drug import agency is located, in accordance with the provisions in the preceding paragraph of this Article.

For publishing an advertisement in a province, autonomous region or municipality directly under the Central Government other than the place where the drug manufacturer or drug import agency is located, any enterprise publishing advertisement shall file a record in advance with the drug regulatory department of the province, autonomous region or municipality directly under the Central Government where the advertisement is to be published. If the drug regulatory department of the province, autonomous region or municipality directly under the Central Government accepting the record finds that the approved contents of the drug advertisement does not conform to the provisions on the control of drug advertisement, it shall turn over the matter to the original verifying and issuing department for handling.

Article 54 For a drug whose production, marketing or use is ordered to be suspended upon decision of the drug regulatory department under the State Council or of the drug regulatory department of the people's government of the province, autonomous region or municipality directly under the Central Government, no advertisement for the drug may be published during the period of suspension; where such an advertisement is already published, the publication shall be discontinued immediately.

Article 55 Any enterprise publishing advertisement, advertising agent or advertisement publisher shall immediately discontinue the publication of any drug advertisement without approval by the drug regulatory department of the people's government of the province, autonomous region or municipality directly under the Central Government, or whose approval number for drug advertisement is forged, or belongs to others, or is expired, or, whose approval number for drug advertisement is canceled because of other illegal advertising activities.

Where a drug advertisement is published in violation of law and the circumstances are serious, the drug regulatory department of the people's government of the province, autonomous region or municipality directly under the Central Government may announce the matter to the public.

Chapter VIII Inspection of Drugs

Article 56 The Drug regulatory department (including the drug regulatory institution legally established by the drug regulatory department of the people's government of the province, autonomous region or municipality directly under the Central Government, the same below) shall supervise and inspect the research and development, production, distribution and use of drugs in accordance with law.

Article 57 Sampling of a drug shall be conducted by two or more persons who are responsible for drug supervision and inspection in accordance with the provisions of the drug regulatory department under the State Council.

The party whose drug is to be sampled shall provide samples of the drug for testing and may not refuse. Where the party whose drug is to be sampled refuses the sampling and testing of the drug without justifiable reasons, the drug regulatory department under the State Council and the drug regulatory department of the people's government of the province, autonomous region or municipality directly under the Central Government where it is located may announce a stop to marketing and use of the drug, of which the sampling and testing are refused.

Article 58 Where a drug is suspected of being impure or adulterated but unable to be tested by testing method and through the testing items prescribed in the national drug standards, the drug testing institution may conduct tests by adding testing methods and items upon approval by the drug regulatory department under the State Council, the testing results obtained by using the additional testing methods and items may be taken as the basis for certifying the quality of the drugs.

Article 59 The drug regulatory department under the State Council and the drug regulatory department of the people's government of the province, autonomous region or municipality directly under the Central Government shall regularly make announcements on drug quality according to the results of sampling and testing. In a drug quality announcement shall be included the names of sampled drugs, sources of the samples, their manufacturers, batch numbers, drug strength, testing institutions, drug specifications, results of testing, and items failing to pass the test, etc. If a drug quality announcement is improperly made, the department making the announcement shall, within 5 days from the date of recognition of the improper announcement, make a correction within the scope in which the original one is made.

Where the party has any objection to the results of testing conducted by the drug testing institution and applies for re-testing, it shall submit a written application and the original testing report to the drug testing institution responsible for re-testing. The sample for re-testing shall be taken form the retaining sample kept by the original testing institution.

Article 60 Where the drug regulatory department takes administrative enforcement measures to seal or seize drugs that have been proved potentially harmful to human health and the related evidentiary materials, it shall, within 7 days from the date it takes such measures, make a decision on whether or not to file a case; where it is necessary to test such drugs, it shall, within 15 days from the date the testing report is issued, make a decision whether or not to file a case; where the conditions for filing a case are not met, the administrative enforcement measures shall be withdrawn; where the marketing and use of such drugs need to be suspended, a decision shall be made by the drug regulatory department under the State Council or the drug regulatory department of the people's government of the province, autonomous region or municipality directly under the Central Government.

Article 61 No fees may be charged for selective drug sampling and testing. Where the party has any objection to the results of testing conducted by the drug testing institution and applies for re-testing, it shall pay in advance the fees for drug testing to the drug testing institution responsible for the re-testing according to the provisions of the drug regulatory department under the State Council or of the drug regulatory department of the people's government of the province, autonomous region or municipality directly under the Central Government. If the results of re-testing are inconsistent with the original testing results, the fees for the re-testing shall be paid by the original testing institution.

Article 62 Fees may be collected for certificate issuance, drug registration, drug certification, drug testing for approval and mandatory drug testing according to the provisions in the Drug Administration Law and in the Regulations. The specific standards for collecting fees shall be formulated by the finance department under the State Council and the competent pricing department under the State Council.

Chapter IX Legal Liabilities

Article 63 A drug manufacturer or distributor shall be punished by the drug regulatory department according to the provisions in Article 79 of the Drug Administration Lawunder any of the following circumstances:

1. where any newly-established drug manufacturer or any manufacturer with a newly-built workshop or with newly-added dosage forms fails in the GMP certification within the time limit prescribed by the drug regulatory department under the State Council but is still engaged in drug production.
2. where any newly-established drug distributor fails in GSP certification within the time limit prescribed by the drug regulatory department under the State Council but is still engaged in drug distribution.

Article 64 Any contract giver or acceptor, in violation of the provisions in Article 13 of the Drug Administration Law, giving or accepting the contract for drug production without authorization shall be punished in accordance with the provisions in Article 74 of the Drug Administration Law.

Article 65 Where, without approval, anyone who sets up a store to sell drugs at the town or country fairs, or sells drugs in a store at the fairs beyond the approved scope of drug distribution, shall be punished according to the provisions in Article 73 of the Drug Administration Law.

Article 66 Any medical institution that uses pharmaceutical preparations dispensed by other medical institutions without approval shall be punished according to the provisions in Article 80 of the Drug Administration Law.

Article 67 Any out-patient department, clinic or any other medical institution, which is set up by individuals, if providing patients with drugs beyond the defined scope or kinds of drugs, shall be punished according to the provisions in Article 73 of the Drug Administration Law.

Article 68 Any medical institution that uses counterfeit and substandard drugs shall be punished according to the provisions in Article 74 and 75 of the Drug Administration Law.

Article 69 Any institution, in violation of the provisions in Article 29 of the Drug Administration Law, conducting a drug clinical trial without approval shall be punished according to the provisions in Article 79 of the Drug Administration Law.

Article 70 Where an applicant, in applying for conducting a drug clinical trail, submits false data on drug production procedures, quality specifications, or results of pharmacological and toxicological studies, etc., or submits fraud samples, the drug regulatory department under the State Council shall disapprove the application and give a warning to the applicant; where the circumstances are serious, no application for clinical trial of the said drug submitted by the said applicant may be accepted within 3 years.

Article 71 Where anyone producing prepared slices of Chinese crude drugs without the national drug standard fails to comply with the processing procedures formulated by the drug regulatory department of the people's government of the province, autonomous region or municipality directly under the Central Government, or any medical institution dispensing pharmaceutical preparations fails to comply with the standards approved by the drug regulatory department of the people's government of the province, autonomous region or municipality directly under the Central Government, punishment shall be imposed thereupon according to the provisions in Article 75 of the Drug Administration Law.

Article 72 Where the drug regulatory department and its staff members, in violation of regulations, release undisclosed experimental data or other materials submitted by a manufacturer or seller for obtaining approval of production or marketing of a drug containing new chemical entities, thus resulting in losses to the applicant, the drug regulatory department shall be liable for compensation in accordance with law. After compensating the losses, the drug regulatory department shall order the staff members who disclose the said data in purpose or have serious negligence to partially or fully bear the compensation and shall also impose administrative sanctions on those who are directly liable.

Article 73 Any drug manufacturer or distributor producing or distributing drugs or any medical institution dispensing pharmaceutical preparations, whose package, labels or inset sheets are in violation of the provisions in the Drug Administration Law and in the Regulations, shall be punished according to the provisions in Article 86 of the Drug Administration Law.

Article 74 Any drug manufacturer, distributor or medical institution altering any items licensed for manufacturing, distributing, or dispensing drugs without completing the formalities for registration of alteration as required shall be given a warning by the original certificate-issuing department and be ordered to complete the said formalities within a time limit. Its Drug Manufacturing Certificate, Drug

Distribution Certificate or Pharmaceutical Preparation Certificate for Medical Institution shall be announced as nullified if it fails to do so within the time limit, and punishment shall be given according to the provisions in Article 73 of the Drug Administration Law if it continues its production and distribution activities.

Article 75 Anyone violating the provisions in Article 48, 49, 50, 51 or 52 of the Regulations concerning the control over drug pricing shall be punished according to the relevant provisions in the Pricing Law.

Article 76 Where the approved content of a drug advertisement is altered without authorization, the advertiser shall be ordered by the drug regulatory department to discontinue publishing the said advertisement without delay, and punishment shall be given by the original approving drug regulatory department according to the provisions in Article 92 of the Drug Administration Law.

After the drug regulatory department withdraws the drug advertisement approval number, it shall notify the organ in charge of advertising supervision and control of the matter within 5 working days from the date the administrative decision is made. The organ in charge of advertising supervision and control shall, within 15 working days from the date it receives the notification from the drug regulatory department, make an administrative decision for handling the matting according to the relevant provisions in the Advertisement Law of the People's Republic of China.

Article 77 Where any enterprise published a drug advertisement outside the province, autonomous region or municipality directly under the Central Government where the drug manufacturer or drug import agency is located without filing a record with the drug regulatory department of the province, autonomous region or municipality directly under the Central Government where the drug advertisement is published, the drug regulatory department of the province, autonomous region or municipality directly under the Central Government shall order the enterprise to make a rectification within the time limit. If the enterprise fails to make any rectification within the time limit, advertising activities carried out in the place for the said drug shall be discontinued.

Article 78 Where the drug regulatory department finds that a drug advertisement is published without approval by the drug regulatory department of the people's government of the province, autonomous region or municipality directly under the Central Government, the drug regulatory department shall notify the organ in charge of advertising supervision and control to investigate and handle the matter in accordance with law.

Article 79 Where anyone that, in violation of the provisions in the Drug Administration Lawand in the Regulations, commits any of the following acts shall be given heavier punishment by the drug regulatory department based on the extent of punishment in the Drug Administration Law and in the Regulations:

1. passing narcotics, psychotropic substances, medicinal toxic drugs and radioactive pharmaceuticals off as other drugs or vice versa;

2. producing or selling counterfeit or substandard drugs of which the main users are pregnant and parturient women, infants and children;
3. producing or selling biological and blood products which are defined as counterfeit or substandard drugs;
4. producing, selling or using counterfeit or substandard drugs, thus inducing harmful results to people;
5. producing, selling or using counterfeit or substandard drugs again after being punished; or
6. refusing or evading supervision and inspection, or forging, destroying or concealing relevant evidentiary materials, or using sealed and seized articles without authorization.

Article 80 Branches of drug regulatory departments shall have the authority to, according to the provisions in the Drug Administration Law and in the Regulations, give administrative punishments such as warning, fine and confiscation of drugs illegally produced or marketed and illegal gains therefrom.

Article 81 Where a drug distributor or medical institution dose not violate the relevant provisions in the Drug Administration Law and in the Regulations and has sufficient evidence to prove its unawareness that the drugs being sold or used are counterfeit or substandard drugs, the said drugs and illegal gains therefrom shall be confiscated; however, it may be exempted from other administrative punishments.

Article 82 Articles confiscated according to the provisions in the Drug Administration Law and in the Regulations shall be dealt with under supervision by drug regulatory departments in accordance with provisions.

Chapter X Supplementary Provisions

Article 83 The terms used in the Regulations are defined as follows:

Drug quality attachment and other marks refer to approval documents for drug production, drug testing reports, drug packages, labels and insert sheets.

New drugs refer to the drugs which have not been marketed within the territory of the People's Republic of China.

Prescription drugs refer to the drugs that may only be purchased, dispensed or used with prescriptions by licensed doctors or licensed assistant doctors.

Non-prescription drugs refer to the drugs announced by the drug regulatory department under the State Council which can be purchased or used by consumers upon their own judgment without prescriptions by licensed doctors or licensed assistance doctors.

Pharmaceutical preparations in medical institutions refer to pharmaceutical preparations based on fixed prescriptions which have been dispensed upon approval by medical institutions according to their own clinical needs for their own use.

Drug certification refers to the process through which the drug regulatory department inspects and evaluates the units engaging in research and development, production, distribution or use of drugs as to their compliance with corresponding requirements, and decides on whether to issue the corresponding certificates.

Drug distribution refers to drug wholesale and/or retail.

Scope for drug distribution refers to the category of drugs reviewed and approved for distribution by the drug regulatory department.

Drug wholesalers refer to the drug distributors who sell the purchased drugs to drug manufacturers, drug distributors or medical institutions.

Drug retailers refer to the drug distributors who sell the purchased drugs to consumers directly.

Article 84 The term "drugs to be marketed in China for the first time" used in Article 41 of the Drug Administration Law refers to the drugs that are marketed for the first time in China by domestic or foreign drug manufacturers, including the same product manufactured by different drug manufacturers.

Article 85 In the second paragraph of Article 59 of the Drug Administration Law, "drug manufacturers, drug distributors or their agents are prohibited from offering, under any pretense, money or things of value or other benefits to leading members, drug purchasers, physicians, or other related persons of the medical institutions where their drugs are used", the term "money or things of value or other benefits" refer to the illegitimate benefits provided by drug manufacturers, drug distributors or their agents to leading members, drug purchasers, physicians, or other related persons of the medical institutions for the purpose of influencing their acts in purchasing or prescribing drugs.

Article 86 The Regulations shall go into effect as of September 15, 2002.

1.3 Regulations

1.3.1 Regulations Related to Registration

1.3.1.1 Provisions for Drug Registration

The State Food and Drug Administration Bureau deliberated and passed the "Provisions for Drug Registration" on June 18, 2007. It has been promulgated and became effective since October 1, 2007.

The SFDA Order No. 28 (Provisions for Drug Registration) is an extremely important legislation to guide the pharmaceutical research and development professionals. This legislation clearly stated the rules for acceptance, review and approval processes for new drug development. The requirements for original data, manufacturing site inspection, product quality inspection are also defined. In addition, it also stated the requirements for monitoring processes, application material/data, and package insert preparation. The legislation includes 15 chapters and six important accessories of 177 (SFDA 2007).

Note: The provisions have six annexes for as listed at the end of this section. Since the annexes have more detailed descriptions about the corresponding topics, they will not be listed in this chapter, but will be discussed in the corresponding chapters of intellectual property right (IPR) and chemical drug or biological product registrations.

Chapter I General Provisions
Chapter II Application for Drug Registration
Chapter III Drug Clinical Trials
Chapter IV Application and Approval of New Drugs
Chapter V Application and Approval of Generic Drugs
Chapter VI Application and Approval of Import Drugs
Chapter VII Application of Non Prescription Drugs
Chapter VIII Submission, Review and Approval of Supplementary Application
Chapter IX Drug Re-Registration
Chapter X Testing for Drug Registration
Chapter XI Drug Registration Specifications and Insert Sheet
Chapter XII Timeline
Chapter XIII Second Review
Chapter XIV Legal Liabilities
Chapter XV Supplementary Provisions

Provisions for Drug Registration (SFDA Order No. 28)
Chapter I General Provisions
Article 1 The Provisions are formulated for the purposes of ensuring the safety, efficacy and quality of drugs and regulating drug registration in accordance with the Drug Administration Law of the People's Republic of China (hereinafter referred to as the Drug Administration Law), Administrative Permission Law of the People's Republic of China (hereinafter referred to as Administrative Permission Law) and the Regulations for Implementation of the Drug Administration Law of the People's Republic of China (hereinafter referred to as the Regulations for Implementation of the Drug Administration Law).

Article 2 The Provisions apply to the applications for drug clinical trial, drug production or import, and conducting drug approval, relevant testing for drug registration, or regulation thereof, within the territory of the People's Republic of China.

Article 3 Drug registration refers to the process of review and approval on which the State Food and Drug Administration, in accordance with the official procedures, evaluates the safety, efficacy and quality of the drugs applied for marketing, and decides whether or not to approve such an application.

Article 4 The State encourages the research and development of new drugs and adopts the special review and approval with respect to innovative drugs, new drugs for serious and life-threatening diseases and to address unmet medical needs and drugs.

Article 5 The State Food and Drug Administration is in charge of drug registration nationwide, and responsible for reviewing and approving the clinical trial, production and importation of drugs.

Article 6 The drug registration shall follow the principles of openness, fairness and justice.

The State Food and Drug Administration adopts the system of collective responsibility of the chief reviewers, the system of publicizing and challenging relevant persons, and the system of responsibility tracing, with social supervision in such procedures as acceptance, inspection, review and approval and sending.

Article 7 In the process of drug registration, the drug regulatory department shall make known to the general public, and hold hearings on, the matters which it deems of vital importance and involving public interests for the granting of permission.

Prior to making the decision of administrative licensing that has a direct bearing on the vital interest between the applicant and the other party, the drug regulatory department shall inform the applicant and the interested party of their rights of requesting for hearings, making statements and argues.

Article 8 The drug regulatory department shall provide the applicant with access to information on the status of the acceptance, examination, inspection, review and approval of drug registration application and the final resolution.

The drug regulatory department shall publicize the following information on its official websites or at the official premises for accepting applications:

1. the items, procedures, fees and their basis, and timelines of the drug registration, index of all the data needed to be submitted and model text of the application form;
2. the name list and other relevant information on the persons involved in the acceptance, examination, inspection, review and approval of drug registration; and
3. general information about categories of approved drugs, etc.

Article 9 The drug regulatory department, relevant institutions and persons involved in the drug registration have an obligation to keep the technical secrets and trial data submitted by the applicant confidential.

Chapter II Application for Drug Registration

Article 10 An applicant for drug registration (hereinafter referred to as applicant) refers to the institution that submits a drug registration application and assumes corresponding legal liability.

A domestic applicant shall be an institution legally registered within the territory of People's Republic of China that independently assumes civil liability and an overseas applicant shall be a legal overseas drug manufacturer. Where an overseas applicant applies for import drug registration, it shall be done by its branch or entrusted agency within the territory of People's Republic of China.

The persons who handle the application for drug registration shall have professional knowledge and be familiar with the laws and regulations on, and the technical requirements for, drug registration.

Article 11 Drug registration applications include applications for new drugs, generic drugs, import drugs and their supplementary applications as well as re-registration applications.

Applications of domestic applicants shall be handled according to the procedures and requirements for new drugs or generic drugs, whereas applications of overseas applicants shall be handled according to those for import drugs.

Article 12 Application for new drugs refers to application for registration of drugs that have not been marketed within the territory of People's Republic of China.

Application for changing dosage form or route of administration, or claiming a new indication for marketed drugs, shall be submitted as the process of new drug application.

Application for generic drugs refers to registration application for producing the drugs having existing national drug standard which is approved to be marketed by the State Food and Drug Administration, whereas the application for biological products shall be submitted as the process of new drug application.

Application for import drugs refers to registration application for drugs manufactured abroad to be marketed within the territory of the People's Republic of China.

Supplementary application refers to application for variation, addition, or cancellation of the items or contents approved in the original application for new drug, generic drug or import drug.

Re-registration application refers to application for continued production or importation of a drug after the expiration of the valid term of the drug approval document.

Article 13 The applicant shall provide sufficient and reliable research data to prove the safety, efficacy and quality of the drug, and be liable for the authenticity of all the dossiers submitted.

Article 14 The cited literature of the dossier of drug registration shall indicate the title of works or the name, volume number, issue and page of the journal. Where the cited references are not published, an author's permission shall be provided. For foreign literatures, Chinese translation shall be provided as required.

Article 15 The State Food and Drug Administration shall obey the development plan and policies on the pharmaceutical industry constituted by the State, and may conduct assessment to the market value of drugs.

Article 16 In the process of drug registration, the drug regulatory department shall conduct on-site inspection and causal inspection to the non-clinical studies and clinical trials, as well as production site inspection for the pre-marketing approval to confirm the authenticity, precision and integrity of the dossier submitted.

Article 17 Where two or more institutions jointly apply for drugs, the application shall be submitted to the drug regulatory department of the province, autonomous region, or municipality directly under the Central Government, in which the drug manufacturer is located; where the applicants are all drug manufacturers, the application shall be submitted to the drug regulatory department of the province, autonomous region, or municipality directly under the Central Government, in which the manufacturer of pharmaceutical preparations is located; where none of the applicants is a drug manufacturer, the application shall be submitted to the drug regulatory department of the province, autonomous region, or municipality directly under the Central Government, in which the site for pilot production of drug samples is located.

Article 18 An applicant shall provide the information on patent and its ownership of the applicant or other parties in China, in respect of the drug applied for registration, its formula, manufacturing processes and/or uses, etc. Where another party owns the patent in China, the applicant shall provide a statement of non-infringement. The drug regulatory department shall publish the information or the statement submitted by the applicant on its official website.

Where a patent dispute occurs in the process of drug registration, it shall be settled in accordance with relevant laws and regulations on patent.

Article 19 For a drug patented in China, applicants other than the patentee may submit the application for registration 2 years prior to the expiry date of the patent. The State Food and Drug Administration shall review the drug application in accordance with the Provisions, and after the expiry date of the patent, check and issue the drug approval number, Import Drug License or a Pharmaceutical Product License if the application conforms with the provisions.

Article 20 In accordance with the provisions in Article 35 of the Regulations for Implementation of the Drug Administration Law, where a manufacturer or distributor submits undisclosed drug experimental and other data which are independently acquired in order to obtain approval for production or marketing of the drug in question which contains any new chemical entity, the State Food and Drug Administration shall, within 6 years from the approval date of the drug, reject any application made by any other applicants by using the undisclosed data of the drug in question without permission of the original applicant who has obtained the drug approval, unless the data submitted are independently acquired by the applicants other than the original one.

Article 21 Pre-clinical drug study for drug registration application includes drug synthetic processes, extraction methods, physical and chemical properties, purity, selection of dosage form, screening of formula, preparing processes, testing methods, quality specifications, stability, pharmacology, toxicology and animal pharmacokinetics, etc. For traditional Chinese medicine preparations, in addition to the above-mentioned items, pre-clinical drug study also includes the study in the source of the crude drugs, and of their pre-treatment and processing, etc. For biological products, it also includes study on the source, quality specifications, storage conditions, biological characteristics and genetic stability of the starting materials such as bacterial and viral seeds/strains, cell lines, bio-tissues, and immunological study, etc.

Article 22 A pre-clinical drug study shall be in conformity with relevant requirements, among which the Good Laboratory Practice for Non-Clinical Laboratory Studies shall be implemented in the study of safety evaluation.

Article 23 The drug research institution shall have relevant staff, premises, equipment, instruments and management system, which are appropriate to the research project, and ensure the authenticity of all experimental data. Experimental animals, reagents and raw materials used in the study shall conform with the provisions of the State.

Article 24 An applicant who entrusts other institutions with a drug research, individual experiment, testing, or pilot production, etc. shall conclude a contract with the trustee, and state it clearly in the registration application. The applicant shall be responsible for the authenticity of the research data in the application dossier.

Article 25 Where the application is only for registration of pharmaceutical preparations, any drug substance used for the study shall have a drug approval number, an Import Drug License or a Pharmaceutical Product License, and be acquired through legitimated means. Where a drug substance used for the study has no drug approval number, Import Drug License or Pharmaceutical Product License, the use of drug substance in study shall be approved by the State Food and Drug Administration.

Article 26 The research data in application dossier for drug registration provided by an overseas drug research institution shall be attached with the items and pages of the information, and with notarized documents proving that the said drug research institution is legally registered overseas. The State Food and Drug Administration may send staff to conduct on-site inspection in needs of drug review.

Article 27 The drug regulatory department may request the applicant or the drug research institution responsible for testing to repeat the test based on the items, methods and data specified in the application documents, and may also authorize a drug testing institute or another drug research institution to repeat the test or conduct methodological verification.

Article 28 The drug study shall be conducted according to the relevant technical guidelines issued by the State Food and Drug Administration. Where an applicant conducts the study by adopting other evaluation methods and techniques, supporting data proving the scientific feasibility of such methods and techniques shall be provided.

Article 29 An applicant who obtains the drug approval number shall manufacture according to the manufacturing processes approved by the State Food and Drug Administration.

The drug regulatory department shall supervise and inspect the applicant's manufacture in accordance with the approved manufacturing processes and quality specifications.

Chapter III Drug Clinical Trials

Article 30 Any drug clinical trial, including bioequivalence study, shall be approved by the State Food and Drug Administration, and shall be in compliance with the Good Clinical Practice.

Drug regulatory department shall supervise and inspect the approved clinical trials.

Article 31 Clinical trials shall be conducted for new drug registration applications. As for generic drug registration applications and supplementary applications, clinical trials shall be conducted in accordance with the requirements in the Annex of the Provisions.

A clinical trial consists of phases I, II, III and IV.

Phase I Clinical Trial: initial clinical pharmacology and safety evaluation studies in humans. These studies are designed to observe tolerability of humans to and pharmacokinetics of a new drug, in order to provide basis for establishing the administration regimen.

Phase II Clinical Trial: preliminary evaluation of therapeutic effectiveness of a drug. The purposes are to preliminarily evaluate the therapeutic effectiveness and safety of the drug for particular indication(s) in patients, and provide evidence for design of Phase III clinical trial and settlement of administrative dose regimen. According to specific trial objectives, this phase of trial may be designed in various forms, including the randomized blind controlled clinical trial.

Phase III Clinical Trial: confirmation of therapeutic effectiveness of a drug. The purposes are to further verify drug therapeutic effectiveness and safety on eligible patients with target indication(s), to evaluate overall benefit-risk relationships of the drug, and to ultimately provide sufficient evidence for the review of drug registration application. The study, in general, shall be a randomized blind controlled trial with an adequate sample size.

Phase IV Clinical Trial: a new drug post-marketing study. The purposes are to assess therapeutic effectiveness and adverse reactions when a drug is widely used, to evaluate overall benefit-risk relationships of the drug when used among general population or specific groups, and to adjust the administration dose, etc.

Bioequivalence study refers to a human study, which applies bioavailability study methods with pharmacokinetic parameters as indicators to compare active ingredient absorption rate and extent of the preparations in the same or different dosage forms of a drug in terms of statistical differences under the same experimental condition.

Article 32 The sample size of a drug clinical trial shall conform to the objectives of the clinical trial and fulfill statistical requirements, and shall be no smaller than the minimum number of subjects required by the Annex of the Provisions. Where there are circumstances, regarding rare or special diseases, etc., which request clinical sample size reduction or clinical trial exemption, a request shall be made with the clinical trial application, and reviewed and approved by the State Food and Drug Administration.

Article 33 As for vaccines prepared during bacterial or viral strain screening or other special drugs, if confirmed without any suitable animal model and laboratory measurement in terms of curative effectiveness, clinical trials may be applied for to the State Food and Drug Administration, subject to ensuring the safety of trial subjects.

Article 34 When a drug clinical trial is approved, the applicant shall select institutions for the clinical trial from those certified for conducting drug clinical trials.

Article 35 Drugs used for clinical trials shall be manufactured in facilities in compliance with the Good Manufacturing Practice for Pharmaceutical Products (GMP). The manufacturing process shall strictly meet the requirements of the GMP.

The applicant shall be responsible for the quality of the drugs used for clinical trials.

Article 36 The applicant may conduct the testing for clinical trial drugs by itself, or entrust a drug testing institute specified in the Provisions to conduct such testing, according to its proposed specifications. Vaccines, blood products and other biological products specified by the State Food and Drug Administration shall be tested by drug testing institutes designated by the State Food and Drug Administration.

A drug can be used for a clinical trial only after tested as qualified.

Drug regulatory departments may conduct sampling and testing on drugs used for clinical trials.

Article 37 Prior to conducting a clinical trial, the applicant shall report to the State Food and Drug Administration for record while copying to the drug regulatory department of the seat of the clinical trial institution and that of the province, autonomous region or municipality directly under the Central Government to receive the application a confirmed clinical trial protocol, the name of the principal investigator at the institution in charge of the clinical trial, a list of participating institutions and names of investigators wherefrom, an ethic committee approval letter, and a template of the informed consent form, etc.

Article 38 Where the applicant finds a clinical trial institution violating relevant regulations or failing to implement the clinical trial protocol, it shall urge the institution to make corrections; if the circumstances are serious, the applicant may demand suspension or termination of the clinical trial, and shall report the matter to the State Food and Drug Administration and the drug regulatory departments of the relevant provinces, autonomous regions or municipalities directly under the Central Government.

Article 39 After completion of a clinical trial, the applicant shall submit a clinical trial final report, a statistical analysis report and its database to the State Food and Drug Administration.

Article 40 A clinical trials shall be implemented within 3 years after approval. If overdue, the original approval documents shall be invalid. If the clinical trial is still needed, the application shall be reapplied for.

Article 41 If any serious adverse event occurs during the clinical trial, the investigators shall report to the drug regulatory departments of the relevant provinces, autonomous regions or municipalities directly under the Central Government and the State Food and Drug Administration and notify the applicant within 24 h, and report to the ethic committee in time.

Article 42 In any of the following circumstances during a clinical trial, the State Food and Drug Administration may order the applicant to modify the protocol, suspend or terminate the clinical trial,:

1. the ethic committee fails to perform its duty;
2. safety of the subjects cannot be adequately ensured;
3. a serious adverse event is not reported within the specified timeline;
4. there is evidence to prove that the drug used for the clinical trial is not effective;
5. a quality problem of the drug used for the clinical trial occurs;
6. there is a fraud in the clinical trial; or
7. there is any other case violating the Good Clinical Practice.

Article 43 Where there is any large-scale of and unexpected adverse reaction or serious adverse event, or there is evidence to prove any serious quality problem of the drug used for a clinical trial, the State Food and Drug Administration or the drug regulatory department of the province, autonomous region or municipality directly under the Central Government may take emergency control measures and order to suspend or terminate the clinical trial. The applicant and clinical trial institution must stop the clinical trial immediately.

Article 44 An overseas applicant intending to conduct an international multi-center clinical trial in China shall submit an application to the State Food and Drug Administration in accordance with the Provisions, and fulfill the following requirements:

1. the drugs used for clinical trials shall be already approved or in phase II or III clinical trial overseas. The State Food and Drug Administration does not accept any overseas applicant's international multi-center clinical trial application for any preventive vaccine not being registered overseas yet;
2. while approving to conduct an international multi-center clinical trial, the State Food and Drug Administration may require the applicant to conduct phase I clinical trial first in China;
3. when conducting an international multi-center clinical trial in China, if there are any observed serious adverse reaction and unexpected adverse reaction associated with the drug in any country, the applicant shall, in accordance with relevant regulations, report to the State Food and Drug Administration in time;
4. the applicant shall submit a complete clinical trial report to the State Food and Drug Administration after the completion of a clinical trial; and
5. the data obtained from an international multi-center clinical trial for drug registration application in China shall be in conformity with the requirements on clinical trial in the Provisions. All the study materials of the international multi-center clinical trial shall be submitted.

Chapter IV Application and Approval of New Drugs

Article 45: The State Food and Drug Administration may implement special review and approval in cases of the following applications:

1. active ingredients extracted from plants, animals and minerals, etc. and their preparations not yet marketed in China, and newly discovered Chinese crude drugs and their preparations;
2. chemical drug substances and their preparations and biological products not yet approved for marketing in China or abroad;
3. new drugs for the treatment of diseases such as AIDS, malignant tumors and rare diseases, etc. with significant clinical advantage; and
4. new drugs for the treatment of diseases, for which effective therapeutic methods are not available.

For drugs specified in the previous clause, applicants may apply for special review and approval in the process of drug registration. The Center for Drug Evaluation of the State Food and Drug Administration shall organize expert meetings to discuss and determine whether or not to conduct special review and approval for the drugs. Specified measures for special review and approval shall be formulated separately.

Article 46 Where a new drug is co-developed by several institutions, the registration can be applied for by one of the institutions, and its duplicate application shall not be made by the others. If a joint application for registration is needed, the institutions shall co-sign as the applicant of the new drug. Each approved new drug, including its different strengths shall be produced by only one institution.

Article 47 For the registration application to change the dosage form without changing administration route of a marketed drug, new techniques shall be employed to improve the drug quality and safety, and the changed dosage form shall have significant clinical advantage compared with the previous dosage form.

Registration applications to change the dosage form without changing the route of administration or to claim any new indication shall be submitted by certified manufacturers, with exceptions for special dosage forms such as targeting delivery, sustained release and controlled release preparations, etc.

Article 48 In the process of the review and approval of a new drug, the registration classification and technical requirements thereof shall not be changed, even though the preparations of the same active ingredients are approved for marketing abroad.

In the process of the review and approval of a new drug, the registration classification and technical requirements thereof shall not be changed, even though the preparations of the same active ingredients applied for by domestic manufacturers are approved for marketing in China.

Article 49 The dossier for drug registration application shall be submitted at one time. No other technical materials should be added by the applicant after a drug registration application is accepted, with the exceptions for applications of special review and approval, new finding regarding drug safety, or supplementary materials as required. Where an applicant deems it integrant for any new technical material to be supplemented, the submitted application shall be withdrawn. Only if no same product is in the new drug observation period, the applicant may re-apply in compliance with the relevant requirements in the Provisions.

Section 1 Clinical Trials for New Drugs

Article 50 After completing the pre-clinical study, the applicant shall fill the Application Form for Drug Registration, and report authentically relevant materials to the drug regulatory department of the province, autonomous region or municipality directly under the Central Government where the applicant is located.

Article 51 Drug regulatory departments of provinces, autonomous regions, or municipalities directly under the Central Government shall conduct the preliminary review of the application dossiers, and issue a acceptance notice of drug registration application if requirements are met, or issue a non-acceptance notice, in which reasons shall be given, of drug registration application if requirements are not met.

Article 52 Drug regulatory departments of provinces, autonomous regions, or municipalities directly under the Central Government shall organize to conduct on-site inspections of the drug research and development conditions and raw data, make preliminary review of the submitted dossiers, and provide review opinions within 5 days from the date it accepts an application. Where the drug for which the registration is applied is a biological product, samples from three production batches thereof shall also be collected for testing, and a notice for the testing for registration shall be issued to the drug testing institute.

Article 53 Drug regulatory departments of provinces, autonomous regions, or municipalities directly under the Central Government shall deliver the review opinions, inspection reports and the application dossiers to the Center for Drug Evaluation of the State Food and Drug Administration within the specified timeline, and notice the applicants.

Article 54 The drug testing institute that receives a notice for the testing for registration shall test the samples according to the drug specifications submitted by the applicant, verify the submitted drug specifications, and submit a certificate of analysis for drug registration to the Center for Drug Evaluation of the State Food and Drug Administration within the specified timeline, and copy to the applicant.

Article 55 After receiving submitted dossiers, the Center for Drug Evaluation of the State Food and Drug Administration shall organize pharmaceutical, medical and other technical personnel to conduct technical review of the submitted dossiers within the specified timeline, and may request, with reasons, applicants to provide supplementary materials when necessary. After completing technical reviews, the Center for Drug Evaluation shall give technical review opinions and report together with relevant documents to the State Food and Drug Administration.

The State Food and Drug Administration shall make review and approval decisions based on the technical review opinions. Where the regulations are conformed to, a Drug Clinical Trial Approval shall be issued; where the regulations are not conformed to, a Disapproval Notice shall be issued with reasons provided.

Section 2 Production of New Drugs

Article 56 After completing drug clinical trials, applicants shall fill the Application Form for Drug Registration, submit production application dossiers to the drug regulatory departments of the provinces, autonomous regions, or municipalities directly under the Central Government where the applicant is located, and at the same time provide the raw materials and research information for preparing reference standards to the National Institute for the Control of Pharmaceutical and Biological Products.

Article 57 Drug regulatory departments of provinces, autonomous regions, or municipalities directly under the Central Government shall conduct the preliminary review of the application dossiers, and issue an acceptance notice of drug registration application if requirements are met, or issue a non-acceptance notice, in which reasons shall be given, of drug registration application if requirements are not met.

Article 58 Drug regulatory departments of provinces, autonomous regions, or municipalities directly under the Central Government shall organize to conduct on-site inspections of the drug research and development conditions and raw data, make preliminary review of the submitted dossiers, and provide review opinions within 5 days from the date it accepts an application. For the other drugs except biological products, samples of three production batches shall also be collected for testing, and a notice of specifications verification shall be issued to the drug testing institute.

Drug regulatory departments of provinces, autonomous regions, or municipalities directly under the Central Government shall deliver the review opinions, inspection reports and the application dossiers to the Center for Drug Evaluation of the State Food and Drug Administration within the specified timeline, and notice the applicants.

Article 59 Drug testing institutes shall verify the submitted drug specifications and give the verification opinions to the Center for Drug Evaluation of the State Food and Drug Administration within the specified timeline, and at the same time copy to the drug regulatory departments of the provinces, autonomous regions, or municipalities directly under the Central Government that notify them to conduct the verification, and the applicants.

Article 60 After receiving submitted dossiers, the Center for Drug Evaluation of the State Food and Drug Administration shall organize pharmaceutical, medical and other technical personnel to conduct technical review of the submitted dossiers within the specified timeline, and may request, with reasons, applicants to provide supplementary materials when necessary.

Where the regulations are conformed to as reviewed, the Center for Drug Evaluation of the State Food and Drug Administration shall notice the applicant to apply for production site inspection and inform the Center for Drug Certification of the State Food and Drug Administration. Where the regulations are not conformed to as reviewed, the Center for Drug Evaluation of the State Food and Drug Administration shall report the review opinions and relevant documents to the State Food and Drug Administration; the State Food and Drug Administration shall make a disapproval decision to the application based on the technical review opinions, and issue a Disapproval Notice with reasons.

Article 61 The applicant shall apply for on-site inspection to the Center for Drug Certification of the State Food and Drug Administration within 6 months from the date it receives the notice of production site inspection.

Article 62 The Center for Drug Certification of the State Food and Drug Administration shall, within 30 days from the date it receives the application for production site inspection, organize on-site inspection of large-scale samples production, verify the applicability of the manufacturing processes and at the same time take samples of one batch of products (samples of three batches of products for biological products), and provide production site inspection report to the Center for Drug Evaluation of the State Food and Drug Administration within 10 days after the site inspection.

Article 63 Samples shall be produced at a plant with the GMP Certificate. As for a new manufacturer, a new workshop established or the production of a dosage form added at an existing manufacturer, the sample production shall meet the GMP requirements.

Article 64 Drug testing institutes shall conduct sample testing according to the verified specifications, and within the specified timeline, provide testing reports to the Center for Drug Evaluation of the State Food and Drug Administration, and copy to the relevant drug regulatory departments of the provinces, autonomous regions, or municipalities directly under the Central Government and the applicants.

Article 65 The Center for Drug Evaluation of the State Food and Drug Administration shall make a general opinion based on the technical review opinions, production site inspection reports and sample testing results, and report the general opinion together with relevant documents to the State Food and Drug Administration. The State Food and Drug Administration shall make a review and approval decision based on the general opinion. Where the regulations are conformed to, a New Drug Certificate shall be issued; if the applicant already has a Drug Manufacturing Certificate and possesses the production conditions, a drug approval number shall be issued at the same time; where the regulations are not conformed to, a Disapproval Notice shall be issued with reasons.
A New Drug Certificate shall not be issued to the approved registration applications for changing dosage forms without changing route of administration or claiming for new indications, with exceptions for special dosage forms such as targeting delivery, sustained release and controlled release preparations, etc.

Section 3 New Drug Observation Period
Article 66 In order to protect the public health, the State Food and Drug Administration may set an observation period for any new drug approved for production. The observation period of a new drug shall be no longer than 5 years from the date the drug is approved for production.

During the observation period of a new drug, the State Food and Drug Administration shall not approve other manufacturers to produce, change dosage form of or import the drug.

Article 67 A drug manufacturer shall investigate the manufacturing processes, quality, stability, therapeutic effect and adverse reactions, etc. of a new drug in the observation period, and report annually to the drug regulatory department of the province, autonomous region, or municipality directly under the Central Government, where it is located. Where a drug manufacturer fails to perform its duties in the observation period, the drug regulatory department of the province, autonomous region, or municipality directly under the Central Government shall order it to make rectifications.

Article 68 Where institutions for drug manufacturing, distribution, use, testing or supervision find any critical quality problem, serious or unexpected adverse reaction of a new drug, they shall report to the drug regulatory department of the province, autonomous region, or municipality directly under the Central Government in time. Once receiving the report, the drug regulatory department of a province, autonomous region, or municipality directly under the Central Government shall organize prompt investigation, and report to the State Food and Drug Administration.

Article 69 Where a drug manufacturer does not conduct production of the new drug, for which an observation period is set, within 2 years from the date of the approval, the State Food and Drug Administration may approve the application of another drug manufacturer to produce the new drug and reset the observation period of the drug.

Article 70 Starting from the date a new drug enters the observation period, any other application for the clinical trial of the same drug already approved by the State Food and Drug Administration may proceed along drug registration application, review and approval procedures; where regulations are conformed to, the State Food and Drug Administration shall approve the production or importation of the same drug. The observations of the drugs produced by the domestic manufacturers should be conducted together with the drug already in the observation period.

Article 71 Starting from the date a new drug enters the observation period, other registration applications for the same drug shall no longer be accepted. The other applicants' applications for the same drug already accepted but not yet approved for clinical trials shall be returned; upon the expiration of the observation period of the drug, the registration of a generic or import drug may be applied for.

Article 72 Where an application for an import drug registration is approved first, the domestic application already approved for clinical trial of the drug may proceed along drug registration application, review and approval procedures; where regulations are conformed to, the State Food and Drug Administration shall approve the production of the drug; or, the applicant may withdraw the application, and submit a generic drug application. The other applications for the same drugs already accepted but not yet approved for clinical trials shall be returned; the registration of a generic drug may be applied for.

Chapter V Application and Approval of Generic Drugs

Article 73 The applicant applying for registration of a generic drug shall be a drug manufacturer. The applied drug shall be within the production scope specified in the Drug Manufacturing Certificate.

Article 74 The generic drug shall have the identical active ingredients, route of administration, dosage form, strength and therapeutic effects with the registered drug. Where a drug has been produced by more than one manufacturer, the selection of registered drugs for comparative study shall be in accordance with relevant technical guidelines.

Article 75 To apply for the registration of a generic drug, the applicant shall fill the Application Form for Drug Registration, submit relevant dossiers and apply for production site inspection to the drug regulatory department of the province, autonomous region, or municipality directly under the Central Government where the applicant is located.

Article 76 Drug regulatory departments of provinces, autonomous regions, or municipalities directly under the Central Government shall conduct the preliminary review of the application dossiers, and issue an acceptance notice of drug registration application if requirements are met, or issue a non-acceptance notice, in which reasons shall be given, of drug registration application if requirements are not met.

As for a drug for which the protection of traditional Chinese medicine preparations has been applied, from the date the application for the protection is accepted through the date an administrative decision is made, the acceptance of the application of its generic drug shall be suspended.

Article 77 Drug regulatory departments of provinces, autonomous regions, or municipalities directly under the Central Government shall organize to conduct on-site inspections of the drug research and development conditions as well as raw data, and production site inspections according to the manufacturing processes and quality specifications provided by the applicant, and take samples of three consecutive batches of products, and send to the drug testing institutes for testing within 5 days starting from the date they accept an application.

The production of samples shall be in conformity with the requirements in Article 63 in the Provisions.

Article 78 Drug regulatory departments of the provinces, autonomous regions, or municipalities directly under the Central Government shall review the submitted dossiers within the specified timeline and give review opinions. Where the regulations are conformed to, they shall provide for the Center for Drug Evaluation of the State Food and Drug Administration with the review opinions, the check report, the production site inspection report and the application dossiers, and inform the applicant. Where the regulations are not conformed to, they shall issue a Disapproval Notice with reasons, and notify the drug testing institute to terminate the testing for registration.

Article 79 Drug testing institutes shall conduct sample testing, provide testing reports to the Center for Drug Evaluation of the State Food and Drug Administration within the specified timeline, and copy to the drug regulatory departments of the provinces, autonomous regions, or municipalities directly under the Central Government that notify them to conduct the verification, and the applicants.

Article 80 The Center for Drug Evaluation of the State Food and Drug Administration shall organize pharmaceutical, medical and other technical personnel to conduct technical review of the submitted dossiers within the specified timeline, and may request, with reasons, applicants to provide supplementary materials when necessary.

Article 81 The Center for Drug Evaluation of the State Food and Drug Administration shall make a general opinion based on the technical review opinions, production site inspection reports and sample testing results, and report the general opinion together with relevant documents to the State Food and Drug Administration. The State Food and Drug Administration shall make a review and approval decision based on the general opinion. Where the regulations are conformed to, it shall issue a drug approval number or a Drug Clinical Trial Approval; where the regulations are not conformed to, it shall issue a Disapproval Notice with reasons.

Article 82 After completing drug clinical trials, applicants shall submit clinical trial data to the Center for Drug Evaluation of the State Food and Drug Administration. The State Food and Drug Administration shall issue a drug approval number or a Disapproval Notice based on the technical review opinions.

Article 83 As for a marketed drug with confirmed safety problems, the State Food and Drug Administration may decide to suspend the acceptance or review and approval of the application of its generic drugs.

Chapter VI Application and Approval of Import Drugs
Section 1: Registration of Import Drugs
Article 84 A drug being applied for importation shall have already obtained the drug marketing authorization in the producing country or region where the overseas pharmaceutical manufacturer is located; those not yet obtained marketing authorization in the producing country or region, however confirmed with safety, efficacy and clinical needs by the State Food and Drug Administration may be approved for importation.

The production of a drug applied for importation shall comply with the GMP requirements of both the producing country or region where the drug manufacturer is located and China.

Article 85 To apply for import drug registration, the applicant shall fill the Application Form for Drug Registration, submit relevant dossiers and samples, provide relevant approval documents, and submit the application to the State Food and Drug Administration.

Article 86 The State Food and Drug Administration shall conduct the preliminary review of the application dossiers, and issue an acceptance notice of drug registration application and notify the National Institute for the Control of Pharmaceutical and Biological Products to conduct testing for registration of samples from three batches if requirements are met; or issue a non-acceptance notice of drug registration application with reasons if requirements are not met.

The State Food and Drug Administration may organize to conduct on-site inspection of development and production conditions, and take samples.

Article 87 The National Institute for the Control of Pharmaceutical and Biological Products shall organize to conduct the testing for drug registration within 5 days from the date it receives the dossiers and samples.

Article 88 The drug testing institutes undertaking the import drug testing shall complete the testing for registration and submit the certificate of analysis for drug registration to the National Institute for the Control of Pharmaceutical and Biological Products within 60 days from the date they receive the documents, samples and relevant reference standards.

Sample testing and verification of specifications for controlled drugs or vaccines shall be completed within 90 days.

Article 89 The National Institute for the Control of Pharmaceutical and Biological Products shall organize experts to conduct technical review within 20 days from the date it receives the certificate of analysis for drug registration and the verified import specifications, and if necessary, conduct further verification according to the review opinions.

Article 90 After completing the testing for import drug registration, the National Institute for the Control of Pharmaceutical and Biological Products shall give the verified specifications, certificate of analysis and opinions thereof to the Center for Drug Evaluation of the State Food and Drug Administration, and copy the applicants.

Article 91 The Center for Drug Evaluation of the State Food and Drug Administration shall organize pharmaceutical, medical and other technical personnel to conduct technical review of the submitted dossiers within the specified timeline, and may request, with reasons, applicants to provide supplementary materials when necessary.

Article 92 The Center for Drug Evaluation of the State Food and Drug Administration shall make a general opinion based on the technical review opinions and sample testing results, and report the general opinion together with relevant documents to the State Food and Drug Administration. The State Food and Drug Administration shall make a review and approval decision based on the general opinion. Where the regulations are conformed to, a Clinical Trial Approval shall be issued; where the regulations are not conformed to, a Disapproval Notice shall be issued with reasons.

Article 93 After a clinical trial application is approved, the applicant shall conduct the trial in accordance with the requirements in Chapter III of the Provisions and the other relevant requirements.

After a clinical trial is completed, the applicant shall fill the Application Form for Drug Registration, submit the clinical trial data, other altered and supplementary data in accordance with regulations, give in detail the basis and reasons, and provide relevant approved documents.

Article 94 The Center for Drug Evaluation of the State Food and Drug Administration shall organize pharmaceutical, medical and other technical personnel to conduct comprehensive review of the submitted clinical trial data within the specified timeline, and may request, with reasons, applicants to provide supplementary materials when necessary.

The State Food and Drug Administration shall make a review and approval decision based on the general opinion. An Import Drug License shall be issued if regulations are conformed to. For a drug applied for registration by a drug manufacturer in Hong Kong, Macao or Taiwan of China, its application shall be handled in reference to the application procedures for import drug registration. If requirements are met, a Pharmaceutical Product License shall be issued; if requirements are not met, a Disapproval Notice shall be issued with reasons.

Article 95 To apply for importation of pharmaceutical preparations, approved documents for the lawful sources of the immediate packaging materials and containers and those of the drug substances and the excipients used for the pharmaceutical preparations shall be provided. Where drug substances and excipients are not yet approved by the State Food and Drug Administration, relevant data of manufacturing processes, specifications and testing methods, etc. shall be submitted.

Section 2 Registration of Import Drug Repackaging

Article 96 The import drug repackaging refers to dividing a large pack into small ones in China or adding outer-package to a drug with inner-package, placing insert sheets and attaching labels, etc., after the production process of the finished pharmaceutical preparations for the drug are completed overseas.

Article 97 To apply for import drug repackaging, the following requirements shall be met:

1. the Import Drug License or Pharmaceutical Product License of the drug is already obtained;
2. the drug shall be one that is not produced within the territory of China, or is produced in China but unable to meet clinical needs;
3. one drug produced by a drug manufacturer shall be repackaged by only one drug manufacturer. The term allowed for repackaging shall not exceed the expiry date of the Import Drug License or Pharmaceutical Product License;
4. the inner–packaging of a drug in any dosage form for repackaging, except tablets and capsules, shall be completed overseas;
5. a drug manufacturer that conducts repackaging shall hold the Drug Manufacturing Certificate. To apply for repackaging of import unpackaged tablets and capsules, the manufacturer shall also hold the GMP certificate covering the dosage forms for repackaging; and
6. An application for drug repackaging shall be made 1 year prior to the expiration of the Import Drug License or the Pharmaceutical Product License.

Article 98 An overseas drug manufacturer shall sign a contract for import drug repackaging with a domestic drug manufacturer, and fill in the Drug Supplementary Application Form.

Article 99 To apply for the repackaging of an import drug, the drug manufacturer entrusted with repackaging of the drug shall submit an application to the drug regulatory department of the province, autonomous region, or municipality directly under the Central Government where it is located. The trustee shall submit the Supplementary Drug Application Form filled in by the truster, the relevant data and samples as well as the contract of entrustment, etc. The drug regulatory department shall conduct the preliminary review of the submitted documents. Where requirements are met, it shall issue a notice of acceptance; where requirements are not met, it shall issue a notice of non-acceptance with reasons.

The drug regulatory department shall make review opinions, then submit the application documents and review opinions to the State Food and Drug Administration and inform the applicant at the same time.

Article 100 The State Food and Drug Administration shall review the submitted documents. Where the regulations are conformed to, it shall issue an Approval for Supplementary Drug Application and a drug approval number; where the regulations are not conformed to, it shall issue a Disapproval Notice with reasons.

Article 101 The repackaged import drugs shall comply with the registration specifications for import drugs.

Article 102 The insert sheets and labels of a repackaged import drug shall be in conformity with those of the import drug, and shall be indicated with the approval number of the repackaging drug and the name of drug manufacturer.

Article 103 The testing for import of overseas pharmaceutical preparation in large package shall be conducted according to the State Food and Drug Administration regulations. The same specifications shall be used for the testing of both repackaged and import products.

Article 104 The overseas drug manufacturer providing the drug shall be responsible for the quality of the repackaged drug. If there is any quality problem, the State Food and Drug Administration may withdraw the approval number of the repackaged drug, revoke the Import Drug License or the Pharmaceutical Product License when necessary according to the requirements of Article 42 of the Drug Administration Law.

Chapter VII Application of Non-Prescription Drugs

Article 105 Where the applied generic drug is regulated as a non-prescription drug, the applicant shall indicate the item of non-prescription drug in the "additional application items" of the Application Form for Drug Registration.

Article 106 Where the applied generic drug is regulated as both a prescription and non-prescription drug, the applicant may submit an application for either a prescription or non-prescription drug according to the respective requirements.

Article 107 For any of the following circumstances, the applicant may indicate the item of non-prescription drug in the "additional application items" of the Application Form for Drug Registration. If relevant requirements for non-prescription drugs apply, the drug shall be reviewed and approved, and regulated as a non-prescription drug; if relevant requirements for non-prescription drugs do not apply, it shall be reviewed and approved, and regulated as a prescription drug:

1. To alter the dosage form of a non-prescription drug determined by the State Food and Drug Administration without changing the indications or functions, dosage and route of administration; or
2. To formulate a new fixed dose combination using active ingredients of non-prescription drugs determined by the State Food and Drug Administration.

Article 108 For the registration application of a non-prescription drug, the insert sheet and package label shall comply with the relevant regulations on non-prescription drugs.

Article 109 For the registration application of an import drug categorized as non-prescription drug, the application, review and approval procedures for import drugs shall apply, and the technological requirements shall be the same as those for the domestically produced non-prescription drugs.

Chapter VIII Submission, Review and Approval of Supplementary Application

Article 110 For the variation of the items specified in the approval document and its attachment for approved new drug development, drug production and import drug, supplementary applications shall be made.

The applicant shall assess the implications of the variation to the safety, efficacy and quality of the drug, and conduct corresponding technical studies in reference to relevant technical guidelines.

Article 111 The applicant shall fill in Supplementary Drug Application Form and submit relevant dossier and explanation to the drug regulatory department of the province, autonomous region, or municipality directly under the Central Government where the applicant is located. Drug regulatory departments of provinces, autonomous regions, or municipalities directly under the Central Government shall conduct the preliminary review of the application dossiers, and issue an acceptance notice of drug registration application if requirements are met, or issue a non-acceptance notice, with reasons, of drug registration application if requirements are not met.

Article 112 For the supplementary application of an import drug, the applicant shall submit relevant dossier and explanations to the State Food and Drug Administration, and provide documents approving the variation issued by the drug regulatory department of the producing country or region. The State Food and Drug Administration shall conduct the preliminary review of the application dossiers, and issue an acceptance notice of drug registration application if requirements are met, or issue a non-acceptance notice, in which reasons shall be given, of drug registration application if requirements are not met.

Article 113 For any supplementary application to amend the drug registration specifications, change excipients for pharmaceutical use in the drug formulation, or modify the manufacturing process that affects the drug quality, etc., the drug regulatory department of the province, autonomous region, or municipality directly under the Central Government shall provide a review opinion, report it to the State Food and Drug Administration for review and approval, and inform the applicant at the same time.

For supplementary application to amend the drug registration specifications, the drug testing institute shall verify the specifications when necessary.

Article 114 For any supplementary application to change the name of a domestic drug manufacturer, the shelf-life of a domestically produced drug, or the production site by a domestic drug manufacturer internally, etc., the drug regulatory departments of the provinces, autonomous regions, or municipalities directly under the Central Government shall conduct the acceptance, review and approval. Where the regulations are conformed to, it shall issue an Approval for Supplementary Drug Application, and report to the State Food and Drug Administration for record; where the regulations are not conformed to, it shall issue a Disapproval Notice with reasons.

Article 115 Any supplementary application to alter drug packaging label in accordance with regulations, or amend the insert sheet as required by the State Food and Drug Administration, etc. shall be filed to the drug regulatory department of the province, autonomous region, or municipality directly under the Central Government for record.

Article 116 Supplementary applications of import drugs shall be reviewed and approved by the State Food and Drug Administration. Those supplementary applications to change the place of production of the drug substance used for any import drug preparation, change the appearance of an import drug not resulting in specification changes, amend the insert sheet of an import drug according to the national specifications or the requirements of the State Food and Drug Administration, update the safety information in the insert sheet of an import drug, alter drug packaging label in accordance with regulations, or change the registration agent shall be filed to the State Food and Drug Administration for record.

Article 117 For supplementary applications of drug manufacturing technology transfer, altering formula or manufacturing process that may affect product quality, etc., the drug regulatory department of the province, autonomous region, or municipality directly under the Central Government shall organize production site inspection, according to the attachment of the Letter of Approval for Drug Registration or the verified manufacturing process. Drug testing institutes shall conduct testing on samples of three batches of product.

Article 118 While reviewing drug supplementary applications, the State Food and Drug Administration may require, with reasons, the applicants to submit additional documents when necessary. Where the regulations are conformed to, it shall issue an Approval for Supplementary Drug Application and a drug approval number;

where the regulations are not conformed to, it shall issue a Disapproval Notice with reasons.

Article 119 After the supplementary application is approved, if a drug approval document is to be renewed, the original one shall be cancelled by the State Food and Drug Administration; if an additional drug approval certificate is to be issued, the original one shall remain valid.

Chapter IX Drug Re-Registration

Article 120 The valid term of a drug approval number, Import Drug License or Pharmaceutical Product License issued by the State Food and Drug Administration is 5 years. To continue its drug production or importation, the applicant shall submit a re-registration application 6 months prior to the expiry date.

Article 121 Within the valid term of a drug approval number, Import Drug License or Pharmaceutical Product License, the applicant shall conduct systematic assessment on the safety, efficacy and quality control of the drug such as relevant research results in the observation period, adverse reaction monitoring, production control and product quality consistency, etc.

Article 122 Where applying for drug re-registration, the holder of a drug approval number shall submit the application to the drug regulatory department of the province, autonomous region, or municipality directly under the Central Government, fill in the Application Form for Drug Re-registration, and provide relevant data.

Where applying for an import drug re-registration, the applicant shall submit the application to the State Food and Drug Administration.

Article 123 Drug regulatory departments of provinces, autonomous regions, or municipalities directly under the Central Government shall review the application dossiers, and issue a acceptance notice of drug re-registration application if requirements are met, or issue a non-acceptance notice, in which reasons shall be given, of drug re-registration application if requirements are not met.

Article 124 Drug regulatory departments of provinces, autonomous regions, or municipalities directly under the Central Government shall review the application dossiers within 6 months starting from the date of acceptance, and approve the re-registration application if regulations are conformed to, or report to the State Food and Drug Administration if regulations are not conformed to.

Article 125 The State Food and Drug Administration shall deal with import drug re-registration applications, complete the review within 6 months, and approve the re-registration application if regulations are conformed to, or issue a non-acceptance notice, in which reasons shall be given, if regulations are not conformed to.

Article 126 In any of the following circumstances, a drug shall not be re-registered:

1. the application for re-registration is not made prior to the expiry date;
2. the relevant requirements set by the State Food and Drug Administration when approved for marketing are not met;
3. the phase IV clinical trial is not completed as required;

4. the adverse drug reaction monitoring is not conducted in accordance with regulations;
5. there are uncertain therapeutic efficacy, serious adverse reaction or other factors harmful to human health upon re-evaluation by the State Food and Drug Administration;
6. the drug approval documents shall be withdrawn in accordance with the provisions of the Drug Administration Law;
7. the production conditions prescribed in the Drug Administration Law are not met;
8. the obligation of observation period is not fulfilled in accordance with regulations; or
9. there are other circumstances not in conformity with relevant regulations.

Article 127 After receiving the opinions from the drug regulatory departments of the provinces, autonomous regions, or municipalities directly under the Central Government, the State Food and Drug Administration shall review the application. Where the regulations on drug re-registration are not conformed to, a notice of rejection for re-registration shall be issued with reasons.

Where a re-registration application has been rejected, except where the drug approval document is withdrawn due to lawfully defined reasons, the drug approval number, Dug Import License or Pharmaceutical Production Certificate shall be withdrawn on the expiry date.

Chapter X Testing for Drug Registration

Article 128 Testing for drug registration consists of sample testing and verification of specifications.

Sample testing refers to the testing of samples conducted by a drug testing institute according to the specifications submitted by an applicant or checked by the State Food and Drug Administration.

Verification of specifications refers to the laboratory testing and review conducted by a drug testing institute on the feasibility and scientific basis of the testing methods and the controllability of the set items and indicators of drug quality in the submitted specifications.

Article 129 The National Institute for the Control of Pharmaceutical and Biological Products or the drug testing institutes of the provinces, autonomous regions, and municipalities directly under the Central Government shall take charge of the testing for drug registration. The National Institute for the Control of Pharmaceutical and Biological Products shall arrange testing for import drug registration.

Article 130 The testing for registration of the following drugs shall be conducted by the National Institute for the Control of Pharmaceutical and Biological Products or the drug testing institutes designated by the State Food and Drug Administration:

1. drugs prescribed in subparagraph (1) and (2) of Article 45 of the Provisions;
2. biological products and radioactive pharmaceuticals; and
3. other drugs specified by the State Food and Drug Administration.

Article 131 Where a drug is permitted entering a special review and approval procedure, the drug testing institute shall give priority to sample testing and specification verification.

Article 132 A drug testing institute engaged in testing for drug registration shall, in compliance with the requirements set forth by the Good Laboratory Practice of drug testing institute and national metrology accreditation, have qualified personnel and adequate equipment, and comply with the quality assurance system and technical requirements of the testing for drug registration.

Article 133 An applicant shall provide the relevant data, samples and reference standards, or assist in sampling, which are required for the testing for drug registration. The amount of samples shall be three times the amount used for testing and, for biological products, manufacturing record for the relevant batches of products shall also be provided.

Article 134 While verifying the specifications of a new drug, the drug testing institute shall, in addition to sample testing, give verification opinions in respect of the specifications and test items, etc., of the drug referring to the study data, the specifications of the same kind of products at home and abroad and relevant requirements.

Article 135 Where the specifications are required to be reestablished, the applicant shall not entrust the drug testing institute that gave verification opinions to conduct the specification study of the drug; and the drug testing institute shall not accept such entrustment.

Chapter XI Drug Registration Specifications and Insert Sheet
Section 1 Drug Registration Specifications

Article 136 National drug standards refer to the Pharmacopoeia of the People's Republic of China, drug registration specifications, etc. published by the State Food and Drug Administration, including the technical requirements such as specifications, testing methods and manufacturing processes, etc.

Drug registration specifications refer to the specified specifications of the applied drug approved by the State Food and Drug Administration to the applicant. The specifications shall be implemented by the drug manufacturer producing the drug.

Drug registration specifications shall not be lower than those required by the Chinese Pharmacopoeia.

Article 137 The establishment of items and the testing methods for drug registration specifications shall be in conformity with the basic requirements of the Chinese Pharmacopoeia, the technical guidelines and rules for compiling the national drug standards published by the State Food and Drug Administration.

Article138 An applicant shall select representative samples for drug registration specifications study.

Section 2 Drug Reference Standards

Article 139 Drug reference standards refer to the materials used in physical, chemical or biological testing specified in specifications and have assigned values of a quantity, and are used for equipment calibration, method validation or value assignment of drugs to be tested, and include reference standards, reference substances, reference crude drugs and reference reagents.

Article 140 The National Institute for the Control of Pharmaceutical and Biological Products shall be responsible for the characterization of national reference standards.

The National Institute for the Control of Pharmaceutical and Biological Products may organize relevant drug testing institute of provinces, autonomous regions, and municipalities directly under the Central Government, drug research institutions or drug manufacturers to undertake collaborative assays of such standards.

Article 141 The National Institute for the Control of Pharmaceutical and Biological Products shall be responsible for the overall technical evaluation of the characterized reference standards in respect of the data of source material selection, preparation methods, testing methods and results, accuracy of value assignment, traceability, stability, filling and packaging conditions, etc. and shall conclude whether or not the candidate materials can be used as national reference standards.

Section 3 Drug Name, Insert Sheet and Label

Article 142 The name, insert sheet and label of any drug for which the registration is applied, shall comply with the provisions of the State Food and Drug Administration.

Article 143 The drug insert sheet and label shall be provided by the applicant. The Center for Drug Evaluation of the State Food and Drug Administration shall review the contents thereof except the manufacturer information, and the State Food and Drug Administration shall review and approve the data when approving the drug production.

The applicant shall be responsible for making the drug insert sheet and label scientific, standard and accurate.

Article 144 The applicant shall monitor the safety and efficacy of a marketed drug, and submit supplementary application to modify the drug insert sheet in time.

Article 145 The applicant shall print the insert sheets and labels according to the format and requirements established by the State Food and Drug Administration, and in conformity with the contents approved.

Chapter XII Timeline

Article 146 The drug regulatory department shall follow the provisions on the timeline for drug registration set forth in the Drug Administration Law, the Administrative Permission Law and the Regulations for Implementation of the Drug Administration Law. The timeline for drug registration in the Provisions refers to the maximum time for acceptance, review and approval of drug registration. The time for the suspension of the review and approval prescribed in laws and regulations or for the applicant to supplement data is not included.

The time for the testing for drug registration and for the review shall be kept in accordance with the Provisions. Where there is a need for time extension in particular situation, it, with reasons provided, shall be reported to the State Food and Drug Administration for approval, and the applicant shall be informed thereof.

Article 147 Drug regulatory departments shall conduct preliminary review on applications, and proceed according to the following circumstances respectively:

1. Where no administrative approval is needed for any application item by law, the non-acceptance of the application thereof shall be informed to the applicant in time;
2. Where an application item is not subject to the jurisdiction of the concerned departments by law, it shall be decided not to accept the application in time and informed to the applicant to apply to the relevant administrative departments;
3. Where there is an error that can be corrected on-site in the dossier, the on-site correction shall be allowed;
4. Where the dossier is incomplete or not conformed with the defined format, the applicant shall be informed on-site or within 5 days at once of what to be supplemented or corrected; if it is not informed to the applicant within the timeline, the application is regarded as accepted on the date the dossier is received; and
5. Where the application item is subject to the jurisdiction of the concerned departments, and the dossier is complete and conformed with the defined format or the applicant has submitted all the required supplementary or corrected data, the application of drug registration shall be accepted.

Where a drug regulatory department accepts or rejects a drug registration application, it shall issue a written receipt on which there shall be a stamp of registration and date.

Article 148 The drug regulatory department of a province, autonomous region, or municipality directly under the Central Government shall complete the check of drug development conditions and raw data, the review of application dossiers, sampling, the notice to drug testing institutes for conducting testing for drug registration, the submission of review opinions, inspection report and application dossiers to the State Food and Drug Administration, and the notice to the applicant of the review opinions within 30 days starting from the date an application is accepted.

Article 149 The time for the testing for drug registration shall be kept in accordance with the following provisions:

1. sample testing: 30 days; sample testing and specifications verification: 60 days; and
2. sample testing of a controlled drug or vaccine: 60 days; sample testing and specifications verification: 90 days.

The sample testing for a drug used for clinical trial conducted by a drug testing institute, as prescribed in Article 36 of the Provisions, shall be completed within the time for sample testing in the previous clause.

Article 150 The time for technical review shall be kept in accordance with the following provisions:

1. new drug application for clinical trial: 90 days; any drug permitted to enter the special review and approval procedures: 80 days;
2. new drug application for production: 150 days; any drug permitted to enter the special review and approval procedures: 120 days;
3. the application for changing the dosage form of a marketed drug or for a generic drug: 160 days; and
4. the supplementary application subject to technical review: 40 days.

The time for the technical review of an import drug registration application shall be kept in accordance with the previous clause.

Article 151 Where the applicant is required to supplement data in the process of technical review, a Deficiency Notice should be issued at one time. Where the applicant disagrees on the contents of the Deficiency Notice, the opinions of the applicant may be heard face to face. The applicant shall provide supplementary data at one time according to the requirements in the notice within 4 months; where an application enters the special review and approval procedures, it shall be handled in conformity with the requirements of the relevant procedures.

After receiving the supplementing data, the technical review shall be completed in no more than one third of the original time; for applications entering the special review and approval procedures, the review shall be completed in no more than one fourth of the original time.

Where an application is recalled by the applicant in the process of drug registration, the review and approval procedure is terminated henceforth.

Article 152 The State Food and Drug Administration shall make the review and approval decision within 20 days; where a decision cannot be made within 20 days, another 10 days may be extended with the approval of the State Food and Drug Administration head in charge, and the applicant shall be informed of the reason of the time extended.

Article 153 The State Food and Drug Administration shall issue and deliver relevant administrative licensing certificates within 10 days from the date the review and approval decision is made.

Chapter XIII Second Review

Article 154 Where there is any of the following circumstances, the State Food and Drug Administration shall not approve the application:

1. different applicants submit the same or almost the same research data without justified reasons;
2. when the application dossier is found false in the process of registration, and the applicant cannot prove the authenticity thereof;

3. the design and performance of the research project are not able to support to evaluate the safety, efficacy and quality of the drug applied for registration;
4. there are critical defects regarding the safety, efficacy and quality in the submitted dossier of the drug applied for registration;
5. an applicant fails to provide supplementary data within the prescribed timeline;
6. the source of drug substances does not meet the requirements;
7. the result of production site inspection or sample testing does not meet the requirements;
8. other circumstances in which applications shall not be approved according to laws and regulations.

Article 155 The written non-acceptance or unapproval decision made by drug regulatory departments by law shall provide the reasons thereof, and inform the applicant of the right to apply for administrative reconsideration or to bring an administrative suit by law.

Article 156 If holding any dispute on the unapproval decision made by the State Food and Drug Administration, an applicant may, within 60 days after receiving the decision, fill in the Application Form for Drug Registration Second Review, and submit the application to the State Food and Drug Administration and provide reasons.

The content of second review shall not exceed the originally applied items and the original application dossier.

Article 157 The State Food and Drug Administration shall make a second review decision, and notify the applicant the decision within 50 days after receiving an application for second review. Where the original decision is affirmed, the State Food and Drug Administration shall not accept any further application for second review thereof.

Article 158 Where there is any need for technical review in second review, the State Food and Drug Administration shall organize relevant technical personnel to conduct review within the timeline as that for the original application.

Chapter XIV Legal Liabilities

Article 159 In any of the circumstances prescribed in Article 69 of the Administrative Permission Law, the State Food and Drug Administration may withdraw the relevant drug approval documents upon the request of any interest party or according to its responsibilities and authorities.

Article 160 Any drug regulatory department or its staff members that violate the provisions of this Provisions and constitute any of the circumstances below shall be instructed by its superior administrative department or supervisory departments to make rectification. If the circumstances are serious, administrative sanctions shall be given to the persons directly in charge and the other persons directly responsible in accordance with law:

1. not accepting a drug registration application that is in conformity with regulatory requirements;
2. not publicizing at the acceptance place the information that shall be publicized by la]w;
3. in the process of acceptance, review and approval, not fulfilling the regulatory informing obligation to the applicant or interest party;
4. not informing the applicant at once of all the contents needed to be supplemented or corrected, where the drug application dossier submitted is incomplete or not conformed with the required format;
5. not stating the reasons of non-acceptance or unapproval of a drug registration application by law; and
6. not holding hearings that shall be held by law.

Article 161 If any drug regulatory department and its staff members request for or accept money or valuable articles from others, or pursue other interests in the process of drug registrations, where a crime is committed, criminal liabilities shall be investigated by law; where a crime is not committed, administrative sanctions shall be given by law.

Article 162 Any drug regulatory department that constitutes any of the following circumstances in the process of drug registration shall be instructed by its superior administrative department or supervisory departments to make rectification, and administrative sanctions shall be given to the persons directly in charge and the other persons directly responsible by law; if a crime is committed, criminal liabilities shall be investigated by law:

1. making a decision to approve any registration application that does not meet the regulatory requirements prescribed in the Provisions or acting beyond regulatory responsibilities and authorities to make such a decision;
2. making a decision to disapprove a registration application conformed with the regulatory requirements, or failing to make a decision to approve a registration application within the regulatory timeline; and
3. failing to perform the confidentiality obligation in violating the requirements prescribed in Article Nine of the Provisions.

Article 163 When undertaking testing for drug review and approval, a drug testing institute that issues a false certificate of analysis shall be punished in accordance with the provisions in Article 87 of the Drug Administration Law.

Article 164 Any drug regulatory department that charges fees without permission or does not charge fees according to set items and rates shall be instructed by its superior administrative department or supervisory departments to return the illegal charges; and administrative sanctions shall be given to the persons directly in charge and the other persons directly responsible by law.

Article 165 Where the Good Laboratory Practice for Non-Clinical Laboratory Studies or the Good Clinical Practice is not executed in the process of drug registration according to regulations, punishments shall be given in accordance with the provisions in Article 79 of the Drug Administration Law.

Article 166 Where an applicant submits false drug registration dossier and samples when applying for clinical trial, the drug regulatory department shall not accept the application or disapprove the applied clinical trial, give a disciplinary warning to the applicant, and not accept any further application for clinical trial of the drug made by the applicant within 1 year; where clinical trial of the drug is already approved, the Drug Clinical Trial Approval shall be withdrawn, a fine of no less than 10,000 yuan but no more than 30,000 yuan shall also be imposed, and no further application for clinical trial of the drug made by the applicant shall be accepted within 3 years.

The State Food and Drug Administration shall keep records of the fraud acts of applicants that submit false dossier and samples, and publicize such records.

Article 167 Where an applicant submits false drug registration dossier and samples when applying for drug production or importation, the State Food and Drug Administration shall not accept or disapprove the application, give a disciplinary warning to the applicant, and not accept any further application made by the applicant within 1 year; where the production or importation of the drug is already approved, the drug approval documents shall be withdrawn, no further application made by the applicant shall be accepted within 5 years, and a fine of no less than 10,000 yuan but no more than 30,000 yuan shall also be imposed.

Article 168 According to the provisions in Article 27 of the Provisions, where a drug testing needs to be repeated but the applicant refuses to do so, the State Food and Drug Administration shall give a warning and instruct to make rectification; if the applicant refuses to make rectification, the application thereof shall not be approved.

Article 169 Where there is any of the following circumstances, the State Food and Drug Administration shall withdraw the drug approval number, and announce to the public:

1. the applicant requests to annul its own drug approval number before the drug approval document expires;
2. the re-registration is not allowed according to provisions in Article 126 of the Provisions;
3. the Drug Manufacturing Certificate is revoked or withdrawn by law;
4. according to provisions in Article 42 of the Drug Administration Law or Article 41 of the Regulations for Implementation of the Drug Administration Law, the drug approval document is withdrawn for any drug with serious adverse reactions or other factors harmful to human health;
5. a decision is made to give an administrative sanction of revoking the drug approval document by law; and
6. other circumstances in which the drug approval documents shall be withdrawn or recalled by law.

Chapter XV Supplementary Provisions

Article 170 The application dossier and requirements of traditional Chinese medicines and natural medicines, pharmaceutical products, biological products, supplementary applications and re-registration application shall be referred to Annex 1, 2, 3, 4, 5 of the Provisions, seriatim. Provisions on observation period are prescribed in Annex 6.

Article 171 The format of drug approval number: Guo Yao Zhun Zi H (or Z/S/J) + four-digit year number + four-digit sequence number; H standing for pharmaceutical products, Z for traditional Chinese medicines, S for biological products and J for repackaged import drugs.

The format of Import Drug License number: H (or Z/S) + four-digit year number + four-digit sequence number; that of Pharmaceutical Product License number: H (or Z/S) C + four-digit year number + four-digit sequence number; H standing for pharmaceutical products, Z for traditional Chinese medicines, S for biological products. For a drug repackaged in China using the license for the large package, the letter B shall be added before the registration number of the original license thereof.

The format of new drug certificate number: Guo Yao Zheng Zi H (or Z/S) +four-digit year number + four-digit sequence number; H standing for pharmaceutical products, Z for traditional Chinese medicines, S for biological products.

Article 172 The acceptance of applications, review and approval of supplementary applications and of re-registration applications undertaken by the drug regulatory departments of provinces, autonomous regions, or municipalities directly under the Central Government prescribed by the Provisions are items delegated by the State Food and Drug Administration. The State Food and Drug Administration may also delegate the drug regulatory departments of provinces, autonomous regions, or municipalities directly under the Central Government to conduct other technical review and review and approval of drug registration.

Article 173 The State Food and Drug Administration adopts the coding management for drugs approved for marketing. The provisions for coding management are separately formulated.

Article 174 The registration applications for narcotic drugs, psychotropic substances, toxic medicines and radioactive pharmaceuticals, besides complying with the Provisions, shall also conform with other relevant State regulations.

Article 175 The provisions for registration of Chinese crude drugs, prepared slices of Chinese crude drugs and import Chinese crude drugs regulated via approval numbers shall be separately formulated by the State Food and Drug Administration.

Article 176 The provisions for drug technology transfer and entrusted manufacturing shall be separately formulated.

Article 177 The Provisions shall go into effect as of October 1, 2007. The Provisions for Drug Registration (Order No. 17 of the State Food and Drug Administration) issued by the State Food and Drug Administration on February 28, 2005 shall be repealed at the same time.

Annex 1 Chinese medicine, natural medicine registration classification and application material requirements
Annex 2 Chemical Drug registration classification and application material requirements
Annex 3 Biologics registration classification and application material requirements
Annex 4 Drug supplementary application—registration matters and application material requirements
Annex 5 Drug re-registration application material requirements
Annex 6 Drug monitoring term table

1.3.1.2 Administrative Measures for the Import of Drugs

Order of the State Food and Drug Administration (No. 4), August 18, 2003
Contents
Chapter I General Provisions
Chapter II Import Record Keeping
Chapter III Port Inspection
Chapter IV Supervision and Administration
Chapter V Annotation

Chapter I General Provisions
Article 1 To regulate the record keeping, customs declaration and port inspection work relating to the import of drugs, guarantee the quality of imported drugs, the present Measures are formulated in accordance with the Pharmaceutical Administration Law of the People's Republic of China, the Customs Law, the Rules for the Implementation of the Pharmaceutical Administration Law of the People's Republic of China and the other relevant laws and regulations (SFDA 2003a, b).

Article 2 The current Measures shall be applicable to the work of record keeping, customs declaration and port inspection relating to the import of drugs.

Article 3 The Drug shall be imported through the ports, which permit the entry of imported drugs upon the approval of the State Council of China.

Article 4 The term "Import Record Keeping" as mentioned in the present Measures refers to the process, in which the import entities file applications to the administrative departments for drugs of the place where the ports are located for customs clearance permit for imported drugs. The import record keeping of narcotics and psychotropic drugs refers to the process that the import entities file applications to the drug administrations where the ports are located for Imported Drugs Port Inspection Notice.

The term "port inspection" means that the medicine inspection institutions determined by the State Food and Drug Administration (SFDA, hereinafter referred to as port drug inspection institutions) conduct examination on the imported Drugs, which have arrived at the ports, in accordance with the law.

Article 5 An import entity shall not go through the formalities for import record keeping and port inspection on imported drugs unless it has acquired the Drug Import Registration Certificate (or Pharmaceutical Products Registration Certificate), or "Drug Import Approval Document ".

In addition, an import entity shall have acquired the Import Permit for the import of narcotics and psychotropic drugs.

Article 6 An import entity shall file a declaration to the customs upon the strength of Customs Clearance Permit for Imported Drugs, while the customs shall handle the procedures for the customs declaration and clearance of the imported drugs.

As to the narcotics and psychotropic drugs, the customs shall handle the procedures for the customs declaration and clearance upon the strength of the Import Permit issued by State Food and Drug Administration.

Article 7 The catalogue of drugs to be imported shall be formulated, amended, and announced by the SFDA jointly with the General Administration of Customs.

Chapter II Import Record Keeping

Article 8 The port drug administrations shall be responsible for the drug import record keeping, which shall be subject to the guidance of the SFDA. Their duties and functions are:

1. To accept the applications for import record keeping, and examine relevant materials;
2. To handle relevant matters related to import record keeping;
3. To contact with the customs for handling matters relating to import record keeping;
4. To notify the port drug inspection offices to make port inspections over the imported drugs;
5. To supervise and address the problems found in import record keeping and port inspection;
6. Other matters as provided for by the Sate Food and Drug Administration.

Article 9 Only as an independent legal person holding a Drug Business License may an entity apply for drug inspection. When a pharmaceutical production enterprise has to import crude drugs and intermediate preparations (including those repackaged within China) needed by this enterprise itself, it shall hold a Pharmaceutical Production License.

Article 10 Under any of the following circumstances, the import record keeping procedures shall not be handled until the imported drugs have been inspected by the port drug inspection offices and have been confirmed as meeting the prescribed standards. For the imported drugs not meeting the prescribed standards, the port drug administrations shall not make import record keeping.

1. The biological products as prescribed by the State Food and Drug Administration;
2. The drugs sold within China for the first time;
3. Other drugs as prescribed by the State Council

Article 11 When an import entity signs a purchase contract, it shall select a port from those permitting the entry of imported drugs as the destination of cargo. The drugs listed in Article 10 shall pass through the ports with a special approval of the state, permitting the entry of imported drugs.

Article 12 An application for import record keeping shall be filed to the destination port drug administration. The imported drugs shall be inspected by the port drug inspection office responsible for the inspection of drugs at the port.

Article 13 When applying for import record keeping, an applicant shall fill in the Imported Drugs Inspection Application Form and submit other relevant materials of the imported drugs (in duplicate) to the local port drug administration upon the strength of the original Drug Import Registration Certificate (or Pharmaceutical Product Registration Certificate (original or duplicate)), and the original Import Permit of narcotics and psychotropic drugs when importing such drugs.

1. Copy of Drug Import Registration Certificate (or Pharmaceutical Product Registration Certificate (original or duplicate)), the Import Permit of narcotics and psychotropic drugs;
2. Copy of the applicant's Drug Business License or Enterprise Legal Person Business License;
3. Copy of certificate of origin;
4. Copy of the purchase contract
5. Copies of the packing lists, bills of lading, and invoices of freight;
6. Copy of the report about the factory inspection;
7. Drug directions and the package and label styles (except for the crude drugs and intermediate preparations);
8. For a biological product within the range of examination, approval and issuance specified by the State Food and Drug Administration, the summary of the production examination records and the original approval issued by the administrative department for drugs of the country or region of origin shall be submitted;
9. For the drugs listed in Article 10, a copy of the recent Report on the Inspection of Imported Drugs and the Customs Clearance Form for Imported Drugs shall be submitted

When a pharmaceutical production enterprise applies for import record keeping for the crude drugs and intermediate preparations needed by itself, it shall submit a copy of both the Pharmaceutical Production License and the Enterprise Legal Person Business License as the materials specified in Item (2) of the present Article.

For the imported drugs transited from other countries or regions, the complete set materials including the purchase contract, packing list, bills of lading, and freight invoices from the place of origin to all the transit places shall be submitted at the same time. Each of the copies of the above-mentioned materials shall be affixed with the seal of the import entity.

Article 14 After a port drug administration has accepted an Imported Drugs InspectionApplication Form and other relevant materials, it shall examine them in compliance with the requirements as below:

1. To examine the above-mentioned materials item by item to see whether they are complete and authentic;
2. To examine the authenticity of the original Drug Import Registration Certificate (or the Pharmaceutical Product Registration Certificate (original or duplicate)), or the original Import Permit for narcotics and psychotropic drugs;
3. If there is no discrepancy upon examination, the original Drug Import Registration Certificate (or the Pharmaceutical Product Registration Certificate (original or duplicate)), or the original Import Permit for narcotics and psychotropic drugs shall be returned to the applicant, and the relevant procedures for import record keeping shall be completed within the same day.

Article 15 For the drugs listed in Article 10 of the present Measures, after the port drug administration has confirmed, upon examination, that there is no discrepancy in the complete set of materials, it shall send an Imported Drugs Port Inspection Notice, attaching a set of the materials as specified in Article 13 of the present Measures, to the competent port drug inspection office, and shall send an Imported Drugs Sampling Notice to the customs office at the same time. The pertinent administrative provisions on the port drug inspection offices' sampling by entering into the supervisory area of the customs office shall be separately formulated by the SFDA and the General Administration of Customs.

The port drug inspection office shall fetch the inspection samples at the sampling place specified in the Imported Drugs Port Inspection Notice, conduct quality inspection on them and shall send the inspection result to the local port drug administration. If the inspection result shows that the imported drugs meet the prescribed standards, the import record keeping shall be approved and a Customs Clearance Form for Imported Drugs shall be issued by the port drug administration; if the inspection shows an adverse result, the import record keeping shall not be approved, and a Notice of Disapproval of Drug Import record keeping shall be issued by the port drug administration.

Article 16 For the drugs other than those listed in Article 10 of the present Measures, after the port drug administration has confirmed that, upon examination, there is no discrepancy in the complete set of materials, it shall approve of the import record keeping and issue a Notice of Customs Clearance for Imported Drugs. At the same time, it shall be responsible for the issuance of Imported Drugs Port Inspection Notice to the port drug inspection office in charge of inspection, and attach to the Notice a complete set of materials as required in Article 13.

For narcotics and psychotropic drugs, after the port drug administration has confirmed, upon examination, that there is no discrepancy in the complete set of materials, it shall issue an Imported Drugs Port Inspection Notice to the port drug inspection office in charge of inspection, and attach to the Notice a complete set materials as required in Article 13 of the present Measures, it needn't issue a Notice of Customs Clearance for Imported Drugs.

The port drug inspection office shall fetch the inspection samples at the sampling place specified in the Imported Drugs Port Inspection Notice, conduct quality inspection on them, and shall deliver the inspection result to the local port drug administration. The drugs confirmed as not meeting the prescribed standards upon inspection shall be dealt with by the port drug administration in accordance with the Pharmaceutical Administration Law and other relevant regulations.

Article 17 Under any of the following circumstances, the imported drugs shall be rejected to be put on import record keeping and a Notice of Disapproval of Putting the Imported Drug on Import Record Keeping shall be issued by the port drug administration; for narcotics and psychotropic drugs, the port drug administration shall not issue an Imported Drugs Port InspectionNotice:

4. An applicant fails to provide the original Drug Import Registration Certificate (or Pharmaceutical Product Registration Certificate (original or duplicate)) or the Import Permit for narcotics and psychotropic drugs;
5. When an applicant goes through the formalities for import record keeping, the valid term of the Drug Import Registration Certificate (or Pharmaceutical Products Registration Certificate) or the Import Permit for narcotics and psychotropic drugs has expired;
6. When an applicant goes through the formalities for import record keeping, the valid term of the drugs is less than 12 months. (For a drug whose valid term is less than 12 months, the valid term of the drugs shall not be less than 6 months when the import record keeping application is handled);
7. The actual production place indicated in the Origin Certification is inconsistent with that specified in the Drug Import Registration Certificate (or in the Pharmaceutical Products Registration Certificate), or the Origin Certification issued by regional international institutions fails to give a clear indication of the production place as specified in the Drug Import Registration Certificate (or in the Pharmaceutical Products Registration Certificate);
8. The import entity fails to obtain a Drug Business License (For the production enterprise, it shall have obtained Pharmaceutical Production License and Enterprise Legal Person Business License);
9. The packages and labels of the drugs that have arrived at the port are inconsistent with the requirements of the State Food and Drug Administration;
10. There is no Chinese language directions for the drug preparations or the Chinese directions is inconsistent with the approved ones;
11. The applicant fails to organize the import at a port permitting the entry of imported drugs upon the approval of the State Council; the destination place of the cargo doesn't fall within the jurisdiction of the local port administration;
12. The applicant fails to provide any evidential document for the biological products within the range of examination, approval and issuance specified by the administrative department for drugs in the production country or region;
13. An applicant forges or alters the relevant documents and vouchers;
14. The Drug Import Registration Certificate (or the Pharmaceutical Registration Certificate) has been canceled;
15. The drugs fall within the scope as specified in Article 10 of the present Measures and shall not be sampled by the port drug inspection office in accordance with Article 25 of the present Measures;

16. The drugs fall within the scope as specified in Article 10 of the present Measures and have confirmed as not meeting the prescribed standards upon port inspection;
17. Other circumstances contrary to the relevant regulations of our country on drug administration.

Article 18 For the imported drugs rejected to be put on import record keeping, they shall be returned to the consignor by the import entity. If unable to be returned, they shall be delivered to and dealt with by the port drug administration.

Article 19 The import of clinical drugs in urgent need, the donated drugs, the samples or comparative drugs needed for the research on new drugs and drug registration shall be subject to the approval of the State Food and Drug Administration, and the import record keeping formalities shall be gone through upon the strength of the Drug Import Approval Document issued by the SFDA in accordance with Article 16 of the present Measures.

Chapter III Port Inspection

Article 20 The port drug inspection offices shall be established by the SFDA in light of the port inspection work related to the imported drugs. A port drug inspection office shall exercise the following functions:

1. To conduct spot inspection on the cargos arrived at the port;
2. To examine the factory inspection report and the Certificate of Origin;
3. To fetch samples under the relevant requirements;
4. To conduct port inspection on the imported drugs;
5. To conduct re-inspection on a disputed inspection result;
6. Other matters as provided for by the State Food and Drug Administration.

Article 21 The National Institute for the Control of Pharmaceutical and Biological Products shall be responsible for the guidance and cooperation of the port inspection on the imported drugs. The standard and comparative samples needed by the port inspection offices shall be examined and labeled by the National Institute for the Control of Pharmaceutical and Biological Products

Article 22 The port drug inspection offices shall conduct inspections on the imported drugs according to the standards specified in the Drug Import Registration Certificate (or the Pharmaceutical Products Registration Certificate).

Article 23 A port inspection office shall contact with the import entity within 2 days from the day it receives the Imported Drugs Port Inspection Notice, and shall fetch samples in the specified storage place of the cargos.

Before sampling, the import entity shall provide the factory inspection report and the original origin certification.

If the port drug inspection office has to fetch samples in the supervisory area of the customs, the port drug inspection office shall, at the same time, contact the customs about the matters related to the sampling, and shall obtain the consent of the customs. When sampling, the personnel of the import entity and those of the customs shall be on the spot at the same time.

Article 24 When a port drug inspection office fetches samples on the spot, it shall pay attention to the imported drugs actually arrived, shall carefully record the samples and fill in the Imported Drugs Sampling Record Form.

For the drugs other than those specified in Article 10, after the port drug inspection office has completed the sampling, it shall give an clear indication of "Sampled" on the original Customs Clearance Permit for the Imported Drugs, and to which it shall affix its official seal.

For narcotics and psychotropic drugs, after the port drug inspection office has completed the sampling, it shall give a clear indication of "Sampled" on the original Import Permit, and to which it shall affix its official seal.

Article 25 A port inspection office shall not fetch samples from the imported drugs under any of the following circumstances:

1. No original factory inspection report or origin certificate has been provided, or the original certificates are inconsistent with the photocopies, which are submitted when the imported drugs are on import record keeping
2. The shipping mark is inconsistent with the documents.
3. The batch number or quantity of the imported drug is inconsistent with the documents.
4. The package and the label of the imported drug are inconsistent with the documents.
5. Other circumstances contrary to the relevant laws, statutes and regulations of our country on drug administration.

As for the drug which needs no sampling, the port drug inspection office shall submit the Imported Drugs sampling recorded form to the port drug administration within 2 days.

Article 26 Port drug inspection office shall in due course conduct inspection on the fetched samples, complete the inspection within 20 days after fetching samples and issue the "Report on the inspection of Imported drugs". When the inspection cannot be completed due to special drugs or to special circumstance, the inspection period can be prolonged accordingly, and the port drug inspection office shall notify import entity and port drug administration. The "Report on the inspection of Imported drugs" shall be with a clear indication of the inspection conclusion, which is marked "To meet the prescribed standards" or "Not to meet the prescribed standards"

For the biological products within the range of examination, approval and issuance specified by the State Food and Drug Administration, if confirmed as meeting the prescribed standards and relevant requirements upon inspection, it shall issue the document for the biological products within the range of examination, approval and issuance at the same time.

Article 27 For the imported drugs as meeting the prescribed standards upon inspection, the port drug inspection office shall deliver the "Report on the Inspection of Imported Drugs" to the port drug administration and the import entity. For the imported drugs as not meeting the prescribed standards upon inspection, the port drug inspection office shall deliver in due course the "Report on the Inspection of Imported Drugs" to the port drug administration and other port drug inspection offices, and to the SFDA and The National Institute for the Control of Pharmaceutical and Biological Products as well.

Article 28 The samples of the imported drugs shall be preserved until the expiry of valid term. If the samples are difficult to be preserved, the preserving period can be adjusted upon actual circumstance. In the case of claim for compensation or return of the imported drugs, the samples shall be preserved until the end of the case. The samples exceeding storage life are dealt with and recorded by the port drug inspection office.

Article 29 If the import entity dissents from the inspection result, it can apply, within 7 days after receiving the inspection result, to the original port drug inspection office for re-inspection and it also can directly apply to The National Institute for the Control of Pharmaceutical and Biological Products for re-inspection. For biological products, the application for re-inspection shall be filed directly to The National Institute for the Control of Pharmaceutical and Biological Products. After accepting the application for re-inspection, the port drug inspection office shall in due course notify port drug administration and make re-inspection conclusion within 10 days which shall be notified to the port drug administration and other port drug inspection offices, and to the SFDA and The National Institute for the Control of Pharmaceutical and Biological Products as well.

Chapter IV Supervision and Administration

Article 30 For the drugs a port drug inspection office shall not fetch samples as prescribed in article 25 of the present Measure but the formalities of customs clearance have been gone through, the port drug inspection office shall adopt administrative coercive measures of sealing and seizing the whole imported drugs

Article 31 For the drugs as not listed in article 10 of this present Measure, which do not meet the prescribed standards upon inspection by port drug inspection office, the import entity shall, within 2 days after receiving the "Report on the Inspection of Imported Drugs", report to the local port drug administration the detailed information of the circulation and use of all imported drugs.

When receiving the "Report on the Inspection of Imported Drugs", the local port drug administration shall in due course adopt administrative coercive measures of sealing and seizing the whole imported drugs and make decision of administrative punishment within 7 days. For the re-inspection application, decision of administrative punishment shall be made within 15 days from the day of the issuance of the inspection report. Pertinent information shall be in due course reported to the SFDA and be notified to drug supervision administration of provinces, autonomous regions, municipalities and other port drug administration.

Article 32 If there is no application for re-inspection within specified period or it is still not consistent with prescribed standards upon re-inspection, port drug administration shall make decision of administrative punishment in accordance with "Pharmaceutical Administration Law" and relevant regulations. Pertinent information shall be reported to the SFDA and be notified to drug supervision administration of provinces, autonomous regions, municipalities and other port drug administration.

If meeting the prescribed standards upon re-inspection, port drug administration shall withdraw administrative coercive measures of sealing and seizing drugs and shall report the decision to the SFDA and notify it to drug supervision administration of provinces, autonomous regions, municipalities and other port drug administration.

Article 33 The other questions found in the process of import report keeping on drugs are dealt with by port drug administration in accordance with "Pharmaceutical Administration Law" and relevant regulations.

Article 34 When a pharmaceutical production or operating enterprise or a medical institution purchases imported drugs, an supplier shall provide the following documents at the same time:

1. Copy of Drug Import Registration Certificate (or Pharmaceutical Product Registration Certificate, copy of Drug Import Approval Document.
2. Copy of "Report on the Inspection of Drug Import" or copy of "Customs Clearance Permit for Imported Drugs" with the indication "Sampled" and to which affixed with the seal.

For a biological product within the range of examination, approval and issuance specified by the State Food and Drug Administration, the document for a biological product within the range of examination, approval and issuance issued by the port drug inspection office shall be submitted at the same time.

For imported narcotics and psychotropic drugs, copy of Drug Import Registration Certificate (or Pharmaceutical Product Registration Certificate, copy of Drug Import Approval Document and copy of Report on the Inspection of Imported Drugs shall be submitted at the same time.

Each of the copies of the above-mentioned materials shall be affixed with the seal of the supplier.

Article 35 Port drug administrations and port drug inspection office shall establish strict administration system for documents of import record keeping and documents of port inspection, and bear secrecy liability for the documents submitted by import entity.

Article 36 If the port drug administration and the port drug inspection office violate relevant regulations as prescribed in import record keeping and port inspection of this present Measure, the SFDA shall give criticism, criticism for general information, if the case is more serious, the SFDA shall stop their qualification for import record keeping and port inspection.

Article 37 If involved in the violation of this present Measure and relevant provisions of the customs, the customs shall deal with it in accordance with the provisions of the Customs Law and The Rules of Administration for the Implementation of the Customs Law of the People's Republic of China

Chapter V Annotation

Article 38 Import entity as mentioned in this present measure includes operating entity, consignee and entity applying for inspection.

Operating entity means the enterprise or entity within China that signs and implements the foreign trade contracts.

Consignee means the consignee or the cargo owner who is indicated in the purchasing contract and the invoice of freight.

Entity applying for inspection means the actual owner of the batch of imported drug or the dealer within China who is specifically responsible for going through the formalities of import record keeping and port inspection. The consignee and the entity applying for inspection can be of the same entity.

Article 39 The pharmaceuticals entering bonded warehouse, bonded area, the special area for processing export products from foreign countries or regions are exempt from handling import formalities of record keeping and port inspection, but are supervised by the customs in compliance with relevant regulations. The pharmaceuticals entering into domestic area from bonded warehouse, export supervisory warehouse, bonded area, the special area for processing export products shall go through formalities of import record keeping and port inspection in compliance with relevant regulations of this present Measure.

The APIs, medicinal materials to be imported in terms of the processing trade under approval are exempt from going through the formalities of import record keeping and port inspection and their pharmaceutical ingredients and medicinal preparation are forbidden to be sold in the domestic area. If they are truly unable to be exported under special circumstance, they shall be delivered as prescribed to local drug supervision and administration department to be disposed of, and be cancelled after verification by the customs.

The small number of drugs carried personally by entering or leaving country personnel should be for personal use and limited to a reasonable amount and accept the supervision from the customs.

Article 40 To import the APIs not listed temporarily in the catalogue of import drugs shall abide by the regulations of this present Measure, and file an application for the import record keeping to the port drug administration.

Article 41 The regulations as regarding the import record keeping and port inspection for the import of medicinal materials are separately formulated by the State Food and Drug Administration.

Article 42 To import narcotics and psychotropic drugs upon the strength of "Drug Import Registration Certificate" (or "Pharmaceutical production Registration Certificate"),import entity shall apply for "Import Permit" in compliance with relevant statutes of the administration of narcotics and psychotropic drugs by the State Council.

Article 43 The narcotics and psychotropic drugs as prescribed in this present Measure refer to the imported narcotic and psychotropic drugs for clinical use, scientific research, teaching, veterinary, etc., which are regulated in compliance with relevant statutes of the administration of narcotics and psychotropic drugs by the State Council.

Article 44 The SFDA and the General Administration of the customs of PRC are responsible for the explanation of this present Measure.

Article 45 This present Measure shall enter into force as of January 1, 2004. The "Administrative measure for the Import of drugs" implemented on the effective date of May 5, 1999 is abolished at the same time.

1.3.1.3 Special Review and Approval Procedure for Drug Registration of the State Food and Drug Administration

The Special Review and Approval Procedure for Drug Registration of the State Food and Drug Administration, adopted at the executive meeting of the State Food and Drug Administration (SFDA) on November 18, 2005, is hereby promulgated and shall go into effect as of the date of promulgation. (SFDA Decree No. 21, 2005)

CONTENTS:

Chapter 1 General Provisions
Chapter 2 Application Acceptance and On-site Inspection
Chapter 3 Testing for Registration
Chapter 4 Technical Review
Chapter 5 Clinical Trial
Chapter 6 Review, Approval and Monitoring of Drug Production
Chapter 7 Supplementary Provisions

Chapter 1 General Provisions

Article 1 This Procedure is formulated for the purpose of effective prevention, timely control and elimination of the hazards of public health emergencies to ensure the health and safety of the public in accordance with the Drug Administration Law of the People's Republic of China, Law of the People's Republic of China on the Prevention and Treatment of Infectious Diseases, Regulations for Implementation of the Drug Administration Law of the People's Republic of China, Regulations on Preparedness for and Response to Emergent Public Health Hazards, and other relevant laws and regulations.

Article 2 The special review and approval procedure for drug registration refers to the procedure and requirements of the State Food and Drug Administration to carry out special review and approval of drugs for handling public heath emergencies under the principle of unified leadership, early involvement, expeditiousness and efficiency, and scientific review and approval, in an effort to approve drugs for the prevention and treatment of public health emergencies as soon as possible under the threat or after the occurrence of public heath emergencies.

Article 3 The State Food and Drug Administration may, according to law, decide to follow the Procedure to conduct special review and approval of drugs for public health emergencies in any of the following circumstances:

1. Where the President of the People's Republic of China declares a state of emergency or the State Council decides that certain areas within a province, autonomous region or municipality directly under the Central Government are in a state of emergency;
2. Where the contingency program for public health emergencies is initiated according to law;
3. Where the drug reserve department or the health administrative department of the State Council proposes a special review and approval for drugs having existing national drug standard;
4. Other circumstances applicable to special review and approval.

Article 4 The State Food and Drug Administration is responsible for the review and approval of clinical trials, production and importation of drugs for the prevention and treatment of public health emergencies.

The (food and) drug regulatory department of a province, autonomous region, or municipality directly under the Central Government shall, upon entrustment of the State Food and Drug Administration, be responsible for on-site inspection and sampling of the pilot products of the drugs for the prevention and treatment of public health emergencies.

Chapter 2 Application Acceptance and On-site Inspection

Article 5 Where the special review and approval procedure for drug registration is initiated, the State Food and Drug Administration is responsible for the acceptance of registration applications for drugs for public health emergencies.

Where a drug or a preventive biological product for public health emergencies has not been marketed in China, the applicant shall, before submission of the registration application, provide the State Food and Drug Administration with relevant research and development information.

Article 6 The applicant shall submit a registration application with relevant technical dossier to the State Food and Drug Administration according to the relevant provisions and requirements on administration of drug registration.

The registration application for drug for public health emergencies may be submitted in electronic form.

Article 7 Before submitting an application for registration, the applicant may provide a feasibility assessment application with general information and relevant explanations. The State Food and Drug Administration shall only comment on the scientific rationality and feasibility of the drug project, and respond within 24 h.

The response to a feasibility assessment application shall be neither deemed as the review and approval opinion nor legally binding on the review and approval result of a registration application.

Article 8 The State Food and Drug Administration shall organize an expert group to evaluate and review the registration application for drug for the prevention and treatment of public health emergencies, make a decision within 24 h on whether or not to accept the application, and notify the applicant.

Article 9 Where a registration application is accepted, the State Food and Drug Administration shall organize technical review of submitted dossier within 24 h and at the same time notify the (food and) drug regulatory department of the province, autonomous region or municipality directly under the Central Government where the applicant is located to conduct an on-site inspection on drug research and development conditions, and organize sampling and testing of pilot products.

The (food and) drug regulatory department of the province, autonomous region, or municipality directly under the Central Government shall, within 5 days, submit the on-site inspection result and relevant opinion to the State Food and Drug Administration.

Article 10 The (food and) drug regulatory department of the province, autonomous region, or municipality directly under the Central Government shall organize staff from the departments of drug registration, drug safety and inspection, etc. to participate in the on-site inspection.

The National Institute for the Control of Pharmaceutical and Biological Products shall be notified to send staff to participate in the on-site inspection and sampling of preventive biological products.

Article 11 For drugs that have existing national standards for the prevention and treatment of public health emergencies, the State Food and Drug Administration may directly review and approve the drug in accordance with the relevant provisions in Chap. 6 of the Procedure when it deems there is no need for a clinical trial in accordance with law.

Article 12 With respect to the registration application for a specific vaccine, where only the original virus strain used in the manufacturing is changed while the manufacturing processes or quality specifications are maintained, the State Food and Drug Administration shall make a decision on whether or not to grant the approval within 3 days after verifying the changed strain used in the manufacturing.

Chapter 3 Testing for Registration

Article 13 After receiving the samples taken by the (food and) drug regulatory department of a province, autonomous region, or municipality directly under the Central Government, the drug testing institution shall immediately organize verification of specifications and laboratory testing on the samples.

The drug testing institution shall complete the testing within the time frame for the drug being applied.

Article 14 For a drug applied first time for marketing, the State Food and Drug Administration may, when necessary, make early involvement by appointing the National Institute for the Control of Pharmaceutical and Biological Products to communicate with the applicant prior to testing for registration so as to timely resolve technical problems which may arise in the process of quality specifications verification and laboratory testing.

With respect to preventive biological products used to prevent and control the epidemic of serious infectious diseases, the State Food and Drug Administration may, depending on the situation, allow the testing for registration and the manufacturer's self-testing to be performed in parallel.

Article 15 After completion of the specifications verification and laboratory testing on a drug, the drug testing institution shall, within 2 days, issue its verification opinion and submit it along with the drug test report to the State Food and Drug Administration.

Chapter 4 Technical Review

Article 16 The State Food and Drug Administration shall, within 15 days after acceptance of the registration application for drug for the prevention and treatment in public health emergencies, complete the first round of technical review.

Article 17 Where the State Food and Drug Administration considers that additional data are needed, it shall immediately inform the applicant of the content and timeline.

Where the applicant submits the supplementary data within the specified timeline, the State Food and Drug Administration shall complete the technical review within 3 days, or, depending on the situations, organize another review meeting within 5 days, and then complete the review report within 2 days.

Chapter 5 Clinical Trial

Article 18 Where the technical review is completed, the State Food and Drug Administration shall, within 3 days, complete the administrative examination, make a decision and inform the applicant.

Where the State Food and Drug Administration decides to approve a clinical trial, it shall issue a Drug Clinical Trial Approval. Where it decides not to approve, it shall issue a Disapproval Notice with reasons.

Article 19 Where an applicant obtains a clinical trial approval, it shall conduct the trial strictly following the relevant requirements in the approval document, and comply with the Good Clinical Practice.

Article 20 Drug clinical trials shall be conducted in institutions legally certified for drug clinical trials. If a clinical trial has to be conducted by an institution not yet certified, a special approval by the State Food and Drug Administration should be obtained.

The application for a clinical trial conducted by an institution not yet certified for drug clinical trials may be submitted along with the application for drug registration.

Article 21 The investigator responsible for a drug clinical trial shall, in accordance with the relevant provisions, timely report adverse events occurred in the process of the clinical trial to the State Food and Drug Administration. If no adverse event occurs, the investigator shall collect relevant information and report to the State Food and Drug Administration monthly.

Article 22 The State Food and Drug Administration shall, in accordance with law, supervise and inspect the clinical trials of drugs for public health emergencies.

Chapter 6 Review, Approval and Monitoring of Drug Production

Article 23 The applicant shall, after completion of the drug clinical trials, submit the relevant data to the State Food and Drug Administration in accordance with the Provisions for Drug Registration.

Article 24 The State Food and Drug Administration shall, within 24 h after receiving data submitted by the applicant, organize technical review, and at the same time notify the (food and) drug regulatory department of the province, autonomous region, or municipality directly under the Central Government where the applicant is located to conduct the on-site inspection on the drug manufacturing conditions, and organize the sampling and testing of pilot products.

The (food and) drug regulatory department of the province, autonomous region, or municipality directly under the Central Government shall, within 5 days, submit the result and opinion of the on-site inspection to the State Food and Drug Administration.

Article 25 Any newly-established drug manufacturer or manufacturer with newly-built manufacturing workshops or newly-added dosage forms for production may apply to the State Food and Drug Administration for a certificate of the Good Manufacturing Practice along with the application for drug registration. The State Food and Drug Administration shall, when conducting the drug registration review, immediately carry out an inspection on the Good Manufacturing Practice certification.

Article 26 The drug testing institution shall, after receiving the samples of three batches taken by the (food and) drug regulatory department of the province, autonomous region, or municipality directly under the Central Government, immediately arrange the testing.

Upon completion of testing, the drug testing institution shall, within 2 days, complete the test report and submit it to the State Food and Drug Administration.

Article 27 The State Food and Drug Administration shall carry out technical review in accordance with Chap. 4 of the Procedure, and shall, within 3 days after the completion of the technical review, complete the administrative examination, make a decision and inform the applicant.

Where the State Food and Drug Administration decides to approve the drug, it shall issue the Letter of Approval for Drug Registration, and may grant an approval number for the drug at the same time if the applicant has appropriate manufacturing conditions; if it decides to disapprove the manufacturing, it shall issue a Disapproval Notice with reasons.

Article 28 Where a drug manufacturer or distributor, or a medical and health institution finds any new or serious adverse drug reaction or cluster adverse reaction relating to a specially approved drug for public health emergencies, it shall immediately report the case to the local (food and) drug regulatory department of the province, autonomous region, or municipality directly under the Central Government, the health administrative department at the provincial level and the professional institution for adverse drug reactions monitoring.

The professional institution for adverse drug reactions monitoring shall regard drugs specially approved for public health emergencies as critically monitored products, analyze the collected case reports in accordance with the relevant provisions and timely report to the (food and) drug regulatory department of the province, autonomous region, or municipality directly under the Central Government and the State Food and Drug Administration.

The State Food and Drug Administration shall reinforce the reevaluation of approved drugs for public health emergencies after they are marketed.

Chapter 7 Supplementary Provisions

Article 29 The measures for special review and approval of the medical devices for public health emergencies shall be separately formulated by the State Food and Drug Administration with reference to the relevant provisions of the Procedure.

Article 30 The Procedure shall go into effect as of the date of promulgation.

1.3.2 Administrative Regulations for Technology Transfer Registration of Drugs

This regulation is issued in 2009 and aiming to facilitate new drug licensing and manufacturing technology transfer. This regulation provides the permission for multinational pharmaceutical companies to transfer the production process of imported drug to domestic manufacturer in China. This regulation provides a new option to multinational pharmaceutical companies during their development process for imported drug license application (SFDA 2009a, b).

Contents:

Chapter I General Provisions

Chapter II Conditions for the Application of New Drug Technology

Chapter III Conditions for the Application of Drug Production Technology Transfer

Chapter IV Application and Examination of Technology Transfer for Drugs

Chapter V Supplementary Provisions

Chapter I General Provisions

Article 1 This Regulation is formulated in accordance with the Provisions for Drug Registration for the purpose of speeding up the transformation of achievements in new drug development, promoting rational transfer of production technologies, encouraging industrial restructuring, optimizing product mix, regulating the registration of drug technology transfer, and assuring the safety, effectiveness and quality controllability of drugs (SFDA 2009a, b).

Article 2 Provisions of this Regulation apply to the application, evaluation, examination, and monitoring of technology transfer for drugs.

Article 3 Drug technology transfer refers to the transfer of drug production technology by the owner to the transferee (a drug manufacturer) according to the provisions of this Regulation and the application of drug registration by the transferee.

Drug technology transfer is classified into new drug technology transfer and drug production technology transfer.

Chapter II Conditions for the Application of New Drug Technology

Article 4 Registration applications for new drug technology transfer may be submitted prior to the expiration date of the monitoring period of the new drug in any of the following circumstances:

1. Drugs with new drug certificates only;
2. Drugs with new drug certificates and drug approval numbers.

For (1) finished products with new drug certificates only and not yet in the monitoring period for new drugs; or (2) APIs with new drug certificates, applications for new drug technology transfer shall be submitted prior to the expiration date of the monitoring period for the corresponding finished products specified in Annex 6 of the Provisions for Drug Registration from the issue date of the new drug certificates.

Article 5 A new drug technology transfer contract shall be signed between the transferor and transferee.

For drugs with new drug certificates but without drug approval numbers, the transferor shall be all the holders of the new drug certificates.

For drugs with new drug certificates and drug approval numbers, the transferor shall be all the holders of the new drug certificates and the drug approval numbers.

Article 6 The transferor shall transfer all the relevant technical dossier of the transferred product such as the manufacturing process and specifications to the transferee and guide the transferee in trial production of 3 consecutive batches of qualified samples.

Article 7 In case changes improving the quality and safety risk control occur in the new drug technology transfer, research shall be conducted in accordance with relevant regulations and technical guidelines. The research information shall be submitted simultaneously with the application dossier.

Article 8 The transferee shall continue to complete the requirements specified in the original drug approval documents issued to the transferor from the approval date of the new drug technology transfer application, for example, to complete the monitoring of ADRs and phase IV clinical trials.

Chapter III Conditions for the Application of Drug Production Technology Transfer

Article 9 Drug production technology transfer may be applied in any of the following circumstances:

1. a. Drugs with new drug certificates only or simultaneously with drug approval numbers, the monitoring periods of which have expired; b. Finished products with new drug certificates only or simultaneously with drug approval numbers,

but without monitoring periods; c. Finished products with new drug certificates only and not yet in the monitoring periods; or APIs with new drug certificates, for which the monitoring periods of the corresponding finished products specified in Annex 6 of the Provisions for Drug Registration have expired from the issue date of the new drug certificates;

2. For drugs without new drug certificates, both the transferor and transferee shall be legally qualified drug manufacturing enterprises, one of which holding over 50 percent of the equity or shares of the other, or both of which being subsidiaries of a same drug manufacturing enterprise, which is the majority shareholder of both sides.
3. For import drugs with IDLs, the production technology may be transferred to local drug manufacturing enterprises by the original appliers for the import drug registration.

Article 10 A drug production technology transfer contract shall be signed between the transferor and transferee.

Article 11 The transferor shall transfer all the relevant dossier and technologies of the transferred product such as the formula, manufacturing process and specifications to the transferee and guide all the work such as the lab-scale production, the pilot-scale production, the validation of manufacturing process parameters, and batch production. The transferor shall also guide the transferee in the trial production of 3 consecutive batches of qualified samples. Drugs manufactured by the transferee shall be consistent with those produced by the transferor in quality.

Article 12 Drugs manufactured by the transferee shall be consistent with those produced by the transferor in formula, manufacturing process, specifications and so on. Changes affecting the drug quality such as changes in API, excipients (kind, quantity and proportion), manufacturing process and process parameters shall not occur.

Article 13 The production scale of the transferee shall be not exceeding 10 fold and not less than one-tenth of the production scale of the transferor, otherwise the relevant manufacturing process parameters shall be revalidated and the validation dossier shall be submitted simultaneously with the application dossier.

Chapter IV Application and Examination of Technology Transfer for Drugs

Article 14 The transferee shall be a drug manufacturing enterprise, the production scope of which specified by the Drug Manufacturing License shall cover the dosage form of the transferred drug.

Article 15 The transferor shall transfer all the strengths of the transferred drug to a same transferee in one transaction.

Article 16 Technology transfers for APIs of narcotic drugs, psychotropic drugs of category I, psychotropic drugs of category II, and drug precursors are forbidden. Finished products for psychotropic drugs of category II shall only be transferred to manufacturers with the qualification for designated production.

Radioactive drugs shall be only transferred to manufacturers with manufacturing licenses for the corresponding drug.

Article 17 For drug technology transfer, a Supplementary Application Form shall be filled in. The dossier and explanation shall be submitted to the provincial food and drug administration where the transferee is located in accordance with the procedure of supplementary application and the attached requirements of this Regulation.

For drugs with drug approval numbers, the application of writing off the original drug approval numbers by the holders shall be submitted simultaneously.

For drugs with IDLs of finished products and simultaneously with IDLs of bulk products for local package in China, the application of writing off the IDLs for bulk drugs by the transferor shall be submitted simultaneously. For drugs with approval documents for local package in China, the application of writing off the above approval documents by the local package enterprises shall be submitted simultaneously.

For drugs with approval of toll manufacture, relevant approval documents for the termination of toll manufacture issued by food and drug administrations shall be submitted simultaneously.

Article 18 In case the transferor and transferee are located in different provinces, autonomous regions or municipalities, the provincial food and drug administration where the transferee is located shall bring forward examination opinions.

Article 19 The provincial food and drug administration where the transferee is located is responsible for the format examination of the application dossier for technology transfer and the organization of site inspection on the transferee. The institute for food and drug control where the transferee is located is responsible for testing 3 batches of samples.

Article 20 The CDE shall evaluate the application dossier, form a technical evaluation opinion and bring forward a comprehensive evaluation opinion according to the site inspection report and the testing result of the samples.

Article 21 The SFDA shall determine whether to approve the application according to the comprehensive evaluation opinion brought forward by the CDE. The Approval Letter of Supplementary Application and a drug approval number will be issued for qualified application.

For drugs having obtained drug approval numbers before the technical transfer, the original drug approval numbers issued to the transferor shall be written off simultaneously.

For drugs having obtained IDLs of bulk drugs for local package in China and the approval documents for local package in China before the transfer, the above certificates and approval documents shall be written off simultaneously.

For finished products for psychotropic drugs of category II, the qualification for designated production previously obtained by the transferor shall be written off at the time of approval of the technology transfer.

In case the new drug technology transfer is approved, the original copy of the new drug certificate shall be returned with added information of the transfer. Otherwise the original copy of the new drug certificate shall be sent back.

In case the technology transfer for drugs with IDLs is approved, the original copy of the IDL shall be returned with added information of the transfer.

An Approval Letter for Clinical Trials is issued when necessary. For unqualified application, a Notification Letter of the Examination Opinions is issued and the reason for rejection is explained.

Article 22 In case clinical trials are necessary deemed by the CDE, the reference drug shall be the marketed products manufactured by the transferor. In case the transferor did not obtain a drug approval number, the reference drug shall be selected in accordance with the Provisions for Drug Registration and relevant technical guidance.

Article 23 After clinical trials are finished, the transferee shall submit the dossier for clinical trials to the CDE and copy to the provincial food and drug administration, which shall organize site inspection on the clinical trials.

Article 24 The application for technology transfer shall not be considered or rejected after consideration in any of the following circumstances:

1. The transferor or transferee is unable to bear civil liability independently due to invalidation of the relevant legal registration documents;
2. The transferor or transferee is unable to provide valid approval documents;
3. The drug is in the state TCM protection period;
4. Relevant information in the application dossier such as the name of the transferor is not in accordance with that of the holder of the new drug certificate or the drug approval number, for which the relevant approval documents are missing;
5. The transferor failed to complete the requirements specified in the approval documents in the prescribed time limit;
6. The SFDA confirms that there are safety problems with the drugs to be transferred;
7. Other circumstances in which the SFDA determines not to consider or to approve.

Chapter V Supplementary Provisions
Article 25 Any dispute occurring in the technology transfer shall be settled by consent or through legal proceedings.

Article 26 This Regulation is in effect from the date of issue and other regulations on technology transfer for drugs previously issued shall be repealed simultaneously.

1.3.2.1 Regulations of Special Examination and Approval in New Drug Registration

Issued by the SFDA on January 7, 2009. No.17 (SFDA 2009a, b)

Article 1 The requirements are developed in accordance with the Provisions for Drug Registration for the purpose to encourage research and development of new drugs and to strengthen risk controls.

Article 2 In accordance with Article 45 of Provisions for Drug Registration, the SFDA may implement special examination and approval in the cases of the following applications of new drugs:

1. active ingredients extracted from plants, animals or minerals, etc. and their preparations not yet marketed in China, and newly discovered Chinese crude drugs and their preparations;
2. chemical drug substance and their preparations and biological products not yet approved for marketing in China or abroad;
3. new drugs for the treatment of diseases, such as AIDS, malignant tumors and rare diseases, etc. with significant clinical advantages;
4. new drugs for the treatment of diseases, for which effective therapeutic method are not available.

The new drugs for the treatment of diseases that are not covered by the state approved "Functions and Indications of TCM preparations", may be considered as new drugs for the treatment of diseases for which effective therapeutic method is not available.

For those drugs specified in items "1)" and "2)", the applicant of drug registration (hereinafter "the Applicant") may apply for the special examination and approval when submitting the application for clinical trials of the new drugs.

For those drugs specified in items "3)" and "4)", the applicants may apply for the special examination and approval only when submitting the production applications.

Article 3 If a registration application meets the requirements specified in Article 2 by review and confirmation of the SFDA in response to the application from the applicant, the SFDA shall give priority to this application in the registration procedures, then, accordingly shall enhance the communication with the applicant.

Article 4 The applicant applying for special examination and approval shall fill out Application Form for Special Examination and Approval of New Drug Registration (see Appendix 1) and submit the relevant required data.

The Application Form for Special Examination and Approval of New Drug Registration and the relevant data should be filed in a separate dossier and be submitted to the acceptance department for drug registration along with the application dossier required by the Provisions for Drug Registration.

Article 5 Upon acceptance, the Acceptance Department shall forward the relevant data of Special Examination and Approval application along with the submitted registration dossier to the Center of Drug Evaluation (CDE), the SFDA.

Article 6 The CDE is in charge of organizing a review and confirmation on the application for Special Examination and Approval, and then informs the applicant with the review results, which will be published on the website of the CDE at the same time.

1. For those specified in items "1)" and "2)" of Article 2, the CDE shall conduct review and confirmation within 5 days after receipt of the application for special examination and approval;
2. For those specified in items "3)" and "4)" of Article 2, the CDE shall organize Expert Meeting for review and confirmation within 20 days after receipt of the application for special examination and approval.

The time used for review and confirmation on an application for special examination and approval is included in the time frame of technical review as specified by Provisions for Drug Registration.

Article 7 Where a drug application is permitted entering a special examination and approval procedure, the CDE shall conduct corresponding technical review on the application in accordance to the relevant procedures and requirements. Authorities responsible for site inspection and lab testing should give priority to the registration application that is permitted entering a special examination and approval procedure.

Article 8 For the registration application permitted entering a special examination and approval procedures, in addition to data supplementation as requested by the CDE, the applicant may also submit new data supplementation under any of the following circumstances:

1. significant safety information newly discovered;
2. data prepared as required by the evaluation meeting;
3. data needed for communication.

For item "1)", if the applicant submits the supplementary data after technical review conclusion is made by the CDE, the time frame of technical review should be extended accordingly, normally 20 days.

Article 9 After receiving the Deficiency Notice issued by the CDE, the applicant should complete the supplementary data within an extended 8 months if it is not possible to submit within 4 months.

Article 10 For applications entering a special examination and approval procedure, the CDE shall establish a working mechanism for communication with the applicant to jointly discuss the concerned technical issues.

Article 11 For the registration application of item "1)" or "2)" of Article 2, provided that the same drug has not yet been granted with special examination and approval, after the basic data of pre-clinical pharmaceutical study, safety and efficacy become available, and before the clinical trial application, the applicant may apply for communication with the CDE, where the topics may be application of special examination and approval, significant technical issues.

Article 12 For the registration applications of Article 2, based on the completion of certain phase of clinical trials and evaluation summary, the applicant may submit to the CDE of the SFDA an application for communication in respect of the following issues:

1. significant safety issues;
2. clinical trial protocol;
3. summary and evaluation on staged results of clinical trials.

Article 13 For the registration application permitted entering a special examination and approval procedure, if any significant changes are necessary during clinical trials such as protocol amendment, indication and specification change, etc., the applicant may submit an application for communication based on the evaluation of the effects of the changes with respect to drug safety, efficacy and quality control.

Article 14 To apply for communication, the applicant should fill out Application Form for Communication of Special Examination approval in New Drug Registration (Appendix 2), and submit relevant data.

Article 15 The CDE shall review Application Form for Communication of Special Examination and Approval of New Drug Registration and the relevant data submitted by the applicant and notify the applicant with the results.

Article 16 When the CDE agrees to any application for communication, it should clearly notify the applicant with the issues to be discussed, and confirm the applicant with method, time, place and attendants of communication, etc., and organize the communication within 1 month after notifying the applicant. However, for the case of Article 11, the communication should be organized within 3 months

Article 17 Communication should be recorded with signatures of both parties to confirm for further reference in the subsequent study and evaluation.

Article 18 The applicant applying for special examination and approval should establish risk control and implementation plan during application for both clinical trials and production.

Article 19 If any registration application granted with special examination and approval for clinical trial application, the applicant shall still need to submit the relevant data as required by this regulation. However, there will be no need for special examination confirmation as the special examination and approval shall apply automatically.

Article 20 Under any of the following circumstances, the SFDA may terminate the special examination and approval procedure, and publicly announce the termination on the website of the CDE:

1. The applicant asks for a termination;
2. The applicant fails to fulfill the required obligation within the specified time frame;
3. Expert Meeting concludes that the special examination and approval procedure is no longer appropriate.

Article 21 When any emergency event occurs that threats the public health, or after occurrence of public healthcare emergency, drug registration needed for such emergency shall follows the special examination and approval as specified by the SFDA Special Examination and Approval Procedures of Drug.

Article 22 This regulation shall become effect as of the date of publication.

Appendix 1: (Table 1.3)

Appendix 2: (Table 1.4)

1.3.2.2 Provisions for Drug Insert Sheets and Labels

The provisions come into force as of June 1, 2006 (SFDA 2006)

Contents

Chapter I General Provisions
Chapter II Drug Insert Sheet
Chapter III Drug Labels
Chapter IV Use of Drug Name and Registered Trademark
Chapter V Other Provisions
Chapter VI Supplementary Provisions

Chapter I General Provisions

Article 1 The Provisions are enacted with a view to regulating drug insert sheets and labels in accordance with the Drug Administration Law of the People's Republic of China and the Regulations for Implementation of the Drug Administration Law of the People's Republic of China.

Article 2 The insert sheets and labels of drugs marketed within the territory of the People's Republic of China shall meet the requirements of the Provisions.

Article 3 Drug insert sheets and labels shall be reviewed and approved by the State Food and Drug Administration.

A drug shall be labeled on the basis of its insert sheet. The content of the label shall be within the scope of the insert sheet. Any words and marks with implied therapeutic effects, misleading information on usage, or inappropriate promotion of the product shall not be printed.

Article 4 A drug label shall be printed on or affixed to the drug package, and no other written words, audio and/or visual materials or other information are attached to introduce or publicize the product or the enterprise.

An insert sheet shall be attached to the smallest package provided by the drug manufacturer for marketing.

Article 5 The wording in drug insert sheets and labels shall be scientific, standardized and accurate. The insert sheet of a non-prescription drug shall be written intelligibly and convenient for patients to judge, choose and use the drug on their own.

Article 6 In the label or insert sheet, the letters or characters shall be clear and easy to be recognized and the marks shall be clear and distinctive. The label and insert sheet shall have no print faded and shall not be affixed unsteadily. Any addition or modification shall not be made by means of pasting, cutting or altering.

Table 1.3 Application form of special examination and approval in new drug registration

INN name		Chemical Name	
Registration		Indication(s)	
Category.			
Registration application meets any of those conditions	□ Active ingredients extracted from plants, animals or minerals, etc. and their preparations not yet marketed in China, and newly discovered Chinese crude drugs and their preparations; □ Chemical drug substance and their preparations and biological products not yet approved for marketing in China or abroad; □ New drugs for the treatment of diseases such as AIDS, malignant tumors and rare diseases, etc. with significant clinical advantages; □ New drugs for the treatment of diseases, for which effective therapeutic method are not available.		
Justification of the application Pages may be attached when needed			
Risk control and implementation plan Pages may be attached when needed			
Applicant 1 (chop) ________ Legal representative (chop)	Applicant 2 (chop) ________ Legal representative (chop)	Applicant 3 (chop) ________ Legal representative (chop) ________	Application date________
________	________		
Contact person of Applicant_______ Telephone No. __________ Fax No._____ Address_____________ e-mail: ______________Mobile Phone No.__________			

Notes to the Form

1. This form is prepared in accordance with REGULATIONS OF SPECIAL EXAMINATION AND APPROVAL IN NEW DRUG REGISTRATION
2. TCM may not need to fill a chemical name

Article 7 Drug insert sheets and labels shall be written in standardized Chinese characters published by the National Language Commission. The versions in other languages shall comply with the Chinese version.

Article 8 With the aim to protect public health and direct the rational use of drugs, drug manufacturers may voluntarily apply to add warnings to drug insert sheets or labels. The State Food and Drug Administration may also request drug manufacturers to add warnings to drug insert sheets or labels.

Chapter II Drug Insert Sheet

Article 9 A drug insert sheet shall include the significant scientific data, conclusions and information concerning drug safety and efficacy in order to direct the safe and rational use of drugs. The specific format, content and writing requirements of drug insert sheet shall be prescribed and issued by the State Food and Drug Administration.

Article 10 Disease names, pharmaceutical terms, drug names, the names and results of clinical testing in drug insert sheets shall be expressed in professional terms published or standardized by the State. The units of measurement shall conform to the national standards.

Article 11 All the active ingredients or medicinal ingredients of traditional Chinese medicines in a prescription shall be listed in the insert sheet. For injections and non-prescription drugs, all excipients shall be listed as well.

---

3. Registration Category should be identical to the Application Form of Registration Application
4. Registration application meets any of those requirements: just to tick off "√" the applicable box "□"
5. Justification of the application: Any corresponding summary data to support that the new drug registration meets any related conditions should be provided according to the specific condition in accordance with Regulations of Special Examination and Approval in New Drug Registration. The major contents in the summary data shall include the followings:
1) Summary data to support that the drugs meet the requirement of Article 2 of Regulations of Special Examination and Approval in New Drug Registration
2) The proposed clinical trial protocol or the summary of any clinical trials that already completed
3) Evaluation of drug safety and efficacy, while considering the pharmacology study and toxicology study and clinical trials
4) Summary of the pharmaceutical research that already completed
5) Summary of other major research. The detailed research data or spectrum will not necessarily be included in this summary. Additional pages can be attached if needed but normally should be not more than 15 pages
6. Risk control and implementation plan: Risk control plan mainly refers to precaution and prevention measures established against those potential risks during the clinical use of the new drug. Please work out specific risk control and implementation plan for clinical trial or post marketing, based on the situation and specific stages of drug development and in accordance with Regulations of Special Examination and Approval in New Drug Registration
7. This Form should be submitted within the specified time frame specified by Regulations of Special Examination and Approval in New Drug Registration
8. This form shall be in four copies with one original and three duplicates

Table 1.4 Application form to apply for communication of regulations of special examination and approval in new drug registration

INN name		Chemical Name	
Registration Category.		Indication(s)	
Registration application meets any of those requirement	□ Active ingredients extracted from plants, animals or minerals, etc. and their preparations not yet marketed in China, and newly discovered Chinese crude drugs and their preparations; □ Chemical drug substance and their preparations and biological prod ucts not approved for marketing in China or abroad; □ New drugs for the treatment of diseases such as AIDS, malignant tumors and rare diseases, etc. with significant clinical advantages; □ New drugs for the treatment of diseases, for which effective therapeutic method are not available.		
The special approval is applicable or not	□ Permitted □ Not yet	Special examination and approval number	
Method of communication	□ round table □ video conference □teleconference		
Study already completed	Before clinical trial application: □pharmaceutical research □pharmacodynamic research □toxicology After clinical trial starting: □Phase I □Phase II □Phase III		
Issues to be communicated	□application for a special examination and approval □significant technical issues □summary and evaluation on the staged results from clinical trials □clinical trial protocol □ significant safety issues □amending of the protocol □change in indication □change in specification □others		
Issue to be discussed and relevant data			

Table 1.4 (continued)

To attach pages if needed					
Attendants applying for communication	Name	Company/Organization	Title	Specialized Field	Responsibility during research
Remarks					
Applicant (chop)____________________ Legal Representative (chop) ________________Application Date__________					
Contact Person________ Telephone No. ____________Fax No._______________ Address_______________ e -mail : ________________Mobile Phone No. _________					

Note to the Form

1) This form is prepared in accordance with Regulations of Special Examination and approval In New Drug Registration
2) TCM may not need a chemical name
3) Registration Category should be identical to the Application Form of Registration Application
4) Registration application meets any of those requirements: just to tick off "√" the applicable box "□"
5) If the new drug registration is already permitted entering a special examination and approval, the applicant should fill the special examination and approval no
6) Method of communication: just to tick off "√" the applicable box "□" to indicate the desired method
7) Study already completed: please choose "Before clinical trial application" or "After clinical trials starting" to indicate the development phase of the new drug, then tick off "√" the applicable box "□"
8) Issues to be communicated: can be multiple choices. Please choose according to Regulations of Special Examination and Approval in New Drug Registration. Application for communication other than those in the scope will not be accepted
9) If the application for communication is submitted before application for clinical trials, the issue(s) for communication should be explained in section of "Issue(s) to be discussed and relevant data", with submission of medical summary and pharmaceutical summary data, along with detailed data and background data related to the issue(s) for communication. Medical summary data: information that can support the drugs meet the Article 2 of Regulations of Special Examina-

The ingredients or excipients included in a prescription, which may cause severe adverse reaction, shall be specified.

Article 12 A drug manufacturer shall trace the safety and efficacy of its marketed drugs. For any modification to the insert sheet, an application shall be submitted timely.

The State Food and Drug Administration may also require a drug manufacturer to make modification to the insert sheet on the basis of the results of adverse drug reaction monitoring and drug re-evaluation.

Article 13 After the modification of the insert sheet is approved, the drug manufacturer shall inform relevant drug distributors, drug users and other departments of the modified content immediately and use the modified insert sheet and label timely as required.

Article 14 The insert sheet shall provide full information on adverse drug reaction and indicate the adverse reactions in detail. A drug manufacturer, who fails to timely modify the insert sheet on the basis of the safety and efficacy data of the marketed drug or to fully explain the adverse reaction in the insert sheet, shall be liable for all the consequences arising therefrom.

Article 15 The approval date and the modification date shall be distinctively shown in the insert sheet.

Chapter III Drug Labels

Article 16 Drug labels refer to the information printed or pasted on drug packaging, including inner labels and outer labels. Inner labels refer to those that appear on immediate packaging; outer labels are those on the other packaging outside of inner labels.

---

tion and Approval in New Drug Registration summary and general evaluation of pre-clinical safety and efficacy, description of the diseases to which the application aimed (pathogenesis mechanisms, current methods of treatment, and overall evaluation on the therapeutic efficacy), proposed protocol of a clinical trial (including subject screening, proposed dose of exposure, and control drug, etc.), clinical trial plan, summary of clinical trial that already completed, summary of previous clinical usage (if any), main preventive measures against any foreseeable risks from clinical use or clinical trial. Pharmaceutical summary data: drug manufacturing process that already completed, quality specification or quality control procedures (including the description and justification of the test items related to safety), summary of stability studies

10) If the application for communication is submitted after obtaining the permit entering a special examination and approval procedure, the issues to be communicated should be explained in the section of "Issue(s) to be discussed and relevant data", and research data and summary data related to the discussion or communication should be provided as attachment to this form in addition to the original registration dossier

11) This form should be submitted within the specified time frame as required by Regulations of Special Examination and Approval in New Drug Registration

12) This form is in 4 copies with one original and 3 duplicates

Article 17 The inner label shall bear such drug information as the adopted name in China, indications or functions, strength, dose and usage, production date, batch number, expiry date and manufacturer. If there is no enough space in the package to include all the information mentioned above, the adopted name in China, strength, batch number and expiry date shall be indicated at least.

Article 18 The outer label of a drug shall indicate such information as the adopted name in China, ingredients, description, indications or functions, strength, dose and usage, adverse reactions, contraindications, precautions, storage, production date, batch number, expiry date, approval number and manufacturer. Where indications or functions, dose and usage, adverse reactions, contraindications and precautions cannot be fully noted, main information plus a "See drug insert sheet for details." notice shall be indicated.

Article 19 The label on the package for transportation and storage shall bear at least the adopted name in China, strength, storage, production date, batch number, expiry date, approval number and manufacturer. Other information such as packaging quantity, precautions for transportation or other marks may be included when necessary.

Article 20 The label for drug substance shall include the adopted name in China, storage, production date, batch number, expiry date, applied specifications, approval number and manufacturer. Other necessary information such as packaging quantity and precautions for transportation shall also be indicated.

Article 21 Where one drug produced by a manufacturer has the same drug strength and packaging specification, the content, format and color of its labels must be the same. Where one drug produced by a manufacturer has different drug strengths or packaging specifications, its labels shall be clearly distinguished from one another, or its specifications shall be notably marked in the corresponding specification items.

Where a drug produced by a manufacturer is administrated as prescription drug and non-prescription drug respectively, their packaging colors shall be distinctly different.

Article 22 For drugs with special requirements on storage, its requirements shall be marked in the notable place of the label.

Article 23 The expiry date in the drug label shall appear in the order of year, month and day, with year shown in four digits, month and day in two digits. Its specific format shall be "Valid till xxxx year xx month" or "Valid till xxxx year xx month xx day". It may be presented with numbers and other symbols as "Valid till xxxx.xx." or "Valid till xxxx/xx/xx".

For the preventive biological product, the expiry date shall be labeled according to the registration specifications approved by the State Food and Drug Administration. The expiry date of the biological product for therapeutic use shall be counted from the filling date. For other drugs, the expiry date shall be counted from the production date.

Where the expiry date is labeled to the day, it shall be marked as 1 day earlier than the actual expiry date; where the expiry date is labeled to the month, it shall be marked as 1 month earlier than the actual expiry month.

Chapter IV Use of Drug Name and Registered Trademark

Article 24 The drug name in insert sheets and labels shall conform to the nomenclature principles on the adopted name in China and trade name of drug announced by the State Food and Drug Administration, and shall be consistent with those appeared in the approval documents of the drug.

Article 25 The adopted name in China shall be conspicuous and prominent, and its typeface, size and color shall be consistent, and meet the following requirements:

1. For horizontal labels, the adopted name in China shall appear in a prominent position within the area of the upper one-third of the label; for vertical labels, it shall appear in a prominent position within the area of the right one-third of the label;
2. No such illegible typefaces as cursive characters and seal characters shall be used, and no such format as italics, margining and shading shall be used to modify the typefaces.
3. The font color of the adopted name in China shall be black or white, in sharp contrast to the light colored or dark-colored background respectively.
4. Writing in separate lines shall be avoided unless limited by the packaging size.

Article 26 The trade name of a drug shall not be placed in the same line with the adopted name in China; its typeface and color shall be no more conspicuous than that of the adopted name in China, and its font area per character shall be no bigger than half of that of the adopted name in China.

Article 27 Unregistered trademarks and other drug names unapproved by the State Food and Drug Administration shall not be used in the drug insert sheets and labels.

Where a registered trademark is used in a drug label, it shall be printed in a corner of the label. Where a registered trademark contains characters, the font area per character shall be no bigger than a quarter of that of the adopted name in China.

Chapter V Other Provisions

Article 28 For narcotic drugs, psychotropic substances, medicinal toxic drugs, radioactive pharmaceuticals, drugs for topical use, non-prescription drugs and other drugs having special marks specified by the State, their special marks shall be printed in the drug insert sheets and labels. Where there are special provisions issued by the State for drug insert sheets and labels, they shall prevail.

Article 29 The labeling provisions for Chinese crude drugs and prepared slices of Chinese crude drugs shall be formulated separately by the State Food and Drug Administration.

Article 30 Where drug insert sheets and labels are not in compliance with the Provisions, a punishment shall be imposed in accordance with the relevant provisions of the Drug Administration Law of the People's Republic of China.

Chapter VI Supplementary Provisions
Article 31 The Provisions shall come into force as of June 1, 2006. the Provisions for Drug Packaging, Labels and Insert Sheets (Provisional) issued by State Food and Drug Administration on October 15, 2000 shall be annulled therefrom.

1.3.2.3 Application Dossier writing Requirements in CTD Format for Chemical Drugs

The implementation of common technical document (CTD) format to assemble all the Quality, Safety and Efficacy information has revolutionized the regulatory review process. It led to harmonized electronic submission and enabled implementation of good review practices in the western world in the past decades. For the pharmaceutical companies, the use of CTD format eliminated the need to reformat the information for submission to the different ICH regulatory authorities, even though there are some differences regarding the module requirement in various regions. In general, the CTD includes five modules. Module 1 is region specific and Modules 2, 3, 4 and 5 are intended to be common for all regions. In July 2003, the CTD became the mandatory format for new drug applications in the EU and Japan, and the strongly recommended format of choice for NDAs submitted to the FDA (Roth 2007).

In recent years, the SFDA has spent significant effort to improve the standards and qualities in pharmaceutical research and development to be in line with international standards. On September 25, 2010, the Department of Drug Registration of the SFDA issued the Notice on Relevant Issues Concerning the Requirements on Application Dossiers in CTD Format for Pharmaceutical Chemicals, No.387. This notice, No. 387, requires that the technology and evaluation department review the registration applications submitted in CTD format separately in sequence to encourage submission of application materials in CTD format. On September 27, 2012, the CDE started to review the registration application submitted in CTD format separately in a sequential process on the basis of actively carrying out various tasks, and elaborated relevant issues (China Pharmaceutical Newsletter 2012). The details are as follows:

1. According to the requirements of the notice, the NDA dossier submitted in CTD format with main research summary of the study information (including electronic version) were listed in the separate CTD sequential process for review. This includes the NDA dossiers in registration category 5 and 6 including category 3+5 and 3+6 drugs. The CTD data were listed and queue up for regulatory review based on the order of submission time to the CDE. The review plan was published on the website of the SFDA. In light of the requirements of the Provisions for Drug Registration, the approved registration for category 3 and

4 drugs shall enter into the monitoring period. In this monitoring period, other applicants' applications for similar varieties that have been accepted but not yet approved for clinical trials shall be rejected. As such, to keep the consistency of review progress for registered category 3 and 4 varieties, applications for both types shall not be included in the separate CTD sequence.

2. To ensure that China's drug registration really keep abreast with international standards, the CDE encourages the application and research carried out in accordance with the research and development concept and technical requirements embodied in the CTD format; and shall not approve the following applications:
   - those which have not been carried out in accordance with the research and development concept and technical requirements embodied in the CTD format;
   - those whose production process research, impurities research and other aspects have serious defects;
   - those whose quality control system has no adequate supportive research data, such as the failure to conduct as required the impurity comparative studies with the products of original research and development pharmaceutical companies, and the failure to conduct the research and control of toxic impurities or degradation products that shall be definitely controlled according to Pharmacopoeias at home and abroad.

In these cases, the applicants can reapply after improvement. The technical standards shall be consistent, be it registration application in CTD format or Annex-2 format.

The CDE shall be on a continuing basis to summarize the common problems found in the review of the application dossiers submitted in CTD format and publish such information on its website in the form of electronic publications for the applicants' attention.

For the multinational pharmaceutical companies who seek to apply for the import drug approval in China, they usually apply for category I or III new drugs. Category I new drugs are defined as the newly developed pharmaceutical products that have not yet received market approval in any country at the time of application. For category I new drug clinical trial approval, the minimum requirement is that the multinational pharmaceutical companies have to have entered phase II clinical trials. Category III drugs are defined as that imported pharmaceutical products already approved overseas but not yet introduced to the Chinese market. All imported pharmaceutical products are subject to the documentation requirements as described under classification I or III.

The multinational pharmaceutical companies can submit all materials using ICH –CTD format; however, the comprehensive introduction part of the dossier needs to follow the Chinese requirements as outlined by the SFDA.

The documentation requirements of the SFDA can be divided into 4 different modules for chemical new drug application as defined in Annex 2 of the Provisions for Drug Registration (Order No. 28). For chemical category I drug application, the four modules contain 32 booklets for documentation. The application package (booklets) depends on the drug category that the new drug belongs to.

- Module 1: Summary
- Module 2: Pharmaceutical information
- Module 3: Pharmacology and toxicology study information
- Module 4: Clinical study Information

The above modules will be described and compared to the CTD in the following corresponding chapters. Once the appropriate classification of the imported pharmaceutical product has been determined, the manufacturer can determine the necessary documentation requirements to support the application.

Briefly, the CMC module in China's CTD format for class 3–6 drugs on marketing authorization application is required, but not for IND submission. The format of submission should in accordance with the booklets required by Appendix 2 of Provisions for Drug Registration. Overall, the ICH-CTD is acceptable by the SFDA. The module 1 for summary should follow the SFDA defined requirements.

1.3.3 Regulations Related to Quality Management, GLP, GMP, GCP Certification

1.3.3.1 Good Laboratory Practice for Non-clinical Laboratory Studies(GLP)

The State Drug Administration Regulation, Order No. 2, Effective Date: on September 1, 2003 (SDA 2003)

Chapter I—General Provisions
Article 1 The provisions are established for improving the quality of non-clinical laboratory studies on new drugs, for assuring the truthfulness, integrity and reliability of experimental data, and for ensuring drug safety for human use pursuant to the stipulations of the Pharmaceutical Administration Law of the People's Republic of China.

Article 2 The provisions shall be adapted to non-clinical laboratory studies for applications of drug registration. All non-clinical research organizations shall follow the provisions.

Chapter II—Organization and Personnel **Article 3** Non-clinical research organizations shall be in compliance with the provisions to establish a well-organized management system. It shall be staffed with a responsible person of the organization, a responsible person of the quality assurance unit and other corresponding personnel.

Article 4 Personnel of non-clinical research organization shall meet the following qualifications:

1. having prudent scientific style, good professional morality and appropriate education and knowledge, receiving professional training, and possessing job experience and capabilities needed for their assignments;
2. familiarizing with the fundamentals of the provisions, strictly performing their assigned duties, skillfully mastering and strictly implementing the Standard Operation Procedures involved in the assignments;
3. making records accurately, clearly and on time, and reporting to the study director in written form on anything happening in the experiment that may affect the experimental results;
4. dressing according to the needs of their work posts, conforming to requirements of personal sanitation and taking health precautions to avoid the contamination of test and control articles and test systems; and
5. taking periodical health examination. Those who are found to have an illness that may adversely affect the reliability of the study shall be excluded from the study.
6. having training, testing, and obtaining job qualifications

Article 5 The responsible person of the non-clinical research organization shall possess a bachelor or a higher degree on medical, pharmaceutical or other relative specialties. Correspondingly professional qualification and abilities are also required. The responsibilities are as follows:

1. taking overall responsibilities and implementing the establishment and organization management of the non-clinical research organization;
2. establishing and maintaining current records of education, professional training and job experience for each individual engaged in the non-clinical laboratory studies;
3. ensuring that there are various facilities, equipment and experimental conditions in compliance with the provisions;
4. ensuring that there are an adequate number of qualified personnel with clear responsibilities and duties and that all of them carry out their work according to the requirements of the provisions;
5. designating a responsible person for the Quality Assurance Unit and ensuring that he or she completes the responsibility defined in the provisions;
6. making master schedule sheet and monitoring the progress in various studies;
7. organizing the establishment and revision of the Standard Operation Procedures and monitoring the personnel to implement the Standard Operation Procedures involved in their assignments;
8. designating a study director before the beginning of each study project. When anyone of them is to be changed, the reasons for and the date of the change shall be recorded;
9. reviewing and approving protocols and final reports;
10. timely dealing with the reports from the Quality Assurance Unit and recording in detail the measures taken;
11. ensuring that the quality and the stability of the test and control articles meet the specification; and

12. signing a written contract with the cooperator or the sponsor.

Article 6 Non-clinical research organizations shall establish an independent quality assurance unit, the number of personnel of which depends on the size of the research organization. The purpose of the establishment is to assure that the facilities, equipment and management system of the research organization are in compliance with the provisions. The responsibilities of the Quality Assurance Unit are:

1. keeping the duplicate of the master schedule sheets, protocols and final reports of the non-clinical research organization;
2. reviewing the protocols, experimental records and final reports according to the provisions;
3. inspecting and supervising every study project and making a plan for reviewing and inspection based on the study project and its duration. Recording in detail inspection, problems existing and measures taken, signing the name and keeping the records for reviewing;
4. inspecting periodically the animal care facilities, experimental instruments and the management of the archives;
5. reporting the problems found during the inspection to the responsible person of the organization and the study director on time, proposing suggestions for solving them and writing down an inspection report; and
6. taking part in the establishment of Standard Operation Procedures and keeping a duplicate of the Standard Operation Procedures.

Article 7 A study director shall be designated in each study project, whose responsibilities are as follows:

1. taking whole responsibilities of the routine operations of the study project;
2. preparing the protocols, proposing the revision or addition of the corresponding Standard Operation Procedures, analyzing the study results and drafting the final reports;
3. complying strictly with thestandard operational procedures. Any changes shall be approved by the responsible person of the organization;
4. assuring that the personnel engaged in the study understand clearly the assignments undertaken and have a good command of the corresponding Standard Operation Procedures;
5. monitoring the progress of the study project and inspecting the various experimental records to assure them to be accurate, direct, clear, and on time;
6. recording in detail the unforeseen cases during the experiment and the measurements taken for remedy;
7. sending the protocols, raw data, specimens which shall be kept, corresponding documentation records and final reports to the archives room after the completion of the experiment; and
8. assuring that each step of the study project is in compliance with the requirements of the provisions.

Chapter III Laboratory Facilities

Article 8 Non-clinical research organizations shall establish corresponding experimental facilities in accordance with the requirements of the provisions and the study project.

All kinds of laboratory facilities shall be kept clean and sanitary, and laid out in a rational way to avoid cross contamination. The environmental conditions Environmental conditions and its justifications should meet the requirements of different facilities.

Article 9 Non-clinical research organizations shall have animal care facilities designed rationally and allocated suitably. The environmental conditions, including temperature, humidity, air cleanness, ventilation, lighting, etc. shall be controlled according to the needs. Animal care facilities mainly include the following:

1. the animal care and management facilities for different genus and species of animals or test systems;
2. the facilities for quarantine of animals and for isolation and treatment of diseased animals;
3. the facilities for collection and disposal of wastes;
4. the facilities for cleaning and disinfection; and
5. the corresponding animal care and management facilities that shall be established when test or control articles contain volatile substance, radioactive materials, biohazardous materials, etc.

Article 10 Non-clinical research organizations shall have storage facilities for feeds, bedding materials, cages and other articles for animal use. Allocation of various facilities shall be rational, preventing contamination with test system. Proper measures shall be taken for easily decayed and deteriorated articles for animal use.

Article 11 Non-clinical research organizations shall have the facilities for handling test and control articles:

1. facilities for receipt and storage of the test and control articles; and
2. facilities for preparing and storing test and control articles.

Article 12 Non-clinical research organizations shall establish corresponding laboratories in accordance with the needs. Specialized laboratories shall be established if biohazardous materials, microorganisms, etc. are handled and used.

Article 13 Non-clinical research organizations shall have facilities for storing protocols, specimens, raw data, final reports, relative documentation and records.

Article 14 Non-clinical research organizations shall establish facilities for environmental monitoring and control.

Chapter IV—Instruments, Equipment and Experimental Supplies

Article 15 Non-clinical research organizations shall be provided with the corresponding instruments and equipment according to the study needs. The instruments and equipment shall be suitably located and managed by the authorized person. To assure the stable and reliable performance of instruments and equipment, they shall be inspected, cleaned, maintained, tested and calibrated periodically.

Article 16 The Standard Operation Procedures, indicating the use, the maintenance and calibration of the instruments and equipment shall be provided in the laboratories where the equipment and instruments are placed. The date, the use and the operator's name on operating, inspecting, testing, calibrating and repairing shall be recorded in detail.

Article 17 Management of the test and control articles of non-clinical research organizations shall be in compliance with the following requirements:

1. The test and control articles of experiments shall be managed by the authorized person and shall be received, registered and distributed according to the procedures. The batch number, stability, content or concentration, purity and other chemical characteristics shall be accurately recorded. In cases where marketed products are used as control articles, such products can be characterized by their labeling or other indications to replace the laboratory analyses.
2. The test and control articles shall be stored under suitable conditions. The container storing test or control articles shall be labeled to indicate the name, abbreviation name, code number, batch number, expiry date, and storage conditions.
3. Contamination or deterioration shall be avoided during the distribution of the test and control articles. The test and control articles distributed shall be accurately labeled on time. Documentation shall be made for the date and quantity distributed and returned for each batch.
4. The uniformity of the mixture shall be determined before administration for each test or control article that is necessary to be mixed with a certain medium. The concentration and stability of the test or control article in the mixture shall also be determined periodically, if necessary. When anyone of the components of the mixture has an expiry date, the date shall be clearly shown on the container. If more than one component have expiry date, the earliest expiry date shall be taken as criterion.

Article 18 The reagents and solutions in laboratories shall be labeled to indicate the name, concentration, storage conditions, preparation date, expiry date, etc. The deteriorated or outdated reagents or solutions shall not be used in the experiments.

Article 19 The animal feeds and drinking water shall be periodically analyzed to ensure that they comply with the nutrition standards and that the contamination adversely affecting the research results shall be less than the limit specified. The analytical results shall be kept as raw data.

Article 20 Research results shall not be adversely affected by the use of detergents, disinfectants, pesticides, etc. in animal care room and the name, concentration, method used, date, etc. shall be recorded in detail.

Chapter V Standard Operation Procedures

Article 21 Non-clinical research organizations shall establish Standard Operation Procedures. The required Standard Operation Procedures should include the following;

1. editing and managing of Standard Operation Procedures.
2. qaulity assurance procedures
3. receipt, labeling, storage, handling, preparing, ordering, sampling and analyzing of test and control articles;
4. animal room and laboratory preparation as well as environmental monitoring and controlling;
5. maintenance, repair, calibration, use and management of experimental facilities, instruments and equipment;
6. operation and management of computer system;
7. transfer, quarantine, numbering and care of test animals;
8. observation records and experimental operations of test animals;
9. operational techniques, such as collection of test samples, examination, determination of various indexes, etc.;
10. examination and handling of animals found to be moribund or dead during study;
11. necropsy of animals as well as histopathological examination;
12. collection, numbering and examination of experimental specimens;
13. management and processing of various experimental data
14. health examination system of personnel;
15. disposal of animal carcasses and other waste;
16. edition and management of Standard Operation Procedures; and other Standard Operation Procedures

Article 22 Standard Operation Procedures shall not be valid until signed and confirmed by the Quality Assurance Unit and approved by the responsible person of research organization. Invalid Standard Operation Procedures shall be destroyed on time except one copy kept.

Article 23 The establishment, revision, valid date as well as distribution and destroying of Standard Operation Procedures shall be recorded and the records shall be well maintained.

Article 24 Standard Operation Procedures shall be stored in the way to assure their convenient use. Any deviations of Standard Operation Procedures shall be approved by the study director and recorded in the raw data. Any significant changes in Standard Operation Procedures shall be confirmed by Quality Assurance Unit and approved by the responsible person of research organization in written form.

Chapter VI Study Implementation

Article 25 Non-clinical research organization shall designate a title or code number for each study project and indicate it uniformly in the documentation and experimental records concerned.

Article 26 Specimens collected from experiment shall be identified by study project title or code number, animal number and collection date.

Article 27 A written protocol shall be prepared and signed by study director. The protocol shall not be implemented until reviewed by the Quality Assurance Unit and approved by the responsible person of non-clinical research organization. The approval date is defined as the initiation date of experiments. If non-clinical study project is commissioned, the protocol shall be also approved by the sponsor.

Article 28 The study protocol shall contain the following:

1. title or code number of the study project and its purpose;
2. the name and address of non-clinical research organization and sponsor;
3. the name of study director and researchers engaged in the study;
4. the name, abbreviation name, code number, batch number, related physicochemical properties and biological characteristics of the test and control articles;
5. justification for selection of the test system;
6. the species, strain, number, age, sex, body weight range, source of supply and grade of the test animals;
7. the method of identification of test animals;
8. the environmental conditions for caring test animals;
9. the name and code number of the feeds;
10. solvents, emulsifiers and other media used in the studies;
11. the route, method, dosage level, frequency and duration of administration of test and control articles as well as the reason for the choice;
12. guiding principle document and literature used in toxicity studies;
13. the frequency and method of tests, analyses and measurements;
14. statistical methods; and
15. the location where all experimental data are to be stored.

Article 29 If the protocol is necessary to be amended during the study, the amendment shall be reviewed by the Quality Assurance Unit and approved by the responsible person of research organization. The amendments, reasons and date thereof shall be recorded and kept together with the original protocol.

Article 30 Study director is responsible for the overall conduction of the study. Personnel engaged in the experiment shall carry out the protocol strictly in compliance with the corresponding Standard Operation Procedures and report on time any abnormalities found during the experiment to the study director.

Article 31 All data shall be recorded directly, accurately, legibly, indelibly and on time and shall be dated and signed by the recorder. If any record is to be corrected, the original record shall be legible and the reason for and date of the correction shall be noted, and the records shall be signed by the corrector.

Article 32 If animals display diseases caused by the factors rather than test articles or abnormalities interfering the research purpose, the animals shall be isolated and quarantined immediately. If the animals are to be treated with drugs, the treatment shall be approved by the study director, and the reasons, approval procedures, examination, drug prescription, date, result, etc. shall be recorded in detail. The treatment shall not interfere with the research.

Article 33 Study director shall prepare a final report and sign it on time after the completion of the study. The final report shall be reviewed by the Quality Assurance Unit and approved by the responsible person of the non-clinical research organization. The approval date is defined as the completion date of the study.

Article 34 The final report shall contain the following:

1. the title or code number of the study project and its purpose;
2. the name and address of non-clinical research organization and sponsor;
3. the date of initiation and completion of the study;
4. the name, abbreviation name, code number, batch number, stability, content, concentration, purity, components and other characteristics of the test and control articles;
5. the species, strain, number, age, sex, body weight range, source of supply, certificate number, certification agency, date of receipt and housing conditions of test animals;
6. the route, dosage, method, frequency and duration of administration of the test and control articles;
7. justification of dosage levels of the test and control articles;
8. the abnormalities that may have affected the reliability of the study and caused the deviation from the protocol;
9. the frequency and method of tests, analyses and measurements;
10. the names and post assignments of the study director and all researchers;
11. statistical methods;
12. study results and conclusion; and
13. the locations where all raw data and specimens are stored.

Article 35 After the final report is signed by the responsible person of non-clinical research organization, if there are corrections or additions to the final report, the parts corrected or added, the date and reasons thereof shall be explained in detail by the responsible person concerned. Such correction or additions shall be confirmed by the study director, reviewed by the Quality Assurance Unit, and approved by the responsible person of non-clinical research organization.

Chapter VII Data and Archives

Article 36 Original protocols, specimens, raw data, records, final reports, documentation concerned with the experiment, inspection report of Quality Assurance Unit, etc. shall be ordered by the study director according to requirements of Standard Operation Procedures and handed to the archives room after completion of the study. They shall be numbered and stored according to Standard Operation Procedures.

Article 37 When the study project is withdrawn or ceased, the study director shall explain the reason in written form and then put in order and keep all the data specified in articles mentioned above in the archives.

Article 38 Archives room shall be under the charge of the authorized persons and shall be managed according to the requirements of Standard Operation Procedures.

Article 39 The retention period of the protocols, specimens, raw data and documentation records, final report and other archives shall last at least 5 years since the drug marketing.

Article 40 Wet specimens, the characteristics of which are liable to be changed, such as tissues, organs, electron microscopic specimens, blood smear, specimens from reproduction toxicity study, etc. shall be retained only as long as the quality of the preparation affords evaluation.

Chapter VIII Supervision and Inspection

Article 41 The State Drug Administration is responsible for supervision, inspection and certification of non-clinical research organizations.

Article 42 All non-clinical research organizations applying for drug registration in the People's Republic of China shall be regulated under the supervision, inspection and certification.

Chapter IX—Supplementary

Article 43 Terms used in this provision are defined as follows:.

1. Non-clinical laboratory study means any toxicity experiments performed under laboratory conditions to evaluate the safety of new drugs, including studies of single dose toxicity, repeated dose toxicity, reproduction toxicity, mutagenic action, carcinogenecity, irritation, dependence and others.
2. Non-clinical research organization means the facility which conducts non-clinical laboratory studies of new drugs, including safety research centers, safety research institutes, research laboratories or teams for safety studies.
3. Test system means animals, plants, microorganisms, cells or genes used to conduct toxicity studies.
4. Quality assurance unit means any unit in non-clinical research organizations that is designed to assure that the study is in compliance with the provisions.
5. Study director means the person who is responsible for the overall conduction of a certain study project.
6. Test article means any drug or substance to be developed into a drug used to conduct a non-clinical laboratory study.
7. Control/reference article means any drug or any other product used in non-clinical laboratory studies for the purpose of establishing a basis for comparison with the test article.
8. Raw data mean any materials and original documents or records which record the original research observations, including worksheets, notes, photographs, microfiche or microfilm copies, microcopies, computer printouts, magnetic media, recorded data from automated instruments, etc.

9. Specimen means any materials derived from a test system for analysis and examination.
10. Sponsor means the unit which commissions the non-clinical research organization to conduct the non-clinical laboratory studies for the test article.

I. Batch number means a distinctive combination of numbers and/or letters which can be used to trace and review the production history of the batch of the test or control articles.

Article 44 Article 44 This provision by The State Food and Drug Administration is responsible for interpretation of this provision.

Article 45 The provisions shall enter into force on September 1, 2003. The former Good Laboratory Practice for Non-clinical Laboratory Studies (GLP) (Trial) issued by State Drug Administration on October 14, 1999 shall be repealed simultaneously.

1.3.3.2 Good Manufacturing Practice for Pharmaceutical Products

Amended in 2010, the SFDA Order No. 79, Order by Ministry of Health of the People's Republic of China (SFDA 2010)
CONTENTS:
Chapter 1 General Provisions
Chapter 2 Quality Control
Chapter 3 Organization and Personnel
Chapter 4 Workshop and Establishment
Chapter 5 Equipment
Chapter 6 Material and Product
Chapter 7 Confirmation and Validation
Chapter 8 Document Management
Chapter 9 Manufacturing Management
Chapter 10 Quality Control and Quality Guarantee
Chapter 11 Consigned Manufacturing and Consigned Inspection
Chapter 12 Product's Delivering and Recall
Chapter 13 Self check
Chapter 14 Supplementary Articles

Chapter 1 General Provisions
Article 1 To standardize good manufacturing for pharmaceutical products, this Regulation is enacted in accordance with the "Drug Administration Law of the People's Republic of China" and "The Regulation on the Implementation of Drug Administration Law of the People's Republic of China".

Article 2 A pharmaceutical enterprise shall establish pharmaceutical goods' quality control system. The system shall contain all factors which may affect the quality of pharmaceutical goods, including all organized and planned activities ensuring pharmaceutical goods' quality in accordance with intending purpose.

Article 3 This Regulation is part of quality control system, is basic requirement for manufacturing and quality control of pharmaceutical products. This Regulation aims to reduce the risks in pharmaceutical goods' manufacturing process at its maximum, such as pollution, cross pollution and confusion, mistake, ensure for continuous stably manufacturing pharmaceutical goods in accordance with intending purpose and registered requirements.

Article 4 The enterprise shall obey this Regulation strictly, insist on honesty and keep faith, prohibit any ostensible and spurious activities.

Chapter 2 Quality Control
Section 1 Principle
Article 5 The enterprise shall establish quality target in accordance with pharmaceutical goods' quality control requirements, carry out all requirements related to safety, effective and quality control into the process of pharmaceutical goods' manufacturing, control and products' discharging, storage, delivering, ensure all pharmaceutical goods are produced in accordance with intending purpose and registered requirements.

Article 6 Senior administrator in enterprise shall ensure the achievement of intending quality target. Personnel in different levels and provider, dealer shall participate in and take each responsibility.

Article 7 The enterprise shall equip adequate personnel, workshop, establishment and equipment in accordance with requirements, and provide essential condition for achieving quality target.

Section 2 Quality Guarantee
Article 8 Quality guarantee is a part of quality control system. The enterprise must establish quality guarantee system, and establish integrate document system at the same time, in order to ensure the system's effective running.

Article 9 Quality guarantee system shall ensure the following

1. Represent the requirements of this Regulation in pharmaceutical goods' design and development.
2. In accordance with the requirements of this Regulation in manufacturing management and quality control activities;
3. Specific management responsibility;
4. Exact stocked and used raw material and wrapper;
5. Effective control in semifinished product;
6. Implement of confirmation and validation;
7. Manufacture, examine, inspect and double examined according to rules strictly;
8. Each batch of products shall only discharge after quality authorizing person's approval;
9. Applicable measures to ensure pharmaceutical goods' quality during the process of storage, delivering and all succedent operation process;
10. According to self-examine rules, examine and evaluate the validity and applicability of the quality guarantee system quality.

Article 10 Basic requirements of pharmaceutical goods' manufacture quality management:

1. Frame manufacturing technique, systemic review and demonstrate it could continuous stably manufacturing products in accordance with requirements;
2. Manufacturing technique and its important changes shall be validated;
3. Equip all required resources, include, but not limited the following:
    1. Hold applicable qualification and the eligible trained personnel;
    2. Adequate workshop and space;
    3. Applicable equipment and maintain guarantee;
    4. Accurate raw material, wrapper and label;
    5. Approved technique rules and operate rules;
    6. Applicable storage and freight condition.
4. Use accurate and easy understand language to frame operate rules;
5. The operate person could accurate operate according to operate rules after training;
6. The whole manufacture process shall be recorded. The windage shall be researched and be recorded;
7. Batch record and delivering record shall be traced back to the whole history of the batch of products, and the records shall be saved appropriately and be easy consult;
8. Reduce the quality risk during the pharmaceutical goods' delivering process;
9. Establish pharmaceutical goods' recall system, and ensure any batch delivered and sold products could be recalled;
10. Survey the reasons leading to pharmaceutical goods' complaints and quality objections, take measures to prevent similar quality objections.

Section 3 Quality Control

Article 11 Quality control includes corresponding organization, document system and sampling, test and so on, to ensure material or products finish necessary examination before delivering, and to verify its quality is in accordance with the requirements.

Article 12 Basic requirements of quality control:

1. Equip applicable establishment, equipment, instrument and trained personnel to effective and reliable finish all related quality control activities;
2. Have approved operate rules, which used to sampling, examine, inspect raw material, wrapper, semifinished product, bulk product and finished product and products' stability, monitor environment when necessary, to ensure the products is in accordance with the requirements of this Regulation;
3. Authorized person shall sampling to raw material, wrapper, semifinished product, bulk product and finished product according to stated methods;
4. Inspect methods shall be confirmed and validated;
5. Sampling, check, inspect shall be recorded, the windage shall be researched and be recorded;

6. Material, semifinished product, bulk product and finished product shall be checked and inspected according to quality standard and be recorded;
7. Material and packaged finished product shall have enough reserved samples so that necessary check or inspect shall be taken; except the finished product with too large package container, the reserved samples' package shall be the same with the final package of the finished product.

Section 4 Quality Risk Management

Article 13 Quality risk management is evaluate, control, communicate, audit system process to quality risk during the whole product life period, via the manner of foresee or review.

Article 14 Quality risk shall evaluate according to science knowledge and experience in order to ensure products' quality.

Article 15 The method, measure, form take during the quality risk management process and the documents formed in the said process shall accommodate to the level of the existent risk.

Chapter 3 Organization and Personnel

Section 1 Principle

Article 16 An enterprise shall establish management organization which accommodate to the pharmaceutical goods' product and have its organization framework chart.

The enterprise shall set up independent quality management department, which carries out the responsibilities of quality guarantee and quality control. The quality management department could set up quality guarantee department and quality control department respectively.

Article 17 Quality management department shall take part in all activities relating to quality, and take responsibility to audit all documents relating to this Regulation. The personnel in quality management department shall not relegate his responsibility to the personnel in other department.

Article 18 The enterprise shall be staffed by an appropriate number of management and technical personnel with appropriate qualification (including education background, training and practice experience), and the responsibilities of each department and each station shall be clarified. Station's responsibility shall not be missed and cross responsibility shall be prescribed specifically. Responsibility taken by each person shall not be overfull.

Every person shall clear and understand his own responsibilities, be familiar with the requirements related to his responsibilities, and accept necessary training, including pre-job training and on-job training.

Article 19 Generally, one shall not relegate his responsibility to other person. If the responsibilities do need to be relegated, the one should relegate his responsibility to the designated person who has equivalent qualification.

Section 2 Important Person

Article 20 The important person shall be the full-time person of the enterprise, at least including the director of the enterprise, director of manufacturing management, director of quality management and authorized person of quality.

Director of quality management and director of manufacturing management shall be independent of each other. Director of quality management and authorized person of quality shall not be independent of each other. Operation procedures shall be established so that authorized person of quality could take his responsibility independently, with no interference from director of enterprise and other person.

Article 21 Director of enterprise

Director of enterprise is the main responsible person of pharmaceutical goods' quality, who comprehensive responsible to the daily management of the enterprise. In order to ensure the enterprise complete quality target and manufacture pharmaceutical goods according to this Regulation, the director of enterprise shall take responsible for providing necessary resources, reasonable plan, organize and correspond to ensure the quality management department could take its responsibility independently.

Article 22 Director of manufacturing management

1. Qualification:
   Director of manufacturing management shall at least have pharmacology or related specialty undergraduate education background (or secondary professional technical title or licensed pharmacist qualification), have at least 3 years' pharmaceutical goods' manufacturing and quality management experience, including at least 1 year's pharmaceutical goods' manufacturing management experience, have taken part in professional knowledge training related to manufacturing products.
2. Main responsibility:
   1. Manufacture and storage the pharmaceutical goods according to approved technology procedure in order to ensure the quality of the pharmaceutical goods;
   2. Ensure every operation procedures related to manufacturing operation are performed strictly;
   3. Ensure batch production record and batch package record are audited by designated person and submitted to quality management department;
   4. Ensure the maintenance of workshop and equipment in order to preserve its good working condition;
   5. Ensure all kind of necessary validation work is completed;
   6. Ensure person related to manufacturing have been trained by pre-job training and on-job training, adjust training content according to actual demands.

Article 23 Director of quality management

1. Qualification:
   Director of quality management shall at least have pharmacology or related specialty undergraduate education background (or secondary professional technical title or licensed pharmacist qualification), have at least 5 years' pharmaceutical goods' manufacturing and quality management experience, including at least 1 year's pharmaceutical goods' quality management experience, have taken part in professional knowledge training related to manufacturing products.
2. Main responsibility:

    1. Ensure the raw material, wrapper, semifinished product, bulk product and finished product are in accordance with the registered approved requirements and quality standard;
    2. Ensure the products are audited to batch record before delivering;
    3. Ensure necessary inspection is finished;
    4. Approve quality standard, sampling method, inspection method and other operation procedures of quality management;
    5. Audit and approve all changes related to quality;
    6. Ensure all important windage and exceed criterion inspection results have been researched and been dealt with in time;
    7. Approve and supervise consigned inspection;
    8. Supervise the maintenance of workshop and equipment in order to maintain its good working condition;
    9. Ensure to finish every necessary confirmation and validation work, checking and approving confirmation or validation scheme and report;
    10. Ensure to finish self-check;
    11. Evaluate and approve material supplier;
    12. Ensure all complaints related to product quality have been researched, and have been dealt with in time and accurately;
    13. Ensure to finish products' persistent stability review plan, provide the data of persistent stability review;
    14. Ensure to finish product quality review analysis;
    15. Ensure quality control and quality guarantee person have been trained by pre-job training and on-job training, adjust training content according to actual demands.

Article 24 Director of manufacturing management and director of quality management often have the following common responsibility:

1. Audit and approve the documents of products' technology procedure, operation procedures;
2. Supervise the sanitation condition of factory;
3. Ensure the key equipment have been confirmed;
4. Ensure to finish the validation of production technology;
5. Ensure all related person in enterprise been trained by pre-job training and on-job training, adjust training content according to actual demands;

6. Approve and supervise consigned manufacture;
7. Ensure and monitor the storage condition of material and goods;
8. Save the record;
9. Supervise the implement condition of this Regulation;
10. Monitor the factors influence the quality of the products.

Article 25 Authorized person of quality

1. Qualification:
   Authorized person of quality shall at least have pharmacology or related specialty undergraduate education background (or secondary professional technical title or licensed pharmacist qualification), have at least 5 years' pharmaceutical goods' manufacturing and quality management experience, have the experience of manufacturing process control and quality check work.
   Authorized person of quality shall have necessary professional theory knowledge, have taken part in the train about product delivering, and could take his responsibility independently.
2. Main responsibility:
   1. Take part in the establishment of enterprise quality system, interior self-check, exterior quality audit, validate and pharmaceutical goods' bad reaction report, product recall and other quality management activities;
   2. Take the responsibility of product delivering, to ensure the manufacturing, checking of every batch of delivered products are all in accordance with corresponding code, pharmaceutical goods' registered requirements and quality standard;
   3. Before delivering the products, authorized person of quality must issue product delivering audit record according to the said item 2 and bring it into batch record.

Section 3 Training

Article 26 The enterprise shall designate department or person to take responsible for training management work, and shall have the training scheme or plan audited or approved by director of manufacture management or director of quality management. The training record shall be preserved.

Article 27 All personnel related to pharmaceutical goods' manufacturing, quality shall be trained, the training content shall accommodate to the post. Except the training of theory and practice of this Regulation, responsibility, skill training about the related code, relevant post shall also be trained, and actual effect shall be periodic evaluated.

Article 28 The working person in high risk operating area (such as: manufacture area of high activity, high toxic, infective, high sensitive material) shall take expert training.

Section 4 Personnel Sanitation

Article 29 All personnel shall take sanitation requirements training, the enterprise shall establish personnel sanitation operation procedures, so that to reduce the pollution risk to pharmaceutical goods taken by person at its maximum.

Article 30 Personnel sanitation operation procedures shall include the content related to health, sanitation practice and personnel dress. Personnel in manufacturing area and quality control area shall correctly understand related personnel sanitation operation procedures. The enterprise shall take measures to ensure the implement of personnel sanitation operation procedures.

Article 31 The enterprise shall manage personnel's health and establish health file. The manufacture personnel contact pharmaceutical goods directly shall receive physical check, and take at least one physical check per year.

Article 32 The enterprise shall take appropriate measure to avoid the person have wound in body surface, have infection disease or other person may pollute pharmaceutical goods to take the manufacture work which directly contact pharmaceutical goods.

Article 33 Visiting person and untrained person shall not enter manufacture area and quality control area, if the persons need to enter in special conditions, the items of their individual sanitation, clothes changing and so on shall be instructed.

Article 34 Any person enters into manufacturing area shall change clothes according to prescription. The material, style and dressing method of work clothes shall be accommodate to the work engaged and the level of air clean degree.

Article 35 The person enters into clean manufacturing area shall not make up and adorn with accouterment.

Article 36 Manufacturing area, storage area shall forbid smoking and having meals, forbid to store food, beverage, cigarette and individual pharmaceutical goods and other non-manufacturing goods.

Article 37 Operation person shall avoid to touch the surface of pharmaceutical goods, wrapper material contact pharmaceutical goods directly and equipment by hand.

Chapter 4 Workshop and Establishment

Section 1 Principle

Article 38 The workshop location's choice, design, overall arrangement, construct, reconstruct and maintenance must in accordance with the pharmaceutical goods' manufacturing requirements, which may avoid pollution, cross pollution, confusion and mistake at its maximum, and may convenient for clean, operate and maintenance.

Article 39 The workshop's location shall consider according to the workshop and manufacturing safety measures. The environment of the workshop shall reduce the pollution risk to material or products at its maximum.

Article 40 The enterprise shall have tidy manufacturing environment. The floor, road surface of the workshop and transport shall not pollute the pharmaceutical goods' manufacturing. The overall arrangement of the manufacturing area, administration area, living area and assistant area shall be reasonable arranged and do not interfere each other. Stream of people and material in factory area and workshop shall reasonable.

Article 41 The workshop shall take appropriate maintenance, and ensure the maintenance activity may not influence the quality of pharmaceutical goods. Clean or take necessary sterilization to workshop according to detailed written operation procedures.

Article 42 The workshop shall have appropriate illumination, temperature, humidity and aeration, to ensure the quality of produced and reserved products and the performance of related equipment shall not be influenced directly or indirectly.

Article 43 The design and installation of workshop, establishment shall effective prevent insect or other animal to enter in. Necessary measures shall be taken to prevent of using raticide, insecticide, smoke fumigant and so on which may pollute equipment, material, goods.

Article 44 Necessary measures shall be taken to prevent unauthorized person to enter in. Manufacturing, storage and quality control area shall not be the direct gate for staffs not in this area.

Article 45 Complete drawing of constructed or reconstructed workshop, public service, fixed pipeline shall be saved.

Section 2 Manufacturing Area

Article 46 In order to reduce pollution and cross pollution risk, workshop, manufacturing establishment and equipment shall reasonable designed, overall arranged and used according to the characteristic, technique process and corresponding clean level, and in accordance with the following requirements:

1. Comprehensive considering the pharmaceutical goods' characteristic, technique and intending purpose and other factors, to confirm feasibility of using workshop, manufacturing establishment and equipment together, and hing related evaluating report;
2. Special and independent workshop, manufacturing establishment and equipment must be used when manufacturing special character pharmaceutical goods, such as high sensitive pharmaceutical goods (i.e. Penicillin) or biologics goods (i.e. bcg vaccine or other pharmaceutical goods prepared by active microorganism). The operating area with large quantity of dust for penicillin species pharmaceutical goods shall keep comparatively negative pressure, the exhaust gas discharged to outdoor shall carry cleanse management and make it be up to the mustard. Air outlet shall be away from air inlet of other air cleanse system;

3. Special establishment (i.e. independent air cleanse system) and equipment must be used when manufacturing β-lactam structure species pharmaceutical goods, sex hormone species prophylactic pharmaceutical goods, and shall be detached with other pharmaceutical goods' manufacturing area strictly;
4. Special establishment (i.e. independent air cleanse system) and equipment shall be used when manufacturing some hormone species, cell toxicity species, high active chemical pharmaceutical goods; under special circumstance, if necessary validation shall be take before taking special protection measures, the above said pharmaceutical goods preparation could use the same establishment and equipment via manufacturing modes in different phases;
5. Ventilation of air cleanse system in the above said item II, III, IV shall take cleanse management;
6. Pharmaceutical goods' manufacturing workshop shall not used for manufacturing non-officinal used products which may have bad influence to pharmaceutical goods' quality.

Article 47 Manufacturing area and storage area shall have enough space to ensure equipment, material, semifinished product, bulk product and finished product could storage in order, to prevent the confusion, cross pollution of different products or material, to prevent missing or mistake during the operation of manufacturing or quality control.

Article 48 Air condition cleanse system shall be equipped according to pharmaceutical goods' variety, manufacturing operation's requirement and exterior environment condition which let the manufacturing area can effective aeration, and have temperature, humidity control and atmosphere cleanse filtration, to ensure the manufacturing environment of pharmaceutical goods is in accordance with the requirements.

The pressure difference between clean area and non-clean area, clean areas in different level shall not lower than 10 Pascal. When necessary, appropriate pressure difference grads shall also be kept in different functional areas (operation area) with same clean level.

Exposure working procedure area for oral liquid and solid preparation, chamber use pharmaceutical goods (including rectal pharmaceutical goods), surface external use pharmaceutical goods and other non-asepsis preparation manufacturing and exposure working procedure area for wrapper material directly contact pharmaceutical goods shall equip according to the requirements of "Asepsis Pharmaceutical Goods" D level clean area in Annex. The enterprise could take appropriate microorganism monitor measures according to products' standard and characteristic.

Article 49 Inner surface of clean area (wall, floor, sunshade) shall be slick, non-crack, narrow joint, non granule fell off, prevent stored dust, convenient for effective clean, and take sterilization when necessary.

Article 50 The design and installation of every kind of pipeline, lighting establishment, place with a draught and other public establishment shall prevent having the part of not easy to clean, and shall try best to maintain outside the manufacturing area.

Article 51 Sewerage shall have appropriate size and install the device of reversing flow. Try best to prevent drain in clear channel, if it is inevitably, the clear channel shall be flat so that it is convenient to clean and sterilize.

Article 52 Quantify of preparation's raw material often carry on in the metage room special designed.

Article 53 Operation rooms which produce dust (such as sampling, metage, mix, package of dry material or products rooms and other operation rooms) shall keep comparatively negative pressure or take special measure, so as to prevent the diffusion of powder dust, avoid cross pollution and easy to keep clean.

Article 54 Pharmaceutical goods' packaging workshop or area shall be reasonable designed and arranged, to prevent confusion or cross pollution. If there are several packaging lines in one area, isolation measures shall be taken.

Article 55 Manufacturing area shall have appropriate light, the light in contact manufacturing area shall satisfy the operation requirements.

Article 56 Manufacturing area could set middle control area. However, middle control operation shall not bring quality risk to pharmaceutical goods.

Section 3 Storage Area

Article 57 Storage area shall have enough space, which ensure the under-examined, qualified, disqualified, withdrew or recalled raw material, wrapper, semifinished product, bulk product and finished product and all kinds of material and products could store in order.

Article 58 The design and construct of storage area shall ensure good storage condition, and have aeration and lighting establishment. Storage area shall satisfy material or products' storage condition (such as temperature, humidity, avoid of light) and safety storage requirements, and check and monitor shall be taken.

Article 59 High active material or product and printing package material shall storage in safe area.

Article 60 Receiving, extending and delivering area shall protect material, product out of influence of weather outside (such as rain, snow). The arrangement and establishment of receiving area shall ensure taking necessary cleaning to the received material's outside packaging.

Article 61 If the under-examined material is stored in separate isolate area, the under-examine area shall have distinct mark, and only authorized person could in and out.

Disqualified, withdrew or recalled material or product shall be stored isolated.

If other method is used for replacing physics isolation, this method shall have equal security.

Article 62 Separate material sampling area is often set up. Air cleaning level of sampling area is the same with the manufacturing requirements. If sample is taken in other area or use other method, pollution or cross pollution shall prevent.

Section 4 Quality Control Area

Article 63 Quality control laboratory is often divided from manufacturing area. Biology examine, microorganism and radioactivity isotope laboratory shall also divided from each other.

Article 64 The design of laboratory shall ensure for applying it's intending purpose, and prevent confusion and cross pollution, enough area shall have for disposing samples, reserved samples and samples for reviewing stability and keeping the records.

Article 65 When necessary, set a special instrument room to prevent static, shaking, humid or other outside factors' disturbance to instrument with high sensitivity.

Article 66 The laboratory disposing special goods such as biology samples or radioactivity samples shall in accordance with the related requirements of the country.

Article 67 Experiment animal room shall be strictly divided from other area. Its design, construct shall in accordance with the related requirements of the country and have independent air disposing establishment and animal's special channel.

Section 5 Assistant Area

Article 68 Retiring room shall not take bad influence to manufacturing area, storage area and quality control area.

Article 69 Bathing room and washing room shall be convenient for person's use, and accommodate with the using number of people. Washing room shall not connect with manufacturing room and storage room.

Article 70 Maintain room shall be away from manufacturing area as far as possible. Spare parts and tools used for maintenance stored in clean area shall be placed in special room or tool cabinet.

Chapter 5 Equipment

Section 1 Principle

Article 71 The design, model choosing, installing, reconstructing and maintenance of equipment shall in accordance with the intending purpose. The risk of pollution, cross pollution, confusion and mistake shall reduce at the maximum. The design shall be easy to operation, clean, maintain and shall take sanitization or sterilization when necessary.

Article 72 Operation procedures for equipment's using, cleaning, maintaining and servicing shall be established. Corresponding operation records shall be kept.

Article 73 The equipment's ordering, installing, confirmation documents and records shall be established and kept.

Section 2 Design and Installation

Article 74 Manufacturing equipment shall not bring any bad influence to pharmaceutical goods' quality. The surface of manufacturing equipment contact with pharmaceutical goods directly shall be neat, smooth, easy to clean or sterilization, be able to bear cauterization. It could not take chemistry reaction with pharmaceutical goods, adsorb pharmaceutical goods or release substance to pharmaceutical goods.

Article 75 Weighing apparatus, measure, apparatus and instrument with appropriate capacity and precision shall be equipped.

Article 76 Appropriate rinse, cleansing device shall be chose, and prevent such devices become pollution resource.

Article 77 Lubricant, refrigerant used for equipment shall not pollute the pharmaceutical goods or container. Try best to use edible lubricant or lubricant at comparative level.

Article 78 The ordering, checking and accepting, keeping, maintaining, extending and discarding of mould for manufacturing shall establish corresponding operation procedures. Set special person and special cabinet to maintain the mould and keep related record.

Section 3 Maintaining and Servicing

Article 79 The maintenance and service of equipment shall not influence the product's quality.

Article 80 Establish the equipment's defending maintain plan and operation procedures. The maintaining and servicing of equipment shall have corresponding record.

Article 81 The equipment with reconstruction or material maintenance shall make reconfirmation. It could only be used after it is confirmed of according with requirements.

Section 4 Usage and Cleansing

Article 82 Main manufacturing and inspection equipment shall have specific operation procedures.

Article 83 Manufacturing equipment shall use between the confirmed parameter scope.

Article 84 Manufacturing equipment shall clean under the operation procedures with detailed prescription.

Manufacturing equipment's clean operation procedures shall prescribe detailed and integrated clean method, clean equipment or tool, cleanser's name and preparation method, the method of wiping the last batch's marker off, the method of protecting the cleaned equipment out of pollution before used, the longest preserve time limit of cleaned equipment, the method of checking the clean condition of the equipment before used, and let the operator could use the repeated, effective method to clean every kind of equipment.

If the equipment needs to be removed, the order and method of removing equipment shall be prescribed; if the equipment needs to be sanitized or sterilized, the detailed method, disinfector's name and preparation method of sanitization or sterilization shall be prescribed. If necessary, the allowed longest interval time limit between end of manufacturing and cleaning shall be prescribed.

Article 85 Cleaned manufacturing equipment shall be preserved in clean, dry condition.

Article 86 The equipment and apparatus used for pharmaceutical goods' manufacturing or inspection shall have using log, the record content includes using, cleaning, maintenance and servicing condition and date, time, the manufactured and inspected pharmaceutical goods' name, specification and batch number and so on.

Article 87 The manufacturing equipment shall have obvious condition identification which indicates the equipment's serial number and content (such as name, specification, batch number); if there is no content in the equipment, the clean condition shall be indicated.

Article 88 Unqualified equipment shall move out of manufacturing and quality control area if possible, before moving, obvious condition identification shall have.

Article 89 The main fixing channel shall indicate the content's name and direction.

Section 5 Adjustment

Article 90 Adjustment and inspection to weighing apparatus, measure, appearance, record and control equipment and apparatus used for manufacturing and inspection shall be done regularly under operation procedures and adjustment plan, and the related records shall be kept. Adjustment's capacity scope shall cover the actual manufacturing and inspection's using scope.

Article 91 Ensure the key weighing apparatus, measure, appearance, record and control equipment and apparatus used for manufacturing and inspection shall be adjusted, and the data shall be accurate and credible.

Article 92 Adjustment shall be done by measure standard instrument, and the measure standard instrument shall in accordance with the related state prescription. The adjustment record shall indicate the name, serial number, adjustment period of validity and measure eligible certificate number of the measure standard instrument, which could ensure the record's traceability.

Article 93 Weighing apparatus, measure, appearance, record and control equipment and apparatus shall have obvious identification, and indicate its adjustment period of validity.

Article 94 Out of adjustment, out of adjustment period of validity, inaccurate weighing apparatus, measure, appearance, record and control equipment and apparatus shall not be used.

Article 95 If an automatic or electron equipment is used during the process of manufacturing, packaging, storage, it shall be regular adjusted and inspected according to operation procedures, to ensure its operation function is normal. Adjustment and inspection shall have corresponding record.

Section 6 Water for Preparation of Pharmaceutical Goods

Article 96 Water used for preparation of pharmaceutical goods shall adapt to its purpose, and in accordance with the quality standard and related requirements of Pharmacopoeia of the Peoples' Republic of China. Water used for preparation of pharmaceutical goods shall use drinking water at least.

Article 97 The design, installation, function and maintenance of water disposal equipment and its transportation system shall ensure the water used for preparation of pharmaceutical goods achieve the set quality standard. The function of water disposal equipment shall not exceed its designed ability.

Article 98 The material used for purified water, injection water store tin and transportation pipe shall be innocuous, bear corruption; the vents of store tin shall install non-desquamating fibrous remove bacterium colander; the design and installation of pipe shall avoid dead angle, blind pipe.

Article 99 The preparation, storage and distribution of purified water, injection water shall prevent the reproduction of microorganism. Purified water could circle, and injection water could heat preservation circle above 70 °C.

Article 100 The water quality of preparation water and original water shall monitor regularly, and do corresponding record.

Article 101 The pipe of purified water, injection water shall be cleaned and sterilized according to operation procedures, and do corresponding record. If the microorganism pollution of preparation water achieves the alarm limit, deviation rectify limit, disposal shall be done under operation procedures.

Chapter 6 Material and Product

Section 1 Principle

Article 102 The raw material used for pharmaceutical goods' manufacturing, wrapper material direct contact with pharmaceutical goods shall in accordance with the quality standard. Printing ink direct printed in pharmaceutical goods shall in accordance with edible standard requirements.

Imported raw material shall in accordance with state related import management rules.

Article 103 Material and product operation procedures shall be constituted, to ensure correct receiving, storage, extending, usage and delivering of material and product, to prevent pollution, cross pollution, confusion and mistake.

Disposal of material and product shall perform in accordance with the operation procedures or technique rules and do corresponding record.

Article 104 The confirmation and changing of material supplier shall take quality evaluation and order after quality management department's approval.

Article 105 The transportation of material and product shall satisfy quality requirement, if the transportation needs special requirements, the transportation condition shall be confirmed.

Article 106 The receiving of raw material, wrapper and printing wrapper direct contact with pharmaceutical goods shall have operation procedures. All material of goods shall be checked to ensure it is the same with the order form, and ensure the supplier is approved by quality management department.

The outer wrapper of material shall have label and indicate the prescribed information. Cleaning shall be done if necessary. If outer wrapper is damaged or have other problems may influence material quality, report to quality management department and do investigation and record.

Receiving every time shall have record, the content includes the following:

1. The name of material indicated in the delivering form and packaging container;
2. Material name and (or) code used in the enterprise;
3. Receiving date;
4. The name of supplier and manufacturer (if different);
5. The batch number of supplier and manufacturer's mark (if different);
6. Total amount of receiving and quantity of packaging container;
7. Designated batch number or running number after receiving by enterprise;
8. Related explanation (i.e. packaging condition).

Article 107 The received material and manufactured finished product shall manage as quarantine, till discharging.

Article 108 The material and product shall store and turnover in order according to its characteristics, its extending and freighting shall in accordance with the principle of early-in-early-out and recent period of validity early out.

Article 109 The material and product managed by computer storage management shall have corresponding operation procedures, to prevent the confusion and mistake bring by system failure, out of service and other special conditions.

If the material and product is identified by complete computer storage management system, the related information may not indicate by written method.

Section 2 Raw Material

Article 110 Corresponding operation procedures shall be constituted, checking or inspection and other appropriate measures shall be done to confirm all raw material in each package is accurate.

Article 111 If material of several batches is received for one time, sampling, inspection, discharging shall be done under batch number.

Article 112 Raw materialstored in storage area shall have appropriate mark, and indicate at least the following contents:

1. The name of designated material and material code in enterprise;
2. Batch number set when the enterprise receiving the raw material;
3. Quality condition of raw material (such as under examination, qualified, unqualified, sampling);
4. Period of validity or period of double examination.

Article 113 Only the raw material approved by quality management department and within the period of validity or period of double examination could be used.

Article 114 The raw material shall be stored according to period of validity or period of double examination. During the period of validity, if there is special condition which influence the quality, the raw material shall be double examined.

Article 115 Material shall be matched by designated person according to operation procedures. After the material is checked, accurate quantify or measure, and make identification.

Article 116 Each material prepared and its weight or volume shall be double examined by other person independently, and do double examination record.

Article 117 All material used in pharmaceutical goods' manufacturing in the same batch shall be concentrated stored and make identification.

Section 3 Semifinished Product and Bulk Product

Article 118 Semifinished product and bulk product shall be stored under appropriate condition.

Article 119 Semifinished productand bulk product shall have obvious identification, and indicate at least the following contents:

1. The name of product and product code in enterprise;
2. Batch number of product;
3. Amount or weight (such as gross weight, net weight and so on);
4. Production working procedure (if necessary);
5. Product's quality condition (if necessary, such as quarantine, qualified, unqualified, sampling).

Section 4 Wrapper

Article 120 The management and control requirements of the wrapper and printing wrapper contact directly with pharmaceutical goods is the same with the raw material.

Article 121 The wrapper shall be extended by assigned person according to operation procedures, and take measures to avoid confusion and mistake, and ensure the wrapper used for manufacturing pharmaceutical goods is accurate.

Article 122 The operation procedures for printing wrapper's design, auditing, and approval shall be constituted, to ensure the printed content of printing wrapper is the same with the approved content by pharmaceutical goods' quality management department, establish special document, keep the original edit sample of approved printing wrapper by execution.

Article 123 When the edition of printing wrapper is changed, measures shall be taken, to ensure the edition used for printing wrapper is accurate. The former printing stencil shall be withdrew, cancelled and destroyed.

Article 124 Special area shall be set for printing wrapper for its appropriate storage. Unauthorized person shall not enter in. Incised label or other bulk printing wrapper shall store in airtight container separately to avoid confusion.

Article 125 Printing wrapper shall be kept by assigned person, and shall be extended according to operation procedures and demanding amount.

Article 126 The wrapper or printing wrapper direct contact with pharmaceutical goods of each batch or extending for each time shall all have identification, which indicate the name and batch number of the used product.

Article 127 Overdue or scrapped printing wrapper shall be destroyed and make records.

Section 5 Finished Product

Article 128 The finished product shall be quarantine storage before discharging.

Article 129 The storage condition for finished product shall in accordance with the requirements of pharmaceutical goods' registration approval.

Section 6 Material and Product under Special Management

Article 130 The checking and accepting, storage, management of stupefacient, mental pharmaceutical goods, toxicity pharmaceutical goods for medical use (including medicinal materials), radioactivity pharmaceutical goods, chemical material which easy to cause toxicity of pharmaceutical goods species, and flammable, explosive and other dangerous material shall perform the related state prescription.

Section 7 Others

Article 131 Each package container for unqualified material, semifinished product, bulk product and finished product shall have obvious symbol, and keep appropriate storage in isolated area.

Article 132 The disposal of unqualified material, semifinished product, bulk product and finished product shall approved by the director of quality management, and do record.

Article 133 Product's callback shall be approved in advance, and take sufficient evaluation to the related quality risk, to decide callback or not according to the evaluation decision. Product's callback shall take according to the scheduled operation procedures, and do corresponding record. The product after callback shall set period of validity according to the production date of the callback products with the earliest batch.

Article 134 The preparation product shall not take renewed process. Generally, unqualified preparation semifinished product, bulk product and finished product shall not come back for manufacturing again. Only when the product does not influence the product's quality, according to corresponding quality standard, and is in accordance with the scheduled, approved operation procedures and after related risk evaluation, it could be disposed by coming back for manufacturing again. The product of coming back for manufacturing again shall have corresponding record.

Article 135 For the products coming back for manufacturing again or manufactured after callback, the quality management department shall consider to do extra related inspection and stability review.

Article 136 The enterprise shall constitute operation procedures for pharmaceutical goods' return back, and do corresponding record. The content shall include at least the following: the product's name, batch number, specification, quantity, unit and address, reason and date, final disposal opinion.

The returned back pharmaceutical goods of same product, same batch number and different channel shall record, store and dispose separately.

Article 137 Only after examination, inspection and investigation, there is evidence proved that the returned back products' quality does not influenced, and after the evaluation of quality management department according to operation procedures, it is considered to re-packaging, re-delivering and selling the returned back products. The factors of evaluation shall at least include the pharmaceutical goods' characteristics, the required storage condition, pharmaceutical goods' current condition, history, and duration between the products' delivering and returning back. If the returned back products do not accord with the storage and transportation requirements, the products shall be destroyed under the supervision of quality management department. If there is doubt on the quality of the returned back products, re-delivering is not allowed.

If the returned back product is called back, the called back products shall in accordance with the intending quality standard and the requirement of Article 133.

The process and result of returning back shall have corresponding record.

Chapter 7 Confirmation and Validation

Article 138 The enterprise shall confirm the required confirmation and validation work, to prove the key factors of related operation could control effectively. The scope and degree of confirmation and validation shall confirm after risk valuation.

Article 139 The workshop, establishment, equipment and inspection apparatus of enterprise shall be confirmed, and manufacturing, operation and inspection shall be done under validated production technology, operation procedures and inspection method, and keep persistent validation condition.

Article 140 Establish the document and record for confirmation and validation, and the document and record shall prove the following intending aims:

1. Design confirmation shall prove the design of workshop, establishment, equipment is in accordance with the intending purpose and the requirements of this Regulation;
2. Installation confirmation shall prove the constructing and installation of workshop, establishment, and equipment is in accordance with designed standard;
3. Running confirmation shall prove the running of workshop, establishment, equipment is in accordance with designed standard;
4. Function confirmation shall prove the workshop, establishment, equipment could persistent according with requirements under normal operation method and technology condition;
5. Technology validation shall prove the production technology according to prescribed technology parameter could persistent produce the product in accordance with the intending purpose and registered requirements.

Article 141 Before using new production prescription or production technology, validate its applicability of routine production. When the production technology is using the prescribed raw material and equipment, the products in accordance with the intending purpose and registered requirement shall be produced.

Article 142 When the main factors influence the products' quality, such as raw material, wrapper direct contact with pharmaceutical goods, production equipment, production environment (or workshop), production technology, inspection method are changed, confirmation and validation shall be done. If necessary, approval shall be done by pharmaceutical goods' supervision management department.

Article 143 The cleansing method shall be validated to approve its cleaning effect, to effective avoid pollution and cross pollution. Cleaning validation shall integrated consider the equipment's using condition, the cleanser and disinfector under used, sampling method and place and corresponding sampling callback rate, leftover's property and limit, sensitive rate of leftover's inspection method and other factors.

Article 144 Confirmation and validation is not a one-off action. After initial confirmation or validation, re-confirmation or re-validation shall be done according to product's quality review analysis condition. The key production technology and operation procedures shall do re-validation regularly, to ensure achieving intending result.

Article 145 The enterprise shall constitute validation overall plan, indicates the key information of confirmation and validation work in the form of document.

Article 146 Validation overall plan or other related document shall have the prescription to ensure workshop, establishment, equipment, inspection apparatus, production technology, operation procedures and inspection method could keep persistent stability.

Article 147 Establish confirmation or validation scheme according to the object of confirmation or validation, and the scheme shall be audited, approved. Confirmation or validation scheme shall have specific responsibility.

Article 148 Confirmation or validation shall perform under the in advance confirmed and approved scheme, and do record. After the confirmation or validation work is finished, write the report, and the work shall be audited, approved. The result and conclusion of confirmation or validation (including evaluation and suggestion) shall be recorded and keep in file.

Article 149 Technology procedure and operation procedures shall be confirmed according to validated result.

Chapter 8 Document Management
Section 1 Principle
Article 150 Document is the basic factor of quality guarantee system. The enterprise must have written quality standard, production prescription and technology procedure, operation procedures and record and other documents with accurate content.

Article 151 The enterprise shall constitute the operation procedures of document management, systemic design, constitute, audit, approve and extending document. The document related to this Regulation shall audit by quality management department.

Article 152 The document's content shall be the same with the requirements of pharmaceutical goods' manufacturing permission, pharmaceutical goods' registration, and help to carry up history condition of products for each batch.

Article 153 Document's drafting, editing, auditing, approving, replacing or removing, reproduction, keeping and destroying shall manage according to operation procedures, and have corresponding record for document's distribution, removing, reproduction, and destroying.

Article 154 Document's drafting, editing, auditing, approving shall execute by appropriate person and indicate the execution date.

Article 155 The document shall indicate title, variety, purpose, and document number and edition number. The characters in the document shall be accurate, clear, understandability, and not on the line.

Article 156 The document shall be stored according to category and have clear consecution, and easy to consult.

Article 157 When reproduction the original document, no mistake could be made; reproduced document shall be clear and easy to be read.

Article 158 The document shall be regular audited, edited; after the document is edited, it shall be managed according to the related regulation, to prevent misusage of former document. The distributing, using document shall be the approved document at current edition. The removed or former edition document could only appear in working locale as keeping file for future reference.

Article 159 Each activity related to this Regulation shall be recorded, to ensure the activities of product's manufacturing, quality control and quality guarantee could be carried up. The record shall remain enough blank for filling data. The record shall be filled in time, have true content, clear handwriting, easy to read, and not easy to erase.

Article 160 Use auto printing record, a collection of illustrative plates and graph and etc of manufacturing and inspection equipment, and indicate the information of product or sample's name, batch number and record the equipment's information, the operator shall indicate his name and date.

Article 161 The record shall keep clean, shall not tear to shreds and altered. Any changes of the record shall indicate name and date, and keep original information clean, if necessary, indicate the reason for changing. If the record shall be copies out again, the original record shall not be tore to shreds, and shall be kept as the annex of the copied out record.

Article 162 Each batch of pharmaceutical goods shall have batch record, including batch production record, batch packaging record, batch inspection record and pharmaceutical goods discharging audit record, and other record related to the batch of products. The batch records shall be managed by quality management department, keep at least 1 year after the pharmaceutical goods' period of validity.

Quality standard, technology procedure, operation procedures, stability review, confirmation, validation, changing and other important document shall keep for a long time.

Article 163 If electric data processing system, picture taking technique or other credible method is used for recording data information, system's operation procedures shall have; accuracy of the record shall be checked.

If electric data processing system is used, only authorized person could input or change data, the change and delete condition shall have records; the system's logging in shall be controlled by the way of inputting password or other methods; after inputting key data, it shall be double examined by other person independently.

For the batch record stored by electric method, shall copy by the way of magnetic tape, microfilm, paper duplicate or other methods, to ensure the safety of the record, and let the data could be convenient to review during the preservation period.

Section 2 Quality Control

Article 164 The material and finished product shall have approved current quality standard; if necessary, semifinished product or bulk product shall also have quality standard.

Article 165 Material's quality standard often includes the following:

1. Basic information of material:

    1. Enterprise designated material's name and inner used material's code;
    2. Gist of quality standard;
    3. Approved supplier;
    4. Actual sample or sample manuscript of printing wrapper.

2. Sampling, inspection method or related operation procedures' serial number;
3. Limit requirements for determination of property and quantity;
4. Storage condition and notice items;
5. Period of validity or period of double examination.

Article 166 Outsourcing or export semifinished product and bulk product shall have quality standard; if the inspection result of semifinished product is used for finished product's quality evaluation, semifinished product's quality standard corresponding to finished product's quality standard shall be constituted.

Article 167 Finished product's quality standard shall include the following:

1. Product's name and product's code;
2. Corresponding product prescription serial number (if any);
3. Product's specification and package's style;
4. Sampling, inspection method or related operation procedures' serial number;
5. Limit requirements for determination of property and quantity;
6. Storage condition and notice items;
7. Period of validity.

Section 3 Technology Procedure

Article 168 Each manufacturing batch of each kind of pharmaceutical goods shall has its technology procedure approved by enterprise. Each kind of packaging style of different pharmaceutical good's specification shall have its own package operation requirements. Technology procedure' constitution shall base on the registered approving craft.

Article 169 Technology procedure shall not change at will. If it needs to be changed, edit, audit, approval shall be done according to related operation procedures.

Article 170 The content of preparation's technology procedure shall include at least the following:

1. Manufacturing prescription:

    1. Product's name and product's code;
    2. Product's type, specification and batch;
    3. List of used raw material (including the material used in manufacturing process, but not appeared in the finished product), indicate each material's designated name, code and dosage; if the dosage of raw material needs to convert, calculate method shall be indicated.

2. Manufacturing operation requirements:

    1. Explanation to manufacturing place and used equipment (such as the place and serial number of the operation room, the level of cleaning level, required requirements to temperature and humidity, the type and serial number of equipment, and so on);

2. The method of preparing key equipment (such as cleaning, assembling, adjustment, sterilization, and so on) or corresponding operation procedures' serial number;
3. Detailed manufacturing procedure and explanation of craft parameter (such as checking, pretreatment of material, order of adding material, mixing time, temperature, and so on);
4. Method and standard of all middle control;
5. Limit of expected ultimately output, if necessary, indicate the limit of semi-finished product's output, and the calculating method and reconciliation of inventory limit;
6. Storage requirement of bulk product, including container, label and special storage condition;
7. Notice items shall be indicated.

3. Package operation requirements:

1. Package type indicated by the amount, weight or volume of products in ultimately packaged container;
2. Full list of all required wrapper material, including the name, amount, specification, type of wrapper and the code of each wrapper related to quality standard;
3. Actual sample or duplicate of printing wrapper, and indicate the printing place of product's batch number, period of validity;
4. Notice items needs to be indicated, including the examination done to manufacturing area and equipment, confirmation of the package manufacturing line's clear work has been done before the package operation is begin, and so on;
5. Package operation procedures' indication, including the important assistant operation and notice items of using equipment, checking of used wrapper;
6. Detailed operation of middle control, including sample method and standard;
7. The calculating method and reconciliation of inventory limit of bulk product, printing wrapper.

Section 4 Batch Production Record

Article 171 Each batch of product shall have corresponding batch production record, which could trace this batch of products' manufacturing history and related information of quality.

Article 172 Batch production record shall be done according to related content to current approved technology procedure. When design the form of record, shall avoid appearing filling mistake. Each page of batch production record shall indicate product's name, specification and batch number.

Article 173 Original blank batch production record shall be audited and approved by the director of manufacturing management and the director of quality management. The duplicate and extending of batch production record shall control and record according to operation procedures. Manufacturing of each batch of products shall only extend one copy of the original blank batch production record.

Article 174 During manufacturing, each operation shall be recorded in time, when the operation has done, manufacturing operator shall confirm and execute his name and date.

Article 175 The content of batch production record shall include the following:

1. The product's name, specification, batch number;
2. Beginning, ending date and time of manufacturing and middle procedure;
3. Signatures of directors in each manufacturing procedure;
4. Signature of manufacturing procedure operator; if necessary, signature of operation (i.e. metage) double examined person shall have;
5. Batch number of each raw material and actual amount (including the batch number and amount of the products devoted for callback or renew disposal);
6. Related manufacturing operation or activity, technology parameter and control scope, and the serial number of main manufacturing equipment;
7. Record of middle control's result and signature of operator;
8. Output in different manufacturing procedure and calculating of reconciliation of inventory when necessary;
9. Record to special problems or abnormity affairs, including detail indication or research report to the windage condition of departure technology procedure, and approved by execution.

Section 5 Batch Package Record

Article 176 Package of each batch of products or part of products in each batch of products shall have batch package record, to trace this batch of products' package operation and related information of quality.

Article 177 Batch package record shall be done according to the content related to package in technology procedure. When design the form of record, shall avoid appearing filling mistake. Each page of batch production record shall indicate wrapped product's name, specification and batch number.

Article 178 Batch package record shall indicate the bulk product's batch number, amount and finished product's batch number and projected amount. The requirement of auditing, approving and extending the original blank batch package record is the same with the requirement of original blank batch production record.

Article 179 During packaging, each operation shall be recorded in time, when the operation has done, packaging operator shall confirm and execute his name and date.

Article 180 The content of batch packaging record shall include the following:

1. The product's name, specification, package type, batch number, date of production, and period of validity;
2. Packageoperation date and time;
3. Signatures of director of packaging operator;
4. Signature of packaging procedure operator;
5. Name, batch number of each wrapper and actual amount;

6. Inspection record done according to technology procedure, including middle control result;
7. Detailed information of package operation, including the serial number of used equipment and package manufacturing line;
8. Actual sample of printed wrapper, and print batch number, period of validity and other printing content; the printing wrapper hard to keep file with batch package record could printing the duplicate of the above said content;
9. Record to special problems or abnormity affairs, including detail indication or research report to the windage condition of departure technology procedure, and approved by execution;
10. Name, code of all printing wrapper and bulk product, and amount of extending, using, destroying or withdrawing product, actual output and inspection of reconciliation of inventory.

Section 6 Operation procedures and Record

Article 181 The content of operation procedures shall include the following: title, serial number, version number, issued department, effective date, distributing department and signatures of constitutor, auditor, authorized person and indicate the date, heading, text and changing history.

Article 182 Workshop, equipment, material, document and record shall have serial number (or code), the operation procedures of serial number (or code) shall be set up, to ensure the serial number (or code) is exclusive.

Article 183 The following activities shall also have corresponding operation procedures, and its process and result shall have records:

1. Confirmation and validation;
2. Installation and adjustment of equipment;
3. Maintenance, cleaning and sterilization of workshop and equipment;
4. Training, changing clothes and sanitation and other matters related to person;
5. Environment monitor;
6. Insect pest control;
7. Alteration control;
8. Windage disposal;
9. Complaint;
10. Recall of pharmaceutical goods;
11. Withdraw of pharmaceutical goods.

Chapter 9 Manufacturing Management

Section 1 Principle

Article 184 All pharmaceutical goods' manufacturing and package shall operate and record according to standard technology procedure and operation procedures, to ensure the pharmaceutical goods' quality standard, and achieve pharmaceutical goods' manufacturing admission and registration approved requirements.

Article 185 Operation procedures of dividing products' manufacturing batch shall be set up. Dividing of products' manufacturing batch shall have the ability to ensure the quality and characteristic of products in one batch are the same.

Article 186 Operation procedures of setting pharmaceutical goods' batch number and confirming manufacturing date shall be set up. Each batch of pharmaceutical goods shall be set with exclusive batch number. Except legal requirements, manufacturing date shall not be later than the beginning date of mixing operation of product moulding or fill installing (enveloping), and shall not take product's package date as the manufacturing date.

Article 187 Output and reconciliation of inventory of each batch of product shall be checked, to ensure the reconciliation of inventory is in accordance with the set limit. If there is diversity, find out the reason, only after confirmation of no potential quality risk, they could be disposed as normal products.

Article 188 Pharmaceutical products of different variety and specification could not manufacture in the same manufacturing operation room, unless there is no possibility of confusion or cross pollution.

Article 189 In every stage of manufacturing, product and material shall be protected to avoid microorganism and other pollution.

Article 190 During the process of manufacturing dry material or product, especially high activity, high toxic or high sensitive material or product, special measures shall be taken, to avoid bringing and diffusing of powder.

Article 191 Container and main equipment, essential operation room used for all material, semifinished product or bulk product during the manufacturing process shall mark label or indicate the name, specification and batch number of the manufactured product or material in other way, if necessary, manufacturing procedure shall also be indicated.

Article 192 Mark used for container, equipment or establishment shall obvious and clear, the format of mark shall approved by related department of the enterprise. Except words explanation could use in the mark, different color could also be used to distinguish the condition of the marked object (such as quarantine, qualified, unqualified or cleaned, and so on).

Article 193 When the product is transporting from one area to another area, the connection between the pipe and other equipment shall be checked, to ensure the connection is accurate.

Article 194 The area shall be cleared after each manufacturing is end, to ensure no material, product and document related to the manufacturing has left in the equipment and working place. Before the beginning of the next manufacturing, the area shall be confirmed again.

Article 195 Avoid any windage of departing technology procedure or operation procedures at the maximum. If any windage appears, perform according to windage disposal operation procedures.

Article 196 Only authorized person could come in and out of the manufacturing workshop.

Section 2 Avoid Pollution and Cross Pollution during Manufacturing Process

Article 197 Take the following measures in manufacturing process to avoid pollution and cross pollution at maximum:

1. Manufacture pharmaceutical goods of different variety in isolated area;
2. Take phase manufacturing method;
3. Set essential air lock and ventilator; press difference control shall be taken in areas with different air cleaning level;
4. Reduce the risk of air not disposed or fully disposed entering manufacturing area to cause pollution;
5. In the manufacturing area which is easy to cross pollute, the operator shall dress special exposure suit in this area;
6. Clean the equipment with validated or the effective cleaning and wiping pollution off operation procedures; if necessary, test the leftover in the surface of equipment which direct contact with material;
7. Manufacture by airtight system;
8. Intake of dry equipment shall have inhaler, outtake shall have the equipment of preventing air flow backwards;
9. Fragile, debris removal, easy to be mouldy apparatus shall avoid to use in manufacturing and cleaning process; when using screen net, take measures to prevent the pollution bringing from the rupture of screen net;
10. The preparation, filtration, fill envelop, sterilization and other procedure of liquid preparation shall finish in prescribed time;
11. Semifinished products of semisolid preparation, such as ointment, cream, jellies and so on and suppository shall prescribe storage period and storage condition.

Article 198 Take regular examination to the measures of preventing pollution and cross pollution and evaluate its applicability and validity.

Section 3 Manufacturing Operation

Article 199 Before the manufacturing is begin, do examination to ensure no product, document and material irrespective to the manufacturing this time has left in the equipment and working place, the equipment is in the cleaned and under used condition. The result of examination shall be recorded.

Before manufacturing operation, the name, code, batch number and mark of material or semifinished product shall be checked to ensure the material or semifinished product used in manufacturing are correct and in accordance with requirements.

Article 200 Middle control and essential environment monitor shall be taken, and take record.

Article 201 The area must be cleared by manufacturing operator after each manufacturing stage of each batch of products is finished, and fill in clear record. The content of clear record includes the following: serial number of operation room, name of the product, batch number, manufacturing procedure, area clearing date, inspection items and result, signatures of director of are clearing and double examined person. Clear record shall bring into batch production record.

Section 4 Package Operation

Article 202 Package operation procedures shall prescribe the measures of reducing the risk of pollution and cross pollution, confusion or mistake.

Article 203 Examination shall be done before the package operation is begin, to ensure working place, package manufacturing line, imprinter and other equipment are in the cleaned or under used condition, there is no product, document or material irrespective to the manufacturing this time has left. The result of examination shall be recorded.

Article 204 Before the package operation is begin, check the wrapper are accurate, check the name, specification, quantity, quality condition of bulk product and the used wrapper, and confirm it is in accordance with the technology procedure.

Article 205 In each package operation room or package manufacturing line, product's name, specification, batch number and batch manufacturing condition shall be indicated in the mark.

Article 206 If there are several packaging lines package at the same time, isolate or take other measures to effective prevent pollution, cross pollution or confusion.

Article 207 The under used load container shall keep clean before loading to prevent there is glass chipping, metal grain and other infectant in the container.

Article 208 Labels shall be marked in time after the product is loaded, enveloped. If labels are not marked in time, operate according to related operation procedures to prevent the mistake of confusion or mislabel.

Article 209 The information of separate printing or online printing during packaging process (i.e. product batch number or period of validity) shall be checked, to ensure it is accurate, and take record. If the information is printed by hand, add the frequency of check.

Article 210 If incision label or separate printing labels outside the package line are used, take special measures to prevent confusion.

Article 211 Check the function of electric code reading machine, label arithmometer or other similar equipment to ensure it could run correctly. Take record to the check.

Article 212 Printing or mould pressing content in the wrapper should be clear, hard to fade and erase.

Article 213 In the manufacturing process, product's middle control examination shall at least include the following:

1. Appearance of package;
2. Integrity of package;
3. Accuracy of product and wrapper;
4. Accuracy of printing information;
5. Whether the function of online monitor equipment is normal.

Sample shall not return after taking away from package manufacturing line, to avoid product's confusion or pollution.

Article 214 If the product needs to re-package due to abnormal condition in package process, special inspection, research and designated person's approval shall be done. Detail record shall be done to re-package.

Article 215 In reconciliation of inventory inspection, if the amount of bulk product, printing wrapper and finished product has obvious difference, investigation shall be done, the finished product shall not be discharged before conclusion is taken.

Article 216 When the package is done, the remained wrapper with printed batch number shall be counted and destroyed by special person, and take the record. If the printing wrapper with no printed batch number is returned to the storage, perform according to operation procedures.

Chapter 10 Quality Control and Quality Guarantee
Section 1 Quality Control Laboratory Management
Article 217 The person, establishment, equipment in quality control laboratory shall accommodate with the product's characteristic and manufacturing scope.

Generally, the enterprise shall not consign other's to check, if consigned check is necessary, the enterprise shall consign exterior laboratory to check according to the prescription of consigned check in Chap. 11, and explanation shall be made in check report.

Article 218 Director of quality control shall have enough qualification and experience of managing laboratory, and could manage one or more laboratories in one enterprise.

Article 219 Inspection person of quality control laboratory shall have education background of technical secondary school with related specialty or senior high school, and have experienced and passed the examination of practice training related to inspection operation.

Article 220 Quality control laboratory shall equipped with Pharmacopoeia, standard illustrative plates collection and necessary reference books, and standard objects or contrast objects and other related standard matter.

Article 221 The document of quality control laboratory shall in accordance with the principle of Chap. 8, and in accordance with the following requirements:

1. Quality control laboratory shall at least have the following detailed documents:
    1. Quality standard;
    2. Sampling operation procedures and record;
    3. Inspection operation procedures and record (including inspection record or laboratory working memo);
    4. Inspection report or certificate;
    5. Essential environment monitor operation procedures, record and report;
    6. Essential inspection method validation report and record;
    7. Apparatus adjustment and equipment's usage, cleaning, maintenance operation procedures and record.
2. Each batch of products' inspection record shall include the quality inspection record to semifinished product, bulk product and finished product, in order to trace the related quality inspection information of this batch of products;
3. Keep certain data (i.e. inspection data, environment monitor data, microorganism in water used for pharmacy monitor data) by the method of easy to do direction analysis;
4. Except the related data of batch record, other source material or record shall also be kept to review.

Article 222 Sampling shall in accordance with at least the following requirements:

1. Person in quality management department could enter in manufacturing area and storage area to take sampling and inspection;
2. Sampling shall in accordance with the approved operation procedures, and the operation procedures shall detailed prescribe the following:
    1. Authorized sampling person;
    2. Sampling method;
    3. Used apparatus;
    4. Quantity of samples;
    5. Method of dividing samples;
    6. Type and condition of sample stored container;
    7. Disposal and mark of remain part after sampling and samples;
    8. Notice items of sampling, includes the prevention measures taken to reduce all kinds of risks produced in sampling process, especially the sampling of asepsis or baleful material, and notice items to prevent pollution and cross pollution during sampling process;
    9. Storage condition;
    10. Cleaning method and storage requirements of sampling apparatus.
3. The method of sampling shall scientific and reasonable to ensure the sample is representative;
4. The reserved sample shall be able to represent the sampled batch of products or material, it is also possible to take out other samples to monitor the most important tache (i.e. the beginning or ending or the manufacturing) of manufacturing;

5. Sample's container shall mark with label, which indicates the sample's name, batch number, sampling date, take from which package container, person of sampling and other information;
6. Samples shall be kept according to prescribed storage requirements.

Article 223 Inspectionto material and products in different manufacturing levels shall in accordance with at least the following requirements:

1. The enterprise shall ensure the pharmaceutical goods are inspected completely under the registered approved method;
2. Inspection method shall be validated if there is one case of the following:
    1. New inspection method is used;
    2. Inspection method shall have changes;
    3. Use the inspection method which is not recorded in Pharmacopoeia of the Peoples' Republic of China or other legal standard;
    4. Inspection method needs to be validated prescribed by this Regulation.
3. For the inspection method does not need to validate, the enterprise shall confirm the inspection method to ensure the inspection data is accurate and credible;
4. Inspection shall have written operation procedures which prescribe the method, apparatus and equipment, the content of inspection operation procedures shall be the same with the confirmed or validated inspection method;
5. Inspection shall have the traceable record and shall be double examined, to ensure the result is the same with the record. All calculation shall have strict check;
6. Inspection record shall include at least the following contents:
    1. Product or material's name, type of preparation, specification, batch number or goods' supplying batch number, if necessary, indicate the name or resource of supplier and manufacturer (if different);
    2. Quality standard and inspection operation procedures based on;
    3. The type and serial number of apparatus or equipment used for inspection;
    4. Confecting serial number of test solution and culture medium used for inspection, resource and serial number of contrast object or standard object;
    5. Related information of animal used for inspection;
    6. Inspection process, including the preparation of contrast liquid, each detailed inspection operation, essential environment temperature and humidity;
    7. Inspection result, including the observed information, calculation and illustrative plates collection or graph, and the serial number of the inspection report based on;
    8. Inspection date;
    9. Signature and date of inspection person;
    10. Signature and date of double examined person for inspection, calculation.
7. All middle control (including middle control take by manufacture person) shall be done under the method approved by quality management department, the inspection shall take record;

8. Quality inspection shall be done to the glass apparatus, reagent, test solution, contrast object and culture medium used for laboratory capability analysis;
9. Experiment animal used for inspection shall be inspected or isolated quarantine before use when necessary. The animal's breeding and management shall in accordance with the related prescription of experiment animal management. The animal shall be marked, and the used history record shall be kept.

Article 224 Quality control laboratory shall set up inspection result of criteria exceeding operation procedures. Any criteria exceeding inspection result must inspect completely according to operation procedures, and take corresponding record.

Article 225 The material, samples of products kept according to enterprise's prescription, used for tracing pharmaceutical goods' quality or investigation are reserved samples. The samples used for products' stability review are not reserved samples.

Reserved samples shall in accordance with at least the following requirements:

1. Management to reserved samples according to operation procedures;
2. Reserved samples could represent the sampled batch of material or product;
3. Reserved samples of finished products:
    1. Each batch of products shall have reserved samples; if one batch of products is packaged for several times, reserve one finished product of smallest commercial package for each package at least;
    2. Package of reserved samples shall be the same with the package of pharmaceutical goods in commercial, if the reserved samples of original pharmaceutical goods could not use the package in commercial, simulated package could be used;
    3. Amount of reserved samples for each batch of products shall ensure two times' full examination of registered and approved quality standard at least (except asepsis inspection and pyrogen inspection);
    4. At least one time visual inspection per year shall be done to reserved samples during storage period if it does not influence reserved samples' package, if there is abnormity, completely investigation shall be done and shall take corresponding measures;
    5. Review to reserved samples shall take record;
    6. Reserved samples shall store under the registered storage condition for at least 1 year after the period of validity of pharmaceutical goods;
    7. If the enterprise stop manufacturing the pharmaceutical goods or is closed, the reserved samples shall deliver to authorized unit for storage, and inform the local pharmaceutical goods' supervision management department, so that the reserved samples could be got when necessary.
4. Reserved samples of material:
    1. Each batch of raw material used for preparation manufacturing and wrapper directly contact with pharmaceutical goods shall have reserved samples.

If the finished products have already have reserved samples, the wrapper directly contact with pharmaceutical goods (i.e. infusion bottle) may not have reserved samples separately;

2. Amount of material's reserved samples shall at least satisfy the requirements of distinguishing;
3. Except the raw material with worse stability, the reserved samples of raw material used for preparation manufacturing (excluding the impregnant, gas or pharmacy water used in manufacturing process) and wrapper directly contact with pharmaceutical goods shall store at least 2 years after the products' discharging. If the material's period of validity is short, the time for storing reserved samples could corresponding shorten;
4. Material's reserved samples shall store according to the prescribed condition, and shall appropriate airproof it when necessary.

Article 226 Management of reagent, test solution, nutrient medium and certified bacterium shall in accordance with at least the following requirements:

1. Reagent and nutrient medium shall order from credible supplier, if necessary, the supplier shall be evaluated;
2. Record of receiving reagent, test solution, nutrient medium shall have, if necessary, receiving date of reagent, test solution, nutrient medium shall be indicated on the container;
3. Reagent, test solution and nutrient medium shall prepare, stored and used according to related prescription or using instruction. In special cases, before receiving or using, distinguish or other inspection shall be done to the reagent;
4. Reagent and prepared nutrient medium shall indicate preparation batch number, preparation date and preparation person's name, and have preparation (including sterilization) record. Unstable reagent, test solution and nutrient medium shall indicate the period of validity and special storage condition. Standardized solution, volumetric solution shall indicate the last standardized date and adjustment gene, and have standardized record;
5. Prepared nutrient medium shall take applicable examination, and take corresponding record. Nutrient medium shall have using record;
6. Inspect all required certified bacterium, and set up certified bacterium's storage, passage, usage, destroying operation procedures and corresponding record;
7. Certified bacterium shall have appropriate mark, its content shall include at least the name of bacterium, serial number, passage number, passage date, passage operator;
8. Certified bacterium shall be stored according to prescribed condition, the method and time of storage shall not have bad influence to the develop characteristics of certified bacterium.

Article 227 Management of standard objects or contrast objects shall in accordance with at least the following requirements:

1. Standard objects or contrast objects shall store and use in accordance with the prescription;
2. Standard objects or contrast objects shall have appropriate mark, the content shall at least include name, batch number, preparation date (if any), period of validity (if any), initial opening date, content or titer, storage condition;
3. If the enterprise needs to prepare working standard objects or contrast objects itself, it shall set up the quality standard of working standard objects or contrast objects and preparation, distinguish, inspection, approval and storage operation procedures, each batch of working standard objects or contrast objects shall standardize using legal standard objects or contrast objects, and confirm the period of validity, and prove working standard objects or contrast objects' titer or content stay stable during the period of validity by regular standardize. The process and result of standardize shall have corresponding record.

Section 2 Discharging of Material and Product

Article 228 Set up the operation procedures of material and product discharging separately, specific indicate the standard, responsibility of approving discharging, and take corresponding record.

Article 229 Dischargingof material shall in accordance with at least the following requirements:

1. Material's quality evaluation content shall at least include manufacturer's inspection report, examination condition and inspection result on integrality and airtightness of material's package;
2. Material's quality evaluation shall have specific conclusion, such as approve to discharge, unqualified or other decision;
3. Material's discharging shall approve by designated person's signature.

Article 230 Dischargingof product shall in accordance with at least the following requirements:

1. Before approving of discharging, each batch of products shall take quality evaluation, to ensure the pharmaceutical goods and its manufacturing are in accordance with the requirements of registration and this Regulation, and confirm the following contents:
    1. Validation of main production technology and inspection method;
    2. All necessary examination, inspection shall be finished, and compositive consider the actual manufacturing condition and manufacturing record;
    3. All necessary manufacturing and quality control are all finished and signed by related directors;
    4. Modification has finished according to related prescription, the modification needs the approval of pharmaceutical goods' supervision management department has been approved;
    5. Modification or windage have finished all necessary sampling, examination, inspection and auditing;

6. All windage related to the batch of products halve specific explanation or indication, or have completely investigated and appropriately disposed; if windage involves other batches of products, the products shall be disposed together.

2. Material's quality evaluation shall have specific conclusion, such as approve to discharge, unqualified or other decision;
3. Each batch of products' discharging shall approve by quality authorized person's signature.
4. Before the discharging of vaccine goods, blood goods, diagnose reagent in vitro used for blood origin screening and other biology goods prescribed by state food and drug administration, qualified certificate shall be issued.

Section 3 Persistent Stability Review

Article 231 The purpose of persistent stability review is to monitor the quality of pharmaceutical goods come into market during the period of validity, to find pharmaceutical goods' stability problems related to manufacture (i.e. the change of impurity content or dissolution characteristic), and confirm the pharmaceutical goods could stored in the indicated storage condition, and in accordance with all requirements of quality standard.

Article 232 Persistent stability review mainly aims to package pharmaceutical goods in commercial, and shall also aim to bulk product. For example, before the bulk product finishes packaging, or there is a long time for storage from manufacturing factory to packaging factory, the influence to package product's stability in corresponding environment condition shall be evaluated. In addition, the semifinished product with longer storage time shall also be reviewed.

Article 233 Persistent stability review shall have review scheme, the result shall have report. The equipment used for persistent stability review (especially the equipment or establishment for stability test) shall confirm and maintain according to the requirements in Chap. 7 and Chap. 5.

Article 234 The time of persistent stability review shall cover the period of validity of pharmaceutical goods, the review scheme shall include at least the following contents:

1. Each specification, each manufacturing batch pharmaceutical goods' review batch number;
2. Related physics, chemistry, microorganism and biology inspection method, special inspection method of persistent stability review could be used;
3. Gist of inspection method;
4. Qualified standard;
5. Description of container airproof system;
6. Examination interval time (test time point);
7. Storage condition (persistent stability test standard condition prescribed by Pharmacopoeia of the Peoples' Republic of China corresponding to pharmaceutical goods' marked storage condition shall be used);

8. Inspection items, if the test items are less than the items of finished products' quality standard, reasons shall be indicated.

Article 235 Review batch number and test frequency shall get enough data for direction analysis. In general, for the pharmaceutical goods of each specification, each kind of inner package, one batch review shall be done for at least per year, unless the products are not manufactured this year.

Article 236 Sometimes, persistent stability review shall add additional batch number, the pharmaceutical goods of important changes or manufacturing and packaging have important windage shall be listed into stability review. In addition, the batch of renew, come back or callback shall also be listed into review, unless the products have already been validated and stability review.

Article 237 Key person, especially quality authorized person, shall know the result of persistent stability review. When the persistent stability review is not doing in the manufacturing enterprise of bulk product and finished product, related parties shall have written agreement, and shall keep the result of persistent stability review for examination of pharmaceutical goods' supervision management department.

Article 238 The result falls short of quality standard or has important abnormity direction shall be investigated. For any confirmed unqualified result to quality standard or important bad direction, the enterprise shall consider whether it influences to pharmaceutical goods in commercial, recall shall be done when necessary, investigated result and measures taken shall report to local pharmaceutical goods' supervision management department.

Article 239 Summarize report shall be made according to the entire data information, including the stage conclusion of review, and shall be kept. Summarize report shall be regular audited.

Section 4 Change Control

Article 240 Enterprise shall set up change control system to evaluate and manage the changes influence to products' quality. The change needs pharmaceutical goods' supervision management department's approval shall perform after approving.

Article 241 Operation procedures shall be set up, which to prescribe the change of application, evaluation, auditing, approval and performance of raw material, wrapper, quality standard, inspection method, operation procedures, workshop, establishment, equipment, apparatus, production technology and computer software. Quality management department shall designate special person to take charge of changing control.

Article 242 Changes shall evaluate its potential influence to products. Enterprise could classify the changes (such as main change, minor changes) according to changes' characteristic, scope, degree of potential influence to products' quality. The required validation, additional inspection and stability review for judgment to changes shall base on science.

Article 243 After the changes related to products' quality is brought forward by application department, evaluation, performance scheme and specific performance responsibility shall be confirmed, and finally audited and approved by quality management department. Performance of changes shall have corresponding complete record.

Article 244 When the raw material, wrapper directly contact with pharmaceutical goods, production technology, main manufacturing equipment and other main factors influence pharmaceutical goods' quality is changed, at least three batches of pharmaceutical goods' quality after the performance of changing shall be evaluated. If the changes may influence the period of validity of pharmaceutical goods, quality evaluation shall include the persistent review of the pharmaceutical goods manufactured after the performance of changing.

Article 245 When the changes are performing, ensure the documents related to changes have already been edited.

Article 246 Quality management department shall keep all documents and records of changing.

Section 5 Windage Disposal

Article 247 Director of each department shall ensure all people perform production technology, quality standard, inspection method and operation procedures correctly, in order to avoid windage.

Article 248 Enterprise shall set up windage disposal operation procedures, prescribe windage's report, record, investigation, disposal and correct measures taken, and have corresponding record.

Article 249 Any windage shall evaluate its potential influence to products' quality. Enterprise could classify the windage (such as important windage, minor windage) according to windage's characteristic, scope, degree of potential influence to products' quality. Evaluation to important windage shall also consider whether additional inspection to products is needed and whether it influences the pharmaceutical goods' period of validity, when necessary, stability review shall be done to important windage products.

Article 250 Any windage production technology, reconciliation of inventory limit, quality standard, inspection method, operation procedures and so on shall take record, and report to director and quality management department, the record shall have clear explanation, important windage shall completely investigate by quality management department and other departments, investigation report shall be issued. Windage investigation report shall be audited and executed by designated person of quality management department.

Enterprise shall take prevention measures to effective prevent similar windage happening again.

Article 251 Quality management department shall be responsible for windage's classification, keep the documents and records of windage investigation, disposal.

Section 6 Correction Measures and Prevention Measures

Article 252 Enterprise shall set up correction measures and prevention measures system, to investigate and take correction and prevention measures to complaint, recall, windage, self-test or exterior examination result, technology performance and quality monitor direction and so on. The depth and form of investigation shall accommodate with the level of risk. Correction measures and prevention measures system shall enhance the understanding to product and technology, improve product and technology.

Article 253 Enterpriseshall set up correction and prevention measures operation procedures, the content shall include at least the following:

1. Analyze to complaint, recall, windage, self-test or exterior examination result, technology performance and quality monitor direction and quality data from other resources to confirm the existent and potential quality problems. If necessary, take appropriate statistic method;
2. Investigate the related reasons to product, technology and quality guarantee system;
3. Confirm the required correction and prevention measures to prevent the problem happening again;
4. Evaluate the rationality, validity and sufficiency of correction and prevention measures;
5. All changes happened in correction and prevention measures shall be recorded;
6. Ensure the related information have transferred to quality authorized person and direct principal preventing the problems happening again;
7. Ensure the related information and correction and prevention measures have passed the approval by senior administrator.

Article 254 Correction and prevention measures' performance shall have document record, and shall keep by quality management department.

Section 7 Supplier's Evaluation and Approval

Article 255 Quality management department shall take quality evaluation to the supplier manufacturing material. Quality management department and related department shall take locale quality audit to the quality system of the main material supplier (especially the manufacturer), and take veto power to unqualified supplier.

The confirmation of main material shall compositive consider the manufactured pharmaceutical goods' quality risk, material dosage and influence degree from material to pharmaceutical goods' quality and other factors.

Legal representative of enterprise, director of enterprise and person in other department could not interfere or disturb the quality management department take quality evaluation independently to material supplier.

Article 256 Material supplier evaluation and approval operation procedures shall be set up, to definite the supplier's qualification, principle of choosing, quality evaluation method, evaluation standard, and material supplier approval procedures.

If quality evaluation takes locale quality audit method, audit content, period, group and qualification of audit person shall be indicated. If trial production of sample small lot production shall be done, manufacturing batch, production technology, product quality standard, stability review scheme shall also be indicated.

Article 257 Quality management department shall designate special person to be responsible for material supplier's quality evaluation and locale quality auditing, distributing the list of approved qualified suppliers. The designated person shall have knowledge on related codes and specialty, and have enough practice experience of quality evaluation and locale quality auditing.

Article 258 Locale quality audit shall verify the accuracy of supplier's qualification approving documents and inspection reports, verify whether the supplier have the condition of inspection. Supplier's personnel institution, workshop establishment and equipment, material management, production technology process and manufacturing management, equipment, apparatus, and document management of quality control laboratory shall be checked, in order to completely evaluate its quality guarantee system. Locale quality audit shall have report.

Article 259 When necessary, samples provided by main material supplier shall take trial production of sample small lot production, and take stability review on the trial produced pharmaceutical goods.

Article 260 Evaluation to material supplier taken by quality management department shall include at least the following:supplier's qualification approving document, quality standard, inspection report, inspection data and report to material's sample. If locale quality audit and samples' small lot production carries on, locale quality audit report and small lot production products' quality inspection report and stability review report shall also include.

Article 261 If material supplier changes, new supplier shall be quality evaluated; if main material supplier changes, related validation and stability review to products shall also be done.

Article 262 Quality management department shall distribute the list of approved qualified supplier to material management department, the list shall include at least material's name, specification, quality standard, manufacturer's name and address, dealer's name (if any) and so on, and the information shall be updated in time.

Article 263 Quality management department shall conclude an agreement with main material supplier, quality responsibilities of two parties shall be indicated in the agreement.

Article 264 Quality management department shall regular evaluate or locale quality audit, review and analyze material quality inspection result, quality complaint and unqualified disposal record to material supplier. If material has quality problems or its manufacturing condition, technology, quality standard and inspection method and key factors may influence quality changes, locale quality audit shall take as soon as possible.

Article 265 Enterprise shall set up quality file to each material supplier, the file shall include supplier's qualification approving document, quality agreement, quality standard, samples' inspection data and report, supplier's inspection report, locale quality audit report, products' stability review report, regular quality review analysis report and so on.

Section 8 Product's Quality Review Analysis

Article 266 Product's quality review analysis shall be done to all manufactured pharmaceutical goods per year according to operation procedures, to ensure the technology is stable and credible, and the applicability of raw material, finished products' quality standard, find bad direction in time, and ensure the improving direction of product and technology. Former review analysis history data shall be considered and validity self-check of products' quality review analysis shall be done.

When there is reasonable science bases, quality review could be done according to product's types, such as sold preparation, liquid preparation and asepsis preparation and so on.

Review analysis shall have report.

Enterprise shall take review analysis to at least the following conditions:

1. All changes to product used raw material, especially raw material supplied by new supplier;
2. Key middle reference point and finished products' inspection result;
3. All batches and investigation fall short of quality standard;
4. Validity of all important windage and related investigation, reform measures and prevention measures taken;
5. Changes on production technology or inspection method and so on;
6. Changes on approved or recorded pharmaceutical goods registration;
7. Result and any bad direction of stability review;
8. All withdraw, complaint, recall and investigation caused by quality reasons;
9. Performance and effect of taking correction measures related to products' technology or equipment;
10. For the new approved pharmaceutical goods or pharmaceutical goods have changes, accomplished working condition after coming into the market according to registration requirements;
11. Confirmed condition of related equipment and establishment, such as air condition cleanse system, water system, compress air and so on;
12. Consign manufacturing or inspection technique contract's performance condition.

Article 267 Review analysis' result shall be evaluated, whether correction and prevention measures need to be taken, or bring forward the evaluation opinions of re-confirmation or re-validation and state reasons, finish correction in time and effectively.

Article 268 When the pharmaceutical goods are consigned for manufacturing, written technique agreement shall conclude between assignor and assignee, which prescribe the responsibilities of two parties in product's quality review analysis, to ensure product's quality review analysis carries on in time and is in accordance with the requirements.

Section 9 Complaint and Bad Reaction Report

Article 269 Pharmaceutical goods' bad reaction report and monitor management system shall be set up, special institution shall be set up and special person shall be designated for management.

Article 270 Collect the bad reaction of pharmaceutical goods actively, specific record, evaluation, investigation and disposal shall be done to bad reaction, take measures in time to control the risk may exist, and report to pharmaceutical goods' supervision management department according to requirements.

Article 271 Set up operation procedures to prescribe the procedure of complaint registration, evaluation, investigation and disposal, and prescribe the measures shall be taken when receiving the complaint may cause by product limitation, including the advisement of whether recalling pharmaceutical goods from market.

Article 272 Special person and enough assistants shall have to be responsible for investigation and disposal to quality complaint, all information about complaint, investigation shall advise to quality authorized person.

Article 273 All complaint shall be registered and audited, the complaint related to product's quality limitation shall record every details of complaint, and taking investigation.

Article 274 If any limitation is found or doubted in some batch of pharmaceutical goods, other batches of products shall consider for checking, and find whether it was influenced.

Article 275 Complaint investigation and disposal shall have record, and indicate the related information of batch of products.

Article 276 Complaint review shall be regular reviewed and analyzed, to find the problems need to be warned, repeated problems and pharmaceutical goods may need to recall, and take corresponding measures.

Article 277 When enterprise has manufacturing mistake, pharmaceutical goods are transformed or other important quality problem, corresponding measures shall be taken in time, when necessary, the enterprise shall report to local pharmaceutical goods' supervision management department.

Chapter 11 Consigned Manufacturing and Consigned Inspection

Section 1 Principle

Article 278 In order to ensure the accuracy and reliability of the quality of consigned manufacturing products and consigned inspection, the assignor and assignee must conclude written agreement, which specific prescribe the responsibilities of each party, content and related technique items of consigned manufacturing or consigned inspection.

Article 279 All activities of consigned manufacturing or consigned inspection, including any changes in technique or other factors, shall in accordance with the related requirements of pharmaceutical goods' manufacturing consent and registration.

Section 2 Assignor

Article 280 The assignor shall evaluate the assignee by locale examination on assignee's condition, technique level, and quality management condition, confirm its ability of finishing assigned job, and ensure to finish in accordance with the requirements of this Regulation.

Article 281 Assignor shall provide all necessary data to assignee, so that the assignee could correct operate the assigned operation according to pharmaceutical goods' registration and other legal requirements.

Assignor shall let the assignee understand all kinds of problems related to product or operation completely, including the possible harms product or operation may caused to assignee's environment, workshop, equipment, person and other material or product.

Article 282 Assignor shall supervise the whole process of consigned manufacturing or inspection.

Article 283 Assignor shall ensure material and products are in accordance with related quality standard.

Section 3 Assignee

Article 284 Assignee shall equip with enough workshop, equipment, knowledge and experience and personnel, to satisfy the consigned manufacturing or inspection work by assignor.

Article 285 Assignee shall ensure the material, semifinished product and bulk product provided by assignor are applicable to the intending purpose.

Article 286 Assignee could not take activities which have bad influence to the consigned manufactured or inspected product quality.

Section 4 Contract

Article 287 The contract conclude between assignor and assignee shall particular prescribe each party's product manufacturing and control responsibility, the technique articles in the contract shall draw out by the directors with pharmacy technology, inspection specialty knowledge and who know this Regulation well. All work of consigned manufacturing and inspection shall in accordance with the requirements of pharmaceutical goods' manufacturing consent and pharmaceutical goods' registration and shall consent by two parties.

Article 288 The contract shall specific prescribe the procedure of approving to discharge each batch of pharmaceutical goods by quality authorized person, to ensure each batch of products have finished manufacturing and inspection according to the requirements of pharmaceutical goods' registration.

Article 289 The contract shall prescribe which party is responsible for material's ordering, inspection, discharging, manufacturing and quality control (including middle control), and shall prescribe which party is responsible for sampling and inspection.

When it is consigned inspection, the contract shall prescribe whether the assignee could sampling in assignor's workshop.

Article 290 The contract shall prescribe that assignor could review or check the manufacturing, inspection and discharging record and samples kept by assignee at any time; if there is complaint, the products may have quality limitation or recall, assignor shall be able to review all records related to product quality evaluation.

Article 291 The contract shall specific prescribe the assignor could check or take locale quality audit to assignee.

Article 292 Consigned inspection contract shall definite that the assignor has duty to receive the check by pharmaceutical goods' supervision management department.

Chapter 12 Product's Delivering and Recall

Section 1 Principle

Article 293 Enterprise shall set up product recall system. It could recall any batch of product with safety problems promptly, effectively when necessary.

Article 294 For the withdrawn and recalled products caused by quality reasons, shall be supervised and destroyed according to prescription, unless the products' quality is proved to be no influence.

Section 2 Delivering

Article 295 Each batch of products shall have delivering record. According to delivering record, sales condition of each batch of products shall be traced, so that all products could be recalled when necessary. The content of delivering record shall include: product's name, specification, batch number, amount, receiving unit and address, contact information, delivering date, transport method and so on.

Article 296 Scattered package of pharmaceutical goods' delivering is limited to two batches as one combined box, the combined box shall indicate all the batch number, and set up combined box record.

Article 297 Delivering record shall keep at least 1 year after the period of validity of pharmaceutical goods.

Section 3 Recall

Article 298 Recall operation procedures shall be set up, to ensure the validity of recall.

Article 299 Special person shall be designated to be responsible for organize and assort with recall, and enough person shall be equipped. The director of product recall shall be independent with sale and market department; if the director of product recall is not the quality authorized person, the information of recall shall be reported to quality authorized person.

Article 300 Recall shall startup at any time, and shall perform promptly.

Article 301 If the product is recalled from market because of safety limitation, the information shall be reported to local pharmaceutical goods' supervision management department immediately.

Article 302 Director of product recall shall review pharmaceutical goods' delivering record immediately.

Article 303 The recalled products shall be marked, and shall storage independent and appropriate to wait for final disposal decision.

Article 304 Development of recall shall have records and have final report. Product's delivering amount, recalled amount and amount balance shall be indicated in the report.

Article 305 Regular evaluation shall be done to the validity of product recall system.

Chapter 13 Self-check

Section 1 Principle

Article 306 Quality management department shall regular organize self-check to enterprise, monitor performance condition of this Regulation, evaluate the enterprise and bring forward essential correction and prevention measures.

Section 2 Self-check

Article 307 Plans shall be done before self-check. Regular check shall be done to organization and personnel, workshop and establishment, equipment, material and product, confirmation and validation, document management, manufacturing management, quality control and quality guarantee, consigned manufacturing and consigned inspection, product delivering and recall and other items.

Article 308 Enterprise shall designate person to take independent, system, complete self-check, and shall take independent quality audit by exterior person or expert.

Article 309 Self-check shall have record. After the self-check is finished, self-check report shall be done, the content shall include at least all condition reviewed in self-check process, evaluated conclusion and advises of correction and prevention measures. The self-check condition shall report to senior administrator of enterprise.

Chapter 14 Supplementary Articles

Article 310 This Regulation is the basic requirements to pharmaceutical goods' manufacturing quality management. For the special requirements on asepsis pharmaceutical goods, biology preparation, blood preparation and other pharmaceutical goods or manufacturing quality management activity, shall constitute by state food and drug administration in appendix.

Article 311 Enterprise could achieve the requirements of this Regulation by a validated substitute method.

Article 312 The meaning of the terms (arranged by Chinese pinyin) in this Regulationare as following:

1. Package
   All operation proceduress from bulk product to finished product, including load, mark with label and so on. However, products' asepsis filling package in asepsis production technology, and finally sterilization products' filling package are not regarding as package.
2. Wrapper
   Material used for wrapper, including wrapper and container, printing wrapper directly contact with pharmaceutical goods, but not including exterior package material used for delivering.
3. Operation procedures
   Currency document approved for instructing equipment's operation, maintenance and cleaning, validation, environment control, sampling and inspection and other pharmaceutical goods' manufacturing activities, is also called as standard operation procedures.
4. Product
   Product includes pharmaceutical goods' semifinished product, bulk product and finished product.
5. Product's lifecycle
   All stages from product's initial develop, coming into the market and withdrawing from market.
6. Finished product
   Product has finished all manufacturing procedures and final package.
7. Reprocessing
   Reprocess by different production technology to part or full of semifinished product or bulk product which one manufacturing procedure does not in accordance with the quality standard, in order to in accordance with the intending quality standard.
8. Bulk product
   Product with no package but have finished all other processing procedures.
9. Quarantine
   The status of raw material, wrapper, semifinished product, bulk product or finished product, use physics method or other effective method to isolate or distinguish them, and it is stored, waited for taking the decision of delivering before it is allowed to manufacture or come into market.
10. Extending
    A series of operations done in the enterprise, such as the operations of material, semifinished product, bulk product, document, mould used for manufacturing.
11. Period of double examination
    After the raw material, wrapper is stored for certain time, for ensuring it is still applicable to intending purpose, the double examined date decided by enterprise.

12. Delivering
    It means a series of operations done from enterprise to dealer or consumer, such as matching goods, transportation and so on.
13. Renew process
    For a batch of semifinished products or bulk products, part of finished products or all products which certain production technology is not in accordance with the quality standard, return the products to the previous procedure, re-process with the same production technology, in order to be accordance with the intending quality standard.
14. Discharging
    Take quality evaluation to a batch of material or product, and take decision of approval for using or approval to come into market, or other decisions.
15. Senior administrator
    It means the person with the power and responsibility of directing and controlling enterprise in the enterprise, and has the power of adjusting resources.
16. Production technology: A document or set of documents setting for manufacturing specified quantity of finished products, including manufacturing prescription, processing instructions (including middle control), notice items and so on.
17. Supplier
    Supplier for material, equipment, apparatus, reagent, service, such as manufacturer, dealer and so on.
18. Callback
    In certain manufacturing stage, add a previous batch or several previous batches of products, partial or whole, which in accordance with quality requirements to the operation of another batch of products.
19. Computer system
    It means the integration system for reporting or auto controlling, including data input, electric disposal and information output.
20. Cross pollution
    Pollution happens between different raw materials, excipient and products.
21. Adjustment
    Confirm a series of activities between the value (especially metage) of measuring, recording, control apparatus or system, or the represented value of practicality measure and corresponding contrast standard measuring value under prescribed condition.
22. Stage manufacturing method
    In common manufacturing area, concentrated manufacturing a kind of product in a period of time, and then completely clean corresponding common manufacturing area, establishment, equipment, apparatus, and change to manufacture another kind of product.
23. Clean Room: A room (area) with defined environmental control of particulates and microbilogical contamination, constructed and used in such a way as to reduce the introduction, generation, and retention of contaminants within the area.

24. Alarm limit
    It means the limit standard when the key parameter of system is above the normal scope, but not achieving the correction limit, the limit shall be alarmed, and may take correction measures.
25. Correction limit
    It means the limit standard when the key parameter of system is above the accepted standard, and needs to investigate and take correction measures.
26. Inspection result exceeding standard
    All situations when inspection result exceeds the legal standard and standard set up by enterprise.
27. Batch
    It means a certain amount of raw material, wrapper or finished product of same intended quality and characteristic by one or several processing procedures. In order to finish some manufacturing operation procedures, a batch of products may need to divide into several batches, and finally combine into one batch. When the products are manufactured in series, batch of product shall correspond to the specific amount of products of same intended characteristic. Batch amount means the amount of products which could fix amount or time when manufacturing.
    Such as: oral or external used solid, semisolid preparation use one combined equipment before moulding or discharging, the manufactured products in same quality are one batch of products; oral or external used liquid preparation combine by medicine liquid before filling load (envelop) in same quality are one batch of products.
28. Batch number: A distinctive combination of numbers and/or letters by which one is able to identify a special batch.
29. Batch production record: All documents and records associated with the manufacture, all history information related to finished products' quality could be traced.
30. Ventilator
    The ventilator shall set between isolated space with two or more doors of two or more rooms (such as between the rooms with different clean level). The aim of setting ventilator is to control air current when person or material is coming in and out of the room. Ventilator divides into person ventilator and material ventilator.
31. Enterprise
    Enterprise means pharmaceutical goods' manufacturing enterprise if there is no special indication in this Regulation.
32. Confirmation
    A series activities confirm workshop, establishment, equipment could run correctly and could achieve intended result.
33. Withdraw of goods
    It means the activity of returning the pharmaceutical goods to enterprise.
34. Document
    The document means in this Regulation include quality standard, technique procedure, operation procedures, record, report and so on.

35. Material
    It means raw material, excipient, packaging materials, and so on.
    Such as: raw material of chemical pharmaceutical goods preparation means raw drug; raw material of biology preparation means raw material; raw material of Chinese tradition medicine means Chinese medicinal plant, Chinese traditional medicine tea and outsourcing Chinese traditional medicine extractive matter; raw material of raw drug means other material in raw drug manufacturing besides wrapper.
36. Reconciliation
    A comparison, making due allowance for normal variation, between the amount actually produced or used and the amount of product or materials theoretically produced or used.
37. Pollution
    Raw material, semifinished product, bulk product, finished product is adversely influenced by impurity or foreign matter with chemistry or microorganism characteristics, during the process of manufacturing, sampling, packaging or re-packaging, storage or transportation.
38. Validation: The documented act of proving that any operation procedures (or method), production technology, or system actually leads to the expected results.
39. Printing wrapper
    It means that the wrapper with special pattern and printing content, such as working aluminum foil, label, instruction, paper box and so on.
40. Raw material
    Any material used in the process of pharmaceutical goods' manufacturing except wrapper.
41. Semifinished product
    Product with part processing procedures finished, and shall take further process to become bulk product.
42. Middle control
    Also named as process control, it means to monitor to production technology during manufacturing, and adjust to take each inspection so that to ensure the product is in accordance with the related standard. Environment or equipment control shall regard as a part of middle control.

Article 313 This Regulation shall be effective from March 1, 2011. According to Article 9 prescribed in "Drug Administration Law of The People's Republic of China", the detailed implement method and implement procedure shall prescribe by State Food and Drug Administration.

1.3.3.3 Good Clinical Practice of Pharmaceutical Products

The SFDA order No. 3, Effective on September 1, 2003 (SFDA 2003a, b)
Contents:

Chapter 1 General Provisions
Chapter 2 Preparations and Prerequisites for Conducting a Clinical Trial
Chapter 3 Protection of a Human Subject's Interests
Chapter 4 Protocol for a Clinical Trial
Chapter 5 The Investigator's Responsibilities
Chapter 6 The Sponsor's Responsibilities
Chapter 7 The Monitor's Responsibilities
Chapter 8 Records and Reports
Chapter 9 Data Management and Statistical Analysis
Chapter 10 Administration of Investigational Product
Chapter 11 Quality Assurance
Chapter 12 Multicenter Trial
Chapter 13 Miscellaneous

Chapter 1: General Provisions

Article 1: This Good Clinical Practice of Pharmaceutical Products (hereinafter "GCP") is promulgated in accordance with the Drug Administration Law of PRC and Implementing Regulation of Drug Administration Law of PRC, making reference to internationally recognized principles to ensure the standardization of clinical trials of drugs which will result in scientific reliability, and the protection of the interests and safety of the human subject.

Article 2 This GCP is a regulation for the standardization of the whole process of a clinical trial, including protocol design, organizing implementation, monitoring, auditing, recording, analysis, summarization and reporting.

Article 3 This GCP is to be observed in all phases of a clinical trial, the bioavailability trial or biological equivalence trial on the human body.

Article 4 All research involving human subjects must conform to the Declaration of Helsinki of World Medical Association (Appendix 1) i.e. fairness, respect of human integrity, maximize the benefits and minimize any harm to the human subject.

Chapter 2: Preparations and Prerequisites for Conducting a Clinical Trial

Article 5 Sufficient scientific basis must be provided for conducting clinical trials of drugs. The purpose of a clinical trial, the problems to be solved, must be considered before conducting a trial on human subjects. The anticipated benefits and risks for the human subjects and public health must be balanced. The anticipated benefits must exceed the possible harm. The selection of clinical trial methods must conform to scientific and ethical criteria.

Article 6 The drugs to be used in a clinical trial shall be prepared and supplied by the sponsor. Before conducting a clinical trial, the sponsor must provide the pre-clinical study documents, including the formulation, manufacturing process and the quality inspection results of the drug. All pre-clinical study information supplied by the sponsor must conform to the requirements of the respective corresponding phase(s) of the clinical trial. The sponsor shall also provide the documents relating to the effectiveness and safety of the drug obtained from clinical trials already completed or being conducted in other places. GMP shall be conformed for manufacturing the investigational product.

Article 7 The equipment and conditions of the institution where the clinical trial will be conducted shall meet requirements for safety and efficacy. All investigators shall be qualified for undertaking the trial by their specialty and ability, and have received training. Before starting a clinical trial, a written agreement shall be reached between the investigator and the sponsor upon trial protocol, monitoring, auditing and standard operating procedures, as well as the responsibilities of each party in the trial.

Chapter 3: Protection of a Human Subject's Interests

Article 8: In a drug clinical trial, the human subject's interests must be fully protected and the trial shall be scientific and reliable. The human subject's interests, safety and health must be higher than the consideration for science and social interests. The use of an Ethics Committee and informed consent form are important methods to protect the human subject.

Article 9 In order to protect the interests of human subjects, an independent Ethics Committee shall be formed and such information filed with the SFDA. The Ethics Committee shall consist of at least five people of different genders including those working in the medical profession, not working in the medical profession, law experts, and members from other units. The structure and work of the Ethics Committee shall not be influenced by those participating in the trial.

Article 10 The protocol of the trial must be reviewed and approved by the Ethics Committee. When conducting a clinical trial, any amendment of the protocol may not be implemented without approval from the Ethics Committee. Any serious adverse events that occur during the trial shall be reported to the Ethics Committee.

Article 11 The decisions regarding review and approval of the protocol by the Ethics Committee shall be decided through discussion and voting. Ethnics Committee members shall avoid participating in the clinical trial. Experts who are not members of the committee may be invited to attend the meeting when necessary, but may not vote. The Ethics Committee shall establish its working procedures. Written records for all meetings and the resolutions adopted during meetings shall be kept for 5 years after the completion of a clinical trial.

Article 12 The Ethics Committee shall strictly examine the following aspects of the protocol in order to protect the interests of human subjects:

the qualifications and experience of investigators and whether they will have enough time to participate in the clinical trial, and whether the staff and equipment conform with the requirements of the trial;

whether the ethical principles are fully considered in the protocol, including the purpose of the investigation, the anticipated risks and benefits to the human subject and other people, and whether the trial is scientifically designed;

whether the method of human subject admission and the information about the trial provided to the human subject, or their families or legal guardians or legal representatives, is complete and easy to understand, and whether the method used to obtain informed consent form is proper;

the treatment or insurance provided to a human subject who is harmed or even dies due to his participation in the clinical trial.

whether the recommendations to modify the protocol are acceptable; and,

periodic examination of the degree of risks to human subjects participating in the clinical trial.

Article 13 After receiving the application, the Ethics Committee shall hold a meeting as soon as possible to review and discuss it. The recommendation shall be issued in writing, including listing the attendance of committee members, their specialties and their signatures. The recommendation may:

- approve;
- approve after necessary modifications;
- disapprove;
- terminate or suspend an already approved trial.

Article 14 The investigator or its designated representative must explain to the human subject the following clinical trial matters in detail:
Participation by the human subject is voluntary. The human subject has the right to withdraw from the trial at any time during any phase and shall not be subject to discrimination or retaliation. The human subject's medical treatment and interests shall not be affected.

The human subject shall be informed that his participation and personal trial data are confidential. The Ethics Committee, drug administration authorities and the sponsor, when necessary, may check the human subject's data according to regulations.

The human subject shall be informed of the purpose of the trial, the procedures and duration of the trial, examination and operational procedures, the predicted possible benefits and risks that the human subject may suffer, and different groups in the trial in which the human subject may be placed.
Enough time must be given to the human subject to consider whether to participate in the trial or not. For a human subject who is unable to express his approval, his legal representative shall be informed of the above introduction and explanations. The explanation regarding the process of obtaining informed consent shall be made to the human subject or his legal representative orally or, in a written language he can understand. During the trial, a human subject has the right to know the trial information concerning himself at any time.

If any harm results because of the trial, the human subject may receive medical treatment and appropriate insurance compensation.

Article 15 The signature on the informed consent form shall be obtained only after the clinical trial has been explained in detail.

The human subject or his legal representative as well as the investigator responsible for the informed consent process shall sign and date the informed consent form.

A human subject who is incompetent may participate in a trial on the condition that the Ethics Committee approves such participation in principle and the investigator considers that the trial will be beneficial for the human subject. The informed consent form must be signed and dated by the legal guardian of the human subject.

If the human subject is a child, the informed consent form must be signed by the legal guardian of the child. If the child can decide whether he is willing to participate, the informed consent form shall also be approved by the child.

If in emergency, the informed consent form has not been obtained from the human subject or legal representative, if an effective treatment is lacking but the investigational product could save life, recover health, or alleviate pain, the clinical trial may be conducted. However, the method used on the human subject shall be explained clearly in the protocol of the trial as well as the relevant file, and approved by the Ethics Committee in advance.

If new information regarding the drug used in the trial is discovered, a written amendment of the informed consent form must be submitted to the Ethics Committee for approval, after which the human subject agreement must be obtained.

Chapter 4: Protocol for a Clinical Trial
Article 16: The protocol for a clinical trial shall be formulated before starting a clinical trial. The protocol shall be jointly discussed and signed by the investigator and sponsor, then submitted to the Ethics Committee for approval before implementation.

Article 17 The protocol for a clinical trial shall contain the following:

1. The topic of the clinical trial.
2. The purpose(s) and objective(s) of the trial, the background for the trial, findings regarding the investigational product before the clinical trial that are of clinical significance; results of other clinical trials related to the proposed trial, the possible risks and benefits for human subjects known to date, and the possible ethnic difference of the investigational product.
3. Name and address of the sponsor; the place where the clinical trial will be conducted; name, qualification and address of the investigator.
4. The type of the design of the clinical trial, the random selection method, and the level of the blinding.
5. The inclusion criteria, exclusion and removal of human subjects, the procedures for human subject inclusion, the method of grouping human subject.
6. The number of cases needed statistically to accomplish the purposes of the trial.
7. Form, dosage, route of administration, method and frequency of administration, period of treatment, order of usage of concomitant medicines, and explanation for package and label.
8. Clinical and laboratory check to be conducted, testing frequency and analysis of pharmacokinetics.
9. The registration, usage record, delivery and handing and storage conditions of the investigational products.
10. Clinical observation, on-site visit and measures to ensure the human subject's compliance of trial procedures.

11. Rules regarding termination of the clinical trial and rules for the completion of the clinical trial.
12. The standards for evaluating therapeutic efficacy, including the method for evaluating parameters, time of observation, recording and analysis.
13. Procedures to maintain the coding of human subject, table of random numbers and case report form.
14. Requirements for the recording of adverse events and methods for serious adverse event reporting; measures to handle, methods and time for monitor and outcome.
15. Establishment and maintenance of trial codes, methods to break the blind and rules concerning how codes may be accessed in emergency situations.
16. The plan of the statistical analysis, the definition and selection for the data package of the statistical analysis.
17. Rules for data administration and data traced to the source.
18. Quality control and quality assurance of clinical trial.
19. Ethics related to trial.
20. Tentative schedule and completion date of clinical trial.
21. On-site visit and medical treatment after the clinical trial is completed.
22. Each party's responsibility and other relevant stipulations.
23. Literature.

Article 18 During the trial, the protocol may be modified according to its procedures, if it is really necessary.

Chapter 5: The Investigator's Responsibilities
Article 19: The investigator responsible for the clinical trial shall:

1. be qualified in a specialized technical position and as a doctor in a medical institution;
2. have the relevant specialized knowledge and experience required in the protocol;
3. have experience in clinical trial research methods or be able to obtain professional assistance from experienced investigator(s) in his institution;
4. be familiar with the relevant information and literature provided by the sponsor of the clinical trial;
5. have authorization to allocate the needed staff and facilities for the clinical trial.

Article 20 The investigator shall read and understand the details of the protocol, and conduct the trial strictly according to the protocol.

Article 21 The investigator shall understand and be familiar with the properties, functions, effects and safety of the drug to be used (including pre-clinical study documents). He shall know well all new information about the product which information is discovered during the clinical trial.

Article 22 The investigator shall conduct the clinical trial in a medical institution with good medical treatment facilities, laboratory equipment and personnel. The institution shall have all necessary facilities to handle emergency situations to ensure the safety of human subjects. The result of laboratory evaluations must be correct and reliable.

Article 23 The investigator must obtain approval from his hospital or governing unit to ensure that he has enough time to undertake and complete the clinical trial within the period stipulated in the protocol. The investigator shall explain the information, regulations and responsibility about the trial to all personnel participating in the clinical trial, and ensure a sufficient number of qualified human subjects in the clinical trial.

Article 24 The investigator shall explain in detail to the human subjects about the trial as approved by the Ethics Committee and obtain the informed consent.

Article 25 The investigator is responsible for making medical treatment decisions about the clinical trial, and shall ensure that the human subjects receive proper treatment when adverse event occurs during the trial.

Article 26 The investigator has an obligation to adopt and make a record of necessary measures to protect the safety of the human subjects. If a serious adverse event occurs during a clinical trial, the investigator shall immediately provide appropriate medical treatment to the human subject and report to drug administration authorities, the sponsor and the Ethics Committee. The investigator shall sign and date this report.

Article 27 The investigator shall ensure that the data is duly written down on the case report form in a correct, complete and legal manner.

Article 28 The investigator shall receive monitors and auditors sent by the sponsor for such purposes and auditing and inspection by drug administration authorities in order to ensure the quality of the clinical trial.

Article 29 The investigator and sponsors shall negotiate and provide for the expenses of the clinical trial in a written contract. The investigator may not charge the human subjects the investigational products expenses during the clinical trial.

Article 30 After the clinical trial is completed, the investigator must prepare the final report with his signature and date, then forward it to the sponsor.

Article 31 For a clinical trial which is terminated, the investigator must inform the human subjects, the sponsor, the Ethics Committee and State Drug Administration and explain the reason.

Chapter 6: The Sponsor's Responsibilities
Article 32: The sponsor is responsible for initiating, applying for, organizing, monitoring, auditing a clinical trial and provides for the expenses of the trial. The sponsor shall submit the application for a clinical trial to the State Drug Administration in accordance with relevant provisions in China's laws, rules and regulations. The sponsor can authorize its contract research organization (CRO) to carry out certain work and obligations regarding the clinical trial.

Article 33 The sponsor shall select the institution and investigator for a clinical trial and confirm their qualifications and conditions to ensure the completion of the trial.

Article 34 The sponsor shall provide the investigator's brochure, containing the chemical, pharmaceutical, toxicological, pharmacological and clinical (including trials already being done or in process) information and data of the investigational product.

Article 35 Upon obtaining approval from the SFDA and agreement by the Ethics Committee, the sponsor shall start to organize the clinical trial in accordance with the protocol.

Article 36 The sponsor and the investigator shall jointly design the clinical trial protocol, stipulate the agreed responsibilities of each party in protocol implementation, data management, statistical analysis, results reporting, thesis publishing, etc. The protocol and contract shall be signed by both the sponsor and the investigator.

Article 37 The sponsor shall provide the investigator with the investigational product, reference product, comparator or placebo. These products shall be easy to recognize, correctly coded and marked with special labels. The sponsor must also ensure the quality of these products. The investigational products shall be properly packed and kept in accordance with the protocol. The sponsor shall establish a management and filing system for the investigational products.

Article 38 The sponsor shall appoint a qualified monitor, who must also be agreed to by the investigator.

Article 39 The sponsor is responsible for the establishment of quality control and quality assurance systems for the clinical trial. The sponsor may organize an audit group for the clinical trial to ensure the quality.

Article 40 The sponsor and the investigator shall study the serious adverse events immediately after occurrence and take necessary measures to ensure the human subject's safety and interests. Adverse events shall be reported to drug administration authorities, health administrative authorities and the other investigators conducting clinical trials on the same drug.

Article 41 If the sponsor terminates a clinical trial, it must immediately inform the investigator, the Ethics Committee and the SFDA and explain the reason.

Article 42 The sponsor shall submit the final report of the clinical trial to the SFDA.

Article 43 The sponsor shall provide the human subject with insurance for harm or death occurring during or caused by the clinical trial, which covers the expenses of the treatment and the economic compensation, and provides the investigator with a legal and economic guarantee, but not including harm and death from medical treatment accidents.

Article 44 If the investigator does not conduct the clinical trial in accordance with the approved protocol, or relevant rules and regulations, the sponsor must identify such and ask for correction. If the situation is serious or the investigator does not correct, the sponsor shall terminate his participation in the clinical trial and report to the SFDA.

Chapter 7: The Monitor's Responsibilities

Article 45: The monitor's responsibility is to protect the human subject's rights and interests in the clinical trial, ensure the record and data of the trial are correct and complete, make certain that the trial is conducted according to the approved protocol, and relevant rules and regulations.

Article 46 The monitor is the major intermediary between the sponsor and the investigator. The number of monitors depends on the complexity of the clinical trial and the number of medical institutions participating in the trial. The monitor shall be qualified in medicine, pharmacy or relevant specialties and properly trained for the trial. He shall be familiar with the relevant drug administration rules and regulations, familiar with the pre-clinical information of investigational product, information concerning the clinical trial, the protocol of the trial and relevant documents.

Article 47 The monitor shall supervise and urge that the clinical trial be conducted according to the standard operating procedures (SOP), in order that the clinical trial comply with the protocol, including:

1. Before the trial starts, confirm that the institution undertaking the trial already meets the appropriate requirements, including recruitment and training of the staff, the equipment of the laboratory is completed, the working conditions are good, all checks related to the trial have been made, estimate whether the number of human subjects is adequate, study and become familiar with the requirements stipulated in the protocol together with the investigator.
2. Monitor the institution and investigator undertaking the trial before, during and after the trial. Confirm that the informed consent form is obtained from all human subjects before the trial. Learn of the recruitment rate of the human subjects and the progress of the trial. Confirm that the records and report of all data are correct and complete.
3. Confirm that all case reports are correctly filled out and in compliance with the source documents. Make certain that all errors or omission have been rectified or marked with the investigator's signature and date. The change of dosage, alternative treatment, concomitant medicine, intercurrent diseases, missed monitoring and checking of every human subject shall be confirmed and written down. The verification of the selected human subject's withdrawal and missed monitoring shall be stated in the case report form.
4. Confirm that all adverse events have been recorded and serious adverse events have been reported within the required time period and filed.
5. Verify whether the investigational product is supplied, stored, distributed and returned in accordance with relevant regulations, and correspondingly recorded.
6. Assist the investigator in providing necessary notices and applications, and report the data and results of the trial to the sponsor.

7. Should record clearly and exactly failures by the investigator during an on-site visit, trial, examination, and whether errors, omissions have been rectified.
8. After every visit, a written report shall be submitted to the sponsor with the date of monitoring, time, monitor's name, the findings of the monitoring.

Chapter 8: Records and Reports

Article 48: The case report form shall be kept completely as original material of the clinical trial. The data of the case report form is from the original material and in compliance with the original material. All observations and results of the trial shall be recorded on the case report immediately, accurately, completely, standardized, truthfully, and be written in the case report form correctly. The case report and case report form may not be changed. In making any modification due to the written mistake, the original record shall be kept easy to recognize and the modification shall be signed and dated by the investigator.

Article 49 The laboratory data of the clinical trial shall be recorded or the copy of the original report shall be pasted onto the case report form. Data within normal ranges must also be recorded. For data that noticeably deviates or data beyond the acceptable range, the investigator must verify it. Each type of test must clearly state the units of measurement.

Article 50 The human subject names should not be on the case report form in order to protect the human subject privacy. The investigator should identify the human subject in accordance with his code and keep record.

Article 51 The final report of the clinical trial shall conform to the protocol and contain the following:

1. The actual number of subjects/cases that randomly participated in each treatment group, and subject dropouts or removed during the trial and the reason.
2. Compare the baseline characteristics among different medical treatment groups in order to determine their comparability.
3. Conduct statistical and clinical analysis for all the indexes of the therapeutic effects evaluation. The explanation of statistical results shall focus on the significance of the clinical trial.
4. The reasonable statistical analysis for adverse events and the laboratory indexes shall be included in the safety evaluation. The adverse events shall be described and evaluated in detail.
5. In assessing therapeutic effects in a multicenter trial, the differences and their effects among each center must be taken into account.
6. Relationship between the therapeutic effects and safety as well as risks and benefits for the investigational products shall be briefly summarized and discussed.

Article 52 All data of the clinical trial shall be kept and managed in accordance with regulations (Appendix 2). The investigator shall keep the documents of the clinical trial for 5 years after the completion of the trial. The sponsor shall keep the clinical trial data for 5 years after the investigational product has been approved for marketing.

Chapter 9: Data Management and Statistical Analysis

Article 53: The purpose of data management is to promptly, completely and accurately record the data. All steps involved in the data management shall be recorded in order to check the quality of the data and the implementation of the trial. The confidentiality of the database shall be protected through appropriate procedures. Maintenance and support programs for computerized databases are required.

Article 54 The human subject in the clinical trial must be grouped according to a randomized plan stipulated in the design of the trial. Either the sponsor or the investigator shall keep the grouping code of each human subject as blinding record. In a blind trial, the condition and the procedure for accessing the code shall be stipulated clearly in the protocol, and a letter with the code to be used in emergencies should be enclosed. In any emergency, the code of a human subject may be accessed in order to know the treatment he received, but the reason must be clearly recorded in the case report form.

Article 55 Standard statistical methods must be applied to express the statistical analysis process and statistical results for the clinical trial data. Professional biostatisticians shall participate in every phase of the clinical trial. The statistical analysis plan shall be included in the protocol and should be confirmed and specified before the formal start of statistical analysis. If an analysis during the middle of trial is needed, the reason and the procedures of analysis must be explained. When evaluating therapeutic efficacy, the reliability range and hypothetic result should be considered together. The selected statistical analysis data package should be explained. The missing, unused or redundant material must be explained clearly. The statistical report of the clinical trial must be in conformity with the final report.

Chapter 10: Administration of Investigational Product

Article 56: Investigational product for a clinical trial may not be sold.

Article 57 The sponsor is responsible for properly packing and labeling the investigational product and marking that the drug is specially to be used in a clinical trial. In a double blind clinical trial, the drug to be investigated and comparator or placebo shall be uniform in shape, smell, packaging, labeling and other features.

Article 58 The use record of the investigational product shall include the information of quantity, loading, shipment, receipt, dispensing/handling, and the reclaim and destruction of unused drug.

Article 59 The investigator is responsible for the administration of the investigational product. He must make certain all investigational products are only administered to the human subjects of the clinical trial, and the dosage and method of use conform to the protocol. The surplus products shall be returned to the sponsor. The above procedures shall be handled and recorded by a specified individual. The investigational product should be managed by a specified individual. The investigator may not transfer the investigational product to any non-participant in the clinical trial.

Article 60 The supply, usage, storage, return of unused investigational product should accept checking from relevant person.

Chapter 11: Quality Assurance

Article 61: The sponsor and investigator shall fulfill respective duty, comply with protocol strictly and adopt Standard Operating Procedure (SOP) to ensure the implementation of the quality control and quality assurance system of the clinical trial.

Article 62 In order to assure the completeness, accurateness, truthfulness and liableness of data, all observation results and findings in the clinical trial must be verified and each phase for data processing must involve quality assurance.

Article 63 Drug administration authorities and the sponsor may authorize an auditor to execute systematic checks for operation and document file of clinical trial in order to evaluate whether the trial is conducted in compliance with the protocol, SOP and relevant regulations, whether the data is recorded timely, factually, accurately and completely. The audit shall be conducted by personnel not directly involved in the clinical trial.

Article 64 Drug administration authorities shall inspect the investigator and sponsor regarding their respective tasks and implementation of such tasks in the trial. All medical institutions participating in the clinical trial and all documents and files (including medical records) shall accept inspection from drug administration authorities.

Chapter 12: Multicenter Trial

Article 65: A multicenter trial consists of several clinical trials conducted by several investigators in different places and institutions in accordance with the same protocol. Each center starts and completes the clinical trial simultaneously. There is a principal investigator who is also the coordinating investigator of every center in the trial with overall responsibility of the multicenter trial.

Article 66 The planning and implementation of a multicenter trial should consider the following:

1. The protocol shall be jointly discussed and made by the principal investigators of each center and sponsor. Before it is implemented, approval from the ethics committee must be obtained.
2. Investigators meetings shall be held during the initial and middle stages of a clinical trial.
3. The clinical trial shall be simultaneously conducted in each center.
4. The sample size and case allocation in each center must meet statistical requirements.
5. The investigational product shall be administered, dispensed and stored, with the same procedures in different centers.
6. The investigators participating in the trial shall be trained in accordance with the same protocol.
7. A standardized assessment method shall be established. The laboratory and clinical methods of assessment applied in the trial shall be of the same quality control system. Laboratory inspection may be conducted by the central laboratory.

8. The data shall be centrally managed and analyzed. A program for data transmission, management, inspection and inquiry shall be established.
9. Ensure that investigators of each trial center observe the protocol and that an investigator's participation is terminated if he violates the protocol.

Article 67 A multicenter trial shall establish a management system based on the number of centers participating in the trial, the requirements of the trial and the familiarity of the drug to be investigated. A coordinating investigator shall be responsible for implementing the whole trial.

Chapter 13: Miscellaneous
Article 68: Explanation of terms of this GCP:

Clinical Trial A Clinical Trial is a systematical investigation of drugs conducted on any human body (patient or healthy volunteer) in order to prove or reveal the function, adverse reaction and/or absorption, distribution, metabolism and excretion of the drug being investigated. The purpose of a clinical trial is to define the therapeutic efficacy and safety of the drug.

Protocol A document that describes the background, rational, objectives design, method and organization of the trial, including statistical considerations and requirements for conducting and completing the trial. The protocol must be signed and dated by sponsor, principal investigator and the institution in which the investigation is conducted.

Investigator's Brochure A compilation of the clinical and non-clinical data on the investigational product already obtained before the clinical trial that will be conducted in human subjects.

Informed Consent A process by which a subject voluntarily confirms his or her willingness to participate in a particular trial, after having been informed of all aspects of the trial that are relevant to the subject's decision to participate. Informed consent is documented by means of a written, signed, and dated informed consent form.

Informed Consent Form An Informed Consent Form is a certification to prove that each human subject is voluntarily participating in a certain trial. The investigator must explain to the human subject about the nature and purpose of the trial, the anticipated risks and benefits, the alternative medical treatments, and the human subject's rights and obligations stipulated in the Declaration of Helsinki, in order that the agreement to participate is based on a good understanding of the trial.

Ethics Committee The Ethics Committee is an independent organization consisting of people specialized in the medical field, legal experts and other people from non-medical fields whose responsibility it is to ensure the protocol and its appendix are ethical and to provide a public guarantee to ensure the protection of the rights, safety and well-being of human subjects. Organizations and persons who conduct the clinical trial shall not interfere or affect the structure and activities of the committee.

Investigator The Investigator is responsible for conducting the clinical trial and for the quality of the trial and the human subject's safety and interests. The investigator must be qualified for conducting the trial by his specialty, qualifications, and capability. In a multicenter clinical trial, a chief investigator is appointed to take charge of the overall implementation of the clinical trial and act as the coordinator among each center.

Coordinating Investigator An investigator assigned the responsibility for the coordination of investigators at different centers participating in a multicenter trial.

Sponsor The Sponsor is a company, institution or organization who initiates a clinical trial and is responsible for initiating, managing, financing and monitoring the trial.

Monitor Person appointed by and responsible to the sponsor who is responsible for monitoring and reporting the situation of the trial which is being conducted and verifying the data.

Audit Audit is a type of systematic check conducted by persons who are not directly involved in the trial. The purpose of an audit is to determine whether the implementation of the trial, the recording and analysis of data comply with the protocol, SOP and relevant regulations.

Inspection The act by drug administration authorities in conducting an official review of documents, facilities, records and other aspects of a clinical trial. Inspection can be done in the institution where the trial is conducted, or in the locality of the sponsor or the contract research organization.

Case Report Form (CRF) The Case Report Form is a kind of document designed according to the protocol to record data of each human subject during the conducting of the trial.

Investigational Product Study drug, comparator and placebo used in a clinical trial.

Adverse Event An untoward medical event in a patient or clinical investigation subject administered a drug and which does not necessarily have a causal relationship with this treatment.

Serious Adverse Event A Serious Adverse Event includes inpatient hospitalization, prolongation of hospitalization, disability/incapacity, effect on work capability, life threatening, death, congenital anomaly etc., which occur during a clinical trial.

Standard Operating Procedures (SOP) Standard and detailed written instructions made to ensure every function in a certain clinical trial is conducted and completed effectively.

Blinding/Masking A procedure in which one or more parties to the trial are kept unaware of the treatment assignments. Single blinding refers to the subjects being unaware, and double-blinding refers to the subjects, investigators, monitor or data analyst being unaware of the treatment assignments.

Contract Research Organization (CRO) Contract Research Organization is technical or commercial institution. The sponsor may authorize the CRO to conduct some work and tasks in a clinical trial. This authorization must be stipulated in writing.

Article 69 The State Food and Drug Administration shall be responsible for interpretation of this GCP.

Article 70 This GCP shall be effective from September 1, 2003, simultaneously, the former GCP issued on September 1, 1999 is annulled.

Appendix 1:
WORLD MEDICAL ASSOCIATION DECLARATION OF HELSINKI
Ethical Principles for Medical Research Involving Human Subjects

Adopted by the 18th World Medical Association (WMA) General Assembly, Helsinki, Finland, June 1964

Amended by the 29th WMA General Assembly, Tokyo, Japan, October 1975

35th WMA General Assembly, Venice, Italy, October 1983

41st WMA General Assembly, Hong Kong, September 1989

48th WMA General Assembly, Somerset West, Republic of South Africa, October 1996

52nd WMA General Assembly, Edinburgh, Scotland, October 2000

A. INTRODUCTION

1. The World Medical Association has developed the Declaration of Helsinki as a statement of ethical principles to provide guidance to physicians and other participants in medical research involving human subjects. Medical research involving human subjects includes research on identifiable human material or identifiable data.
2. It is the duty of the physician to promote and safeguard the health of the people. The physician's knowledge and conscience are dedicated to the fulfillment of this duty.
3. The Declaration of Geneva of the World Medical Association binds the physician with the words, "The health of my patient will be my first consideration," and the International Code of Medical Ethics declares that, "A physician shall act only in the patient's interest when providing medical care which might have the effect of weakening the physical and mental condition of the patient."
4. Medical progress is based on research which ultimately must rest in part on experimentation involving human subjects.
5. In medical research on human subjects, considerations related to the well-being of the human subject should take precedence over the interests of science and society.
6. The primary purpose of medical research involving human subjects is to improve prophylactic, diagnostic and therapeutic procedures and the understanding of the etiology and pathogenesis of disease. Even the best proven prophylactic, diagnostic, and therapeutic methods must continuously be challenged through research for their effectiveness, efficiency, accessibility and quality.

7. In current medical practice and in medical research, most prophylactic, diagnostic and therapeutic procedures involve risks and burdens.
8. Medical research is subject to ethical standards that promote respect for all human beings and protect their health and rights. Some research populations are vulnerable and need special protection. The particular needs of the economically and medically disadvantaged must be recognized. Special attention is also required for those who cannot give or refuse consent for themselves, for those who may be subject to giving consent under duress, for those who will not benefit personally from the research and for those for whom the research is combined with care.
9. Research Investigators should be aware of the ethical, legal and regulatory requirements for research on human subjects in their own countries as well as applicable international requirements. No national ethical, legal or regulatory requirement should be allowed to reduce or eliminate any of the protections for human subjects set forth in this Declaration.

B. BASIC PRINCIPLES FOR ALL MEDICAL RESEARCH

10. It is the duty of the physician in medical research to protect the life, health, privacy, and dignity of the human subject.
11. Medical research involving human subjects must conform to generally accepted scientific principles, be based on a thorough knowledge of the scientific literature, other relevant sources of information, and on adequate laboratory and, where appropriate, animal experimentation.
12. Appropriate caution must be exercised in the conduct of research which may affect the environment, and the welfare of animals used for research must be respected.
13. The design and performance of each experimental procedure involving human subjects should be clearly formulated in an experimental protocol. This protocol should be submitted for consideration, comment, guidance, and where appropriate, approval to a specially appointed ethical review committee, which must be independent of the investigator, the sponsor or any other kind of undue influence. This independent committee should be in conformity with the laws and regulations of the country in which the research experiment is performed. The committee has the right to monitor ongoing trials. The researcher has the obligation to provide monitoring information to the committee, especially any serious adverse events. The researcher should also submit to the committee, for review, information regarding funding, sponsors, institutional affiliations, other potential conflicts of interest and incentives for subjects.
14. The research protocol should always contain a statement of the ethical considerations involved and should indicate that there is compliance with the principles enunciated in this Declaration.
15. Medical research involving human subjects should be conducted only by scientifically qualified persons and under the supervision of a clinically competent medical person. The responsibility for the human subject must always rest with

a medically qualified person and never rest on the subject of the research, even though the subject has given consent.

16. Every medical research project involving human subjects should be preceded by careful assessment of predictable risks and burdens in comparison with foreseeable benefits to the subject or to others. This does not preclude the participation of healthy volunteers in medical research. The design of all studies should be publicly available.
17. Physicians should abstain from engaging in research projects involving human subjects unless they are confident that the risks involved have been adequately assessed and can be satisfactorily managed. Physicians should cease any investigation if the risks are found to outweigh the potential benefits or if there is conclusive proof of positive and beneficial results.
18. Medical research involving human subjects should only be conducted if the importance of the objective outweighs the inherent risks and burdens to the subject. This is especially important when the human subjects are healthy volunteers.
19. Medical research is only justified if there is a reasonable likelihood that the populations in which the research is carried out stand to benefit from the results of the research.
20. The subjects must be volunteers and informed participants in the research project.
21. The right of research subjects to safeguard their integrity must always be respected. Every precaution should be taken to respect the privacy of the subject, the confidentiality of the patient's information and to minimize the impact of the study on the subject's physical and mental integrity and on the personality of the subject.
22. In any research on human beings, each potential subject must be adequately informed of the aims, methods, sources of funding, any possible conflicts of interest, institutional affiliations of the researcher, the anticipated benefits and potential risks of the study and the discomfort it may entail. The subject should be informed of the right to abstain from participation in the study or to withdraw consent to participate at any time without reprisal. After ensuring that the subject has understood the information, the physician should then obtain the subject's freely-given informed consent, preferably in writing. If the consent cannot be obtained in writing, the non-written consent must be formally documented and witnessed.
23. When obtaining informed consent for the research project the physician should be particularly cautious if the subject is in a dependent relationship with the physician or may consent under duress. In that case the informed consent should be obtained by a well-informed physician who is not engaged in the investigation and who is completely independent of this relationship.
24. For a research subject who is legally incompetent, physically or mentally incapable of giving consent or is a legally incompetent minor, the investigator must obtain informed consent from the legally authorized representative in accordance with applicable law. These groups should not be included in research

unless the research is necessary to promote the health of the population represented and this research cannot instead be performed on legally competent persons.

25. When a subject deemed legally incompetent, such as a minor child, is able to give assent to decisions about participation in research, the investigator must obtain that assent in addition to the consent of the legally authorized representative.
26. Research on individuals from whom it is not possible to obtain consent, including proxy or advance consent, should be done only if the physical/mental condition that prevents obtaining informed consent is a necessary characteristic of the research population. The specific reasons for involving research subjects with a condition that renders them unable to give informed consent should be stated in the experimental protocol for consideration and approval of the review committee. The protocol should state that consent to remain in the research should be obtained as soon as possible from the individual or a legally authorized surrogate.
27. Both authors and publishers have ethical obligations. In publication of the results of research, the investigators are obliged to preserve the accuracy of the results. Negative as well as positive results should be published or otherwise publicly available. Sources of funding, institutional affiliations and any possible conflicts of interest should be declared in the publication. Reports of experimentation not in accordance with the principles laid down in this Declaration should not be accepted for publication.

C. ADDITIONAL PRINCIPLES FOR MEDICAL RESEARCH COMBINED WITH MEDICAL CARE

28. The physician may combine medical research with medical care, only to the extent that the research is justified by its potential prophylactic, diagnostic or therapeutic value. When medical research is combined with medical care, additional standards apply to protect the patients who are research subjects.

29. The benefits, risks, burdens and effectiveness of a new method should be tested against those of the best current prophylactic, diagnostic, and therapeutic methods. This does not exclude the use of placebo, or no treatment, in studies where no proven prophylactic, diagnostic or therapeutic method exists.
30. At the conclusion of the study, every patient entered into the study should be assured of access to the best proven prophylactic, diagnostic and therapeutic methods identified by the study.
31. The physician should fully inform the patient which aspects of the care are related to the research. The refusal of a patient to participate in a study must never interfere with the patient-physician relationship.
32. In the treatment of a patient, where proven prophylactic, diagnostic and therapeutic methods do not exist or have been ineffective, the physician, with informed consent from the patient, must be free to use unproven or new pro-

phylactic, diagnostic and therapeutic measures, if in the physician's judgment it offers hope of saving life, re-establishing health or alleviating suffering. Where possible, these measures should be made the object of research, designed to evaluate their safety and efficacy. In all cases, new information should be recorded and, where appropriate, published. The other relevant guidelines of this Declaration should be followed.

Appendix 2:
Record Keeping for a Clinical Trial (Tables 1.5, 1.6 and 1.7)

1.3.3.4 Examination and Approval for Import of Packaging Materials and Containers in Direct Contact with Drugs

Issued by the China Food and Drug Administration, December 6, 2013 (CFDA 2013)

Table 1.5 For preparation phase of the clinical trial

Document to be kept		Investigator	Sponsor
1	Investigator's brochure	Keep	Keep
2	Protocol and its amendment (signed)	Keep original	Keep
3	Case report form (sample form)	Keep	Keep
4	Informed consent form	Keep original	Keep
5	Financial rules	Keep	Keep
6	Multi-party agreement (signed) (Investigator, sponsor, contract research organization)	Keep	Keep
7	Written approval from ethics committee	Keep original	Keep
8	List of ethics committee members	Keep original	Keep
9	Application for the clinical trial		Keep original
10	Laboratory information prior to the clinical trial		Keep original
11	Written approval from State Food and Drug Administration		Keep original
12	Investigator's resume and relevant documents	Keep	Keep original
13	Normal value range of laboratory testing related to clinical trial	Keep	Keep
14	Quality control certificate for medical or laboratory operation	Keep original	Keep
15	Label of drug to be investigated		Keep original
16	Shipping order for drug to be investigated and relevant materials of the trial	Keep	Keep
17	Testing certificate of investigational product		Keep original
18	Procedures of breaking blind of trial		Keep original
19	General randomization list		Keep original
20	Monitoring report		Keep original

Table 1.6 During the conducting phase of the clinical trial

Document to be kept		Investigator	Sponsor
21	Updated investigator's brochure	Keep	Keep
22	Updated version of other documents (protocol, case report form, informed consent form, written situation notice)	Keep	Keep
23	Curriculum vitae of new investigator	Keep	Keep original
24	Updated normal value range of medical and laboratory tests	Keep	Keep
25	Shipping order for investigational products and relevant materials for clinical trial	Keep	Keep
26	Testing certificate of investigational product with new commission number		Keep original
27	Monitor's visiting report		Keep original
28	Signed informed consent form	Keep original	
29	Original documents of medical treatment	Keep original	
30	Case report form (filled out, signed and dated)	Keep original	Keep the copy
31	Investigator's report of serious adverse event submitted to the sponsor	Keep original	Keep
32	Investigator's report of unexpected serious adverse event submitted to State Drug Administration and ethics committee	Keep	Keep original
33	Mid-term or annual report	Keep	Keep
34	List of codes confirmed by human subject	Keep original	
35	Form of subject screening and inclusion	Keep	Keep
36	Registration form of investigational product	Keep	Keep
37	Signature sample of investigator	Keep	Keep

Table 1.7 After completion of the clinical trial

Document to be kept		Investigator	Sponsor
38	Certificate for destruction of investigational product	Keep	Keep
39	Category of codes of the human subject who completed the trial	Keep	Keep
40	Audit certificate		Keep original
41	Final monitoring report		Keep original
42	Certificate of treatment group and accessing the code		Keep original
43	Report of the completion of the trial submitted to the ethics committee and State Food and Drug Administration		Keep original
44	Final report	Keep	Keep original

I. Project name

Examination and approval for packaging materials and containers in direct contact with drugs

II. Content of licensing

Approval of import (incl. from Hong Kong, Macao and Taiwan) of packaging materials and containers in direct contact with drugs

Product catalog of packaging materials and containers (referred to as "PMC") in direct contact with drugs under registration management

(I) Infusion bottles (bags, film and accessories);
(II) Ampoule
(III) Medicinal (injection, oral or topical dosage form) bottles (tube, cap);
(IV) Medicinal stopper;
(V) Medicinal prefilled syringes;
(VI) Medicinal eye (nose, ears) drops bottle (tube);
(VII) Medicinal rigid plate (film);
(VIII) Medicinal aluminum foil;
(IX) Medicinal ointment tube (box);
(X) Medicinal spray (gas) aerosol pump (valves, tanks, cylinders);
(XI) Medicinal desiccant.

III. Legal basis

"Drug Administration Law," " Regulations for Implementation of Drug Administration Law", " Regulations for Management of Packaging Materials and Containers in Direct Contact with Drugs"

IV. Charges

No charge

V. Quantity restrictions

No quantity limit for the licensing

VI. List of application dossiers

"Registration Application Form for Packaging Materials and Containers of Imported Drugs ":

Information Number (1) Manufacturer' legal production qualification documents, notarized documents and their Chinese translations;

Information No (2) Overseas Pharmaceutical Manufacturers' entrustment of Chinese agents for application shall provide entrustment documents, notarized documents and Chinese translations. Chinese agents' Business License or "Registration Certificate of Foreign Enterprises Permanent Representative in China" of Overseas Pharmaceutical Manufacturers' Chinese Permanent Representatives;

Information No (3) Review of applied products' overseas production, sales and application, and special reasons for registration application in China;

Information No (4) Quality inspection report of three batches of applied product issued by drug packaging inspection agency set or determined by the CFDA;

Information No (5) Clean room (area) cleanliness inspection reports and self-test report of three batches of products;

Information No (6) Formulations of applied product;

Information No (7) Elaborations of applied products' production process and main production and testing equipment;

Information No (8) Quality standards of applied products;

Information No (9) Research data of stability testing (drug compatibility test) of applied packaging materials jointly with drugs contained;

Information No (10) Floor plan of production plant and clean room (area) of applied products.

Specific requirements for the above application dossiers are detailed in Annex III of "Regulations for the management of packaging materials and containers in direct contact with drugs"

VII. Requirements for application dossiers

(I) General requirement for aApplication dossiers

1. The first page of the application dossiers should be a project directory in which the application items shall be arranged in the order specified in Annex III of the "Regulations for the management of packaging materials and containers in direct contact with drugs" (CFDA Order No. 13). Each data shall indicate on the cover: PMC names, data item number, item name, applicant's contact name, phone, address.
2. The Dossier should use A4 paper to print or copy, the contents should be clear and not to be altered. The Information should be complete and standardized the data truthful and reliable.
3. The dossiers should be enclosed in sets into a Portfolio, whose envelope shall be marked with:
   Application classification, registration category, PMC name, X set/Xth bags/X in total, original/copy, the contact person, telephone, and name of the agency for registration application.
4. Submit two sets of complete application dossiers (1 set of originals, one set of copies), 3 copies of the application forms (2 in the originals, 1 in the copies).
5. "PMC Registration Application Form": Download from the CFDA website (www.cfda.gov.cn) The "Application Form for Developing the Offer Program ", fill in as required for print and filing.
6. Along with the submission or mail of the application dossiers, their electronic version shall be sent to the following Administrative Center by e-mail. e-mail address: slzx@cfda.gov.cn.
7. The data verification code of the electronic application forms should be consistent with paper application forms.
8. All application materials should be in Chinese accompanied by English translations, or other languages for reference. Chinese translation should be consistent with the original content.

(II) Specific requirements for application dossiers

1. "PMC Registration Application Form": should be filled according to the explanatory notes, with signatures or seals (if any) of all the applicants.

2. Proof documents:
   (1) Manufacturer' legal production qualification documents, notarized documents and their Chinese Translations
   The applicant shall submit copies of the proof documents issued by the government departments of country of origin to approve its engagement in the production and distribution of drug PMC (similar to Chinese Business License, Production License or Registration Certificate, etc.), the original copy of notarized documents issued by public notary office and their Chinese translation. If the above-mentioned special approval documents are not required by the government of the country of origin, such information need not to be submitted after explanation of related information.
   (2) Originals of the entrustment documents from overseas manufacturers to Chinese agencies for registration application, originals and Chinese translations of notarized documents issued by public notary offices of the country of origin
   (3) Copies of Chinese domestic agency's "Business License" or "Registration Certificate of Foreign Enterprises' Permanent representative office in China"
3. Review of applied products' overseas production, sales and application, and special reasons for registration application in China.
4. Test reports:
   (1) Original copy of quality inspection report of three batches of the applied product issued by drug PMC inspection agencies set or determined by the CFDA, that may be submitted separately after the technical review process.
   (2) Original of Clean room (area) cleanliness inspection reports within 1 year of the application date shall be submitted.
   (3) the self-test report of three batches of the applied products shall be submitted
5. Quality standards:
   If the quality standards of drug PMC are new standards or corporate standards, the instructions for the drafting of standards should be provided.
6. Other information shall be filed in accordance with Annex III of the "Provisions for the management of packaging materials and containers in direct contact with drugs" (CFDA Order No.13).

VIII. Diagram of application procedures (Fig. 1.2)

IX. Licensing procedures

(I) Acceptance:

After the Application is made to the Administrative Service Center, and the application dossiers submitted in order listed in Article VI of this "TIPS", the work staff shall review the format. If the application items are not subject to administrative examination and approval according to law, the decision of non-acceptance shall be immediately made. If the application items are not within the purview of the executive authorities, the decision of non-acceptance shall be immediately made

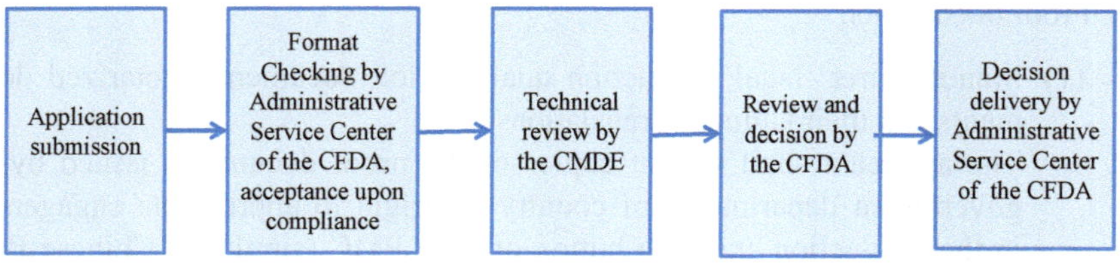

Fig. 1.2 Application procedures

and the applicant shall be informed to apply to related administrative institutions; If the application dossiers have errors that can be corrected on the spot, the applicant shall be allowed to correct on the sport; if the application dossiers are incomplete or do not meet the statutory form, the applicant should be informed in full to enrich or rectify the relevant contents on the spot or within 5 days. If they are not informed, the application dossiers shall be deemed accepted from date of receipt. If the application dossiers are within the scope of the administrative institutions, the application materials are complete and comply with the statutory form, or the applicant has submitted all application materials in accordance with the requirements of the administrative authorities for enrichment or correction, the application shall be accepted for administrative examination and approval.

(II) PMC Registration inspection:

The applicants shall submit three consecutive batches of samples to drug PMC inspection agencies set or determined by the CFDA. Drug PMC inspection agency shall perform test within 60 days after receiving the registration notice and samples, issue test report and submit to the CFDA. The CFDA shall conduct on-site inspection of the development of imported drug PMC and production conditions, and take samples.

(III) Technical review:

The CFDA shall organize and complete the technical review within 90 days after receiving the test report and opinions, if additional information is needed, the CFDA shall issue a notice for supplementary information to inform in full the applicant of the required supplementary information. The applicants shall complete once for all the required information within 4 months, if they failed to do so, the application for review shall be rejected.

(IV) Administrative licensing decision:

The CFDA shall complete the examination and approval within 20 days after completion of the technical review.

If a decision cannot be made within 20 days, an extension of 10 days may be granted upon approval of competent the CFDA leaders. "Registration Certificate for Import of Drug PMC" shall be issued upon compliance; if the requirements are not met, a "Notice of approval opinion" shall be issued.

(V) Delivery:

Within 10 days from the date of decision making of administrative examination and approval, the CFDA Administrative Service Center shall deliver the decision to the applicants.

(VI) Re-review:

If the applicants disagree with the decision of disapproval, they can apply to the CFDA for reconsideration within 10 days upon receipt of the disapproval decision. The contents of the reconsideration shall be limited to the original application items and the original dossiers and samples submitted. After receiving the application for reconsideration, the CFDA shall make the decision for re-review within 50 days. If the original disapproval decision is canceled after re-review, the appropriate Drug PMC approval documents shall be issued; if the original decision is maintained, repeated application for reconsideration shall not be accepted by the CFDA.

X. Commitment time frame

Administrative licensing decision shall be made within 170 days from the date of acceptance. (Note: the CFDA shall complete the examination and approval within 20 days after completion of the technical review, if not, an extension of 10 days can be granted upon approval of competent the CFDA leaders; application for an extension above 10 days shall be submitted to the State Council for approval.)

The above timeframe does not include the time for supplementary information and the corresponding review.

XI. License validity and renewal

"Registration Certificate for Import of Drug PMC" is valid for 5 years. If the import is still necessary upon expiry of the Registration Certificate, the applicant shall apply for renewal 6 months before the expiry.

XI. Annual inspection or annual review of the license

None

XIII. Authority of implementation

Authority of implementation: the CFDA

Location for acceptance: the CFDA Administrative Service Center

XIV. Institutions for inquiries and complaints

Inquiries: the CFDA

Complaints: the CFDA Bureau of Investigation and Enforcement, Department of Legal affairs

Note: The time frame of the TIPS counts on working days, excluding legal holidays.

1.3.4 Regulations Related to Inspection

1.3.4.1 General Regulation Requirements for On-site Verification, inspection and sampling procedure for Drug Registration

Regulations Requirements for On-Site Verification for Drug Registration

Provisions for Drug Registration on-site verification, No. 255 was issued and became effective on May 23, 2008 by State Food and Drug Administration. This provision contains 7 chapters as listed below:

Chapter I General Provisions
Chapter II Drug Registration develop on-site verification
Chapter III drug registration production site inspection
Chapter IV Implementation Organization
Chapter V drug registration inspection sampling requirements
Chapter VI inspectors Management
Chapter VII Supplementary Provisions
The provision includes a total of 59 articles and 5 Annexes as listed below:

1. Key points and judgment rules for drug registration site verification
2. Application form for drug research and development situation
3. On-site verification report for drug registration development
4. Application form for drug registration production on-site inspection
5. On-site inspection report for drug registration production

The On-Site Inspection and Sampling Procedure and Requirements for Drug Registration

Drug registration site verification and sampling procedures and requirements (Trial) was issued on July 19, 2005 by State Food and Drug Administration. The provision includes 16 articles and 5 Annexes:

1. DrugWW research and development status declaration form (non-clinical testing)
2. Drug research and development status declaration form (after clinical trials)
3. Drug research and development verification report form (non-clinical testing)
4. Drug research and development verification report form (after clinical trials)
5. Drug registration test sample Seals (model)

Notice on the Related Convergence Problems to the Implementation of On-Site Verification of Drug Registration Regulations

(Food and Drug Administration Office [2008] No. 151)

This notice provided directions to provinces, autonomous regions and municipalities Food and Drug Administration regarding the newly revised "Drug Registration" and "drug registration site verification regulations". The implementation of this notice started on May 23, 2008. The aim of this notice is to better accomplish the verification process for the drugs accepted for drug registration application after the implementation of the "registration measures" and before the implementation of the "verification provisions", the relevant interface issues are clarified and explained in this notice. The above inspection associated regulations were developed mainly for the domestic pharmaceutical manufactures, which have no significant impact for the overseas multinational pharmaceutical companies.

1.3.4.2 Inspection of Overseas Drug Manufacturers by the SFDA

In recent years, overseas pharmaceutical manufacturers have started to face on-site inspection. On August 20, the State Food and Drug Administration (SFDA now CFDA) issued the draft version of Administrative Measures for the Inspection of Overseas Drug Manufacturers for seeking public comments and feedback with a closing date of October 8th, 2012.

According to the draft administrative measures, if an overseas drug manufacturer is concluded as "con-complaint" after inspection, the SFDA will take the following potential actions:

- issue a Warning Letter to its agency in China, or
- issue an order to suspend the import of the drug, or
- suspend its drug registration evaluation process, or
- suspend the import drug declaration at entry port
- order the enterprise to recall the drug or take other appropriate measures for the drugs already imported,

Under special circumstances, the SFDA may make the above decisions immediately if an overseas pharmaceutical manufacturer has serious defects that largely jeopardizing the safety of the public.

According to the draft Measures, any overseas pharmaceutical manufacturers fail the on-site inspection will face a severe penalty, including the situations that any manufacturer refuses to take the inspection without any due reasons or don't cooperate with the SFDA's inspectors will be determined as it fails the inspection directly.

If the manufacturer fails the inspection, its representative agency in China will receive a Warning Letter from the SFDA, which orders a suspension of the drug import or the drug registration in China. At the same time, the SFDA will inform all the drug administrative agencies at ports to stop the issue of relevant Drug Import Note. The drug will be prohibited for importation until it passes the next on-site inspection.

The Measures applies to the overseas pharmaceutical manufacturers having gained or applying for Imported Drug License (for overseas pharmaceutical manufacturers) or the Pharmaceutical Product License (for pharmaceutical manufacturers of HK, Macau and Taiwan of China). The on-site inspection covers whether the actual production process is in accordance with the pharmaceutical registration application dossiers and the required materials submitted by the corresponding representative agency in China of the overseas manufacturer after receiving SFDA's inspection notice; whether the production process complies with the GMP requirements (2010 Revision).

Based on Article 15, inspection conclusions are divided into "Compliant", "Compliant after rectification" and "Non-compliant". The judgment principles are listed in the following Table 1.8 for reference:

Table 1.8 Inspection conclusion and its judgment principles

On-site inspection conclusion	Judgment principles
Compliant	The drug production and quality control is consistent with the application dossiers, and the manufacturer can organize production as required by the drug GMP including the situation that defects can be rectified immediately
Compliant after rectification	Several major defects are discovered during the on-site inspection and the subsequent submitted rectification report shows that the manufacturing process can comply with the GMP requirements after rectification
Non-compliant	During the inspection, it is discovered that:
	1) falsifying act or any key element affecting product quality is inconsistent with the application dossier;
	2) significant defect or several major defects, showing that the inspected manufacturer is unable to manage drug production in compliance with the GMP
	When necessary, the Drug Certification Management Center of the CFDA may organize inspectors to check and verify the rectification of the manufacturer again

Administrative Measures for Inspection of Overseas Drug Manufacturers (for trial implementation), the SFDA, October 8, 2012 (SFDA 2012)

Article 1 According to the Drug Administration Law, the Implementing Regulations of the Drug Administration Law, the Special Rules of the State Council on Strengthening the Supervision and Administration over the Safety of Food and Other Products and other relevant provisions, for the purpose of regulating the inspection of overseas drug manufacturers, these Measures are hereby enacted.

Article 2 The inspection of overseas drug manufacturers is an inspection, organized by the State Food and Drug Administration, of the manufacturing sites of imported drugs that are in the process of registration review or approval or for which a marketing license has been obtained, with a view to strengthening the supervision and administration over the imported drugs, regulating the manufacture of the imported drugs and ensuring the quality safety of the imported drugs.

Article 3 These Measures are applicable to all overseas drug manufacturers who have obtained an Imported Drug License or a Pharmaceutical Product License issued by the State Food and Drug Administration, and overseas drug manufacturers who are applying for an Imported Drug License or a Pharmaceutical Product License to be issued by the State Food and Drug Administration.

Article 4 The State Food and Drug Administration determines the overseas drug manufacturers subject to an on-site inspection and the lists of varieties of products based on information in various aspects, such as the registration review, the routine supervision and administration, the inspections at ports and the reports by the general public, and inform the relevant information such as the inspection time in advance to the offices of the overseas drug manufacturers in China or the agents appointed by them in China (hereinafter referred to as an “Agent” or “Agents”).

Article 5 The Agents are responsible for communicating and contacting with the overseas drug manufacturers, and are responsible for submitting required materials to the Drug Certification Management Center of the State Food and Drug Administration in a timely manner. See the Appendix for the specific requirements for the materials.

Article 6 When an overseas drug manufacturer receives a notice of onsite inspection, if there is a real special reason for postponing the on-site inspection, its Agent shall submit a written application, explaining the reason, to the Drug Certification Management Center of the State Food and Drug Administration. Any manufacturer who refuses the on-site inspection without reason or fails to cooperate with the on-site inspection shall be deemed to have failed to pass the inspection.

Article 7 During the on-site inspection, the inspected overseas drug manufacturer shall arrange for mass production of the products to be inspected.

Article 8 A team leader of the responsibility system will be implemented for the on-site inspections. Generally, an inspection team consists of 2–5 inspectors.

Article 9 The first meeting for an on-site inspection shall be presided over by the team leader of the inspection team and shall confirm the scope of inspection, the inspection schedule and the accompanying personnel of the manufacturer and declare inspection disciplines and points for attention.

Article 10 The main contents of the on-site inspection include: the submissions for drug registration, the consistency between the on-site materials and the actual manufacture process, and the compliance of the drug manufacture process with the Good Manufacture Practice (as amended in 2010).

Article 11 The inspected overseas drug manufacturer shall provide the relevant materials necessary for the inspection in a timely manner. According to the need of the inspection, the inspectors may collect evidence by taking such measures as photographing and camera shooting. If the manufacturer refuses photographing or camera shooting, the inspectors shall describe in detail the relevant circumstances in an inspection report. When necessary, the inspectors may take samples and bring them to China for inspection.

Article 12 After the on-site inspection ends, the inspection team shall analyze and summarize the on-site inspection to identify the defective items of the manufacturer. During the analysis and summarization, the accompanying personnel of the manufacturer shall withdraw.

Article 13 At the last meeting, the inspection team shall orally feedback the defective items found in the inspection to the inspected overseas drug manufacturer. If the inspected overseas drug manufacturer disputes such items, it may make an explanation and when necessary, the inspection team may further verify the relevant circumstances and modify the defective items according to the result of verification.

Article 14 Within 2 months after the on-site inspection ends, the Drug Certification Management Center of the State Food and Drug Administration shall feed back a written on-site inspection report to the Agent. For any manufacturer for whom no obvious defective item is found in the on-site inspection or who can immediately rectify the defective items in a proper manner, the Drug Certification Management Center of the State Food and Drug Administration will act directly according to the relevant provisions of Article 15 hereof, instead of feeding back the written on-site inspection report to the Agent. Within 1 month after receiving the on-site inspection report, the Agent shall be responsible for submitting a rectification report for the inspected manufacturer to the Drug Certification Management Center of the State Food and Drug Administration. If the Agent is unable to submit the rectification report within the specified time limit for any special reason, it shall file an application to the Drug Certification Management Center of the State Food and Drug Administration in advance, specifying a time limit for submitting the rectification report, provided, however, that the extension may not exceed 1 month.

Article 15 Within 1 month after receiving the rectification report submitted by the Agent, the Drug Certification Management Center of the State Food and Drug Administration shall make a comprehensive judgment regarding the inspection according to the risk management principle. Inspection conclusions are divided into "Compliant", "Compliant after rectification" and "Non-compliant". The judgment principles are as follows:

I. If the drug production and quality control is consistent with the submissions, and the manufacturer can organize production as required by the drug GMP, the manufacturer is determined to be "compliant".

II. If several major defects are found in the on-site inspection and the submitted rectification report shows that after the rectification, the manufacturer can organize production as required by the drug GMP, the manufacturer is determined to be "compliant after rectification".

III. If in the inspection, it is found that the manufacturer has committed any falsifying act or any key element affecting product quality is inconsistent with the submissions; there is a significant defect or several major defects, showing that the inspected manufacturer is unable to organize production as required by the drug GMP, the inspection conclusion is determined to be "non-compliant". When necessary, the Drug Certification Management Center of the State Food and Drug Administration may organize inspectors to check and verify the rectification of the manufacturer again.

Article 16 For any manufacturer for whom the inspection conclusion is "compliant" or "compliant after rectification", the State Food and Drug Administration shall feedback written opinions to its Agent within 1 month after the inspection conclusion is made. For any manufacturer for whom the inspection conclusion is "noncompliant", the State Food and Drug Administration shall issue a warning letter to its Agent, ordering it to suspend importation of the drug, or to suspend the registration review and approval process for the drug, until the manufacturer is compliant in the next on-site inspection. Meanwhile, a notice will be issued to each port administration of food and drug, requiring it to suspend issuance of a Customs Clearance Form for Imported Drugs for the drug. For any drug that has been imported, the State Food and Drug Administration shall order the manufacturer to recall the drug or make other decisions, depending on the severity of the circumstance.

Article 17 Under a special circumstance, when it is found in the on-site inspection that the inspected overseas drug manufacturer has any significant defect, seriously jeopardizing the safety of the public in using the drug, the State Food and Drug Administration may immediately make a relevant decision under paragraph 2 of Article 16 hereof.

Article 18 These Measures shall become effective as of ___________, and the State Food and Drug Administration shall be responsible for interpreting these Measures.

Appendix
Specific Requirements for Materials:

The following materials are required to be in duplicate, printed using A4 papers and bound.

I. Site Master File: The contents of the site master file include nine aspects, i.e., the general information of the manufacturer, the quality management system of the manufacturer, the personnel, the premises and equipment, the documentation, the production, the quality control, the distribution, complaints, product defects and recalls, and the self-inspections. The specific requirements shall be drafted according to the most recent requirements of PIC/S regarding the site master file. This item of materials is required to be expressed in Chinese and a part of charts and tables are allowed to be filled in English.

II. Basic Information on Importation of the Imported Drug into China over the Last 3 Years including the importation quantity, the port inspection, the adverse reaction, the product complaints and the product recalls of this variety of drug in each of the last 3 years. In the case of a complaint against or recall of the product for any quality reason, the reason for such complaint or recall and the final settlement shall be set forth in detail. This item of materials is required to be expressed in Chinese. If this variety of product is in the process of applying for an Imported Drug License or a Pharmaceutical Product License from the State Food and Drug Administration, this item of materials is not required to be submitted.

III. Basic Information on Production and Sale of the Imported Drug in Other Countries across the Globe over the Last 3 Years including whether its importation and sale is stopped due to noncompliance with GMP or whether the product is recalled for a quality reason in other countries. If any of the aforesaid circumstances occurs, the specific reason and the final settlement shall be set forth in detail. This item of materials is required to be expressed in Chinese. If this product is not marketed in other countries, this item of materials is not required to be submitted.

1.4 Guidance

All guidances related to chemical new drug applications will be discussed with corresponding booklets in the following chapters. The following figures provide a chronologically brief summary of the guidances for chemical drug (Fig. 1.3) development issued by Chinese regulatory agencies.

Regarding biological product applications, they are very different from the chemical new drug applications. Biological products have their own classifications. Provisions for Drug Registration provide detailed description and definitions for the biological products classification in Annex 3 "Biologics registration classification and application material requirements". In Fig. 1.4 below, the corresponding guidances issued by Chinese regulatory agencies are listed in a chronological order.

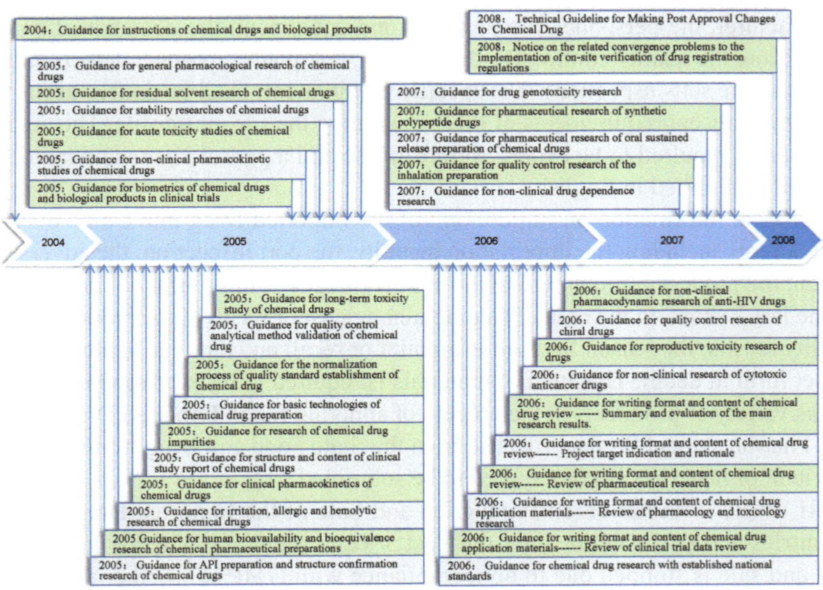

Fig. 1.3 The major CFDA guidance development for chemical drugs in China

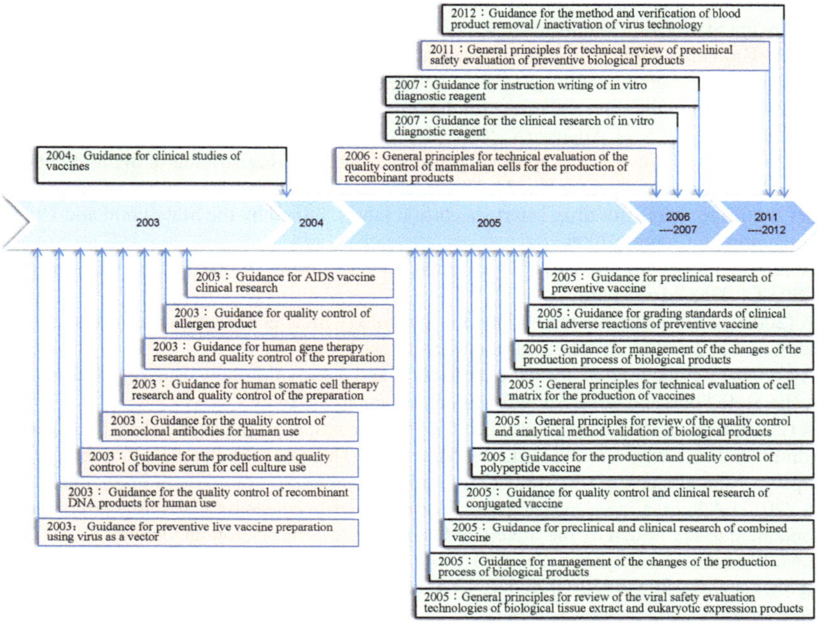

Fig. 1.4 The major CFDA guidance development for biological products in China

References

Bian YW, An J et al (15 July 2002) Interpretation of Drug Administration Law of People's Republic of China. Legislative Affairs Commission of the NPC Standing Committee. http://www.npc.gov.cn/npc/flsyywd/xingzheng/node_2179.htm

CFDA (6 December 2013) Examination and approval for import of packaging materials and containers in direct contact with drugs; Issued by the China Food and Drug Administration, http://eng.sfda.gov.cn/WS03/CL0769/98096.html

China Pharmaceutical Newsletter (2012) Center for drug evaluation issued the "relevant instructions for separate sequential review of varieties applied in CTD format". Volume XIII 2012

Huang Y (2010) ZUIXIN YAOPIN ZHUCE FAGUI JI ZHIDAO YUANZE. Chinese medical science and technology press, Beijing, p 3–250

National People's Congress (2001) Pharmaceutical Administration Law of the People's Republic of China. No. 45, Feb. 28, 2001 http://eng.sfda.gov.cn/WS03/CL0766/61638.html

Roth RI (2007) Preparing the common technical document for registration of pharmaceuticals for human use (CTD)—insights and recommendations. Therapeutic Innovation and Regulatory Science March 2008, 42(2):149–15 doi:10.1177/009286150804200207

SDA (2002) Regulations for implementation of the Drug Administration Law of the People's Republic of China, Decree of the State Council of the People's Republic of China, No. 360; issued by the State Drug Administration on August 4, 2002 http://eng.sfda.gov.cn/WS03/CL0767/61640.html

SDA (2003a) Good laboratory practice for non-clinical laboratory studies (glp), Order No. 2, isuued by the State Drug Administration, effective on September 1, 2003
SFDA (2003a) Good clinical practice of pharmaceutical products. Order No. 3, issued by the State Food and Drug Administration, Effective on September 1, 2003
SFDA (2003b) Administrative measures for the import of drugs. Order of the State Food and Drug Administration (No. 4), August 18, 2003
SFDA (2005) Special review and approval procedure for Drug Registration of the State Food and Drug Administration, Decree No. 21, November 18, 2005
SFDA (2006) Provisions for drug insert sheets and labels, issued by the State Food and Drug Administration on June 1, 2006
SFDA (2007) Provisions for Drug Registration, No. 28. June 18, 2007 http://eng.sfda.gov.cn/WS03/CL0768/61647.html
SFDA (2009a) Administrative regulations for technology transfer registration of drugs, issued by the State Food and Drug Administration on August 19, 2009
SFDA (2009b) Regulations of special examination and approval in new drug registration. Issued by the State Food and Drug Administration on January 7, 2009
SFDA (2010) Good manufacturing practice for pharmaceutical products, the State Food and Drug Administration Order No. 79; Order by Ministry of Health of the People's Republic of China http://www.doc88.com/p-991218878276.html
SFDA (2012) Administrative measures for inspection of overseas drug manufacturers (for trial implementation), issued by the State Food and Drug Administration on October 8, 2012 http://hi.baidu.com/eaxnaifxbjbduwr?page=1
Zhang SS, Cao ZS, Hui QS (2007) ZUIXIN YAO PIN ZHUCE ZHINAN. Chinese medical science and technology press, Beijing, p 1–11

Chapter 2
Pharmaceutical Intellectual Property Rights in China

Ming Q. Lu, Sandy Bai, Yuyuan Tan and Cheng Xu

2.1 Introduction

Based on the market size and its fast-growing rate, China is expected to become the second largest drug market in the world by 2015 with a growth rate over 25 % per annum in the next 3 years. Therefore, China is expected to attract more overseas pharmaceutical companies. At the same time, pharmaceutical products rely heavily on the protection of intellectual property rights (IPR), so it is essential for those overseas pharmaceutical companies to have a comprehensive understanding of the corresponding laws and regulations, to adjust their strategy for IPR protection to better benefit from their products in the Chinese market. Up to date, China has gone through a few milestone IPR changes and has established a relatively comprehensive legal system in relation to IPR protection. The core IPR protection is through the implementation of the patent laws and regulations. The state IP office of China and its branches are the key IPR executing agents (Liu 2009) . The intellectual assets are protected by patents, administrative regulations (Table 2.2), trademarks, copyrights, and trade secrets (Qu 2010) . The patent law (Amendment to Patent Law 2008) is the most important one for IPR protection, which adopted the international standard of novelty examination to conduct drug patent review and approval. In terms of drug patent administration, new articles of parallel importing,

M. Q. Lu (✉)
Helsinn Therapeutics (U.S.), Inc., 1140 US Highway 22, Suite 101, Bridgewater, NJ 08807, USA
e-mail: Mingqilu@verizon.net

S. Bai
Group Investment Company Beijing of China, 138 Building B-538, Zhang Hua Road, Hai Dian District, 100036 Beijing, P. R. China

Y. Tan
Beijing PRI BioScience Development Co, Ltd., C-505 Building 102, Zhu Jiang Di Jing No.28, Guangqu Road, Chao Yang District, 100022 Beijing, P. R. China

C. Xu
Shanghai Zhangjiang Center for Translational Medicine, Shanghai Biotecan Co., Ltd., Building 3, 899 Zuchongzhi Road, 201203 Shanghai, P. R. China

M. Q. Lu (ed.), *Approaching China's Pharmaceutical Market*,
DOI 10.1007/978-3-319-15576-0_2

compulsory licensing, and the exemption (Bolar exemption) for drug clinical trial and its dossier application are added. To enforce drug patent protection, the new patent law increased administrative penalties for patent violations. These newly added articles provide stronger protection for the IPR.

The Chinese environment for the protection of intellectual property right is considered complicated by many companies, especially for the small to medium-sized companies or those just entered into Chinese territory recently; Many overseas and multinational pharmaceutical companies are concerned that their imported or locally manufactured pharmaceuticals produced in China will be imitated or copied, or their intellectual property will be infringed. However, there are many similarities between the Chinese IPR compared to the western world IPR protection.

2.2 Historic Milestones of Patent and New Drug Protection Regulation Changes in China

In 1984, China issued the Patent Law. On April 1, 1985, the Chinese Patent Law entered into effect (Patent Law 1984). However, the Patent Law did not provide patent protection for pharmaceuticals until it was amended in 1993. During the period from 1984 to 1993, drugs were primarily protected by administrative measures (Fig. 2.1, Tables 2.1 and 2.2).

In 1993, China issued patent protection law for pharmaceuticals. The patent law was revised on September 4, 1992 for the first time and the revised Patent Law became effective on January 1, 1993. The duration of patent was extended for regular

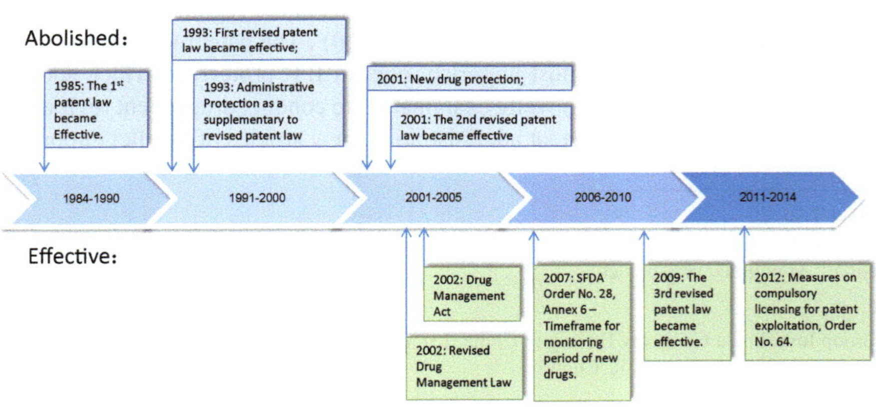

Fig. 2.1 Historic development outline of intellectual property protection in China

Table 2.1 Patent protection in China

Drug listing date	Protection period (Years)
1987–1993	15
1993–Present	20

Table 2.2 Administrative new drug protection in China

Drug listing date	Protection period (Class I) (Years)
1985–1999	8
1999–2002	12
2002–Present	5

patents from 15 to 20 years, and for utility model and design patents from 5 to 10 years, with no further extensions. Chemicals and pharmaceuticals were removed from the list of unpatentable subject matter. Some of the administrative protection measures remained effective in addition to patent protection for pharmaceuticals due to specific historical reasons. This patent law significantly stimulated local pharmaceuticals' innovative activities for new drug (The Amendment of the Patent Law 1993).

In August, 2000, the Patent Law was revised on August 25, 2000, for the second time and the revised Patent Law came into force on July 1, 2001. As the result of the negotiations with WTO, China committed again to review and revise the Patent Law. Accordingly, the Standing Committee of the People's Congress passed the second amendment bill on August 25, 2000, and the amendment became effective on July 1, 2001. China succeeded in making accession into WTO on November 12, 2001. This second amendment made the Patent Law in compliance with the TRIPS Agreement, the Patent Law was revised to grant patentee the right to prevent others from "offering for sale" patented products or products obtained directly by patented processes (The Amendment of the Patent Law 2000).

In October, 2001, to encourage the local pharmaceuticals innovation of new drugs, the Chinese government provided a great incentive to take up innovation activities. The State Food and Drug Administration (SFDA) extended the drug protection period: Class I of drugs protected period extended from 8 to 12 years; the protection periods of Class II and III new drugs extended their protected periods from 6 and 4 years to 8 years; Class IV drugs extended their protected period from 3 years to 6 years; For Class V new drugs, SFDA increased the protection period to 6 years.

The implementation of a certain period of protection for the production of new drugs is similar to and consistent with the international standards. During the protection period, only the manufacturer, who had the drug license approved by SFDA could make the exclusive product with the same formulation and dosage form.

In addition, to encourage pharmaceuticals to develop new drugs, SFDA is to establish a new drug review system: including (1) Class I confidential drug, anti-cancer drugs, and anti-AIDS drugs will be approved under expedited procedures; (2) The evaluation process for the first in class drugs for the treatment of difficult or severe diseases will be accelerated; (3) the approval process will also be accelerated for technological innovation, that may significantly reduce the generic drug costs or improve their qualities.

In 2002, the administrative "New drug protection" issued in 2001 was replaced with the "Revised Drug management Law" and "Drug Management Act", i.e., "New Drug Monitoring Scheme". Part of the reasons is that upon re-entry into the WTO, new drug protection became inconsistent with the intellectual property protection systems under Trade-Related Aspects of Intellectual Property Rights (TRIPs).

The New Monitoring Scheme focuses on monitoring new drugs for safety and effectiveness by providing market exclusivity to the supplier of that new drug. The period of market exclusivity was reduced from 12 years to 5 years for the Class I new drugs, and less than 5 years for other Classes of new drugs. Overall, the intellectual property protection becomes more consistent with the current international standards. It should be noted that this Monitoring Scheme only applies to drugs manufactured in China, see Tables 2.3 and 2.4.

In December 2008, the Patent Law was revised (The Amendment to Patent Law 2008) for the third time and the revised Patent Law came into force on October 1, 2009 (Table 2.1). This amendment further strengthened the legal protection to inventors in China. The new contents are designed to shift China's economy patterns from manufacturing and exports towards technology and innovation.

The revised Patent Law made the definitions of invention, utility model and design much clearer. China's patent law requires that invention patents and utility model patents to possess novelty, creativity and practical applicability. The required standards were further raised in the revised Patent Law. To grant a Chinese patent, China patent office adopted the "absolute novelty" standard that is used internationally, i.e. the invention is not known publicly either inside or outside China prior to the date of application for a patent. For the invention patent, a finished drug must be defined in terms of usage, i.e. the applicant must clearly state in the application for the diagnostic or therapeutic indications of the drug (Zhang 2008) . A finished drug or biological product or API is eligible for product invention patent application.

In general, the revised patent law in 2008 brings the Chinese standards closer into conformance with international practice. For the multinational pharmaceutical companies, this patent law is even more important since it becomes the only protection for imported drugs.

2.3 Current Effective Rules for New Drug Protection

Patent Protection

In China, the accepted types of patents include inventions, utility models, and industrial designs. Invention patents are available to both product and method inventions. The term for invention patents (compound patent) is 20 years and the term for utility model and design patents is 10 years, from the filing date of patent application (Standing Committee of the National People's Congress 2008). A product patent for a drug entitles the patentee the exclusive right to manufacture, market, and sell the drug. The measurements of the patent acceptance are based on the novelty, inventiveness, and industrial applicability. A finished medicinal product typically consisting of active ingredients is generally eligible for product invention patents (Fig. 2.2). Active ingredients in a drug are also eligible for separate product patents.

Table 2.3 Historical market exclusivity under the administrative new drug and patent protection for chemical drugs

Classification of new drugs	1985 Drug controlling law (Years)	1999 "New drug registration act" and "Notice on new drug protection and technology transfer" (Years)	2002 New drug protection in "revised drug management law," "Drug Management Act" (Years)	Patent protection
New chemical entity that has not been approved anywhere in the world	8	12	Transitory protection 5	15 Years (–1993) 20 Years (1993–)
Approved abroad, but not in the foreign pharmacopoeia, not imported to China	6	8	4	None
New combination of registered drug	4	8	3	None
Approved on the foreign pharmacopoeia, imported in China, but not produced in China (not approved in China since 2002)	3	6	3	None
New use of already registered drug	3	6	3	None

Note 1: On introduction of the "Revised Drug Management Law" and "Drug Management Act" in 2002, "new drug protection" was repealed. The "new drug monitoring" period was introduced in 2002 and become effective in May 1, 2002

1. Drugs that passed clinical test on September 15, 2002 were given market exclusivity for the period of "new drug protection" in the 1999 scheme

2. Drugs that applied for to the government, but had not passed a clinical test yet, nor sold in China, were given a "monitoring period" in the new 2002 scheme

Note 2: The classification of drug categories is unique in China. In history, the classification was modified a few times, e.g. it has been classified into 5 categories in 1999, 6 categories in 2002, 2005 and 2007. The contents of the categories are also different depending on the versions of the Act (Deng 2004; Chen 2007) `

The product invention patent for a finished drug must be defined in terms of usage (indication), i.e. the diagnostic or therapeutic use of the product. In China, a new drug usually will satisfy the inventiveness requirement if its active ingredients are novel or it delivers new beneficial effects compare to the existing treatments.

Table 2.4 New drug monitoring period

Monitoring period	Chemical drug	Therapeutic biological product	Preventative biological products
5 (Year)	1. Among those not yet marketed domestically or oversea:	1. Biological products not yet Marked domestically or oversea	1. Vaccine not yet marketed domestically or oversea
	1.1 Drug substance and its preparations made by synthesis or semi-synthesis		
	1.2 Preparation of new active chemical monomer extracted from natural sources or by fermentation		
	1.3 Preparation of optical isomer obtained from known drugs by chiral separation or synthesis		
4 (Year)	1. among drugs not yet marketed domestically or oversea:	2. Mono-clonal antibody	2. DNA vaccine
	1.4 Drug with fewer Components derived from Marketed multi-component drug;	3. Gene therapy, somatic cell therapy as well as the preparations	3. An already marketed vaccine with new adjuvant. Change of carrier of combined vaccine
	1.5 New compound formula preparation;	4. Allergen products	4. Non-purified vaccine, or full cell vaccine (bacteria, virus) changed into purified vaccine, or combined vaccine
	2. Preparation with change in route of administration but not yet marketed domestically or oversea	5. Multi component products with bioactivity extracted from, or by fermentation from human and/ or animal tissues and/ or body fluid,	5. Vaccine with strains not yet approved in China (except for vaccine for influenza, vaccine for leplospirosis and others)
	3. Among the drug marketed overseas but not domestically:	6. New combination product made from the already marketed biological products	6. Vaccine already marketed overseas but not yet marketed domestic
		7. A product that is marketed already overseas but not yet marketed domestic	7. Combined vaccine prepared with vaccine already marketed domestic
	3.1 preparation marketed overseas, and/or preparation with change in dosage form of the preparation but without change in route of administration	8. Micro ecological product, where some of the strains used for preparing of micro-ecological products not yet approved	8. Re-combination vaccine with protective antigen spectrum different with the marketed one

Table 2.4 (continued)

Monitoring period	Chemical drug	Therapeutic biological product	Preventative biological products
		9. Products with not completely same structure products and not yet marketed at domestic or overseas (including amino acid locus mutation/ absence, modification caused by a different expression system, deletion, changed interpretation, as well as chemical modifications of the product) with the already marketed	
		10. Products with a method of preparation different with the already marketed one, (such as use of different expression system, host cells)	
		11. Products first time made with DNA recombination technology (such as use of recombination technology to replace the synthesis technology, tissue extraction or fermentation technology)	
3 (Year)	3. Amongst the drug marketed overseas but not in China:	14. Biological products with change in route of administration (excluding 12)	9. Vaccine manufactured with the change of the other approved expression or the other approved cellular stroma. Vaccine using new process, which is proved to improve the safety and effectiveness of the vaccine based on the data of laboratory
	3.2 Combination preparations, and/or with changed dose form, but no change of administration route		

Table 2.4 (continued)

Monitoring period	Chemical drug	Therapeutic biological product	Preventative biological products
	3.3 Preparations with changed administration route and marketed ex-China;		10. Vaccine with change of de-activator (method of deactivation) or de-toxicitor (method of de-toxicity)
	4. Drug substance and itspreparation with changed acid or alkaline radicals (or metallic elements), but without any pharmacological change, and the original drug entity already approved in China		
	5. Change in dosage form of existing drugs marketed in China, but without change in route of administration, where special technology is used, such as targeted delivery preparation, sustain or controlled release preparation		11. Vaccine with change in the route of administration

Note: This table is simplified based on Provisions for Drug Registration (SFDA Order No. 28)—Annex 6: Timeframe for monitoring period of New Drugs. No monitoring period will be established for the drugs other than those listed

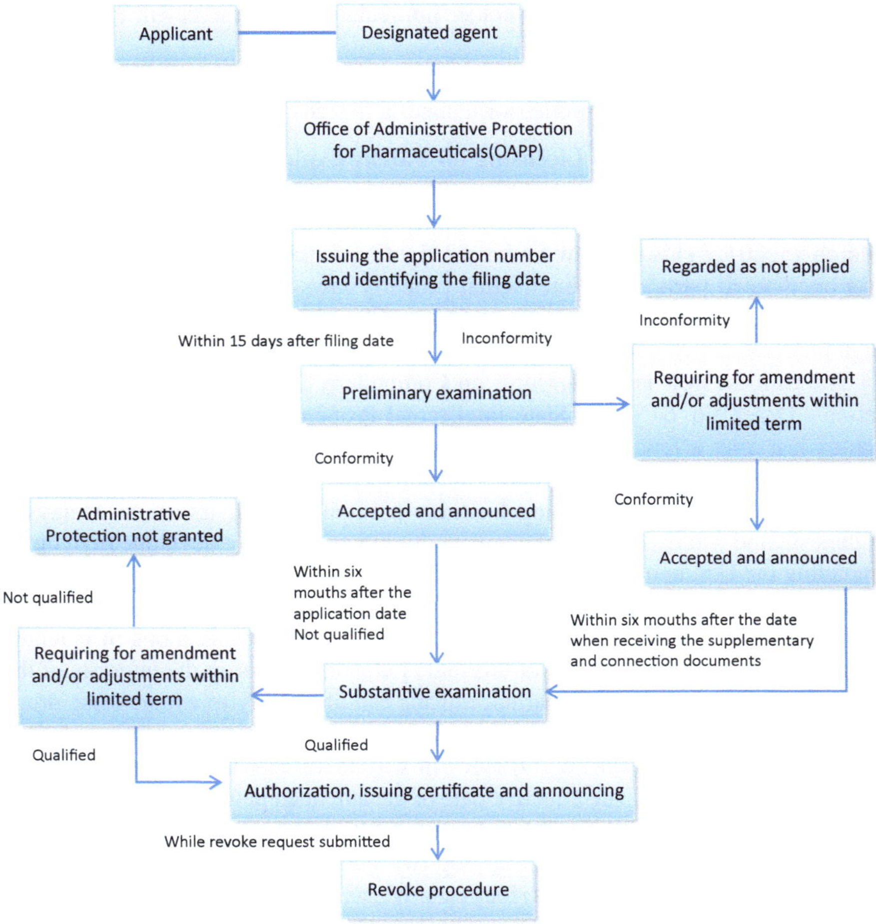

Fig. 2.2 Examination and approval procedure of administrative protection for pharmaceuticals. (Source: China Food and Drug Administration website with modifications)

In the US, European Union, and Japan, the pharmaceutical drug patent terms have been extended due to its long development process before marketing. However, such patent extension has not been accepted in China.

The 2008 Amendments to the Patent Law became effective on October 1, 2009, also specifically provides an infringement exemption for local generic drug manufacturers. The amendments are similar to the "Bolar exemption" in the United States, namely, "manufacturing, using or importing patented drugs or medical devices solely for the purpose of acquiring information necessary for obtaining administrative approval, and manufacturing or importing patented drugs or medical devices for an enterprise for the purpose of seeking administrative approval, shall not constitute patent infringement." This enables local manufacturer to embark upon the preparation for manufacturing of a patented drug well before the patent expires and to be ready to compete with the patent holder immediately after the patent expires (see details in the following section).

The innovations of medical devices and instruments and drug packaging are usually protected under utility models or industrial designs.

Measures on Compulsory Licensing for Patent Exploitation—Order No. 64 of the State Intellectual Property Office (2012)
State Intellectual Property Office of China issued a patent law amendment on March 15, 2012. This new law favors the fighting for cheaper drugs. This new law has overhauled parts of its intellectual property laws to allow the Chinese local manufacturers to make cheap generic drugs still under patent protection from foreign pharmaceutical companies.

The Chinese new law "Measures on Compulsory Licensing for Patent Exploitation—Order No. 64 of the State Intellectual Property Office" (SIPO 2012) was issued just after a few months of a similar move called "compulsory license" by India to effectively end the monopoly on an expensive cancer drug made by Bayer AG. Such compulsory Licensing has also previously been issued in Malaysia, Indonesia and Thailand, as well as on multiple occasions by developed countries including the U.S. and EU member countries.

Based on the new patent law, the Chinese government may issue compulsory licenses to eligible local pharmaceuticals to produce generic versions of patented drugs during state emergencies, or unusual circumstances, or in the interests of the public. In addition, the local pharmaceuticals can also apply to export these drugs to other countries. Compulsory licenses are available to nations to issue under the World Trade Organization (WTO) rules in certain cases where life-saving treatments are unaffordable. The effective date of the amended patent law "Measures for the Compulsory Licensing for Patent Implementation" was May 1, 2012.

China and India are ranked as the top two countries for manufacturing active pharmaceutical ingredients (APIs) for years. Western countries buy those APIs from China, and then sell the patented drugs back to China at prices only a very limited Chinese can afford. Technically, it is not a hard work for local Chinese pharmaceuticals to make the generic versions of the majority of the patented drugs. However, the current patent laws still provide a very reliable way for drug protection. This patent law amendment is more likely to affect the drugs for the treatment of medical emergencies or unusual circumstances, or in the interests of the public, such as SARS or AIDS etc. A reasonable balance between the patented drug prices and medical needs may also play a role for the measure on compulsory licensing decision by the Chinese government.

Administrative Protection—Monitoring Period (Marketing Exclusivity)—3–5 years for new drug and new formulation after first approval in China. Only apply for locally manufactured products (SFDA 2007).

In addition to patent protection, China also established a special administrative protection system (monitoring period protection, see Figs. 2.3 and 2.4) for new drugs. SFDA provide administrative protection to pharmaceutical companies by granting licenses and permits, which gives these companies certain exclusive rights. The current administrative protection policies for drugs have become effective since

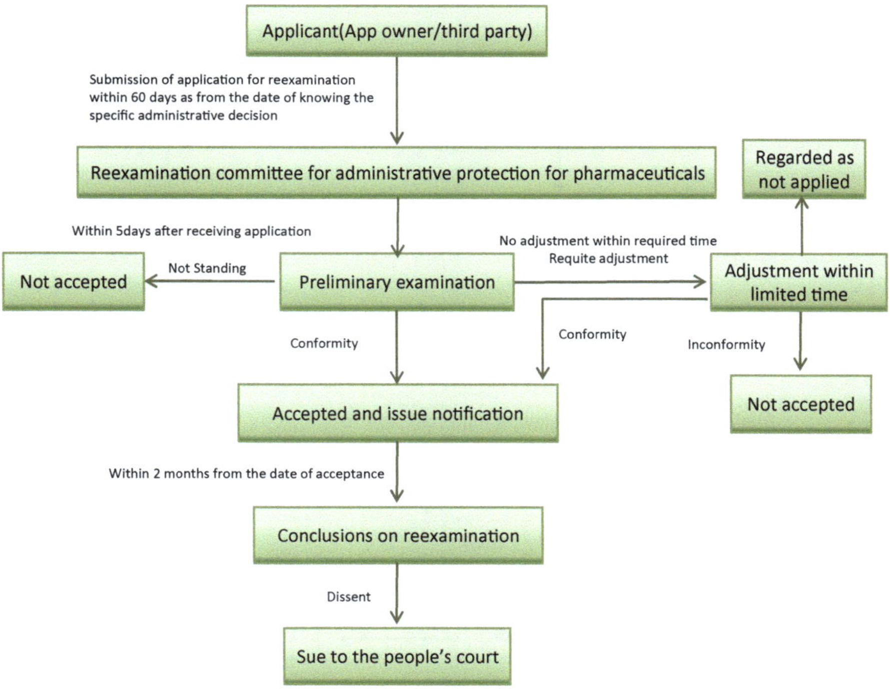

Fig. 2.3 Reexamination procedure of administrative protection for pharmaceuticals. (Source: China Food and Drug Administration website with modifications)

2002. The monitoring period of a new drug is 5 years from the date of approval to manufacturing the drug. During a new drug's monitoring period, the SFDA will not give permission to other enterprises to make, modify or import drugs of the same type to ensure that the protected drug manufacture enjoys certain degree of exclusivity (Figs. 2.3 and 2.4).

Trade Secret

In China, trade secrets are protected mainly under the *PRC Anti-Unfair Competition Law* (Standing Committee of the National People's Congress 1993); The protections under this law provide the advantages to the entitled pharmaceutical companies to prohibit others from the following acts: (a) any attempt to obtain trade secrets from their rights holders by theft, coaxing, coercion or any other unlawful means; (b) disclosing, using or allowing others to use trade secrets being obtained through any of the above means; (c) in breach of confidentiality obligations to the right holders regarding the trade secrets, disclosing, using or allowing others to use the trade secrets; or (d) prohibiting any third party from obtaining, using, or disclosing of other party's trade secrets when the third party is or should have been aware of the existence of any illegal acts mentioned above. Trade secret provides intellectual property protection in the biological and pharmaceutical sectors from other angle.

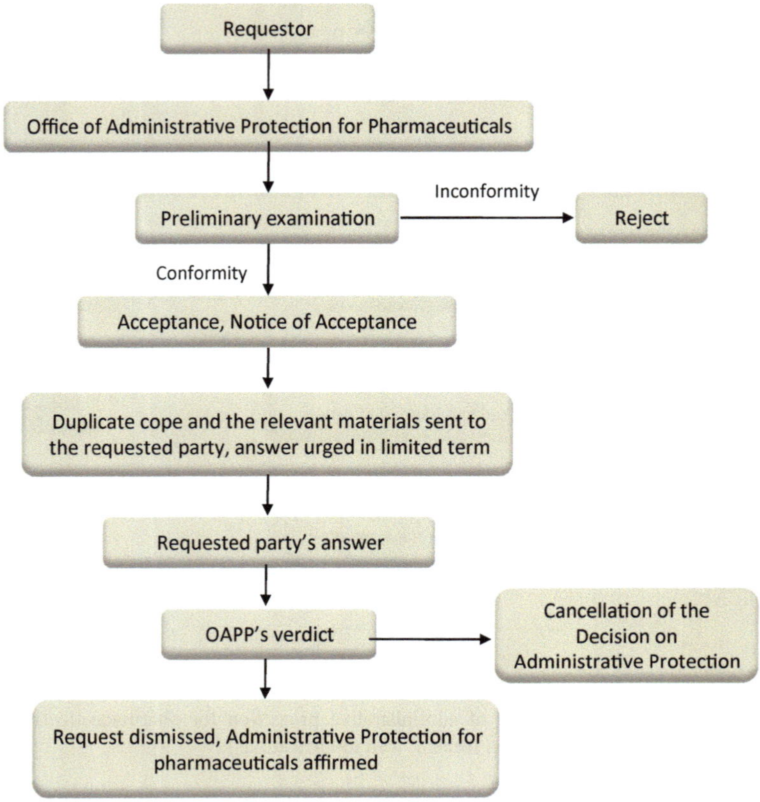

Fig. 2.4 Revoke procedure of administrative protection for pharmaceuticals. (Source: China Food and Drug Administration website with modifications)

A Registered Trademark

A registered trademark in China is valid for 10 years starting from the registration date of the trademark. The term of validity of a registered trademark can be extended infinitely upon renewal. In addition to trademarks, some drugs which satisfy certain requirements may also distinguish themselves from comparable products by using a unique drug "commodity name". However, such drug commodity names must follow the naming rules imposed by the pharmaceutical administrative supervision department.

Data Exclusivity

Based on China's Regulations on Drug Registration, data submitted to the SFDA for approval containing a new chemical entity is protected for 6 years from the date of marketing approval. As such, other companies must create their own data (the full NDA package—following Class I or III new drug requirement) to support a competing drug registration.

2.4 Strategic Consideration of Pharmaceutical Product Protection

Strategic thinking of the pharmaceutical product protection needs integrated information. For the products still have a long period of patent protection, the protection path seems very straight forward. However, many foreign companies often concerns about how to protect their pharmaceutical products with only a limited patent protection period left, or simply facing a patent expiration, or without a patent protection.

Up to date, many international companies selected not to apply for patents in China. The consequence is that their pharmaceutical products are not protected by patents in China.

For the drug without a patent or patent already expired, the companies should consider whether there is still a market need, or whether they can still make it as the first in class drug in China since they may still take the favor to set the price high, to block or influence the profit of the latter potential generic versions.

Alternatively, the companies may consider the following strategies:

Monitoring Period Exclusivity If the new drug is manufactured in China, the monitoring period exclusivity imposed by SFDA may provide an up to 5 years protective period.

This period may vary from 3 to 5 years depending on the category of the new drug. During the this period, the SFDA will not approve any other companies to manufacture, distribute, or import this drug, unless the competing investigational product has been approved for entering clinical trials in China prior to the beginning of the monitoring period. Since this protection will not apply to the imported drugs, the foreign pharmaceutical companies may consider local manufacturing, or partnering strategies to take the advantage of this protection policy.

Data Exclusivity Due to the 6 years data protection, other companies must create their own data (the full NDA package—following Class I or III new drug requirement) to support a competing drug registration. Foreign pharmaceutical companies without a valid patent protection may market their new chemical entity drug in China to take the advantage of this approach. New drugs in the Class I category may leave significant hurdles for competitors to develop their generic version, especially for the drugs without many available publications. Comparatively, new drugs in the Class III category may be easier for other applicants due to the much open policies of the western regulation.

Other Considerations In addition to the above thought, the foreign pharmaceutical companies may also take the following factors for consideration including: difficulty factors for manufacturing the new chemical or biological entity, trade secrets, registered trademark etc.

2.5 Pharmaceutical Patent Litigation

China surpassed the United States to become the top patent filing country in the world in 2011 by obtaining 526,412 invention patent applications, compared to 503,582 utility patent applications in the US. One of the major reasons is the attractive incentives originated from the Chinese government (Zhao 2012) . In 2008, the Chinese government issued the National Intellectual Property Strategy and various incentive programs. Those programs provided generous funding to encourage domestic companies, research institutes, and universities to seek patent protection for their innovations. These incentives have significantly boosted the new patent filings by Chinese domestic companies. While at the same time, China has become the world's top litigious country for intellectual property disputes since 2005 with a total of 13,424 cases filed with Chinese courts (Figs. 2.5 and 2.6) versus 10,905 cases filed in the U.S. during the same period (SIPO 2006).

China's Regulations on Drug Registration require a drug manufacturer to declare that it does not infringe any third-party patent when filing a registration application.

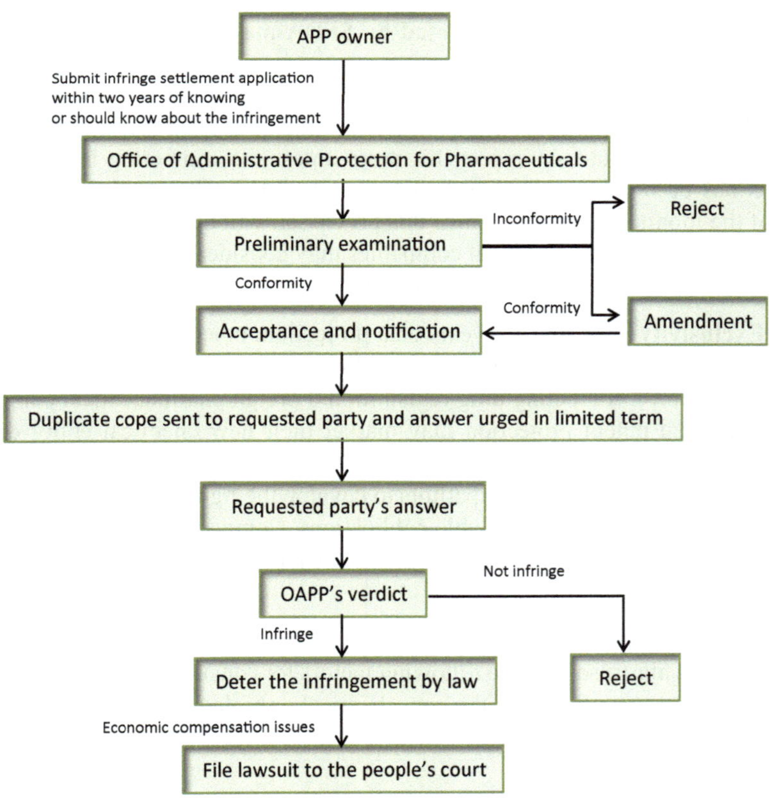

Fig. 2.5 Infringe settlement procedure of Administrative Protection for Pharmaceuticals (APP). (Source: China Food and Drug Administration website with modifications)

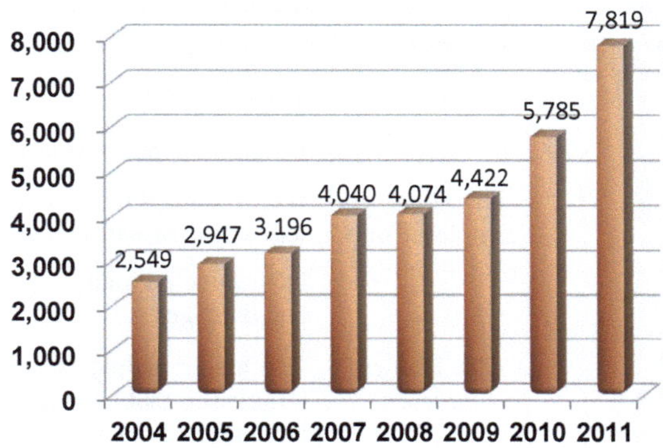

Fig. 2.6 Patent lawsuits in China, 2004–2011. (*Source:* PRC *State Intellectual Property Office White Papers*, 2004–2011)

A generic drug manufacturer may file for registration with the SFDA 2 years prior to the expiration of a patent. The SFDA will review the application but withhold approval until patent expiration in China. In addition, a patentee may, on the basis of an infringement judgment, request the SFDA to revoke an approved drug registration.

However, there are still a significant number of international companies have selected not to apply for patents in China. As such, many of their pharmaceutical products are not protected by patents in China.

Once a dispute on infringement happens in China, as in other countries, litigation instituted by intellectual property owners is the most effective way to solve the problem. In general, China has two routes for enforcing IP rights: administrative procedures and judicial actions (Fig. 2.5).

Administrative Procedures Depending on the nature of intellectual property rights and infringement, the IP owner can ask the State Administration for Industry and Commerce, the Public Security Department, the Copyright Office, the Trademark Office, or the State Intellectual Property Office (SIPO) to enforce intellectual property rights through inspection, seizure, reprimand, and fines. The administrative decisions in China are subject to judicial review.

It is suggested that upon identifying infringing products, the intellectual property owners can request Chinese customs to seize such products in an effort to prevent their export. To facilitate customs enforcement, the IP owner should record its copyrights, trademarks, and patents with the General Office of Chinese Customs.

Judicial Actions China has a four-level court system: (1) the Basic People's Court; (2) the Intermediate People's Court; (3) the Higher People's Court; and (4) the Supreme People's Court (Bai 2007). See Table 2.5.

The Supreme People's Court is the highest court in China. It handles appeals from lower courts and issues judicial interpretations and guidelines to clarify legislation or to harmonize lower-court procedures. The Supreme People's Court has its own intellectual property chambers within the courts to hear patent cases. These chambers have the power to determine permanent injunction, preliminary injunction, and damages.

Table 2.5 The four-tier court system and their functions

Pharma	Court System	Function
	The Supreme People's Court	The highest court in China; Handling appeals from Higher People's Courts; Issues judicial interpretations and guidelines to clarify legislation or harmonize lower-court procedures. Determine permanent injunction, preliminary injunction, and damages.
	↕	
	The Higher People's Court	One higher people's court in each province and certain large cities that have the rank of a province, such as Beijing, Shanghai, and Tianjin.
	↕	
Infringe Law Suit→	The Intermediate People's Court	Each major Chinese city has one or two Intermediate People's Courts.
	↕	
Infringe Law Suit→	the Basic People's Court	Each county or district in each major city has one Basic People's Court.

There is one higher people's court in each province, autonomous region, and certain large cities that have the rank of a province, such as Beijing, Shanghai, and Tianjin.

Each major city has one or two Intermediate People's Courts, which have jurisdiction over first-instance patent-related civil disputes.

Each county or district in each major city has one Basic People's Court. China has a "two instance" judicial system—the decisions of the court of first instance can be appealed to the court at the higher level, which makes what essentially is a final decision.

The court has authority to order pretrial injunctions to stop infringement and collect infringement evidence. The court may impose statutory damages, award to the patentee reasonable expenses incurred in halting the infringing act. Upon winning a lawsuit, the IP owner is entitled to an injunction to deter infringement in China. China has become a major ground for patent disputes. More and more Chinese companies and foreign companies are likely to resort to the counts to resolve patent disputes.

References

Bai BJ, Wang PJ, Cheng H (2007) What multinational companies need to know about patent enforcement and patent litigation in China. Northwest J Tech Intellect Prop 5(3):449. http://scholarlycommons.law.northwestern.edu/njtip/vol5/iss3/4. Accessed 18 Oct 2014

Chen X, Watanabe M (2007) Pharmaceutical industry in China—intellectual property protection, pricing and innovation. Institute of Developing Economies, Japan External Trade Organization

Deng R, Kaitin K (2004) The regulation and approval of new drugs in China. Ther Innov Regul Sci 38(1):29–39. doi:10.1177/009286150403800105

Ding J et al (2011) From imitation to innovation: a study of China's drug R & D and relevant national policies. J Technol Manage Innov 6(2):1–13

Liu C (2009) Law of intellectual property. Publishing House of Renmin University of China, Beijing

Patent Law (1984) Patent law of the people's republic of China. Adopted at the Fourth Meeting of the Standing Committee of the Sixth National People's Congress and promulgated by order No. 11 of the President of the People's Republic of China on March 12, 1984, and effective as of April 1, 1985

Qu M, Ye B (2010) Protecting pharmaceutical intellectual property rights in China, King and Wood Beijing

SFDA (2007) Provisions for Drug Registration, No. 28. June 18, 2007; Annex 6: Timeframe for monitoring period of New Drugs. http://eng.sfda.gov.cn/WS03/CL0768/61647.html. Accessed 12 Dec 2013

SIPO (2006) State intellectual property office of the P.R. China. China's intellectual property protection in 2005. http://english.sipo.gov.cn/laws/whitepapers/200804/t20080416_380356.html. Accessed 5 Sept 2006

SIPO (2012) Measures on compulsory licensing for patent implementation—Order No. 64 of the State Intellectual Property Office, May 1, 2012

Standing Committee of the National People's Congress (1993a) Anti-unfair competition law of the People's Republic of China. September 2, 1993

Standing Committee of the National People's Congress (1993b) The amendment of the patent law. Standing committee of the people's congress passed the amendment on September 4, 1992, and the amended patent law came into force on January 1, 1993

Standing Committee of the National People's Congress (2008) The amendment to patent law. P.R.C. Exec. Order No. 8 (2008), promulgated by the Standing Comm. Nat'l People's Cong., Dec. 27, 2008, effective on Oct. 1, 2009

Zhang Q (2008) Implementation of intellectual property strategies in the medicine and bio-technology sphere. Intellectual Property Publishing House, Page 59

Zhao Y (2012) China's patent litigation landscape shifts. Intellectual Property and Technology News (Sept. 5, 2012)

Chapter 3
The China Food and Drug Administration (CFDA)

Yuyuan Tan, Yanbin Xie, Xianchao Qiao and Sandy Bai

3.1 Overview of Chinese Drug Safety Supervision History

In September) 1984, the National People's Congress (NPC) Standing Committee passed China's first "Drug Administration Law." This law became effective on July 1, 1985. The implementation of this law put drug production, business activities and the state of drug supervision and management on the legal track. Since then, China's regulatory system experienced significant changes as marked by the following milestone evolutions (Table 3.1):

- Establishment of the State Drug Administration (SDA) in 1998;
- Establishment of the State Food and Drug Administration (SFDA) in 2003;
- The State Food and Drug Administration merged into the Ministry of Health (SFDA) in 2008;
- Establishment the China Food and Drug Administration (CFDA) in 2013.

---

http://eng.sfda.gov.cn/WS03/CL0756/

Y. Tan (✉)
Beijing PRI BioScience Development Co, Ltd., C-505 Building 102, Zhu Jiang Di Jing No. 28, Guangqu Road, Chao Yang District, 100022 Beijing, P. R. China
e-mail: tanyuyuan1991@163.com

Y. Xie
China ICON PLC., Room 1502-1506, Tower B Global Trade Center, No. 36, North Ring East Road, Dongcheng District, 100013 Beijing, P. R. China

X. Qiao
Konney Science and Technology Co., Ltd., 14 Songshan Road, Qingdao, 266021 Shandong, P. R. China

S. Bai
Group Investment Company Beijing of China, 138 Building B-538, Zhang Hua Road, Hai Dian District, 100036 Beijing, P. R. China

M. Q. Lu (ed.), *Approaching China's Pharmaceutical Market*,
DOI 10.1007/978-3-319-15576-0_3

Table 3.1 Chinese drug safety supervision history

Regulatory authorities	Established	Summary
The State Drug Administration (SDA)	1998	Constituted by the former State Pharmaceutical Administration of National Economic Council, Pharmaceutical Affairs Division of Ministry of Health, and part of the State Administration of Traditional Chinese Medicine
The State Food and Drug Administration (SFDA)	2003	The SFDA was formed by merging of State Drug Administration and State Food Administration
The State Food and Drug Administration merged into the Ministry of Health (SFDA)	2008	The SFDA merged into the Ministry of Health.
The China Food and Drug Administration (CFDA)	2013	The CFDA was established and become an independent regulatory authority with the same level of Ministry of Health.

In March 2013, the CFDA was established on the basis of the former SFDA (China Daily 2013). The difference between the CFDA and the SFDA is that the administrative level of CFDA was promoted to a ministerial-level authority, i.e. on the same level as Ministry of Health (NPC 2013). Looking at the CFDA structurally, it made significant strides in the replacement of the overlapping department and streamlining the regulatory processes for food and drug administration. The establishment of the CFDA made the organization structure-wise similar to the US FDA. The CFDA as a ministerial-level authority now is directly under the State Council of the People's Republic of China (McKenna 2013).

3.1.1 The Establishment of State Drug Administration (SDA, 1998)

In 1998, the State Drug Administration (SDA) was established, which was constituted by the former State Pharmaceutical Administration of National Economic Council, Pharmaceutical Affairs Division of Ministry of Health, and part of the State Administration of Traditional Chinese Medicine. Since then, it catapulted modern Chinese drug safety regulation. Although the aim of this institutional reform is to solve the issue of regulatory bull management and overlapping responsibilities, the bull management appears to have been present through the regulatory history.

3.1.2 The Establishment of State Drug and Food Administration (SFDA 2003)

In 2003, the SFDA was formed by merging of State Drug Administration and State Food Administration. Referring to the US Food and Drug Administration (US FDA) system, China began to build its own version of the FDA.

The SFDA's management scope includes both drug and food categories. This structure set up the foundation for the unified management as the US FDA does. However, the reality was that the SFDA could not function as the US FDA, considering several cultural and legal disparities. For example, bull management became protected by national regulation of "Decision on Further Strengthening food safety" issued in 2004 by the State Council. It was clearly stated that for food safety management, it must take the principal of "Segment-based supervision as the major one" i.e. the local government is the one overall responsible, while the corresponding individual supervision department is responsible for its own functional duties and management. At the same time, variety management is supplemented. This food regulation also "spread" to the field of drug management. As such, the SFDA was held responsible for production and quality of drugs, and the transportation sector of the middle belonged to the Ministry of Commerce Management, and jurisdiction scope of hospital drug use belongs to the Ministry of health. In addition, in the same segment, drug management also involved multiple functional departments: for example, the Industrial and Commercial Departments are held responsible for safety in the drug distribution.

Even though the SFDA was given the comprehensive power to coordinate various departments for law enforcement, the position level of the SFDA was only at the vice-ministerial level. Therefore, it was hard to coordinate with other ministerial departments, such as agriculture, industry and commerce, quality inspection departments etc. In such a regulatory environment, many gray areas existed among the various departments; repeated supervision could not be avoided. In addition, it was easy to produce the phenomenon of mutual responsibility situations. Therefore, the SFDA had difficulties implementing their responsibilities.

3.1.3 The SFDA Merged into the Ministry of Health (SFDA, 2008)

During the SFDA era, before 2008, many problems of drug supervision and administration existed, and frequent safety-related accidents occurred. Food and drug administration is critical to public safety. However, such heavy responsibilities were poorly managed and could not meet the public's expectations. In 2008, the SFDA merged into the Ministry of Health—another milestone of reform. Using the experience of the US FDA for reference, China initiated unified management, and the SFDA acquired a functional role in "Segment-based supervision and comprehensive coordination."

However, the merger of the SFDA into Ministry of Health still could not avoid the frequent occurrence of medical safety accidents. In accordance with the regulations of the drug administration law, pharmaceutical supervisory and administrative departments were authorized to conduct supervision and inspection over the research, development, production and trade of pharmaceuticals, as well as the medical organizations' use of pharmaceuticals (Meng 2013).

Before 2008, according to the division of management field, the Ministry of Health was responsible for the management of the hospitals and the medical personals and the SFDA was responsible for drugs and medical devices. The reality was that the SFDA had a lack of effective regulation, even though the hospitals accounted for more than 70 % of drug circulation and was the most important link in the drug use.

Although the merger of the SFDA into Ministry of Health in 2008 required their mutual cooperation, it was still more like a formality merger or integration of forms, rather than a functional integration. The hospital management authority remained under the Ministry of health. One manifestation of this phenomenon was that in the actual supervision, the SFDA as a vice ministerial level unit was still below the Ministry of health and other ministerial level organization. Therefore, operation between these two bodies was not smooth.

3.1.4 Establishment of the CFDA—An Independent Regulatory Authority Parallels to Ministry of Health (2013)

Under the SFDA system, there were several regulatory disadvantages, indicating the need for reform. In 2013, the original SFDA was separated from the Ministry of Health, becoming an independent authority with the same ministerial level as others. The new and current State Food and Drug Administration (CFDA), became the first independent food and drug supervision authority at ministerial level.

Based on the current reformed authority, various regulatory functions will be integrated under the supervision of the CFDA and distributed into its different functional departments. The jurisdiction of the drug and hospital administrations is separated once more. The CFDA structure and responsibilities not only conform to the public expectations, but also fall in line with international trends.

According to the plan, the CFDA will integrate the responsibilities of the food safety office, as well as food and drug administration. The overall safety supervisions of food and drug from the production, circulation to consumption are fully the responsibilities of the CFDA.

This unified management is considered a true emulation of the US FDA. People don't expect that this one simple reform can solve China's food and drug safety issues. After all, the China's FDA only has about 10 years of history; the US FDA experienced a century of innovation and improvement to reach today's system.

This reform will set the CFDA in parallel with the Ministry of Health. It is expected that it will still, despite these changes, be difficult for the CFDA to intervene and influence the drug use processes since hospitals remain under the supervision of Ministry of Health.

3.2 The CFDA Reform Layout

3.2.1 The Functional Integration

The establishment of the CFDA aims to combine the food and drug regulatory functions together under the supervision of the same organization. Based on the recent disclosed document "The main duties, internal structure, staffing requirements of the CFDA", (hereinafter referred to as the" three fixed program"), the future of the CFDA layout is more focused on the field of food and drugs. Regarding drug-related management, it emphasizes the decentralization of authority (SCOPSR 2013).

Since its establishment, the CFDA has held these as its top priorities: the integration of functions, the optimal combination, and the straightening out of mechanisms. According to the CFDA's issued "three fixed program," this new authority has set up 17 internal departments, and 345 administrative personnel (SCOPSR 2013). Overall, going according to plan, the employee number has decreased, and departmental agencies also have streamlined. The new structure includes three divisions with their main focus on production, market and distribution, and monitoring and evaluation processes and other comprehensive functions.

In the field of pharmaceuticals, the previous medical device division of the SFDA was divided into two divisions, i.e. division of medical device registration management, and Division of medical devices supervision), other temporary use the SFDA settings.

At the same time, the CFDA separated the division of policies and regulations into three divisions: the first is a legal division—specialized in laws and regulations; the second is a policy research office (comprehensive division), to strengthen the research function; the third is a news propaganda division. The corresponding organization adjustment reflects the promotion of the CFDA's macro design ability in its planning, standardization and implementation of its regulations.

The number of people involved in the reform and adjustment was estimated near a million people only in the field of food safety supervision at the grassroots level.

The whole reform process was carried out in accordance with the "three, six, nine, twelve" principle, i.e.,(1) by the end of March 2013, realizing the establishing administration level, (2) by the end of June 2013, implementation of the provincial agency set up, (3) by the end of September 2013, local municipal institutions set up; (4) by the end December 2013, with the county level set up, thoroughly complete the implementation of food and drug system countrywide reform.

3.2.2 Streamline Administration and Institute Decentralization

The rationalization of the organizational structure helps for the clarification of each departmental function. The future of the CFDA is headed towards the direction of "simplification, decentralization, integration, and strengthening" to realize the transformation of functions (Meng 2013). This is particularly reflected in the regulation of drugs and devices.

In the "three fixed program," the two administrative approvals, (i.e., the pharmaceutical production of administrative license and pharmaceutical production quality management authentication) were gradually integrated as one administrative license; the two administrative approvals (i.e., drug business administrative license and GSP certification) were gradually integrated as one administrative license. Such simplification can reduce the pharmaceutical enterprises cost. The examination and approval authority delegated to the provincial GMP, also can mobilize the enthusiasm of the local government. Therefore, it is the embodiment of decentralization (SCOPSR 2013).

At the same time, many duties were delegated to the provincial food and drug regulatory authorities, including the standards for quality control of pharmaceutical, medical device authentication; supplement and re-registration of drugs; application of administrative licensing for drugs without change in the intrinsic quality; application regarding change for administrative license of domestic class III medical devices without change in the inherent quality of the products; commissioned drug production license, etc.

For architectural changes in the field of medical devices mentioned above, the two divisions were considered better to avoid the previously excessive concentration of power. Specifically, the medical device registration division has the responsibilities for medical device registration strictly in accordance with the conditions and procedures of the laws and regulations. The division of medical equipment supervision is mainly responsible for safety aspect, problems, proposing mechanisms to improve the system and providing improvement suggestions.

After the reform of the Chinese regulatory authority, the CFDA has been elevated to the ministerial level and become more efficient and powerful. A total of 104 new standards for the CFDA certification of medical devices have been issued in 2013 (CFDA 2013). All of them became effective as of October 1, 2014.

3.3 China's Drug Regulatory Outlook in the Future

3.3.1 Absorbing Foreign Advanced Management Concept

From the beginning, the food and drug supervision system of China has been trying to emulate the US FDA. However, it is not possible to directly copy the US FDA model in China due to the differences in system, economy, culture and many other factors. In reference to the past 10-plus years of practice, people realized that the establishment of rational organization is important; however, the formation of scientific supervision concepts seems even more critical. It is almost impossible to establish a top-level regulatory authority, without fully understanding the current regulatory environment, the regulatory agencies on the top list of the world, and the pros and cons of those agencies. China is actively absorbing the world's advanced regulatory concept. Its regulatory system is getting closer to the world regulatory standards.

3.3.2 Business Interests Must be Concessive to Science

The US FDA established in 1906 as a unified and responsible authority for food and drug safety supervision. Since then, the agency has continuously improved and updated its capabilities and optimized its organizational structures through practice.

In the food and drug supervision field, it is believed that it should never be dominated by any commercial and political forces, but should give way to science and ethics. To protect people's safe use of food and drugs, scientific principles must be in a dominant position in the FDA's decision. However, the fact is that the FDA will be challenged from politics, business, the most typical one of which is the food and pharmaceutical application lobbying organization. In general, lobbying all has ended in failure.

3.3.3 Open and Transparent Mechanisms Ensure Operation

Whether it is related to punishment or remedial measures, the FDA (what is "it"?) always follows the open and transparent mode of operation. It is understood that the FDA must accept supervision from three aspects: the supervision of the Ministry of Health, the Commission and the Parliament regularly held hearings or investigations, and supervision of civil societies. When the FDA appears negligent, consumer and public organizations will issue their lawsuit. This determines that the FDA in the meeting, voting and decision-making process must maintain open and transparent operation.

Based on the practical experience of the US FDA for nearly a century, it is essential to continue its improvement based on changes in science and to keep an open and transparent mechanism to maintain the agency's status at the top and its optimized regulatory condition. The CFDA has kept its open attitude and good communication with the top regulatory agencies in the world in recent years. It is getting more global and closing to world standards.

3.4 The CFDA Structure and Function

3.4.1 Responsibilities

The major responsibilities of the CFDA include the following ten aspects (CFDA 2013):

1. Responsible for drafting laws, regulations and policy plans on the administration and supervision of food (including food additives and health food, the same below) safety, drugs (including traditional Chinese medicines and ethno-medicines, the same below), medical devices and cosmetics; formulate normative

documents, and facilitating the establishment and implementation of the food safety responsibility mechanism, under which food companies shall bear the main responsibility and local people's governments shall take integrated responsibility; establishing the direct reporting system for critical food and drug information and supervise its implementation; taking measures to reduce risks on regional and systemic food and drug safety;

2. Responsible for formulating the regulations on food administrative licensing and supervise their implementation; establishing food safety risk management mechanism, formulating annual plans for nation-wide inspection for food safety and programs for major control actions, and organizing their implementation; establishing the unified food safety information release system and releasing information on important food safety issues; participating in formulating food safety risk monitoring plans and food safety standards, and undertaking food safety risk monitoring thereon;
3. Responsible for organizing the formulation and publication of the national pharmacopeia, other drug and medical device standards and classification system, and supervising their implementation; developing good practices on research, production, distribution and use of drugs and medical devices, and supervising their implementation; undertaking drug and medical device registration, supervision and inspection; establishing monitoring system for adverse drug reactions, adverse events of medical devices, and undertaking monitoring and response activities; drawing up and improve regulations and qualifications for licensed pharmacists, guide and supervising the registration work; participating in formulating national essential medicine list and assisting its implementation; formulating administrative provisions for cosmetics administration and supervising their implementation;
4. Responsible for formulating the investigation and enforcement system for food, drugs, medical devices and cosmetics, and organizing their implementation; organizing the investigation and punishment on major violations; establishing recall and disposal system for defect products, and supervising the implementation;
5. Responsible for establishing food and drug emergency response system, organizing and guiding the emergency response and investigation on food and drug safety incident, and supervising the implementation of investigation and punishment;
6. Responsible for formulating science and technology development plans for food and drug safety, and organizing their implementation; accelerating the construction of food and drug testing system, electronic supervision tracking system, and information system;
7. Responsible for undertaking the public communication, education and training, and international exchanges and cooperation in the field of food and drug safety; promoting the establishment of credibility system;
8. Responsible for guiding food and drug administration works of local governments, regulate administrative activities, and improving the interlocking mechanism between administrative enforcement and criminal justice;

9. Responsible for undertaking the routine work of the Food Safety Commission of the State Council; taking charge of comprehensive coordination on food safety administration, facilitating and improve the cooperation and coordination mechanism; supervising the work of provincial people's governments on food safety administration, and evaluating their performance;
10. Responsible for undertaking other work assigned by the State Council and the Food Safety Commission of the State Council.

3.4.2 Structure

See Fig. 3.1 for the CFDA organization structure. http://eng.sfda.gov.cn/WS03/CL0756/

3.4.2.1 Major Divisions of the CFDA and Their Function

General Office

The General Office of the CFDA is responsible for routine operation of documentation and communication, meeting affairs, confidential work, archive management, superintendence, and government information disclosure, security and confidentiality affairs, as well as dealing with letters and calls, etc.

There are five divisions:

- Division of General Affairs
- Division of Secretariat I (Office of Duty)
- Division of Secretariat II
- Division of Documentation & Communication
- Division of Superintendence (Office of Letters and Calls)

Department of Legal Affairs

To organize the drafting of laws, regulations and provisions; to examine and verify the legality of normative documents; to undertake the administrative enforcement, administrative reconsideration, and administrative despondence, etc.

There are four divisions:

- Division of General Affairs
- Division of Regulations I
- Division of Regulations II
- Division of Enforcement Supervision (Office of Administrative Reconsideration)

Department of Food Safety Supervision II

To track and analyze food safety situation and existing problems at distribution and consumption stages, and to put forward recommendations on system, mechanism and performance improvement; to supervise the low-level administrative

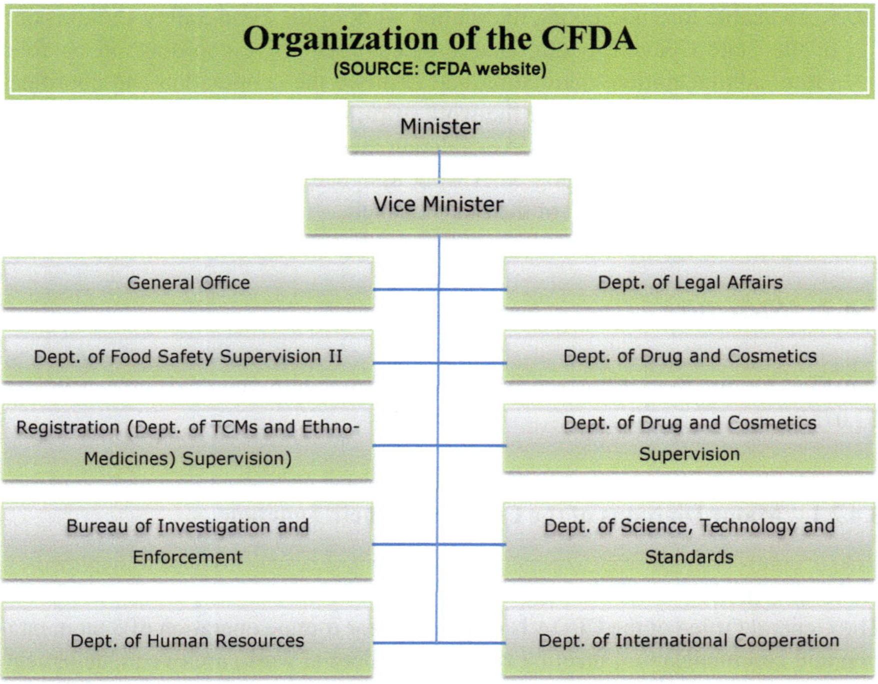

Fig. 3.1 Organization of the CFDA. (Source: the CFDA website modified)

departments in conducting administrative licensing by law, in performing the administrative duty, in detecting and rectifying illegal and improper acts in time.

There are five divisions:

- Division of General Affairs
- Division of Supervision I
- Division of Supervision II
- Division of Supervision III
- Division of Supervision IV

Department of Drug and Cosmetics Registration (Department of TCMs and Ethno-Medicines Supervision)

To conduct drug registration and issue administrative licenses for certain categories of cosmetics in strict accordance with the conditions and procedures prescribed by law, take the correspondent responsibilities, optimize registration and administrative licensing control procedures, supervise the implementation of good practices for drug non-clinical studies, drug clinical trials, and TCM preparation slices processing, and implement the TCM species protection system.

There are six divisions:

- Division of General Affairs
- Division of Traditional Chinese Medicines and Ethno-Medicines

- Division of Biological Products
- Division of Drug Research Supervision
- Division of Cosmetics

Department of Drug and Cosmetics Supervision
To track and analyze drug and cosmetics safety situation and existing problems, and to put forward recommendations on system, mechanism and performance improvement; to supervise the low-level administrative departments in conducting administrative licensing by law, in performing the administrative duty, in detecting and rectifying illegal and improper acts in time; to undertake supervision of radio-active drugs, narcotics, toxics and psychotropics, and pharmaceutical precursor chemicals, etc.; to organize and conduct adverse drug reaction monitoring and drug reevaluation.

There are six divisions:

- Division of General Affairs
- Division of Drug Manufacturing Supervision
- Division of Drug Distribution Supervision
- Division of Drug Monitoring and Re-evaluation
- Division of Controlled Drug Supervision
- Division of Cosmetics Supervision

Bureau of Investigation and Enforcement
To organize the investigation and punishment on major and serious cases pertaining to food and drug safety; guide and supervise investigation and enforcement of local governments, regulate administrative activities, and improve the interlocking mechanism between administrative enforcement and criminal justice; supervise recall and disposal for defect products; to guide the local governments in examining and approving advertisements for drugs, medical devices, and health food.

There are four divisions:

- Division of General Affairs
- Division of Investigation and Enforcement I
- Division of Investigation and Enforcement II
- Division of Investigation and Enforcement III

Department of Science, Technology and Standards
To organize and implement major science and technology programs for food and drug supervision, accelerate the construction of food and drug testing system, electronic supervision tracking system, and information system; to draft qualification requirements and testing norms governing food and drug testing institutions, and supervise their implementation; to organize the drafting of standards for drugs, medical devices, cosmetics, and catalogues, pharmaceutical use requirements, standards for immediate packaging materials and containers, and participate in the drafting of food safety standards.

There are four divisions:

- Division of General Affairs (Division of Informationalization)
- Division of Science and Technology

- Division of Standard Management
- Division of Testing Institutes Instruction

Department of Human Resources
To manage human resources, authorized institutional strength, capacity building and training of the head office and its affiliated institutions; draw up and improve regulations and qualifications for licensed pharmacists, guide and supervise the registration work.

There are four divisions:

- Division of General Affairs (Division of Personnel Supervision)
- Division of Personnel
- Division of Talents
- Division of Affiliated Institutions (Division of Compensation)

Department of International Cooperation
(Office of Hong Kong, Macao and Taiwan Affairs)

To organize and carry out international exchanges and cooperation, and exchanges and cooperation with Hong Kong, Macao, Taiwan in food and drug administration.

There are four divisions:

- Division of General Affairs
- Division of International Organizations
- Division of Bilateral Cooperation
- Division of Hong Kong, Macao and Taiwan Affairs

3.4.2.2 The Relationship Between Department of Drug and Cosmetics Registration and Technical Support Centers

Drug and cosmetics registration is one of the important responsibilities of the CFDA. For drug registration, the department of drug registration has the overall responsibilities. To conduct such duty, this department has to work with various technical support centers. The relationship of this department with other support centers is illustrated in Fig. 3.2.

3.4.2.3 Function of Technical Support Centers

Acceptance Center

Review all submission packages for fileability

- CPP/CMP
- POA/LOA
- GMP

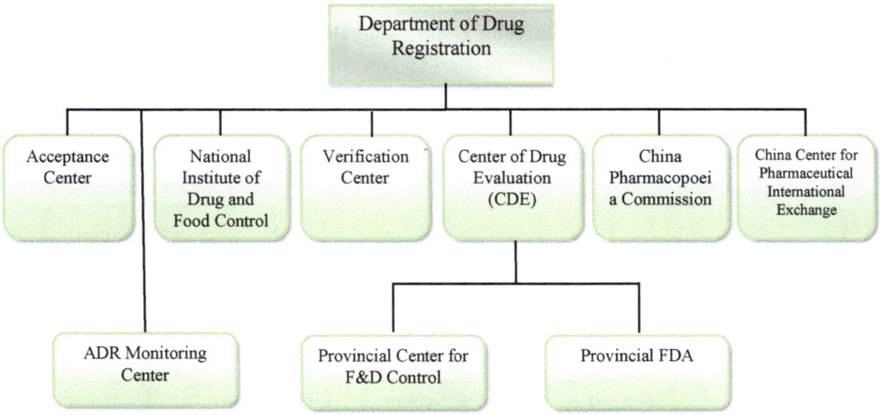

Fig. 3.2 Relationship of Department of Drug Registration and other support centers. (Source: The fifth China clinical trial outsourcing congress, March 4–5, 2013 (Salako 2013) modified)

- Patent statement
- TSE certificate
- Container statement
- Business license (local)

NOTE: Consistency of all information on the certificates against those on the application form; e.g. drug name should be consistent on all certificates, internal code vs. product name

Issues the approval letter and license to sponsor

The Center of Drug Evaluation (CDE)

For the CDE structure, please see Fig. 3.3. The functions of the CDE include technical review of CTA, NDA and various applications, providing review conclusion, approval of package insert and labeling, and collaboration on the SFDA projects and issuing guidance on drug registration etc., as listed below, see Fig. 3.3.

Technical Review

- CTA
- NDA
- Supplementary Application
- License renewal with supplementary application

Technical Approval

- Reviews conclusion
- Issues final Specification, Package Insert and Labeling

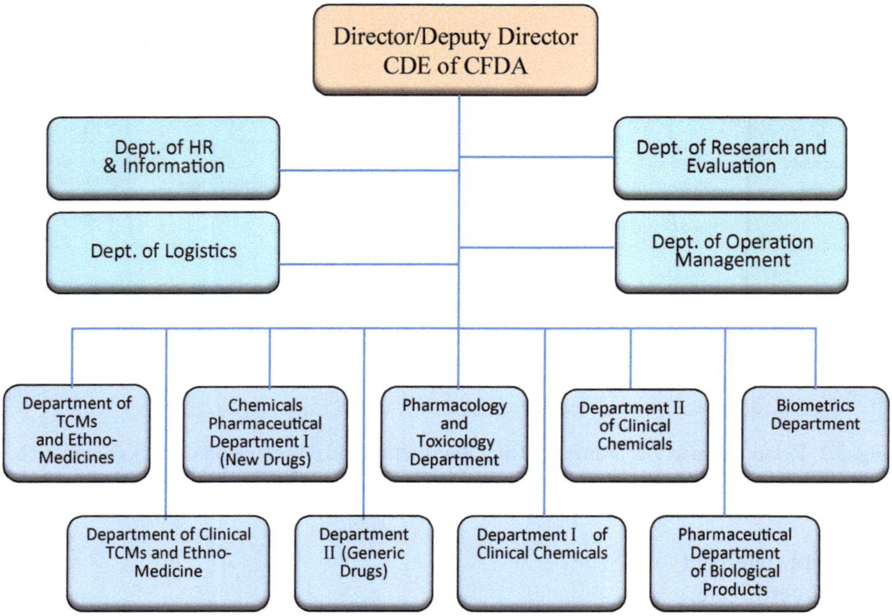

Fig. 3.3 The CDE's organizational chart. (Source: Modified based on SFDA (2012), China pharmaceutical newsletter, Vol. VIII, 2012)

Project Collaboration

- Issues technical guidelines on drug registration
- Collaborates on SFDA project

Offices of Clinical Evaluation

Through the institutional reform, the functions of the new formed offices are similar to FDA's evaluation system.

Office of Clinical Evaluation I

- Cancer
- Endocrine
- Respiration
- Psychosis

Office of Clinical Evaluation II

- Cardiovascular
- Antimicrobial
- Gastrointestinal
- Neurological

National Institute of Drug and Food Control (NIDFC)

Drug Testing

- Sample test for registration
- Creates the test reports and specifications
- Samples test for imported chemicals/biologicals
- Causal inspection in the market

Other Items for Testing at NIDFC

- Medical Devices
- Food
- Cosmetics

China Pharmacopoeia Commission (ChPC)

Establishes the Pharmacopoeia of the People's Republic of China
Issues and revises SFDA specification for local manufactured drugs
Approves the INN name of new drug

3.5 Difference of the China Pharmaceutical Regulatory Environment from Western Countries—The FDA

China has an extensive regulatory process for drug development. Therefore, there is a huge potential for significant drug lag. Part of the technical or logistic reasons could be the significantly smaller work force in the regulatory agencies compared to that of the western world. Up until 2013, the China FDA (CFDA), i.e. SFDA in the past, had about 120 employees to oversee drug review and registration and 500 inspectors at provincial level for onsite pre-approval inspections versus about 3000 US FDA employees in similar positions (Salako 2013). Regarding the pharmaceutical companies, the registered pharmaceutical companies in China are 4749 in 2008 versus 413 in the US.

For IND filing and approval, the CFDA must approve an IND before a trial can start and it takes 12–15 months; in the US, sponsors can start clinical trial 30 days after submitting an IND unless FDA objects. At the IND stage, CFDA requires extensive and validated CMC data for the active pharmaceutical ingredient just going into early phase clinical trial. In the US, such information could be fulfilled during the clinical development process before NDA filing.

There are about 550 CFDA approved clinical sites in China and a little more than 1000 research institutions registered for preclinical research. In order to conduct clinical trials, all the clinical sites have to be certified by the CFDA for specific therapeutic area (Salako 2013). This leads to intense competition among foreign and local companies for the best sites, especially in major cities like Beijing, Shanghai, Guanzhou and Nanjing.

3.6 The State Bases for Clinical Research of Pharmaceutics and Principle Investigators (PIs)

3.6.1 Introduction

Compared to the clinical trial unit in the West, a pharmaceutical clinical trial unit in China is called a clinical research base. As part of this base, the clinical trial units in China are quite different from the clinical sites in the western world. Those clinical trial units must be accredited by the China Food and Drug Administration (CFDA) to be qualified to conduct clinical trials (CFDA 2013).

As of December 2014, a total of 823 clinical trial units were listed as the qualified units according to the CFDA data query (Table 3.2). For each listed hospital, the date of expiry and certification are listed as well as the qualified medical specialties. Re-certifications are needed every 3 years. A total of 115 phase I units with 8–24 beds per unit are certified in China. About 20 centers focus on anticancer drug clinical phase II and III trials (Wei 2013). However, only a few centers are able to conduct all phases from I to III. Approximately 13,500 clinical investigators and their staffs were trained for GCP by 2013.

http://app1.sfda.gov.cn/datasearch/face3/base.jsp?tableId=19&tableName=TABLE19&title=%D2%A9%CE%EF%C1%D9%B4%B2%CA%D4%D1%E9%BB%FA%B9%B9%C3%FB%B5%A5&bcId=118714941832181502104731901420

3.6.2 The State Bases for Clinical Research of Pharmaceutics

The information in the following tables (Tables 3.2 and 3.3) is collected from the China Food and Drug Administration website, *China Pharmaceutical Newsletter* and various publications (CFDA 2013). The numbers are increasing annually. The certification status of the sites may change as time goes on.

3.6.3 The Certified Investigators and Clinical Sites

As of 2013, there was an estimated total of 1600 investigators at over 600 sites. However, this is only a fraction of 10,550 investigators and 2103 sites that have contributable clinical trial history in China (Thoelke 2013).

Table 3.2 The state pharmaceutical clinical research base

Medical institutions	Certificate no	Accredited specialties
Peking University First Hospital	417	Immunization, pediatric intensive care medicine, medical imaging (cure), orthopedics
Pingxiang City People's Hospital	418	Pingxiang City People's Hospital
First Affiliated Hospital of Kunming	419	Tumors, endocrine, rheumatology, ENT, blood
Nantong Cancer Hospital	420	Tumor
Second Affiliated Hospital of Anhui Medical University	421	Cancer, kidney disease, infection, respiratory
Jiangxi Cancer Hospital (Second People's Hospital of Jiangxi Province)	422	Blood, orthopedics, gynecology, oncology, medical imaging (radiation therapy, nuclear medicine), TCM oncology
Dongzhimen Hospital, Beijing University of Chinese Medicine	423	TCM Cardiovascular medicine, TCM neurology, TCM respiratory medicine, TCM digestive medicine, TCM kidney diseases, TCM gynecology, TCM pediatric medicine, endocrine (breast), TCM surgery, infection, TCM geriatric medicine, TCM endocrine, TCM oncology, TCM anorectal medicine, TCM peripheral vascular medicine, TCM skin medicine, TCM Orthopedic medicine, TCM ENT, TCM ophthalmology
Cancer Center of Guangzhou Medical University	424	Tumor
Henan Tumor Hospital	425	Blood, tumor
People's Hospital of Xinjiang Uygur Autonomous Region	426	Cardiovascular (hypertension), immune, digestive, skin, oncology, endocrine
Zhongshan Hospital of Hubei Province	427	Infection, neurology, digestive
Affiliated Hospital of Binzhou Medical College	428	Respiratory, digestive, endocrine, oncology, general surgery (gastrointestinal)
Zhejiang Hospital	429	Intensive care medicine, respiratory, geriatric (elderly cardiovascular, urinary elderly, senile endocrinology)
Xinhua Hospital Affiliated to Shanghai Jiao Tong University School of Medicine	430	Cardiovascular, respiratory, ophthalmology, otolaryngology, endocrine, digestive, hematology, urinary, pediatric hematology, pediatric kidney disease, pediatric endocrinology, pediatric neurology, pediatric cardiology, ultrasound diagnosis
Shenzhen Second People's Hospital	431	Blood, endocrine, nephrology, respiratory, orthopedics, neurosurgery, urology, general surgery (thyroid and breast, liver and gallbladder), burns, chest surgery, integrative medicine, intensive care medicine
Second Hospital of Jilin University	432	Digestive, neurology, blood, cancer, ophthalmology, general surgery
The Second Hospital of Shandong University	XF20120139	Cardiovascular, hematology, respiratory, neurology, neurosurgery, orthopedics, urology, ophthalmology

Table 3.2 (continued)

Medical institutions	Certificate no	Accredited specialties
First People's Hospital of Changzhou	XF20120140	Digestive, hematology, oncology, cardiovascular, respiratory, nephrology, urology, cardiothoracic surgery, neurosurgery, orthopedics
The People's Hospital of Guangxi Zhuang Autonomous Region	XF20120141	Cardiovascular, endocrinology, respiratory, hematology, digestive, nephrology, neurology, otolaryngology, obstetrics and gynecology, cardiothoracic surgery, general surgery, urology
Academy of Military Medical Sciences Affiliated Hospital	XF20120142	Anti-radiation, antitoxic, detoxification, hematology, oncology
First Hospital of Shanxi Medical University	XZF20120143	Respiratory, digestive, endocrinology, hematology, rheumatology and immunology, neurology, dermatology, otolaryngology, medical imaging (nuclear medicine), traditional Chinese medicine (digestive), mental health, infection
The First Affiliated Hospital of Henan University of TCM	ZF20120144	Chinese medicine for cardiovascular, Chinese medicine for digestive, Chinese medicine for pediatrics, Chinese medicine for anorectal, Chinese medicine for nephrology, Chinese medicine for peripheral angiopathy, Chinese medicine for respiratory, Chinese medicine for neurology, Chinese medicine for dermatology, Chinese medicine for gynecology, Chinese medicine for orthopedics and traumatology, Chinese medicine for endocrinology, Chinese medicine for oncology, Chinese medicine for rheumatology and immunology
The Military General Hospital of Beijing PLA	XZF20120145	Chinese medicine for cardiovascular, pediatric oncology, anesthesiology, general surgery, oncology, cardiovascular, endocrinology, dermatology, hematology, immunology, neurology, traumatology, urology, respiratory, obstetrics and gynecology, otolaryngology, nephrology, medical imaging (diagnosis), digestive
Haikou People's Hospital	XF20120146	General surgery, neurology, neurosurgery, cardiovascular, urology
Gansu Tumor Hospital	XF20120147	Oncology
Stomatology Hospital of the Fourth Military Medical University	XF20120148	Stomatology
Shanghai Municipal Hospital of Traditional Chinese Medicine	ZF20120149	Chinese medicine for oncology, Chinese medicine for digestive, Chinese medicine for cardiovascular, Chinese medicine for orthopedics and traumatology, Chinese medicine for anorectal, Chinese medicine for respiratory, Chinese medicine for hematology

Table 3.2 (continued)

Medical institutions	Certificate no	Accredited specialties
Affiliated Hospital of Guiyang Medical College	XF20120150	Infectious diseases, dermatology, general surgery, endocrinology
Anhui Provincial Hospital	XZF20120151	Rheumatology, endocrinology, respiratory, Chinese medicine for oncology
The Second Hospital of Nanjing	XF20120152	Liver, infection
General Hospital of Ningxia Medical University	XF20120153	Respiratory, cardiovascular, digestive, oncology
Hengshui People's Hospital (Harrison International Peace Hospital)	XF20120154	Cardiovascular, neurology
First Hospital of Xi'an Jiao-tong University	XF20120155	Cardiovascular, respiratory, oncology, psychiatry, neurology, general surgery, infection, hematology, obstetrics and gynecology, nephrology, dermatology, endocrinology
Affiliated Hospital of Jiangsu University	XF20120156	Cardiovascular, endocrinology, digestive, oncology, burns
The First Affiliated Hospital, Sun Yat-sen University	XF20120157	Cardiovascular, hematology, digestive, burns, cardiovascular surgery, anesthesiology, orthopedics, endocrinology, nephrology, neurology, respiratory
Beijing Shijitan Hospital, CMU	XF20120158	Oncology, cardiovascular, respiratory, neurology, obstetrics and gynecology, general surgery
The Second Hospital of Third Military Medical University	XF20120159	Respiratory, cardiovascular, oncology, digestive, nephrology, neurology, hematology, anesthesiology, dermatology, urology
Beijing Ditan Hospital Capital Medical University	XF20120160	Liver, AIDS
The Second Hospital of Zhejiang University School of Medicine	XF20120161	Cardiovascular, respiratory, oncology, neurology, digestive, hematology, endocrinology, rheumatology, psychiatry, dermatology, ophthalmology, urology, anesthesiology
Sun Yat-Sen Memorial Hospital, Sun Yat-Sen University	XF20120162	Cardiovascular, endocrinology, digestive, dermatology, obstetrics and gynecology, orthopedics, respiratory, neurology, medical imaging (diagnosis)
China-Japan Friendship Hospital	XF20120163	Oncology, cardiovascular, endocrinology, respiratory, immunology, nephrology, obstetrics and gynecology
The First Hospital of Jilin University	XF20120164	Neurology, digestive, oncology, infection, orthopedics, cardiovascular, urology, obstetrics and gynecology, nephrology, cardiovascular surgery, ophthalmology, pediatric respiratory, pediatric neurology, pediatric digestive, pediatric cardiovascular
Orient Liver-Gallbladder Surgery Hospital	XF20120165	General surgery, digestive, medical imaging (diagnosis)

Table 3.2 (continued)

Medical institutions	Certificate no	Accredited specialties
Zhongshan Hospital Fudan University	XZF20120166	General surgery, orthopedics, thoracic surgery, Chinese medicine for neurology, neurology, immunology, ophthalmology, cardiovascular, respiratory, digestive, nephrology, endocrinology, hematology, dermatology, medical imaging (diagnosis, treatment), anesthesiology
Traditional Chinese Medicine Hospital of Xinjiang Uygur Autonomous Region	ZF20120167	Chinese medicine for cardiovascular, Chinese medicine for neurology, Chinese medicine for nephrology, Chinese medicine for orthopedics and traumatology, Chinese medicine for gynecology, Chinese medicine for pediatrics, Chinese medicine for oncology, Chinese medicine for digestive, Chinese medicine for respiratory, Chinese medicine for endocrinology, Chinese medicine for rheumatology, general surgery, Chinese medicine for dermatology
West China Hospital, Sichuan University	XZF20120168	Cardiovascular, respiratory, digestive, endocrinology, hematology, dermatology, neurology, oncology, infection, psychiatry, detoxification, Chinese medicine for respiratory, Chinese medicine for digestive, immunology, otolaryngology, anesthesiology, general surgery (hepatobiliary, ophthalmology, nephrology, medical imaging (nuclear medicine), orthopedics, Chinese medicine for oncology, Chinese medicine for encephalopathy
Guangdong General Hospital	XF20120169	Cardiovascular, oncology, dermatology, rheumatology and immunology, respiratory, endocrinology, hematology, burns, nephrology, medical imaging (diagnosis)
Xin Hua Hospital Affiliated to Shanghai Jiao Tong University School of Medicine	XF20120170	Pediatric respiratory, pediatric general surgery, oncology, nephrology, general surgery, dermatology
Yue Bei People's Hospital	XF20120171	Cardiovascular, oncology
Shanghai Shuguang Hospital	ZF20120172	Chinese medicine for liver, Chinese medicine for orthopedics and traumatology, Chinese medicine for nephrology, Chinese medicine for cardiovascular, Chinese medicine for endocrinology, Chinese medicine for neurology, Chinese medicine for oncology, Chinese medicine for digestive, Chinese medicine for respiratory, Chinese medicine for surgery, Chinese medicine for gynecology, Chinese medicine for anorectal

Table 3.2 (continued)

Medical institutions	Certificate no	Accredited specialties
Beijing Hospital of Traditional Chinese Medicine	ZF20120173	Chinese medicine for cardiovascular, Chinese medicine for respiratory, Chinese medicine for digestive, Chinese medicine for nephrology, Chinese medicine for oncology, Chinese medicine for dermatology, Chinese medicine for cerebrovascular disease, Chinese medicine for cerebrovascular disease, Chinese medicine for surgery, Chinese medicine for gynecology, Chinese medicine for anorectal, Chinese medicine for orthopedics
Ruikang Hospital Affiliated to Guangxi University of Chinese Medicine	ZF20120174	Chinese medicine for neurology, Chinese medicine for nephrology, Chinese medicine for respiratory, Chinese medicine for orthopedics, Chinese medicine for digestive, Chinese medicine for endocrinology, Chinese medicine for cardiovascular, Chinese medicine for oncology, Chinese medicine for obstetrics and gynecology
Longhua Hospital Shanghai University of TCM	ZF20120175	Chinese medicine for oncology, Chinese medicine for surgery, Chinese medicine for urology, Chinese medicine for rheumatology, Chinese medicine for anorectal, Chinese medicine for orthopedics and traumatology, Chinese medicine for respiratory, Chinese medicine for neurology, Chinese medicine for nephrology, Chinese medicine for endocrinology (Chinese medicine for diabetes mellitus), Chinese medicine for digestive, Chinese medicine for cardiovascular
Fujian Medical University Union Hospital	XF20120176	Urology, cardiovascular, otolaryngology, oncology, hematology, digestive, endocrinology, orthopedics
Huashan Hospital Fudan University	XF20120177	Infection, cardiovascular, endocrinology, hematology, neurology, neurosurgery, dermatology, urology, medical imaging (diagnosis, treatment, nuclear medicine), general surgery
Beijing Friendship Hospital, Capital Medical University	XF20120178	Respiratory, obstetrics and gynecology, ophthalmology, dermatology, anesthesiology, digestive, cardiovascular, neurology, nephrology, urology, parenteral nutrition, oncology, orthopedics, tropical diseases, hematology
Beijing Hospital	XZF20120179	Oncology, respiratory, cardiovascular, endocrinology, hematology, neurology, obstetrics and gynecology, orthopedics, urology, dermatology, digestive, medical imaging (diagnosis, treatment), Chinese medicine for diabetes mellitus

Table 3.2 (continued)

Medical institutions	Certificate no	Accredited specialties
Hunan Provincial People's Hospital	XF20120180	General surgery, hepatobiliary surgery, orthopedics, urology, otolaryngology head and neck surgery, cardiovascular, digestive, respiratory, neurology, nephrology, pediatric respiratory, obstetrics and gynecology
The First Teaching Hospital Of Xinjiang Medical University	XF20120181	Cardiovascular, liver, gynecology, digestive, respiratory, dermatology, orthopedics, general surgery
The Central Hospital of China Aerospace Corporation	XF20120182	Cardiovascular, digestive, respiratory, nephrology, neurology
Wuxi People's Hospital	XF20120183	Respiratory, digestive, cardiovascular, hematology, nephrology, endocrinology, general surgery, orthopedics, urology, pediatric respiratory, pediatric nephrology
The First Affiliated Hospital of Chongqing Medical University	XF20120184	Infection, respiratory, neurology, endocrinology, otolaryngology, digestive, obstetrics and gynecology, liver
The Third Hospital of Hebei Medical University	XF20120185	Orthopedics, endocrinology, liver, neurology, obstetrics and gynecology, nephrology
The Second Hospital of Shanxi Medical University	XF20120186	Cardiovascular, respiratory, hematology, nephrology, neurology, orthopedics, urology, general surgery, obstetrics and gynecology, otolaryngology, anesthesiology
Guangzhou Red Cross Hospital	XF20120187	Cardiovascular, endocrinology, digestive, respiratory, burns
Hainan Hospital of Traditional Chinese Medicine	ZF20120188	Chinese medicine for cerebrovascular disease, Chinese medicine for urology, Chinese medicine for orthopedics and traumatology
Yunnan Tumor Hospital (The Third Hospital of Kunming Medical University)	XF20120189	Cancer
Tongji Medical College Reproductive Medicine Center	XF20120190	Reproductive health and infertility
The Fifth Affiliated Hospital, Sun Yat-Sen University	XF20120191	Nephrology, cancer
Subei People's Hospital	XF20120192	Respiratory, digestive, cardiovascular, endocrinology, neurology, hematology, orthopedics, gynecology, cancer
The Third Affiliated Hospital, Sun Yat-Sen University	XF20120193	Infection, rheumatology and immunology, respiratory, obstetrics and gynecology, neurology, endocrinology, psychiatry, dermatology
Sun Yat-Sen University Cancer Center	XF20120194	Cancer
The First Affiliated Hospital of Dalian Medical University	XF20120195	Cancer, cardiovascular, nephrology, endocrinology, urology, obstetrics and gynecology, dermatology

Table 3.2 (continued)

Medical institutions	Certificate no	Accredited specialties
Xuanwu Hospital Capital Medical University	XF20120196	Hematology, obstetrics and gynecology, ophthalmology, pain, neurology, dermatology, cardiovascular, digestive, vascular surgery, neurosurgery
Ruijin Hospital, Shanghai Jiao Tong University	XF20120197	Digestive, cardiovascular, endocrinology, hematology, burns, orthopedics, medical imaging (diagnosis, treatment, nuclear medicine), respiratory, infection (liver), nephrology, neurology, urology, dermatology, cancer, obstetrics and gynecology, anesthesiology
Taihe Hospital (Affiliated Hospital of Hubei University Of Medicine)	XF20120198	Stomatology, endocrinology, neurology, digestive, cardiovascular, cancer
Baiqiuen International Peace Hospital	XF20120199	Cardiovascular, digestive, nephrology, cancer, endocrinology
Jingzhou Central Hospital	XF20120200	Infection, digestive, neurology, cardiovascular, cancer
Xiangya Hospital Central South University	XZF20120201	Infection (liver), digestive, respiratory, hematology, rheumatology, nephrology, general surgery, otolaryngology, burns, anesthesiology, ophthalmology, cancer, cardiothoracic surgery, dermatology, orthopedics, Chinese medicine for neurology, Chinese medicine for digestive, Chinese medicine for rheumatology and immunology
The Second Affiliated Hospital to Nanchang University	XF20120083	Cardiovascular, hematology, neurology, cancer, respiratory, digestive, obstetrics and gynecology, nephrology, endocrinology
Xi'an Mental Health Center	XF20120084	Psychiatry
The First Affiliated Hospital of Guangzhou Medical University	XF20120085	Respiratory
Hospital of Stomatology Wuhan University	XF20120086	Stomatology
Zhejiang Hospital	XF20120087	Cardiovascular, cancer, digestive, neurology, endocrinology
First Affiliated Hospital of Kunming Medical University	XZF20120088	Psychiatry, neurology, liver, digestive, cardiovascular, respiratory, orthopedics, dermatology, Chinese medicine for rheumatology
Beijing Children's Hospital	XZF20120089	Pediatric endocrinology, pediatric nephrology, pediatric cardiovascular, pediatric respiratory, Chinese medicine for pediatrics, pediatric hematology, pediatric neurology, dermatology
The First Affiliated Hospital of Guangxi Medical University	XF20120090	Cardiovascular, endocrinology, digestive, hematology, dermatology, otolaryngology, infection, neurology, nephrology, burns, respiratory, orthopedics, urology, ophthalmology
Tianjin Nankai Hospital	XF20120091	General surgery

Table 3.2 (continued)

Medical institutions	Certificate no	Accredited specialties
Hebei Hospital of Traditional Chinese Medicine	ZF20120092	Chinese medicine for digestive, Chinese medicine for nephrology, Chinese medicine for anorectal, Chinese medicine for orthopedics and traumatology
Daqing Oilfield General Hospital	XF20120093	Respiratory, digestive, cardiovascular
Fuzhou General Hospital of Nanjing Military Command	XF20120094	Respiratory, cardiovascular, nephrology, endocrinology, cancer, general surgery, urology
West China Second University Hospital	XF20120095	Obstetrics and gynecology
Baotou Central Hospital	XF20120096	Neurology, cardiovascular, respiratory, digestive, general surgery
Jiangxi Hospital of Traditional Chinese And Western Medicine	ZF20120097	Chinese medicine for respiratory, Chinese medicine for cardiovascular, Chinese medicine for cancer, Chinese medicine for obstetrics and gynecology, Chinese medicine for encephalopathy, Chinese medicine for orthopedics and traumatology, Chinese medicine for urology
Beijing Chest Hospital, Capital Medical University	XF20120098	Tuberculosis, cancer
Nanjing Drum Tower Hospital The Affiliated Hospital of Nanjing University Medical School	XF20120099	Obstetrics and gynecology, cardiovascular, respiratory, cancer, neurology, digestive, endocrinology, general surgery, urology
Tangdu Hospital, The Fourth Military Medical University	XF20120100	Infection, digestive, respiratory, hematology, neurology, cancer, neurosurgery, thoracic surgery, general surgery
The Second Hospital of Haerbin Medical University	XF20120101	Cardiovascular, neurology, immunology, respiratory, endocrinology, hematology, infection, digestive, cardiovascular surgery, dermatology, ophthalmology
The First Affiliated Hospital of Liaoning University of Traditional Chinese Medicine	ZF20120102	Chinese medicine for hematology, Chinese medicine for liver, Chinese medicine for nephrology, Chinese medicine for surgery, Chinese medicine for orthopedics, Chinese medicine for obstetrics and gynecology, Chinese medicine for neurology, Chinese medicine for digestive, Chinese medicine for cancer, Chinese medicine for endocrinology, Chinese medicine for respiratory, Chinese medicine for cardiovascular, Chinese medicine for rheumatology, Chinese medical for otolaryngology, Chinese medicine for pediatrics, Chinese medicine for anorectal, Chinese medicine for geriatrics senile dementia)
Beijing Anzhen Hospital, Capital Medical University	XF20120103	Cardiovascular, cardiothoracic surgery, respiratory, anesthesiology, neurology, general surgery, urology, medical imaging (nuclear medicine)

Table 3.2 (continued)

Medical institutions	Certificate no	Accredited specialties
Guizhou Province Hospital of Traditional Chinese Medicine	ZF20120104	Chinese medicine for cardiovascular, Chinese medicine for orthopedics and traumatology, Chinese medicine for anorectal, Chinese medicine for endocrinology
Guangzhou Hospital of Traditional Chinese Medicine	ZF20120105	Chinese medicine for cancer, Chinese medicine for cardiovascular, Chinese medicine for neurology, Chinese medicine for digestive, Chinese medicine for orthopedics
The Second Hospital of Wenzhou Medical University	XZF20120106	Orthopedics, anesthesiology, obstetrics and gynecology, cardiovascular, respiratory, digestive, pediatric respiratory, Chinese medicine for anorectal
Zhongda Hospital Southeast University	XF20120107	Cardiovascular, respiratory, digestive, hematology, nephrology, obstetrics and gynecology, neurology, orthopedics, medical imaging (diagnosis, treatment)
The Second Affiliated Hospital of Shantou University Medical College	XF20120108	Orthopedics, endocrinology, obstetrics and gynecology, urology
Peking University School of Stomatology	XF20120109	Stomatology
Nanjing Brain Hospital	XF20120110	Neurology, psychiatry
Hebei General Hospital	XZF20120111	Cardiovascular, respiratory, digestive, endocrinology, neurology, thoracic surgery, hematology, obstetrics and gynecology, immunology, orthopedics, anesthesiology, general surgery, Chinese medicine for cerebrovascular disease, otolaryngology
Jiangsu Cancer Hospital	XF20120112	Cancer
The Second Affiliated Hospital of Guangzhou Medical University	XF20120113	Neurology, cardiovascular, rheumatology and immunology, anesthesiology, medical imaging (diagnosis)
Eye & ENT Hospital of Fudan University	XF20120114	Ophthalmology, otolaryngology
Luoyang Orthopedic-Traumatological Hospital	ZF20120115	Chinese medicine for orthopedics, Chinese medicine for rheumatology
The Affiliated Hospital of Hunan Traditional Chinese Medicine Institute	ZF20120116	Chinese medicine for cancer, Chinese medicine for liver, Chinese medicine for cardiovascular, Chinese medicine for cerebrovascular disease, Chinese medicine for nephrology
Cancer Hospital of Shantou University Medical College	XF20120117	Cancer
Dermatology Hospital of Chinese Academy of Medical Sciences	XF20120118	Dermatology
Hebei Mental Health Center	XF20120119	Psychiatry
Affiliated Hospital of Guilin Medical University	XF20120120	Hepatobiliary surgery, respiratory, nephrology, neurology, digestive

Table 3.2 (continued)

Medical institutions	Certificate no	Accredited specialties
Liaoning People's Hospital	XF20120121	Cardiovascular, dermatology
Shandong Cancer Hospital	XF20120122	Cancer
Henan Ophthalmology Center	XF20120123	Ophthalmology
Hematology Hospital of Chinese Academy of Medical Sciences	XF20120124	Hematology
The First Affiliated Hospital of Chinese PLA General Hospital	XF20120125	Respiratory, burns and plastic surgery, orthopedics
General Hospital of Guang-zhou Military Command of PLA	XF20120126	Cardiovascular, digestive, respiratory, neu-rology, cancer, hematology, anesthesiology, dermatology
Suzhou Hospital of Traditional Chinese Medicine	ZF20120127	Chinese medicine for orthopedics and traumatology
The Eye Hospital of Wenzhou Medical University	XF20120128	Ophthalmology
Guangxing Hospital Affiliated to Zhejiang Traditional Chi-nese Medicine University	ZF20120129	Chinese medicine for cardiovascular, Chinese medicine for nephrology, Chinese medicine for gynecology, Chinese medicine for pediatrics
The Second Hospital of Jilin University	XF20120130	Dermatology, obstetrics and gynecology, respiratory, nephrology, endocrinology, cardiovascular
The Second Hospital of Dalian Medical University	XF20120131	Cancer, cardiovascular, respiratory, diges-tive, neurology, endocrinology, nephrology, ophthalmology, urology, general surgery, dermatology
The First Affiliated Hospital of Wenzhou Medical University	XF20120132	Neurology, cardiovascular, digestive, hematology, infection (liver), endocrinol-ogy, stomatology, general surgery, urology, orthopedics
Beijing You An Hospital, Capi-tal Medical University	XZF20120133	Liver, AIDS, Chinese medicine for liver
Shanghai Changhai Hospital	XF20120134	Digestive, hematology, cancer, respiratory, cardiovascular, rheumatology, otolaryngol-ogy, general surgery, urology, dermatology and venereology, anesthesiology, medical imaging (diagnosis, nuclear medicine)
302 Military Hospital of China	XF20120135	Digestive, liver, infection, AIDS
NO. 3 People Hospital Affili-ated to Shanghai Jiao Tong University School of Medicine	XF20120136	Infection (liver), cancer, general surgery
General Hospital of Shenyang Military Command	XZF20120137	Cardiovascular, digestive, nephrology, can-cer, neurology, respiratory, anesthesia and analgesia, dermatology and venereology, ophthalmology, general surgery, urology, Chinese medicine for digestive,
The First Hospital of Harbin Medical University	XF20120138	Cardiovascular, respiratory, neurology, digestive, hematology, rheumatology and immunology, infection, endocrinology, psychiatry

Table 3.2 (continued)

Medical institutions	Certificate no	Accredited specialties
The Second Hospital of Suzhou University	XF20120001	Neurology, cardiovascular, endocrinology, respiratory, digestive, orthopedics, urology, general surgery, hematology, cancer, medical imaging (nuclear medicine)
The First Affiliated Hospital of Soochow University	XF20120002	Cardiovascular, neurology, infection (liver), cancer, obstetrics and gynecology, hematology, digestive, respiratory, rheumatology, anesthesiology, neurosurgery, dermatology, ophthalmology, urology, orthopedics, general surgery, medical imaging (diagnosis, treatment, nuclear medicine)
Affiliated Hospital of Hainan Medical University	XF20120003	Respiratory, cardiovascular, neurology, obstetrics and gynecology, urology
Qingdao Ophthalmology Hospital	XF20120004	Ophthalmology
Nanjing Hospital of Traditional Chinese Medicine	ZF20120005	Chinese medicine for anorectal, Chinese medicine for gynecology, Chinese medicine for orthopedics and traumatology, Chinese medicine for cerebrovascular disease, Chinese medicine for cardiovascular, Chinese medicine for digestive
Shanghai NO. 6 People's Hospital	ZXF20120006	Endocrinology, cardiovascular, respiratory, digestive, orthopedics, nephrology, hematology, cancer, infection, anesthesiology, general surgery, Chinese medicine for encephalopathy, medical imaging (diagnosis)
Zhujiang Hospital of Southern Medical University	ZXF20120007	Cancer, cardiovascular, neurosurgery, Chinese medicine for nephrology
Tongji Hospital, Tongji University	XF20120008	Psychiatry, cardiovascular, neurology, digestive, endocrinology, orthopedics, otolaryngology
Jiangsu Province Hospital of Traditional Chinese Medicine	ZF20120009	Chinese medicine for pediatrics, Chinese medicine for digestive, Chinese medicine for respiratory, Chinese medicine for otolaryngology, Chinese medicine for endocrinology, Chinese medicine for rheumatology, Chinese medicine for geriatrics (senile dementia, senile sequelae of cerebral infarction), Chinese medicine for cardiovascular, Chinese medicine for cancer, Chinese medicine for neurology, Chinese medicine for hematology, Chinese medicine for surgery, Chinese medicine for dermatology, Chinese medicine for ophthalmology, Chinese medicine for gynecology, Chinese medicine for orthopedics and traumatology, Chinese medicine for anorectal, Chinese medicine for andrology

Table 3.2 (continued)

Medical institutions	Certificate no	Accredited specialties
Gansu Provincial University	XF20120010	Respiratory, digestive, cardiovascular
The Second Affiliated Hospital of Chongqing Medical University	XF20120011	Liver, digestive, obstetrics and gynecology, nephrology, neurology, cardiovascular, endocrinology, general surgery, urology
Shaanxi Cancer Hospital	XF20120012	Cancer
Guangdong Second Traditional Chinese Medicine Hospital	ZF20120013	Chinese medicine for cardiovascular, Chinese medicine for neurology, Chinese medicine for digestive, Chinese medicine for orthopedics and traumatology
Shanghai Xuhui District Central Hospital	ZXF20120014	Cardiovascular, urology, Chinese medicine for cerebrovascular disease
Shanghai Pulmonary Hospital	ZXF20120015	Cancer, tuberculosis, respiratory, Chinese medicine for cancer
Hainan General Hospital	XF20120016	Respiratory, digestive, cardiovascular, endocrinology, liver
Wuhan General Hospital of Guangzhou Military	XF20120017	Neurology, respiratory, cardiovascular, digestive, cancer
Sir Run Run Shaw Hospital School of Medicine Zhejiang University	XF20120018	Respiratory, cardiovascular, neurology, digestive, cancer, medical imaging (diagnosis)
Dongfang Hospital, Beijing University of Chinese Medicine	ZF20120019	Chinese medicine for respiratory, Chinese medicine for cardiovascular, Chinese medicine for neurology, Chinese medicine for endocrinology, Chinese medicine for digestive, Chinese medicine for cancer, Chinese medicine for surgery, Chinese medicine for obstetrics and gynecology, Chinese medicine for ophthalmology, Chinese medical for otolaryngology, Chinese medicine for dermatology
Second Artillery General Hospital of PLA	XF20120020	Respiratory, endocrinology, cardiovascular, neurology
General Hospital of Beijing Military Command	XF20120021	Digestive, neurology, liver, endocrinology, cancer, cardiovascular, respiratory, orthopedics
201 Military Hospital of China	ZXF20120022	Digestive, cardiovascular, Chinese medicine for hematology
Fudan University Shanghai Cancer Center	XF20120023	Cancer, medical imaging (diagnosis), medical imaging (nuclear medicine)
401 Military Hospital of Jinan Military Command	XF20120024	Traumatology
306 Military Hospital of China	XF20120025	Endocrinology, cardiovascular, orthopedics, stomatology
The Inner Mongolia Autonomous Region Sino-Mongolian Medicine Hospital	ZF20120026	National medicine for cardiovascular (Mongolian medicine), national medicine for cerebrovascular diseases (Mongolian medicine), national medicine for hematology (Mongolian medicine), Chinese medicine for cardiovascular

Table 3.2 (continued)

Medical institutions	Certificate no	Accredited specialties
Guangzhou First People's Hospital	XF20120027	Digestive, respiratory, cardiovascular, nephrology, hematology, neurology, obstetrics and gynecology, anesthesiology, dermatology, burns, orthopedics, urology
Nan Fang Hospital of Southern Medical University	ZXF20120028	Digestive, nephrology, hematology, infection, cancer, cardiovascular, endocrinology, respiratory, Chinese medicine for nephrology, rheumatology, Chinese medicine for cerebrovascular diseases, Chinese medicine for cardiovascular, medical imaging (diagnosis)
Affiliated Hospital of Nantong University	XF20120029	Digestive, hematology, cardiovascular, nephrology, obstetrics and gynecology, respiratory, cancer, neurology, infection (liver), dermatology, ophthalmology, orthopedics
Union Hospital Tongji Medical College Huazhong University of Science And Technology	ZXF20120030	Respiratory, digestive, cardiovascular, hematology, infection, dermatology, orthopedics, anesthesiology, general surgery, otolaryngology, neurology, endocrinology, cancer, obstetrics and gynecology, ophthalmology, stomatology, rheumatology, nephrology, Chinese medicine for orthopedics and traumatology
Sichuan Academy of Medical Sciences & Sichuan Provincial People's Hospital	ZXF20120031	Neurology, cardiovascular, digestive, dermatology, obstetrics and gynecology, infection, cancer, endocrinology, nephrology, Chinese medicine for orthopedics and traumatology
The Second Affiliated Hospital of Kunming Medical University	XF20120032	Neurology, digestive, endocrinology, cardiovascular, respiratory, hematology, obstetrics and gynecology, pediatric respiratory, burns, dermatology
85 Hospital of People's Liberation Army	XF20120033	Liver
The First Affiliated Hospital of Guangxi University of Chinese Medicine	ZF20120034	Chinese medicine for orthopedics and traumatology, Chinese medicine for obstetrics and gynecology, Chinese medicine for anorectal, Chinese medicine for cardiovascular, Chinese medicine for neurology, Chinese medicine for endocrinology, Chinese medicine for cancer, Chinese medicine for digestive, Chinese medicine for nephrology
Jinan Infectious Disease Hospital	XF20120035	Liver

Table 3.2 (continued)

Medical institutions	Certificate no	Accredited specialties
Hubei Provincial Hospital of Traditional Chinese Medicine	ZF20120036	Chinese medicine for cardiovascular, Chinese medicine for cerebrovascular disease, Chinese medicine for liver, Chinese medicine for stomatology, Chinese medicine for respiratory, Chinese medicine for obstetrics and gynecology, Chinese medicine for pediatrics, Chinese medicine for surgery (hepatobiliary), Chinese medicine for orthopedics and traumatology, Chinese medicine for rheumatology, Chinese medicine for nephrology
Shantou Central Hospital	XF20120037	Cardiovascular, cancer
The First Affiliated Hospital of Shantou University School of Medicine	XF20120038	Cancer, respiratory, rheumatology, general surgery
The First Affiliated Hospital of Guangzhou Chinese Medicine University	ZF20120039	Chinese medicine for orthopedics and traumatology, Chinese medicine for digestive, Chinese medicine for surgery, Chinese medicine for anorectal, Chinese medicine for gynecology, Chinese medicine for ophthalmology, Chinese medicine for cancer, Chinese medicine for cardiovascular, Chinese medicine for respiratory, Chinese medicine for nephrology, Chinese medical for otolaryngology, Chinese medicine for neurology
The Third Affiliated Hospital of Third Military Medical University	XF20120040	Otolaryngology, traumatology, respiratory, obstetrics and gynecology, cardiovascular, ophthalmology, neurology, cancer, digestive,
Tongde Hospital of Zhejiang Province	ZF20120041	Chinese medicine for cancer, Chinese medicine for digestive, Chinese medicine for nephrology, Chinese medicine for orthopedics and traumatology
Affiliated Hospital of Inner Mongolia University for The Nationalities	ZF20120042	National medicine for hematology (Mongolian medicine), national medicine for cardiovascular (Mongolian medicine), national medicine for cerebrovascular disease (Mongolian medicine), national medicine for orthopedics and traumatology (Mongolian medicine), national medicine for rheumatology (Mongolian medicine), national medicine for endocrinology (Mongolian medicine)
Tongji Hospital of Tongji Medical College of HUST	ZXF20120043	Cardiovascular, respiratory, digestive, infection, dermatology, nephrology, rheumatology, endocrinology, allergy, cancer, neurology, obstetrics and gynecology, transplantation, traumatology, general surgery, urology, stomatology, pediatric genetic metabolism, pediatric endocrinology, pediatric infection, otolaryngology, ophthalmology, Chinese medicine for rheumatology, Chinese medicine for endocrinology

Table 3.2 (continued)

Medical institutions	Certificate no	Accredited specialties
Hangzhou No. 6 People's Hospital	XF20120044	Liver, infection
Zhongnan Hospital of Wuhan University	XF20120045	Cancer, respiratory, cardiovascular, endocrinology, neurology, obstetrics and gynecology, stomatology, nephrology, Chinese medicine for nephrology, dermatology, digestive, urology, infection
Guangdong Chinese Medical Hospital (The Second Affiliated Hospital of Guangzhou Chinese Medical University)	ZF20120046	Chinese medicine for ophthalmology, Chinese medicine for digestive, Chinese medicine for surgery, Chinese medicine for orthopedics, Chinese medicine for gynecology, Chinese medicine for anorectal, Chinese medicine for dermatology, Chinese medicine for cardiovascular, Chinese medicine for neurology, Chinese medicine for respiratory, Chinese medicine for nephrology, Chinese medicine for endocrinology, Chinese medicine for cancer, Chinese medical for otolaryngology, Chinese medicine for pediatrics, Chinese medicine for stomatology
The Third Xiangya Hospital of Central South University	XF20120047	Respiratory, cardiovascular, digestive, infection (liver), dermatology, otolaryngology, general surgery
Shanghai Ninth People's Hospital Affiliated Shanghai Jiao Tong University School of Medicine	XF20120048	Stomatology, cardiovascular, neurology, otolaryngology, plastic surgery, orthopedics
Tso-ngon Tibetan Medicine Hospital	ZF20120049	National medicine for hepatobiliary (Tibetan medicine), national medicine for rheumatology (Tibetan medicine), national medicine for cerebrovascular disease (Tibetan medicine)
Hanzhou First People's Hospital	ZXF20120050	Cardiovascular, respiratory, Chinese medicine for cancer
Kunming General Hospital of Chengdu Military Command	ZXF20120051	Detoxification, cardiovascular, digestive, respiratory, nephrology, cancer, neurology, orthopedics, Chinese medicine for orthopedics
Shanghai Changzheng Hospital	XF20120052	Respiratory, cardiovascular, digestive, neurology, endocrinology, nephrology, infection (liver), cancer, dermatology, immunology, ophthalmology, otolaryngology
Shengjing Hospital of China Medical University	XF20120053	Obstetrics and gynecology, respiratory, cardiovascular, endocrinology, nephrology, digestive, liver, anesthesiology, dermatology, pediatric respiratory, pediatric nephrology
The First Affiliated Hospital, Zhejiang University	XF20120054	Infection, cardiovascular, urology, ophthalmology, hematology, digestive, respiratory, endocrinology, cancer, nephrology, otolaryngology, dermatology, psychiatry, AIDS

Table 3.2 (continued)

Medical institutions	Certificate no	Accredited specialties
The First Hospital of Third Military Medical University	ZXF20120055	Digestive, liver, respiratory, dermatology, obstetrics and gynecology, ophthalmology, cardiovascular, neurology, anesthesiology, cancer, nephrology, otolaryngology, orthopedics, urology, plastic surgery, Chinese medicine for rheumatology
General Hospital of Chengdu Military Command of PLA	XF20120056	Digestive, endocrinology, nephrology, respiratory, hematology, cancer, cardiovascular, urology, neurosurgery, general surgery
The Second Xiangya Hospital of Central South University	XF20120057	Endocrinology, cardiovascular, urology, ophthalmology, digestive, respiratory, liver, dermatology, cancer, psychiatry, detoxification
The Affiliated Hospital of Xuzhou Medical College	XF20120058	Cardiovascular, respiratory, hematology, anesthesiology, dermatology, neurosurgery, urology, medical imaging (treatment)
The First Affiliated Hospital of Nanchang University	XF20120059	Digestive, burns, obstetrics and gynecology, orthopedics, urology, general surgery, endocrinology, neurology, nephrology, cardiovascular, hematology, cancer, infection, respiratory, ophthalmology
Chenzhou No. 1 People's Hospital	XF20120060	Neurology
Beijing Tongren Hospital, Capital Medical University	XF20120061	Cardiovascular, endocrinology, ophthalmology, otolaryngology
81 Hospital of People's Liberation Army	XF20120062	Cancer, liver
The First Hospital of Lanzhou University	XF20120063	Hematology, cardiovascular, respiratory, infection, nephrology, urology, neurology, digestive, obstetrics and gynecology, endocrinology
The Cancer Hospital of Guangxi Zhuang Autonomous Region	XF20120064	Cancer
254 Hospital of People's Liberation Army	XF20120065	Cardiovascular
Renmin Hospital of Wuhan University	XF20120066	Cardiovascular, digestive, neurology, psychiatry, respiratory, nephrology, infection, obstetrics and gynecology, endocrinology, ophthalmology, urology, otolaryngology, reproductive medicine, dermatology
Shandong Provincial Hospital of Dermatology	XF20120067	Dermatology
Xijing Hospital (The First Affiliated Hospital of The Fourth Military Medical University)	ZXF20120068	Digestive, respiratory, cancer, cardiovascular, endocrinology, neurology, hematology, obstetrics and gynecology, nephrology, immunology, psychiatry, pediatric infection, dermatology, ophthalmology, anesthesiology, burns, neurosurgery, orthopedics, Chinese medicine for cardiovascular, medical imaging (diagnosis)

Table 3.2 (continued)

Medical institutions	Certificate no	Accredited specialties
Joint Shantou Eye International Center of Shantou University and The Chinese University of Hong Kong	XF20120069	Ophthalmology
Jilin Provincial Cancer Hospital	XF20120070	Cancer
The Second Hospital of Liaoning Chinese Medicine University	ZF20120071	Chinese medicine for cardiovascular, Chinese medicine for endocrinology, Chinese medicine for neurology, Chinese medicine for obstetrics and gynecology, Chinese medicine for anorectal
Tianjin First Center Hospital	XF20120072	Transplantation (heart, liver, kidney, lung)
Hunan Cancer Hospital	ZXF20120073	Cancer, Chinese medicine for cancer, anesthesiology, medical imaging (diagnosis, nuclear medicine)
First Teaching Hospital of Tianjin University of TCM	ZF20120074	Chinese medicine for cardiovascular, Chinese medicine for pediatrics, Chinese medicine for surgery, Chinese medicine for respiratory, Chinese medicine for obstetrics and gynecology, Chinese medicine for neurology, Chinese medicine for endocrinology, hepatobiliary internal medicine, Chinese medicine for orthopedics and traumatology, Chinese medicine for digestive, Chinese medicine for nephrology, Chinese medicine for rheumatology, Chinese medicine for hematology, Chinese medical for otolaryngology
The Affiliated Hospital of Inner Mongolia Medical University	XF20120075	Cardiovascular, respiratory, hematology, obstetrics and gynecology
Brains Hospital of Hunan Province	XF20120076	Psychiatry, detoxification
Second Affiliated Hospital of Tianjin University of TCM	ZF20120077	Chinese medicine for obstetrics and gynecology, Chinese medicine for cardiovascular, Chinese medicine for respiratory, Chinese medicine for nephrology, Chinese medicine for rheumatology, Chinese medicine for digestive, Chinese medicine for surgery (urology), Chinese medicine for pediatrics, Chinese medicine for orthopedics and traumatology, Chinese medicine for cerebrovascular disease, Chinese medical for otolaryngology

Table 3.2 (continued)

Medical institutions	Certificate no	Accredited specialties
First Affiliated Hospital of Huan University of TCM	ZF20120078	Chinese medicine for cardiovascular, Chinese medicine for liver, Chinese medicine for orthopedics and traumatology, Chinese medicine for respiratory, Chinese medicine for ophthalmology, Chinese medicine for endocrinology, Chinese medicine for digestive, Chinese medicine for neurology, Chinese medicine for obstetrics and gynecology, Chinese medical for otolaryngology, Chinese medicine for stomatology, Chinese medicine for cancer, Chinese medicine for surgery
Beijing Jishuitan Hospital	XF20120079	Cardiovascular, digestive, respiratory, neurology, rheumatology, burns, orthopedics
Guangzhou Eighth People's Hospital	XF20120080	Liver, AIDS
Affiliated Orthopedic-Traumatological Hospital of Guangzhou University of TCM	ZF20120081	Chinese medicine for orthopedics and traumatology
Peking University People's Hospital	XF20120082	Cardiovascular, respiratory, hematology, liver, general surgery, orthopedics, digestive, endocrinology, immunology, nephrology, cancer, urology, obstetrics and gynecology, ophthalmology, otolaryngology, dermatology, anesthesiology

It is different from the western world in the fact that all clinical sites have to be accredited by CFDA to be able to conduct any clinical trials. All investigators have to go through the GCP training and get the certification to be legally to conduct a clinical trial. In 2013, there was an estimated 550 CFDA-accredited clinical research sites in China. Those clinical sites are accredited by therapeutic area (see Chap. 2 for more details). This limitation set by CFDA results in intense competition among multinational pharmaceutical drug developers for the best clinical sites, especially in big cities. Comparatively, the registered preclinical research institutions are almost double versus clinical sites in China (Fig. 3.4).

3.7 Differences Between the CFDA and Western Regulatory Agencies

Coupled with the fast-growing pharmaceutical market in China, the regulatory policies and guidance are also constantly under modification. The extensive regulatory processes play a significant role in the drug lag in IND/CTA and NDA stages compared to the western world.

Table 3.3 The state pharmaceutical clinical cancer research base

Location	Hospital name	Beds	Yearly outpatients	Class	Physicians
Shanghai	Ruijin Hospital Affiliated to Medical College of Shanghai Jiaotong University	1682	2,063,531	3-A	1504
	The sixth People's Hospital of Shanghai	1650	1,693,097	3-A	1455
	RenjiHospital (West Branch) Affiliated to Medical College of Shanghai Jiaotong University	1605	2,161,292	3-A	1298
	The First People's Hospital of Shanghai, Shanghai Red Cross Hospital	1580	1,805,623	3-A	1690
	Zhongshan Hospital Fudan University	1575	2,074,402	3-A	1360
	Changhai Hospital Affiliated to the Second Military Medical University	1500		3-A	
	Xinhua Hospital Affiliated to Shanghai Jiaotong University	1228	2,018,892	3-A	1529
	Shanghai Changzheng Hospital	1000		3-A	
	Shanghai Pneumology Hospital (Shanghai Occupational Diseases Hospital)	980	448,500	3-A	368
	Tumor Hospital Affiliated to Fudan University	923	514,797	3-A	540
	Shanghai Tenth People's Hospital	911	1,055,161	3-A	922
	Shanghai Chest Hospital Affiliated to Shanghai Jiaotong University	676	191,382	3-A	330
	Jing'an District Red Cross Hospital of Shanghai	513	637,075	2-A	406
	The Third People's Hospital Affiliated to Medical College of Shanghai Jiaotong University (Shanghai Baogang Hospital)	502	417,294	3-B	400
Jiangsu-Nanjing	People's Hospital of Jiangsu Province	1887	2,605,121	3-A	1030
	Gulou Hospital of Nanjing	1406	1,696,771	3-A	759
	Nanjing First Hospital	1215	1,180,177	3-A	550
	Jiangsu Provincial Tumor Hospital, Jiangsu Provincial Tumor Prevention & Treatment Institute	588	161,447	3-A	277
	The 81st Hospital of PLA			3-A	
Jiangsu-Suzhou	The First Affiliated Hospital of Soochow University	1494	1,388,617	3-A	763
	The Second Affiliated Hospital under Suzhou University, The sixth People's Hospital under Suzhou Municipality, China-France Friendship Hospital	851	862,301	3	502

Table 3.3 (continued)

Location	Hospital name	Beds	Yearly outpatients	Class	Physicians
Jiangsu-Wuxi	Jiangyin City People's Hospital	1450	1,067,522	2-A	569
	Wuxi Fourth People's Hospital, Fourth Affiliated Hospital of Suzhou University, Wuxi Tumor Hospital	887	583,448	3-B	315
Jiangsu-Yangzhou	Subei People's Hospital of Jiangsu Province, Yangzhou Red Cross Central Hospital	1550	992,170	3-A	773
	Yangzhou City, Jiangsu Province People's Hospital	925	543,953	3-A	288
Jiangsu-Nantong	Affiliated Hospital of Nantong University	1537	995,735	3-A	664
Jiangsu-Zhenjiang	Hospital Affiliated Jiangsu University	730	736,130	3-A	421
Jiangsu-Changzhou	The Third Affiliated Hospital under Medical College of Suzhou University, The first People's Hospital of Changzhou	1316	1,114,263	3-A	578
Jiangsu-Huaian	The First People's Hospital of Huaian, The fIRSTst Red Cross Hospital of Huaian	1200	998,255	3-A	559
Zhejiang-Hangzhou	The First Affiliated Hospital under Medical College of Zhejiang University, The First Hospital of Zhejiang Province	2687	2,365,222	3-A	1225
	The Second Affiliated Hospital under Medical College of Zhejiang University	1899	1,523,571	3-A	1063
	Zhejiang Cancer Hospital	1372	170,296	3-A	379
	Sir Run Run Shaw Hospital Affiliated to Medical College of Zhejiang University	1200	730,882	3-A	647
	Zhejiang Hospital of Hangzhou	500	188,363	3-A	375
Zhejiang-Wenzhou	The First Affiliated Hospital under Wenzhou Medical College	1615	1,793,757	3-A	1036
Shandong-Jinan	Qilu Hospital of Shandong University	1740	1,641,705	3-A	958
	General Hospital of Jinan Military Region	1147		3-A	
	Ji'nan Central Hospital, Clinical Hospital under Shandong University	960	811,334	3-A	549
	Cancer Hospital of Shandong Province	897	39,478	3-A	254
Shandong-Qingdao	Affiliated Hospital under Medical College of Qingdao University	1945	1,596,910	3-A	885
Shandong-Yantai	Yantai Yuhuangding Hospital, Yantai Yuhuangding Hospital Affiliated to Medical College of Qingdao University	1613	1,134,234	3-A	648

Table 3.3 (continued)

Location	Hospital name	Beds	Yearly outpatients	Class	Physicians
Shandong-Linyi	Linyi Cancer Hospital	500	53,885		189
Anhui-Hefei	The First Affiliated Hospital of Anhui Medical University	1884	1,533,220	3-A	962
Anhui-Bengbu	Affiliated Hospital of Bengbu Medical College, Anhui Provincial Tumor Hospital	1400	618,648	3-A	669
Anhui-Wuhu	Affiliated Yijishan Hospital of Wannan Medical College	1161	591,717	3-A	599
Chongqing	The First Affiliated Hospital under the Third Military Medical University, Chongqing Southwest Hospital	2200		3-A	7
	Xinqiao Hospital of Chongqing Municipality	1100		3-A	3
	Chongqing Daping Hospital	960		3-A	1
	Chongqing Cancer Hospital& Institute	469	110,297	1-A	206
	The First People's Hospital of Chongqing Municipality, Chongqing TCM-WM Hospital	332	385,998	3-A	181
Sichuan-Chengdu	West China Hospital of Sichuan University	4300	3,147,492	3-A	1818
	People's Hospital of Sichuan Province	2300	3,029,000	3-A	1128
	The Second People's Hospital of Sichuan	1200	84,413	3-A	295
	Chengdu Military General Hospital	850		3-A	
Sichuan-Luzhou	Affiliated Hospital of Luzhou Medical College	2500	1,000,000	3-A	777
Sichuan-Yibin	The NO. 2 People's Hospital of Yibin	1700	612,877	3-A	488
Yunnan-Kunming	General Hospital of Kunming, Chengdu Military Region, Chinese People's Liberation Army	1500		3-A	9
	Oncology Hospital of Yunnan province	1003	82,216	3-A	311
Shaanxi-Xian	Xijing Hospital of Xi'an	3128	2,000,000	3-A	3
	First Affiliated Hospital of Medical College of Jiaotong University	2300	1,200,000	3-A	720
	Xi'an Affiliated Jiaotong College of Medicine	950	817,793	3-A	673
	The Third People's Hospital, Shaanxi Provincial Tumor Hospital	610	18,387	3-A	176
	Tangdu Hospital affiliated to fourth Military University	150		3-A	3
Xinjiang-Urumqi	Xinjiang Oncology Hospital	2000	100,000	3-A	212

Table 3.3 (continued)

Location	Hospital name	Beds	Yearly outpatients	Class	Physicians
Beijing	Peking Union Medical College Hospital	1836	1,788,825	3-A	1550
	PLA General Hospital	1739		3-A	3
	The Military General Hospital of Beijing PLA	1600		3-A	
	Beijing Chaoyang Hospital	1498	2,090,722	3-A	1025
	Peking University People's Hospital	1381	1,559,870	3-A	1086
	Beijing China-Japan Friendship Hospital	1298	1,475,581	3-A	972
	Chinese Academy of Medical Sciences Cancer Hospital Cancer Institute	1249	412,804	3-A	510
	The Third Hospital of Peking University	1190	2,088,776	3-A	1346
	PLA Navy General Hospital	980		3-A	
	Beijing Hospital of Ministry of Health	948	1,066,221	3-A	760
	Beijing Friendship Hospital Affiliated to Capital Medical University	872	1,581,000	3-A	963
	Beijing Railway General Hospital, The Ninth Clinical Medical College of Peking University	858	749,820	3-A	691
	Beijing Tumor Hospital, Clinical Tumor College of Peking University	635	233,551	3-A	375
	Beijing Chest Tumor & Tuberculosis Hospital	533	117,139	3-A	206
	The 307th Hospital of PLA	50	41,624	3-A	
Tianjin	Tianjin Medical University Cancer Institute and Hospital (TMUCIH), Tianjin Tumor Hospital	1483	343,093	3-A	508
	Nankai University Affiliated Hospital	1000	613,245	3-A	560
Hebei-Shijiazhuang	The Fourth Hospital under Heibei Medical University, Heibei Provincial Tumor Hospital	920	469,793	3-A	519
	Bethune International Peace Hospital, PLA	900		3-A	
Hebei-Zhangjiakou	The 251st Hospital of PLA	600		3-A	
Hebei-Hengshui	Harrison International Peace Hospital of Hengshui City	531	255,173	3-A	408
Shanxi-Taiyuan	Shanxi Tumor Hospital, Shanxi Third People's Hospital	1519	207,007	3-A	358
Ningxia-Yinchuan	Affiliated Hospital of Ningxia Medical University	1900	720,000	3-A	785

Table 3.3 (continued)

Location	Hospital name	Beds	Yearly outpatients	Class	Physicians
Inner Mongolia-Baotou	Third Affiliated Hospital of Inner Mongolia Medical College (Baotou Hospital)	729	466,953	3-A	358
Gansu-Lanzhou	General Hospital of Lanzhou Military Region	910		3-A	
	Oncology Hospital of Gansu Province	506	43,478	3-A	186
Guangdong-Guangzhou	Guangdong Provincial People's Hospital, Guangdong Provincial Mental Health Institute	2500	3,463,000	3-A	1064
	Nanfang Hospital under Nanfang Medical University	1800	1,893,176	3-A	713
	Zhujiang Hospital of Southern Medical University	1800	578,635	3-A	390
	Guangzhou General Hospital of Guangzhou Military Region, Chinese People's Liberation Army	1200		3-A	
	Tumor Hospital under Sun Yat-sen University	1055	346,904	3-A	374
	First Affiliated Hospital of Guangzhou Medical College	816	938,301	3-A	546
	The Second People's Hospital of Guangzhou Municipality	784	844,922	3-A	366
Guangdong-Shenzhen	Shenzhen People's Hospital, The Second Affiliated Hospital under Medical College of Jinan University	1100	2,009,126	3-A	648
Guangdong-Shantou	First Affiliated Hospital of Medical School of Shantou University	668	496,381	3-A	434
	Affiliated Cancer Hospital of Medical School of Shantou University	400	35,819	3	140
	Ophthalmic Center of Shantou University Medical College	91	114,148	3-A	23
	Shantou Central Hospital	973	603,862	3-A	369
Guangdong-Shaoguan	Yuebei People's Hospital	1575	561,077	3-A	428
Guangdong-Foshan	First People's Hospital of Foshan City	1474	2,391,586	3-A	533
Guangdong-Zhongshan	People's Hospital of Zhongshan City	1356	1,851,494	3-A	449
Guangdong-Zhuhai	The Fifth Affiliated Hospital of Sun Yat-sen University	1300	446,000	3-A	279
Guangdong-Zhanjiang	Affiliated Hospital under Guangdong Medical College	1209	700,781	3-A	504

Table 3.3 (continued)

Location	Hospital name	Beds	Yearly outpatients	Class	Physicians
Fujian-Fuzhou	Xiehe Hospital Affiliated to Fujian Medical University	1830	1,182,857	3-A	643
	The First Affiliated Hospital Fujian Medical University	1301	1,199,972	3-A	702
	Fuzhou General Hospital of Nanjing Military Command	1200		3-A	2
	Fujian Provincial Tumor Hospital	1099	106,995	3-A	301
Guangxi-Nanning	Affiliated Tumor Hospital under Guangxi Medical University, Guangxi Tumor Prevention & Treatment Institute	522	26,128	3-A	179
Hubei-Wuhan	Tongji hospital affiliated to Tongji Medical College of HUST	2500	2,556,000	3-A	982
	Union hospital affiliated to Tongji Medical College of HUST	2401	1,865,184	3-A	921
	Zhongnan Hospital under Wuhan University	2000	686,879	3-A	482
	Wuhan General Hospital of Guangzhou Military	1800	1,000,000	3-A	
	Hubei Cancer Hospital	1000	70,000	3-A	203
	Pu Ai Hospital of Wuhan City	910	522,724	3-A	201
Hubei-Shiyan	Taihe Hospital of Shibu	2300	846,149	3-A	600
Hubei-Jingzhou	Central Hospital of Jingzhou City	1100	597,370	3-A	377
Hunan-Changsha	The Second Xiangya Hospital of Central South University	3500	1,662,500	3-A	1034
	Xiangya Hospital of Central-South University	3500	1,500,000	3-A	1065
	The Third Xiangya Hospital of Central South University	1800	470,531	3-A	445
	Changsha Central Hospital	1376	356,343	2-A	393
	Hunan Provincial Tumor Hospital	802	107,395	3-A	263
Hunan-Hengyang	The First Affiliated Hospital under the University of South China (Former: The First Affiliated Hospital under Hengyang Medical College)	1200	777,073	3-A	362
Hunan-Yueyang	The First People Hospital of Yueyang	1029	550,000	3-A	289
Hunan-Chenzhou	Chenzhou City People's Hospital Group	1475	1,307,008	3-A	505
Jiangxi-Nanchang	The First Affiliated Hospital of Nanchang University	1600	1,025,080	3-A	663
	People's Hospital of Jiangxi Province	1112	427,644	3-A	526
	The Second Affiliated Hospital under Jiangxi Medical College	763	500,866	3-A	472
Henan-Zhengzhou	The First Affiliated Hospital of Henan University of TCM	1200	881,983	3-A	598

Table 3.3 (continued)

Location	Hospital name	Beds	Yearly outpatients	Class	Physicians
Henan-Xinxiang	First Affiliated Hospital of Xinxiang Medical University	2800	245,696	3-A	547
Liaoning-Shenyang	The First Affiliated Hospital under China Medical University	1586	1,503,450	3-A	1219
	The General Hospital of Shenyang Military Region	1228			
Liaoning-Dalian	First Affiliated Hospital of Dalian Medicine University	1848	1,374,352	3-A	931
	Second Affiliated Hospital of Dalian Medicine University	1250	835,938	3-A	693
Jilin-Changchun	First Hospital of Jilin University	1960	1,467,164	3-A	985
	Jilin Provincial People's Hospital	1517	506,770	3-A	717
	Jilin Provincial Tumor Hospital	1110	29,250	3-A	233
Jilin-Siping	Central People's Hospital of Siping City	700	350,865	2-A	384
Heilongjiang-Haerbin	The Third Affiliated Hospital under Harbin Medical University, Heilongjiang Provincial Tumor Hospital	2135	166,580	3-A	480

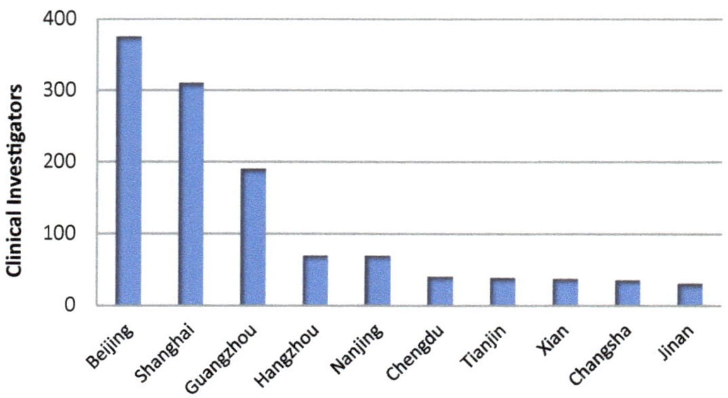

Fig. 3.4 Clinical Investigator Distribution in major cities. (Source: The fifth China clinical trial outsourcing congress, March 4–5, 2013 (Modified))

The CFDA faces other changes, as well, as it currently rests in a developing regulatory environment. The CFDA is keenly aware that the current capacity and capabilities of the CDE are not compatible with what is needed to fulfill China's public health mission. In the past few years, China has made significant reforms toward establishing a regulatory system that will be more in line with that of western agencies. Overall, the data from clinical trials in the past few years conducted in China are compatible with the global trials and have been routinely included in global clinical trials.

In early 2013, China made a significant change in regulatory agencies. They consolidated six of China's food and drug regulatory organizations into one ministry-level agency and named it as the China Food and Drug Administration (CFDA). The new organization, the CFDA, aims to improve its effectiveness and possesses more integrated and powerful functions.

The major differences between the CFDA and the US FDA could be summarized in the following aspects:

- Work force for drug review and registration: It is estimated that roughly 120 employees oversee drug review and registration process in central the CFDA and about 500 inspectors work at the provincial level for onsite pre-approval inspections. In the US, there is an estimated 3000 FDA employees in similar positions for such processes.
- Pharmaceutical companies: As of 2008, there were about 4749 registered pharmaceutical companies in China, versus 413 in the US based on the fifth China Clinical Trials Outsourcing Congress data.
- IND/CTA timeframe for approval: In the US, pharmaceutical companies can initiate their clinical trial 30 days after an IND filing if no rejection is heard from the FDA; in China, it usually takes a significantly long time to get approval and approval from the CFDA is mandatory before the trial can start.

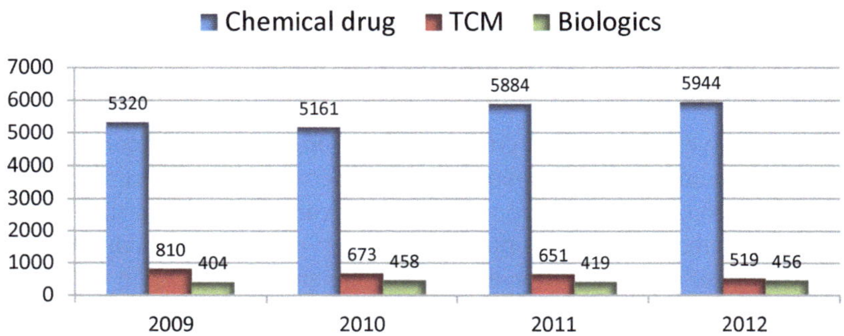

Fig. 3.5 Drug applications by acceptance numbers from 2009 to 2012. (Source: 2012 China drug review annual report, the CFDA website)

Table 3.4 Approval of drug clinical research in 2012. (Source: 2012 China drug review annual report, the CFDA website)

Registration category	Clinical trial	Bioequivalence study	Sub-total
Chemical drug	425	178	603
TCM	37	2	39
Biologics	62	/	62
Total	704		

TCM Traditional Chinese Medicine

- CMC data requirement: For the IND stage, the requirements for CMC data are more numerous than in the western world. Extensive and validated CMC data, such as API manufacturing process, impurity, or formulation stability specification, are often required before the clinical trial approval.

From the following data, table and figure (Fig. 3.5; Table 3.4), it is easy to see the imbalance of the workload versus the labor force (number of workers) of the CFDA.

In 2012, the CDE has accepted a total of 6919 new registrations. The Fig. 3.5 below shows the comparison between current, accepted drug applications with those of previous years. Over the past 4 years, the accepted applications of chemical drugs were generally accounted for 80–85 % of the total accepted cases. In the same year, the CDE completed 4941 drug review tasks and submitted them for review and approval by the CFDA. Of which, 3323 are suggested for approval and 1618 are suggested for disapproval.

3.8 Communication with China Regulatory Agencies and Regulatory Information Tracking

In the past few years, the CFDA emphasized and openly endorsed core values with the CDE, including openness, innovation, fairness, data-driven, teamwork and responsibility. From the annual reports of recent years, it is evident that one of the many efforts is that the CFDA is open to the supervision by its stakeholders.

The pattern of communication and developing and implementing Quality Management Practice for the Communication between the Drug Registration Applicants and the CDE was transformed to ensure that all decisions of the CDE are made on the basis of integrated information collection to improve the quality and efficiency of decision-making. Now, both the pharmaceutical company and the CDE may request communication on key technical issues, exchange information and opinions, and develop meeting minutes to be signed and recognized by both parties.

The other new feature is that the CFDA has been more proactively open to public media organizations and receiving media supervision as well as other approaches. Basically, those approaches include:

- The CDE continued to improve the system of technical guidance for drug R&D, e.g., they initiated 36 drafting guidance and 7 revision guidance in 2012.
- The CDE has established a special column of "Answers to Common Questions" on its official website, which addresses 103 questions in 2012; regarding the new problems and questions, the CDE has been using electronic publications to share its forward-looking views on these questions. The CDE addressed more questions through the information feedback platform of the CDE's website and the CDE director's mailbox in the past few years.
- The CDE held more open day activities, workshops on drug technical review to share the technical requirements and standards with the industry regarding drug research, development and evaluation,
- One of the most important new features that may benefit the multinational pharmaceutical companies is the openness of drug review and extensive incorporation of national and international experts into the deliberation and decision-making under the strict qualification screening, the avoidance of conflict of interest and the confidentiality management.

The above functional adjustments of China's regulatory agencies will make the pharmaceutical regulatory environment more compatible to western standards, and make it much easier for the global pharmaceutical companies to adapt to China's system.

Regulatory Status Tracking by Center for Drug Evaluation, the CFDA
Even though there are many regulatory consultation companies in China, the multinational pharmaceutical companies can always check their regulatory application status through the CDE/CFDA website. Unfortunately, a majority of the contents are still not available in English. However, the updated information is very timely on the CDE/CFDA websites in Chinese. On the websites, you may track the updated

Table 3.5 Online regulatory status tracking by

No.	Acceptance number	Time of acceptance	Review status	Pharmacology toxicology	Clinical	CMC	Note
1	CXHL1002209	2013-03-05					
2	CXHL1000112	2012-03-04					
3	CXHL1000344	2013-03-11					
4	CXHL1000212	2011-03-03					

The status in the above table (Table 3.5) could indicate that the corresponding field is: (a) undergoing review; (b) waiting in the queue for review; (c) finished with the review process; (d) review not initiated yet by professional reviewers. After completion of the review for each of the fields, the dossier will enter the integrated/joint review stage

information about IND, NDA, ANDA, confirmatory clinical, supplementary application, or Import re-registration status.

The followings are the procedures:

- Open the CDE website by clicking: http://www.cde.org.cn/
- Under "Information disclosure" select "Review status—New application task publicity" or by clicking: http://www.cde.org.cn/news.do?method=changePage&pageName=service&frameStr=4

Based on your drug category, i.e. TCM, Chemical drug or Biologics, IND or NDA etc., you may see the all application drugs or simply put your acceptance number to check the status.

References

CFDA (2013a) CFDA issued the announcement for accreditation of drug clinical trial institutions (No. 1). China Pharmaceutical Newsletter, Vol. VI, 2013

CFDA (2013b) CFDA: more than 100 new industry standards released by CFDA. China Certification, November 26, 2013. http://www.china-certification.com/en/cfda-more-than-100-new-industry-standards-released-by-cfda. Accessed 15 Sept 2014

CFDA (2013c) Main responsibilities of China food and drug administration. http://www.sda.gov.cn/WS01/CL0003/. Accessed 16 Sept 2014

China Daily (22 March 2013) China gets stronger food, drug regulator. China Daily, Xinhua. http://www.chinadaily.com.cn/business/2013-03/22. Accessed 8 June 2014

McKenna C et al (3 June 2013) Consolidation of the China food and drug administration. CMS. http://www.lexology.com/library/detail.aspx?g=20a4e134-7414-4f4d-88d5-d7dd36d800a7. Accessed 6 March 2014

Meng L (21 May 2013) China's FDA dream—Chinese drug safety regulators in the modern sense. Sina Blog. http://blog.sina.com.cn/s/blog_6b812ae10102egmj.html. Accessed 18 March 2014

NPC (10 March 2013) China to elevate food, drug agency to general administration. NPC, CPPCC annual sessions. http://news.xinhuanet.com/english/china/2013-03/10/c_132221729.htm. Accessed 6 March 2014

Salako Q (2013) Navigating the Chinese regulatory system for drugs for rare diseases. The 5th China clinical trial outsourcing congress, March 4–5, 2013

SCOPSR (15 May 2013) China food and drug administration main responsibilities, internal organs, and staffing requirements, Source: SFDA, comprehensive division. http://www.scopsr.gov.cn/zxdd/zdxw/201305/t20130515_221349.html. Accessed 4 Feb 2014
SFDA (2012) SFDA promulgated annual report on drug registration approval 2011, China. Pharmaceutical Newsletter VIII, 2012. http://www.ccpie.org/news/download/2012pharm-13.pdf. Accessed 12 Feb 2013
SFDA (2013) Center for drug evaluation, SFDA released the "2012 China Annual Drug Evaluation Report". China Pharmaceutical Newsletter IV, 2013. http://www.ccpie.org/news/download/2013pharm-4.pdf. Accessed 22 Jan 2014
Thoelke KR (2013) Including China in your global clinical development strategy why, when and how. The 5th China clinical trial outsourcing congress, March 4–5, 2013
Wei J (2013) Regulatory highlights and drug development in China. The 5th China clinical trial outsourcing congress, March 4–5, 2013

Chapter 4
Registration

Ming Q. Lu, Yanbin Xie and Sandy Bai

4.1 Introduction

The pharmaceutical regulations in China have changed dramatically over the past 15 years. Since the first registration regulation issued in 1985, four revisions have been implemented in 1999, 2002, 2005 and 2007.

Provisions for Drug Registration (SFDA 2007) Order No. 28, issued on July 10, 2007 and enacted on October 1 2007 are the most important regulations regarding new drug application process. In this regulation, the application, review and approval processes have been clearly defined. In addition, the requirements for the source data, the production site inspection, testing and quality of products were also described in detail.

Currently the Provisions for Drug Registration issued in 2007 are under the process of revision. The CFDA published a draft amendment to the Drug Registration Regulation for public comment by December 13, 2013. The significant changes include the deletion of Article 19 of the SFDA Order No.28, i.e. "Generic companies may submit the application for registration 2 years prior to the expiry date of the patent. The CFDA shall review the drug application in accordance with the Provisions, and after the expiry date of the patent, check and issue the drug approval number, Import Drug License (IDL) or a Pharmaceutical Product License if the application conforms to the provisions." This deletion is made to be in line with Article 69 of the PRC Patent Law, which contains a clause similar to the Bolar Exemption. Based on this deletion, the CFDA may accept generic applications made

M. Q. Lu (✉)
Helsinn Therapeutics (U.S.), Inc., 1140 US Highway 22, Suite 101, Bridgewater, NJ 08807, USA
e-mail: mingqilu@verizon.net

Y. Xie
China ICON PLC., Room 1502–1506, Tower B Global Trade Center, No. 36,
North Ring East Road, Dongcheng District, 100013 Beijing, P. R. China

S. Bai
138 Building B-538, Zhang Hua Road, Hai Dian District, 100036 Beijing, P. R. China

M. Q. Lu (ed.), *Approaching China's Pharmaceutical Market*,
DOI 10.1007/978-3-319-15576-0_4

for research purposes during the validity term of the relevant patents, and review and approve those applications in reliance upon a non-infringement affidavit of the filing party.

New requirements could include that, in case of a change of applicant during clinical studies for new drugs, or a change in manufacturing process, formulation, specification or manufacturing site for chemical drugs or biological products prior to phase III studies, pharmaceutical companies have to get the CFDA's approval through a supplementary application. In case of such multiple filings of the same drug, once a local new get New Drug Monitoring Period approval, the CFDA will no longer accept an application for registering the same drug regardless of its dosage forms. In the case of those applications that had already been in the review process prior to the approval, the CFDA may continue to review and approve those applications; once those new drugs get approval, they would also get the same New Drug Monitoring Period. The SFDA Order No. 28 is still the effective provisions to follow. Upon new provisions, publication and implementation, this chapter will be renewed in the next edition.

Drug registration refers to the process of review and approval on which the CFDA, in accordance with the official procedures, evaluates the safety, efficacy and quality of the drugs applied for marketing, and decides whether or not to approve such an application.

Therefore, multinational pharmaceutical companies need to accomplish the application to the CFDA and get approval for clinical trials, drug manufacturing, drug importation, and change/modification of drug approval document before proceeding to reach safety, efficacy and quality control outcome.

4.2 Applicant Requirement for Drug Registration

The following listed items provide detailed explanations for foreign pharmaceutical applicants regarding the requirement as an applicant:

1. An applicant for drug registration refers to the institution that submits a drug registration application and assumes corresponding legal liability.
2. A domestic applicant shall be an institution legally registered within the territory of People's Republic of China that independently assumes civil liability and an overseas applicant shall be a legal overseas drug manufacturer. Where an overseas applicant applies for import drug registration, it shall be done by its branch or entrusted agency within the territory of People's Republic of China. The people who handle the application for drug registration shall have professional knowledge and be familiar with the laws and regulations on, and the technical requirements for, drug registration
3. Applications of domestic applicants shall be handled according to the procedures and requirements for new drugs or generic drugs, whereas applications of overseas applicants shall be handled according to those for import drugs.
4. The applicant shall provide sufficient and reliable research data to prove the safety, efficacy and quality of the drug, and be liable for the authenticity of all the dossiers submitted.

4.3 The Drug Registration Scope

Drug registration applications include applications for new drugs, generic drugs, import drugs and their supplementary applications as well as re-registration applications.

Applications of domestic applicants shall be handled according to the procedures and requirements for new drugs or generic drugs, whereas applications of overseas applicants shall be handled according to those for import drugs.

4.3.1 New Drug Application

Application for new drugs refers to application for registration of drugs that have not been marketed within the territory of People's Republic of China. Application for changing dosage form or route of administration, or claiming a new indication for marketed drugs, shall be submitted as the process of new drug application.

There are two applications, i.e. CTA/IND and NDA. Two approvals are needed, i.e. CTA/IND letter and drug license with Appendix.

4.3.2 Generic Drug Application

Application for generic drugs refers to registration application for producing the drugs having existing national drug standard which is approved to be marketed by the State Food and Drug Administration, whereas the application for biological products shall be submitted as the process of new drug application.

4.3.3 Import Drug Application

Application for import drugs refers to registration application for drugs manufactured abroad to be marketed within the territory of the People's Republic of China.

4.3.4 Supplementary Application

Supplementary application refers to application for variation, addition, or cancellation of the items or contents approved in the original application for new drug, generic drug or import drug. Supplementary application apples to any changes to approved documents (dossier), their appendices (pharmaceutical ingredient and specification) or major changes including supplement, requires in-country testing.

4.3.5 Re-registration Application

Re-registration application refers to application for continued production or importation of a drug after the expiration of the valid term of the drug approval document.

4.4 Drug Registration Application Acceptance Status

1. New drug applications and generic drug application shall be accepted by the local provincial Food and Drug Administration. The applicants should submit relevant information and the application shall be submitted to apply for the production site inspection.
2. The relevant information and samples for imported drug applications shall be filed directly to the administrative acceptance service center of the SFDA.
3. An overseas applicant intending to conduct an international multi-center clinical trial in China shall submit an application to the SFDA:

    i. the drugs used for clinical trials shall be already approved or in phase II or III clinical trial overseas. The SFDA does not accept any overseas applicant's international multi-center clinical trial application for any preventive vaccine not being registered overseas yet;
    ii. while approving to conduct an international multi-center clinical trial, the SFDA may require the applicant to conduct phase I clinical trial first in China;
    iii. when conducting an international multi-center clinical trial in China, if there are any observed serious adverse reaction and unexpected adverse reaction associated with the drug in any country, the applicant shall, in accordance with relevant regulations, report to the SFDA in time;
    iv. the applicant shall submit a complete clinical trial report to the SFDA after the completion of a clinical trial; and
    v. the data obtained from an international multi-center clinical trial for drug registration application in China shall be in conformity with the requirements on clinical trial in the Provisions. All the study materials of the international multi-center clinical trial shall be submitted.

4.5 Registration Categories of Chemical Drugs, Therapeutic and preventive Biological Products

Chemical Drugs are six registration categories or some time called classes. The clinical trial requirements are very different as listed briefly below (SFDA Annex 2 and 3 2007) (Table 4.1):

Table 4.1 Registration categories of chemical drugs and the corresponding clinical trial requirement

Class 1	Definition	New chemical entity never marketed in any country
		i. Drug substance and its preparations made by synthesis or semi-synthesis
		ii. Chemical monomer (including drug substance and preparation) extracted from natural sources or by fermentation
		iii. Optical isomer (including drug substance and preparation) obtained by chiral separation or synthesis
		iv. Drug with fewer components derived from marketed multi-component drug
		v. New combination products
		vi. A preparation already marketed in China but with a newly added indication not yet approved in any country
	Clinical requirement	Phase I: 20–30 cases/group for single and multiple ascending dose trials
		Phase II: >100 cases/group
		Phase III: >300 plus statistically significant consideration
		Phase IV: >2000
Class 2	Definition	Drug preparation with changed administration route and not marketed in any country
	Clinical requirement	Phase I: 20–30 cases/group for single and multiple ascending dose trials
		Phase II: >100 cases/group
		Phase III: >300 plus statistically significant consideration
		Phase IV: >2000
Class 3	Definition	Drug marketed ex-China, including:
		i. Drug substance and its preparations, and/or with changed dose form, but no change of administration route
		ii. Combination preparations, and/or with changed dose form, but no change of administration route
		iii. Preparations with changed administration route and marketed ex-China
		iv. A preparation already marketed in China but with a newly added indication approved ex-China
	Clinical requirement	PK: 20–30 cases
		Phase III: >100 pairs
		Multiple indications: >60 pairs
Class 4	Definition	Drug substance and its preparation with changed acid or alkaline radicals (or metallic elements), but without any pharmacological change, and the original drug entity already approved in China
	Clinical requirement	PK: 20–30 cases
		Phase III: >100 pairs
		For multiple indication: >60 pairs

Table 4.1 (continued)

Class 5	Definition	Drug preparation with changed dose form, but no change of administration route, and the original preparation already approved in China
	Clinical requirement	Oral solid preparation bioequivalence trials: 18–24 cases
		Non-oral preparation: clinical trial needed, > 100 pairs
		Sustained and controlled released preparations: PK of single and repeated doses needed; clinical trial: > 100 pairs
		Single active component Injection: > 100 pairs;
		Multiple component injection: > 300 pairs;
		Microemulsions and liposome: Refer to Class 1 and 2.
Class 6	Definition	Drug substance or preparation following national standard
	Clinical requirement	Oral solid preparation bioequivalence trials: 18–24 cases;
		If the quality of drug needs to be controlled by process and standards, clinical tests need 100 cases

From the following Fig. 4.1, it is clear that the classifications of the new drug for both local and import drug are consistent following Provisions for Drug Registration (SFDA Order No. 28) issued on July 10, 2007. The Imported Drug Administration Measures (Order No. 6) issued on March 12, 1999 with the effective date on May 1, 1999 was annulled (Tables 4.2 and 4.3).

If the drug registration falls in supplemental application category, the pharmaceutical companies should provide the following items to meet the registration requirements (Table 4.4).

4.6 Classification of Investigational Product—Chemical

(Annex 2: Registration Categories and Application Information Requirements of Chemical Drugs, Provisions for Drug Registration the *SFDA Order No. 28, 2007)*

I Registration Categories

1. New chemical entity never marketed in any country.

   i. Drug substance and its preparations made by synthesis or semi-synthesis.
   ii. Chemical monomer (including drug substance and preparation) extracted from natural sources or by fermentation.
   iii. Optical isomer (including drug substance and preparation) obtained by chiral separation or synthesis.
   iv. Drug with fewer components derived from marketed multi-component drug.
   v. New combination products.

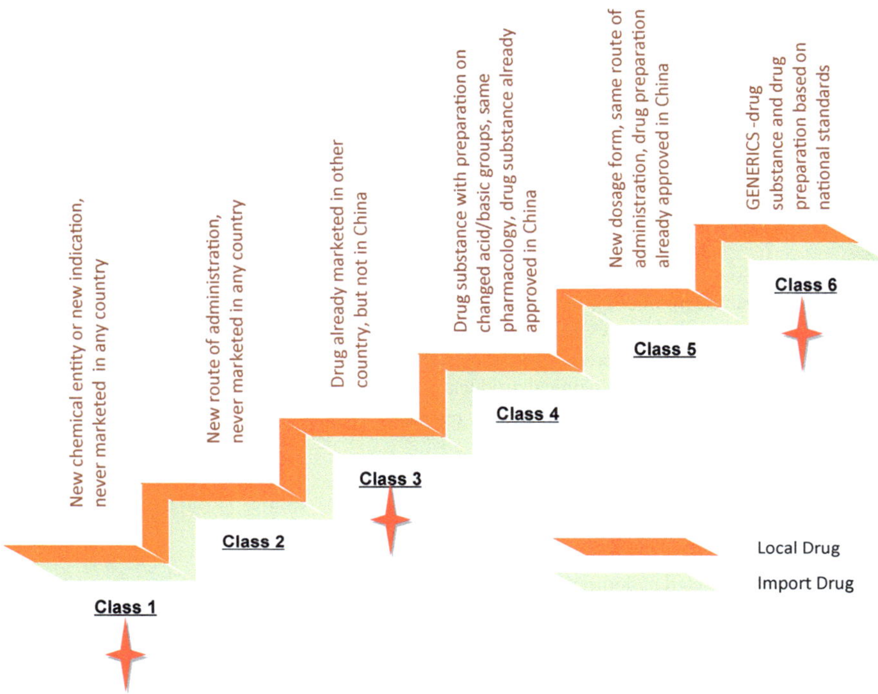

Fig. 4.1 Classifications of local and import drugs

vi. A preparation already marketed in China but with a newly added indication not yet approved in any country.

2. Drug preparation with changed administration route and not marketed in any country
3. Drug marketed ex-China, including:
   i. Drug substance and its preparations, and/or with changed dose form, but no change of administration route.
   ii. Combination preparations, and/or with changed dose form, but no change of administration route.
   iii. Preparations with changed administration route and marketed ex-China.
   iv. A preparation already marketed in China but with a newly added indication approved ex-China.
4. Drug substance and its preparation with changed acid or alkaline radicals (or metallic elements), but without any pharmacological change, and the original drug entity already approved in China.
5. Drug preparation with changed dose form, but no change of administration route, and the original preparation already approved in China,
6. Drug substance or preparation following national standard.

Table 4.2 Registration categories of therapeutic biological products

Category	Description	Clinical requirement
1	Biological products not yet marketed at domestic or overseas	Phase I: >20
2	Mono-clonal antibody	Phase II: >100
3	Gene therapy, somatic cell therapy as well as the preparations	Phase III: >300 and statistically significant
4	Allergen products	Phase III: >300 and statistically significant
5	Multi component products with bioactivity extracted from, or by fermentation from human and/or animal tissues and/or body fluid	
6	New combination product made from the already marketed biological products	
7	A product that is marketed already overseas but not yet marketed domestic	
8	Some of the strains used for preparing of micro-ecological products not yet approved	
9	Products with not completely same structure with the already marketed products and not yet marketed at domestic or overseas (including Amino Acid Locus Mutation/Absence, modification caused by a different expression system, deletion, changed interpretation, as well as chemical modifications of the product)	
10	Products with a method of preparation different with the already marketed one, (such as use of different expression system, host cells)	
11	Products first time made with DNA recombination technology (such as use of recombination technology to replace the synthesis technology, tissue extraction or fermentation technology)	
12	Products transformed from non-injection into injection, or topical use into systemic use, and not yet marketed at domestic or overseas	
13	The marketed products with a change in dosage form but no change in route of administration	
14	Products with a change in route of administration (excluding the above Category 12)	
15	Biological products admitted with National Standards	

II Application Dossier Items

A. Summary

1. Name of the drugs.
2. Certified Documents.
3. Objectives and basis for R & D.
4. Summary of main study work.

Table 4.3 Registration categories of preventive biological products

Category	Description	Clinical requirement
1	Vaccine not yet marketed at domestic or overseas	Trials should be conducted in accordance with the requirement for new drugs.
2	DNA vaccine	Phase I: >20
3	A already marketed vaccine with new adjuvant. Change of carrier of combined vaccine	Phase II: >300
4	Non-purified vaccine, or full cell vaccine (bacteria, virus) changed into purified vaccine, or combined vaccine	Phase III: >500 and statistically significant
5	Vaccine with strains not yet approved in China (except for vaccine for influenza, vaccine for leplospirosis and others)	
6	Vaccine already marketed overseas but not yet marketed domestic	
7	Combined vaccine prepared with vaccine already marketed domestic	
8	Re-combination vaccine with protective antigen spectrum different with the marketed one	
9	Vaccine manufactured with the change of the other approved expression or the other approved cellular stroma. Vaccine using new process, which is proved to improve the safety and effectiveness of the vaccine based on the data of laboratory	
10	Vaccine with change of de-activator (method of deactivation) or de-toxicitor (method of de-toxicity)	If no change in the safety and effectiveness, trails may be exempted
11	Vaccine with change in the route of administration	Trials normally should be as for new drugs. But the Phase I trial may be exempted if the route change is from injections into non injections
12	A domestic marketed vaccine with change in dosage form but no change in route of administration	Only phase III trial needed
13	Vaccine with dosage of immunity or immunity procedure	Phase I may be exempted if it is due to immunity procedure change
14	Vaccine with an enlarged group of people (enlarged age range)	The same as categories 1–9
15	Vaccine admitted with National Standards	Only phase III trial needed

Table 4.4 Registration items of supplemental application of drug registration

A. Supplemental application of drug registration involved in the following review and approval at provincial (PDA) and national Food and Drug Administration (SFDA Annex 4 2007). Specific requirements are as follows:
1) Application for Drug Approval Number of a new drug by the New Drug Certificate holder of the drug
2) Use of the name of the Trade Name of drugs
3) Additional indications or functions of TCM or natural drug, or the indication approved in China for chemical drug or biological products
4) Change in the usage or dosage of the drugs, or the group of patient to use the drug, but without change in route of administration
5) Change of strength of drugs
6) Change of the supplementive in the formula of the drugs, where there is a medial requirement for it
7) A change in the drug manufacture technology and process affecting drug quality
8) Amendment of drug registration standards
9) Substitute or removal of the drug material listed in formula of National Drug Standards as toxic or endangered
10) Change of the immediate packing material or container of the import drugs, domestic injection, ophthalmologic, spray, powder Aerosol, Inhaler and Spray. Use of new immediate packing material or container
11) Application for combined packing of drug
12) The transfer of new drug technology
13) Addition or amendment of items in insert sheet of TCM or natural drug, such as pharmacology and toxicology, clinical trial and Pharmacokinetic
14) A change in items within the import drug registration certificate, such as name of the drug, drug enterprise name, registered location, packing specification
15) Change of the location where the import drug is manufactured
16) Change of the location where the import drug is packed overseas
17) Repacking of import drugs in China
18) Change of the location where the raw material for import preparation is manufactured
B. Supplemental applications to be approved by PDA and be filed for record at the SFDA, or directly be filed for record at the SFDA
19) Change of the name of a domestic drug manufacturer
20) Internal change of the manufacture workshop of a domestic drug manufacturer
21) Change of immediate packing material or container (except for the item 10 as above)
22) Change of valid period of domestic drugs
23) Change of manufacture location of import drugs
24) Change of appearance of the drug without change of drug standards
25) Amendment of insert sheet of the drugs according to national drug standards or required by the SFDA
26) Supplementing and perfecting of the drug safety part of the insert sheet
27) Modification of design of packing and label of the drugs according to the regulation
28) Change of the agent for import drug registration
29) Others
C. Supplemental applications to be filed for record at PDA
30) Amendment of insert sheet of the domestic drugs according to national drug standards or required by the SFDA

Table 4.4 (continued)

31) Supplementing and perfecting of the domestic drug safety part of the insert sheet
32) Modification of design of packing and label of the domestic drugs according to the regulation
33) Change of the packing specification of domestic drugs
34) Change of manufacture location of domestic drugs
35) Change of appearance of the domestic drug without change of drug standards
36) Others

5. Draft of packaging insert, note to the draft, and latest literature.
6. Design of packaging and labeling.

B Pharmaceutical information

7. Summary of Pharmaceutical Study,
8. Research information and relevant literature of the production process of the drug substance, research information and relevant literature of formula and process of the preparations.
9. Study information and relevant literature for the chemical structure and components determination.
10. Study information and literature for quality specification.
11. Draft of quality specification and notes, and providing reference standard.
12. Test report of drug sample.
13. The source, test report and quality specification of drug substance and excipient.
14. Stability study and relevant literature.
15. Selection basis and quality specification of immediate packing material and container.

C Pharmacology and toxicology study information.

16. Summary of pharmacology and toxicology study.
17. Primary pharmacodynamics study and literature.
18. General pharmacology study and literature.
19. Acute/single dose toxicity study and literature.
20. Repeated dose toxicity study and literature.
21. Special safety study and literature of hypersensitive (topical, systemic and photo-toxicity), hemolytic and topical irritative (blood vessel, skin, mucous membrane, and muscle) reaction related to topical and systemic use of the drugs.
22. Study and relevant literature on Pharmacodynamics, toxicity and pharmacokinetics change caused by the interactions amongst multiple components in the combination products.
23. Study and literature of mutagenicity test.
24. Study and literature of reproductive toxicity.
25. Study and literature of carcinogenicity test.
26. Study and literature of drug dependence.
27. Study and literature of pre-clinical pharmacokinetics.

a. **Clinical Study Information**

28. Summary of global clinical study information.
29. Clinical study protocol.
30. Investigator's Brochure.
31. Draft of Informed Consent Form, approval of the Ethics Committee.
32. Clinical study report.

III Notes to Application Information Items/Booklets

1. Information Item 1, Name of the drugs, includes International Nonproprietary Name (INN), Chemical Name, English Name, and Chinese Phonetics. Chemical structure, Molecular Weight, Molecular Formula shall be noted. The Nomenclature of the drug should be explained for any new name.

2. Information Item 2, Certified Documents, includes,

   i. Certified Documents of lawful registration of the Applicant, copies of Drug Manufacturing License, GMP Certificate. For the application of production of new drugs, copies of GMP Certificate for the workshop where the sample product of the drugs was manufactured should be provided.
   ii. Certified Documents stating patent status and ownership of this entity and formula, production process of the drug, and letter of guarantee stating that no infringement upon the patent rights of others.
   iii. Copies of official approvals of the research proposal of narcotics, psychotropic, medical-use toxic drugs and radioactive drugs.
   iv. For the application of production of new drugs, copy of Approval of Clinical Study of New Drugs and the quality standard of investigational drugs should be provided for the market authorization approval.
   v. For the application of production of preparation, certified documents to evidence the legal channels of drug substance should be provided, including copies of certified approval document of drug substance, drug standards, test report, business licenses of manufacturers of drug substance, Drug Manufacturing License, GMP Certificate, sales invoice, and supply contract.
   vi. Copies of the Drug Packing Material and Container Certificate or Import Drug Packing Material and Container Certificate for the immediate packing material and container.

3. Information Item 3, objectives and basis of the application, includes R&D, marketing status, and the related literature of the drugs, as well as the summary of the use and production of the drugs, domestically and overseas,
4. Information Item 4, summary and evaluation of main research results, includes the summary of main research results by the Applicant, and a comprehensive analysis of safety, efficacy, and quality controllability of the drugs of the application.

5. Information Item 5, draft of insert sheet, notes to the draft and latest literature, includes the sample of draft of packaging insert sheet drafted in accordance with the relevant regulations, notes on how each items of the insert sheet were drafted, latest relevant literature.
6. Information Item 7, Summary of Pharmaceutical Study, refers to the summary of experiment and global literature of Pharmaceutical Study of the drug in the application (synthesis process, selection of dosage form, screening of formula, determination of structure, quality study and determination of quality standards, and stability study).
7. Information Item 8, research information of the production process of the drug substance, includes technology process and chemical reaction equation, initial raw material and organic menstruum, reaction conditions (temperature, pressure, duration, catalyst) and operation procedure, refining method and main physical-chemical constants. The raw material input, and output yield, as well as possible impurities or other by-products produced or mixed during the production process should be explained.
8. Information Item 10, experiments information and literature for quality research, includes physical-chemical properties, purity inspection, dissolution, assay, and methodology validation, as well as the data and results collected at various stages.
9. Information Item 11, draft of drug quality specification and notes, and reference standard shall be provided: Quality specification shall comply with the format of the current version of Chinese Pharmacopoeia, and the terminology and units of measure of Chinese Pharmacopoeia should be used. Reagents, reagent solution, buffer solution, titrant and others used and their concentration should follow the current version of Chinese Pharmacopoeia. In the event of a different one was used, detailed explanations should be provided. Reference standard shall be provided with separate information attached to explain the source, physical-chemical constants, purity, content, and measurement method and data of the drugs. Notes to the draft of drug standards shall include the selection of items to be controlled, selection of method, inspection and purity and limitation range, as well as the basis to decide each item.
10. Information Item 12, the test report of the sample products, means the self-test report of the sample products of the drugs in the application. Self-test report for at least one batch of sample product should be provided before the clinical study. Self-test reports of the consecutive 3 batches of sample products should be provided for the market authorization approval after completion of the clinical study.
11. Information item 14, experiments information and literature of the stability study of the drugs, includes stability test conducted together with the use of the immediate packing material and container.
12. Information item 16, Summary of pharmacology and toxicology study, refers to the summary of experiment and global literature of pharmacology and toxicology study of the drug in the application (including pharmacodynamics, mechanism of action, general pharmacology and toxicology, and pharmacokinetics).

13. Information item 27, summary of pre-clinical pharmacokinetics, refer to the summary of experiment and literature of pre-clinical pharmacokinetics (animal) of the drug in application (absorption, metabolite, distribution, execration)
14. Information item 28, Summary of global clinical study information, refers to summary of global literature, abstract and latest updating regarding the clinical trial of the drug in the application.
15. Information item 29, Clinical study protocol: Clinical study protocol should cover details to deal with the critical items including proposed indication, usage and dosage, which should be supported with submission of study information. Clinical study protocol should be scientific, complete and there should be a comprehensive summary of pre-clinical and clinical information related to the key analysis of the potential risks and benefit of proposed trials.
16. Information item 29, Investigator's Brochure, refers to summary of existing pre-clinical and clinical information of the drug in the application, for the purpose to provide Investigator and other participators with information to aid them in understanding the characteristic of the drug and Clinical study protocol. Investigator's Brochure should be concise and objective.

IV Table of Application Information Item and Notes

B Notes

1. Information item 1–30 (except for item 6) of Table of Application Information Item (Table 4.5) should be submitted for Application of Drugs under Registration Categories 1–5. Re-compiled summary Information Items 1–6, Information Item 12 and 14, clinical Information Items 28–32 and other changes and supplemental information shall be submitted and numbered with the numbers of Information Items upon the completion of the clinical study.
   For the drugs under Registration Category 1, upon the completion of the clinical study, all the required information of Information Items 1–30 should be re-edited according to the result of trails conducted during clinical study, and then be re-submitted.
   When the registration of drug substance and registration of preparation of the chemical drug under Registration Category 3 and 4 are applied at the same time, the registration of drug substance should comply with the requirement for production.
2. Information Items 1–16 and 28–30 shall be submitted for the application for drugs under Registration Category 6 the Table of Application Information Items. If the clinical study was required, upon completion of the clinical study, Information Items 28–32 and other changes and supplemental information shall be submitted and numbered with the numbers of Information Items.
3. During the registration of drugs under Registration Category 6, there should be a comprehensive quality study of the process and formula of the drug, and quality comparison with the already marketed drugs according to the national standards. When it is not possible to conduct the quality comparison with the already marketed drugs according to the national standards, a quality study should be

Table 4.5 Application information item

Information Category	Information item	Registration category and information item requirement					
		1	2	3	4	5	6
Summary information	1	+	+	+	+	+	+
	2	+	+	+	+	+	+
	3	+	+	+	+	+	+
	4	+	+	+	+	+	+
	5	+	+	+	+	+	+
	6	+	+	+	+	+	+
Pharmaceutical Information	7	+	+	+	+	+	+
	8	+	*4	+	+	*4	*4
	9	+	+	+	+	+	+
	10	+	+	+	+	+	+
	11	+	+	+	+	+	+
	12	+	+	+	+	+	+
	13	+	+	+	+	+	+
	14	+	+	+	+	+	+
	15	+	+	+	+	+	+
Pharmacology and toxicology study information	16	+	+	+	+	+	+
	17	+	*14	±	*16	–	–
	18	+	*14	±	*16	–	–
	19	+	*14	±	*16	–	–
	20	+	*14	±	*16	–	–
	21	*17	*17	*17	*17	*17	*17
	22	*11	–	–	–	–	–
	23	+	±	±	±	–	–
	24	+	±	±	±	–	–
	25	*6	–	*6	*6	–	–
	26	*7	–	–	–	–	–
	27	+	*18	*18	+	*18	–
Clinical Study information	28	+	+	+	+	+	+
	29	+	+	+	+	+	Δ
	30	+	+	+	+	+	Δ
	31	+	+	+	+	+	Δ
	32	+	+	+	+	+	Δ

6 + Denote the information must be submitted
7 ± Denote literature can be used instead of test information,
8 – Denote the information may be exempted
9 *Denote the information shall be submitted according to the requirement, *6 refer to note 6
10 ΔDenote that the provisions 4 of "V, Requirement For Clinical Study" shall apply
11 Literature refers to literature and/or summary of literature of all Pharmacology and toxicology study information of the drug in the application (including pharmacodynamics, mechanism of action, general pharmacology and toxicology and pharmacokinetics)

conducted according to the requirement for registration of new drug, and if necessary, quality provisions in the national standard can be appended and/or revised.

4. During the application only for preparations, the lawful Certified Documents to evidence the lawful sourcing of the drug substances shall be provided in 2 duplicates, which should be respectively categorized into information item 2 (certified document) and information item 13 (The source, test report and quality specification of drug substance and excipient). For the applicant using domestic drug substance, the documents that should be provided include copies of certified approval document of drug substance, drug standards, test report, business licenses of manufacturers of drug substance, Drug Manufacturing Certificate, and GMP Certificate, supply contract signed with manufacturers of drug substance, purchasing receipts. When the import drug substances were used, copies of supply contract signed with manufacturers of drug substance or its legal domestic agent, Import Drug Certificate, or Pharmaceutical Product Certificate, test report from Drug Control Institute of the local Customs, and drug standards shall be provided. During drug registration, use of investigative preparation with the drug substances without Import Drug Certificate, or Pharmaceutical Product Certificate must be approved by the SFDA.
5. The reproductive toxicity research information corresponding to the drug used for the people at child-bearing age should be submitted based on the natures of the indications and characteristic of the new drug.
6. For any of the drugs with expected treatment period longer than 6 months inclusive, or used for treatment of chronic and recurrent disease, or intermittent use for a regular period of time, experiment information or literature on Carcinogenicity should be provided, and information of carcinogenicity test or literature should be submitted for the following new drugs, based on the indication and characteristic of action:

   i. New drugs with chemical structure relating to the known carcinogen or the metabolite of the new drugs are similar to the known carcinogen.
   ii. During long-term toxicity experiment, cytotoxic effects were shown or extraordinary activation on the growth of cells in certain visceral organs and tissues were caused.
   iii. Drug with a positive test result during mutagenicity test.

7. For new drugs acting on central nervous system, such as analgesics, depressants, stimulants, and drugs with chemical structure related to those compounds liable to cause drug dependence, experiment information of drug dependence should be submitted.
8. For the new drug under Registration Category 1, toxicokinetics study should usually be conducted during the repeated doses toxicity study.
9. Under the Registration Category 1, the optical isomer obtained from a known drug through chiral separation or synthetic method and its preparation, the research information and relevant literature compared between racemate and mono-isomer in areas on pharmacodynamics, pharmacokinetics and toxicology

(normally acute toxicity) should be provided to indicate the justification of the R&D. When the safety range of racemate is narrow, and the available information indicates that the unexpected toxicology (irrelevant to pharmacology) is considerably high, the toxicology test of mono isomer with repeated doses (normally lasting for 3 months) or other toxicology tests (such as reproductive toxicology) shall be provided based on the comprehensive information such as clinical course of treatment, dosage, and indications of the drugs, as well as the people using the drugs.

10. For drugs under Registration Category 1 with fewer components derived from already marketed multi-component drugs, if the component did not include the substance explained in note 6 herein, then Information Items 23–25 may be exempted.
11. For the new combination products under Registration Category 1, Information Item 22 should be submitted.
12. For the new combination products under Registration Category 1, information of toxicity test of repeated dosage compared with single dosage should be provided, and if the—toxicity test of repeated dosage indicated no increase in toxicity, and no change in the target tissue, Information Item 27 should be exempted.
13. For the new combination products under Registration Category 1, if there is no significant change in animal pharmacokinetic study results, then Item 23–25 should be exempted.
14. For the new drugs under Registration Category 2, the route of administration during the pharmacology and toxicology study should be the same with that to be used in clinical study. Generally, the pharmacokinetic test or the related toxicology study information (such as topical and repeated dose toxicity) compared with the original route of administration should be provided.
15. For the drugs under Registration Category 3, the preparations with change in route of administration and already marketed overseas, emphasis should be focused more on the drug absorption or topical toxicity influenced by the excipient, and if necessary, the pharmacokinetic test or other toxicology study should be provided.
16. For the new drugs under Registration Category 4, pharmacokinetic, main pharmacodynamic, normal pharmacology and acute toxicity test information compared with the already marketed drugs should be provided to reflect the difference before and after the changes, and if necessary, the research information on repeated doses toxicity and other relevant pharmacology and toxicology study should be provided. If the preparation is made by changing the acidic or alkaline radicals (or metallic elements) of the salt of a marketed drug, it has been already marketed overseas, then the application information requirement under Registration Category 3 shall be provided.
17. For the drugs for topical use, in addition to the information required under the relevant Registration Category and Information Items, the information under Information Item 21 should also be submitted; topical absorption test should be conducted, if necessary.

18. When there is an obvious safety concerns in the immediate, sustained and controlled released preparations (narrow safety range, significant increase in dosage), animal pharmacokinetic study information compared with the marketed immediate, sustained and controlled released preparations regular preparations should also be provided at single dose.

V Requirement for Clinical Study

1. For the new drugs under Registration Category 1 and 2, clinical trials should be conducted.

    i. Cases of patients for clinical trials should meet the statistical requirement and the minimal cases required.
    ii. The minimal cases required (trial group) of clinical trials are as following, 20–30 for Phase I, 100 for Phase II, 300 for Phase III, 2000 for Phase IV,
    iii. Phase I clinical trial of the contraceptives should be conducted following this Regulation. In Phase II clinical trial, a randomized controlled clinical study should be conducted on at least 100 pairs of subjects for at least 6 menstruation cycles. In Phase III trial, an open trial on at least 1000 cases for 12 menstruation cycles should be accomplished. In Phase IV trial, variable factors of such kind of drugs should be carefully considered to finish the trial with adequate numbers of cases.

2. For the new drugs under the Registration Categories 3 and 4, human pharmacokinetic study and randomized controlled clinical trials on at least 100 pairs of subjects should be conducted. In the event of more than one indication, cases for each main indication shall not be less than 60 pairs. Human pharmacokinetics study and an open trial on at least 500 cases for 12 menstruation cycles should be accomplished for contraceptives.
    Human pharmacokinetics study may be exempted for the following 2 cases:

    i. Preparation of topical use with only topical treatment effect.
    ii. Oral preparation that not be absorbed.

3. The clinical study for the new drug under Registration Category 5 should be conducted in accordance with the following principles,

    i. Bioequivalence trials should be conducted for oral solid preparations on normally 18–24 cases.
    ii. When a bioequivalence trial is difficult to be conducted for oral solid preparations or other non- oral solid preparations, clinical trails should be conducted, and cases for the clinical trials should be at least 100 pairs.
    iii. For the preparations of sustained and controlled released preparations, controlled human pharmacokinetic study and clinical trials related to therapeutics should be conducted on single dose and repeated doses of the drugs, and the cases for clinical trials should be at least 100 pairs.

iv. Necessary clinical trials should be conducted for injection. When clinical trials are needed, clinical case should be at least 100 pairs for single active component injection, and at least 300 pairs for multiple component injection. For microcapsule, microemulsions and liposome, clinical trials should be conducted according to requirement for category 1 and 2.

4. For the oral solid preparations under the Registration Category 6, bioequivalence tests should be conducted on normally 18–24 cases. If the quality of drug needs to be controlled by process and standards, clinical tests should be conducted on normally 100 cases.
5. Application for reduction or exemption of clinical trial should be made during the application of drug registration with detail of reasons and information for reduction or exemption of clinical trials. If a clinical trial is already approved, with exception of the case where reduction or exemption of clinical trial is allowed by this Regulation, reduction or exemption of clinical trial generally should not be allowed. If there is indeed difficulty to complete the clinical trial, application should be made with detail of the basis and plan for reduction or exemption of clinical trial, where the rational should be justified in term of clinical statistic, status of group of patients in the clinical trials.
6. The comparative drug used for the controlled clinical trials shall be already marketed in China. If the comparative drug must be imported, there need to be approval from the SFDA. Priority in choosing the comparative drug of positive clinical test should according to the following:

   i. Drug from the original innovative manufacturer
   ii. The same drug of definite clinical test data
   iii. Drug of the same active substance and route of administration but different dosage form
   iv. Other drug of similar mechanism of action effect and the same indication.

VI Requirement on Import Chemical Drug
A. Requirement of Application Information Items

1. Application Information should be submitted in accordance with the requirement under Table of the Application Information Items of Chemical Drugs. For the application of the new chemical entity not yet marketed in any country, Application Information should be submitted in accordance with the Registration Category 1. For other drugs, Application Information should be submitted in accordance with the Registration Category 3. CTD data as specified by ICH may also be submitted, however, summary general information should be submitted according to requirement of Application Information Items. Drug under Registration Category 1 should be those that are at least in the stage of Phase II Clinical Trials ex-China.

2. Information Item 5, include draft of packaging insert sheet, notes to the draft and the updated literature, the original PI from the manufacturing country, the actual commercial sample of PI used in the manufacturing country and the Chinese

translation. The original commercial packaging and labeling should also be provided for Registration Category 6.

3. All the clinical study information used for the market authorization approval in the original manufacturing countries shall be submitted for Information Item 28.
4. All the application information shall be in Chinese with the original text attached, information in other language (ex-English) may be attached as reference. The Chinese translation shall be consistent with the original language.
5. The Chinese translation of quality specification must comply with the format of the National Drug Standards of China.

B. Requirement and Notes to the Information Item 2, Certified Documents

1. Information Item 2, Certified Documents, includes,

    i. Certified documents, notarized document for the free sale certificate (FSC) issued from the competent authorities of the local country or region where the manufacturer is located, and the GMP Certificate of the manufacturer, and the Chinese translation. Application for the drugs under Registration Category 1, the above Certified Documents can be submitted together with the clinical study report upon the completion of the clinical study in China. However, during the application of Clinical Trails, certified documents of GMP Certificate of the manufacturer issued by local competent drug administration where the drug is manufactured must be provided.
    ii. When the registration of a foreign drug manufacturer is conducted by manufacturer's office in China, copies of Registration Certificate of Resident Office of Foreign Enterprise should be provided. When a foreign drug manufacturer authorizes domestic agent to conduct the registration, copies of the authorization document, notarized document and the Chinese translation, as well as the Business License of the domestic agent shall be provided.
    iii. Documents and explanations to evidence the patent status and ownership of the drugs of the application, the formula of the drugs, the production technology and process of the drugs, as well as letters of statement stating that the new drug will not infringe upon the patent rights of others.

2. Notes,

    i. Certified Documents, notarized document for the FSC and GMP Certificate of the manufacturer should comply with the recommended format by World Health Organization (WHO). The document in other format must be legalized by the Chinese embassy in the original country.
    ii. When the manufacturing site and packaging site separated, the Certified GMP Certificates of manufacturing and packaging site issued by the corresponding countries should be provided.
    iii. In the event that the products not yet approved in the manufacturing country or region, the Certified Documents from the country where the products being marketed and GMP Certificates from this country could be provided. The Certified Documents from the country where the products being marketed and GMP Certificates from this country should be recognized by the SFDA.

iv. For the drug substance, the Certified Documents for the approval of the marketing for the drug substance or its preparation issued by the competent authorities of the original manufacturing country, and the GMP Certificate of the manufacturer should be provided. Drug Master File (DMF) or Certificate of Suitability to the Monographs of the European Pharmacopoeia of the drug substance may also be accepted.
v. To apply for an international multi–center clinical study, certified document of GMP Certificate of the drug manufacturer issued by local drug administration where the manufacturer is located must be provided.
vi. For drug substance or preparation, whenever applicable, certified document of GMP Certificate of the drug manufacturer issued by local food and drug administration where the manufacturer is located, ISO9000 quality assurance certificate issued by the competent organization, and/or free sale certificate (FSC) issued from the competent authorities of the local country or region where the manufacturer is located should be provided

C. Requirement for the Clinical Study Conducted in China

1. During application of drug never marketed in any country, clinical trials should be conducted according to clinical study requirement of Registration Category 1.
2. During application of drug that marketed ex-China but not in China, clinical trials should be conducted according to clinical study requirement of Registration Category III.
3. During application of drug with same route of administration but different dosage form of that of the drug marketed in China, if information item 28 of the application meets the requirement, clinical trials should be conducted according to clinical study requirement of Registration Category 5. If information item 28 of the application did not meet the requirement, clinical trials should be conducted according to clinical study requirement of Registration Category 3.
4. During application of drug already with National Standards, if information item 28 of the application meet the requirement, clinical trials should be conducted according to clinical study requirement of Registration Category 6. If information item 28 of the application did not meet the requirement, clinical trials should be conducted according to clinical study requirement of Registration Category 3. No clinical trial is needed for application of drug substance already with National Standards.
5. For the application only for the importation of the drug substance without available National Drug Standards in China, the clinical study shall be conducted with the use of the preparations of the drug substance.

VII Application Information and Requirement for Radioactive Drugs
A Requirement of Information Items

1. For the application of radioactive drugs: the application information shall be prepared for nuclide, drug substance, packing case and preparations respectively, and be in accordance with the corresponding Category of chemical drugs, and

the Requirement of Application Information Items. Information Items 22 and 26 may be exempted.
2. For the application of diagnosis radioactive drugs, Information Items 24 and 25 may be exempted.
3. For the application of radioactive chemicals and packing case, Information Item 17 and 18 may be exempted. Information required under preparation should also be provided for the application of packing case.

B Notes to the Information Items

1. Information Item 8 shall be submitted in accordance with the following,

    i. Radioactive chemicals: the selection of the production method of the nuclide, irradiation condition, nuclear reaction equation, chemical processing technology after target material eradiated (with the chemical reaction equation and production process attached), detailed operation procedure, possible nuclear impurity introduced, refining (purifying) method, and the specification, standards and analysis of the other chemical reagent (in particular target material), relevant literature and information at domestic and overseas should be provided.
    ii. Packing case: the experiment basis for the determining of packing case, the preparation process, route, reaction condition, operation steps and quality standards of all components of the packing case shall be provided. If any components was made by the manufacturer, then the basis of determining of the detailed synthesis route, synthesis process flow, reaction equation, chemical equation, reaction condition, operation procedure, material input, output ratio, and possible impurity introduced and mixed, quality control of the intermediate products at each steps, refining (purifying) method of finished product, quality standard of the raw material, literature and information at domestic and overseas shall be provided.
    iii. Preparation: basis to choose the formula of the preparation, preparation process, reaction condition, operation procedure, refining or purifying method, quality standards and analysis and test data of raw material, and literature and information at domestic and overseas shall be provided.

2. Information Item 9 shall be submitted in accordance with the following,

    i. Radioactive chemicals: global literature and experiment data (illustrating spectrum and a comprehensive interpretation) used to determine the structure should be provided. If the radioactive nuclide of the radioactive drug is not yet listed in the Chinese Pharmacopoeia, then the decay illustrating chart of the nuclide, experiment data (or spectrum) to determine the nuclear characteristic, as well as experiment information and literature compared with the nuclear characteristic of the nuclide widely recognized at domestic and overseas should be provided.
    ii. Packing case: The detailed component and usage of the packing case should be provided, with explanation of the function of each and every components of the packing case. If any component was made by the manufacturer, then global literature and the detailed experiment data (illustrating spectrum and

a comprehensive interpretation) used to determine the structure should be provided.

iii. Preparation: Experiment data to determine the chemical structure should be provided. If there is a difficulty to provide, the reason should be explained and reasonable logic can be used to conclude the possible chemical structure or quote the relevant literature that can be used as basis.

3. Information Item 10 shall be submitted in accordance with the following,

   i. Radioactive chemicals: research items for the physical-chemical constants, items of the purity testing, the screening of the method to measure the content, and the basis to determine the method should be provided with details of the measuring method, and measuring data.
   ii. Packing case: the analyzing and measuring method, principle and data of the characteristic, determination, clarity, and PH value of the solutions should be provided. Determining of the content measuring method, the experiment data, testing method for bacteria, intracellular toxicity, and the research information to decide the limitation should be provided.
   iii. Preparation: determining method and experiment data of the physical-chemical properties, characteristic, determining and principle, PH value, radioactive nuclear purity (including main nuclear impurity), radioactive chemical purity, radioactivity, chemical purity of the drug should be provided. For the injection, methods used for testing for bacteria, intracellular toxicity, data, basis to determine the limitation of intracellular toxicity should be provided.

4. Information Item 17 shall be submitted in accordance with the following,

   i. For the diagnosis radioactive drug, information about the testing and measuring method, testing conditions and result explanation of image of the target organ and whole body planar image should be provided. The image picture or its copies of the development at all phase of test, as well as the function measuring result should be provided.
   ii. For the therapeutically radioactive drug, experiment information of animal experimental model within the main indications should be provided, detailed global literature of pharmacodynamic study of the drug or other similar drug should also be provided.

5. Information Item 19 shall be submitted in accordance with the following,

Acute toxicity test should be conducted on mouse for the drug substance of radioactive drug under Registration Categories 1 and 3, while packing case and preparations should be tested with abnormal toxicity test. If there is only a limited quantity produced from refining and synthesis of the drug substance and there is only a trivial clinical usage, then the abnormal toxicity test may also be adopted.

6. Information Item 20 shall be submitted in accordance with the following,

   i. For the radioactive drug under Registration Category 1, experiment information and literature of long-term toxicity test and medical internal irradiation absorption dose (MIRD) on rat and dog should be provided.

ii. For the radioactive diagnosis and therapeutic radioactive drug under Registration Category 1, internal irradiation absorption dose after the full decay of the radioactive nuclide of the drug, estimation of absorption dose of the human target organ and non-target organ, or the literature of the drug or similar drug at domestic and overseas should be provided.

C Requirement of Clinical Study
The clinical study of the radioactive drug should be conducted in accordance with the corresponding Category of the chemical drugs. In some special case, cases of clinical trials may be adjusted to an appropriate level subject to the statistical requirement.

D Definition
Radioactive chemicals, packing case and preparation referred in this provision have the following definition:

Radioactive chemicals: means the material of Radioactive Nuclide, which will be directly used for the preparation of radioactive drug preparation.

Packing case: a collective name for unidentified ligand, reducing agent, oxidant, separator, which will be used as auxiliary of the radioactive chemicals for the purpose of quick preparation before any application.

Preparation: refers to the radioactive drug made of Radioactive Nuclide and other substance.

4.7 Classification of Investigational Product—Therapeutic Biological Products

(Annex 3: Registration Categories and Application Information Items
Requirements of Biological Products, Provisions for Drug Registration the SFDA Order No. 28, 2007)

Part I Therapeutic Biological Products

I Registration Categories

1. Biological products not yet marketed at domestic or overseas.
2. Mono-Clonal Antibody.
3. Gene therapy, somatic cell therapy as well as the preparations.
4. Allergen products.
5. Multi component products with bioactivity extracted from, or by fermentation from human and/or animal tissues and/or body fluid,
6. New combination product made from the already marketed biological products.
7. A product that is marketed already overseas but not yet marketed domestic.
8. Some of the strains used for preparing of micro-ecological products not yet approved.

9. Products with not completely same structure with the already marketed products and not yet marketed at domestic or overseas (including Amino Acid Locus Mutation/Absence, modification caused by a different expression system, deletion, changed interpretation, as well as chemical modifications of the product).
10. Products with a method of preparation different with the already marketed one, (such as use of different expression system, host cells).
11. Products first time made with DNA recombination technology (such as use of recombination technology to replace the synthesis technology, tissue extraction or fermentation technology).
12. Products transformed from non-injection into injection, or topical use into systemic use, and not yet marketed at domestic or overseas.
13. The marketed products with a change in dosage form but no change in route of administration.
14. Products with a change in route of administration (excluding the above Category 12).
15. Biological products admitted with National Standards.

II Application Dossier Items
A Summary

1. Name of the drugs.
2. Certified Documents.
3. Objectives and basis for the application.
4. Summary and evaluation of main research results.
5. Sample draft of insert sheet, notes to the draft, and literature.
6. Sample design for packing, label.

B Pharmaceutical Study Information

7. Summary of Pharmaceutical Study Information.
8. Research information of the raw material used for production.

    i. Research information about the sourcing, collection, and quality control of the animal or plant tissues or cells, unprocessed blood plasma.
    ii. Research information about the sourcing, collection (or selection) process, and determining of cells used for production.
    iii. Information about the establishment, determination, and storage of the strains banks, as well as the stability of transfer of culture.
    iv. Research information about the sourcing, quality control of other raw materials used for production.

9. Research information about the production process of the raw materials or the unprocessed fluids.
10. Research information of the formula and process of the preparations, source and quality standards of the supplementives, as well as the relevant literatures.
11. Experiment information and literature of the quality study of the products, including the preparing and standardizing of the Standard Material or Controls,

as well as the comparison information with those similar product already marketed at domestic or overseas.

12. Record of manufacturing and testing of the sample products to be used for application of clinical study.
13. Draft of the manufacture and test standards, with notes to the draft and verification information of the test method.
14. Preliminary research information about the stability.
15. Basis for selection and quality standards of immediate packing material and container.

C Pharmacology and Toxicology Study Information

16. Summary about the pharmacology and toxicology study information.
17. Experiments information and literature of pharmacodynamic.
18. Experiments information and literature of regular pharmacology study.
19. Experiments information and literature of acute toxicity.
20. Experiments information and literature of long term toxicity.
21. Experiments information and literature of animal pharmacokinetics.
22. Experimental data and literature of mutations test.
23. Experimental data and literature of reproductive toxicity.
24. Experimental data and literature of carcinogenicity test.
25. Research information and literature of immunotoxicity and/or immunogenticity.
26. Experiments information and literature on major special safety test information related to topical and systemic use of the drugs, such as hemolysis and topical (blood vessel, skin, mucous membrane, endometium, tunica and muscle) irritation.
27. Experiments information and literature of the efficacy, toxicity and pharmacokinetics caused by the interactions between multiple components in the combination products.
28. Experiment information and literature of drug dependence.

D Clinical Study Information

29. Summary of clinical study at domestic and overseas.
30. Clinical study plan and protocol.
31. Investigator's Brochure.
32. Sample draft of Informed Consent Form, approval of the ethics committee.
33. Summary report of the clinical study.

E Others

34. Brief summary of the pre-clinical study.
35. Experiments and study information and summary of the production process improvement, quality perfection, the pharmacology and toxicology study and other works conducted during the clinical study.
36. Amendments and basis to amend of the approved manufacturing and testing standards.

37. Research and study information of the stability test.
38. Manufacturing and testing records of the 3 consecutive batches of trial products.

III Requirement of the application information (Tables 4.6 and 4.7)

VI Notes to the Application Information
A Item 1–31 are required for Clinical Trial application, Item 1–6, 15 and 29–38 are to be submitted after the completion of clinical trials.

B Notes to General Information Requirements

1. Information Item 1, Name of the new drug, including International Nonproprietary Name, English name, China adopted name and its Chinese phonetics, molecular weight. The nomenclature of the drug should be explained for any new name.
2. Item 2, Certified Documents includes,

    i. Copies of Certified Documents of lawful registration of the Applicant (business licenses), Drug Manufacturing License and change registration, GMP Certificate.
    ii. Documents stating patent status and ownership or the biological products of application, or the formula used, process used, and letters of statement stating that no infringement upon the patent rights of others.
    iii. Copy of Approval of Clinical Study of New Drugs and drug standard of investigative drugs should be provided for application of the production of new biological product.
    iv. Copies of the Drug Packing Material and Container Certificate or Import Drug Packing Material and Container Certificate for the immediate packing material and container.

3. Information Item 3, objective and basis for the application, includes the current status and relevant literature of the research, marketing, and the relevant literature of the products, or the summary of production, the use of the products at domestic and overseas, analysis of the renovation, and feasibility of the products.
4. Information Item 4, summary and evaluation of main research results include the summary of the main research results of the products, and a comprehensive evaluation of the safety, efficacy, and quality controllability of the products.
5. Information Item 5, sample draft of insert sheet, notes to the draft, and literature, includes the sample draft of the insert sheet drafted in accordance with the relevant regulations, notes to all the items of the draft of the insert sheet, relevant literature or the latest version of the insert sheet from the original manufactures in the original language and the translations.

C Note to Requirement of Pharmaceutical Study Information

1. For any production use of raw materials sourced from cows, relevant material required by SFDA should be provided.
2. For products extracted from human and/or animal tissues and body fluid, and/or for the re-combination products by expression of McAb and eukaryote,

Table 4.6 Application information items for therapeutic biological products, (Information Items 1–15, 29–38)

Information category	Information item	Registration category and information item requirement														
		1	2	3	4	5	6	7	8	9	10	11	12	13	14	15
Summary information	1	+	+	Refer to Technical guidance	Refer to Technical guidance	+	+	+	+	+	+	+	+	+	+	+
	2	+	+			+	+	+	+	+	+	+	+	+	+	+
	3	+	+			+	+	+	+	+	+	+	+	+	+	+
	4	+	+			+	+	+	+	+	+	+	+	+	+	+
	5	+	+			+	+	+	+	+	+	+	+	+	+	+
	6	+	+			+	+	+	+	+	+	+	+	+	+	+
Pharmaceutical Information	7	+	+			+	+	+	+	+	+	+	−	+	−	+
	8	+	+			+	−	+	+	+	+	+	−	−	−	+
	9	+	+			+	−	+	+	+	+	+	−	−	−	+
	10	+	+			+	+	+	+	+	+	+	−	+	−	+
	11	+	+			+	+	+	+	+	+	+	−	+	−	+
	12	+	+			+	+	+	+	+	+	+	−	+	−	+
	13	+	+			+	+	+	+	+	+	+	−	+	−	+
	14	+	+			+	+	+	+	+	+	+	−	+	−	+
	15	+	+			+	+	+	+	+	+	+	−	+	−	+
Clinical Study information	29	+	+			+	+	+	+	+	+	+	+	+	+	+
	30	+	+			+	+	+	+	+	+	+	+	+	+	+
	31	+	+			+	+	+	+	+	+	+	+	+	+	+
	32	+	+			+	+	+	+	+	+	+	+	+	+	+
	33	+	+			+	+	+	+	+	+	+	+	+	+	+
Other	34	+	+			+	+	+	+	+	+	+	+	+	+	+
	35	+	+			+	+	+	+	+	+	+	+	+	+	+
	36	+	+			+	+	+	+	+	+	+	−	+	−	+
	37	+	+			+	+	+	+	+	+	+	−	+	−	+
	38	+	+			+	+	+	+	+	+	+	−	+	−	+

1 + denote the information must be submitted
2 − denote the information may be exempted
3 ± denote the information required or not required based on the particular case

Table 4.7 Application information item requirements for pharmacology and toxicology of therapeutic biological product (Information items 16–28)

Cat.	Item	Registration category and requirement for information														
		1	2	3	4	5	6	7	8	9	10	11	12	13	14	15
Pharmacology & Toxicology	16	+	+	Refer to Technical guidance	Refer to Technical guidance	+	+	+	+	+	+	+	+	+	+	+
	17	+	+			+	+	+	+	+	+	+	+	+	+	+
	18	+	+			+	+	+	+	+	+	+	+	+	+	+
	19	+	+			+	+	+	+	+	+	+	+	+	+	±
	20	+	+			+	+	+	+	+	+	+	+	+	+	+
	21	+	+			±	±	±	−	+	±	+	+	±	+	±
	22	±	±			±	±	±	−	±	±	±	±	−	±	−
	23	±	±			±	±	±	−	±	±	±	±	−	±	−
	24	±	±			±	±	±	−	±	±	±	±	−	±	−
	25	+	+			+	+	+	−	+	+	+	+	−	+	±
	26	+	+			+	+	+	−	+	+	+	+	+	+	±
	27	−	−			−	+	−	−	−	−	−	−	−	−	−
	28	±	±			±	−	−	−	±	−	−	±	−	−	−

4 + denote the information must be submitted
5 − denote the information may be exempted
6 ± denote the information required or not required based on the particular case

additional information for the verification of de-activation process of virus should be added.

3. For any potential human toxic material introduced during the production process, the research information about the removal effect of process should be provided, and the standard to control the material within the limit should be established, and basis for the standards should be provided.
4. Information item 11, information of quality study of the product, includes analysis of physical-chemical characteristic, determining of the structure, verification test, purity measuring, content measuring, and bioactivity measuring of the product. Additional research information on analysis of impurity should be provided for the purified products.
5. For the biological product under registration category 15, in principle, the quality standard should not lower than the similar products already marketed.
6. Production scale of that during the production of 3 consecutive batches of trial products should be to the designed production capacity, production scale before and after marketing should be consistent, if there is significant change in production scale before and after marketing, a supplemental application should be applied.

D Note to Requirement of Pharmacology and Toxicology Study Information

1. Because of the diversity and complication of the biological products, requirement of pharmacology and toxicology study information may not be applicable for all therapeutic products, so applicant should provide information with scientific and reasonable reference to the relevant guiding principle, taking the particular characteristic of the biological products, to meet the requirement of drugs evaluation during the application of a particular biological product. If the above requirement is not applicable for the products to be registered, applicant should make notes in the application dossier, and if necessary, provide other relevant information.

2. In principle, the related animal should be used for pharmacology and toxicology study. Attention should be paid during the study to how the immunogenic of the product may impact the design, results and assessment of animal experiment. If some of the standardized research method is not applicable for the products to be registered, applicant should make notes in the application dossier, and if necessary, provide other relevant information.
3. The standardized genotoxicity study is generally not applicable for biological products, therefore, the study is usually not required, however, if there is any particular safety concerns in the products, related research data should be submitted.
4. For those product used for child bearing group, the registration applicant should assess the Reproductive toxicity taking consideration of the specification and indication of the products, and if necessary, provide the research information related to Reproductive toxicity.

5. The standardized carcinogenicity tests are generally not applicable for most of biological products, however, the registration applicant should assess the carcinogenicity risks taking into consideration the bioactivity, clinical duration, group to use the products. If there is any possibility in carcinogenicity caused by the products, related research information should be provided.
6. Topical Irritation research information should be provided for Injection, Suppositories, ophthalmologic, spray, Ointment, cream, and gel. Hemolysis test should be conducted for injection and biological products with tendency of hemolysis.
7. When there is any concerns with drug dependence (need for repetitive use, possibly acting on central nerve system), applicant should assess the possibility of drug dependence based on the functioning mechanism of the product, and if necessary, provide with research data on drug dependence.
8. For the products under Registration Category 2, (Mono-Clonal Antibody)

   i. When there is antibody combination information to indicate that the quadruman shall be the most correlated specie, for the uncoupled Mono-Clonal Antibody test, the animal of this specie shall be used to conduct the main pharmacology and pharmacokinetic study.
   ii. For toxicology and pharmacokinetic study, the test should best be conducted on the animal experimental model with the same target antigen with human. If there is neither suitable animal experimental model nor animal with relevant antigen, and the cross-reaction test result with human tissue is negative, then toxicology study information may be exempted. Immuno-toxicity study should focus on the potential toxicity reaction when combining the non-target tissues, such as the cross reaction with the human tissues/cells or the combination with non-target tissue. If there is a suitable experimental model, cross-reaction tests should be conducted with animal in vivo, in addition to being conducted in vitro. In particular for immunity combination product with cytolysis or the antibody with Antibody Dependent Cell-mediated Cytotoxicity (ADCC), additional animal toxicity tests on more than one kind of animal at over-dosage or multi doses should be considered.

9. For the products under Registration Category 3, (Gene therapy products), pharmacology and toxicology study should focus on:

   i. Related animal should be used for study. In principle, biological reaction of related animal to the expression of gene therapy products should be relevant to that of human body. When the virus carrier is used in the products, the animal should also susceptible to wild virus.
   ii. Standardized pharmacokinetics study is not applicable for gene therapy products, where the focus of pharmacokinetics study of gene therapy products should be the introduction, distribution and elimination of the gene, if or not the gene act on host cell and reproductive cell group, pharmacokinetics action of the gene expression, distribution and elimination of carrier.
   iii. The possibility of genotoxicity, carcinogenicity, Reproductive toxicity should be assessed based on the data related to distribution and elimination of introduced gene and its expression, and if necessary, the related research data should be provided.

10. For the human blood products under Registration Category 5, safety research information (item 19–28) may be exempted, once related information or evidence is provided, if the dosage is not to exceed the biologically tolerance dosage, and if there is no special process is used to treat the product, and there is no special solution is used.
11. For the biological product under category 7, 10 and 15, consistency with the marketed products should be firstly assessed for the areas of preparation process, quality standards, and bioactivity (it should include pharmacokinetics data if necessary), by using of method of comparison study. If there is great similarity with the marketed product in the above areas, and if the marketed products have a definite clinical safety and effectiveness record, only one animal is required for the toxicology study, where the duration of long term toxicology study may be only 1 month. Major pharmacodynamic study may just conduct 1–2 items of study, or be part of the Activity Assays of quality standards as general. If the applicant can sufficiently evidence the consistency of the product with the marketed products, it can be the reason to apply for reduction or exemption of related pharmacology and toxicology study items.
12. For products under Registration Category 8, the research information used for the determining of the dosage and the research information about the influence that the products impose on the normal bacteria should be provided.
13. For the biological products under Registration Category 13, choosing of the items to be tested should be based on a comprehensive consideration of the characteristic of the changed dosage form of the product and the relevant pharmaceutical and clinical requirements possibly arisen from such change,

    i. For the transforming between injections, powder for injection, and intravenous infusion, if there is no change in the clinical usage and dosage, there is usually only a need for research information on hemolysis test and local irritation test. Subject to the change in formula, if necessary, other related toxicology study information should be provided.
    ii. For other special preparation such as liposome, which can change the original Pharmacokinetic behavior, pharmacology and toxicology study should be designed based on comparison study data of animal Pharmacokinetic between old and new dosage, taking consideration of identity, safety tolerance clinical indication and patient group to use the products, and the related data should be submitted.

14. For the preparations under Registration Category 14, if there are sufficient reasons and/or literature to evidence the in vivo metabolite and safety of the products are similar before and after the change of the route of administration, and then reduction or exemption of some of the items required for this biological product may be applied.

E Others

1. Requirements for therapeutic biological products shall be applicable for in vivo diagnosis biological product; the data should be submitted under the applicable category.

2. For any new indication of biological products, the registration should follow the new drug registration category with submission the related dossier. If there is no change in pharmaceutical aspect, and there is no increase in clinical dosage and duration, the related Pharmacokinetic, pharmacology and toxicology data may be exempted.

V Notes to the Clinical Study

1. Clinical trials should be conducted for the application of new drug.
2. Cases of patient for clinical trials should meet the statistical requirement and minimal cases requirement.
3. The minimal sample size requirements for clinical trials are, Phase I: 20, Phase II: 100, Phase III: 300.
4. Clinical trials for the products under Registration Categories 1–12 should be conducted in accordance with requirement for new drugs.
5. Only Phase III clinical trials are usually required for the products under Registration Categories 13–15.
6. For the renovated sustained released preparation, comparisons study of human pharmacokinetic study and clinical trials shall be conducted.

VI Application Information and requirement for Import Therapeutic Biological Products

A Requirement for Application Information Items

Application information shall be submitted in accordance with the Registration Application Information Items. For the application of the preparations not yet marketed at domestic or overseas, information shall be submitted in accordance with Registration Category 1. For application of products marketed overseas but not in China, information shall be submitted in accordance with Registration Category 7. For application of products already marketed in China, information shall be submitted in accordance with Registration Category 15.

B Requirement and Notes to the Information Item 2, Certified Documents

1. Information Item 2, Certified Documents includes,

   i. Certified Documents, notarized documents for the approval of the marketing of the products issued from the competent authorities at the local country or region where the manufactured is located, and the GMP Certificate of the manufacturer, and the Chinese translation.
   ii. For application for the product not yet marketed at domestic or overseas, the above Certified Documents can be submitted together with the clinical study report upon the completion of the clinical study in China.
   iii. When the registration of a foreign drug manufacturer is conducted by manufacturer's office in China, copies of Registration Certificate of Resident Office of Foreign Enterprise should be provided.
   iv. When a foreign drug manufacturer authorizes at domestic agent to conduct the registration, copies of the authorization document, notarized documents and the Chinese translation, as well as the Business License of the domestic agent shall be provided.

v. Documents and explanations to evidence the patent status and ownership of the product, the formula of the product, the production technology and process of the product, as well as letters of guarantee stating no infringement upon the patent rights of others.

2. Notes

   i. The GMP Certificate and approval for the marketing of the product issued by the competent authorities at the local countries or region where the manufacturer is located should be acknowledged by the Chinese embassy in the local countries and the public notaries in the countries.
   ii. When the preparations are manufactured in one location and packed in another location, then the Certified Documents of GMP Certificates of the preparations manufacturer and packing manufacturer issued by the countries where the manufacturers are located should be provided.
   iii. In the event that the products have not yet been approved to be marketed by the country or the region where the products are manufactured, then the Certified Documents from the other country where the products is approved to be marketed should be provided, and should be recognized by the SFDA. But the GMP certificates must be issued by the competent authorities from the country where the manufacturer is located.

C Requirement for other Information Items

1. All the clinical study information used during the application for marketing in the local countries or region where the manufacturer is located should be submitted as Information Item 29.
2. All the application information should be translated into Chinese with the original language attached. The Chinese translation shall be consistent with the original language.
3. The Chinese translation of biological products standards must comply with the format required by the National Drug Standards of China.

D Requirements for clinical study conducted in China

1. A clinical study should be applied for in accordance with Registration Category 1 for the application of the biological products not yet marketed at domestic or overseas.
2. A clinical study should be applied for in accordance with Registration Category 7 for the application of the biological products already marketed overseas but not yet marketed domestic.
3. A clinical study should be applied for in accordance with Registration Category 15 for the application of the biological products admitted with National Standards.

4.8 Classification of Investigational Product—Preventive Biological Products

(Annex 3: Registration Categories and Application Information Items Requirements of Biological Products, Provisions for Drug Registration the SFDA Order No. 28, 2007)

Part II
Preventive Biological Products

I Registration Categories

1. Vaccine not yet marketed at domestic or overseas.
2. DNA vaccine.
3. An already marketed vaccine with new adjuvant. Change of carrier of combined vaccine.
4. Non-purified vaccine, or full cell vaccine (bacteria, virus) changed into purified vaccine, or combined vaccine.
5. Vaccine with strains not yet approved in China (except for vaccine for influenza, vaccine for leplospirosis and others).
6. Vaccine already marketed overseas but not yet marketed domestic.
7. Combined vaccine prepared with vaccine already marketed domestic.
8. Re-combination vaccine with protective antigen spectrum different with the marketed one.
9. Vaccine manufactured with the change of the other approved expression or the other approved cellular stroma. Vaccine using new process, which is proved to improve the safety and effectiveness of the vaccine based on the data of laboratory.
10. Vaccine with change of de-activator (method of deactivation) or de-toxicitor (method of de-toxicity).
11. Vaccine with change in the route of administration.
12. A domestic marketed vaccine with change in dosage form but no change in route of administration.
13. Vaccine with dosage of immunity or immunity procedure.
14. Vaccine with an enlarged group of people (enlarged age range).
15. Vaccine admitted with National Standards.

II Application Information Items

1. Summary information

    i. Name of the new products.
    ii. Certified Documents.
    iii. Objective and basis for the application.
    iv. Sample draft of the insert sheet, notes to the draft and literature.
    v. Sample design of the packing, label.

2. Research information summary and the evaluation information.
3. Research information of the production bacterial and toxicity strains.

   i. Source and characteristics and Certified Documents.
   ii. Information on establishment and determination of Batches of the strains.
   iii. Information on Stability during transfer of culture.
   iv. Test report of batches of bacterial and toxicity strains used for production from NICPBP.

4. Research information of the cellular stroma for production.

   i. Information on Source, characteristic and determination of cellular stroma.
   ii. Information on establishment and determination of Cell bank.
   iii. Information on Stability of transfer of culture.
   iv. NICPBP test report of the production cells bank for cellular stroma used for manufacture.
   v. Source and quality standards of culture fluid, addictive and others.

5. Research information of production process and technology.

   i. Research data of the production process of original fluid of the vaccine, theoretical and experiment basis and verification data.
   ii. Formula and production process of the preparations, and the basis to determine shall be provided.

6. Research information of the quality of the product: non-clinical efficacy and safety research data.

   i. Research data on quality study and registration standard study.
   ii. Research and verification information of the test method.
   iii. Comparison analysis with similar products.
   iv. Analysis information of product antigencity, product immunocity and protectiveness of the animal test
   v. Research information of animal hypersensitivity test.
   vi. Information of animal safety evaluation of the product.

7. Draft of manufacturing and testing standards drafted in accordance with relevant regulations, attached with the notes on how each items were drafted, and the relevant literature.
8. Record of the manufacturing and testing of sample product to be used for application of clinical study.
9. Preliminary stability test information.
10. Quality certificate of the animal used for production, research and test.
11. Draft of Informed Consent, the clinical study plan and study protocol.
12. Summary of the pre-clinical study.
13. Summary information of the relevant clinical study at domestic and overseas.
14. Summary of clinical study report including sample of Informed Consent Form, approval from the Ethics Committee.

15. Summary of work, experiment and study information on the improvement of the production technology and the perfection of quality standards during clinical study.
16. Stability research information to determine the storage and validity period of the vaccine.
17. Amendments and basis to amend of the approved manufacturing and test standards.
18. Record of production and testing of the 3 consecutive batches of the trial products.

III Application Information Items Table (Table 4.8)

IV Notes to the Application Information Items

1. Items 1–11 shall be submitted for application of clinical study. Items 1, 2 and 12–18 shall be submitted upon completion of clinical study.
2. Information item 1

    i. Name of the new drug, including International Nonproprietary Name, English name, China adopted name and its Chinese phonetics, basis for the name. The nomenclature of the drug should be explained for any new name.

    Certified Documents includes,

    a. Certified Documents of lawful registration of the Applicant (business licenses), copies of Drug Manufacturing License and change registration, GMP Certificate. For the application of production, copies of GMP Certificate for the workshop where the sample product of the drug was manufactured should be provided.
    b. Notes stating patent status and ownership or the biological product in the application, or the formula, process to be used, and letters of guarantee stating that no infringement upon the patent rights of others.
    c. Copy of Approval of Clinical Study of New Drugs and drug standards of investigative drugs should be provided for the production of new biological product.
    d. Copies of the Drug Packing Material and Container Certificate or Import Drug Packing Material and Container Certificate for the immediate packing material and container.

    ii. Objective and basis for the application includes the relevant literature of the current research and marketing status of the products, or summary of the production, and inoculation use at domestic and overseas, and the analysis information of renovation and feasibility of the vaccine.
    iii. Sample of insert sheet, notes to the draft and literature includes sample draft of insert sheet drafted in accordance with the relevant regulations, notes on how all items of the draft of the insert sheet were drafted and the latest relevant literature or the latest version of the insert sheet in the original language from the original manufacturer and the translation.

Table 4.8 Application information item

Info Item	Registration category and requirement for information														
	1	2	3	4	5	6	7	8	9	10	11	12	13	14	15
1	+	+	+	+	+	+	+	+	+	+	+	+	+	+	+
2	+	+	+	+	+	+	+	+	+	+	+	+	+	+	+
3	+	+	−	−	+	+	+	+	±	−	−	−	−	−	+
4	+	+	−	−	+	+	+	+	±	−	−	−	−	−	+
5(1)	+	+	+	+	+	+	+	+	+	+	−	−	−	−	+
5(2)	+	+	+	+	+	+	+	+	+	+	+	+	−	−	+
6	+	+	+	+	+	+	+	+	+	+	+	+	+	+	+
7	+	+	+	+	+	+	+	+	+	+	+	+	+	+	+
8	+	+	+	+	+	+	+	+	+	+	+	+	+	+	+
9	+	+	+	+	+	+	+	+	+	+	+	+	+	+	+
10	+	+	+	+	+	+	+	+	+	+	+	+	+	+	+
11	+	+	+	+	+	+	+	+	+	+	+	+	+	+	+
12	+	+	+	+	+	+	+	+	+	+	+	+	+	+	+
13	+	+	+	+	+	+	+	+	+	+	+	+	+	+	+
14	+	+	+	+	+	+	+	+	+	+	+	+	+	+	+
15	+	+	+	+	+	+	+	+	+	+	+	+	+	+	+
16	+	+	+	+	+	+	+	+	+	+	+	+	+	+	+
17	+	+	+	+	+	+	+	+	+	+	+	+	+	+	±
18	+	+	+	+	+	+	+	+	+	+	+	+	+	+	+

1 + denote the information must be submitted
2 − denote the information may be exempted
3 ± denote the information may or may not be required based on the particular case

3. Information Item 3

    i. Research information of Source and characteristics: including source of the production bacterial and toxicity strains, research information or Certified Documents to show the bacterial and toxicity strains can be used for production, history including history of separation, determination and de-toxicity, characteristic, research information on the adaptability to cellular stroma, infective titer, antigenocity, immuno-genecity, toxic (or toxicity).
    ii. Research information of establishment and determination of Batches of the strains: including relevant information on initial batch of the production bacterial and toxicity strains, primary generation batch, information of the establishment of production batch bank, including generation numbers, the preparation, storage of sub-batch of production strains, test report of each batch of production bacterial and toxicity strains, items to be tested including exogenesis factors, determination test, characteristic, infective titer, antigenocity, immunocity. For strain of primary generation, gene sequence should be determined.
    iii. Research information of Stability during transfer of culture includes determining of the limitation of last generation number to be used. For items to be tested, refer to the test items of batches of strains.

4. Information Item 4

    i. Information on Source and characteristic: including source of cellular stroma used for production, Certified Documents and research information to show that the cellular stroma can be used for production, history (including the history of establishment of cells system, determining, and history of transfer of culture), biological characteristic, exogenesis factors test, analysis of karyotype, tumorigencity test and other study. For those vaccines with change of cellular stroma, in principle, the safety risks of new cellular stroma should not be higher than the marketed vaccine.
    ii. Information on Cell bank: including information on the establishment of production cellular stroma initial cell bank, primary cell bank, production cell bank, including the generation number, preparation, storage and administration of the various production cell banks, comprehensive tests of cell banks. Items to be tested include biological characteristic, karyotype analysis and exogenesis factors inspection.
    iii. Information on Stability of transfer of culture: including determining of the limitation of last generation number to be used. For items to be tested, refer to items to be tested of the cell bank, with addition of tumorigencity.
    iv. In the event that material sourced from cows is used, relevant information should be provided in accordance with requirements of SFDA.
    v. The above information may be exempted for bacteria vaccine

5. Information Item 5

Information on Research of the production process of original fluid of the vaccine: including the main technical parameters to optimize the production process, including inoculation quantity of bacteria (or virus), culture conditions, fermentation condition, de-activity and crack process conditions, extraction and purifying of the bioactive material, removal of the potential toxic material to human, activation, coupling and combination technology of antigen and carrier for the combined vaccine, research information of the percentage of various bioactive components, compatibility of antigen and etc. Summary of the materials input, output of various intermediary products and the quality during the production process, finished product output and quality should be provided. Quality of the products under the production process should be assessed and verified.

When there is possible substance with potential harm to human going into production process, verification data with the removal process shall be provided. Limit standard of harmful substance and basis should be provided.

6. Information item 6 (1)

For purified vaccine, quality study should usually include Measuring of antigen components, contents, molecular weight, purity; specificity determination; and measure and test of the content (or residual) of the non-effective component.

Quality standards and test results of the products, including quality standards and test results of the each single component of the combined vaccine

After the production process is defined, the registration standards of the products should be defined based on test results of trial product of multiple batches by using of statistical analysis methodology.

7. Information item 6 (3)

If there is already similar vaccine in the market, there is a need to compare with this vaccine, if the new vaccine is developed based on the marketed one, comparison study should be conducted to the quality of the old vaccine. For a combined vaccine, the quality comparison should be conducted to each single vaccine.

8. Information item 6 (6)

Toxicity reversion test study information should be provided for toxoid vaccine or vaccine used toxoid as carrier.

Toxicity test study information should be provided based on the group of people to use the vaccine, characteristic of the vaccine, immunity dosage, and immunity procedure.

9. Information item 9 and 16 Stability test of vaccine should be conducted in such way that one than 3 batches of product are stored under the proposed storage condition, the efficacy and activity of the vaccine shall be checked out periodically and the trend should be analyzed, where an overall inspection is conducted at critical point of time. In addition, accelerated Stability should also be conducted.
10. Information item 18, production scale of that during the production of 3 consecutive batches of trial products should be to the designed production capacity, production scale before and after marketing should be consistent, if there is significant change in production scale before and after marketing, a supplemental application should be applied

V Notes to the Clinical Study

1. Cases of patients (subject) for the clinical trials should meet the statistical requirement and minimal cases requirement. Minimal cases include both trial group and control group.
2. The minimal cases requirement for a clinical trial is, Phase I: 20, Phase II: 300, Phase III: 500.
3. For vaccine under Registration Categories 1–9 and 14, the clinical trials should be conducted in accordance with the requirement for new drugs.
4. For vaccine under Registration Category 10, if the research information is provided to evidence no change in the safety and effectiveness of the vaccine after the deactivation or de-toxicity of the vaccine, then normally clinical trials may be exempted.
5. For vaccine under Registration Category 11, a clinical trial normally should be conducted in accordance with requirement for new drugs. But the Phase I clinical trials may be exempted for the vaccine with the route of administration changed from injections into non-injections.
6. Only the phase III clinical trials are needed for the vaccine under Registration Categories 12 and 15.
7. For the vaccine under Registration Category 13, the Phase I clinical trials may be exempted for the vaccine where the immunity procedure is changed.
8. For the preventive products used in infants, in principle, the sequence of Phase I clinical trials should be adults first, then children and then infants.
9. Each phase of clinical trial should be conducted after the completion of previous phase in accordance with the prescribed immunity procedures.
10. For the vaccine applied for marketing first time in China, Epidemiology Protective Test should be conducted,

VI Application Information and requirement for Import Preventive Biological Products

A Requirement with information items

Application information shall be submitted in accordance with the Registration Application Information Items. For the application of the vaccines not yet marketed at domestic or overseas, information shall be submitted in accordance with Registration Category 1. For the application of the vaccines marketed overseas but not yet marketed at domestic, information shall be submitted in accordance with Registration Category 6. For the application of the vaccines already marketed at domestic, information shall be submitted in accordance with Registration Category 15.

B Requirement and Notes to the Information Item 2 (Certified Documents)

1. Information Item 2 (Certified Documents) includes the following,
    i. Certified Document, Notarized Document for the approval of the marketing for the vaccine issued from the competent authorities at the local country or region where the manufacturer is located, and the GMP Certificate of the manufacturer, and the Chinese translation. For application for the vaccine not yet marketed at domestic or overseas, the above Certified Documents can be submitted together with the clinical study report upon the completion of the clinical study in China.
    ii. When the registration of a foreign drug manufacturer is conducted by manufacturer's office in China, copies of Registration Certificate of Resident Office of Foreign Enterprise should be provided. When a foreign drug manufacturer authorizes domestic agent to conduct the registration, copies of the authorization document, notarized document and the Chinese translation, as well as the Business License of the domestic agent shall be provided.
    iii. Documents and explanations to evidence the patent status and ownership of the biological product, the formula of the biological product, the production technology and process of the biological product, as well as letters of guarantee stating that the new drug will not infringe upon the patent rights of others.
2. Notes
    1. The GMP Certificate and approvals for the marketing of the product issued by the competent authorities at the local countries or region where the manufacturer is located should be acknowledged by the Chinese embassy in the local countries and the public notaries in the countries.
        i. When the preparations are manufactured in one location and packed in another location, then the Certified Documents of GMP Certificates of the preparation manufacturer and packing manufacturer issued by the countries where the preparation manufacturer and packing manufacturer are located should be provided.
        ii. In the event that the products have not yet been approved to be marketed by the country or the region where the products are manufactured, then the Certified Documents from the other country where the products are approved to be marketed should be provided, and should be recognized by the SFDA. But the GMP Certificates must be issued by the competent authorities from the country or region where the manufacturer is located.

C Requirement for Other Information Items

1. All the clinical study information used during the application for marketing in the local countries or region where the manufacturer is located should be submitted as Information Item 13.
2. All the application information should be translated into Chinese with the original language attached. The Chinese translation shall be consistent with the original language.
3. The Chinese translation of vaccine standards must comply with the format required by the National Drug Standards of China.

D Requirements for Clinical Study Conducted in China

1. A clinical study should be applied for in accordance with Registration Category 1 for the application of the vaccine not yet marketed at domestic or overseas.
2. A clinical study should be applied for in accordance with Registration Category 6 for the application of the vaccine already marketed overseas but not yet marketed at domestic.
3. A clinical study should be applied for in accordance with Registration Category 15 for the application of the vaccine admitted with National Standards.

Reference

SFDA (2007a) Provisions for drug registration, No. 28. June 18, 2007 http://eng.sfda.gov.cn/WS03/CL0768/61647.html. Accessed 12 Dec 2013

SFDA (2007b) Provisions for drug registration, No. 28. June 18, 2007; Annex 2: Registration categories and application information requirements of chemical drugs

SFDA (2007c) Provisions for drug registration, No. 28. June 18, 2007; Annex 3: registration categories and application information items requirements of biological products

SFDA (2007d) Provisions for drug registration, No. 28. June 18, 2007; Annex 4: registration categories and application information items requirements of biological products

Chapter 5
Guidance for Application Materials/Booklets (Chemical)

Ming Q. Lu, Yuan Qiao, Edbert D. Lu and Yuyuan Tan

5.1 Introduction

The following are the major guidelines/guidance related to the CFDA dossier content preparation. For new investigational chemical drug dossier, including IND/CTA and NDA preparation, there are 32 items/booklets (SFDA 2007). These booklets are divided into 4 modules, i.e. Summary, Pharmaceutical, Pharmacology and Toxicology, and Clinical Study information. For the dossier submission, the applicants from multinational pharmaceutical companies need to fill out the CFDA drug registration application form required for overseas applicants. Usually, international pharmaceutical companies may, based on their investigational drug status, submit a separate summary document for special review and approval, i.e., "The Special Review Procedure (SRP) application" (SFDA 2009). In this document, the content mainly include: drug basic information, drug research background, pharmaceutical research, safety and effectiveness assessment, planned clinical trials, risk control and management of the clinical trials, and conclusion/discussion sections. For convenience, some applicants simply name it Booklet 0. The guidelines listed below will be discussed in corresponding to the booklets in this chapter. In this chapter, we

M. Q. Lu (✉)
Helsinn Therapeutics (U.S.), Inc., 1140 US Highway 22, Suite 101, Bridgewater, NJ 08807, USA
e-mail: Mingqilu@verizon.net

Y. Qiao
Neurophysiology and Orthopedics, School of Medicine, Shandong University, 44 Wenhua Xi Road, Shandong, Ji'nan 250012, P. R. China

E. D. Lu
Molecular and Cellular Biology, University of California, Berkeley, CA 94720, USA

Y. Tan
Beijing PRI BioScience Development Co, Ltd., C-505 Building 102, Zhu Jiang Di Jing No. 28, Guangqu Road, Chao Yang District, 100022 Beijing, P. R. China

M. Q. Lu (ed.), *Approaching China's Pharmaceutical Market*,
DOI 10.1007/978-3-319-15576-0_5

will provide a brief outline of the requirements of each of the dossier booklets based on the major regulatory guidelines.

5.2 Guidance for Summary Preparation

- Guidance for writing format and content of chemical drug review—Summary and evaluation of the main research results
- Guidance for writing format and content of chemical drug review—Project target indication and rationale
- Guidance for writing format and content of chemical drug review—Review of pharmaceutical research
- Guidance for writing format and content of chemical drug application materials—Review of pharmacology and toxicology research
- Guidance for chemical drug research with established national standards
- Guidance for writing format and content of chemical drug application materials—Review of clinical trial data review

5.3 Guidance for Pharmaceutics Research

- Guidance for pharmaceutical research of oral sustained release preparation of chemical drugs
- Guidance for stability research of chemical drugs
- Guidance for basic technology research of chemical drug preparation
- Guidance for research of chemical drug impurities
- Guidance for quality control research of chiral drugs
- Guidance for pharmaceutical research of synthetic polypeptide drugs
- Guidance for residual solvent research of Chemical drugs
- Guidance for the normalization process of quality standard establishment of chemical drugs
- Guidance for API preparation and structure confirmation research of chemical drugs
- Guidance for quality control analytical method validation of chemical drugs

5.4 Guidance for Pharmacology and Toxicology Research

- Guidance for non-clinical research of cytotoxic anticancer drugs
- Guidance for general pharmacological research of chemical drugs
- Guidance for non-clinical drug dependence research

- Guidance for human bioavailability and bioequivalence research of chemical pharmaceutical preparations
- Guidance for short-term toxicity study of chemical drugs
- Guidance for long-term toxicity study of chemical drugs
- Guidance for irritation, allergic and hemolytic research of chemical drugs
- Guidance for drug reproductive toxicity study
- Guidance for drug genotoxicity research
- Guidance for non-clinical research of drug dependence
- Guidance for the necessity of carcinogenicity test

5.5 Guidance for Clinical Trials

- Guidance for clinical pharmacokinetics of chemical drugs
- Administrative Guidelines for Phase I Drug Clinical Trials (Provisional)
- Guidance for clinical trial biostatistics of Chemical drugs and biological products
- Ethical Guidelines for Ethical Review Work of Drug Clinical Trials
- Guidance for clinical research of anticancer drugs
- Guidance for clinical research of antibacterial drugs
- Good Clinical Practice (GCP 2003)
- Guidance for structure and content of clinical study report of chemical drugs

5.6 Content and Technical Guidance for Review Material/Booklet Preparation and Format

5.6.1 Requirements for the Application Booklets

In this section, we will focus on the application booklets that are unique or different from the western standards—CTD requirements. The booklets needed for chemical drug IND and NDA submission are listed below.

IND
Submit application item 1–30 except item 6 based on Application Item Table:

A. Summary

1. Name of the drugs
2. Certified Documents
3. Objectives and basis for R & D
4. Summary of main study work
5. Draft of packaging insert, note to the draft, and latest literature
6. Design of packaging and labeling

B. Pharmaceutical information

7. Summary of Pharmaceutical Study
8. Research information and relevant literature of the production process of the drug substance, research information and relevant literature of formula and process of the preparations
9. Study information and relevant literature for the chemical structure and components determination
10. Study information and literature for quality specification
11. Draft of quality specification and notes, and providing reference standard
12. Test report of drug sample
13. The source, test report and quality specification of drug substance and excipient
14. Stability study and relevant literature
15. Selection basis and quality specification of immediate packing material and container

C. Pharmacology and toxicology study information.

16. Summary of pharmacology and toxicology study
17. Primary pharmacodynamics study and literature
18. General Pharmacology study and literature
19. Acute/single dose toxicity study and literature
20. Repeated dose toxicity study and literature
21. Special safety study and literature of hypersensitive (topical, systemic and photo-toxicity), hemolytic and topical irritative (blood vessel, skin, mucous membrane, and muscle) reaction related to topical and systemic use of the drugs
22. Study and relevant literature on Pharmacodynamics, toxicity and pharmacokinetics change caused by the interactions amongst multiple components in the combination products
23. Study and literature of mutagenicity test
24. Study and literature of reproductive toxicity
25. Study and literature of carcinogenicity test
26. Study and literature of drug dependence
27. Study and literature of pre-clinical pharmacokinetics

D. Clinical Study Information

28. Summary of global clinical study information
29. Clinical study protocol
30. Investigator's Brochure
31. Draft of Informed Consent Form, approval of the Ethics Committee (No)
32. Clinical study report (No)

NDA

After completion of clinical trials, submit the following items:

Updated review items 1 ~ 6:

A. Summary

1. Name of the drugs
2. Certified Documents
3. Objectives and basis for R & D
4. Summary of main study work
5. Draft of packaging insert, note to the draft, and latest literature
6. Design of packaging and labeling

Updated item 12 and 14:

B. Pharmaceutical information

11. Draft of quality specification and notes, and providing reference standard
12. Test report of drug sample
14. Stability study and relevant literature

Note: To facilitate review and comparison, the Center for Drug Evaluation (CDE) requires Item 11 to be provided. Under general circumstances, after having submitted quality standards of clinical use, the Institute for Drug Control shall make some modifications for the quality standards. Sponsors should make the response if it is accepted or not when declaring the production quality standards. Generally speaking, there will be some modifications to Item 11; therefore, sponsors need to submit it.

Clinical trial data—items 28–32 and updated data, including changed, added or supplemented information should be submitted according to the dossier order.

C. Clinical Study Information

28. Summary of global clinical study information
29. Clinical study protocol
30. Investigator's Brochure
31. Draft of Informed Consent Form, approval of the Ethics Committee
32. Clinical study report

For class 1 new drug dossier, after completion of the clinical trials, all the research outcomes related to the corresponding dossier items from 1 to 30 during the clinical trial period should be updated and submitted.

When applying for registration of the active pharmaceutical ingredient (API) and preparation under category 3 and 6 simultaneously, the registration application for the API should conform to the requirements of NDA.

Application for Registration of the Drugs with National Standards: Generic Drug Application

Submit items 1–16 and 28–30 according to the requirements listed in the Application Item Table. For those that require clinical trials, after the completion of clinical trials, if there is no change in Summary Items (1–6), and Pharmaceutical information (12, 14), resubmission is not necessary. Submit items 28–32 and other updated data, including changed, added or supplemented information according to the dossier order.

5.6.2 Module I—Summary Information

In Module I, there are a total of six booklets about the summary information of the drug name, certified documents, objectives and basis for R & D, main study work, draft of packaging insert, and design of packaging and labeling. Regarding the requirements of these booklets, SFDA issued a series of the corresponding guidance (CFDA 2006; Huang 2010; Zhang 2007).

5.6.2.1 Booklet 1—Drug Name

Include the drug's generic name, trade name, chemical name, English name, and Chinese Pinyin. Indicate their chemical structure, molecular weight, molecular formula, etc., (according to the CDE requirements). If they are new dosage forms or new nomenclature, Pharmacopoeia Commission's response letter should be attached. For the generic drug application, the application package should include national standards. Trade names are not acceptable.

5.6.2.2 Booklet 2—Certified Documents

For New Drug IND/CTA Application, the Following Should be Provided

1. The drug manufacturer: "three certificates" (GMP should be in accordance with the name and address of production license)
   Drug certificate applicant: valid business license, certificate of legal institutions and registration change certificate
2. Patent search reports, non-infringement guarantee
3. Special drugs: SFDA Safety Supervision Division's project approval documents
4. Legitimate sources of APIs for preparation (one set)

   1. To purchase directly from raw materials manufacturers

      a. Three certificates of raw materials manufacturers (the three certificates must in accordance with the name and address in the approval documents of raw material)
      b. The certificates of approval documents of raw materials (drug registration document; drug registration certificate; documents with issued renewal, etc.)

c. Reports of quality standards and APIs manufacturing inspection reports
d. Purchase receipts (For complimentary APIs, provide the relevant certificates)
e. Copies of the purchase and sale contracts or supply agreements
f. Internal-Test Report (full inspection)

2. Purchased from distributers of raw materials
   In addition to providing the documents above, the supply agreements with the distributers and raw material manufacturers are needed.
   Newly added: When applying for production approval, the application cannot be approved if APIs are acquired by a complementary pathway, or proof of a legitimate source and the supply agreement cannot be provided,
3. The simultaneous raw materials and preparation application for registration
   When the raw material manufacturer is different from the preparation manufacturer, the supply agreements or cooperative development agreements of raw materials and preparation manufacturers should be provided (the source of APIs of the same preparation applied cannot be the same API applicant.)
4. Use of imported raw materials

5. Trademark inquiry form or trademark registration certification (the submission can be postponed to the NDA application)
6. The certification or acceptance notice of packaging materials and containers which contact directly with drugs (In pharmacopoeia 2005 edition, capsule has been classified as packaging materials)
7. Commissioned tests and the commission contract shall be provided together with proof of legal registration of the institution and the necessary proof of qualification.
8. The proof documents related to the changes of the original proof documents
9. The proof documents for OTC application, etc.
10. Those needed to be signed by a non-statutory representative shall provide the signature of the legal representative and provide the original letter of authorization.

For New Drug NDA, the Following Should be Provided

1. Clinical trial authorization/IND approval letter
2. Quality standards for drugs to be used in clinical trials
3. The raw material acceptance form in the preparation of standard inspection issued by NIFDC (raw material)
4. For the new companies, new workshops or new preparations, it is allowed to apply for NDA only if they get the *Production Certificate with the corresponding permitted production scope.*

5.6.2.3 Booklet 3—Objectives and Basis for Research and Development

This booklet is very important and is special for the CFDA dossier since it may be directly related to the acceptance decision. Generally, the rejection causes could include: the rationale is denied; insufficient justification of specifications; safety cannot be warranted or; the effectiveness has not been proven.

This booklet could include the following six parts (according to the content of chemical drug application dossier written format and the technical guidelines of the content: the written format and content of the purpose and basis of the project. Special attention should be given to the statement of the basis of specifications and preparations. Emphasis varies depending on different kinds of applications.

Format and Content of the Booklet

1. **Basic Information of Drugs** Name, structure, mechanism of action, preparation specification, usage and dosage intended for clinic, registration classification and the rationale.

When applying for market approval, approval certificate number of clinical trials and approval time should be indicated. When applying for APIs, basic information of the preparations which are applied simultaneously should be stated.

When applying for preparations, the source of raw materials and quality standards should be indicated.

2. **The Background of the Project (the statement of "marketed overseas" is not acceptable as the basis of the project). Generally this Section Should Include the Following Information**

- Briefly state clinical features of indication, including possible etiology, pathogenesis, epidemiology features.
- Briefly state the current conditions and commonly used drugs of the indication; elaborate the main characteristics of different types of drugs.
- Briefly state the scientific basis, clinical significance and positioning of the drug development, such as efficacy, safety, tolerability, compliance and other characteristics.
- Indicate whether the drug research information has been published domestically (China) or abroad; the current research and development stage; whether it has approved for marketing, post-marketing clinical use conditions, etc.

3. **Drug Characteristics** Generally, it should be considered from the following aspects:

- Chemical structure, physical and chemical nature of characteristics. (If no special features, no statement is needed.)
- Characteristics of pharmacological effects, targets and mechanisms of action, including non-clinical and clinical pharmacology studies.

- Pharmacokinetic characteristics, including animal and/or human pharmacokinetic parameters, plasma protein binding, drug distribution, metabolism pathways, excretion pathways, and bioavailability.
- The main toxicity test results and adverse reaction characteristics, acute toxicity from animals, long-term toxicity, special safety (such as allergic, hemolytic, local irritation, etc.), genetic toxicity, reproductive toxicity, drug dependence, carcinogenicity, and other types of clinical adverse reactions, etc.
- In addition to the above information, the other information relates to the characteristics of the product and the rational basis of the project, such as the pharmacoeconomics of the drug should be considered.

4. Intellectual Property Status of the Drug Domestically and Abroad
Briefly state the intellectual property status of the drug domestically and abroad (including application, authorization, patent life, legal status, etc.). Make clear whether there are explicitly declared drug issues or involvement in infringement.

5. Comprehensive Analysis
On the basis of the elaboration of the aforementioned legislation on drugs declared by project background, drug characteristics, and intellectual property status, explain the project rationale and basis from the aspects of the safety, effectiveness, quality controllability, clinical positioning, clinical benefit/risk ratio, pharmacoeconomics, etc. Highlight the advantages of this drug.

6. References
List references in the order cited in the text, along with the original text and Chinese literature abstracts (do not include the literature cited in other booklets). The relevant references from top domestic and international authoritative journals are preferred.

Newly Added Requirements

- Review of the preparation research and the necessity of its clinical use
- Description of the status of marketed new drugs in the same category for its protection periods, the transition periods, and the monitoring periods, etc.

5.6.2.4 Booklet 4—Summary of Main Study Work

According to the requirements of Provisions for Drug Registration, Annex 2, this booklet should provide the summary and assessment for the main study outcome. The booklet should provide the important, comprehensive, and integrated information to support the registration application. The regulatory agency reviewers will use this booklet as the basis of comprehensive evaluation of drug safety, effectiveness and quality.

In accordance with “Guidance for writing format and content of chemical drug review—Summary and evaluation of the main research results”, this section provides the general principle for the content and format preparation. This guidance applies to the registration application of chemicals. For drugs of different registration categories, at different stages of registration, “the summary and evaluation of the main research results” may just refer to the general requirements of this guidance to write the applicant booklet. There are different emphases and specific content requirements depending on the drug category and application stages.

This Booklet can be Divided into the Following Five Parts for Preparation

- The basic status of the drug
- Major outcome and assessment of its pharmaceutical research
- Major outcome and assessment of its pharmacology and toxicology research
- Major outcome and assessment of its clinical trials
- Integrated analysis and evaluation

Description of the Booklet Content

1. The Basic Status of the Drug
Briefly state the basic status of the drug, including drug name, dosage form and specifications of the preparation, the clinical indications, usage and dosage form, pharmacological effects, mechanism of action, market conditions of the drug domestically and abroad, and drug registration classification. For the drug applying for NDA approval, the certificate number of clinical trial approval and its approval time should also be indicated.

2. Pharmaceutical Major Research Outcome and Evaluation
This section summarizes, analyzes and evaluates the pharmaceutical research results of the drug.

- API: briefly state the preparation art, structure confirmation, quality of research and quality standards, the findings of stability and other researches; the results should be analyzed and evaluated.
- Preparation: briefly state the selection of the preparation, prescription and preparation art, quality of research and quality standards, the findings of stability and other researches; the results should be analyzed and evaluated.

Based on the summary above, comprehensive analysis and evaluation of the results of the pharmaceutical research should be conducted. The analysis should mainly focus on the scientificity and standardability of the test process. The test results will be compared with the relevant literature; the analysis should be focused on interlinkages between research results, e.g. the interlinkages of API intermediates involved in the preparation process, by-products, the relationship between the quality of research in organic solvents and related substances, residual solvents check, relationship between quality assessment method involved in the screening process of preparation, the quality of research methods, quality standards established in technology, quality research, and relationship stability studies.

3. The Main Research Results and Evaluation of Pharmacology and Toxicology

In this section, the research results in pharmacology and toxicology should be summarized, and a comprehensive analysis and evaluation of the results should be conducted.

According to the registration classification and characteristics of the drug, applicants should briefly state the results of pharmaceutical and toxicology studies and literature, including the main pharmacodynamics, general pharmacology, acute toxicity, chronic toxicity, special safety (such as allergic, hemolysis, local irritation, etc.), genetic toxicity, reproductive toxicity, carcinogenicity, drug dependence, and non-clinical pharmacokinetic aspects. If some research is not carried out, the reason should be explained.

When applying for NDA, in addition to clarifying the above required contents, this document should also indicate the issues related to clinical trials and additional research in pharmacology and toxicology, as well as other complementary research in toxicology during the clinical trials conducting period.

Based on the summary of the research results, a comprehensive analysis and evaluation should be carried out, including a relevant comparison of study results and related literature as well as one between the various toxicological findings to obtain a comprehensive evaluation of the drug toxicology studies.

Regarding effectiveness, the registration applicant should analyze the possible roles of drug targets, mechanisms and treatment characteristics (onset and duration, activity intensity, dose-effect relationship and the effective dose, etc.) in animal models, and according to the results of animal research, predict drug characteristics and effects of the potential advantages and disadvantages compared to the conventional drug in clinical practice.

Regarding safety, applicants should analyze drug toxicities in target organ or tissue of the experimental animals, the nature, extent and recoverability of the toxicities to determine the NOAEL (no-observed-adverse-effect level). The applicant should also predict the toxicities of the drug in the clinical target organ or tissue, the toxicity nature, extent and recoverability, and the safe range, etc., based on the results of animal research. In addition, the toxicities should be compared with existing drugs to predict the potential advantages and disadvantages of the drug.

For drugs applying for clinical trials, i.e. IND or CTA, the outcome of the pharmacology and toxicology studies should be analyzed for whether the data supports clinical trials and the safety issues of clinical trials.

For drugs applying for NDA approval, the attention should be focused on the correlation among pharmacology and toxicology studies and clinical trial results. According to the requirements of the relevant guidelines, non-clinical efficacy and safety information are required for the preparation of instructions.

The requirements of this section for content and format are based on the following ICH and FDA Guidance:

- U.S. Department of Health and Human Services & Food and Drug Administration Guidance for Reviewers Pharmacology/Toxicology Review Format. May, 2001.
- ICH/M4S: The CTD—Safety. August, 2001.

According to regulatory requirements, the preparation for the review of pharmacology and toxicology research data may basically be based on the guiding principles; however the focus may vary based on the drug characteristics, registration stage, and drug registration categories.

Review of pharmacology and toxicology research data contains four parts: preface, toxicology study summary, analysis and evaluation of research outcomes, and reference materials.

4. The Main Results and Evaluation of Clinical Trials

This section should summarize and analyze the results of the drug clinical trials and literature research outcomes.

When applying for IND or CTA, the literature about the clinical trials of the drug should be briefly stated. The efficacy and safety characteristics should be summarized, analyzed and evaluated. The rationale of the clinical trial design should be illustrated.

When applying for market/NDA approval, a list to illustrate the completed clinical trial types, phases, and the project contents are required. In this list, it should mainly summarize and evaluate the results of clinical trials with the focus on the effectiveness and safety in comparison to the drugs in the same class worldwide.

A comprehensive analysis of the methods and results of clinical trials should be made, especially with the focus on study design, inclusion and exclusion criteria, control drug selection, dosage and method of administration, efficacy and safety evaluation, and statistical analysis. Meanwhile, the efficacy and safety of the drug should be analyzed, compared, and evaluated in addition to the existing integrated information of the drug domestically and abroad. The content of the instruction (package insert) related to the clinical trials should be clarified.

5. Comprehensive Analysis and Evaluation

In this section, comprehensive pharmaceutical, pharmacological and toxicological analyses and clinical trial results should be included. To summarize the above results of the overall research and literature, the drug safety, effectiveness, quality controllability, including the evaluation of the scientificity, standardability and integrity of the research, should be evaluated. Please also explain if the research outcomes support the project rationale and the existing issues.

The comprehensive evaluation of the major findings should also take the corresponding pharmacology, toxicology, clinical study results into consideration and determine if those results do not conflict, and support each other instead. For example: when the same drug is applied to treat different implications, the requirements for drug toxicity could be different; the relationship between the toxicological findings and pharmaceutical impurities should be explored to make sure there aren't any conflicting findings; the consistency between the sample quality used in clinical trials and the sample quality for pharmacology and toxicology studies should also be explored; and the relationships between quality standard specification (limitation set up) and safety research and clinical trial outcome should be addressed, etc.

When applying for IND/CTA, the integrated information (including pharmaceutical characteristics, pharmacology and toxicology studies, clinical indications, clinical research in the population using the drug, the literature, the feasibility of the drug in clinical trials, and the safety and efficacy) should be analyzed and evaluated comprehensively. The safety concerns and focused parameters that need special monitoring attention during the clinical trial should be proposed.

When applying for NDA, a comprehensive summary and analysis of the safety, effectiveness and quality controllability should be provided. The potential post market benefit/risk of the drugs should be comprehensively evaluated.

The review of clinical trial data is the summary and evaluation of the integrated clinical information that is needed for drug registration. This document includes two parts, i.e. (a) clinical trials and literature summary and (b) the overall evaluation of clinical trials. The content of the review of clinical trial data varies depending on different drug registration categories and registration stages.

The requirements of this section for content and format are based on "The common technical document for the registration of pharmaceuticals for human use efficacy—M4e: clinical overview and clinical summary of module 2".

Format and Content of Booklet

A: Clinical Trials and Literature Summary

1. Clinical trial summary
    - 1.1 Biopharmaceutical research summary
    - 1.2 Summary of clinical pharmacology research
    - 1.3 Summary of the clinical effectiveness
        - 1.3.1 The study population
        - 1.3.2 The validity of the results and comparison
        - 1.3.3 Comparison the results among different study populations
        - 1.3.4 Clinical information related to the recommended dose and method of administration
        - 1.3.5 Long-term efficacy and tolerability issues
    - 1.4 Summary of clinical safety
        - 1.4.1 Drug use/exposure
        - 1.4.2 Adverse events
        - 1.4.3 Evaluation of laboratory parameters
        - 1.4.4 Safety-related symptoms, signs, and other findings
        - 1.4.5 Safety in special populations
        - 1.4.6 Post market data

2. Clinical trial literature summary

B: The Overall Evaluation of Clinical Trials

1. Project analysis
2. The overall evaluation of bio-pharmaceutics
3. The overall evaluation of clinical pharmacology
4. The overall evaluation of the effectiveness
5. The overall safety evaluation
6. Benefit and risk assessment

C. Explanation of terms
D. References
E. The Author

5.6.2.5 Booklet 5—Draft of Packaging Insert, Note to the Draft, and Latest Literature

This booklet may be exempted for APIs.

The draft items of drug instruction should follow the following orders in the relevant regulations (Table 5.1):

Precautions
The order should be:

1. For Class I new drugs, it should use the term "the product"
2. "Clinical research" item is for new drugs in Class 1 category and drugs with added new indications
3. The "warning" item is mandatory
4. [Drug Name], [Character], [Indications], [Usage and Dosage], [Specifications], [Storage], [Expiration] content items should be according to the national drug standards. [Approval no.], [Manufacturer] content items should be written in reference of the approved content.[Pharmacology and Toxicology], [Pharmacokinetics], [Adverse reactions], [Contraindications], [Precautions], [Pediatric use], [Medication in elderly patients], [Overdose] items should be objectively and scientifically described according to the actual situation; if some items are lack reliable experimental or literature basis, they should be marked "not clear."

Describe the "indication" accurately.

5.6.2.6 Booklet 6—Design of Packaging and Labeling (not required for IND)

For the IND application, it is not required. For NDA, the design should follow the Provisions for Drug Insert Sheets and Labels (SFDA Decree No. 24, 2006). It is acceptable in word file and no color or market version is required. For generic drugs, a registered trademark can be added.

Table 5.1 Items of drug instruction

No.	Project	No.	Project
1	Drug instruction title	15	Precautions
2	Warnings	16	Medication in pregnant women and lactating women
3	Drug Name, Generic Name, Pinyin, English Name ,Product Name	17	Pediatric Use
4	Ingredients	18	Medication in elderly patients
5	Characters	19	Drug Interactions
6	Content of preparation	20	Overdose
7	Pharmacology and Toxicology	21	Specifications
8	Pharmacokinetics	22	Storage
9	Clinical studies	23	Packaging
10	Indications	24	Expiration date
11	Usage and dosage	25	Approval Number
12	Adverse reactions	26	Manufacturer or company name: Address: Postcode: Telephone and fax numbers (shall be marked with the country and area code): Web site or e-mail:
13	Contraindications	27	References
14	Caveat	28	Publication and revision date of the instruction

5.6.3 Module II—Pharmaceutics Research Information

In Module II, there is a total of nine booklets (7–15) regarding requirements for pharmaceutical information, including requirements for the summary of pharmaceutical study, production process of the drug substance, formula and process of the preparations; chemical structure and components determination; quality specification, reference standard; test report of drug sample; the source, test report and quality specification of drug substance and excipient; stability study and relevant literature; and selection basis and quality specification of immediate packing material and container. Regarding the requirements of these booklets, SFDA issued a series of the corresponding guidance (SFDA 2005, 2006, 2007).

5.6.3.1 Booklet 7—Summary of Pharmaceutical Study

IND Booklet format and content are consistent with the requirements of CDE (Guidance for writing format and content of chemical drug review—Review of pharmaceutical research:), including, synthesis, dosage form selection, formulation selection, structure confirmation, quality research and quality standard specification, stability studies, and review of domestic and abroad literature.

NDA If some pharmaceutical changes are made in the clinical trial period, this booklet needs to be re-submitted with the modified content.

Note: It is better to not make adjustments in the production process and prescriptions, etc. during clinical trial period; otherwise, it will not be consistent with clinical samples unless clinical samples are produced after the adjustments.

This guideline applies to the chemical drug registration. The applicant may have different emphases for different classifications or categories of the drug according to the specific conditions of the guidance and different stages of registration.

The requirements of this section for content and format are based on the following ICH and FDA Guidance:

- ICH: Organization of the common technical document for the registration of pharmaceuticals for human use M4.
- ICH: The common technical document for the registration of pharmaceuticals for human use: Quality-M4Q Quality overall summary of module 2 module 3: Quality.
- FDA: Guidance for industry—Guideline for the format and content of the chemistry, manufacturing, and controls section of an application.
- FDA: Guidance for industry—Format and content for the CMC section of an annual report.

1. Basis Characteristics of Drug

1.1 Nomenclature
1.2 Structure
1.3 General Properties

2. The Format and Content of the Review of APIs Pharmaceutical Research

2.1 Manufacturing art research
2.2 Structure validation research
2.3 The quality research and quality standard development
2.4 Stability research
2.5 Packaging materials or containers with direct contact of the drug
2.6 Comprehensive Analysis and Assessment
2.7 References

3. The Format and Content of the Review for Pharmaceutical Research of Preparation

3.1 Dosage form, formulation, and manufacturing art research
3.2 The quality research and quality standard development
3.3 Stability research
3.4 Packaging materials or containers with direct contact of the drug
3.5 Comprehensive analysis and assessment
3.6 References

5.6.3.2 Booklet 8—Research Information and Relevant Literature of the Production Process of the Drug Substance and Formula as well as Process of its Preparations

For the preparation of this booklet, the following contents should be provided (SFDA 2005, 2007):

A. Raw Materials Include

1. Preparation process and chemical equation (Reason of the cooperation and choice of multiple synthetic routes)
2. Starting materials and organic solvents, etc. (National Bureau has strict supervision and management of starting material, and high attention should be paid among corresponding professionals!)
3. The reaction conditions (temperature, pressure, time, catalyst, etc.)
4. The operational procedures
5. Refining methods
6. The main physical and chemical constants, periodic accumulated data and literature
7. The impact on the environment and its evaluation (for 3-waste treatment)

Newly added: Process validation data (needed for NDA application)

Please pay attention to the centralized review for transition period varieties "technical standards for chemicals shall not be approved" relevant content in the C part.

B. Preparations Include

1. Formulation basis (For multiple formulation choices, formulation selection processes should be provided.)
2. Rationale of dosage selection
3. Specification basis
4. The proceses of manufacturing art (text + flowchart)
5. The basis for establishment of the process parameters (including conditions)
6. The relevant atlas

C. Common Process Parameters

1. The specific method of crushing the drug—size requirements
2. Method of mixing the drug with excipients—equipment used, mixing time
3. The amount of binder and its method of adding in the method of wet production of tablets
4. The drying temperature and time of the wet granules
5. Tableting pressure of tablets
6. The temperature of the coating operation, the coating liquid atomization pressure, liquid jet method and speed, drying temperature and time
7. Sterilization temperature and time of injection, the freeze-dried curve

D. Raw Excipient Function and the Rationale of its Amount
Excipient specification is required.

The supplier's full inspection report and internal report for entering the plant (full review) of raw excipients must be attached. Please state clearly how to control the quality of raw materials.

E. Process Validation
It should include the starting material, formulation selection, production processes, equipment and other verification information (CDE website published some verification related guidance)

1. Aseptic and sterilization process validation
2. Indicate the feeding amount and yield
3. Impurities or other intermediate products which may be introduced in the process
4. Trials for impact factors. Light, high temperature, high humidity (if some items were eliminated, please explain why)

Technology Research Data Should be Clearly Stated
During the preparation stage of this booklet, the applicants should ensure if the documents properly address the following questions, for example:

What are the formulations, processes, procedures, parameters in laboratory scale study?

Are there any adjustments to the scale amplification, batch, formulation, process, procedures, and parameters in the pilot scale?

Please identify the permissible range for the operating procedures and parameters.

For NDA filing, the booklet should be different from the original IND package. This booklet relates to the NDA, and may serve as the basic reference for strict on-site inspection of the production; therefore, it is the most important information for the NDA.

It is required to submit large-scale research data. This is also related to "drug registration site inspection". The research data on the basis of pilot scale study should focus on the changes of each steps and parameters in the amplification process, which requests for a full-scale production process. The applicants need to explain the research of the production process during the clinical research period and indicate the production and inspection conditions of clinical trial samples.

In summary, the manufacturing processes are related to the later stage on-site inspection. Therefore, it is extremely important for the final market approval.

For a generic drug application, it is the same as the IND/CTA application. The related research projects should be studied comparatively to imitations (batch) to demonstrate the equivalence with products on the market. For information regarding the specific test, please refer to "Guidance for generic chemical research".

5.6.3.3 Booklet 9—Study Information and Relevant Literature of the Chemical Structure and Components Determination

For the requirements of this booklet, please see details in "Guidance for API preparation and structure confirmation research of chemical drugs". This Guidance is developed in reference to (a) FDA: Guidance for Industry Drug Substance, Chemistry Manufacturing, and Controls Information, 2004 and, (b) EMEA: Note for Guidance on Chemistry of the New Active Substance, 2003. Therefore, the requirements are similar in many ways to the requirements in western Guidance.

This guidance is intended to describe the basic laws of research of APIs development, follow the laws to conduct the research and development of APIs and determine the basic technical requirements in compliance with the relevant laws and regulations. Therefore, the guidance may provide the basic technical direction to the researchers for APIs research. It may help them become aware of the problems in the drug evaluation process.

The main contents of this guidance include the overview, the general processes of the research, the basic content of the study, glossary, references, etc. The overview should introduce the purpose, significance, and the scope of the guidance.

- The general process of research for API development provides a common rule to the researchers and gives them an overall understanding of the drug development process.
- The basic contents of research for APIs development are the elaboration of the selection of process, requirements of starting materials and reagents, the accumulation of process data, requirements of intermediates, optimization of process test and pilot scale, analysis of impurities, "three wastes" treatment and comprehensive analysis of process. Its contents are basically in accordance with the preparation of APIs development process. From the laboratory stage to the stage of industrial production, corresponding requirements were made. It emphasizes the importance of process control. The aim is that researchers could develop a reasonable and feasible production process in accordance with the above requirements.
- The general process of confirmatory study of APIs mainly elaborate the basic rules of drug structure confirmatory research, and help drug developers have an overall understanding.
- The basic content illustrates the requirements of samples, drug name, molecular structure, physical and chemical constants, methods frequently used to confirm the structure and its purpose and meaning, the different requirements of various structural types of drugs, and comprehensive analysis.

Basic Content of Research of APIs Development

1. Selection of the manufacturing process
2. The starting materials and reagents requirements
3. The accumulation of process data

4. Research and quality control of intermediates (SFDA 2006)
5. Process optimization and pilot scale
6. The analysis of impurities
7. The "three wastes" treatment
8. Comprehensive analysis of process

The Basic Content of Structure Confirmatory Research of APIs

1. Develop research protocol
2. Requirements of the test sample
3. General content of structure confirmatory studies
4. References, significance and requirements of comparison products for structure confirmatory studies
5. Comprehensive analysis
6. Drug name, structure and physicochemical constants

1. For IND commissioned for clinical study, a commission contract must be signed and the report and atlas must be stamped. Special attention should be paid to the authenticity of proof of qualification and the applicant, because the "measures" Article 13 clearly stated that the applicant is responsible for the authenticity of all information.
2. During the NDA stage, if there is no supplementary content, there is no need to provide.

5.6.3.4 Booklet 10—Study Information and Literature for Quality Specification

For IND, please see details in "Guidance for research of chemical drug impurities" and "Guidance for residual solvent research of chemical drugs". These Guidance are developed in reference to the ICH, FDA and EMA's Guidance:

- ICH:Q3A(R):Impurities in New Drug Substances. 2002
- ICH:Q3B(R):Impurities in New drug Products. 2003
- ICH:Q3C(M):Impurities: Guideline for Residual Solvents(Maintenance). 2002
- EMEA: Position paper on specification for class 1 and class 2 residual solvents in active substances. 2003
- FDA: Guidance for Industry—INDs for Phase 2 and Phase 3 Studies Chemistry, Manufacturing, and Controls Information. 2003
- ICH:Q6A:Specification:Test Procedures

Therefore, the requirements are very similar to the existing Guidance in the western world.

This booklet should include physical and chemical properties, a purity test, dissolution, microbiological examination, sterile examination, assay validation, periodic data accumulation results, the source of standard reference, and an atlas.

API Quality Research

- Quality Standards
- General characteristics
- Impurities research
- Analytical methods
- Analytical method validation
- API batch analysis

Drug quality research

- Quality Standards
- Analysis methods
- Analytical method validation
- Analytical method validation (appearance, identification, quantitative determination, relevant substrates and content, uniformity, dissolution, microbial limit)
- Batch inspection report

Note: pay attention to detail. For example, ask yourself: what kind of materials and models are used for filtering? What is the rational basis? The processes and results of the tests should be provided.

For an NDA, if there are no modifications or changes, there is no need to provide it; if there are some modifications, please explain them one by one and pay attention to the convergence.

For generic drugs, note the national standard. All of the research should be run in parallel with the imitations. When a drug has both import standards and national drug standards, it is preferred to refer to import standards (see full text of the normal procedure) to establish the standard for registration application.

5.6.3.5 Booklet 11—Draft of Quality Specification and Notes, and Providing Reference Standard

A. For details please see "Guidance for the normalization process of quality standard establishment of chemical drug".

1. Quality standards should be consistent with the format of "Chinese Pharmacopoeia"—the current version, and use its terminology and measurement units.
2. The reagents, test solution, buffers, titration solutions, etc., should adopt the concentrations stated in the current version of "Chinese Pharmacopoeia". if there are differences, it should be explained in details.
3. For the standard drug or drug for comparison, the references should be attached to provide information on their sources, physical and chemical constants, purity, content, measurement methods and data.

Note: In addition to the experimental data on which the draft instructions are prepared, the results of at least three batches of samples in the pilot scale and the data from clinical samples should be provided, or should be added together with the validation data from multiple batches of samples. Draft instructions should include the focused procedures during the implementation of the standards.

B: In some circumstances, even if there is no modification, you may need to submit the data to facilitate the review if the CDE requests you to submit it.

If there are modifications to the content, please briefly state the changes in a logical order. This section contains the core elements for manufacturing on-site inspection.

5.6.3.6 Booklet 12—Test Report of Drug Sample

IND: Test report of drug samples refers to the internal test report for the samples (1 ~ 3 batches)

NDA: Test report of drug samples is needed to provide an internal-test report for three consecutive batches of samples for NDA filing after clinical trials. The three batches of samples for NDA submission must meet the GMP requirements (SFDA 2010).

Applicants should pay attention to whether the results reported from the Institute for Drug Control are similar to the internal-test results. If the difference is significant, applicants should identify the causes before sending the re-check report; otherwise at the time of the review, there would be unnecessary delay or questions to be raised.

Emphasis: the clinical samples must be the samples confirmed with the corresponding processes and preparation in the dossier, and are the products of pilot-scale; otherwise it will be inconsistent, especially for solid preparations.

Pilot-scale sample: those samples have to be able to represent the samples in the mass production scale with the same quality, and simulate the samples produced under actual production conditions.

Scale (samples for stability study should reach a certain size)

1. Chinese Pharmacopoeia (2005 edition): For tablets, capsules and other solid dosage preparations, normally about 10,000 units are needed; For a special preparation, or special drugs, it may be flexible.
2. Chinese Pharmacopoeia (2005 edition Appendix): For bulky packaged preparation (such as intravenous fluids, oral, etc.), it should take at least 10 times the total amount required for the stability test.
3. APIs
   1000 times more than a single dose;
   The final product yield should reach kg class;
   Unit reactor volume should be no less than 20 l.
4. Import drug Requirements: At least two batches in three should be pilot-scale batches; as proven, the third batch can be smaller, e.g. oral solid dosage tablets and capsules could be 25,000–50,000 tablets or capsules.
5. Preparations: one output of the production should reach 1/10 of the production scale.

In summary, on the premise of your own manufacturing equipment, on-site verification of the production will be closely linked to the "equipment match" condition to conduct the inspections.

5.6.3.7 Booklet 13—The Source, Test Report and Quality Specification of Drug Substance and Excipient

IND Proof documents for legitimate source of raw materials are required and depend on the following conditions.

Using APIs made in China, the applicant should provide the API approval documents, inspection reports, drug standards, license for pharmaceutical raw material manufacturing, drug production license, GMP certificate, a copy of the raw material supply agreement signed between drug manufacturers, sales invoices, etc.

Using imported APIs, the applicant should provide the raw material supply agreements with drug manufacturers or domestic legal sales agents signed, Import Drug License or Pharmaceutical Product Registration Certificate, port drug testing report, and drug specification copies, etc. During the drug registration process, the imported APIs used in the preparation of drugs without the Import Drug License or Pharmaceutical Product Registration Certificate must be approved by the State Food and Drug Administration.

For source of excipients, the manufacturing plants, approval number, inspection reports, and the product quality standards should be included.

NDA If there is no change, then resubmission not needed. For the purpose of facilitating the regulatory review, however, it is recommended to provide (provide what?) once again.

5.6.3.8 Booklet 14—Stability Study and Relevant Literature (SFDA 2005)

IND: For details, please refer to "Guidance for stability research of chemical drugs". This Guidance is developed in accordance to the ICH and FDA corresponding Guidance. Therefore, the requirements are very consistent with the western world standards.

Stability testing of packaging materials with direct contact to the drug should be jointly conducted with the drug.

Note: It refers to the impact factor test (high-temperature test, humidity test, light), accelerated testing, and long-term trial (the three parts).

NDA: The long-term stability study content and results (three batches) should be added. It should be clearly stated the period of validity and its basis. At the same time, the compatibility of the drug and packaging materials should be evaluated. If you accepted the transfer of clinical approval documents and clinical samples were produced in the enterprise, it requires that these samples shall be used in stability tests in pilot scale. Such stability study outcomes need to be reported in this dossier.

General Content of Stability Study Report
In general, stability study outcomes should include the following:

1. The test drug name, specifications, dosage form, batch number, manufacturer, source of API, manufacturing date, and the test start time. The output amount of each batch should be explicitly given in the stability test.
2. The conditions of stability tests, such as temperature, light intensity, relative humidity, container etc. The properties of packaging/seal system should be clarified, e.g. packaging material types, shapes, and colors.
3. The requirements for the limits in each quality testing method and indicators of stability studies.
4. The actual analytic data acquired at each sampling points of the start and middle of the study generally should be submitted in tabular form. Together with the corresponding atlas.
5. The results of the test should truthfully reflect the data and should avoid the use of "meet the requirements" and other expressions. Test results should be stated by the percentage amount of active ingredient or each unit containing a labeled amount of the active ingredient, such as μg, mg, g, and other representations, and should give the percentage of the results compared with the results at the start. If the test repeats several times at some points of time, it should provide all the test results and the relative standard deviation (RSD).
6. The test results should be analyzed with preliminary conclusions.

5.6.3.9 Booklet 15—Selection Basis and Quality Specification of Immediate Packing Material and Container

IND: Based on the results of the stability test and previous impact factor study, provide the rationale and basis for the selection of the drug packaging materials. The source and quality standards of the drug packaging materials should be attached.

NDA: The content of the 6 months follow-up stability test should be provided.

5.6.4 Module III—Pharmacology and Toxicology Research Information

In Module III, there are a total of 12 booklets (16–27) about pharmacology and toxicology information, including summary of pharmacology and toxicology; primary pharmacodynamics; general pharmacology; acute/single dose toxicity; repeated dose toxicity study and literature; special safety of hemolytic and topical irritative reaction; pharmacodynamics, toxicity and pharmacokinetics change caused by the interactions amongst multiple components in the combination products;

mutagenicity test; reproductive toxicity; carcinogenicity test; drug dependence; and pre-clinical pharmacokinetics. Regarding the requirements of these booklets, SFDA issued a series of the corresponding guidance (SFDA 2005, 2006, 2007).

All the booklets (16–27) are accomplished by external CRO or institutions. The following attention should be noted:

- Sign a contract of commissioned tests
- Sample batch number provided have to be one of the previous mentioned samples in the manufacturing process, quality, and stability studies (one of the three batches).
- Qualified Report
- Control samples (positive drug): it is recommended to provide them to the test institute after full inspection
- Carefully check the test report (animal species, quantity, weight, feeding requirements, anatomy photos, etc.)

5.6.4.1 Booklet 16—Summary of Pharmacology and Toxicology Study

The Corresponding Guidances are Aiming

1. to raise the attention for the important relationship between the toxicology research and the project rationale;
2. to study the relevance among pharmacodynamics, pharmacokinetics/toxicokinetics, and toxicology;
3. to explore the relevance among pharmacology, toxicology and pharmaceutical research and clinical trials;
4. through the comprehensive evaluation of drug efficacy and safety, to establish the comprehensive and standard analysis and evaluation processes in drug development;
5. to improve the quality of pharmacology and toxicology research documentations, and
6. to standardize pharmacology and toxicology studies to further improve the efficiency of new drug registration.

The preparation of the summary of pharmacology and toxicology study booklet depends on the drug classifications in registration categories, the corresponding regulation requirements, drug characteristics, and registration stages. In other words, it may need different emphasis on different sections based on the above factors stated in the guidance.

This booklet should consist four major sections, i.e. (a) preface, (b) pharmacology and toxicology study summary, (c) analysis and evaluation of research, and (d) reference.

Booklet Format and Content

A. Preface
The preface should provide the background of the drug development related to the research and evaluation of the pharmacology and toxicology of the drug. In general, it should include the followings:

- Name of active pharmaceutical ingredients (including the Chinese name and the English name), structure type or characteristics.
- Clarify drug clinical indications: Briefly state the drug related disease pathogenesis, clinical symptoms, disease courses, outcome, etc., as well as the existing drugs in the same drug class in clinical practice.
- Possible drug mechanism of actions.
- Briefly state the development progress of the drug or drugs in the same class domestically and overseas, as well as the primary efficacy and safety issues observed in non-clinical trials and clinical practice.
- Clarify the project rationale and basis.
- Drug preparation and specifications: For drugs in the process for clinical trial application, the draft clinical protocol and its comparisons with the marketed drugs in the same class world widely should be briefly stated.
- Applicants for registration, drug registration purposes, registration class and topics need special emphasis.

B. Pharmacology and Toxicology Study Summary
This section includes the summary of pharmacology and toxicology studies as well as literature that supports the application for registration. Applicants should summarize the study protocols, main results of test and literature in the following order: pharmacodynamics, pharmacokinetics and toxicology.

1. Pharmacodynamic trials and literature
2. Pharmacokinetic trials and literature

The test results generally include the following:

- Absorption rate (time to peak and peak concentrations) and extent (area under the curve of the plasma concentration and bioavailability), and the relationship between the absorption and dose.
- Tissue distribution, plasma protein binding rate and volume of distribution.
- Metabolic pathways, the major metabolite, and metabolism-related enzymes.
- Ways and extent of excretion, clearance, half-life, the material balance.
- Drug-drug interactions based on pharmacokinetics.

3. Toxicology tests and literature
Applicants should summarize the toxicology tests and literature in the following order:

- General Pharmacology (safety pharmacology) tests and literature
- Acute toxicity test and literature

- Long-term toxicity (if necessary including toxicokinetic) tests and literature
- Allergic (topical, systemic and sensitive toxicity), hemolytic and local (blood vessels, skin, mucous membranes, muscles, etc.) irritating special safety tests and literature, which mainly related to topical, systemic administration
- Test data and literature about toxic mutual influence among various ingredients in preparation
- Mutagenicity tests and literature
- Reproductive toxicity tests and literature
- Carcinogenicity studies and literature
- Dependence test and literature

In vitro tests summary should include test methods, the drug concentration and the main test results. The in vivo test summary should include species and strains of the experimental animals, dosage regimen, and the main test results.

C. Comprehensive Analysis and Evaluation for Pharmacology and Toxicology Studies

This section is not a repeated statement or a simple pile-up of pharmacology and toxicology findings; it should be an integrated analysis and comprehensive summary of the corresponding pharmacological and toxicological data of the drug.

- The rationale and selection basis of the research project
- The effectiveness of the drug
- The safety of the drug
- Comprehensive evaluation

D. References

5.6.4.2 Booklet 17—Primary Pharmacodynamics Study and Literature

This booklet is a summary of primary pharmacodynamic studies and literature. It should summarize the test methods and the main results of each tests and/or literature. Pharmacodynamics includes the basic type of drug action, dose-effect relationship of the drug action, therapeutic effect, adverse reactions and mechanism of action of the drug.

Pharmacodynamic Study and Literature

Applicants should briefly summarize the main pharmacodynamics, mechanism of action studies and literature following the order of in vitro studies first and then in vivo studies next. In vitro tests should briefly state the test methods, drug concentration, and main test results. In vivo tests should briefly state the animal models, administered programs (including dose, route, frequency, duration, etc.) and the main results. Applicants should summarize the main results of pharmacodynamic tests and literature in tabulated format (Table 5.2).

Table 5.2 Pharmacodynamic studies and literature summary

Research Project	Testing System	Dosage and Vehicle	Dose / Concentration	Route of Administration	Duration and Frequency of Administration	Primary Findings

The booklet of pharmacodynamic studies should include: preface, materials, methods, results, discussion, conclusions, references, and study leaders, participants, unit, time, and the competent departments.

5.6.4.3 Booklet 18—General Pharmacology study and literature

"Guidance for general pharmacological research of chemical drugs" Issued by State Food and Drug Administration on March 18, 2005, provided the general pharmacological definitions, the basic principles of the tests, the trial design, and the main research contents (SFDA 2005).

This guidance is prepared in reference to (1) the ICH Guidance for Industry ICH S7A: Safety Pharmacology Studies for Human Pharmaceuticals. 2001; (2) the ICH Guidance for Industry ICH S7B: Safety Pharmacology Studies for assessing the potential for delayed ventricular repolarization (QT interval prolongation) by Human Pharmaceuticals 2002.

Broad general pharmacology (General Phannacology) refers to a wide range of pharmacological studies conducted aside from the main pharmacodynamics, including safety pharmacology and secondary studies. General pharmacology referred herein, is limited to the contents of safety pharmacology studies.

Safety Pharmacology mainly indicates the study of the drug (within the therapeutic range or above the therapeutic range of doses) for its potential, undesirable adverse effects on physiological functions, i.e. the effects of drugs on the central nervous system, cardiovascular system and respiratory system. If necessary, safety pharmacology research may be added and/or supplemented.

Basic Principles

1. Test Method

It should be based on the drug characteristics and clinical objectives to make a reasonable test design. The commonly accepted methods domestically and abroad, should be selected, including scientific and effective sound new technologies and methods. Some safety pharmacology studies can select the methods based on the available pharmacodynamic response model, pharmacokinetic characteristics, types of animals. Both in vivo in vitro tests can be accepted.

2. Study Stages
General pharmacology studies in drug research throughout the whole development processes can be conducted in different stages. Prior to the clinical trials, the core battery studies unrelated to the central nervous system, cardiovascular system, and respiratory effects should be completed. Additional and/or supplemental safety pharmacology studies could be completed before the NDA submission.

3. The Implementation of GLP Requirements (SFDA 2003)
The safety evaluation studies of the drug must be conducted in compliance with GLP.

4. Drugs Which Could be Exempted from General Pharmacology Studies Include

- Topical administrative drugs with low blood concentration in vivo, or with low distribution in other tissues and organs (such as skin, eye medication, etc.).
- Cytotoxic drugs which only for the treatment of patients with advanced cancer, can be exempted for general pharmaceutical research before its first use in clinics; however, this does not include drugs with a new mechanism of action.

The Basic Requirements for Test Design

The basic requirements are consistent with the ones in the western world. The following content should be included in the report.

1. Biological Materials
There are several biomaterials: whole animals, isolated organs and tissues, in vitro cultured cells, cell fragments, organelles, receptors, ion channels, and enzymes. Whole animals often mean mice, rats, guinea pigs, rabbits, dogs and so on. Animal selection should match the test methods and also the factors related to strains, sex, age and other factors. For the selection of biological materials, the sensitivity, reproducibility and feasibility, as well as the correlation with human should be considered. Conscious animals are recommended in studies in vivo. If using anesthetized animals, the selection of narcotic drugs and the depth of anesthesia should be considered.

2. The test Substance
For externally used medications and injections, preparations are generally used as the test substance. Test substances should be consistent with the pharmacodynamic or toxicological studies as possible, attached with the internal test report of the research unit.

3. The Sample Size
The number of test groups and the number of animals in each group should be set properly so that it be used to interpret the test results scientifically and rationally, to

appropriately reflect biologically meaningful effect, and be in accordance with the principle of statistical requirements.

For small animals, each group generally consists of no less than 10; for large animals each group is generally no less than 6. Generally male and female animals are one-to-one by ratio.

4. Dose

In vivo safety pharmacology tests should study the observed dose-response relationship of adverse reactions. Also, if possible, the relationship between time and effect should also be studied. In general, the dose which can cause adverse reactions should be compared with the effective dose in animal or the effective dose intended to be used for humans.

Different species of animals have different pharmacodynamic response sensitivities; therefore, the dose of safety pharmacology tests should include or exceed the effective dose or the therapeutic range of main pharmacodynamics. If it lacks results of adverse reactions in safety pharmacology studies, the highest dose tested should be set to the dose, which produces medium level of adverse reactions in other toxicity tests with a similar route of administration and similar time of administration. In the actual work, toxic effects in the toxic dose range may affect the observation of adverse reactions in safety pharmacology, limiting the increase of the dose level. When safety pharmacology indicators don't cause adverse reactions, a single dose could be used in condition of limiting the dose.

In vitro studies should determine the concentration-effect relationship of the test substance. If no significant influence is observed, the selection of the concentration range should be explained.

5. Control

Generally, solvents and/or excipients are used as controls. To illustrate the similarities and differences between the characteristics of the test substance and known drug, positive control drugs can also be used.

6. Route of Administration

For whole animal experiments, the route should first be consistent with the intended clinical administrative pathway. If there are multiple intended clinical pathways, separate corresponding routes should be used. For specific clinical routes of administration which are difficult to implement in animal experiments, the route can be chosen according to the characteristics of the test substance, and explain the reasons.

7. Times of Administration

Generally, a single time of administration is used. However, if the main pharmacodynamic studies indicate that test substance will work sometime after administration, or there are safety issues or concern from the non-clinical study results and/or clinical studies with repeated administration, the repeated administration should be designed reasonably based on specific circumstances.

8. Observation Time
The observation time points and the observation period should be selected in combination with pharmacodynamic and pharmacokinetic properties of the test substance, the test animal and clinical research programs, etc.

The Main Content of Research

Impact on Important Vital Functional System
The purpose of safety pharmacology core portfolio experiments is to study the effects of the test substance on important vital functions. The central nervous system, cardiovascular system, and respiratory system are usually considered as important systems, which is the study content of core portfolio experiments.

The Additional and/or Supplementary Safety Pharmacology Tests
When core portfolio experiments, clinical trials, epidemiology, in vivo experiments or literature suggest that the drug has potential adverse reactions related to human safety, safety pharmacology studies should be added and/or complemented. Additional safety pharmacology experiments, in addition to the core portfolio, reflect in-depth study of the test substance on the central nervous system, cardiovascular system and respiratory system should be considered. For additional safety pharmacology experiments, the specific analytic method based on existing information should be selected. Supplementary safety pharmacology experiments are those which are not conducted on the urinary/renal system, autonomic nervous system, gastrointestinal system in the core portfolio experiment or repeated dose toxicity test, but need to be conducted due to the concerns about safety.

Data Processing and Results Evaluation

According to the detailed test records, choose the appropriate statistical methods to conduct qualitative and quantitative analysis of the data. Comprehensive evaluation should be conducted in combination with drug efficacy, toxicology, pharmacokinetics, and other research materials to propose suggestions for clinical study design.

5.6.4.4 Booklet 19—Acute/Single Dose Toxicity Study and Literature

Animal acute toxicity tests study the toxicity reaction in a certain time range after one or more administration of the test substance within 24 h.

"Guidance for acute toxicity studies of chemical drugs" was issued by State Food and Drug Administration on March 18, 2005. This guidance applies to animal acute toxicity tests of chemical drugs. It states the basic principles of animal selection, dose, route of administration in the acute toxicity test, analysis and evaluation requirements of obtained data, the scientific principles involved, and the development background of the guidance (SFDA 2005).

This guidance development is referenced (in)? ICH, FDA and European Union's guidelines. Therefore, it is generally consistent with international registration requirement.

1. Content of the Study

1. Test substance: the test substance should be able to represent the test substance of clinical trials and marketed drugs, and meet the same quality standards with the test substance of clinical trials and marketed drugs.
2. Animals: species, sex, age, number of animals, body weight.
3. Route of administration: the route of administration should at least include the intended clinical administration pathway and a way which enables the prototype drug to go into the circulation more completely (such as intravenous).
4. Dose levels: generally, the dosing groups should be divided from no toxicity dose to severe toxicity (life-threatening) doses; the negative control group should be also be set (solvent control group).
5. Observation time and indicators: After administration, continuous observation for at least 14 days, interval and frequency of observation should be appropriate to observe the toxicity onset time, recovery time, and the death time, etc. Observation indicators include general indicators. (Such as animal appearance, behavior, secretions, excretions, etc.), animal deaths (the time of death, before dying reaction, etc.), animal body weight changes (animals are weighted each time before administration to the end of the test; they can be weighted repeatedly during the observation) and so on.
6. Pathology examination.

2. Data Analysis and Evaluation

1. Results processing and analysis
   - According to various reactions' onset time, severity, duration, analyze the incidence rate and severity of various reactions at different doses. Summarize and analyze the observations to determine the dose-effect relationship and changes over time for each reaction.
   - Determine the organ, tissue and system possibly involved in each reaction.
   - According to the results of the visible lesion and histopathological examination of the gross anatomy, make the initial judgment of the possible toxicity target organ.
   - According to the incidence and animal deaths at different doses, determine the animal's maximum no reaction dose, the minimum toxicity dose, maximum tolerated dose, the minimum lethal dose, etc., determine the initial safe scope of the drug.
   - For the drug which need to determine LD50 value, use reasonable statistical methods to calculate LD50 value
   - Clarify the calculation and statistical methods; provide the basis for the reasonable method chosen.

2. Comprehensive evaluation
   - According to the onset time, incidence, dose-reaction relationship, different species of animals, laboratory historical background data, the results of the pathological examination, and characteristics of the drugs in the same class, determine the correlation between the reactions and drug action. Summarize the safety range of the test substance, toxicity severity and recoverability; according to the possible sites involved in toxicity, together with gross anatomy and histopathology results, determine the toxicity target organs.
   - Acute toxicity test results can be used as reference for further toxicology dose selection, and it can also prompt some indicators needed in subsequent toxicity studies. In addition, according to different reactions of animals with different routes of administration, it can determine initially the bioavailability of the test substance, and provide reference for preparation development

5.6.4.5 Booklet 20—Repeated Dose Toxicity Study and Literature

The purpose of the long-term toxicity study was to characterize the toxicity of the test substance by repeated dose toxicity in animal tests to predict the possible adverse reactions to the human body and reduce the risk of the human subjects in clinical trials and in postmarket public populations. It includes the following five areas (SFDA 2005):

- Clinical adverse reactions may be caused by test substance, including adverse reactions' nature, extent, dose-response relationship and time-response relationship, reversibility, etc.;
- Determines the toxicity target organ or target tissue by repeated administration of the test substance;
- Presume the starting dose of clinical trials and safety range of repeated drug dosing;
- Prompt safety indicators of the clinical trials which need specific monitoring attentions;
- Provide reference for detoxification or rescue measures in clinical trials.

State Food and Drug Administration issued the "Guidance for long-term toxicity study of chemical drugs" on March 18, 2005, to support clinical trials respectively. For some drugs with long clinical courses, the applicants can submit the long-term toxicity studies to support the different stages of clinical studies prior to clinical phase I, phase II or phase III, according to the actual situation of drug development.

1. Project Rationale
In principle, if the existing data does not meet the long-term toxicity testing requirements, long-term toxicity tests should be performed from the perspective of ensuring clinical drug safety.

2. The Basic Principles

Integrity

Long-term toxicity tests cannot be separated from pharmacodynamics and pharmacokinetics. The test design should take full account of the test design and results of other studies and toxicology studies. The results of long-term toxicity tests should be the verification, addition and supplement with other pharmacology and toxicology test results.

Analysis of Specific Issues

Experimental design should be comprehensively considered based on the structural characteristics and physicochemical properties of the compounds, similar compounds' domestic or abroad clinical usage, clinical indications and treatment groups, clinical drug programs, related pharmacodynamic, and pharmacokinetic and toxicological studies and information.

Randomized, Controlled and Repeated

Long-term toxicity testing experimental design should follow the "randomized, controlled and repeated" principle.

3. The Basic Content

3.1 The test substance

Long-term toxicity tests should use samples which have stabilized preparation process and accord with the quality standards of clinical trial. Test substance should indicate the name, origin, batch number, the content (or specifications), storage conditions and preparation methods, along with the internal-test report of the study unit. Used materials, solvents, etc. should indicate batch number, size and manufacturer, and meet the test requirements.

In the drug development process, if the preparation process of the test substance may affect their safety changes, the appropriate safety studies should be conducted.

3.2 Experimental Animals—the Choice of Animal Species or Strain

Long-term toxicity tests of chemical drugs usually adopt two kinds of experimental animals: rodents and non-rodents. Ideal animals should have the following characteristics: (a) biotransformation for the test substance is similar with human body; (b) sensitive to the test substance; and (c) with a lot of historical control data.

- **Quality control of experimental animals**

Long-term toxicity tests generally choose normal, healthy, and not pregnant animals. Animal weight difference should be within 20% of the average weight. Animals should comply with national level requirements of the relevant provisions and sources. The strains and genetic background should be clear and they should have experimental animal quality certification.

Animal age should be determined according to the length of study and the patient population of the clinical application of test substances. The age of the animal should be consistent, usually 6–9 weeks for rats, 6–12 months for Beagle dogs.

- **Sex and the number of experimental animals**

Under normal circumstances, in the long-term toxicity tests, each test group should have an equal number of male and female animals. The number of animals in each group should be able to meet the analysis and evaluation needs of test results. The general number for rats is 10～30 for female and male respectively; for Beagle dogs or monkeys, 3–6 for female and male respectively.

3.3 Administration Regimen
Dose of administration

Generally long-term toxicity tests set at least high, medium and low dose groups; When necessary, a vehicle (or excipients) as the control group, a blank control group or a positive control group could be used. Due to the increase of theoretical population incidence of toxicity with increased drug exposure, it is expected that animal with high-dose produces significant higher toxicity by principle, and even individual animal death. Low doses should be higher than the equivalent dose in pharmacodynamic tests on animals by principle, and does not make the animal exhibit toxicity effects. In order to investigate the toxicity dose-response relationship, a middle dose should be set between the high dose and low dose.

- **Route of administration**

By principle, the route should be consistent with the clinical route of administration; if not, an explanation should be given.

- **Dosing frequency**

By principle, animals of long-term toxicity tests should be administered daily. For the drugs with a long-term administration (3 months or more), the drugs should be administered at least 6 days a week. For special type of test substance, due to its toxicity characteristics and clinical administration programs, the frequency of administration should be designed according to the characteristics of specific drugs.

- **The period of administration**

The long-term toxicity test administration period is usually associated with the proposed clinical administration course, clinical indications, and drug related populations.

For drugs with single-dose administration in a clinic, long-term toxicity tests with a period of 2 weeks generally can support its clinical trial (IND) and production application (NDA).

For drugs with a clinical course of no more than 2 weeks, long-term toxicity tests with period of a month generally can cover its IND and NDA application.

For drugs with a clinical course of more than 2 weeks, the sponsor can conduct the long-term toxicity test which supports it to enter stage 3 of the clinical trial (and production); alternatively, the sponsor can also conduct long-term toxicity studies with different administration periods to support the corresponding phases I, II or III, clinical trials, and NDA. Generally, long-term toxicity tests with a period of 1 month can support clinical trials with a drug dosing time of no more than 2 weeks. For details, please see the Appendix of this section.

The information obtained by toxicity studies with a short period of administration can provide a reference for dose, frequency of administration, etc. for a long-term of administration for toxicity studies; meanwhile, the information obtained in clinical trials can help the design of animal toxicity studies with longer administration terms and reduce the risk of drug development. When using long-term toxicity tests with different dosing periods to support the drug in Phase 1, 2 or 3 clinical trials and production license application, the contents of long-term toxicity tests with different dosing periods should be complete and normative.

3.4 Test Indicators and Time

Indicators which must be examined in long-term toxicity tests are described in Appendix II of this section. In addition to the required test indicators, long-term toxicity tests should increase the corresponding test indicators specifically based on the characteristics of the test substance.

Prior to the test, the rodents should be observed for at least 5 days for the adaptation; non-rodents should be observed for at least 1–2 weeks; the appearance, signs, behavior, food intake and body weight should be checked; non-rodents should also be checked for their body temperature, ECG, hematology and blood chemistry indicators twice. In addition, historical background data related to indicators in experimental animals also have important reference value in the long-term toxicity tests.

During the test, the appearance, signs, behavioral activity, food intake, body weight, stool, administration local reactions, hematology, blood chemistry and other indicators should be observed.

Body temperature, ECG, eye examinations and urine analysis of non-rodents should be conducted. Detection times and period should be determined according to the characteristics of the test substance and the length of the test period. By principle, toxic reactions should be found as soon as possible, and reflect the relationship between the observed changes of indicators or parameters and the administration period.

After the completion of the administration, a comprehensive gross anatomy should be conducted for the animals (except convalescent animals being observed), major organs should be weighed and the organ coefficient should be calculated. Histopathological examination is significant for judging toxicity target organs or tissues of the animals; pathology reports should be signed by the examiner and be stamped by the inspection institute; if there are unusual changes, corresponding histopathology photos should be attached. The main organ tissue of the non-rodent control group and treatment group should be histopathologically examined; rodent control and high-dose groups of animals, as well as autopsy abnormalities should be carefully checked, if there is pathology change in one group, other dose groups should also be histopathologically examined.

In long-term toxicity tests, part of the animals should be observed for their recovery period after the end of administration to understand the extent of reversible toxicity and delayed toxicity that may occur. The length of the recovery period should be determined based on pharmacokinetic characteristics of the test substance, the target organ or tissue toxicity, and recovery situations.

3.5 Toxicokinetics

Toxicokinetics in the guidance refers to the study which inspects drug systemic exposure combined with long-term toxicity test. Toxicokinetics can describe the relationship between systemic exposure and exposure dose, exposure time and the results of toxicology. The main purpose of toxicokinetic study in this section is to explain the results of long-term toxicity tests.

Toxicokinetic tests should select the appropriate time points to sample and measure, to get the area under the curve (AUC), peak plasma concentration (Cmax), time to peak (Tmax) and other parameters. Certain drugs should be combined with an evaluation of the drug plasma protein binding rate to evaluate the systemic exposure. Toxicokinetic data can come from all of the animals in long-term toxicity tests, and can also come from a fraction of the animals. It is recommend in this section to include low, medium, and high dose groups of animals in order to estimate whether the kinetic process of the high dose drug in animals exhibits non-linear dynamics.

4. Analysis and Evaluation of the Results

The ultimate aim of long-term toxicity is to predict the possible toxicity reaction in human body. Only through the scientific analysis and evaluation of the research data can the toxicity of animals and its correlation with human body be fully understand and clearly described. Analysis and evaluation of the long-term toxicity test results is an essential part of the long-term toxicity tests; therefore, the comprehensive analysis and evaluation of the research outcome must be conducted.

4.1 Analysis of Research Results

The purpose of the analysis of long-term toxicity test results is to determine whether there is toxic reaction happening in animals, to describe its nature and extent (including toxicity onset time, extent, duration, and reversibility, etc.), to determine target organ toxicity, to determine the safety range, and to explore possible mechanisms of toxicity.

- **Correctly understand the significance of the test data**

When analyzing the long-term toxicity test results, one should correctly understand the significance of the mean data and individual data. In long-term toxicity studies of rodent groups, the mean data usually has greater significance than the individual animal data. Laboratory background data and literature data can provide references for the analysis of the results. Non-rodents are small in number and have big individual differences; therefore, the test data of individual animals often have important toxicological significance. In addition, non-rodent test results must be compared with the data before administration, data of the control group, and the laboratory historical background data. The reference value of literature data is limited.

When analyzing the long-term toxicity test results, the statistical and biological significance of data should be comprehensively considered. The correct use of statistical hypothesis testing helps to determine the biological significance of the test results, but the statistical significance does not necessarily represent a biological significance. When determining the biological significance, the dose-response relationship of the parameter changes, the changes of other relevant parameters, and the comparison with the historical background data should be taken into consideration.

Furthermore, when analyzing the long-term toxicity test results, abnormal data should be explained carefully.

- **Determine toxic response**

The parameter differences between the treatment group and the control group may result from the test substance-related toxicity, animal's adaptability to drugs or normal physiological fluctuations. When evaluating test results, one should carefully analyze the parameter's dose-response relationship, the range of parameter's changes and gender differences within the animal group, multiple test results of toxicology indicators, and the relevance and role of mechanisms to correctly judge toxicity of the drug. The change of individual parameter is often not sufficient to determine whether the compounds cause toxic reactions. Therefore, further research may be needed. In addition, toxicokinetic studies can provide important reference for determining the toxic reactions and toxicity target organ or tissue.

4.2 The Significance of Animal Toxicity Responses for Clinical Trials

When applying the long-term toxicity test results to the human body, there will inevitably be differences in the toxicity reactions of the test substance between animals and humans. Firstly, there may be toxicity reaction differences between different animal species or even individuals within the same species. Secondly, because the long-term toxicity tests generally use a higher dose of the test substance, the test substance can present nonlinear dynamic and metabolic processes in animals, leading to a toxicity irrelevant to humans. In addition, some toxicity reactions with low incidence and some idiosyncratic reactions which occur only in a small part of the population are difficult to predict by long-term toxicity tests, while some toxicity reactions are difficult to detect in animals, such as headache, dizziness, bloating, skin itching, blurred vision and so on. In light of these reasons, the results of long-term animal toxicity tests are generally not completely reproduced in human clinical trials. However, if there is no test result or literature proving that the toxicity of the test substance in animals has no relationship with that of humans; it must be assumed that human is most sensitive to the toxic effects, and the toxicity reaction in long-term toxicity tests of animals will reappear in clinical trials. (this highlighted part does not seem to flow with the first part; people might not see the connection due to the grammar. Talk to me about what you're trying to say)

4.3 Comprehensive Evaluation

Long-term toxicity testing is an integral part of the drug's non-clinical safety studies. Long-term toxicological studies have maximum comprehensiveness, the most information, and the biggest clinical significance in drug non-clinical toxicology studies. When evaluating the results, one should integrate information such as the characteristics of the test substance, pharmacodynamics, pharmacokinetics and other toxicology studies, as well as the results of clinical studies which have been

Table 5.3 Drug administration period in long-term toxicity tests

Courses of drug clinical treatment	Drug administration period in long-term toxicity test		Supported clinical phases
	Rodent animal (month)	Non-rodent animal (month)	
2-week to 1 month	1	1	Phase II
	3	3	Phase III(and production)
≤3 month	3	3	Phase II
	6	6	Phase II (and production)
≤6 month	6	6	Phase II
	6	9	Phase III (and production)
>6 month	6	9	Phase II
	6	9	Phase III (and production)

obtained for evaluation comprehensively. The evaluation of long-term toxicity test results should finally be implemented in clinical adverse reactions of the test substance, clinical toxicity target organs or tissues, the safety range, clinical key indicators for observation, and the necessary clinical care or rescue measures.

5. Conclusion

The long-term toxicity test design, analysis, and evaluation of its results should be conducted based on its purpose. Through long-term toxicity tests, one should be able to make reasonable predictions and judgments for the clinical adverse reactions of test substances, clinical toxicity target organs or tissues, the safety range, clinical key indicators for observation, and the necessary clinical care or rescue measures (Table 5.3).

5.6.4.6 Booklet 21—Special Safety Study and Literature of Hypersensitive (topical, systemic and photo-toxicity), Hemolytic and Topical Irritative (blood vessel, skin, mucous membrane, and muscle) Reaction Related to Topical and Systemic Use of the Drugs

General requirements of local injections safety tests for drugs with existing national standards (SFDA 2005):

- for intravenous administration: vascular irritation test, allergy test, hemolytic test
- for intramuscular injection: muscle irritation test, allergy test, hemolytic test
- for subcutaneous injection: skin irritation test, allergy test
- for injections with several routes of administration: the need to simultaneously conduct safety tests in multiple pathways.

Chemical drug irritations and allergic and hemolytic reactions refer to the local toxicities (e.g., irritation and sensitization, etc.) and/or systemic toxicities, such as allergic and hemolytic, etc.). Those toxicities can be caused by chemical drug preparations which are administrated through the eye, ear, nose, mouth, respiratory, joint cavity, skin, rectal, vagina, or intravenously, intraarterially, intramuscularly, subcutaneously, intrathecally or other non-oral methods. It is part of the preclinical safety evaluation components.

Active ingredients of drugs and their metabolites, excipients, related substances and physical and chemical properties (such as pH, osmotic pressure, etc.) are all likely to cause irritation and/or allergic and/or hemolysis. Therefore, prior to the clinical use, the drug should be studied for its local and/or systemic toxicity of its preparation at the administration site after administration, to prompt the possible toxicity in clinical applications, target organ toxicity, safety range, clinical research and clinical monitoring indicators, and offer reference for clinical detoxification or rescue measures to protect the safety and effect of clinical medicine.

State Food and Drug Administration issued "Guidance for irritation, allergic and hemolytic research of chemical drugs" on March 18, 2005. The guidance applies to chemical drugs. The main contents include the general principles and common test methods of chemicals irritation, general principles for allergic and hemolytic research and evaluation. This guidance is developed in reference to the relevant technical guidelines under the framework of ICH tripartite (EU, Japan and the United States) and other nations, as well as the research progress about the irritation, allergic, and hemolytic effect of drugs with non-oral administration, domestic and abroad. This guidance also includes the general rules of non-clinical drug safety evaluation and the practice of drug research technology in China. The main references of the western literature include:

- FDA Guidance for Industry Skin irritation and sensitization testing of generic transdermal drug products
- FDA Guidance for Industry Photo safety testing
- FDA Guidance for Industry Immunotoxicology evaluation of investigation new drug
- EPA Health effects test guidelines OPPTS 870.7800 Immunotoxicity
- EPA Health effects test guidelines OPPTS 870.2500 Acute dermal irritation
- EPA Health effects test guidelines OPPTS 870.2600 Skin sensitization
- EPA Health effects test guidelines OPPTS 870.2400 Acute eye irritation
- EMEA Non-clinical local tolerance testing of medicinal products
- ISO 10993-10:2002(E) Biological evaluation of medical devices- Part 10- Tests for irritation and delayed-type hypersensitivity

Thus, studies conducted overseas are generally consistent with the registration requirements in China.

1. General Provisions

According to the "Drug Registration" (Trial), chemical drugs irritation, allergic and hemolytic research must be conducted in compliance with "non-clinical studies of drug quality management practices" (GLP). Experimental design should follow the randomized, controlled, repeatable principles.

Chemical irritation and allergic and hemolytic reaction research designs should involve the consideration of the following factors and aspects: the mechanism of toxicity, affecting factors, clinical significance, method of administration of drugs, and indications of clinical application.

Animal species should be selected based on the experimental models to be used and the indicators of observation. Animal sex, age and physiological status should be in accordance with the requirements of the test animal models. Test substances should be in accordance with the preparations of clinical use. Administration regimen should be determined according to the test model and the proposed clinical application conditions.

In addition to the administration site, the observation region should also include the surrounding tissues or parts which may be exposed to the test substance.

If the test substance is the same or can be compared to the proposed preparation in the clinical studies, and other non-clinical safety (such as long-term toxicity) study results can fully reflect the irritant, allergic and hemolytic toxicity of the test substance, the relevant toxicity studies can be excused.

Chemical drug irritant, allergic and hemolytic studies should use the test substance consistent with the preparations of clinical use and in line with the clinical quality standards, and indicate their name, origin, batch number, the content (or specifications), storage conditions and preparation methods. The names and amount of the excipients and impurities should be stated as clear as possible, along with the internal-test report of research unit. Excipients and solvents should be marked with the batch number, size, and manufacturer, and meet the test requirements.

Research should be carried out using reasonable methods and means to avoid false negative or false positive test results.

When irritation and/or allergic and/or hemolysis tests of the test substance prompts a certain toxicity, there should be a comparative study with marketed preparation with the same route of administration. The determination of the sample cases in comparative studies should follow the basic statistics principle.

When evaluating the irritation, allergy and hemolysis of the test substance, the pharmaceutical, pharmacology, toxicology and clinical applications should be considered for a comprehensive study. Based on the integrated knowledge, decide whether the test substance is qualified for clinical trial and what the concerned problems are in clinical use.

2. Chemical Drug Irritation, Allergic and Hemolytic Test Method and Content

- **Irritation test methods**
  Skin irritation test
  Injection site irritation test
  Eye irritation test

- **Allergic test methods**
  Passive cutaneous anaphylaxis test
  Active systemic allergy test
  Guinea pig maximization test and the Buehler test

Skin phototoxicity test
Light skin allergy test

- **Hemolytic test methods**
  Conventional in vitro test tube method (visual inspection method)
  Improved in vitro hemolysis test method (spectrophotometry)

5.6.4.7 Booklet 22—Study and Relevant Literature on Pharmacodynamics, Toxicity and Pharmacokinetics Change Caused by the Interactions Amongst Multiple Components in the Combination Products

Compound medicines are the preparations made of two or more drugs. They belong to "new compound preparations" in the Class 1 drug category for registration. For compound preparation, booklet 22 should be submitted. "Drug Registration" made some principled requirements for innovation of combined (?) drug research, mainly in terms of animal testing requirements. Test data and literature of multiple ingredients' efficacy, toxicity, and pharmacokinetic interactions in compound preparation should be provided. For the requirements of clinical trials, there is no significant difference between compound drugs and monotherapy.

Over the years, in the development of a new compound preparation, the ratio and dose of monotherapy in the compound are determined by animal studies. The composition of compound is determined through efficacy trials in animals. The confirmed compound is used to conduct long-term animal toxicity tests. After obtaining the approval to conduct clinical trials, the compound determined in animal efficacy tests will be used in humans to observe its effectiveness and safety without studying if the monotherapy dose and ratio in the compound are suitable for the target indication crowd.

In the United States and European countries, the compound is heavily dependent on research and development results in the target indication of the crowd. Its research and development emphasize that the single drug in the compound generally should have the basis of the combination therapy in human body. The needed animal studies depend on the combination therapy data. The research institution could discuss it with the Drug Administration Authorities. The requirements of clinical research are clearly different from monotherapy. As indicated in the compound drug clinical research guidelines issued by the FDA and EMEA, clinical research requirements generally include:

1. To determine the appropriate proportion and amount of each components in the compound;
2. To explore the dosing regimen;
3. To determine the suitable application crowd;
4. To clarify its short-term and long-term safety and effectiveness;
5. To make clear of the compound advantages.

Theoretically, the compound formulation does not represent that it has the proper proportions and dosage in human. Due to the ratio and doses of each ingredient in the compound are screened out by animal tests. The requirements for combination preparation in clinical trials include:

1. Compound preparation dose-finding studies should be conducted to determine the appropriate dose combinations and proportions of each component.
2. Compound preparations dose-finding study content should include both exploration of different proportions of monotherapy, and exploration of different doses of single-agent;
3. Generally, according to the factorial analysis to design clinical studies, sponsors should compare synchronously the efficacy and safety among the compound preparations consisting of different doses and proportions and the respective monotherapy or placebo;
4. Based on factorial results of the study, sponsors should select a reasonable ratio and dose of the composition of the compound preparation;
5. In the confirmatory clinical studies, sponsors should further study the safety and efficacy of compound formulations in the crowd with target indications.

The traditional animal testing uses a single specification compound with a fixed ratio and dose. Therefore, to solve the problems over the above five aspects in compound drug clinical trials, the results of traditional animal testing do not suit to the requirements for compound drug clinical trials when applied to directly humans. For the innovative combination drugs, after obtaining clinical trial approval, sponsors need to prepare their compound preparations with different proportions, different doses with a variety of specifications, and conduct the exploratory studies in a certain proportion and dose range.

5.6.4.8 Booklet 23—Study and Literature of Mutagenicity Test

Mutagenicity Tests Mainly Include the Following

- Microbial reverse mutation assay
- Description of strain, dose groups (including the blank control, vehicle control, positive control, with S9 or without S9 and test substance group), test methods and test results, etc.
- Chromosome aberration test
- Description of cell, dose groups (including the blank control, vehicle control, positive control, with S9 or without S9 and test substance group), test methods and test results, etc.
- Micronucleus test
- Description of animals, the dose groups (including the control, vehicle control, positive control), the route of administration, the test method (such as bone marrow sampling), and the test results, etc.

The evaluations of mutagenicity and genotoxicity testings are very similar. Since inducibility and carcinogenicity are relevant, the mutagenicity and genotoxicity tests can be used for the evaluation of the new drug carcinogenicity.

Genetic toxicity tests include various methods with a variety of biological models. Sponsors can use prokaryotic cells or eukaryotic cells, or even mammalian cells to conduct in vitro tests with or without metabolic activation substances. The tests can also be carried out in vivo in whole animals. Based on genetic endpoint detection methods, detection tests can be divided into three categories, i.e. gene mutations, chromosomal aberrations, DNA damage and repair; in terms of the test system, genotoxicity tests can be divided into in vivo tests and in vitro tests.

This booklet should be prepared in accordance with the information given in "Guidance for drug genotoxicity research", which is based on the following major western guidances:

- ICH Steering Committee. Harmonized Tripartite Guideline S2A:
- Guidance on specific aspects of regulatory genotoxicity tests. 1995
- ICH Steering Committee. Harmonized Tripartite GuidelineS2B:Genotoxicity: A standard battery for genotoxicity testing ofpharmaceuticals. 1997
- ICH Steering Committee. Harmonized Tripartite Guideline M3:
- Non-clinical safety studies for the conduct of human clinical trials forpharmaceuticals. 2000
- FDA. Guidance for industry and review staff: Recommended approaches to integration of genetic toxicology study results. 2006
- OECD Guideline for Testing of Chemicals.471Bacterial reverse mutation test. 1997
- OECD Guideline for Testing of Chemicals.473 *In Vitro* Mammalian chromosome aberration test. 1997
- OECD Guideline for Testing of Chemicals.474 Mammalian erythrocyte micronucleus test. 1997
- OECD Guideline for Testing of Chemicals.476 *In Vitro*
- Mammalian cell gene mutation test. 1997

"The new compound preparation" in registration category 1, if its animal pharmacokinetic studies showed no significant changes, booklet 23 could be exempted.

5.6.4.9 Booklet 24—Study and Literature of Reproductive Toxicity

Reproductive toxicity studies are an important part of non-clinical drug safety evaluation. They are closely related to toxicological studies of acute toxicity, chronic toxicity, genotoxicity and other studies, which are important parts in the process of entering the drug into clinical research and the market.

On December 19, 2006, the State Food and Drug Administration issued "Guidance for reproductive toxicity research of drugs" Note [2006] No. 639. This booklet preparation should not be unfamiliar to most foreign manufacturers, since the guidance is developed in reference to the following western standard guidance (SFDA 2006):

- ICH Steering Committee. Harmonized Tripartite Guideline S5A: Detection of toxicity to reproduction for medicinal products.

- ICH Steering Committee. Harmonized Tripartite Guideline S5B: Maintenance of the ICH guideline on toxicity to male fertility.
- ICH Steering Committee. Harmonized Tripartite Guideline M3: Non-clinical safety studies for the conduct of human clinical trials for pharmaceuticals.
- Omori Y. Principles and guidelines a review of recommendations (on detection of toxicity) in the three regions. In: P.F. D'Arcy and D.W.G. Harron edited, Proceedings of the First International Conference on Harmonization. Brussels 1991: 256–266
- EEC guidelines: Detection of toxicity to reproduction for medicinal products including toxicity to male fertility.
- FDA. Reviewer guidance: Integration of study results to assess concerns about human reproductive and developmental toxicities.

This guidance focuses on the basic principles of the animal, dosage, administration method, and selection of the test in animal reproductive toxicity, and introduces some commonly used test protocols, analyzes and evaluates the obtained data along with the relevant scientific principles and background.

1. The Basic Principles

Reproductive toxicity tests of drugs belong to non-clinical safety evaluation studies and must be performed in compliance with "non-clinical studies of drug quality management practices". Reproductive toxicity tests should comply with the basic principles of general animal testing, which are randomized, controlled, and repeatable.

2. The Basic Content

a) General considerations

- **Test substance**

The test substance of reproductive toxicity tests should be the samples with stable preparation processes, be in line with the quality standards of clinical research, and indicate the name, origin, batch number, the content (or specifications), storage conditions and preparation methods of the test substance, and be attached to the internal-test report of research and development units. The materials and solvents used should be marked with the batch number, size, and manufacturer, and should meet the test requirements.

- **Pharmacokinetic study of the test substance**

Prior to starting the reproductive toxicity test, the existing pharmacokinetics information may be derived from non-pregnant and non-lactating animals. When conducting the evaluation of the results, there is a need for further research of the pregnant or lactating animal pharmacokinetic status.

- **Test System**

Reproductive toxicity testing should be conducted using mammalian animals. While using animal species and strains, the background information, availability, and the correlation with humans should be considered. Generally, the same animal species and strains with other toxicological tests should be used so that the results of toxicology tests are comparable with others, and excessive pre-trials may be avoided. Rats are good subjects and are highly comparable with other test results, and a lot of background information about rats has accumulated; therefore, rats can be used as the preferred rodent animals for reproductive toxicity testing.

In embryo-fetal developmental toxicity studies, a second mammalian animal species generally needs to be adopted. A wealth of background information has accumulated on rabbits, which are easily available and practical for use. Therefore, rabbits are the preferred non-rodent animals. When rabbits are not suitable, it depends on the circumstances to choose another alternative non-rodent or a second rodent. Usually, choosing young, sexually mature adult, and nulliparous female animals is practical. The initial weight of individual animals should not exceed the average weight of 20 %. Animals should comply with the relevant provisions of the State level requirements. The sources, strains, and genetic background should be clear and the experimental animals should have quality certification.

b) Administration

- **Dose selection.**

Generally, the selection of high dose should be in accordance with existing research data (pharmacology, acute toxicity and long-term toxicity, pharmacokinetic studies) or the pre-tests and physicochemical properties of the test substance and route of administration. Slight maternal toxicity reactions should appear within the high-dose range. In most cases, l g/kg daily is the maximum dose limit. The low dose amount should be the reproductive toxicity NOAEL. Between high-dose and low-dose, 1–2 doses can be set according to the specific circumstances in order to observe the possible dose-response relationship.

- **Route of administration.**

Under normal circumstances, the route of administration should be consistent with the intended use of clinical pathways. If there are multiple intended uses and the studies suggest that pharmacokinetic characteristics (including street distribution) of different routes of administration are similar, the route of administration using a higher amount of exposure is recommended. In addition, intraperitoneal injection may have direct effects on the uterus and fetus; therefore, this route is usually not utilized when using pregnant animals for study.

- **Frequency of administration.**

Usually, one administration daily is practical. However, the pharmacokinetic parameters and expected clinical administration should be considered to increase or decrease the times of administrations.

- **Control groups.**

A vehicle control group should be set, and its route and frequency of administration should be the same as that of the test substance group. If the excipient may have an effect or influence on the test substance, a blank control group should be set.

Furthermore, setting a positive control group should be considered. It may be necessary depending on circumstances such as a new animal system, how long it been since the system was used, or a new testing facility.

- **Test program**

General considerations of test protocol selection

The choice of the test protocol should consider existing pharmacology, toxicology and pharmacokinetic data of the test substance or the similar drugs, especially information in terms of reproductive toxicity. It is recommended to adopt more mature experimental designs. For most drugs, the three stages of the test protocol (commonly used test protocol) are usually more appropriate and can recognize the potential reproductive and developmental stage damages.

- **General reproductive toxicity test**

Description of animals, dose groups (the multiple relationship with pharmacodynamic dose and proposed clinical dose), route of administration, time of administration (such as continuous administration time before male and female mating and continues administration time after mating), observed indicators and the test results etc. should be provided.

- **Teratogenic sensitive period toxicity test**

Description of animals, dose groups (the multiple relationship with pharmacodynamics dose and proposed clinical dose), route of administration and time, observed indicators and test results, etc. should be provided.

- **Perinatal toxicity test**

Description of the animal, dose groups (the multiple relationship with pharmacodynamics dose and proposed clinical dose), the route of administration and time, observed indicators and test results, etc. should be provided.

- **Toxicokinetics**

Toxicokinetics in this booklet and its guidelines refer to the pharmacokinetics studies which inspect drug systemic exposure combined with reproductive toxicity studies. Toxicokinetics can describe the relationship between systemic exposure and the exposure dose, exposure time, and the results of toxicology. The main purpose of a toxicokinetic study in this booklet is to analyze the results of genotoxicity tests and scientifically compare different toxicological test results to provide reference for risk assessments of clinical use.

Toxicokinetic tests should involve the appropriate sampling time points to get the area under the curve (AUC), the peak concentration (Cmax.), peak time (Tmax) and other parameters. Certain drugs should take the drug plasma protein binding rate into consideration to evaluate systemic exposure. Toxicokinetic data can come from all animal reproductive toxicity studies and can also come from part of the animals. Toxicokinetic data should include fetuses/pups data to evaluate if drugs and/or metabolites can pass through the placenta barrier and whether they can be secreted through milk. This part of the animal tests may include low, medium and high dose groups to estimate if the dynamic process of the drug in high doses is a nonlinear dynamical process in animals.

3. Analysis and Evaluation of the Results

The ultimate goal of the animal reproductive toxicity test is to predict the possible reproduction- and developmental-related toxicity in humans. Analysis and evaluation of test results are necessary parts of the test. The study results should be comprehensively analyzed and evaluated.

- **Statistical analysis**

Choose the appropriate statistical methods to analyze the data. The reasonability of the chosen statistical methods should be stated.

Significance tests can help analyze the test results. The result explanation itself must be based on the rationality in biology. The inference may be wrong in the cases that the difference with the control group result is considered not to be caused by biological factors, just because there is no statistical significance. To some extent, the thought may also be wrong in the cases that the differences with the statistical significance must be related to biological factors. Especially for the abnormalities with low incidence and showing a skewed distribution (e. g, embryonic death, birth defects), the confidence intervals of the variables associated may indicate the possible size of effect. When using statistic program, the indicator unit used in the comparison between groups should be considered: usually nest rather than fetal individual units, if the parental animals of both sexes were administered, use the mating pair (i. e. two generations of experimental study of parental pairing) as the unit.

- **Data Report**

It is recommended that the test data is tabulated to show the test results for each animal. The expression form of overall test group data is reasonable from a biological standpoint (i. e., avoid false precision), and reflects the distribution of variables. The appendix or form made out of all test data (such as body weight, food intake, litter the corresponding data) should be as concise as possible, instead of calculated values using the absolute value to represent each data; avoid unnecessary repeats.

When making the form of the observation results with low incidence (such as signs, autopsy findings, malformations, etc.), it is recommended to list the several positive test data together. Especially, the data of the structural changes (fetal malformations) should be clearly marked as the abnormal fetal nest numbers and each nest affected fetuses (number) in the table and stated all the observed changes of each affected fetus. If necessary, other derived forms can be summarized out of the original form according to the type of abnormalities.

- **Analysis of results**

Under normal circumstances, analysis and evaluation should be conducted for the toxicity of the test substance manifested in animal reproductive and developmental aspects. If positive reproductive toxicity or developmental toxicity results appear, the possibility of reproductive toxicity and developmental toxicity risk in humans should be assessed. These positive toxicity results may appear in reproductive toxicity, general toxicity test or also may appear in human studies. The following is the toxicity routine analysis and evaluation:

a. **Reproductive toxicity**
   Reproductive toxicity leads to structural and functional changes which may affect the reproductive capacity of P0-generation, including toxic effects on fertility, childbirth and breast-feeding and so on.
b. **Developmental toxicity**
   Developmental toxicity is the toxic effects on the F1 generation, including death, malformations (structural abnormalities), abnormal growth, and functional toxicity.
c. **Others**
   In many cases, the reproductive toxicity shown by the parent and progeny may be secondary to maternal toxicity. The results should be combined with related toxicity results, such as the long-term toxicity studies, to determine whether reproductive toxicity shown is the secondary result of maternal toxicity.

- **Comprehensive evaluation**

Reproductive toxicity study is an integral part of drug safety evaluation and the drug overall concurrency process. Reproductive toxicity studies cannot be separated from pharmacodynamics, pharmacokinetics and other toxicological studies. The test results with other toxicology test results should be the confirmation, instruction and additions to each other.

When evaluating the reproductive toxicity test results, the following information should be combined to conduct a comprehensive analysis: (a) pharmaceutical characteristics of the test substance; (b) pharmacodynamics, pharmacokinetics and other toxicological studies, especially the long-term toxicity tests and genotoxicity tests results; and (c) population characteristics of study subjects in clinical study results which have been achieved.

4. Phased Reproductive Toxicity Studies

According to the characteristics of the test substance and proposed indications, especially the clinical research study population characteristics, it can be phased to provide reproductive toxicity study data to support clinical research in different phases. Under normal circumstances, it should be prior to the start of clinical studies to provide complete fertility and early embryonic developmental toxicity and embryo-fetal developmental toxicity test data. Perinatal toxicity test data can be provided at the time of application for market.

For "The new compound preparation" in registration category 1, if its animal pharmacokinetic studies show no significant changes, it could be excused from booklet 24.

5.6.4.10 Booklet 25—Study and Literature of Carcinogenicity Test

The purpose of the carcinogenic test is to investigate the potential carcinogenic effects of drugs in animals to evaluate and predict the possible harm to humans.

Any potential carcinogenic factors appeared in in vitro tests, animal toxicity tests, and human application can prompt carcinogenicity studies, Internationally, for the expected long-term use drugs, it has been requested to conduct rodent carcinogenicity tests. In the study of potential carcinogenic effects of drugs, the carcinogenicity tests are more meaningful than existing genotoxicity tests and systems exposure evaluation techniques.

Since carcinogenicity tests cost a significant amount of time and animal resources, carcinogenicity studies should be carried out only when they are really needed to evaluate the potential carcinogenicity caused by drug exposure in humans through long-term administration studies in animals (SFDA 2005, 2007, 2010).

Considerations of Conducting Carcinogenicity Tests

- **Duration and exposure**

Drugs with expected clinical use duration for at least 6 consecutive months generally necessitates carcinogenic tests.

Some types of compounds may not be continuous used over 6 months, but may be reused in an intermittent manner. The drugs which need regular medication intermittently for treatment of chronic and recurrent disease usually need carcinogenicity tests. Some drug delivery systems which may lead to prolonged exposure should also be considered for carcinogenicity tests. Unless there are potential carcinogenic factors, drugs with short-term contact or not used frequently usually do not need carcinogenicity tests.

- **Potential carcinogenic factors**

Drugs have potential carcinogenic concerns that may need carcinogenicity tests. Several factors needed for considering include:

1. There is evidence that these drugs have human-related potentially carcinogenicity
2. Its structure-function relationship prompt risk of cancer;
3. There is evidence of precancerous lesions in repeated dose toxicity studies;
4. The compound or its metabolites which lead to local tissue reactions or other pathophysiological changes got long-term retention in the tissue.

- **Indications and patient populations**

When life expectancy is short in specific target populations (e. g., within 2–3 years), it long-term carcinogenicity tests may not be required.

Anticancer drugs for systemic advanced cancer usually do not need carcinogenicity tests. When anticancer drugs are quite effective and can significantly prolong life, there are concerns of the late secondary tumors. When these drugs are intended for the adjuvant treatment of patients without tumors or the non-tumor indications of long-term use, carcinogenicity tests are usually needed.

- **Route of administration**

The route of administration should be as possible as consistent with the intended use of clinical pathways; if the degree of metabolism and systemic exposure are similar to the system under different routes of administration, one of the routes of administration can be used to carry out carcinogenicity tests; In such cases, it should get full attention if the test drugs get adequate exposure in the tissues and organs (such as the lung associated with inhalant use) related to the clinical route of administration. Pharmacokinetic distribution data can provide evidence for whether the drugs get sufficient exposure.

- **The degree of systemic exposure**

Topical medication (such as skin and eye medication) may require carcinogenicity tests. For the topical medication with very little systemic exposure, oral route of administration is not required to evaluate the potential carcinogenic effects of internal organs; if there is potential light carcinogenic concern, conducting percutaneous carcinogenicity tests may be necessary. Unless there is significant systemic exposure or relevant concerns, ophthalmic drugs usually do not need carcinogenicity tests.

In the case of compounds changing the salt, acid radical, or modified bases, if there already has been the original compound carcinogenicity test data, the data should be provided with the evidence that there is no significant change of the pharmacokinetics, pharmacodynamics, or toxicity in relation to the original compounds. The bridging studies to determine the need for new carcinogenicity tests may be necessary when drug exposure and toxicity changes,

- **Endogenous peptides, protein substances and their analogs**

Endogenous substances of replacement therapy (concentration at physiological levels), when there are clinical experience, usually do not need carcinogenicity test.

If there are factors of concerns in the course of treatment, clinical indications, or patient population, long-term carcinogenicity needs to be evaluated:

1. Their biological activity is significantly different from that of natural materials;
2. The structure after the modification shows significant changes compared with natural substances.
3. The amount of the drug exposed exceeds the normal level in the blood or tissues.

- **Carcinogenicity testing schedule**

Carcinogenicity tests should usually be completed before the application for market approval. If there are particular concerns about patient populations, rodent carcinogenicity tests need to be completed before performing large-scale clinical trials.

For developing the drugs to treat some serious diseases (such as AIDS), animal carcinogenicity tests need not to be carried out before the application for market approval, but these tests should be carried out after marketing.

Carcinogenicity tests measure the risk of drug potential carcinogenicity in the life of the test animals with one or more exposure with the test drug. Currently it can be divided into short-term and long-term carcinogenicity tests. Short-term experiments can be divided into mutagenicity tests and cell transformation tests. The short-term evaluation tests of mutagenicity and genotoxicity are similar. Because induction and carcinogenicity have some relevance, these tests can be used to evaluate the carcinogenicity of new drugs. For cell transformation experiments, the cells are cultured in liquid. The cancer cells lose the contact capacity so the cells in malignant transformation clones arrange messily and overlap; while cells of normal clones arranged orderly and only form a single-layer of cells. Animal carcinogenicity experiments are divided into two kinds: short-term and long-term. Short-term animal carcinogenicity experiments mainly include experiments induced skin tumors in mice, experiments induced lung tumors in mice, rat liver foci induced experiment, experimental induced breast cancer in female rats, cancer-promoting agents tests. Long-term animal carcinogenicity experiments include long-term animal carcinogenicity studies, and combined chronic toxicity carcinogenicity tests. This booklet "carcinogenicity studies and literature" requires long-term animal carcinogenicity experiments.

5.6.4.11 Booklet 26—Study and Literature of Drug Dependence

Drug dependence means that the drug interacts with the body for a long time, so that the specific, compensatory, and adaptive changes of the body occur in the physiology and biochemical processes and/or morphology. Stopping the medication can cause the body's discomfort and/or psychological desire. Dependence can be divided into physical dependence and psychological dependence. Physical dependence is an adaptation state of the body produced by long-term use of use-dependent drugs, including tolerance and withdrawal symptoms after stopping. Psychological dependence is a special spiritual effect produced by drug's effect on the central nervous system, showing a strong desire for the drug and compulsive drug-seeking behavior. Dependence liability can be reflected during the drug study of animal or human (SFDA 2007).

Physical dependence and psychological dependence may exist at the same time, and may also be isolated. Like stimulants usually presents psychological dependence, but physical withdrawal symptoms are not obvious.

Tolerance and sensitivity (sensitization) are two different forms of adaptive changes in the central nervous system. Tolerance means that after repeated use of certain drugs, the body's sensitivity to the drug reduces, and increasing the dose is required to produce the original effect. On the contrast of tolerability, sensitization is that after repeated use of drugs, the body's sensitivity to the drug improves, and the drug effect is enhanced. The sensitization phenomenon of addictive drugs appears as enhanced behavioral reactions and drug-seeking motives.

Currently the compounds known to produce dependence mainly include opioid, cocaine, amphetamines, cannabinoids, benzodiazepines, barbiturates, and some steroid hormones, and so on.

Drug dependence research is part of the non-clinical safety studies; it must be performed by "non-clinical studies of drug quality management practices." Dependence research should be combined with the pharmaceutical, pharmacokinetics, pharmacodynamics, general pharmacology and toxicology test results of the test substance to comprehensively analyzed and evaluated. Experimental design should be consistent with randomized, controlled, blinded and repeated principles.

Basic Content

A. Scope

1. The novel compounds with similar structure of the known compounds having the potential dependence;
2. Drugs acting on the central nervous system, resulting in significant analgesic, sedative, hypnotic and stimulant effects
3. Compounds containing the known ingredients with strong dependence;
4. Drugs with direct or indirect effects on the central opioid receptor, cannabinoid receptor, dopamine receptor, norepinephrine receptor, 5-serotonin receptor, N-cholinergic receptor, 7-aminobutyric acid receptor, benzodiazepine receptor;
5. Known metabolites with dependence ingredients
6. Drugs intended for detoxification;
7. Drugs which are thought non-dependent originally, but are found to have dependence liability in clinical studies or in clinical applications.

B. The Test Substance

The test substance of dependence tests should adopt the samples with a stable preparation process and in line with quality standards for clinical trials, and indicate the name, origin, batch number, the content (or specifications), storage conditions, and preparation methods of the test substance, along with the self-test report of the research institute. The materials and solvents used should be marked with batch number, size and manufacturer, and meet the test requirements.

C. Test System

1. The basis of the selection of the test system
   Factors of the selection of the test system include pharmacodynamic response of test system, such as sensitivity, specificity and reproducibility, background of the test substance, such as pharmacodynamic, pharmacokinetic characteristics, species, strain, sex, and age of experimental animals. If you select a special test system, please explain the reasons.
2. Experimental animals
   Commonly used experimental animals include mice, rats, monkeys, etc. Under normal circumstances, use male animals, and add female animals when necessary. Usually rats and mice are used. For the drugs with highly suspicion of the potential for drug-induced dependence and rodent test result is negative, primate animals should be used. Animals should comply with the relevant provisions of the state level requirements.
3. Test systems in vitro
   In vitro test systems can be used in supportive research (such as the study of activity characteristics and action mechanism of the drug). Commonly used in vitro test systems include: isolated organs, tissues, cells, subcellular organelles, receptors, ion channels and enzymes.

D. Dose of Administration

Dependence study should be conducted over a wide range of the doses. Different doses can be chosen depending on different test method and purpose. Multiple increment of the main efficacy ED50 or the minimum effective dose is commonly used, and the dose is designed combined with the drug's solubility, toxicity and effects on motor function, learning ability and memory. Each test should set at least three dose groups.

E. Route of Administration
In principle, the route of administration should be consistent with the clinic and increase venous route of administration as possible.

F. Control Groups
The positive control and vehicle control groups should be set up. If the test substance need to be dissolved using a special solvent, an additional blank control should also be set. If a test substance is a relatively pure single compound with similar structure of its mother nuclear which has significant dependency, then, the mother compound should be selected as positive control drug.

G. Test Requirements
Drug dependence trials generally include three parts: the neuropharmacology test, the physical dependence test, and the psychological dependence test.

1. Neuropharmacology Test
If there is an early in vitro dependent test, positive results obtained should be further confirmed by in vivo studies

A neuropharmacology method can be used for the measurement of behavioral effects and neurotransmitters to initially judge whether the test substance has dependent tendencies. These elements can be observed through pharmacodynamic tests, general pharmacology or toxicology tests. The specific method is no longer listed.

Generally, after fully revealing the pharmacological properties of the drug, further research of the potential physical dependence and psychological dependence needs to be conducted. Except for the case when the following three conditions occur simultaneously:

- In the effective concentration range, the drug does not interact with the target molecule associated with dependence, or even if it is observed that the drug binds with the relevant target, this combination does not cause corresponding changes in function.
- In vivo studies show no dependence potential.
- It is not found that the drug has new possible mechanism of action associated with reliance.

When the type and extent of potential dependence have been fully exposed from in vitro experiments, further studies are not necessary.

If it is found that this drug has a new mechanism of action possibly associated with reliance, further research is required.

2. Physical Dependence Test

A variety of drugs with potential dependence produce different symptoms of physical dependence, and there is no ideal single indicator reflecting the physical dependence;

Therefore, a variety of indicators are needed to evaluate physical dependence comprehensively. Physiological indicators can include body weight, body temperature, respiration, food intake, etc. In behavioral tests, indicators which can reflect motor function, learning ability, memory ability, and motivation behavior changes can be used. The suitable indicators should be able to observe the dynamic changes before, during, and after drug administration since such indicators may help to describe the degree, characteristics, and development process of the tolerance and sensitization of the body.

2.1 Method

There are three ways to use general test methods for the evaluation of drug physical dependence: natural withdrawal tests, urging withdrawal tests, and alternative tests. Whether natural or urging withdrawal, animals will exhibit a series of behavior changes with different levels, but not all the withdrawal symptoms will appear in one animal. Since the indications are not the same for each method of observation, physical dependence test can be combined with pharmacodynamics, general pharmacology performance to choose the appropriate method in combination with China's specific situation.

2.2 Major notes in the observation of withdrawal reactions

a. Dose, frequency and period of administration should make the animal produce neural adaptive response.
b. Observation of the withdrawal response should be given appropriate time and frequency, and draw attention to the changes before and after administration.
c. Both natural withdrawal and urged withdrawal are needed, but they can be performed on different animal models.
d. Use the instruments available to detect objective indicators.
e. Rebound phenomenon often appears after withdrawal of addictive drugs (acute pharmacological effect of the drug opposite symptoms), and attention should be paid when choosing observational indicators.

3. Psychological Dependence Test

Drugs which can induce psychological dependence could prompt the drug users to exhibit periodic or continuous desire for the drug in order to feel the euphoric effects. This is a subjective experience, only can be reflected indirectly by animal behavior change caused by drug use. Methods often used include a self-administration test, drug discrimination test, conditioned place preference test, and a behavioral sensitization test.

3.1 Method

The common methods may include the following:

- Monkey self-administration test
- Rats self-administration test
- Conditioned place preference in rats or mice
- Conditioned place preference test
- The drug discrimination tests in rats or mice
- Behavioral sensitization test
- Rats behavioral sensitization test

Other methods may also be used but need to be explained.

3.2 Psychological dependence study notes:

a. In the self-administration experiment, non-response period (a period of time before the animals showed a drug-seeking behavior), the point of time to increase doses, and alternative procedures associated with the side effects of drugs should be noted.
b. In the self-administration test, integrate information of the physical dependence test results as available Design a suitable dose and change the dose at least three times.
c. In the conditioned place preference test, balanced experimental design should be used to avoid the impact of the natural tendency of animals.

4. In Vitro Test of Dependence

H. The selection of dependent research projects

In order to obtain sufficient information about drug dependence, the selection of drug dependence research needs to refer to pharmacodynamics, general pharmacology, and other toxicology test results. There should at least be a physical dependence test (natural withdrawal and urged withdrawal) and a psychological dependence test. For the drugs that have strong spiritual activity and are intended to be used to change the spirit and neural activity, there should be primate animal test data.

I. Phased Dependence Study

1. For the Single Compound Which May Present Dependence

In vivo neural pharmacology studies should be completed before Phase I clinical trials. The safety information observed in early non-clinical or early clinical studies could provide reference for further non-clinical dependent studies. Further evaluation of physical dependence and psychological dependence should be completed before the beginning of phase II trials. If necessary, the mechanism of in vitro tests and dependence need to be discussed.

2. For Effective Part of Traditional Chinese Medicine (TMC) or Compound Preparation of Traditional Chinese Medicine

TCM effective parts or components of TCM compound preparation are complex. The targets are enormous and in vitro test results have limited reference value. In vivo neuropharmacology pharmacology study results have some meaning in determining whether there is dependence, but there is great difficulty and limitation for the result evaluation. In vivo dependence test should be used as the primary method to investigate TCM effective parts or dependence of TCM compound preparation.

Tor the TCM effective parts or TCM compound preparation which need drug dependence trial, comprehensive in vivo dependent trials data should be provided before Phase II clinical begins.

J. Analysis and Evaluation of Results

When analyzing and evaluating the obtained non-clinical trial data, generally, the following aspects should be considered:

1. Problems of statistical differences and biological differences: Statistical differences can be used to determine whether the test substance has impact on the test results of examining. Due to the sample size, it may sometimes mask the true biological differences, so there should be fully adequate samples. Note that each of the test sample results should be analyzed. The statistical difference should be considered in combination with the normal reaction of animals to analyze.
2. The selection of the positive drug: Choose the appropriate positive drug with similar structure and/or similar mechanism of action as possible.
3. The observation of the appearance time, duration and action, strength of the abnormal behaviors of animals.
4. Whether the selected animal is appropriate and whether the animal model is reliable.
5. Analysis of the sensitivity, specificity and reliability of the selected indicators.
6. Assessment of the specific test results and overall assessment.
7. The relationship between the doses produced dependence, and the effective and toxic dose.
8. To analyze whether there is tolerance, and the relationship between tolerance and dependence.
9. To analyze comprehensively the feasibility of continuing the clinical study, according to the proposed indications and effectiveness of drugs.

In summary, the risk assessment of the drug potential dependence should take full advantage of all the non-clinical research data by combining pharmaceutical, pharmacological and clinical research information to conduct scientific and objective analysis and evaluation in order to determine whether there is potential dependency.

5.6.4.12 Booklet 27—Study and Literature of Pre-Clinical Pharmacokinetics

"Guidance for Non-Clinical Pharmacokinetic Study of Chemical Drugs", issued by the State Food and Drug Administration on March 18, 2005, is the reference for drug research and development institutions to perform non-clinical pharmacokinetic studies of new chemical drugs, and not the requirements of new drug application. Referring to this guidance, researchers can scientifically and rationally design their experiments according to the characteristics of different drugs and comprehensively evaluate the test results.

The main content of this booklet should include the basic principles of a non-clinical pharmacokinetic study, the general requirements of test design, drug analysis method of biological samples, research projects (plasma concentration-time curve, absorption, distribution, excretion, plasma protein combined, biotransformation, and effects on activity of drug metabolism enzyme), data processing and analysis, results and evaluation. In addition, it analyzes some common problems and their resolution pathways in the studies.

The Test Design

A. General Requirements

1. Test substance

The name, dosage, batch number, source, purity, storage conditions and preparation methods of the test substance should be provided. The test substance and dosage forms should be consistent with the pharmacodynamic or toxicological studies, and the quality inspection report of the research units should be attached.

2. Test Animals

Generally, adult and healthy animals are used. Commonly used animals are mice, rats, rabbits, guinea pigs, dogs, miniature pigs and monkeys, etc. General principles for animal selection are listed as following:

1. Preferred animals: as consistent as possible with the pharmacodynamic and toxicology studies
2. Performing the test under the awake condition of animal as possible–for pharmacokenatic studies, it is highly recommended to take multiple samples from the same animal
3. Two or more kinds of animals should be used for innovative drugs; usually one of which is rodent, and the other is non-rodent (such as dogs, monkeys or mini-pigs, etc.). For other drugs, one kind of animal could be proper to meet the goal, and the first recommended choice is non-rodent
4. Rabbits and other herbivores are not suitable for oral administration.

3. Dose Selection

In vivo pharmacokinetic studies in animals should be designed to have at least three dosing groups. For the high dose, it should be close to the maximum tolerated dose. The medium and small dose should be selected according to the upper and lower limits of the effective range. The primary objectives are to investigate that the in vivo pharmacokinetics of the drug belongs to a linear or non-linear model within the range of the doses, to facilitate interpretation of pharmacodynamics and toxicology research findings, and to provide information for the further research and development of new drugs.

4. Route of Administration

The route of administration should be as consistent as possible with the clinical use of drug.

B. Analysis Methods of Biological Samples of Drugs

Analysis methods of biological samples include chromatography, radionuclide labeling, immunology and microbiology methods. The key of biological sample measurement is methodology validation. Methodology validation is the basis for the entire pharmacokinetic study.

C. Research Project

1. The plasma concentration-time curve

1. The number of tested animals: each sample point of the plasma concentration-time curve is limited to no less than 5 data to calculate the number of animals needed. It is highly recommended to take multiple samples from the same individual animal. If the data from several animals together constitute one plasma concentration-time curve, the number of animals should be increased correspondingly to reflect the impact of individual differences in the test results. It is recommended that the number of male and female test animals is fifty-fifty. If significant gender differences are found in pharmacodynamics studies, the number of animals should be increased to recognize gender differences of the test substance. For single-sex treatment, you can choose the gender consistent with clinical drug administration.
2. Sampling points: The determination of the sampling points has a significant impact on the results of pharmacokinetic studies. If the sampling points are too few or inappropriate, the plasma concentration-time curve obtained may vary significantly with the real situation of the drug in the body. A blood sample is needed before administration as a baseline reference. To obtain a complete plasma concentration-time curve, the design of the sampling time points should take into account the drug absorption, equilibrium phase (near the peak concentration) and the elimination phases.
3. Oral administration: Generally, study subjects should be fasted over 12 h before administration to eliminate the effect of food on drug absorption. The fasting time after administration should be unified according to the specific circumstances to avoid the impact of the data fluctuations and the food effect.
4. The pharmacokinetic parameters: To obtain the main pharmacokinetic parameters of the test substance based on the plasma concentration-time data measured in each test animal.
5. Data needed to be provided: a single administration and multiple administrations.

2. Absorption

For the new drugs with oral administration, the whole animal test should be carried out, together with the intravascular administration as possible to provide absolute bioavailability.

3. Distribution

It is convenient to perform tissue distribution test using rats or mice. After the administration with a certain dose (generally effective dose is appropriate), the drug concentration should be measured at least in heart, liver, spleen, lung, kidney, gastrointestinal tract, gonads, brain, fat, skeletal muscle, and other tissues to know the main tissue distribution of the drug in the body.

4. Excretion

1. The urine and fecal excretion of the drug: Generally, mice or rats are used. The animals are placed in metabolic cages. After the administration of an effective dose, all the urine and feces are collected by a certain time interval segment to determine the drug concentrations.
2. Biliary excretion: Generally, biliary catheter drainage is used in rats under ether anesthesia; Administrate the drug after the animals wake up and collect the bile segmented at appropriate intervals to determine the drug excretion in bile.
3. Record the rate and total amount (percentage of total administered dose) of drugs excreted from feces, urine, and bile to provide substrate balance data.

5. Binding with Plasma Proteins

The study of drug and plasma protein binding can be carried out in a variety of methods, such as equilibrium dialysis, ultra-filtration, distribution equilibrium, the gel filtration method, and spectral method. According to the physicochemical properties of drugs and laboratory conditions, one method can be selected to conduct plasma protein binding experiments by at least three concentrations (including effective concentration). Experiment for each concentration was repeated at least three times to know if the drug's plasma protein binding rate is concentration dependent.

6. Biotransformation

For innovative drugs, it still needs to know the condition about biotransformation in vivo, including its conversion type, its major transformation pathways and metabolic enzymes possibly involved. For new prodrugs, in addition to studying its main metabolic pathways and the structure of the active metabolite, it needs to perform systematic pharmacokinetic study about the prototype drug and active metabolites. For the drugs which are eliminated mainly by metabolism in the body (prototype drug excretion $<50\,\%$), biotransformation studies can be divided into two phases:

a. In pre-clinical stage, chromatographic method or radionuclide label method can be adopted to analyze and separate the metabolites that may exist; In addition, chromatography-mass spectrometry can be used to speculate the preliminary structure.
b. If Phase II clinical studies suggest that they have development prospects in aspects of efficacy and safety, further research and elaboration of the possible metabolic pathways, structure and metabolic enzymes of the major metabolite should be conducted before the NDA.

If many signs suggest the existence of a strong active metabolite, research about active metabolites should be carried out as soon as possible to determine the necessity of metabolite pharmacodynamics tests.

7. Impact on Drug Metabolic Enzyme Activities
For innovative drugs, the drug should be observed for its metabolizing enzymes, especially for the induction or inhibition effects of cytochrome P450 isozymes. In the pre-clinical stage, the substrate method can be used to observe the inhibition effect on animal and human liver microsomal P450 enzymes, to compare the differences between species. The induction effect of the drug on enzyme can be observed through the change of hepatic P450 enzyme activity after multiple administrations in whole animals or repeated action of the drug to know whether there is a potential metabolic interaction of the drug.

Data Processing and Analysis

The test data should be effectively integrated, using scientific and rational data processing and statistical methods. If using computer to process the data, the name, version, and sources of the program should be indicated and its reliability should be confirmed.

Results and Evaluation

The obtained data should be scientifically and comprehensively analyzed and evaluated. The comprehensive discussion of the drug pharmacokinetic characteristics in animals include: absorption, distribution, and elimination characteristics of the drug; excretion through urine, feces and bile; the plasma protein binding extent; extent of drug accumulation in the body and major accumulation organ or tissue. For innovative medicines, sponsors also needs to clarify the drug's biotransformation, elimination process and material balance in vivo.

In the process of evaluation, a comprehensive evaluation should be conducted to analyze the relationship between the pharmacokinetic characteristics and the preparation selection, the efficacy and safety, to provide more valuable information for the overall evaluation and clinical studies of drugs.

Common Problems and Dealing Strategies

A. Pharmacokinetic and Preparation Studies
The new delivery system is in continuous development, with innovations such as liposomes, nano drug delivery systems, transdermal drug delivery system, local drug delivery system, and pulse dosing systems. Depending on different needs of delivery along with the characteristics of drugs and their preparations, researchers can formulate a reasonable and feasible pharmacokinetic study program.

B. The Repeated Drug Administration
For the drugs which need long-term clinical administration and have the tendency to accumulate in the body, the pharmacokinetic studies about multiple administrations should be considered.

Generally, in multiple administration trials, a selected dose (effective dose) can be used. According to the pharmacokinetic study outcome of a single administration, calculate the half-life of elimination. From the pharmacodynamic data obtained from the reference, determine the selected dose, dosing interval, and the number of days of administration.

For the following cases, the study about drug concentration in specific tissues after multiple dosing may be considered:

1. The half-life of drug/metabolite in the tissues significantly exceeds the half-life of plasma elimination and more than twice of the dosing interval of toxicity studies;
2. The histopathological changes, which are not observed in the short-term toxicity studies, the single dose tissue distribution studies or other pharmacological studies, have great significance to the safety evaluation;
3. Drugs with positioned and targeted release.

C. About Compound Drugs

For a new compound, its interaction should be studied through comparing the pharmacokinetics of single-agents with compounds to investigate the reasonability of the prescription. If the drug belongs to the new compound preparation in registered class 1, generally, the repeated dose toxicity test data compared with monotherapy should be provided. If the repeated dose toxicity tests show that its toxicity does not increase and the toxicity target organ has no change, Booklet 27 can be excused.

D. About Chiral Drugs

If the racemate has been marketed and the researchers hope to develop a single enantiomer, the pharmacokinetic curve of the single enantiomer in animals should be obtained for the monitoring of the enantiomers' transformation into each other and the disposition in the body. The comparison with the pharmacokinetic curve obtained in phase I clinical trials should be conducted.

E. Pharmacokinetics and Toxicokinetics

In the pharmacokinetics test of three doses, the highest dose uses the pharmacokinetic parameters close to the maximum tolerated dose of animals, which has a direct reference value to the toxicokinetic trial design. Drug tissue distribution studies may provide a basis for evaluating the toxicity in target organ. The results of drug plasma protein binding tests are also the basis for estimating the relationship between the plasma concentration and toxicity. The reason is mainly due to the fact that the correlation between toxic reactions and the area under blood free drug-time curve is better than the correlation between toxic reactions and the area under the total drug-time curve. The data provided by a biotransformation study can help determine the possible ingredients that cause toxicity, and the ingredients that should be studied in toxicokinetic tests.

F. Controlled and Sustained Release Preparations

If the drugs for registration application are controlled and sustained release preparations, the preparation of this booklet should refer to the "Guidance for pharmaceutical research of oral sustained release preparation of chemical drugs". Sustained release preparation of the drug is a slow release by an appropriate speed while the peak of plasma concentration has small fluctuation, so that the toxic and side effects beyond the plasma concentration range for treatment can be avoided while the concentration can be maintained within the effective range for a long time to maintain the effectiveness. Compared to the common preparations, sustained release preparations can extend the duration of the therapeutic effect, reduce toxicity and number of drug administrations, and improve the medication compliance.

There are differences in pharmaceutical research aspects between oral sustained release preparation and general oral solid dosage. The pre-clinical animal pharmacokinetic study of oral sustained release preparation is generally only used as the reference to determine whether it has the characteristics of sustained release. It is used to investigate whether the sustained release preparations have a burst release phenomenon, to ensure the safety of clinical trials. Oral sustained release preparation is designed to slow the rate of drug release in vivo, to maintain stable blood concentration. In clinical trial stage, selection of two or three preparations with different release rates to conduct in vivo experiments and to compare their plasma concentration-time curves are the common practice. It can help to determine the prescription with appropriate release rate in vivo, and can also help to study the correlation between the in vitro and in vivo data.

5.6.5 Module IV—Clinical Study Information

5.6.5.1 Booklet 28—Summary of Global Clinical Study Information

The review of relevant clinical trial data domestically and abroad for Booklet 28 refers to the review of literature and summary of clinical trials and the recent follow-up reports. For this booklet, the main references are the clinical requirements in Common Technical Document (CTD) of ICH guidelines. On the basis of full consideration of the China's present condition of drug registration, guidance for the writing of the review of relevant clinical trial is formulated. Its format and content should be in reference with the two guidance: "Guidance for writing format and content of chemical drug review—Summary and evaluation of the main research results" and "Guidance for structure and content of clinical study report of chemical drugs" of the series of guiding principles. At different stages of registration, the review of clinical trial content provided in this booklet has some differences.

- When applying for clinical trial approval (IND/CTA), a literature summary and total evaluation of clinical trials should be provided.
- When applying for production and marketing (NDA), in addition to providing a clinical trial literature summary and total evaluation of clinical trials, the clinical trial summary of the research drug should be provided.

In this booklet, the applicant should provide complete summary and evaluation of clinical information, which fully reflects the characteristics of drug development program. The content convergence should be logical and the idea should be clear.

Review of Clinical Trial Dossier

Review of the clinical trial dossier is the necessary process of summary and evaluation of clinical information for drug registration, involving two parts: a summary of clinical trials and literature, and the overall evaluation of clinical trials. For different drug registration categories and different registration phases, the emphasis of the review for the clinical trial dossier has some differences.

A. Clinical Trials and Literature Summary
It refers to the detailed factual summary of clinical trials and literature information related to the study drug. According to China's registration reality, clinical trials and the literature summary are divided into two parts: (a) Clinical trial summary of the study drug; (b) Clinical trial literature summary.

For drugs in different registration categories, the clinical trial literature summaries may be different.

1. Drugs that are not marketed domestically (in China) and abroad are defined as drugs of drug category I. If there is relevant clinical literature, the possible clinical trials literature summary based on your best knowledge should be provided; If there is no relevant clinical trial literature indeed, the situation should be explained. In addition, the biopharmaceutical research or literature summary closely related to clinical trials should also be provided.
2. For drugs which are marketed overseas but not in the domestic (China) market, a domestic and international clinical trial literature summary in as much detail as possible should be provided. The summary should include the post market clinical application information as possible.
3. For drugs with the national standards, a brief summary of the clinical trial literature should be provided; meanwhile, the summary should include as much post market clinical application information as possible.

B. The Overall Evaluation of Clinical Trials
According to the clinical trial summary, clinical trial literature summary, information of clinical trial reports, and related non-clinical trial information, a comprehensive evaluation should be conducted. Based on the analysis and evaluation, the advantages and disadvantages should be weighed to draw appropriate conclusions.

The Writing Format and Content of the Review of Clinical Trial Data

A. Summary of Clinical Trials and Literature
The summary of clinical trials and summary of clinical trial literature are both written using the following frame and logical order:

- Summary of the bio-pharmaceutical research.
- Summary of the clinical pharmacology studies.
- Summary of the clinical effectiveness.
- Clinical safety summary.

- Study report listing and literature.

In addition, the writing of this dossier shall provide the basis for the clinical trial protocol and the content of the drug instruction.

1. Clinical Trial Summary

1.1 Biopharmaceutical research summary

The purpose of this section is to provide a basis for the dosage form design. First, the test results or the literature are listed, including: (a) In vitro dissolution studies; (b) bioavailability (BA) or bioequivalence (BE) research or literature. (these may make more sense without the a and b labeling) Then, based on the above tests and literature, a summary should be written. The key points of the summary are listed as follows:

- The evidence about the formulation and process changes to show the impact on dissolution in vitro, BA and BE;
- The evidence of the food effect on BA and BE;
- The evidence of the dissolution in vitro showing correlation with BA;
- Comparison of BA with BE in different formulations.
- According to the analysis of the drug in vitro dissolution studies and literature, and the analysis of BA or BE studies or literature, provide rationale and basis for the determination of the formulation.

1.2 Summary of Clinical Pharmacology Studies

The purpose of clinical pharmacology studies (or literature) is to provide guidance for clinical trials. According to the following written content, first, list the test results and literature results. Then, provide the summary.

1. For human biological material research (or literature), the key points are the permeability studies (such as intestinal absorption, the transition of blood-brain barrier), protein binding, liver metabolism, and drug interactions related to the metabolism.
2. Human pharmacokinetic (PK) and pharmacodynamic (PD) studies: Summarize the impact of different study populations, intrinsic factors, and extrinsic factors on PK and PD to provide basis for the drug dose and dose adjustments for different target indication populations (such as children, elderly, liver, and kidney dysfunction patients).
3. Bridging study: Summarize and analyze the effectiveness information among regions or races, to provide the evidence of bridging studies abroad.

1.3 Summary of the Clinical Effectiveness

Describes respectively the effectiveness of the study drug for each applied indications; List the clinical trials related to efficacy evaluation, including dose-effect relationship research, comparative effectiveness research, long-term effectiveness research, and effectiveness studies in different populations.

Analyze the key points and special points of test design, such as randomization, double-blind, control drug selection and basis, subject selection, special points of trial design, primary and secondary endpoints, treatment and observation period, and established analytical methods for research outcomes.

Non-clinical trial data and clinical pharmacology data can be cited when necessary, as the basis to support the usage and dosage.

In the writing process, it is suggested to adopt appropriate text, figures, and tables. For drugs with several clinical trials, all the data for effectiveness should be summarized, including whether the data supports or does not support the conclusion. Usually, two methods are adopted: the pooled analysis of clinical trial results and the comparison between the results of clinical trials. For drugs with only one clinical trial, the summary is conducted with the effectiveness data of the single trial.

The specific content of the summary includes:

1.3.1 The study population

Briefly describe the baseline demographic and other characteristics, including disease characteristics (such as severity and duration), treatment, inclusion and exclusion criteria, differences of the baseline levels of various study populations, the differences between the study population and post marketing intended population, evaluation of the number, time, and reason of the discontinued patients.

1.3.2 The writing focus of the effectiveness research outcomes and comparison is listed as the followings:

1. Analyze and compare all the clinical trial results used for the evaluation of the effectiveness (including negative results and results which do not support the conclusions of the study). Key points of the analysis include the study endpoint, control group, treatment and observation period, statistical methods, study population, doses, etc.
2. The key point of the comparison between clinical trials are the primary endpoint. If the primary endpoints involve in different variables or time points, all the important information obtained from clinical trials should be comprehensively compared.
3. Provide the confidence interval of efficacy.
4. If there are important differences between the results of the clinical trials with the same design, they should be described and discussed.
5. If there is a meta-analysis of clinical trials, its design and analysis program should be explained.
6. Bridging study: Summarize and analyze the effectiveness information between regions or races to provide evidence for bridging studies.

1.3.3 Comparison of the results between different study populations

The purpose is to investigate whether the treatment outcomes between different groups of people are consistent.

Conduct transverse comparative analysis between multiple clinical trials to evaluate the influence of demographic factors (such age, gender, and ethnicity) and other established or related internal factors or external factors on efficacy. For clinical trials whose subjects are children, the effectiveness in the child population should be routinely analyzed.

1.3.4 Clinical information related to the recommended dose and methods of administration

With the non-clinical trial results, summarize the data of pharmacokinetics, pharmacology and toxicology studies. Compare the controlled clinical trials and non-controlled clinical trials, provide the basis of the support for the recommended dose (first administration dose, maximum dose, individualized medication guide, etc.) and method of administration.

1.3.5 Long-term efficacy and tolerability

The purpose is to know the long-term efficacy condition of drugs, and the existence of tolerability issues.

Provide the number of the patients with long-term efficacy data and the clinical data of drug exposure time, and analyze the data on whether the efficacy will sustain or diminish with the prolonged treatment time. This kind of analysis mainly aims at clinical trials with controls, especially those which collect long-term efficacy data. In clinical trials with long-term efficacy observations, the influence of the early treatment interruption or the switch to other treatments on the effectiveness results should be considered.

1.4 Summary of Clinical Safety

Summary of all the clinical trial data and literature related to safety: All the subjects, even those with just one-time use of the test drug, should be included in the safety analysis. For safety-related data, the following four aspects should be considered:

- Drug use/exposure (dose, time of administration, the number of drug users).
- General adverse events and laboratory abnormalities.
- Serious adverse events and important adverse events.
- Adverse reactions.

1.4.1 Drug use/exposure

First, list the analysis data, including that of non-clinical trials and literature as well as clinical results associated with clinical safety and special safety issues.

- Drug use/exposure
- Characteristics of the study population and the number of users

1.4.2 Adverse events

- General adverse events
- Death
- Serious adverse events
- Important adverse events
- Analysis of adverse events by organ system classification
- Analysis of adverse events

The clinical trials which can use combined safety analysis include:

- Controlled studies: Combination is the best source of the information for most common adverse events, and can distinguish drug-related adverse events and spontaneous events.
- All studies: Combination can facilitate the evaluation of rare adverse events.

- The specific route of administration, or dosing regimen, or all the study of the specific concomitant medication.
- The clinical trials to collect adverse events through voluntary questionnaires or direct questions.
- Clinical trials in the same geographic areas.

The first two of the above combinations are most commonly used.

In some cases, the combined safety analysis cannot provide valuable information, e.g., the incidence of adverse events vary greatly between the different clinical trials, or some cases are very difficult to interpret, and combination may mask the real differences. Those which are inappropriate to adopt the combined safety analysis can use an individual study report.

1.4.3 Evaluation of laboratory examination parameters

Briefly state the main changes of laboratory examination parameters in clinical trials, including blood cell examination, blood biochemistry, urinalysis, and other appropriate data. It will be described mainly from the following three aspects:

The number of subjects that exhibit abnormal laboratory parameters;

Abnormalities of important laboratory parameters (including those that cause drug withdrawal);

Central tendency (such as the group mean or median) of laboratory parameters.

Evaluation of the first two of the above aspects may be more clinically meaningful.

When evaluating the laboratory parameters, attention should be given to the consistency of each laboratory values and the combination condition should be explained.

- Analyze the meaning of the changes of laboratory parameters and its possible relationship with the study drug, such as the relationship with dosage and drug concentrations (for example: if the parameters will return to normal with continuing treatment or if there is a need for concomitant medication).
- Analyze the relationship between laboratory index abnormalities and the above adverse event related factors.

1.4.4 Symptoms and signs and other discoveries related to safety

Provide the summary of safety related symptoms, signs, ECG, imaging results, etc. The analytical methods are the same as laboratory parameter analysis methods.

1.4.5 Safety in special populations

- Internal factors
- External factors
- Drug interactions
- Pregnant and lactating women
- Overdose
- Drug abuse
- Withdrawal and rebounce
- Impact on the operation control or damage to the cognitive ability

1.4.6 Post marketing data

If the drug has already been put on the market, the applicant should provide the post market clinical data summary.

2. Clinical Trial Literature Summary

This part is the writing based on literature (foreign and domestic). Its format and content requirements are the same as the ones in the "clinical trial summary" section.

B. The Overall Evaluation of Clinical Trials

The writing should include the following aspects:

- A description and explanation of the progress of all the clinical trials of the study drug;
- An evaluation of the quality of clinical design and implementation, including the implementation of GCP;
- A brief statement of the clinical positive findings;
- A benefit and risk assessment based on the conclusions of relevant clinical trials;
- A list of concerns related to effectiveness or safety and an explanation of how these concerns are evaluated and resolved;
- A summary of unresolved concerns and an explanation of why the unresolved concerns do not affect the review, and, lastly, the plans to solve these concerns;
- An outline of some important or unusual prescription information.

1. Project Rationale Analysis

The purpose is to provide the basis to support the project rationale.

Specifically, analyze and discuss the following items (and provide the conclusive evaluation for the project rationale of the study drug) (maybe the part in parentheses should be included in the list):

1. Pharmaceutical classification confirmation of the study drug;
2. The target indications which the study drug is intended to treat, prevent or diagnose;
3. The scientific background of the study drugs;
4. The clinical trial projects (including clinical trials which are ongoing or will be conducted, as well as the basis of regulatory applications) and overseas clinical trial data which are planned to use;
5. When analyzing the study design and implementation process, attention should be paid to whether they are consistent with the current theory and research progress. If not, the corresponding analysis should be made. Explain whether the regulatory requirements and recommendation from the registration department have been considered.

(Why is this list numbered, while others are bulleted and some are even not bulleted at all? Choose a format!)

2. Biopharmaceutics Overall Evaluation

The purpose is to provide the basis for determining the dosage form. Since the dosage form design is directly related to the effectiveness and safety, the important issues related to bioavailability of the proposed marketing dosage forms should be analyzed, e.g., formulation, dosage, the similarities and differences between proposed marketing preparation and the preparation for clinical trials, the food effect. The appropriate conclusions should be provided.

3. Clinical Pharmacology Overall Evaluation
Through the study of drug pharmacokinetics, pharmacodynamics, analysis, and evaluation of in vitro tests related data, provide the basis for clinical trials. During the analysis, all relevant data should be considered and the level of support for conclusions should be commented on.

4. The Overall Evaluation of Effectiveness
Provide the clinical efficacy analysis of the study drug in the targeted population for the indication of effectiveness, and indicate the supportive extent of these data for the indications and prescribing information.

The following factors shouldbe comprehensively considered for the evaluation of effectiveness:

1. Study population characteristics, including demographic characteristics, disease classification, other potential important variation, important populations excluded from the study, as well as the selection condition of children or the elderly. Discuss the differences between the study population and the proposed post market population.
2. Experimental design, including patient choice, the administration time and observation period, the control group and the selection of the endpoints. Be careful when using uncommon clinical trial endpoints. When using alternative study endpoints, there should be evidence that the alternative endpoint is appropriate.
3. When using equivalence or non-inferiority tests to prove the validity of the studies, the evidence that the testing boundary values are set properly should be provided.
4. Statistical analysis methods and any problems, which need explanation due to the impact on the results.
5. When there are significant differences between the study results and literature, the reasons for the differences should be analyzed and explained.
6. The relationship between efficacy and dose or drug administration for each indication in overall and different subset subject populations.
7. The supportive level of the clinical data from other geographic districts.
8. Drugs with long-term use should be considered for its long-term efficacy and drug resistance.
9. Evidence that the efficacy is related to plasma concentration.
10. The clinical meaningfulness of the study results.
11. If a surrogate endpoint is used, indicate the degree of clinical benefit.
12. If the effectiveness for a specific population in clinical trial is insufficient, the effectiveness should use extrapolation of the effectiveness of the general population to judge.

5. Overall Safety Evaluation

It is important that the safety analysis considers the following points:

1. Adverse reactions related to pharmacological classification of the study drug.
2. Special adverse reactions (such as QT prolongation).
3. Adverse reaction information related to animal toxicology and product quality.
4. The study population characteristics and the exposure extent of drugs of the experimental groups and the control groups. Due to the limitations of safety data, a proper evaluation should be made regarding the forecasting of the product safety in post marketing stage.
5. For common adverse reactions, only the adverse reactions with high incidence should be briefly discussed. For serious adverse reactions, important adverse reactions and abnormal laboratory parameters with important clinical significance, the absolute patient number, and incidence should be analyzed and evaluated.
6. If there are obvious differences between the test results and the literature, interpretation should be made accordingly.
7. Analyze the differences of the incidence of any adverse events in patient subgroups (demographic factors, body weight, comorbidities, concomitant medications, genetic polymorphisms, etc.).
8. The relationship between adverse reactions and dose, dosing interval, medication cycle and its administrative methods.
9. The safety of long-term drug use.
10. Methods to prevent, mitigate, or treat adverse reactions.
11. Overdose reaction, rebounce phenomenon, drug dependence, abuse status.
12. Worldwide post marketing clinical application condition, any proven new or different safety issues, and the response of administration department to safety issues.
13. The support degree of study data from other regions for this trial.

6. Benefit and Risk Assessment

Summarize the aforementioned biological pharmacology, clinical pharmacology, efficacy, and safety, and assess the overall benefit and risk of the study drug. The following aspects in the analysis should be discussed:

1. The effectiveness of each target indications.
2. The obvious safety issues and preventive measures that can be taken.
3. Dose-effect relationship, the relationship between dose and toxicity, suitable dose range, and drug administration methods.
4. The safety and effectiveness in different populations (age, gender, race, organ functional status, severity of the disease, genetic polymorphisms).
5. Safety data in different age groups of children.
6. Any of the known and potential risk factors of food effects, drug-drug interactions. Provide the recommended usage of the study drug.
7. The effect on the controlling and operating capabilities.

5.6.5.2 Booklet 29—Clinical Study Plan and Study Protocols

Clinical study plan and study protocols should describe the important contents of the clinical trials in detail, including the proposed indications, usage, and dosage, with the support of submitted research data. The clinical study plan and study protocol should be scientifically sound and complete. There should be a comprehensive summary of the important analysis of the non-clinical and clinical data related to the potential risks and benefits of the proposed trials (SFDA 2003).

For multinational pharmaceutical companies, it is important to study and fully understand the CFDA regulations and guidance, especially the requirements regarding different categories/classes of drugs when they prepare their clinical study plan, whereas for the clinical study protocol, the content and format are very consistent with the western world.

5.6.5.3 Booklet 30—Investigator's brochure

This booklet refers to the summary compilation of the existing clinical and non-clinical research data of the investigational drugs. The purpose of the brochure is to provide information to investigators and other members involved in the trials and help them understand the characteristics of the investigational drug and clinical trial protocol. The content of the investigator's brochure should be concise and objective.

5.6.5.4 Booklet 31—Draft of Informed Consent Form and Approval of the Ethics Committee

This dossier should be prepared based on "Guidance for ethical review of investigational drug clinical trials". "Ethical review of clinical trials of drugs guiding principles" is prepared according to GCP (GCP 2003), and "Declaration of Helsinki" of the World Medical Association. Applicants for ethical review should submit the application to the Ethics Committee according to the provisions and requirements the Ethics Committee (SFDA 2010).

A. The Application Documents Submitted to Ethical Review Should Include (but not be limited to) the Following Contents

1. Ethical review application form (signed and dated);
2. Clinical trial protocol (annotated version number and date);
3. Informed consent (annotated version number and date);
4. Materials related the recruitment of subjects;
5. Case report form;
6. The investigator's brochure;
7. The principal investigator's resume;
8. The state food and drug administration "drug clinical trial approval document";

9. Explanation of the important decisions of applied research projects by other ethics committees, providing reasons of previous negative/rejected conclusions;
10. Qualified inspection report of investigational drugs.

B. The Application Documents Submitted for Ethical Review Should Include (but not be limited to) the Following file Contents
1. Design and implementation of the clinical trial protocol

1. The trials conform to accepted scientific principles, based on the literature and adequate laboratory studies and animal experiments.
2. The trial design related to trial purposes and the rationality of control settings.
3. Criteria for the early withdrawal of trial subjects, and criteria for the suspension or termination of the trials.
4. The monitoring and inspection plan during the trial implementation process, including establishing an independent data and safety monitoring committee if necessary.
5. Qualifications and experience of investigators, sufficient time to carry out clinical trials, staffing and equipment conditions complying with the trial requirements.
6. Report on the results of clinical trials and the way for publication.

2. The Risks and Benefits of Trials

1. Assessment of the properties, degree and incidence of the trial risks.
2. Minimizing risks within a possible extent
3. Assessment of expected benefit: the benefit of participants and society.
4. The reasonableness of risk and benefit of trials:
   - For trials with a direct benefit prospect on the subjects, the expected benefit and risk should be at least equivalent to that of the alternative, currently available treatment. Trial risk must be relatively reasonable compared to the expected benefits of subjects;
   - For trials without a direct benefit prospect on subjects, the risk must be relatively reasonable compared to the expected social benefit.

3. Recruitment of Subjects

1. Population characteristics of subjects (including gender, age, race, etc.).
2. Benefits and risks of trials are distributed fairly and equitably in the target disease population.
3. Intended recruitment pathways and methods.
4. The methods to inform the trial subjects or their representatives.
5. Patient inclusion and exclusion criteria.

4. Information Provided by the Informed Consent

1. The purpose of the test, the test procedure to be followed (including all invasive procedures), the test duration.
2. The expected risks and inconvenience to subjects.
3. The expected benefit: If there is no direct benefit to the subjects, the subjects should be informed.

4. Alternative treatment available for subjects, as well as the important potential risks and benefit of the alternative treatment.
5. Whether the subjects are paid for participating in trials.
6. Whether the trial requires expense from subjects.
7. The confidentiality of the relevant records which can identify the subjects' identity. It is explained that if necessary, the trial investigators, the ethics committee, and the government administration departments can get access to the information of the trial subjects.
8. Whether the subject would get treatment and appropriate compensation if damage associated with the trial occurs.
9. It should be stated that the participation in the trial is voluntary, subjects can refuse to participate in or have the right to withdraw from the trial at any time, any stage of the trial and will not face discrimination or retaliation, and their medical treatment and interests are not affected.
10. When there are questions about the trial or about and the right of the subjects, as well as the event of trial related injury, there should be available contacts and contact information to address the concerns.

5. Informed Consent Process

1. Informed consent should comply with the principles of fully informing, full understanding, and voluntary selection. (this part can use a little clarification)
2. Informed consent should be expressed in plain and understandable language to the subject population.
3. How to obtain informed consent is described with details including who is responsible for obtaining informed consent and signing informed consent provisions.
4. If subjects who cannot express informed consent are included, the reasons should be proper and rightful; there should be a detailed description of how to obtain informed consent or a licensed agreement.
5. Regulations about listening and responding to the questions and opinions of the trial subjects, or their representatives in the trial process.

6. Medical Care and Protection of Subjects Should Involve/Include

1. Investigators' qualifications and experience must meet the requirements of the trial.
2. Reasons for not giving the standard treatment due to trial purposes.
3. Providing medical care for subjects during and after the trial (what about it?)
4. Providing appropriate medical monitoring, psychological and social support for subjects.
5. Measures to be taken when subjects withdraw from the trial voluntarily.
6. The standards for prolonged use, emergency use, or offers out of sympathy of the investigational drug.
7. Instructions about whether to continue to provide trial subject drugs after the trial.
8. Instructions about the expense that the subjects need to pay.
9. Compensation provided to subjects (including cash, services, and/or gifts).
10. Compensation or treatment provided at the subjects' damage, disability, death caused by participation in the trial.

11. Insurance and damage compensation.

7. Privacy and Confidentiality

1. Provisions about the personnel who can access the subject's personal information (including medical records, biological samples)
2. Measures to ensure the confidentiality and safety of personal information of the subjects.

8. Trials Involving Vulnerable Groups

1. Only with the vulnerable people as subjects, the trial can be carried out well.
2. Trials specific to the particular illness or health problems of the vulnerable group.
3. When the trial cannot provide a direct benefit to the subjects for vulnerable groups, the trial risk should not be greater than the generally minimal risk, unless the Ethics Committee agreed that the degree of risk may increase slightly.
4. When the subjects cannot give full informed consent, it needs to obtain the informed consent from his legal representative; if possible, the consent of the subject himself should also be obtained.

9. Trials Involving Specific Diseases Population, Specific Geographic Area Population/or Ethnics

1. The trial's impact on specific disease population, specific area population or ethnics.
2. External factors' impact on individual informed consent.
3. During the trial, planning the consultation to the crowd.
4. The trial is conducive to local development, such as the strengthening of local health care services, enhancing research capacity, and responding to public health needs.

5.6.5.5 Booklet 32—Clinical Study Report

The contents of this dossier refer to "Guidance for structure and content of clinical study report of chemical drugs". This guideline is derived from the following major regulations:

- FDA: Guideline for the Format and Content of the Clinical and Statistical Sections of an Application, 1988
- ICH-E3:"Structure and Content of Clinical Study Reports", 1995
- EMEA: "Day 70 Critical Assessment Report", 2002

Clinical Study Report format

1. Phase I Clinical Trial

1.1 Format of tolerance study report

1. Front matter
2. Introduction

3. Study objectives
4. Study management
5. The description of the overall study design and protocol
6. Consideration of the study design
7. Subject selection (inclusion criteria: age, gender, ethnicity, body weight, physical examination, exclusion criteria, the sample size)
8. Investigational drugs (name, dosage form, source, batch number, size, expiration date, storage conditions)
9. Routes of administration (including the basis for determining the route of administration)
10. Dose setting (the first dose, the maximum test dose, dosing groups) and its rationale
11. Study process/procedures
12. Table of the indicators to be observed (symptoms, signs, laboratory examinations, special examinations)
13. Data quality assurance
14. Statistical disposition plan
15. Amendment during the trial
16. Trial results and analysis (the general condition and analysis of the subjects, comparability analysis between each dose groups, the results of each observation indicators, data processing and analysis, observation and analysis of adverse events)
17. Conclusion
18. Description of the particular circumstances of the trial
19. The main reference lists
20. Accessories (1,2,3,4,5,7,9,11,12,14)

1.2 Clinical Pharmacokinetic Study Report Format

1. The front matter
2. Introduction
3. Trial purposes
4. Trial Management
5. The description of the overall design and protocol
6. Consideration of the trial design
7. Subject selection (inclusion criteria,: age, gender, ethnicity, body weight, physical examination, laboratory examination, exclusion criteria, sample size)
8. Investigational drugs (name, dosage form, source, batch number, size, expiration date, storage conditions)
9. Routes of administration and its rationale
10. Dose setting and its rationale
11. The biological sample collection (sample name, acquisition time, and disposal methods) and trial procedures
12. Determination of drugs in biological samples
13. Detailed description of analysis methods and selection basis (equipment, analytical conditions, the control substrate used, such as the drug, metabolites,

purity of internal standard substrate) and confirmation (the lowest limit of quantitation, specificity, precision, accuracy, extraction recycling rate, the standard curve)
14. Inspection of the stability of samples and the quality control of measuring methods
15. Data quality assurance
16. Statistical disposition plan
17. Amendment during the trial
18. Data of the study results (the sample chromatogram of 20% subjects and accompanying control sample chromatogram, measured data of various biological samples, data processing, statistical methods and results, pharmacokinetic parameters, concentration-time curve)
19. Observation and analysis of adverse events (including laboratory examination results)
20. Analysis and evaluation of the results (including observation of adverse reactions)
21. Conclusion
22. Description of the particular circumstances in the relevant trial
23. Main reference list
24. Accessories (1,2,3,4,5,7,9,10,11,12,14)

2. Phase II/III Clinical Study Report Format

1. The front page
2. Introduction
3. Study objectives
4. Study management
5. Study design and process
   - The description of the overall design and protocol
   - The consideration of the trial design and the selection of control groups
   - Indication scope and its rationale
   - Subject selection (diagnostic criteria and its rationale, inclusion criteria, exclusion criteria, sample size and its rationale)
   - Grouping method
   - Investigational drugs (including the name, dosage form, source, batch number, size, expiration date, storage conditions and control drugs)
   - Administrative regimen and its rationale (including the dose and its rationale, route of administration, manner and timing of administration, etc.)
   - Trial procedures (including visit plan)
   - Indicators and the time of observation (including primary and secondary efficacy indicators and safety indicators)
   - The evaluation criteria for efficacy
   - Data quality assurance
   - Statistical analysis plan
   - Amendment during the trial and interim analysis

6. Trial results
   - The description of subjects allocation, withdrawal and discontinuation condition
   - Study protocol deviation
   - Subjects demography, baseline conditions and comparability analysis
   - Compliance analysis
   - Combination therapy results and analysis
   - Efficacy analysis (the primary and secondary efficacy results and analysis, efficacy evaluation) and summary
   - Safety analysis (analysis of the use of medication, description and analysis of all adverse events, description and analysis of serious and important adverse events, laboratory examinations related to safety, the results analysis of vital signs and physical examination) and summary
7. Discussion and conclusions of the trial
8. The description of the particular circumstances in the trial
9. Summary of each participating clinical institutions
10. The main reference lists
11. Accessories (1,2,3,4,5,6,7,8,9,11,12,13,14)

3. Bioavailability/Bioequivalence Study Report Format

1. The front matter
2. Introduction
3. Study objectives
4. Study Management
5. The description of the overall design and protocol
6. The consideration of the control trial design and the selection of reference drug
7. Subject selection (inclusion criteria: age, sex, weight, physical examination, laboratory examination, exclusion criteria, sample size)
8. Investigational drugs (including the name, dosage form, source, batch number, size, expiration date, storage conditions and the reference drug)
9. Route of administration and its rationale
10. Dose and its retinae
11. The biological sample collection (sample name, acquisition time, and disposal methods) and trial procedures
12. Determination of drugs in biological samples
    - Determination methods (instruments, reagents) and confirmation (LOQ, specificity, precision, accuracy, recycling rate, standard curves, etc.)
    - The inspection of sample stability
    - Quality control of the determination methods
13. Data quality assurance
14. Modifications and analysis during the trial
15. The results data
    - The sample chromatogram of 20 % subjects and accompanying control sample chromatogram
    - Plasma concentration-time curve (individual and average)

- Measured data, data processing, statistical methods and results
- Pharmacokinetic parameters

16. Bioequivalence analysis
17. Observation and analysis of adverse events (including laboratory examination results)
18. Description of the particular circumstances in the relevant trial
19. Main references
20. Accessories (1,2,3,4,5,6,7,8,9,10,11,12,14)

4. Accessories

1. The approval documents of Ethics Committee
2. The research information introduced to the subjects and informed consent sample of subjects
3. Conditions and qualifications of the clinical research institution, the name, institution, qualifications, responsibilities in the trial and resume of the main investigators
4. Clinical trial protocol, modified content of the protocol; and Ethics Committee's approval documents for modifications
5. Case report form (CRF) sample
6. The total random table
7. Inspection reports and probation production record of the investigational drug (including placebo)
8. Instructions of positive control drug and the investigational drug (if it is already marketed) instruction
9. The registration form of the drug batch number for each subject, if the investigational drugs include multiple batch numbers
10. The chromatogram copies of 20 % of the subjects tested sample, including the standard curve of corresponding analysis batch and chromatogram copies of QC samples, concentration-time curve of subject individual
11. Case reports of serious adverse events and important adverse events that the principal investigator considered needing to be reported
12. Statistical analysis report
13. Summary table of each center of multi-center clinical trial
14. The copy of the main references of the clinical research literature

Note: In addition to the requirements for the submission of statistical analysis, sponsors still need to provide the database. This should be explicitly provided to the relevant personnel of the statistical unit in the clinical study kickoff meeting.

5.7 Drug Labeling and Package Insert Management

The dossier document should be written according to regulations of drug instruction and labeling, No. 24, issued in June 1, 2006, by the SFDA. In addition, the writing format and content of the instructions and labeling of chemicals should also be consistent with the requirements of SFDA. For details, please refer to the "Notice About Further Standardize Drug Names Management" (State Food and Drug Administration Note [2006] No. 99), "the announcement about matters related to the implementation of the regulations of drug instruction and labeling" (State Food and Drug Administration Note [2006] No. 100), "Specific rules of chemicals and therapeutic biologics instruction" on May 10, 2006, and "Specific rules of non-prescription chemical drugs instrction" on October 20, 2006.

5.7.1 Provisions for Drug Insert Sheets and Labels

Refer to SFDA Regulations; Order No. 24; Promulgation Date: 2006-03-15; Effective Date: 2006-06-01

Chapter I
General Provisions

Article 1 The Provisions are enacted with an aim to regulate drug insert sheets and labels in accordance with the Drug Administration Law of the People's Republic of China and the Regulations for Implementation of the Drug Administration Law of the People's Republic of China.

Article 2 The insert sheets and labels of drugs marketed within the territory of the People's Republic of China shall meet the requirements of the Provisions.

Article 3 Drug insert sheets and labels shall be reviewed and approved by the State Food and Drug Administration.

A drug shall be labeled on the basis of its insert sheet. The content of the label shall be within the scope of the insert sheet. Any words and marks with implied therapeutic effects, misleading information on usage, or inappropriate promotion of the product shall not be printed.

Article 4 A drug label shall be printed on or affixed to the drug package, and no other written words, audio and/or visual materials or other information shall be attached to introduce or publicize the product or the enterprise.

An insert sheet shall be attached to the smallest package provided by the drug manufacturer for marketing.

Article 5 The wording in drug insert sheets and labels shall be scientific, standardized and accurate. The insert sheet of a non-prescription drug shall be written intelligibly and convenient for patients to judge, choose, and use the drug on their own.

Article 6 In the label or insert sheet, the letters or characters shall be clear and easy to be recognized and the marks shall be clear and distinctive. The label and insert sheet shall have no print faded and shall not be affixed unsteadily. Any addition or modification shall not be made by means of pasting, cutting or altering.

Article 7 Drug insert sheets and labels shall be written in standardized Chinese characters published by the National Language Commission. The versions in other languages shall correspond to the Chinese version.

Article 8 With the aim to protect public health and direct the rational use of drugs, drug manufacturers may voluntarily apply to add warnings to drug insert sheets or labels. The State Food and Drug Administration may also request drug manufacturers to add warnings to drug insert sheets or labels.

Chapter II Drug Insert Sheet

Article 9 A drug insert sheet shall include the significant scientific data, conclusions and information concerning drug safety and efficacy in order to direct the safe and rational use of drugs. The specific format, content and writing requirements of the drug insert sheet shall be prescribed and issued by the State Food and Drug Administration.

Article 10 Disease names, pharmaceutical terms, drug names, the names and results of clinical testing in drug insert sheets shall be expressed in professional terms published or standardized by the State. The units of measurement shall conform to the national standards.

Article 11 All the active ingredients or medicinal ingredients of traditional Chinese medicines in a prescription shall be listed in the insert sheet. For injections and non-prescription drugs, all excipients shall be listed as well.

The ingredients or excipients included in a prescription, which may cause severe adverse reactions, shall be specified.

Article 12 A drug manufacturer shall trace the safety and efficacy of its marketed drugs. For any modification to the insert sheet, an application shall be submitted promptly.

The State Food and Drug Administration may also require a drug manufacturer to make modifications to the insert sheet on the basis of the results of adverse drug reaction monitoring and drug re-evaluation.

Article 13 After the modifications to the insert sheet are approved, the drug manufacturer shall inform relevant drug distributors, drug users and other departments of the modified content immediately and use the modified insert sheet and label promptly as required.

Article 14 The insert sheet shall provide full information on adverse drug reaction and indicate the adverse reactions in detail. A drug manufacturer that fails to timely modify the insert sheet on the basis of the safety and efficacy data of the marketed drug or to fully explain the adverse reaction in the insert sheet shall be liable for all the consequences arising therefrom.

Article 15 The approval date and the modification date shall be distinctively shown in the insert sheet.

Chapter III Drug Labels

Article 16 Drug labels refer to the information printed or pasted on drug packaging, including inner labels and outer labels. Inner labels refer to those that appear on immediate packaging; outer labels are those on the other packaging outside of inner labels.

Article 17 The inner label shall bear such drug information as the adopted name in China, indications or functions, strength, dose and usage, production date, batch number, expiration date and manufacturer. If there is no enough space in the package to include all the information mentioned above, the adopted name in China, strength, batch number and expiration date shall be indicated at least.

Article 18 The outer label of a drug shall indicate such information as the adopted name in China, ingredients, description, indications or functions, strength, dose and usage, adverse reactions, contraindications, precautions, storage, production date, batch number, expiration date, approval number, and manufacturer. Where indications or functions, dose and usage, adverse reactions, contraindications and precautions cannot be fully noted, main information plus a "See drug insert sheet for details." notice shall be indicated.

Article 19 The label on the package for transportation and storage shall bear at least the adopted name in China, strength, storage, production date, batch number, expiration date, approval number, and manufacturer. Other information such as packaging quantity, precautions for transportation, or other marks may be included when necessary.

Article 20 The label for drug substance shall include the adopted name in China, storage, production date, batch number, expiration date, applied specifications, approval number, and manufacturer. Other necessary information such as packaging quantity and precautions for transportation shall also be indicated.

Article 21 Where one drug produced by a manufacturer has the same drug strength and packaging specification, the content, format, and color of its labels must be the same. Where one drug produced by a manufacturer has different drug strengths or packaging specifications, its labels shall be clearly distinguished from one another, or its specifications shall be notably marked in the corresponding specification items.

Where a drug produced by a manufacturer is administrated as either a prescription drug or a non-prescription drug, their packaging colors shall be distinctly different.

Article 22 For drugs with special requirements on storage, its requirements shall be marked in the notable place of the label.

Article 23 The expiration date in the drug label shall appear in the order of year, month and day, with the year shown in four digits, and the month and day in two digits. Its specific format shall be "Valid till XXXX year XX month" or "Valid till XXXX year XX month XX day". It may be presented with numbers and other symbols as "Valid till XXXX.XX." or "Valid till XXXX/XX/XX".

For the preventive biological product, the expiration date shall be labeled according to the registration specifications approved by the State Food and Drug Administration. The expiration date of the biological product for therapeutic use shall be counted from the filling date. For other drugs, the expiration date shall be counted from the production date.

Where the expiration date is labeled to the day, it shall be marked as 1 day earlier than the actual expiration date; where the expiration date is labeled to the month, it shall be marked as 1 month earlier than the actual expiration month.

Chapter IV
Use of Drug Name and Registered Trademark

Article 24 The drug name in insert sheets and labels shall conform to the nomenclature principles on the adopted name in China and trade name of drug announced by the State Food and Drug Administration, and shall be consistent with those appeared in the approval documents of the drug.

Article 25 The adopted name in China shall be conspicuous and prominent, and its typeface, size and color shall be consistent, and meet the following requirements:

1. For horizontal labels, the adopted name in China shall appear in a prominent position within the area of the upper one-third of the label; for vertical labels, it shall appear in a prominent position within the area of the right one-third of the label;
2. No such illegible typefaces as cursive characters and seal characters shall be used, and no such format as italics, margining and shading shall be used to modify the typefaces.
3. The font color of the adopted name in China shall be black or white, in sharp contrast to the light-colored or dark-colored background respectively.
4. Writing in separate lines shall be avoided unless limited by the packaging size.

Article 26 The trade name of a drug shall not be placed in the same line with the adopted name in China; its typeface and color shall be no more conspicuous than that of the adopted name in China, and its font area per character shall be no bigger than half of that of the adopted name in China.

Article 27 Unregistered trademarks and other drug names unapproved by the State Food and Drug Administration shall not be used in the drug insert sheets and labels.

Where a registered trademark is used in a drug label, it shall be printed in a corner of the label. Where a registered trademark contains characters, the font area per character shall be no bigger than a quarter of that of the adopted name in China.

Chapter V Other Provisions

Article 28 For narcotic drugs, psychotropic substances, medicinal toxic drugs, radioactive pharmaceuticals, drugs for topical use, non-prescription drugs and other drugs having special marks specified by the State, their special marks shall be printed in the drug insert sheets and labels. Where there are special provisions issued by the State for drug insert sheets and labels, they shall hold authority.

Article 29 The labeling provisions for Chinese crude drugs and prepared slices of Chinese crude drugs shall be formulated separately by the State Food and Drug Administration.

Article 30 Where drug insert sheets and labels are not in compliance with the Provisions, a punishment shall be imposed in accordance with the relevant provisions of the Drug Administration Law of the People's Republic of China.

Chapter VI Supplementary Provisions

Article 31 These Provisions shall come into force as of June 1, 2006. The Provisions for Drug Packaging, Labels and Insert Sheets (Provisional) issued by State Food and Drug Administration on October 15, 2000 shall be annulled therefrom.

5.7.2 Provisions on Drug Trade Names

On March 15, 2006, the SFDA issued a notice regarding further standardization of the management of drug names (State Food and Drug Administration Note [2006] No. 99). This regulation set up the principles for trade name nomenclature.

5.7.3 Provisions on Drug Trade Names

1. The drugs must use their generic names; the drug names should comply with the "Provisions of the drug generic name nomenclature principles".
2. Drug trade names cannot have exaggerated propaganda and/or suggestion of the efficacy. It should comply with the requirements of "Drug trade name nomenclature principles", and can only be used after obtaining the approval from the SFDA.
3. The applicable range of the drug trade name should strictly accord with the "Provisions for Drug Registration". In addition to drugs with new chemical structures, new active ingredients, drugs with compound patents, and other varieties are not allowed to use the trade names.
   The same drugs produced by the same drug manufacturers, with same ingredient but different specifications and formulations, should use the same trade name.
4. The drug trade name cannot be used alone in advertising. The same applies to the use of a text trademark unauthorized as trade name.
5. Since June 1, 2006, for new registered drugs, the use of its name and trademark should meet the requirements of "Provisions for Drug Insert Sheets and Labels" (Order No. 24).
   On January 24, 2007, the SFDA issued a notice of the explanation of related questions about the "Provisions for Drug Insert Sheets and Labels" (State Food

and Drug Administration Note [2007] No. 49) for drug names and trademarks, explaining:

Since June 1, 2006, drugs consistent with the following circumstances may apply to use trade names: (a) drugs with new chemical structures, new active ingredients and in the protection, transition and monitoring period; or (b) drugs with compound patent in China, and the patent is within the validity period.

6. Use of trademarks

   Based on Article 27 of "Provisions for Drug Insert Sheets and Labels", unregistered trademarks and other drug names unapproved by SFDA shall not be used in the drug insert sheets and labels.

   Notice about regulating "The Use of Drug Name in Advertising" (State Drug Administration City [2006] No. 216) stipulates that the advertisements publicizing registered trademarks must also use the generic names of drugs.

Drug Trade Name Nomenclature

1. The names must be composed of Chinese characters. Do not use Graphics, letters, numbers, symbols and other signs.
2. Do not use the characters banned by People's Republic of China Trademark Law.
3. Do not use the following characters:
   - Expand or imply drug efficacy;
   - Express the treatment site;
   - Directly express the drug's formulations, quality, materials, function, use, and other characteristics;
   - Directly express the characteristics of the use object;
   - Involve in pharmacology, anatomy, physiology, pathology or therapeutics;
   - Use the Chinese translation and its main terms of International Nonproprietary Name (INN);
   - Cite those with similar sound or shape of drug generic name;
   - Cite drug habit name or formerly used name;
   - Same or similar with the trade name used by others;
   - Names of people, places, drug manufacturers or other words with specific meaning.

5.7.4 Regulation Details of Chemicals and Biological Products Instruction

On May 10, 2006, the "Regulation Details of Chemicals and Biological Products Instruction" and "Regulation Details of Preventive Biological Products Instruction" were issued by the State Food and Drug Administration, Note [2006], No. 202. The provisions are as follows:

1. Effective on June 1, 2006, for the drugs approved by State Board or submitted for supplement application, the instruction format and content should comply with the requirements of the "Announcement about the Implementation of

Related Matters" of "Provisions for Drug Insert Sheets and Labels" by the State Food and Drug Administration, Note [2006] No. 100).
2. Drugs approved for registration before June 1, 2006 and its instruction without the content of clinical trials are allowed to not list clinical trial item.
3. For drugs with approval for registration before June 1, 2006, its approval date should be the date recorded by the drug regulatory authority.
4. External use drug is identified with the red box background marked white word "outside". The external use drug label logo should be printed in color. Monochrome printing is allowed in instruction.

5.7.4.1 Instruction and Content Item Requirements of Chemicals and Therapeutic Biological Products

Approval and modification date: The approval date is the time that the SFDA approved the drug registration. The modification date is the time of each change made.

The approval and modification dates should be printed in the upper left corner of the instructions page. The modification date is located below the approval date, and written line-by-line in chronological order.

Special drugs, external use drugs ID: For narcotic drugs, psychotropic drugs, medical use toxic drugs, radioactive drugs, and external use drugs, a special identification mark should be put in the first page of instruction at the top right.

Instructions title: the "XXX" in "XXX instruction" refers to the generic name of the drug.

"Please read the instructions carefully and use under the guidance of the physician": the content must be marked, and be printed under the instruction title.

Warnings refer to the warnings of serious adverse reactions and potential safety issues. They can also include contraindications, precautions, overdose and other matters, which need special attention from the drug administration population.

If there are contents listed, it should be indicated by obvious bold text under the instruction title. If there are none, do not list them.

Drug Name

The drug names should be listed in the following order:

1. Generic name: for a drug recorded in the Chinese Pharmacopoeia, its generic name should be consistent with the pharmacopoeia; for a drug not recorded in the pharmacopoeia, its name should be in line with the generic drug nomenclature.
2. Product Name: for drugs with unauthorized trade names, this item is not listed.
3. English Name: for drugs without English name, this item is not listed.
4. Chinese Pinyin:

Ingredient

1. list the chemical name, chemical structure, molecular formula, and the molecular weight of active ingredient. Write in the following ways:
   - Chemical name:
   - Chemical structural formula:

– Formula:
– Molecular weight:

2. Compound preparations are allowed to not list the chemical name, chemical structure, molecular formula, molecular weight content of each active ingredient. This item can be expressed as all the active ingredients contained and their amount of the components is listed in terms of preparation unit (e.g., per tablet, granule, stick, bottle, etc.).
3. For chemicals or biological products with multi-components or unclear chemical structure, the main ingredients should be listed and active ingredient sources should be briefly described.
4. If the prescription contains excipients which may cause serious adverse reactions, the excipients should be listed in this item.
5. For injections, all excipients should be listed.

Character
Including the appearance, smell, taste, solubility, and physical constants of the drug

Indication
Based on the use of the drug, the accurate way of expression should be used, specifically for prevention, treatment, diagnosis, mitigation, or adjuvant treatment of a disease (condition) or symptoms.

Specification It refers to weight, content, or PCS of the main drug (or potency) in the preparations per stick, per tablet, or per other unit. The active ingredient potency (or content and potency) and loading capacity (or volume after reconstitution of lyophilized formulations) per stick (bottle) of biological products should be marked.

The representation generally is written in accordance with the Chinese Pharmacopoeia requirements. If there are two or more specifications, they should be listed separately.

Usage and Dosage This item should include two parts: usage and dosage. For those with a medication basis having drug treatment or medication prescribed period, the treatment course and time limit must be indicated. The drug administration method should be described in detail. Special attention should be paid to accurately listing the dose, measurement methods, medication times and treatment period, and the relations with the specification.

If there are special requirements on the usage, they should be detailed according to the actual situation.

Adverse Reactions The adverse reactions of the drug should be realistically detailed, and listed in order of the severity, frequency, and symptoms.

Contraindications The populations or diseases that should be prohibited from this drug use should be listed.

Precautions The issues that call for attention must be listed, including situations that require caution for use (such as problems of liver or kidney function), factors that influence drug efficacy (such as food, smoking, alcohol), conditions that require observation during the medication process (such as allergic reactions, regular blood examination, liver function, or kidney function), and influence of medication on clinical examinations.

Abuse or drug dependence content can be listed under this item.

Pregnant and Lactating Women This item highlights the influence of the drug on women and fetus or baby during pregnancy, childbirth, and maternal lactation periods, and indicates if the drug can be used and the precautions about the medication use.

If no experiment was conducted and/or there no reliable references, it should be stated under this item.

Pediatric Use This item mainly includes the differences between children and adults in the pharmacological, toxicological, or pharmacokinetic aspects due to children's growth and development, and indicates if the drug can be used and outlines precautions about the medication use.

If no experiment was conducted and/or there are no reliable references, it should be stated under this item.

Geriatric Use This item mainly includes the differences between elderly and adults in the pharmacological, toxicological, or pharmacokinetic aspects due to the decline of various body functions, and indicates if the drug can be used and outlines precautions about the medication use.

If no experiment was conducted and/or there are no reliable references, it should be stated under this item.

Drug Interactions Drugs or drug classes that interact with this drug should be listed, and the results of drug interaction and outlines precautions for combination medication use should be described.

If no experiment was conducted and/or there are no reliable references, it should be stated under this item.

Overdosage List in detail the possible toxicity reaction, dosage, and treatment methods due to an overdosage of this drug.

If no experiment was conducted and/or there are no reliable references, it should be stated under this item.

Clinical Trial It is the overview of the clinical trials of this drug. The description should be accurate and objective. It includes the method of administration, study subjects, the main observation parameters, adverse reactions, and the results of the clinical trials.

There is no need to write this item for drug without clinical trials.

Pharmacology and Toxicology Include two parts: pharmacological action and toxicological studies.

Pharmacological action is the relevant information about the drug's action on human body in clinical pharmacology. It can also list the results of in vitro tests and/or animal experiments related to clinical parameters or contributing to elaborating clinical/pharmacological action. Pharmacological action of compound preparation can be the pharmacological action of each component.

The content involved in toxicological studies is the non-clinical toxicological study results associated with clinical applications that will help to determine the clinical safety of the drug. Important information like animal species, method of administration (dose, dosing period, route of administration) and major toxic manifestations should be described. Toxicological study content of compound preparation should include toxicological study results of compound administration if possible; if there is no information, the toxicological content of single drug should be written and included.

If no experiment was conducted and/or there are no reliable references, it should be stated under this item.

Pharmacokinetics It should include the whole process of absorption, distribution, metabolism, and excretion of drug in the body, and its main pharmacokinetic parameters, as well as pharmacokinetic parameters or characteristics in special populations. It should describe that whether the drug is secreted through breast milk and whether the drug can go through the placental barrier and the blood-brain barrier and so on. Human clinical trial results should be listed. If there is a lack of human clinical trial data, the results of non-clinical trials can be listed and explained.

If no experiment was conducted and/or there are no reliable references, it should be stated under this item.

Storage The representation of the detailed conditions should be written according to Chinese Pharmacopoeia, and the specific temperature should be indicated. For example, it can say "saved in a cool place (not exceeding 20 C)".

For biological products, sponsors should also indicate the environmental conditions of product preservation and transportation. In particular, the specific temperature should be indicated clearly.

Packaging This includes packaging materials and containers with direct contact to the drug and the packaging specifications, and stating in this order.

Validity Stating with month as unit.

Executive Standard List the standard, version of implementation, such as '"Chinese Pharmacopoeia" 2005 edition', or the drug standard number, such as 'WS-10001 (HD-0001) -2002'.

Approval No. It refers to the drug approval number, imported drug registration No., or registration No. of pharmaceutical products.

For narcotic drugs, the psychotropic drugs, anabolic agents, peptide hormones, and the drug permit card number need to be indicated.

Manufacturers The content of this item of drugs made in China should be consistent with the content stated in Drug Production Licenses. For the imported drugs, manufacturers should be consistent with the documentation provided by the government. Provide the information in the following order:

- Company name
- Production address
- Postal Code
- Telephone and fax numbers (the area code must be indicated)
- Web site (If no web site, no need to write. This item is not retained)

5.7.5 Regulation Detail of the Instruction of Chemical Non-Prescription Drugs

On October 20, 2006, the State Food and Drug Administration issued "Regulation Details of the Instruction of Chemical Non-Prescription Drugs" and "the instructions Notice on the issuance of performing the conversion of prescription drugs into Over-the-Counter drugs and related issues", No. 540 (SFDA 2006]. In these regulations, the instruction format and writing requirements of chemical non-prescription drug are specified.

5.7.5.1 Instruction Format and Content Requirements for Chemical Non-Prescription Drugs

Drugs for external use are identified with the red box background marked with white word "outside". The label logo of drugs for external use should be printed in color, and monochrome printing is allowed in instruction.

The identification of non-prescription drugs and external use drugs are marked in the right corner of the first instruction page.

Specific identification of non-prescription drug use is based on "Notice about the Disclosure of Non-Prescription Drug Specific Identification and Management Requirements". Instruction title: the "XXX" in "XXX instruction" refers to the generic name of the drug.

Please read the instructions carefully and follow the instructions. The advice for a nonprescription drug shall be: "Please purchase and use in accordance with the drug instructions or under the guidance of pharmacist".

The advice must be marked and printed with heavier font.

Warnings refer to the need to remind people to pay special attention to the safety of the medication use.

If there is content under "Warnings", it should be indicated with obvious bolded text under the instruction title.

Drug Name
The drug names should be listed in the following order:

- Generic name: For drug listed in Chinese Pharmacopoeia, its generic name should be consistent with the pharmacopoeia; For drug not listed in Pharmacopoeia, its name should be in line with the generic drug nomenclature.
- Product Name:

- English Name: for drugs with no English name, this item is not listed.
- Chinese Pinyin:

Ingredient

Prescription composition and the amount of various ingredients should be consistent with the drug registration approval documents. The amount of ingredients is counted per preparation unit (e.g.; per tablet, granule, bag, stick, bottle).

The generic name and content of single-component formulation should be indicated, as well as all excipients.

For compound preparation, it must specify for the composition of all the active ingredients and the content of each ingredient, as well as all excipients.

Character

Include the drug appearance (color, shape), gas, taste, etc. Characters should comply with pharmaceutical standards.

Action Category

This should be written in accordance with the non-prescription drug category of this drug published by the State Food and Drug Administration, such as "antipyretic analgesics". (I don't understand this sentence)

Indications

This should be written according to the non-prescription drug indications published by the State Food and Drug Administration. It shall not exceed the range of indications published by the State Food and Drug Administration.

Specification

This refers to the weight, content, or PCS of the main drug in the preparations per stick, per tablet or per other unit. The active ingredient potency (or content) and loading capacity (or volume after reconstitution of lyophilized formulations) per stick (bottle) of biological products, should be marked. Measurement units must be expressed in Chinese.

Only one specification can be written in each instruction.

Usage and Dosage

Dosage is written following the non-prescription drug dosage of this drug published by the State Food and Drug Administration. The number is written with Arabic numerals, and all of the weight or volume units must be expressed in Chinese characters.

According to the specific situation, usage can be described in the range of non-prescription drug usage, dosage, and indications published by the State Food and Drug Administration. The usage cannot mislead the medication users in other aspects.

The special usage and dosage that need special attention should be stated in precautions. The usage and dosage for special populations, such as the elderly or children should not use the wording of "children reduce" or "elderly reduce" and other expression methods. For example, it could be indicated in precautions: "for the amount of children (or elderly dosage) to consult a physician or pharmacist."

Adverse Reactions Adverse reactions refer to the harmful reactions of qualified drugs unrelated to the drug treatment purpose or unexpected under normal usage and dosage.

Under this item, the adverse reactions known or known to possibly occur should be realistically detailed and be listed in the order of the severity of the adverse reactions, the frequency of occurrence, or the systematicness of symptoms.

The adverse reactions published by the State Food and Drug Administration are not allowed to be deleted or reduced.

Contraindications The various situations that the drug cannot be applied to should be listed, such as the population or disease to which the drug cannot be applied. The drug contraindications' content issued by the State Food and Drug Administration are not allowed to be deleted. The content of contraindications should use overstriking font for printing.

Precautions The issues that must be noted should be listed when using the drug. Such issues may include:

a. the situations require caution (e.g., problems with liver and kidney function);
b. factors that influence drug efficacy (e.g., food, tobacco, alcohol, etc.);
c. pregnant women, lactating women, children, elderly and other special populations;
d. the influence of medication on clinical examination; or
e. abuse or drug dependence, as well as other related content.

It must be indicated that "People allergic to this product are prohibited to use it", "People with irritable physique must be cautious when using it", "Do not use this product when its characteristics changes", "If you are using other drugs, please consult your physician before using this product", or "Please place this product where children cannot reach."

The drug which can be used in children must be marked with "Use by children must be under adult's supervision." Drugs containing stimulants should be marked "Athletes should be use under the guidance of doctors."

For the drugs with risk if taken by pregnant women, lactating women, children, the elderly, and other special populations that is unclear, it must be indicated that the relevant population should be used under the guidance of doctors.

The precautions of this product published by the national Food and Drug Administration cannot be deleted. [Precautions] should be printed with an obvious font.

Drug Interactions The drugs that have interactions with this drug and precautions of combination therapies should be listed. If no experiment was conducted and/or there are no reliable references, it should be stated under this item.

It must be marked that "Drug interactions may occur if used with other drugs; for details, please consult your physician or pharmacist".

Storage This is written according to pharmaceutical standards. If there are special requirements, the appropriate temperature should be indicated.

Packaging Include packaging materials and containers with direct contact to the drug, and the packaging specifications, and provide statement in the required order.

Validity It refers to the period of time in which the quality can be maintained under the specified storage conditions of this drug.

Validity should be described in months. It can be expressed as 'XX' months, where 'X' is represented by Arabic numerals.

Executive Standards List the name, version or drug standard code of the executive standard, such as "Chinese Pharmacopoeia" 2000 edition, National Drug Standards WS—10001 (HD-0001) -2002.

Approval No. It refers to the drug approval No., imported drug registration No., or pharmaceutical product registration No.

Instruction Revision Date It refers to the date when the revised instruction is approved for use.

Manufacturers This item for drugs made in China should be consistent with the content in "drug manufacturing licenses". For imported drugs, it should be consistent with the documentary evidence provided by the government. Please follow the list in the following manner:

- Company Name
- Manufacturer's Address
- Postal Code
- Telephone (The area code must be indicated)
- Fax number (The area code must be indicated)
- Website (If no website, no need to write. This item is not retained)
- If there is any question, contact the manufacturer.

5.8 Comparison of Application Material Correspondence Between CFDA Required Format and FDA CTD Format

Most of the western pharmaceutical companies' applications fall in the category of either 1 or 3, i.e. the new chemical entity is not yet marketed in any country or drug marketed ex-China. CTD data as specified by ICH may also be submitted; however, summary general information should be submitted according to requirement of Application Information Items. Drugs under Registration Category 1 should be those that are at least in the stage of Phase II Clinical Trials overseas. Based on the Provisions for Drug Registration (SFDA Order No. 28), in general, the IND/CTA and NDA requirements for China are almost identical to the document requirements in CTD format (Roth 2007) in the Western world (Fig. 5.1) (Table 5.4).

In this section, one special topic that should be mentioned is the Special Review Procedure (SRP) application. If the candidate drug meets the criteria and gets the approval for SRP from the CFRDA, it is a significant advantage for the applicant company.

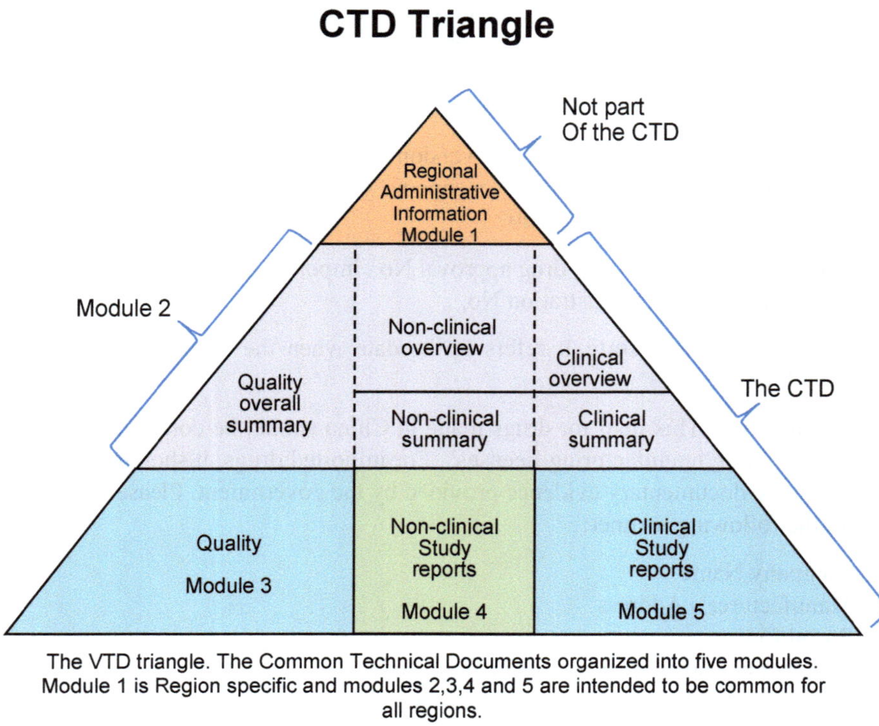

Fig. 5.1 The Common Technical Documents triangle

Table 5.4 Comparison of China Application Dossier modules with CTD modules

China Application Dossier modules	CTD modules
0. Application tables Note: The preparation of standard-alone documents for Special Review Procedure (SRP) application may apply	1. Regional administrative documents (Not Part of the CTD)
A. Summary information	2. Summary/Overview
B. Pharmaceutical information	3. Quality/CMC
C. Pharmacology and toxicology study information	4. Nonclinical study reports/Pharmacology and toxicology reports
D. Clinical study information	5. Clinical documents

5.8.1 Administrative Documents

5.8.1.1 General Forms and Tables

The administrative document section is neither defined as part of the CTD in the Western world since the requirement in the FDA and European regulatory agencies are different, nor as the items in the application dossier in China. Therefore, the applicant should fill in the corresponding tables based on the requirements.

5.8.1.2 The Special Review Procedure (SRP) Application

In this section, one special topic that should be mentioned is the Special Review Procedure (SRP) application. If the candidate drug meets the criteria and gets the approval for SRP from the CFRDA, it is a significant advantage for the applicant company (For details, see Section 3. Under Regulations of Special Examination and Approval in New Drug Registration, State Food and Drug Administration Note [2009] No. 17).

A. Background

The SFDA issued the Notification to Publish the Regulation of New Drug Registration Special Review Procedure on January 9th, 2009 (No.17). The Article 4 States that "the applicant applying for a special review procedure should fill in the Application Form for New Drug Registration Special Review Procedure and submit relevant data. The Application Form for New Drug Registration Special Review Procedure and relevant data should be filed in a separate dossier and submitted to the acceptance department for drug registration along with the application dossier in accordance with the Provisions for Drug Registration". Therefore, the separated, filed summaries are important documents to be submitted for a drug applying for special review process. Whether an application can be reviewed and approved via SRP is based on if the Separated Filed Dossier can scientifically and logically elucidate the research data and meet the criteria in the regulation (SFDA 2009).

The following basic principles are important and construct the foundations for authorizing the dossier:

- General information and target profile of the product;
- Indications (or usage);
- Completed studies;
- Purpose of this application and supporting data; and
- Risk control plan and implementation scheme.

The following instructions are prepared for new chemical drug applications. However, for biological products, it can be prepared with reference to the similar format in combination with their respective product characteristics.

B. Basic Contents of the "Standard-alone documents"

- Overview to justify the applied drug in accordance with Article 2 in Regulation of New Drug Registration Special Review Procedure;
- Protocol for planned clinical trial(s) or summary of completed clinical trials;
- Evaluation of safety and efficacy based on the completed studies (pre-clinical and clinical);
- Summary of finished pharmaceutical researches;
- Summary of other major studies;

- Risk control plan and implementation scheme;
- Conclusion and discussion.

A) Overview to Justify the Applied Drug in Accordance with Article 2 of Regulation of New Drug Registration Special Review Procedure.

General Information of the Product

Briefly describe the drug name, structure, molecular formula, and the major mechanisms of action, etc.

To describe what the treatment objective of the drug is, you must answer questions including: Is this treatment targeted as the first-line or second-line treatment in clinical practice? Are there any other factors that need to be considered related to the expected treatment outcome?

Characteristics of Target Diseases

Briefly describe the epidemiology of the target disease, including the incidence, prevalence, mortality, and related concomitant diseases. If data is available, the differences of epidemiology in different regions should be discussed.

Discuss the characteristics of the disease, including:

- What is the hazardless of this disease?
- Is it lethal or caused disability?
- Is this disease (such as hypercholesterolemia, hypertension) a precursor or risk factor for other diseases (such as coronary artery disease, stroke)?

If yes, how will this risk factor prognosticate the occurrence of more serious diseases? What are the expected outcomes for the early intervention of this disease?

Existing Treatments

To introduce if there are any other treatments for the disease including drug and non-drug treatments.

If there are other treatments existing, the following aspects should be considered:

- What are the characteristics of the existing treatment? Attention should be paid to whether the data comes from well-controlled studies to reach scientific conclusions.
- Is there any comparison on the efficacy and safety of treatments, and how can you conduct the comparison? What about the comparison results?
- Is there any other factors impacting the efficacy of existing treatment, such as tolerability, convenience, or patient preference?

If there is no treatment yet, analyze what the consequences without treatment are?

B) Protocols for Planned Clinical Trials or Summary of Completed Clinical Trials

Introduction of Protocol for Planned Clinical Trials

This section is mainly required for applications of the clinical trials.

Table 5.5 Example of description on the clinical trials to be conducted

Study No.	Study Name	Study Objective	Study Design	Dosage and Its Regimen	Control Treatment	Study Endpoints	Number of Subjects

Description of the Overall Study Design and Protocol
The description of overall study design and protocol should be clear and concise. It is recommended to use tables, charts, and other visual methods to describe the clinical trials to be conducted (see Table 5.5).

Selection of Study Subjects (study population)
Define the reasonable inclusion criteria, exclusion criteria, and criteria to remove patients from treatment or assessment. Based on the study objective, determine the inclusion criteria for the indication scope with justification to select the generally accepted diagnostic criteria, and pay attention to the severity and course of the disease, medical history characteristics, score of physical examination, the laboratory test results, previous treatment, possible prognostic factors, age, sex, weight, race, and so on.

The reasons for defining the criteria should be justified.

Determination of Dosage Regimen
Indicate the dosage regimen, including the starting dose, route of administration, dose interval, dose exploration plan, and the possible modification of dosage regimen. Rationales for dosage regimen should be justified.

Considerations on the Selection of Control Group
The basis and justification for selection of the control group should be indicated.

If there is no control group in the study, the reasons should be provided; if randomized gis not adopted, detailed reasons should be provided to explain any other technical measures applied to effectively minimize the selection bias.

Determination and Justification for Efficacy and Safety Variables
For the determination of efficacy variables: the primary endpoint shall be clearly explained, and corresponding justifications should be provided (such as literature, guidelines, etc.); if surrogated variables are used, corresponding justification should be provided. Other important secondary endpoints should also be explained.

For the determination of safety variables: include the specific safety variables, the laboratory examinations, precautions, reasons for the determination of important safety variables. Describe the method of collecting the adverse event data, adverse events assessment criteria, and management.

If the efficacy or safety variables are unconventional and/or are non-standardized parameters, the accuracy, reliability, and relevance should be justified.

Table 5.6 Example of description of the completed clinical trials

Study Name	Study Location	Objective and Design	Dosage and Its Regimen	Control Treatment	Number of Subjects	Primary Findings

Statistical Plan and Determination of Sample Size

The statistical design and types of analysis should be clearly listed and explained with justification, such as superiority, equivalence or non-inferiority, the definition of primary and secondary endpoints, and statistical analysis methods for endpoints.

Sponsors need to provide detail calculation method and calculation process of sample size, as well as the statistics estimations used in the calculation process and the basis of the estimation.

Any protocol amendment for on-going studies and information outside of protocol should also be described, and the statistical consideration involved in protocol amendment should be explained. It should be indicated whether an interim analysis will be conducted. If there is an interim analysis planned, it should be conducted according to the protocol and the calculation methods for consumption should be explained.

Quality Assurance of Data

Briefly describe the quality control process to ensure the accurate and reliable measurement of data, including the audit/inspection situation, the consistency of data entry, numerical range and logical inspection, and blind review process, etc.

Situation for Completed Clinical Trials

This section is designed for the applications that relevant clinical trials finished.

It is recommended to use tables, charts, and other visual methods to describe the completed clinical trials (see Table 5.6).

Provide brief and clear description and evaluation to the completed clinical trials, such as design methodology, endpoint variables, statistical methods, efficacy, and safety, etc.

C) Evaluation of safety and Efficacy Based on Completed Studies (pre-clinical and clinical)

Safety

This section mainly describes the safety issues found in research. According to the objectives and research phase of the application, the focuses would be different to support the future research (or application).

Non-Clinical

Describe the general situation of non-clinical studies, such as the title of the studies, purpose, time, research institutions, and responsible person, GLP implementation situation, batch number of test drug, quality specification of related bathes and the differences to the batches used in CMC researches, study protocol (animal, dosage, route of administration, period, etc.), and test results. It is recommended to describe the studies by visual methods such as table and charts.

The non-clinical findings, which need to be emphasized in the clinical trials or cannot be sufficiently explained by clinical trial data should be highlighted, such as genetic toxicity, reproductive toxicity, carcinogenicity, and drug interactions, etc.

It is recommended to provide a description and evaluation on liver toxicity, cardiovascular toxicity, and renal toxicity, etc. If the product will be used in special populations (such as pregnant women, children), it should be considered whether specific non-clinical data is needed.

If the drug has not yet been used in humans, the justification and determination of first dose in humans (first human dose) on the basis of animal test results should be indicated.

Clinical

Adverse events (AEs)/adverse drug reactions (ADRs): list the important risks already identified in clinical trials and the potential risks. If possible, this information should include evidences of exposure, incidence, severity, reversibility and risk population. It is recommended to describe with tables, charts, and other visual methods (see Table 5.7).

Limitations of safety database: the limitations of the database of safety should be indicated (for example, the sample size of study population, populations excluded from the study (pregnancy or breast-feeding women, children, etc.), and related inclusion/exclusion criteria). The limitations predicating the safety in future clinical trials or post-marketing safety should be clearly discussed, especially for populations intended or potentially exposed to future studies and clinical application.

Identified and potential interactions: include food-drug and drug-drug interactions to discuss the identified and potential pharmacokinetic and pharmacodynamic interactions. Summarize the evidence supporting the interaction and its possible

Table 5.7 Example of treatment-emergent adverse events/adverse reactions

System organ class Preferred term	Number (%) of patients reporting AE's by treatment arm				
	10 mg (*N*=318) n (%)	20 mg (*N*=370) n (%)	50 mg (*N*=336) n (%)	100 mg (*N*=412) n (%)	Placebo (*N*=355) n (%)
Cardiac disorders (Total)	11 (16.7%)	10 (0.0%)	12 (16.7%)	14 (66.7%)	5 (0.0%)
Conduction disorder	3 (0.0%)	5 (0.0%)	7 (16.7%)	8 (50.0%)	3 (0.0%)
….					
Nervous system disorders (Total)	3 (0.0%)	6 (16.7%)	7 (0.0%)	10 (16.7%)	5 (0.0%)
Headache	1(0.0%)	4 (0.0%)	4 (0.0%)	6 (16.7%)	3 (0.0%)
…					

mechanisms, and discuss the potential risks to the health of patients for different indications and in different populations.

Efficacy

Describe the results of efficacy evaluation, including the comparison of differences between groups for primary and secondary efficacy endpoints, and pharmacokinetic parameters. Conduct the FAS analysis and PP analysis according to the scheme defined in the study design.

With analysis on primary and secondary endpoints, briefly summarize and evaluate the effectiveness and clinical significance of test drugs.

Compliance

Provide the summary and analysis for patients' compliance. Describe the methods/indicators of compliance, such as drug counting, dairy cards, and testing of drug concentrations in blood, urine, and other body fluid samples.

Others

This section focuses on other important information reflecting the advantages of the clinical treatment.

Evaluation of Whether the Results of Clinical Trials can Support the Advantages of the Clinical Treatment in the Application

Discuss the advantages of the applied clinical treatment, such as indications (and/or patient population) without effective treatment and methods, or defects in existing treatment and methods combining the above-mentioned safety, efficacy, and compliance analyses, in comparison to the control treatment and/or the existing treatment,. Discuss the clinical characteristics or benefit of the applied drug.

The evaluation and discussion could be derived from the benefits/risk assessment, but should not be too extensive; the evaluation should still be based on the analysis of research data.

D) Summary for Finished Pharmaceutical Researches

According to the type and purpose of the application, the description and evaluation of the research process and results for drug substances and drug products should be provided with quality control as the core, such as: production conditions of pre-clinical samples, whether the clinical trial samples are produced in GMP workshop, the relevance of its quality, and production scale of drug substance and drug product; indicate whether the product quality can be controlled well by the process, quality specification and stability, the existing impurities limits and justifications, etc.

For the above contents, the drug substance and the drug product should be described separately.

E) Summaries of Other Major Studies

If there is other research and results included in the previous studies, it can be explained and evaluated in this section.

F) If the Risk Control Plan and Implementation Scheme Adequate for the Application?

Summary of safety issues

At the beginning of the risk control plan and implementation scheme, an abstract should be prepared, including: (1) important confirmed risks that have been identified; (2) important potential risks; and (3) important missing data.

It is encouraged to outline the important and special safety issues that already happened or potentially can happen, including the non-clinical and clinical data related to the safety issues.

Risk Control Plan and Implementation Scheme

The routine risk control plan should include: (1) internal assessment and reporting systems for suspected adverse reactions in the study and (2) reports to be submitted to health authorities, including expedited reports of adverse drug reactions (ADR) and periodic safety update reports (PSURs).

The Separated Filed Dossier should include the risk control plan to address the plan to each important safety issue and assess its rationality:

- Safety issues already identified in previous studies (or safety issues expected to be happened or need to pay attention);
- Safety issues monitored by the sponsors and related plans;
- Assessment and report for significant events.

It should be clearly indicated whether the investigator brochure (IB) is available; any target toxicity organs found in the previous studies and level of the toxicity; any monitoring measures for these toxicity taken into consideration in the clinical trial protocol; if the principle investigator (PI) has experience for clinical trials, and the situation of Ethics Committees (EC). Insurance situation for the clinical trial could also be included into the document.

Important potential risks should be discussed, such as potential risks caused by changes to the course of treatment (for long-term treatment), the target patient population (pregnant women, children), and drug interactions.

It is recommended to include the following events in the risk control plan: studies, evaluation, control and significant safety event reporting. When establishing these significant events, considerations should include: the exposure to the product reached a level, which is sufficient to identify the concerned AEs/ADRs, and/or obtain expected safety results.

Other Information

Risk control is always specific to individual products, indications, target populations, and issues to be addressed. For a drug in clinical research stage, the current drug regulatory system and the measures are all effective measures to control the risks. The risk control plan in this guidance is to require the sponsors to apply administrative methods and measures in the drug development process based on their understanding of the investigational products.

Conclusion and Discussion

This section is intended to be a high-level summary and analysis to the abovementioned contents based on the type and purpose of application to discuss if the application submitted conforms to the requirement for corresponding type in SRP.

Modified based on the Source: www.baidu.com/p/guihuaxz2012

Table 5.8 Module I: Summary

Item	CTD module number/title equivalent
1. Names of drugs	3.2.S.1 General information
	2.3.S1 General information
2. Certified documents	1.3 Administrative information
	1.3.1 Contact/sponsor/applicant information
	1.3.2 Field copy certification
	1.3.5 Patent and exclusivity
	3.2.S.4 Control of drug substance
3. Objectives and basis for R&D	2.2 Introduction to summary
	1.14.4.1 Investigator brochure
4. Summary of main study work	2.2 Introduction to summary
	2.3 Quality overall summary
	2.4 Nonclinical overview
	2.5 Clinical overview
	2.6 Nonclinical written and tabulated summaries
	2.6.1 Introduction
	2.6.2 Pharmacology written summary
	2.6.3 Pharmacology tabulated summary
	2.6.4 Pharmacokinetic written summary
	2.6.5 Pharmacokinetic tabulated summary
	2.6.6 Toxicology written summary
	2.6.7 Toxicology tabulated summary
	2.7 Clinical summary
	2.7.1 Summary of biopharmaceutic studies and associated analytical methods
	2.7.2 Summary of clinical pharmacology studies
	2.7.3 Summary of clinical efficacy [indication]
	2.7.4 Summary of clinical safety
	2.7.5 References
	2.7.6 Synopses of individual studies
5. Draft of packaging insert, note to the draft, and latest literature	1.14.1 Draft labeling
	1.14.2 Final labeling
	1.14.2.2 Final package insert (package inserts, patient information, medication guides)
6. Design of packaging and labeling.	1.14.1.1 Draft carton and container labels
	1.14.2.1 Final carton or container labels
	1.14.2.3 Final labeling text

Summary

Documents/items needed for CTA/IND and NDA submission in China have many similarities in comparison to the western dossier documents in CTD format as well. Therefore, we listed the China booklets/Items with the corresponding items in the CTD module side by side to make it easier for the Chinese regulatory filing. The following tables listed the corresponding documents as well as their basic requirements (FDA 2014) (Table 5.8 und 5.9).

Table 5.9 Module II: CMC

Item	CTD module number/Title equivalent
7. Summary of CMC	2.3 Quality overall summary
8. Research information and relevant literature of the production process of the drug substance, research information and relevant literature of formula and process of the preparations	3.2.S.2.2 Description of Manufacturing Process and Process Controls
	3.2.P.1 Description and composition of the drug product
	3.2.P.2 Pharmaceutical development
	3.2.P.3 Manufacture
	3.2.P.3.2 Batch Formula
	3.2.P.3.3 Description of manufacturing process and process controls
	3.2.P.3.4 Controls of critical steps and intermediates
9. Study information and relevant literature for the chemical structure and components determination	*3.2.S.3.1 Elucidation of structure and other characteristics*
10. Study information and literature for quality specification	3.2.S.1.3 General properties
	3.2.S.4.3 Validation of analytical procedures
	3.2.P.5.1 Specification(s)
	3.2.P.5.2 Analytical procedures
	3.2.P.5.3 Validation of analytical procedures
11. Draft of quality specification and notes, and providing reference standard.	3.2.S.4.1 Specification
	3.2.S.4.2 Analytical Procedures
	3.2.S.4.5 Justification of Specification
	3.2.S.5 Reference standards or materials
	3.2.P.5.1 Specification(s)
	3.2.P.5.2 Analytical procedures
	3.2.P.5.6 Justification of specification(s)
	3.2.P.6 Reference standards or materials
12. Test report of drug sample.	3.2.S.4.4 Batch analyses
	3.2.P.5.4 Batch analyses
13. The source, test report and quality specification of drug substance and excipient.	3.2.S.2.1 Manufacturer(s)
	3.2.S.3 Characterization
	3.2.S.4.1 Specification
	3.2.P.3.1 Manufacturer(s)
	3.2.P.4.1 Specification(s)
14. Stability study and relevant literature	3.2.S.7.1 Stability summary and conclusions
	3.2.S.7.3 Stability data
	3.2.P.8.1 Stability summary and conclusion
	3.2.P.8.3 Stability data
15. Selection basis and quality specification of immediate packing material and container.	3.2.P.7 Container closure system

5.8.1.3 Pharmaceutical Information (Table 5.9)

5.8.2 Pharmacology and Toxicology Study Information (Table 5.10)

5.8.3 Clinical Study Information (Table 5.11)

Table 5.10 Module III: Pharmacology and toxicology

Item	CTD module number/Title equivalent
16. Summary of pharmacology and toxicology studies	2.4 Nonclinical overview
17. Primary pharmacodynamics study and literature	4.2.1.1 Primary pharmacodynamics
18. General Pharmacology study and literature	4.2.1.3 Safety pharmacology
19. Acute/single dose toxicity study and literature	4.2.3.1 Single dose toxicity [Species and route]
20. Repeated dose toxicity study and literature	4.2.3.2 Repeat dose toxicity [Species, route, duration]
21. Special safety study and literature of hypersensitive (topical, systemic and photo-toxicity), hemolytic and topical irritative (blood vessel, skin, mucous membrane, and muscle) reaction related to topical and systemic use of the drugs	4.2.3.6 Local tolerance 4.2.3.7 Other toxicity studies
22. Study and relevant literature on Pharmacodynamics, toxicity and pharmacokinetics change caused by the interactions amongst multiple components in the combination products	4.2.1.4. Pharmacodynamic Drug Interactions
23. Study and literature of mutagenicity test	4.2.3.3 Genotoxicity
24. Study and literature of reproductive toxicity	4.2.3.5 Reproductive and developmental toxicity
25. Study and literature of carcinogenicity test	4.2.3.4 Carcinogenicity
26. Study and literature of drug dependence	4.2.3.7.4. Dependence
27. Study and literature of pre-clinical pharmacokinetics	4.2.2 Pharmacokinetics

Table 5.11 Module IV: Clinical documents

Item	CTD module number/Title equivalent
28. Summary of global clinical study information	2.5 Clinical overview 2.7 Clinical summary
29. Clinical study protocol	5.3 Protocol [under specific study]
30. Investigator Brochure	1.14.4.1 Investigational brochure
31. Draft of Informed Consent Form, approval of the Ethics Committee	5.3 List of IECs or IRBs and consent forms [under specific study]
32. Clinical study report	5 Clinical study reports

References

FDA (2014) The comprehensive table of contents headings and hierarchy, Version 2.3 Feb. 27, 2014

Huang Y (November 2010) ZUIXIN YAOPIN ZHUCE FAGUI JI ZHIDAO YUANZE, 1st edn. Chinese Medical Science and Technology Press, Beijing, pp 3–250

Roth RI (2007). Preparing the Common Technical Document for registration of pharmaceuticals for human use (CTD)—insights and recommendations. Ther Innov Regul Sci 42(2):149–159. doi:10.1177/009286150804200207

SFDA (2003a) Good Laboratory Practice for non-clinical laboratory studies (GLP)

SFDA (2003b) Regulation, Order No. 2, Effective Date: on September 1, 2003

SFDA (2003c) Good clinical practice of pharmaceutical products. SFDA order No. 3, Effective on September 1, 2003

SFDA (2005a) Guidance for stability research of chemical drugs

SFDA (2005b) Guidance for basic technology research of chemical drug preparation

SFDA (2005c) Guidance for research of chemical drug impurities

SFDA (2005d) Guidance for residual solvent research of Chemical drugs

SFDA (2005e) Guidance for the normalization process of quality standard establishment of chemical drugs

SFDA (2005f) Guidance for API preparation and structure confirmation research of chemical drugs

SFDA (2005g) Guidance for quality control analytical method validation of chemical drugs

SFDA (2005h) Guidance for non-clinical research of cytotoxic anticancer drugs

SFDA (2005i) Guidance for general pharmacological research of chemical drugs

SFDA (2005j) Guidance for human bioavailability and bioequivalence research of chemical pharmaceutical preparations

SFDA (2005k) Guidance for acute toxicity studies of chemical drugs

SFDA (2005l) Guidance for long-term toxicity study of chemical drugs

SFDA (2005m) Guidance for irritation, allergic and hemolytic research of chemical drugs

SFDA (2005n) Guidance for clinical pharmacokinetics of chemical drugs

SFDA (2005o) Guidance for structure and content of clinical study report of chemical SFDA (2006). Guidance for clinical research of anticancer drugs

SFDA (2006a) Guidance for drug reproductive toxicity study

SFDA (2006b) Guidance for writing format and content of chemical drug review—Summary and evaluation of the main research results

SFDA (2006c) Guidance for writing format and content of chemical drug review—Project target indication and rationale

SFDA (2006d) Guidance for writing format and content of chemical drug review—Review of pharmaceutical research

SFDA (2006e) Guidance for writing format and content of chemical drug application materials—Review of pharmacology and toxicology research

SFDA (2006f) Guidance for chemical drug research with established national standards

SFDA (2006g) Guidance for writing format and content of chemical drug application materials—Review of clinical trial data review

SFDA (2006h) Guidance for quality control research of chiral drugs

SFDA (2007a) Guidance for pharmaceutical research of oral sustained release preparation of chemical drugs

SFDA (2007b) Guidance for pharmaceutical research of synthetic polypeptide drugs

SFDA (2007c) Guidance for non-clinical drug dependence research

SFDA (2007d) Guidance for drug genotoxicity research

SFDA (2007e) Guidance for non-clinical research of drug dependence

SFDA Order No. 28 (2007f) Provisions for drug registration

SFDA Order No. 17 (2009) The Special Review Procedure (SRP) application

SFDA (2010a) Good manufacturing practice for pharmaceutical products, SFDA Order No. 79 Order by Ministry of Health of the People's Republic of China
SFDA (2010b) Guidance for the necessity of carcinogenicity test
SFDA (2010c) Ethical guidelines for ethical review work of drug clinical trials drugs
SFDA (2011) Administrative guidelines for phase I drug clinical trials (Provisional)
Zhang SS, Cao ZS, Hui QS (October 2007) ZUIXIN YAO PIN ZHUCE ZHINAN, 1st edn. Chinese Medical Science and Technology Press, Beijing, pp 1–11

Chapter 6
New Investivational Drug Application

Yanbin Xie, Sandy Bai and Ming Q. Lu

6.1 Acceptance of New Investigational Product Application

6.1.1 Clinical Trials for New Drugs (IND)

The local applicant (manufacturer) shall fill the Application package to the drug regulatory department of the province, autonomous region or municipality (PDA) directly where the applicant is located.

PDA shall conduct the preliminary review of the application dossiers, and issue a acceptance notice of drug registration application if requirements are met, or issue a non-acceptance notice with the corresponding reasons.

PDA shall organize to conduct on-site inspections of the drug research and development conditions and raw data, make preliminary review of the submitted dossiers, and provide review opinions within 5 days from the date it accepts an application. For biological product, samples from three production batches shall also be collected for testing, and a notice for the testing for registration shall be issued to the drug testing institute.

PDA shall deliver the review opinions, inspection reports and the application dossiers to the Center for Drug Evaluation the CDE of the SFDA within the specified timeline, and notice the applicants.

The drug testing institute shall verify the submitted drug specifications, and submit a certificate of analysis for drug registration to the CDE within the specified timeline, and copy to the applicant.

M. Q. Lu (✉)
Helsinn Therapeutics (U.S.), Inc., 1140 US Highway 22, Suite 101, Bridgewater, NJ 08807, USA
e-mail: mingqilu@verizon.net

Y. Xie
China ICON PLC., Room 1502–1506, Tower B Global Trade Center, No. 36, North Ring East Road, Dongcheng District, 100013 Beijing, P. R. China

S. Bai
138 Building B-538, Zhang Hua Road, Hai Dian District, 100036 Beijing, P. R. China

M. Q. Lu (ed.), *Approaching China's Pharmaceutical Market,*
DOI 10.1007/978-3-319-15576-0_6

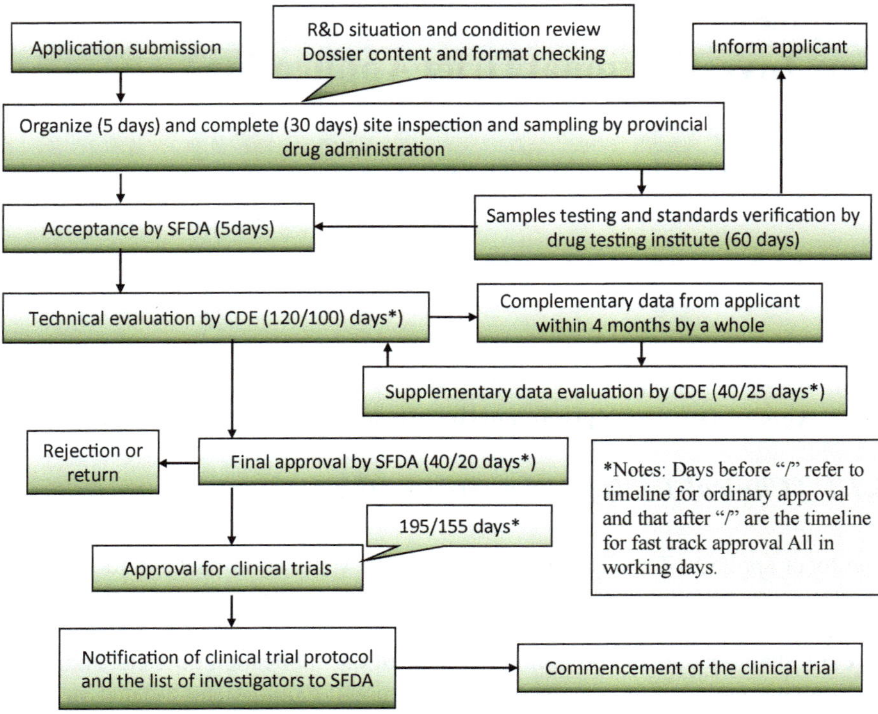

Fig. 6.1 CTA (IND) application and approval process for new drugs. (Modified based on CFDA Website: http://eng.sfda.gov.cn/WS03/CL0769/61659.html)

After receiving submitted dossiers, the CDE shall organize pharmaceutical, medical and other technical personnel to conduct technical review of the submitted dossiers within the specified timeline, and may request, with reasons, applicants to provide supplementary materials when necessary.

After completing technical reviews, the CDE shall give technical review opinions and report together with relevant documents to the SFDA.

SFDA shall make review and approval decisions based on the technical review opinions.

6.1.2 Production of New Drugs (NDA)

PDA shall conduct the preliminary review of the application dossiers, and issue an acceptance notice of drug registration application if requirements are met, or issue a non-acceptance notice, in which reasons shall be given, of drug registration application if requirements are not met.

After receiving submitted dossiers, the CDE shall organize pharmaceutical, medical and other technical personnel to conduct technical review of the submitted dossiers within the specified timeline, and may request, with reasons, applicants to provide supplementary materials when necessary.

If the regulations are conformed to as reviewed, the CDE shall notice the applicant to apply for production site inspection and inform SFDA. If the regulations are not conformed to as reviewed, the CDE shall report the review opinions and relevant documents the SFDA. The SFDA shall make a disapproval decision to the application based on the technical review opinions, and issue a Disapproval Notice with reasons.

Prior to making the decision of administrative licensing, the regulatory agency shall inform the applicant and the interested party of their rights of requesting for hearings, making statements and argues.

The agency shall provide the applicant with access to information on the status of the acceptance, examination, inspection, review and approval of drug registration application and the final resolution.

The agency shall publicize the following information on its official websites or at the official premises for accepting applications:

1. the items, procedures, fees and their basis, and timelines of the drug registration, index of all the data needed to be submitted and model text of the application form;
2. the name list and other relevant information on the persons involved in the acceptance, examination, inspection, review and approval of drug registration; and
3. general information about categories of approved drugs, etc.

6.1.3 Application and Approval of Generic Drugs (Generic)

PDA shall review the submitted dossiers within the specified timeline and give review opinions. If the regulations are conformed to, they shall provide for the CDE with the review opinions, the check report, the production site inspection report and the application dossiers, and inform the applicant. If the regulations are not conformed to, they shall issue a Disapproval Notice with reasons, and notify the drug testing institute to terminate the testing for registration

After receiving submitted dossiers, the CDE shall organize pharmaceutical, medical and other technical personnel to conduct technical review of the submitted dossiers within the specified timeline, and may request, with reasons, applicants to provide supplementary materials when necessary.

If the regulations are conformed to as reviewed, the CDE shall notice the applicant to apply for production site inspection and inform the SFDA. Where the regulations are not conformed to as reviewed, the CDE shall report the review opinions and relevant documents to the SFDA; the SFDA shall make a disapproval decision to the application based on the technical review opinions, and issue a Disapproval Notice with reasons.

6.1.4 Application and Approval of Import Drugs

The SFDA shall conduct the preliminary review of the application dossiers, and issue an acceptance notice of drug registration application and notify the National Institute for the Control of Pharmaceutical and Biological Products to conduct testing for registration of samples from three batches if requirements are met; or issue a non-acceptance notice of drug registration application with reasons if requirements are not met.

The SFDA may organize to conduct on-site inspection of development and production conditions, and take samples.

6.1.5 Import Drug Repackaging

To apply for the repackaging of an import drug, the drug manufacturer entrusted with repackaging of the drug shall submit an application to PDA where it is located. The trustee shall submit the Supplementary Drug Application Form filled in by the trustier, the relevant data and samples as well as the contract of entrustment, etc. The drug regulatory department of PDA shall conduct the preliminary review of the submitted documents. If requirements are met, it shall issue a notice of acceptance; if requirements are not met, it shall issue a notice of non-acceptance with reasons.

The drug regulatory department shall make review opinions, then submit the application documents and review opinions to the SFDA and inform the applicant at the same time.

6.2 Application Path

Based on Provisions for Drug Registration (SFDA Order No. 28) issued on July 10, 2007, the classifications of the new drug for both local and import drug are consistent and follow the same standard requirements.

6.2.1 Local Drug Registration Application (Fig. 6.1)

6.2.2 Management of Import Drugs

See 5.1.4 (Application and Approval of Import Drugs) and 3.6 [Provisions for Drug Registration (SFDA Order No. 28)—Chap. VI (Application and Approval of Import Drugs)] for details.

In general, for the clinical trial application of import drugs, the foreign pharmaceutical companies have to have accomplished minimum a phase II clinical trial overseas. If the companies already have the their drug approved for the corresponding indication overseas, they may follow the category 3 drug application, i.e. to conduct a PK bridging study, 20–30 cases, and a phase III trial with >100 pairs of patients. If it is for application of multiple indications, the sample size has to be >60 pairs of patients. If the pharmaceutical products are in the development stage of phase II or III, and are not yet approved for marketing, the companies have to follow the requirements for category 1.1 new drug application path. They could apply for the global/international multi-center trial with a few sites in China or multi-regional trial to meet their goal of their marketing application.

6.2.2.1 Application and Approval Procedure for Imported Drugs

A General Requirements for Import Chemical Drug Registration Dossiers

1. The applicant shall submit an application for drug registration by electronic and paper documents created by the new version of "Programs for drug registration application form". Regarding this program, please visit www.cfda.gov.cn
2. The first page of the application dossiers should be the index, arranged in accordance with the listed order of Provisions for Drug Registration (State Food and Drug Administration Order No. 28)—Annex II. The following should be marked on the cover page of each dossier item/booklet including drug name, dossier item number, item name, applicant contact name, phone number, and address.
3. Application dossiers should be printed or copied with A4 size paper. The following should be marked on the file envelope: application classification, registration classification, drug name, contact person, telephone number, the name of registration agency and other information requested. The number of sets of dossiers and application forms should be provided as required. Stamps or signatures of overseas applicants and domestic agency are required.
4. The electronic version of part of the drug application dossiers should be submitted simultaneously as required. After the State Food and Drug Administration receives electronic dossiers, the paper version of application dossiers should be submitted or mailed to the State Food and Drug Administration.
5. Drug Registration Application Form should be filled according to Provisions for Drug Registration (State Food and Drug Administration Order No. 28). The specifications and packaging specifications should be filled as required. On the application form Institution 1 and Institution 2 are overseas certification holder and manufacturer information. Business name, address etc. should be filled in English; Institution 3 is overseas packaging plant information; the information of domestic agency must be filled in Chinese.
6. The product cannot be used to apply for import registration if some drug with the same active ingredient is in the monitoring period,

B Requirements for Import Chemical Drug Application Items

1. The application dossiers should be submitted in accordance with chemical drugs Application Dossiers requirement. To apply for the drugs which are not permitted to market domestic and abroad, dossiers should be submitted in accordance with Registration Category I drug requirements; for the other drugs, the dossiers should be submitted in accordance with Registration Category 3 drug. requirements
2. For dossier Item 5, package insert sample, drafting rationale of the package insert, and the latest references are required
   In addition, it is required to provide original package insert with the Chinese translation approved in the original manufacturing country or region by the regulatory agencies. For Dossier Item 6, it is required to provide the original packaging and labeling information approved for the original manufacturing country or region.
3. For dossier Item 28, all the clinical trial data used for the market approval in the original manufacturing country or region should be submitted.
4. All application dossiers should be in Chinese and attached with its original documents. Other languages should be attached as reference. The Chinese translation should be consistent with the original content.
5. The Chinese version of the drug standards must conform to the format of the Chinese national drug standards.

C Requirements and Description of Certification Documents of Dossier Item 2 –

1. Dossier Item 2 proof documents include the following:
   - Proof documents, notary document and its Chinese translation, which indicate the GMP compliance of the pharmaceutical manufacturing enterprises and prove the drugs to go to the market issued by the drug regulatory authorities in drug manufacturing countries or regions, are required. Applications for the drug without marketing approval in domestic market and abroad, this marketing approval document can be submitted together with the clinical study report after the completion of the clinical trial in China.
   - If registration affairs are managed by the resident representative office of overseas pharmaceutical manufacturers in China, a copy of the registration certificate of the representative office should be provided. If overseas pharmaceutical manufacturers authorize Chinese agents to handle the registration affairs, the overseas foreign enterprises should provide the authorization document, notary document and its Chinese translation as well as the copy of Chinese agency's business license.
   - The descriptions of application drug, formulation, technology and other patent condition, its ownership status and the guarantee of no infringement to patents of others should be provided.

2. Instructions:
   - Proof documents, which indicate the GMP compliance of the pharmaceutical manufacturing enterprises and prove the drugs to go to the market issued by the drug regulatory authorities in drug manufacturing countries or regions, should comply with the unified format recommended by World Health Organization. Documents of other format must be notarized by the notary office of the host country and certificated by Chinese embassies and consulates in the corresponding countries.
   - If the drug preparation is produced in one place and the packaging in another place, the proof documents issued by Drug Regulatory Authorities in the country or region of the preparation and packaging plants, which prove that the pharmaceutical manufacturing enterprises are in compliance with the GMP norms, should be provided.
   - If the drugs don't have the marketing approval in the drug manufacturing country or region, they can provide documents for marketing approval in other countries or regions, which are subject to the State Drug Administration approval. However, the proof documents which prove that the pharmaceutical manufacturing enterprises comply with the GMP should be issued by drug regulatory authorities in drug manufacturing country or region.
   - For APIs, the proof documents, which issued by drug regulatory authorities of the drug manufacturing country or region, approve the drug to go to market and prove that the pharmaceutical manufacturing enterprises are in compliance with the GMP, should be provided. The data and documents of bulk drug master system files—DMF (Drug Master File) can also be provided.

D The Requirements of Clinical Research in China

1. For the application for drugs, which don't have the marketing approval domestically and abroad, clinical research should be conducted according to the requirements of classification 1. The application of drug should be the drug which has entered Phase II or Phase III of clinical trial.
2. For the application of drug, which has been marketed abroad, but not yet marketed in China, clinical research should be conducted according to the requirements of category 3.
3. For the application of API or its preparation, which has existing national drug standards, if the dossier item 28 meets the requirements, clinical trials could carried out in accordance with the requirements of category 6; if it does not meet the requirements, clinical trials should be carried out in accordance with requirements of classification 3.
4. A separate application for the import of API with no national drug standards, clinical research should be conducted with its preparations.

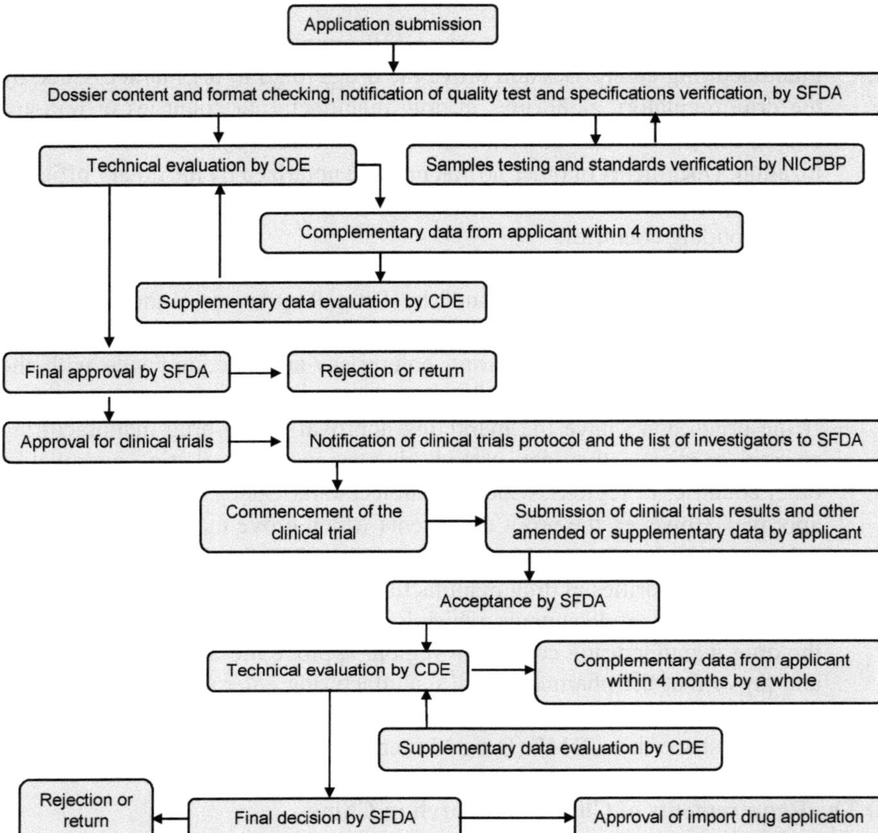

Fig. 6.2 Application and approval procedure for imported drugs. (Modified based on the CFDA website figures http://eng.sfda.gov.cn/WS03/CL0769/61658.html http://eng.sfda.gov.cn/WS03/CL0769/61657.html)

In the following Fig. 6.2, approval process for import drugs is divided into four stages:

- First stage: from application submission to the accomplishment of dossier checking and verification. The time needed is 30 days.
- Second stage: from dossier acceptance through technical evaluation process by the CDE. The time needed is 120 days. If complementary data needed, extra time will be added.
- Third stage: from final approval of clinical study to the Commencement of the clinical trial. The time needed is 30 days.
- Forth stage: From the submission of clinical trials results to the approval of import drug application.

The process for the approval of import drug application highly depends on if any complementary data is needed. The days before "/"line refer to timeline for ordinary approval and that after "/" line are the timeline for fast track approval. All timelines are calculated in working days.

6.2.2.2 Supplementary Application and Approval Procedure

The following are the description of the supplementary application items:

1. Copies of drug approval certificate and appendixes.

Include all the approval documents related to the application, such as drug registration approval, approval for supplemental application, approval for trade name, publishing document of drug standards, approval for amendment of drug standards and uniformly renewed drug approval number, New Drug Certificate, Import Drug Licensor Drug Product License. Annex should include all the annexes to the above approval, such as drug standards, insert sheet, design of packing and label and other annex.

2. Certified Documents:

   - If the Applicant is a drug manufacture enterprise, copies of the drug manufacture certificate, business licenses, and GMP Certificate should be provided. If the Applicant is not a drug manufacture enterprise, copies of the certified document of legal registration of the Applicant should be provided. If the drug registration is conducted by the resident office of the foreign manufacturer, copy of Registration Certificate of Resident Office of Foreign Enterprise should be submitted. If drug registration is conducted by a Chinese agent with authorization from the foreign manufacturer, the certified documents of the authorizations, notarized documents and the Chinese translation should be submitted together with the copy of Business License of the domestic agent.
   - For different application items, the certified document should be provided according to the Table of Application Information Items respectively for each item.
   - For import drug, the certified documents, notarized documents of the approval of the changes of the drugs issued by the competent drug administration authorities at the local country or region and the Chinese translation should by provided. The form of the documents should comply to the requirements for certified document set out in the application information items of TCM, natural drugs, chemical drugs, biological products, except for change in strength of drugs, change of manufacture location, change of manufacturer name or legal location, if the local drug authorities can not provide relate certified document, notes should be explain according to the local laws and regulation.

3. Draft of the amended design of the insert sheet of the drugs, attached with detailed notes for the amendments.

4. Draft of the amended design of the packing and label of the drugs, attached with detailed notes for the amendments.
5. Pharmaceutical study information. Part or all the experiment information of Pharmaceutical study and necessary global literature should be provided respectively for the different registration category, information items should be provided according to the corresponding application information items of Annexes 1–3.
6. Pharmacology and toxicology study information. Part or all the experiment information of Pharmacology and toxicology study and necessary global literature should be provided respectively for the different registration category, information items should be provided according to the corresponding application information items of Annexes 1–3.
7. Clinical study information: If there is a need for a clinical study, the information items should be provided according to the corresponding application information items of Annexes 1–3. Information should be provided respectively before and after clinical trial. If there is no need for clinical study, the literature of the clinical study may be provided instead (Figs. 6.3 and 6.4).

6.2.2.3 Import Drug Repackaging Application and approval

The import drug repackaging refers to dividing a large pack into small ones in China or adding outer-package to a drug with inner-package, placing insert sheets and

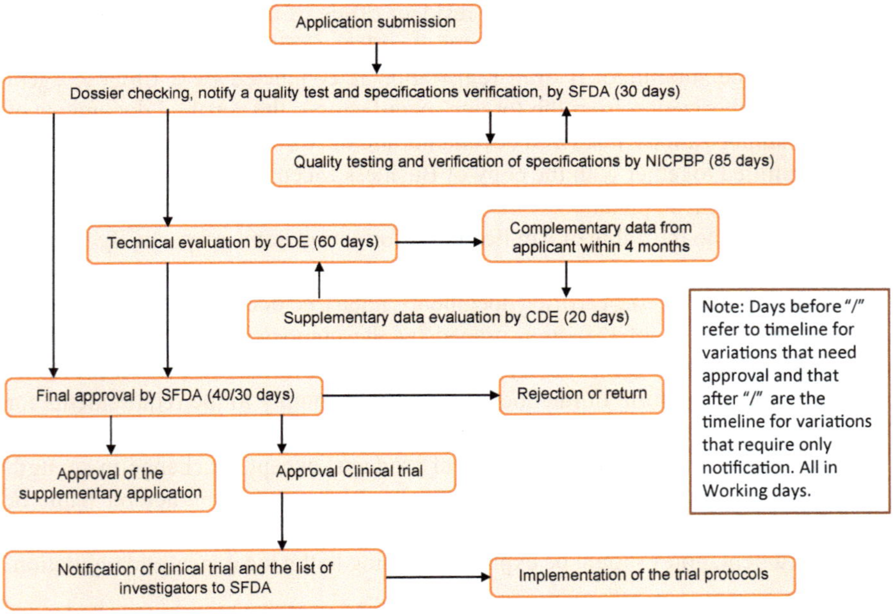

Fig. 6.3 Supplementary application and approval process for clinical trials. (Adopted and modified from the CFDA website)

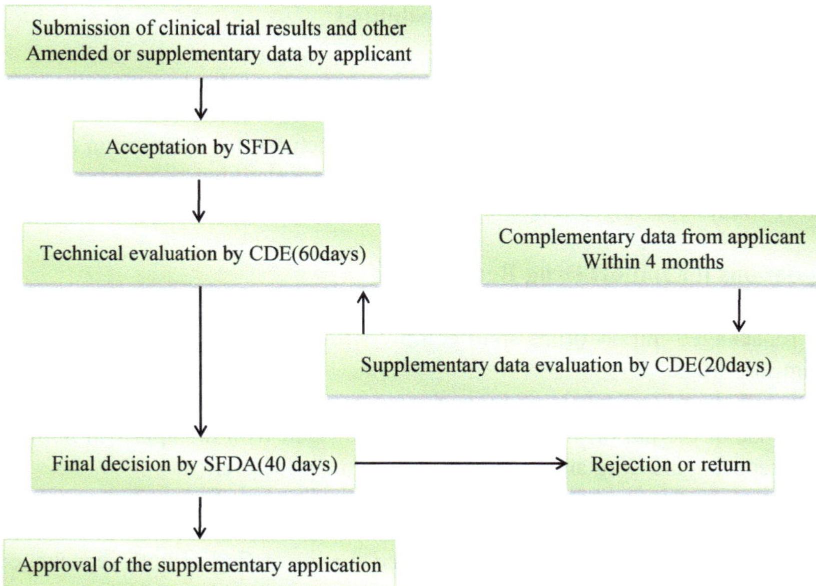

Fig. 6.4 Supplementary application and approval process for NDA. (Adopted and modified from the CFDA website)

attaching labels, etc., after the production process of the finished pharmaceutical preparations for the drug are completed overseas. Items 96–104 in Section 2 (Registration of Import Drug Repackaging) of Provisions for Drug Registration (SFDA Order No. 28) provide detailed description for import drug repackaging application and approval.

A Requirements for Application of Import Drug Repackaging

1. The Import Drug License or Pharmaceutical Product License of the drug is already obtained;
2. The drug shall be one that is not produced within the territory of China, or is produced in China but unable to meet clinical needs;
3. One drug produced by a drug manufacturer shall be repackaged by only one drug manufacturer. The term allowed for repackaging shall not exceed the expiry date of the Import Drug License or Pharmaceutical Product License;
4. The inner–packaging of a drug in any dosage form for repackaging, except tablets and capsules, shall be completed overseas;
5. A drug manufacturer that conducts repackaging shall hold the Drug Manufacturing Certificate. To apply for repackaging of import unpackaged tablets and capsules, the manufacturer shall also hold the GMP certificate covering the dosage forms for repackaging; and
6. An application for drug repackaging shall be made 1 year prior to the expiration of the Import Drug License or the Pharmaceutical Product License.

B Overseas Drug Manufacturer Responsibilities

1. To sign a contract for import drug repackaging with a domestic drug manufacturer;
2. To fill in the Drug Supplementary Application Form;
3. To prepare the samples for domestic drug manufacturer, for submission use;
4. The overseas drug manufacturer providing the drug shall be responsible for the quality of the repackaged drug.

C Regulations for Import Drug Repackaging

1. The repackaged import drugs shall comply with the registration specifications for import drugs.
2. The insert sheets and labels of a repackaged import drug shall be in conformity with those of the import drug, and shall be indicated with the approval number of the repackaging drug and the name of drug manufacturer.
3. The testing for import of overseas pharmaceutical preparation in large package shall be conducted according to the State Food and Drug Administration regulations. The same specifications shall be used for the testing of both repackaged and import products.
4. If there is any quality problem, the State Food and Drug Administration may withdraw the approval number of the repackaged drug, revoke the Import Drug License or the Pharmaceutical Product License when necessary according to the requirements of Article 42 of the Drug Administration Law.

D Import Drug Repackaging Application and Approval Process

1. The drug manufacturer entrusted, i.e. a domestic drug manufacturer, with repackaging of the drug shall submit an application to the drug regulatory department of the province, autonomous region, or municipality directly under the Central Government where it is located.
2. The trustee shall submit the Supplementary Drug Application Form filled in by the overseas drug manufacturer, the relevant data and samples as well as the contract of entrustment, etc. The drug regulatory department shall conduct the preliminary review of the submitted documents. Where requirements are met, it shall issue a notice of acceptance; where requirements are not met, it shall issue a notice of non-acceptance with reasons.
3. The drug regulatory department shall make review opinions, then submit the application documents and review opinions to the State Food and Drug Administration and inform the applicant at the same time.
4. The State Food and Drug Administration shall review the submitted documents. Where the regulations are conformed to, it shall issue an Approval for Supplementary Drug Application and a drug approval number; where the regulations are not conformed to, it shall issue a Disapproval Notice with reasons.

6.2.3 Special Review and Approval for Drug Registration

The State encourages the research and development of new drugs and adopts the special review and approval with respect to innovative drugs, new drugs for serious and life-threatening diseases and to address unmet medical needs and drugs (SFDA 2005)

In the recently years, regulatory approval timelines for clinical trial application are greatly shortened to 6–12 months. All IND and NDA submission packages from overseas companies are required in Chinese. CTD format in compliance with ICH guidance for application package has been accepted. The minimal patient sample size and statistical significance requirement have to meet the regulatory requirements.

The shortening of the approval timeline by the CDE are mainly related to the following factors:

1. Factors from the CDE Aspect:

   – Green channel approach which shortened the approval time
   – Establishment of in-house statistical division
   – Participating in more major international conferences
   – Expanding review team
   – Implementing good review practice: more science based approach; openness, fairness, rightfulness.

2. Factors from Industry Aspect:

   – Increased Pre-IND consultation
   – Participating in more training workshops to promote GMP, GLP, GCP and new drug development
   – Participating in major international conferences
   – Acceptance of CTD format and ICH guidance make it easier for western companies

6.2.3.1 Special Review and Approval Procedure for Drug Registration of the State Food and Drug Administration

State Food and Drug Administration (2005), Decree No. 21

The Special Review and Approval Procedure for Drug Registration of the State Food and Drug Administration, adopted at the executive meeting of the State Food and Drug Administration (SFDA) on November 18, 2005, has become effective as of the date of promulgation, SFDA

Chapter 1
General Provisions

Article 1 This Procedure is formulated for the purpose of effective prevention, timely control and elimination of the hazards of public health emergencies to ensure the health and safety of the public in accordance with the Drug Administration Law of the People's Republic of China, Law of the People's Republic of China on the Prevention and Treatment of Infectious Diseases, Regulations for Implementation of the Drug Administration Law of the People's Republic of China, Regulations on Preparedness for and Response to Emergent Public Health Hazards, and other relevant laws and regulations.

Article 2 The special review and approval procedure for drug registration refers to the procedure and requirements of the State Food and Drug Administration to carry out special review and approval of drugs for handling public heath emergencies under the principle of unified leadership, early involvement, expeditiousness and efficiency, and scientific review and approval, in an effort to approve drugs for the prevention and treatment of public health emergencies as soon as possible under the threat or after the occurrence of public health emergencies.

Article 3 The State Food and Drug Administration may, according to law, decide to follow the Procedure to conduct special review and approval of drugs for public health emergencies in any of the following circumstances:

1. Where the President of the People's Republic of China declares a state of emergency or the State Council decides that certain areas within a province, autonomous region or municipality directly under the Central Government are in a state of emergency;
2. Where the contingency program for public health emergencies is initiated according to law;
3. Where the drug reserve department or the health administrative department of the State Council proposes a special review and approval for drugs having existing national drug standard;
4. Other circumstances applicable to special review and approval.

Article 4 The State Food and Drug Administration is responsible for the review and approval of clinical trials, production and importation of drugs for the prevention and treatment of public health emergencies.

The (food and) drug regulatory department of a province, autonomous region, or municipality directly under the Central Government shall, upon entrustment of the State Food and Drug Administration, be responsible for on-site inspection and sampling of the pilot products of the drugs for the prevention and treatment of public health emergencies.

Chapter 2
Application Acceptance and On-site Inspection

Article 5
Where the special review and approval procedure for drug registration is initiated, the State Food and Drug Administration is responsible for the acceptance of registration applications for drugs for public health emergencies.

Where a drug or a preventive biological product for public health emergencies has not been marketed in China, the applicant shall, before submission of the registration application, provide the State Food and Drug Administration with relevant research and development information.

Article 6 The applicant shall submit a registration application with relevant technical dossier to the State Food and Drug Administration according to the relevant provisions and requirements on administration of drug registration.

The registration application for drug for public health emergencies may be submitted in electronic form.

Article 7 Before submitting an application for registration, the applicant may provide a feasibility assessment application with general information and relevant explanations. The State Food and Drug Administration shall only comment on the scientific rationality and feasibility of the drug project, and respond within 24 h.

The response to a feasibility assessment application shall be neither deemed as the review and approval opinion nor legally binding on the review and approval result of a registration application.

Article 8 The State Food and Drug Administration shall organize an expert group to evaluate and review the registration application for drug for the prevention and treatment of public health emergencies, make a decision within 24 h on whether or not to accept the application, and notify the applicant.

Article 9 Where a registration application is accepted, the State Food and Drug Administration shall organize technical review of submitted dossier within 24 h and at the same time notify the (food and) drug regulatory department of the province, autonomous region or municipality directly under the Central Government where the applicant is located to conduct an on-site inspection on drug research and development conditions, and organize sampling and testing of pilot products.

The (food and) drug regulatory department of the province, autonomous region, or municipality directly under the Central Government shall, within 5 days, submit the on-site inspection result and relevant opinion to the State Food and Drug Administration.

Article 10 The (food and) drug regulatory department of the province, autonomous region, or municipality directly under the Central Government shall organize staff from the departments of drug registration, drug safety and inspection, etc. to participate in the on-site inspection.

The National Institute for the Control of Pharmaceutical and Biological Products shall be notified to send staff to participate in the on-site inspection and sampling of preventive biological products.

Article 11 For drugs that have existing national standards for the prevention and treatment of public health emergencies, the State Food and Drug Administration may directly review and approve the drug in accordance with the relevant provisions in Chap. 6 of the Procedure when it deems there is no need for a clinical trial in accordance with law.

Article 12 With respect to the registration application for a specific vaccine, where only the original virus strain used in the manufacturing is changed while the manufacturing processes or quality specifications are maintained, the State Food and Drug Administration shall make a decision on whether or not to grant the approval within 3 days after verifying the changed strain used in the manufacturing.

Chapter 3
Testing for Registration

Article 13 After receiving the samples taken by the (food and) drug regulatory department of a province, autonomous region, or municipality directly under the Central Government, the drug testing institution shall immediately organize verification of specifications and laboratory testing on the samples.

The drug testing institution shall complete the testing within the time frame for the drug being applied.

Article 14 For a drug applied first time for marketing, the State Food and Drug Administration may, when necessary, make early involvement by appointing the National Institute for the Control of Pharmaceutical and Biological Products to communicate with the applicant prior to testing for registration so as to timely resolve technical problems which may arise in the process of quality specifications verification and laboratory testing.

With respect to preventive biological products used to prevent and control the epidemic of serious infectious diseases, the State Food and Drug Administration may, depending on the situation, allow the testing for registration and the manufacturer's self-testing to be performed in parallel.

Article 15 After completion of the specifications verification and laboratory testing on a drug, the drug testing institution shall, within 2 days, issue its verification opinion and submit it along with the drug test report to the State Food and Drug Administration.

Chapter 4
Technical Review

Article 16 The State Food and Drug Administration shall, within 15 days after acceptance of the registration application for drug for the prevention and treatment in public health emergencies, complete the first round of technical review.

Article 17 Where the State Food and Drug Administration considers that additional data are needed, it shall immediately inform the applicant of the content and timeline.

Where the applicant submits the supplementary data within the specified timeline, the State Food and Drug Administration shall complete the technical review within 3 days, or, depending on the situations, organize another review meeting within 5 days, and then complete the review report within 2 days.

Chapter 5
Clinical Trial

Article 18 Where the technical review is completed, the State Food and Drug Administration shall, within 3 days, complete the administrative examination, make a decision and inform the applicant.

Where the State Food and Drug Administration decides to approve a clinical trial, it shall issue a Drug Clinical Trial Approval. Where it decides not to approve, it shall issue a Disapproval Notice with reasons.

Article 19 Where an applicant obtains a clinical trial approval, it shall conduct the trial strictly following the relevant requirements in the approval document, and comply with the Good Clinical Practice.

Article 20 Drug clinical trials shall be conducted in institutions legally certified for drug clinical trials. If a clinical trial has to be conducted by an institution not yet certified, a special approval by the State Food and Drug Administration should be obtained.

The application for a clinical trial conducted by an institution not yet certified for drug clinical trials may be submitted along with the application for drug registration.

Article 21 The investigator responsible for a drug clinical trial shall, in accordance with the relevant provisions, timely report adverse events occurred in the process of the clinical trial to the State Food and Drug Administration. If no adverse event occurs, the investigator shall collect relevant information and report to the State Food and Drug Administration monthly.

Article 22 The State Food and Drug Administration shall, in accordance with law, supervise and inspect the clinical trials of drugs for public health emergencies.

Chapter 6
Review, Approval and Monitoring of Drug Production

Article 23 The applicant shall, after completion of the drug clinical trials, submit the relevant data to the State Food and Drug Administration in accordance with the Provisions for Drug Registration.

Article 24 The State Food and Drug Administration shall, within 24 h after receiving data submitted by the applicant, organize technical review, and at the same time notify the (food and) drug regulatory department of the province, autonomous region, or municipality directly under the Central Government where the applicant is located to conduct the on-site inspection on the drug manufacturing conditions, and organize the sampling and testing of pilot products.

The (food and) drug regulatory department of the province, autonomous region, or municipality directly under the Central Government shall, within 5 days, submit the result and opinion of the on-site inspection to the State Food and Drug Administration.

Article 25 Any newly-established drug manufacturer or manufacturer with newly-built manufacturing workshops or newly-added dosage forms for production may apply to the State Food and Drug Administration for a certificate of the Good Manufacturing Practice along with the application for drug registration. The State Food and Drug Administration shall, when conducting the drug registration review, immediately carry out an inspection on the Good Manufacturing Practice certification.

Article 26 The drug testing institution shall, after receiving the samples of three batches taken by the (food and) drug regulatory department of the province, autonomous region, or municipality directly under the Central Government, immediately arrange the testing.

Upon completion of testing, the drug testing institution shall, within 2 days, complete the test report and submit it to the State Food and Drug Administration.

Article 27 The State Food and Drug Administration shall carry out technical review in accordance with Chap. 4 of the Procedure, and shall, within 3 days after the completion of the technical review, complete the administrative examination, make a decision and inform the applicant.

Where the State Food and Drug Administration decides to approve the drug, it shall issue the Letter of Approval for Drug Registration, and may grant an approval number for the drug at the same time if the applicant has appropriate manufacturing conditions; if it decides to disapprove the manufacturing, it shall issue a Disapproval Notice with reasons.

Article 28 Where a drug manufacturer or distributor, or a medical and health institution finds any new or serious adverse drug reaction or cluster adverse reaction relating to a specially approved drug for public health emergencies, it shall immediately report the case to the local (food and) drug regulatory department of the province, autonomous region, or municipality directly under the Central Government, the health administrative department at the provincial level and the professional institution for adverse drug reactions monitoring.

The professional institution for adverse drug reactions monitoring shall regard drugs specially approved for public health emergencies as critically monitored products, analyze the collected case reports in accordance with the relevant provisions and timely report to the (food and) drug regulatory department of the province, autonomous region, or municipality directly under the Central Government and the State Food and Drug Administration.

The State Food and Drug Administration shall reinforce the reevaluation of approved drugs for public health emergencies after they are marketed.

Chapter 7
Supplementary Provisions

Article 29 The measures for special review and approval of the medical devices for public health emergencies shall be separately formulated by the State Food and Drug Administration with reference to the relevant provisions of the Procedure.

Article 30 The Procedure shall go into effect as of the date of promulgation.

6.2.4 Special Review and Approval for New Drug Registration

This new regulation published in 2009 has the following intentions:

1. Encourage drug innovation in China
2. Develop the principles of 'early involvement, priority evaluation, multiple channel communication, and dynamic submission of supplemental information'.

3. Stipulate relevant provisions on the conditions, procedures, and requirements of the special approval process for new drugs
4. Specify rights and obligations of applicants in the special approval process

This new regulation includes the following categories:

1. Active ingredients extracted from plants and animal or mineral resources and their formulations that have never been marketed in China.
2. Active pharmaceutical ingredients (APIs) and their formulations or biological products that have not yet been approved for domestic and foreign markets.
3. New drugs showing clear therapeutic advantages in the treatment of AIDS, malignant tumors, and rare or orphan diseases.
4. New drugs that may be used to potentially treat diseases for which no known effective therapy is yet available.

The following tables showed that significant improvement for approval time in the past years (SFDA 2013) (Table 6.1):

From 2012 China Annual Drug Evaluation Report, China Pharmaceutical Newsletter, Vol. IV, 2013

In comparison to the average industry experience in the previous years, the IND time is greatly shortened, see data below (Table 6.2):

From Jan. 1 to Dec. 10 of 2012, the CDE accomplished a total of 47 chemical drug IND reviews, including Class 1 and 2. The listed time in the following table was calculated from the formal application package submission to the accomplishment of the review with conclusion (Fig. 6.5).

Among the initial 47 reviewed chemical drug applications, 34 applications were in the Class 1.1 category new drug, i.e. 72 % of the total INDs. The following table shows the percentage of the applications in the therapeutic fields (Tables 6.3 and 6.4).

Table 6.1 The average of the review time

Sequence	January 2012		December 2012	
	Reception date	Waiting time (month)	Reception date	Waiting time (month)
IND	May 2011	6	August 2012	4
Bridging clinical trial	December 2010	12	August 2011	15
NDA	January 2011	11	November 2011	12
ANDA	October 2010	14	December 2010	24
Supplementary application	July 2011	5	August 2012	3
Import re-registration	September 2011	4	June 2012	5

Table 6.2 The average timeline before 2012

Review timelines in the previous years					
Category	IND/CTA	NDA	Supplementary	Sample Test (Registration)	Sample Test (Import Drug)
Month	12–15	15–18	10–12	6–8	3–4

Table 6.3 Distribution of the Class 1.1 new applications in various therapeutic fields

Indication	Percent (%)	Average Time (Mouth)	Shortest Time (Mouth)
Anti-cancer	32	6.1	4.2
Endocrine	17	6.7	5.8
Psychiatry/CNS	15	7.3	5.8
GI	13	7.6	5.6

Table 6.4 Registration application from 2009–2012—Number of various registration applications

	2009	2010	2011	2012
Category1.1. new drugs	42	69	79	78
Other new drugs above category 3	656	718	793	942
Category 4–6	1314	1358	1806	1852
Global multi-centered clinical trial	157	150	179	138
Imported drug	365	410	459	442

Table 6.5 Major reforms to drug regulatory process in 2013

Significance	This new the SFDA regulation would establish a fast-track review process for drugs that are in great clinical need. This reform is needed as the CDE currently struggles under the weight of repeat applications for generics already available in the market
Implications	Innovative drugs, especially those China-based intellectual property and/or government-directed research and development, will be encouraged through fast-track reviews and regulatory approvals. The incentives within the tendering, pricing and reimbursement processes will be used to encourage greater development of drugs for pediatric use
Prospect	The reforms will be cheered by the industry, with further potentially significant changes on the horizon including greater involvement of local authorities in drug registrations

The SFDA published the processes of fast-track drug registration for China-based innovation, clinical priorities to promote the development of Chinese local pharmaceutical companies

- The number of Category 1.1 (New Drug) applications was around 70
- Very small portion compared with other Categories
- From 2012 China Annual Drug Evaluation Report, China Pharmaceutical Newsletter, Vol. IV, 2013 (Table 6.5)

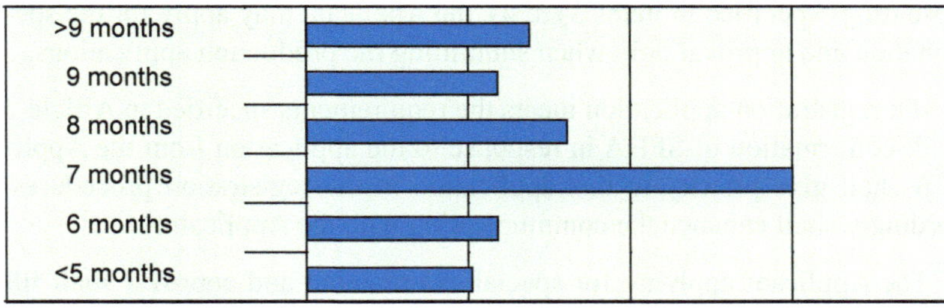

Fig. 6.5 Review time needed for first-round evaluation of initial IND in 2012

6.2.4.1 Regulations of Special Examination and Approval in New Drug Registration

State Food and Drug Administration Note (2009), No. 17

To encourage research and development of new drugs and strengthen risk control, the State Food and Drug Administration (SFDA 2009) has developed Regulations of Special Examination and Approval in New Drug Registration in accordance with the Drug Registration regulation. This regulation has become effective as of the date of promulgation on January 7, 2009.

Article 1 The requirements are developed in accordance with the Drug Registration Regulation for the purpose of encouraging research and development of new drugs and strengthening risk control.

Article 2 In accordance with Article 45 of Drug Registration Regulation, the SFDA may implement special examination and approval in the cases of the following applications of new drugs:

1. Active ingredients extracted from plants, animals or minerals, etc. and their preparations not yet marketed in China, and newly discovered Chinese crude drugs and their preparations;
2. Chemical drug substance and their preparations and biological products not yet approved for marketing in China or abroad;
3. New drugs for the treatment of diseases such as AIDS, malignant tumors and rare diseases, etc. with significant clinical advantages; and
4. New drugs for the treatment of diseases, for which effective therapeutic method are not available.

The new drugs for the treatment of diseases that are not covered by the state approved "Functions & Indications of TCM preparations", may be considered as new drugs for the treatment of diseases for which effective therapeutic method is not available.

For those drugs specified in items 1) & 2), the applicant of drug registration (hereinafter "the Applicant") may apply for the special examination and approval when submitting the application for clinical trials of the new drugs.

For those drugs specified in items 3) & 4), the Applicant may apply for the special examination and approval only when submitting the production applications.

Article 3 If a registration application meets the requirements specified in Article 2 by review & confirmation of SFDA in response to the application from the Applicant, SFDA shall give priority to this application in the registration procedures, then, accordingly shall enhance the communication with the Applicant.

Article 4 The Applicant applying for special examination and approval shall fill out Application Form for Special Examination and Approval of New Drug Registration (Appendix 1) and submit the relevant data.

The Application Form for Special Examination and Approval of New Drug Registration and the relevant data should be filed in a separate dossier and be submitted to the acceptance department for drug registration along with the application dossier required by the Drug Registration Regulation.

Article 5 Upon acceptance, the acceptance department shall forward the relevant data of Special Examination and Approval application along with the submitted registration dossier to the Center of Drug Evaluation (hereinafter the CDE), the SFDA.

Article 6 the CDE of the SFDA is in charge of organizing a review & confirmation on the application for Special Examination and Approval, and then informs the Applicant with the review results, which will be published on the website of the CDE of the SFDA at the same time.

1. For those specified in items 1) & 2) of Article 2, the CDE of the SFDA shall conduct review & confirmation within 5 days after receipt of the application for special examination and approval;
2. For those specified in items 3) & 4) of Article 2, the CDE of the SFDA shall organize Expert Meeting for review & confirmation within 20 days after receipt of the application for special examination and approval.

The time used for review & confirmation on an application for special examination and approval is included in the time frame of technical review as specified by Drug Registration Regulation.

Article 7 Where a drug application is permitted entering a special examination and approval procedure, the CDE of the SFDA shall conduct corresponding technical review on the application according to the relevant procedures and requirements. Authorities responsible for site inspection and lab testing should give priority to the registration application that is permitted entering a special examination and approval procedure.

Article 8 For the registration application permitted entering a special examination and approval procedure, in addition to data supplementation as requested by the CDE of the SFDA, the Applicant may also submit new data supplementation under any of the following circumstances:

1. Significant safety information newly discovered
2. Data prepared as required by the Evaluation Meeting;

3. Data needed for communication.

For item 1), if the Applicant submits the supplementary data after technical review conclusion is made by the CDE of the SFDA, the time frame of technical review should accordingly be extended, normally 20 days.

Article 9 After receiving the Deficiency Notice issued by the CDE of the SFDA, the applicant should complete the data supplementation within an extended 8 months if it is not possible to submit within 4 months.

Article 10 For applications entering a special examination and approval procedure, the CDE of the SFDA shall establish a working mechanism for communication with the Applicant to jointly discuss the concerned technical issues.

Article 11 For the registration application of item 1) or 2) of Article 2, provided that the same drug has not yet been granted with special examination and approval, after the basic data of pre-clinical pharmaceutical study, safety and efficacy become available, and before the clinical trial application, the Applicant may apply for communication with the CDE of the SFDA, where the topics may be application of special examination and approval, significant technical issues.

Article 12 For the registration applications of Article 2, based on the completion of certain phase of clinical trials and evaluation summary, the Applicant may submit to the CDE of the SFDA an application for communication in respect of the following issues:

1. Significant safety issues;
2. Clinical trial protocol;
3. Summary and evaluation on staged results of clinical trials.

Article 13 For the registration application permitted entering a special examination and approval procedure, if any significant changes are necessary during clinical trials such as protocol amendment, indication and specification change, etc., the Applicant may submit an application for communication based on the evaluation of the effects of the changes with respect to drug safety, efficacy and quality control.

Article 14 To apply for communication, the Applicant should fill out Application Form for Communication of Special Examination Approval in New Drug Registration (Appendix 2), and submit relevant data.

Article 15 The CDE of the SFDA shall review Application Form for Communication of Special Examination and Approval of New Drug Registration and the relevant data submitted by the Applicant and notify the Applicant with the results.

Article 16 When the CDE of the SFDA agrees to any Application for Communication, it should clearly notify the Applicant with the issues to be discussed, and confirm the Applicant with method, time, place and attendants of communication, etc., and organize the communication within 1 month after notifying the Applicant. However, for the case of Article 11, the communication should be organized within 3 months

Article 17 Communication should be recorded with signatures of both parties to confirm for further reference in the subsequent study and evaluation.

Article 18 The Applicant applying for special examination and approval should establish risk control and implementation plan during application for both clinical trials and production.

Article 19 If any registration application granted with special examination and approval for clinical trial application, then, while the Applicant shall still need to submit the relevant data as required by this regulation, but there will be no need for special examination confirmation as the special examination and approval shall apply automatically.

Article 20 Under any of the following circumstances, the SFDA may terminate the special examination and approval procedure, and publicly announce the termination on the website of the CDE.

1. The Applicant asks for a termination;
2. The Applicant fails to fulfill the required obligation within the specified time frame;
3. Expert Meeting concludes that the special examination and approval procedure is no longer appropriate.

Article 21 When there is any emergency event occurs that threats the public health, as well as after occurrence of public healthcare emergency, registration of the drugs needed for such emergency shall follow the special examination and approval as specified by SFDA Special Examination and Approval Procedures of Drug.

Article 22 This regulation shall go into effect as of the date of publication.

Appendix 1 (Table 6.6)

Notes to the Form

1. This form is prepared in accordance with Regulations of Special Examination and Approval in New Drug Registration
2. TCM may not need to fill a chemical name.
3. Registration Category should be identical to the Application Form of Registration Application.
4. Registration application meets any of those requirements: just to tick off "√" the applicable box "□".
5. Justification of the application: Any corresponding summary data to support that the new drug registration meets any related conditions should be provided according to the specific condition in accordance with Regulations of Special Examination and Approval in New Drug Registration. The major contents in the summary data shall include the followings:

    1. Summary data to support that the drugs meet the requirement of Article 2 of Regulations of Special Examination and Approval in New Drug Registration.
    2. The proposed clinical trial protocol or the summary of any clinical trials that already completed.

<table>
<tr><td>INN name</td><td></td><td>Chemical Name</td><td></td></tr>
<tr><td>Registration Category</td><td></td><td>Indication(s)</td><td></td></tr>
<tr><td>Registration application meets any of those conditions</td><td colspan="3">□ Active ingredients extracted from plants, animals or minerals, etc. and their preparations not yet marketed in China, and newly discovered Chinese crude drugs and their preparations;
□ Chemical drug substance and their preparations and biological products not yet approved for marketing in China or abroad;
□ New drugs for the treatment of diseases such as AIDS, malignant tumors and rare diseases, etc. with significant clinical advantages;
□ New drugs for the treatment of diseases, for which effective therapeutic method are not available.</td></tr>
<tr><td colspan="4">Justification of the application

Pages may be attached when needed</td></tr>
<tr><td colspan="4">Risk control and implementation plan

Pages may be attached when needed</td></tr>
<tr><td>Applicant 1
(chop)
____
Legal representative
(chop)
________</td><td>Applicant 2
(chop)
____
Legal representative
(chop)
________</td><td>Applicant 3
(chop)
____
Legal representative
(chop)
________</td><td>Application date________</td></tr>
<tr><td colspan="4">Contact person of Applicant________ Telephone No. ____________ Fax No.______
Address______________ e-mail: _______________Mobile Phone No.___________</td></tr>
</table>

Table 6.6 Application form of special examination and approval in new drug registration

3. Evaluation of drug safety and efficacy, while considering the pharmacology study and toxicology study and clinical trials.
4. Summary of the pharmaceutical research that already completed.
5. Summary of other major research. The detailed research data or spectrum will not necessarily be included in this summary. Additional pages can be attached if needed but normally should be not more than 15 pages.

6. Risk control and implementation plan: Risk control plan mainly refers to precaution and prevention measures established against those potential risks during the clinical use of the new drug. Please work out specific risk control and implementation plan for clinical trial or post marketing, based on the situation and specific stages of drug development and in accordance with Regulations of Special Examination and Approval in New Drug Registration.
7. This Form should be submitted within the specified time frame specified by Regulations of Special Examination and Approval in New Drug Registration.
8. This form shall be in 4 copies with one original and three duplicates.

Appendix 2 (Table 6.7)

Note to the Form:

1. This form is prepared in accordance with Regulations of Special Examination and Approval in New Drug Registration.
2. TCM may not need a chemical name.
3. Registration Category should be identical to the Application Form of Registration Application.
4. Registration application meets any of those requirements: just to tick off "√" the applicable box 5. If the new drug registration is already permitted entering a special examination and approval, the Applicant should fill the special examination and approval no.
5. Method of communication: just to tick off "√" the applicable box "□" to indicate the desired method.
6. Study already completed: please choose "Before clinical trial application" or "After clinical trials starting" to indicate the development phase of the new drug, then tick off "√" the applicable box "□".
7. Issues to be communicated: can be multiple choices. Please choose according to Regulations of Special Examination and Approval in New Drug Registration. Application for communication other than those in the scope will not be accepted.
8. If the application for communication is submitted before application for clinical trials, the issue(s) for communication should be explained in section of "Issue(s) to be discussed and relevant data", with submission of medical summary and pharmaceutical summary data, along with detailed data and background data related to the issue(s) for communication.

INN name		Chemical Name	
Registration Category.		Indication(s)	
Registration application meets any of those requirement	□ Active ingredients extracted from plants, animals or minerals, etc. and their preparations not yet marketed in China, and newly discovered Chinese crude drugs and their preparations; □ Chemical drug substance and their preparations and biological products not yet approved for marketing in China or abroad; □ New drugs for the treatment of diseases such as AIDS, malignant tumors and rare diseases, etc. with significant clinical advantages; □ New drugs for the treatment of diseases, for which effective therapeutic method are not available.		
The special approval is applicable or not	□ Permitted □ not yet	Special examination and approval number	
Method of communication	□ round table □ video conference □ teleconference		
Study already completed	Before clinical trial application: □ pharmaceutical research □ pharmacodynamic research □ toxicology After clinical trial starting: □ Phase I □ Phase II □Phase III		
Issues to be communicated	□ application for a special examination and approval □ significant technical issues □ summary and evaluation on the staged results from clinical trials □ clinical trial protocol □ significant safety issues □ amending of the protocol □ change in indication □ change in specification □ others		
Issue to be discussed and relevant data			

Table 6.7 Application form to apply for communication of regulations of special examination and approval in new drug registration

Medical summary data: information that can support the drugs meet the Article 2 of Regulations of Special Examination and Approval in New Drug Registration summary and general evaluation of preclinical safety and efficacy, description of the diseases to which the application aimed (pathogenesis mechanisms, current methods of treatment, and overall evaluation on the therapeutic efficacy), proposed protocol of a clinical trial (including subject screening, proposed dose of exposure, and control drug, etc.), clinical trial plan, summary of clinical trial that already

To attach pages if needed					
Attendants applying for communication	Name	Company/Organization	Title	Specialized Field	Responsibility during research
Remarks					
Applicant (chop)_________________ Legal Representative (chop) ______________Application Date__________					
Contact Person_______ Telephone No. __________Fax No._____________ Address______________ e-mail: ______________Mobile Phone No. ________					

Table 6.7 (*Continued*)

completed, summary of previous clinical usage (if any), main preventive measures against any foreseeable risks from clinical use or clinical trial.

Pharmaceutical summary data: drug manufacturing process that already completed, quality specification or quality control procedures (including the description and justification of the test items related to safety), summary of stability studies.

9. If the application for communication is submitted after obtaining the permit entering a special examination and approval procedure, the issues to be communicated should be explained in the section of “Issue(s) to be discussed and relevant data”, and research data and summary data related to the discussion or communication should be provided as attachment to this form in addition to the original registration dossier.
10. This form should be submitted within the specified time frame as required by Regulations of Special Examination and Approval in New Drug Registration.
11. This form is in four copies with one original and three duplicates.

6.3 Application for Special Drug Categories

6.3.1 Rare disease/Orphan drug

In the US, orphan drug definition and application mechanism are well established. In the past 5 years, 39 orphan drugs were launched in the US across numerous therapeutic categories, e.g. chronic myelogenous leukemia, hemophilia, homozygous familial hypercholesterolemia, and cystic fibrosis (Biotech 2013).

In 2013 alone, nine orphan drugs were approved. The growing number of commercially available orphan drugs and the high cost of various orphan treatments have led to reconsideration of payer reimbursement policies. Comparatively, there is no official rare disease or orphan drug definition (Salako 2013) . no orphan drug application mechanism, and no biologic has been granted any clinical waiver at registration yet in China.

In Order No. 28, Article 32, regarding the sample size of a drug clinical trial, the minimum number of subjects and statistical requirement have to be met (SFDA 2007). Where for rare or special diseases, request for clinical sample size reduction or clinical trial exemption in the clinical trial application could be reviewed and approved by the SFDA.

In Article 45 and Special Examination and Approval in New Drug Registration Regulation (SFDA 2009), the statements indicate that the SFDA may implement special review and approval in cases of rare disease or orphan drug.

In the very recent years, the China National Congress has been lobbying for the establishment of few rare disease associations and patient groups. Since 2011, government has provided more research grant support. The healthcare policies are getting more and more favorable for the rare disease treatment. The SFDA also initiated orphan drug green channel projects initiated in 2012 (Gong and Jin 2012). Orphan drug is granted to apply for fast tract review, sample size reduction, and clinical trial waiver, even though there is still lack of detailed description.

6.3.2 Fast Track Mechanism Allows the Sponsors to Have the Following Advantages

1. The regulatory agency will involve earlier in the approval process and provision of stage-based guidance to enhance communication with sponsors. The review process could be more efficient due to the allowance of simultaneous reviews of IND applications and the ethical committee evaluation.
2. During the drug development process, submissions of supplementary materials are granted.
3. The review time is shortened with the adjusted regulatory technical requirements and standards.
4. The sponsor may incorporate risk-control strategies during the CMC review process

5. Even though the approval of a clinical trial waiver (CTW) is theoretically possible, the SFDA rarely grants CTW. It is more practical to apply for the reduction of clinical sample size. Currently, the average pharmaceutical company experience for the review timelines are 12–15 months for IND, 15–18 months for NDA, 10–12 months for Supplementary, 6–8 months for Sample Test (Registration), 3–4 months for Sample Test (Import drug).

6.4 Categories of Drug Licenses in China

There are mainly three different required drug licenses in China. It is different from the western world that after the NDA approval, you still need to acquire the corresponding license to eventually put your drug in the China market.

1. Manufacturing License: If your drug is manufactured in China, you need to apply for the manufacturing license. This license applies to the drug manufacturers located in China, including a. Wholly Foreign Owned Enterprise; b. Joint Venture and c. Domestic Drug pharmaceuticals. Manufacturing license is valid for 5 years and it should be renewed 6 months before its expiry. Marketing authorization is required before drug launch.
2. Import Drug License (IDL): IDL is the drug marketing permit issued by the CFDA. All the overseas pharmaceutical companies must obtain IDL for their products before being marketed in China according to the Drug Administration Law of People's Republic of China. All pharmaceuticals including API, and excipient, must be registered in China before being marketed in China. Only after being obtained IDL, the pharmaceutical companies are allowed to distribute their corresponding products in China. It should be noted that to obtain the import drug marketing authorization, one of the critical milestone is to successfully register your imported drugs. It is important to know that a. CTA/IND dossier approval is valid for 3 years; b. CPP (Certificate of a pharmaceutical product) from the original country is necessary; c. NDA approval and the license are valid for 5 years.
3. Drug Wholesale License: This license applies to the wholesalers located in China. Similar to the manufacturing license, the license is valid for 5 years and it should be renewed 6 months before its expiry.

Reference

Biotech (2013) Life sciences: capturing value Burrill & Company's 27th Annual Report on the Life Sciences Industry, p 45–52

Gong S, Jin S (2012) Current progress in the management of rare diseases and orphan drugs in China. Intractable Rare Dis Res 1(2):45–52

Salako Q (2013) Navigating the Chinese regulatory system for drugs for rare diseases. The 5th China clinical trial outsourcing congress, March 4–5, 2013.
SFDA (2005) Special review and approval procedure for drug registration of the State Food and Drug Administration. SFDA Decree No. 21; Effective on Nov. 18, 2005
SFDA (2007) Provisions for drug registration, No. 28. June 18, 2007. http://eng.sfda.gov.cn/WS03/CL0768/61647.html. Accessed 12 Dec 2013
SFDA (2009) Regulations of special examination and approval in new drug registration. Issued by SFDA on January 7, 2009. http://wenku.baidu.com/link?url=uxkOSjVhDzHri_ODNd5p-tqE8j4lBfDABoZLEPXiNrDxLFV3wRC58LDRvnNwBq9EvE1uGdSSmS8WNJSLu4Gog. Accessed 17 March 2013
SFDA (2013) 2012 China annual drug evaluation report, China Pharmaceutical Newsletter, Vol. IV

Chapter 7
Clinical Development of Investigational New Drug

Qinping Liao, Tao Lv, Yuan Qiao and Jianpeng Wang

7.1 Introduction

Clinical development in China is a complicated process, which needs integrated, logical, rigorous and critical thinking as well as a comprehensive planning. In addition to a though understanding of the regulations, it is also essential to know the local health care and current treatment standards, the pipelines under development, the market and unmet medical need information.

Prior to the initiation of the clinical development process, the following factors should be measured:

- Local standard health care and treatment of the target indication
- Unmet medical and market needs
- Local investigational drugs under development for the same indication
- Drugs with the same API under monitoring protective periods
- New drug application category/classification per the CFDA regulations
- Competitors' trials and trials compete with the same study population
- Clinical development and ethics requirements and timeline
- Availability of the positive control drug to be used in your trials
- The CFDA certified clinical sites and investigators in the therapeutic field
- Local CRO with good capability, reputation and experience
- Perceptions and expectations of target patient population toward clinical trials

Q. Liao (✉) · T. Lv
Division of Gynecology/Obstetrics and Pediatrics, Beijing Tsinghua Chang Gung Hospital, Changping Tiantongyuan, No. 168 Litang Road, Beijing 102218, P. R. China
e-mail: 13701124527@163.com

Y. Qiao
Neurophysiology and Orthopedics, School of Medicine, Shandong University, 44 Wenhua Xi Road, Ji'nan, Shandong 250012, P. R. China

J. Wang
Echocardiography, Cardiovascular Institute and Fuwai Hospital, Chinese Academy of Medical Sciences, Beijing 100037, P. R. China

M. Q. Lu (ed.), *Approaching China's Pharmaceutical Market*,
DOI 10.1007/978-3-319-15576-0_7

- Key opinion leaders and investigators in your therapeutic field
- Issues related to import of study medications and export of clinical samples
- Central versus local laboratory standards
- Numbers of clinical sites and Contingent plan for recruitment
- Patient medical insurance and reimbursement of adverse events

Prior to clinical trials, the sponsors have to accomplish the following preparations and fulfil the prerequisites for conducting a clinical trial,

Sufficient scientific basis must be provided for conducting clinical trials of drugs. The purpose of a clinical trial, the problems to be solved, must be considered before conducting a trial on subjects. The anticipated benefits and risks for the subjects and public health must be balanced. The anticipated benefits must exceed the possible harm. The selection of clinical trial methods must conform to scientific and ethical criteria.

The drugs to be used in a clinical trial shall be prepared and supplied by the sponsor. Before conducting a clinical trial, the sponsor must provide the pre-clinical study documents, including the formulation, manufacturing process and the quality inspection results of the drug. All pre-clinical study information supplied by the sponsor must conform to the requirements of the respective corresponding phase(s) of the clinical trial. The sponsor shall also provide the documents relating to the effectiveness and safety of the drug obtained from clinical trials already completed or being conducted in other places. GMP shall be conformed for manufacturing the investigational product (SFDA 2010b).

The equipment and conditions of the institution where the clinical trial will be conducted shall meet requirements for safety and efficacy. All investigators shall be qualified for undertaking the trial by their specialty and ability, and have received training. Before starting a clinical trial, a written agreement shall be reached between the investigator and the sponsor upon trial protocol, monitoring, auditing and standard operating procedures, as well as the responsibilities of each party in the trial.

7.2 Clinical Development Plan and Trial Protocols

7.2.1 Clinical Development Plan

The overall clinical development plan and trial protocols should be described in details in Booklet 29, Clinical trial and research programs, of the IND package, including the target indication, purpose of the study, dosage and administration etc. with supportive research data.

The clinical development plan and clinical trials should be scientifically sound and complete. A comprehensive summary and analysis of the non-clinical and clinical data associated with the potential risks and benefits should be provided.

7.2.2 Clinical Trial Protocols

The clinical trial protocol should be prepared and finalized before starting a clinical trial. The protocol shall be jointly discussed and signed by the principal investigator and sponsor, then submitted to the EC for approval before implementation.

The protocol design should meet the requirement of the CFDA based on its drug category, classification and phases. The standard CTD format is acceptable and the content of the protocol for a clinical trial shall contain the following essential sections:

1. The title of the clinical trial.
2. The purpose(s) and objective(s) of the trial, the background for the trial, findings regarding the investigational product before the clinical trial that are of clinical significance; results of other clinical trials related to the proposed trial, the possible risks and benefits for subjects known to date, and the possible ethnic difference of the investigational product.
3. Name and address of the sponsor; the place where the clinical trial will be conducted; name, qualification and address of the principal investigator.
4. The type of the design of the clinical trial, the random selection method, and the level of the blinding.
5. The inclusion and exclusion criteria, removal of subjects, the procedures for subject inclusion, the method of grouping subjects.
6. The sample size needed statistically to accomplish the purposes of the trial.
7. Form, dosage, route of administration, method and frequency of administration, period of treatment, order of usage of concomitant medicines, and explanation for package and label.
8. Clinical and laboratory check to be conducted, testing frequency and analysis of pharmacokinetics.
9. The registration, usage record, delivery, handing and storage conditions of the investigational products.
10. Clinical observation, onsite visit and measures to ensure the subjects compliance of trial procedures.
11. Rules regarding termination of the clinical trial and rules for the completion of the clinical trial.
12. The standards for evaluating therapeutic efficacy, including the method for evaluating parameters, time of observation, recording and analysis.
13. Procedures to maintain the coding of subject, table of random numbers and case report form.
14. Requirements for the recording of adverse events and methods for serious adverse event reporting, treatment, follow-up and recovery.
15. Establishment and maintenance of trial codes, methods to break the blind and rules concerning how codes may be accessed in emergency situations.
16. The plan of the statistical analysis, the definition and selection for the data package of the statistical analysis.
17. Rules for data administration and data traced to the source.

18. Quality control and quality assurance of clinical trial.
19. Ethics related to trial.
20. Tentative schedule and completion date of clinical trial.
21. Onsite visit and medical treatment after the clinical trial is completed.
22. Each party's responsibility and other relevant stipulations.
23. Literature.

During the trial, the protocol may be modified according to its procedures, if it is deemed necessary.

7.2.3 General Requirements for Clinical Phases

Any drug clinical trial, including bioequivalence study, shall be approved by the CFDA, and shall be in compliance with the Good Clinical Practice.

Drug regulatory department shall supervise and inspect the approved clinical trials.

Clinical trials shall be conducted for new drug registration applications. As for generic drug registration applications and supplementary applications, clinical trials shall be conducted in accordance with the requirements in the Annex of the Provisions.

Clinical trials consist of phases 1, 2, 3, and 4. New drug application for market approval should accomplish phase 1, 2 and 3 clinical trials. Before market approval, some new drug may get the execution to conduct phase 2 and 3 clinical trials, or only conduct phase 3 trial. Generic drugs and supplementary drug application should follow "Provisions for Drug Registration (SFDA Order No. 28)" to conduct their clinical trials.

A. Phase 1 Clinical Trials

Phase 1 clinical trials are the initial clinical pharmacology and safety evaluation studies in humans. These studies are designed to observe tolerability of humans to and pharmacokinetics of a new drug, to provide basis for establishing the administration regimen.

Phase I trials are the first stage of testing in human. Based on the CFDA regulation, a minimum of 20–30 healthy volunteers in the testing group should be recruited. Occasionally, real patients may be used, such as patients who have terminal cancer or HIV and the treatment is likely to make healthy individuals ill. For new drug development, phase 1 is aimed to assess the safety, tolerability, pharmacokinetics, and pharmacodynamics of a drug. These trials are usually conducted in clinical phase 1 units, where the subject can be observed by full-time staff. Phase 1 clinical trials are run in the CFDA certified units in 3A hospitals or contract research organization (CROs) research units. The CROs conduct these studies on behalf of pharmaceutical companies. Phase I trials normally include dose-ranging studies. Healthy volunteers are paid an fee for their time spent in the volunteer center.

Phase 1 trials may include single ascending dose and multiple ascending dose studies. In these studies, blood or other fluid samples of the subjects are collected at various time points and analyzed to acquire information on how the drug is processed within the body. Food effect study is a short trial designed to investigate any differences in absorption of the drug by the body, caused by eating before the drug is given. These studies are usually run as a crossover study, with volunteers being given two identical doses of the drug while fasted, and after being fed. For the new drug application from overseas companies, pharmacokinetic comparison among ethnic groups is needed. In addition, pharmacokinetic research in special population or drug interaction studies should be considered.

B. Phase 2 Clinical Trials

The purposes are to preliminarily evaluate the therapeutic effectiveness and safety of the drug for particular indication(s) in patients, and provide evidence for design of Phase 3 clinical trials and settlement of administrative dose regimen. According to specific trial objectives, phase 3 trials may be designed in various forms, including the randomized blind controlled clinical trials.

The goals of phase 2 are to evaluate whether the drug has any biological activity or effect, and how well the drug works and [1] Phase II trials are performed as well as how safe the drug is in a larger group of volunteers and patients. The minimum sample size of patients should be above 100 cases.

Phase 2 clinical trials are divided into two stages. The first stage is dose exploratory stage. In this stage, it should be started with the minimum dose, and gradually increase the dose with small sample size in each group. After the confirmation of the safe and effective dose range, the second stage could be initiated. In the second stage, the study should adopt the randomized, double blinded, placebo or positive drug controlled design. Through the clinical trials, the preliminary effectiveness and adverse reactions of the investigational drug should be determined.

A randomized controlled trial is the gold standard for a clinical trial. Randomized controlled trials are often used to test the efficacy of various types of medical intervention within a patient population and may also provide an opportunity to gather useful information about drug adverse reactions.

The key feature of the randomized controlled trial is that study subjects are randomly allocated to receive one or other of the alternative treatments under study. The most important advantage of proper randomization is that it minimizes allocation bias, balancing both known and unknown prognostic factors, in the assignment of treatments.

A randomized controlled trial may be blinded by "procedures that prevent study participants, investigators or outcome assessors from knowing which intervention was received". Blinded randomized controlled trials are usually classified as "single-blind", "double-blind" or "triple-blind".

Randomized controlled trials without blinding are referred to as open-label. Such open-label trials tend to be biased toward beneficial effects only if the randomized controlled trial outcomes were subjective as opposed to objective;

Control is a method used to compare the effects of treatment efficacy and safety. Most of the clinical trials select a control group, e.g. placebo or positive drug control. Placebo-control is usually limited to that the target indication has no effective drug treatment or the target indication is mild that could recover without treatment. Most of the clinical trials select positive drug as their control.

Placebo-controlled trials are designed to have no real effect. Placebos are most commonly used in blinded trials, where subjects do not know if they are receiving real or placebo treatment. The purpose of the placebo group is to account for the placebo effect, that is, effects from treatment that do not depend on the treatment itself. Without a placebo group to compare against, it is not possible to know whether the treatment itself had any effect.

Positive controls are groups where a phenomenon is expected, i.e., they ensure that there is an effect when there should be an effect, by using an experimental treatment that is already known to produce that effect.

C Phase 3 Clinical Trials

Phase 3 clinical trials are confirmation of therapeutic effectiveness of a drug. The purposes are to further verify drug therapeutic effectiveness and safety on eligible patients with target indication(s), to evaluate overall benefit-risk relationships of the drug, and to ultimately provide sufficient evidence for the review of drug registration application. The study, in general, shall be a randomized blind controlled trial with an adequate sample size with a minimum clinical sample size no less than 300 cases.

D. Phase 4 Clinical Trials

Phase 4 clinical trials are new drug post-marketing studies. The purposes are to assess therapeutic effectiveness and adverse reactions when a drug is widely used, to evaluate overall benefit-risk relationships of the drug when used among general population or specific groups, and to adjust the administration dose, etc. The minimum phase 4 sample size is 2000 cases.

E. Bioequivalence Study Bioequivalence study refers to a human study, which applies bioavailability study methods with pharmacokinetic parameters as indicators to compare active ingredient absorption rate and extent of the preparations in the same or different dosage forms of a drug in terms of statistical differences under the same experimental condition.

To determine bioequivalence, between a commercially-available brand product and a potential to-be-marketed generic product, pharmacokinetic studies are needed in a cross-over study in healthy volunteers, but occasionally in patients. Serum/plasma samples are obtained at regular intervals and assayed for parent drug (or occasionally metabolite) concentration. For comparison, the plasma concentration data are usually used to assess key pharmacokinetic parameters including area under the curve (AUC), peak concentration (C_{max}), time to peak concentration (T_{max}), and absorption lag time (t_{lag}). Testing should be conducted at several different doses, especially when the drug displays non-linear pharmacokinetics.

In the case that blood concentration levels are neither feasible nor possible to compare the two products (e.g. inhaled corticosteroids), then pharmacodynamic endpoints, e.g. comprehensive clinical efficacy or in vitro tests, should be used for comparison. In addition to data from bioequivalence studies, other data may need to be submitted to meet regulatory requirements for bioequivalence, including (a) analytical method validation; (b) *in vitro-in vivo* correlation studies

For Category 5 new drugs, i.e. drug preparation with changed dose form, but no change of administration route, and the original preparation already approved in China, bioequivalence trials should be conducted for oral solid preparations on normally 18–24 cases. When a bioequivalence trial is difficult to be conducted for oral solid preparations or other non- oral solid preparations, clinical trials should be conducted, and cases for the clinical trials should be at least 100 pairs.

Similar to the western standards, two products are considered bioequivalent if the 90% CI of the relative mean Cmax, AUC (0-t) and AUC (0-∞) of the test (e.g. generic formulation) to reference (e.g. innovator brand formulation) are within 80–125%.

7.2.4 Clinical Requirements Related to New Drug Categories and Classifications

7.2.4.1 Clinical Study Requirements for Chemical Drugs

a. **Clinical Study Requirements for Chemical Drugs Manufactured in China** (SFDA 2007a)

    1. For the new drugs under Registration Category 1 and 2, clinical trials should be conducted.

        - Cases of patients for clinical trials should meet the statistical requirement and the minimal cases required.
        - The minimal cases required (trial group) of clinical trials are as following, 20–30 for Phase I, 100 for Phase II, 300 for Phase III, 2000 for Phase IV,
        - Phase 1 clinical trial of the contraceptives should be conducted following this Regulation. In Phase 2 clinical trial, a randomized controlled clinical study should be conducted on at least 100 pairs of subjects for at least 6 menstruation cycles. In Phase 3 trial, an open trial on at least 1000 cases for 12 menstruation cycles should be accomplished. In Phase IV trial, variable factors of such kind of drugs should be carefully considered to finish the trial with adequate numbers of cases.

    2. For the new drugs under the Registration Categories 3 and 4, human pharmacokinetic study and randomized controlled clinical trials on at least 100 pairs of subjects should be conducted. In the event of more than one indication, cases for each main indication shall not be less than 60 pairs. Human

pharmacokinetics study and an open trial on at least 500 cases for 12 menstruation cycles should be accomplished for contraceptives.
Human pharmacokinetics study may be exempted for the following two cases:

- Preparation of topical use with only topical treatment effect.
- Oral preparation that not be absorbed.

3. The clinical study for the new drug under Registration Category 5 should be conducted in accordance with the following principles,

   - Bioequivalence trials should be conducted for oral solid preparations on normally 18–24 cases.
   - When a bioequivalence trial is difficult to be conducted for oral solid preparations or other non- oral solid preparations, clinical trails should be conducted, and cases for the clinical trials should be at least 100 pairs.
   - For the preparations of sustained and controlled released preparations, controlled human pharmacokinetic study and clinical trials related to therapeutics should be conducted on single dose and repeated doses of the drugs, and the cases for clinical trials should be at least 100 pairs.
   - Necessary clinical trials should be conducted for injection. When clinical trials are needed, clinical case should be at least 100 pairs for single active component injection, and at least 300 pairs for multiple component injection. For microcapsule, Microemulsions and liposome, clinical trials should be conducted according to requirement for category 1 and 2.

4. For the oral solid preparations under the Registration Category 6, bioequivalence tests should be conducted on normally 18–24 cases. If the quality of drug needs to be controlled by process and standards, clinical tests should be conducted on normally 100 cases.
5. Application for reduction or exemption of clinical trial should be made during the application of drug registration with detail of reasons and information for reduction or exemption of clinical trials. If a clinical trial is already approved, with exception of the case where reduction or exemption of clinical trial is allowed by this Regulation, reduction or exemption of clinical trial generally should not be allowed. If there is indeed difficulty to complete the clinical trial, application should be made with detail of the basis and plan for reduction or exemption of clinical trial, where the rational should be justified in term of clinical statistic, status of group of patients in the clinical trials.
6. The comparative drug used for the controlled clinical trails shall be already marketed in China. If the comparative drug must be imported, there need to be approval from the SFDA. Priority in choosing the comparative drug of positive clinical test should according to the following:

   - Drug from the original innovative manufacturer
   - The same drug of definite clinical test data

- Drug of the same active substance and route of administration but different dosage form
- Other drug of similar mechanism of action effect and the same indication.

b. **Clinical Study Requirements for Import Chemical Drugs** (SFDA 2007b)

1. During application of drug never marketed in any country, clinical trials should be conducted according to CT study requirement of Registration Category 1.
2. During application of drug that marketed ex-China but not in China, clinical trials should be conducted according to CT study requirement of Registration Category 3.
3. During application of drug with same route of administration but different dosage form of that of the drug marketed in China, if information item 28 of the application meet the requirement, clinical trials should be conducted according to CT study requirement of Registration Category 5. If information item 28 of the application did not meet the requirement, clinical trials should be conducted according to CT study requirement of Registration Category 3.
4. During application of drug already with National Standards, if information item 28 of the application meet the requirement, clinical trials should be conducted according to CT study requirement of Registration Category 6. If information item 28 of the application did not meet the requirement, clinical trials should be conducted according to CT study requirement of Registration Category 3. No clinical trial is needed for application of drug substance already with National Standards.
5. For the application only for the importation of the drug substance without available National Drug Standards in China, the clinical study shall be conducted with the use of the preparations of the drug substance.

7.2.4.2 Clinical Study Requirements for Therapeutic Biological Products

a. **Clinical Study Requirements for Therapeutic Biological Products Manufactured in China**

1. A clinical trials should be conducted for the application of new drug.
2. Cases of patients for a clinical trial should meet the statistical requirement and minimal cases requirement.
3. The minimal cases requirement for a clinical trial is, Phase I: 20, Phase II: 100, Phase III: 300 (SFDA 2011a,b).
4. Clinical trials for the products under Registration Categories 1–12 should be conducted in accordance with requirement for new drugs.
5. Only Phase III clinical trials are usually required for the products under Registration Categories 13–15.
6. For the renovated sustained released preparation, comparisons study of human pharmacokinetic study and clinical trials shall be conducted.

b. **Clinical Study Requirements for Import Therapeutic Biological Products** (SFDA 2007c)

1. A clinical study should be applied for in accordance with Registration Category 1 for the application of the biological products not yet marketed at domestic or overseas.
2. A clinical study should be applied for in accordance with Registration Category 3 for the application of the biological products already marketed overseas but not yet marketed domestic.
3. A clinical study should be applied for in accordance with Registration Category 15 for the application of the biological products admitted with National Standards.

7.2.4.3 Clinical Study Requirements for Preventive Biological Products.

a. **Clinical Study Requirements for Preventive Biological Products Manufactured in China** (SFDA 2007c)

1. Cases of patients (subjects) for the clinical trials should meet the statistical requirement and minimal cases requirement. Minimal cases include both trial group and control group.
2. The minimal case requirement for a clinical trial is, Phase I: 20, Phase II: 300, Phase III: 500.
3. For vaccine under Registration Categories 1–9 and 14, the clinical trials should be conducted in accordance with the requirement for new drugs.
4. For vaccine under Registration Category 10, if the research information is provided to evidence no change in the safety and effectiveness of the vaccine after the deactivation or de-toxicity of the vaccine, then normally clinical trials may be exempted.
5. For vaccine under Registration Category 11, a clinical trial normally should be conducted in accordance with requirement for new drugs. But the Phase I clinical trials may be exempted for the vaccine with the route of administration changed from injections into non-injections.
6. Only the phase III clinical trial is needed for the vaccine under Registration Categories 12 and 15.
7. For the vaccine under Registration Category 13, the Phase I clinical trials may be exempted for the vaccine where the immunity procedure is changed.
8. For the preventive products used in infants, in principle, the sequence of Phase I clinical trials should be adults first, then children and then infants.
9. Each phase of clinical trial should be conducted after the completion of previous phase in accordance with the prescribed immunity procedures.
10. For the vaccine applied for marketing first time in China, Epidemiology Protective Test should be conducted,

b. **Clinical Study Requirements for Import Preventive Biological Products**

1. A clinical study should be applied for in accordance with Registration Category 1 for the application of the vaccine not yet marketed at domestic or overseas.
2. A clinical study should be applied for in accordance with Registration Category 6 for the application of the vaccine already marketed overseas but not yet marketed at domestic.
3. A clinical study should be applied for in accordance with Registration Category 15 for the application of the vaccine admitted with National Standards

7.3 Responsibilities of the Related Parties

7.3.1 The Sponsor's Responsibilities

The following responsibilities are defined by Chinese regulatory authority (SFDA order No. 3):

- The sponsor is responsible for initiating, applying for, organizing, monitoring, auditing a clinical trial and provides for the expenses of the trial. The sponsor shall submit the application for a clinical trial to the CFDA in accordance with relevant provisions in China's laws, rules and regulations. The sponsor can authorize its contract research organization (CRO) to carry out certain work and obligations regarding the clinical trial.
- The sponsor shall select the institution and investigator for a clinical trial and confirm their qualifications and conditions to ensure the completion of the trial.
- The sponsor shall provide the investigator's brochure, containing the chemical, pharmaceutical, toxicological, pharmacological and clinical (including trials already being done or in process) information and data of the investigational product.
- Upon obtaining approval from the CFDA and agreement by the EC, the sponsor shall start to organize the clinical trial in accordance with the protocol.
- The sponsor and the investigator shall jointly design the clinical trial protocol, stipulate the agreed responsibilities of each party in protocol implementation, data management, statistical analysis, results reporting, thesis publishing, etc. The protocol and contract shall be signed by both the sponsor and the investigator.
- The sponsor shall provide the investigator with the investigational product, reference product, comparator or placebo. These products shall be easy to recognize, correctly coded and marked with special labels. The sponsor must also ensure the quality of these products. The investigational products shall be properly packed and kept in accordance with the protocol. The sponsor shall establish a management and filing system for the investigational products.
- The sponsor shall appoint a qualified monitor, who must also be agreed to by the investigator.

- The sponsor is responsible for the establishment of quality control and quality assurance systems for the clinical trial. The sponsor may organize an audit group for the clinical trial to ensure the quality.
- The sponsor and the investigator shall study the SAEs immediately after occurrence and take necessary measures to ensure the subject's safety and interests. Adverse events shall be reported to drug administration authorities, health administrative authorities and the other investigators conducting clinical trials on the same drug.
- If the sponsor terminates a clinical trial, it must immediately inform the investigator, the EC and the CFDA and explain the reason.
- The sponsor shall submit the final report of the clinical trial to the CFDA.
- The sponsor shall provide the subject with insurance for harm or death occurring during or caused by the clinical trial, which covers the expenses of the treatment and the economic compensation, and provides the investigator with a legal and economic guarantee, but not including harm and death from medical treatment accidents.
- If the investigator does not conduct the clinical trial in accordance with the approved protocol, or relevant rules and regulations, the sponsor must identify such and ask for correction. If the situation is serious or the investigator does not correct, the sponsor shall terminate his participation in the clinical trial and report to the SFDA.

In addition to the above responsibilities defined by Chinese regulatory authority, the sponsors should also follow the ICH requirements including:

- The sponsor is responsible for implementing and maintaining quality assurance and quality control systems with written SOPs to ensure that trials are conducted and data are generated, documented (recorded), and reported in compliance with the protocol, GCP, and the applicable regulatory requirement(s).
- The sponsor is responsible for securing agreement from all involved parties to ensure direct access (see 1.21) to all trial related sites, source data/documents, and reports for the purpose of monitoring and auditing by the sponsor, and inspection by domestic and foreign regulatory authorities.
- Quality control should be applied to each stage of data handling to ensure that all data are reliable and have been processed correctly.
- Agreements, made by the sponsor with the investigator/institution and any other parties involved with the clinical trial, should be in writing, as part of the protocol or in a separate agreement.

7.3.2 The Investigator's Responsibilities

To be a clinical investigator for the clinical trial in China, it is very different from the western world. Based on the Chinese regulation, the investigators have the following responsibilities when conducting clinical trials:

- The investigator responsible for the clinical trial shall:
  - be qualified in a specialized technical position and as a doctor in a medical institution; has the relevant specialized knowledge and experience required in the protocol;
  - have experience in clinical trial research methods or be able to obtain professional assistance from experienced investigator(s) in his/her institution;
  - be familiar with the relevant information and literature provided by the sponsor of the clinical trial;
  - have authorization to allocate the needed staff and facilities for the clinical trial.
- The investigator shall read and understand the details of the protocol, and conduct the trial strictly according to the protocol.
- The investigator shall understand and be familiar with the properties, functions, effects and safety of the drug to be used (including pre-clinical study documents). He shall know well all new information about the product which information is discovered during the clinical trial.
- The investigator shall conduct the clinical trial in a medical institution with good medical treatment facilities, laboratory equipment and personnel. The institution shall have all necessary facilities to handle emergency situations to ensure the safety of subjects. The result of laboratory evaluations must be correct and reliable.
- The investigator must obtain approval from his hospital or governing unit to ensure that he has enough time to undertake and complete the clinical trial within the period stipulated in the protocol. The investigator shall explain the information, regulations and responsibility about the trial to all personnel participating in the clinical trial, and ensure a sufficient number of qualified subjects in the clinical trial.
- The investigator shall explain in detail to the subjects about the trial as approved by the EC and obtain the informed consent.
- The investigator is responsible for making medical treatment decisions about the clinical trial, and shall ensure that the subjects receive proper treatment when adverse event occurs during the trial.
- The investigator has an obligation to adopt and make a record of necessary measures to protect the safety of the subjects. If a serious adverse event occurs during a clinical trial, the investigator shall immediately provide appropriate medical treatment to the subject and report to drug administration authorities, the sponsor and the EC. The investigator shall sign and date this report.
- The investigator shall ensure that the data is duly written down on the case report form in a correct, complete and legal manner.
- The investigator shall receive monitors and auditors sent by the sponsor for such purposes and auditing and inspection by drug administration authorities in order to ensure the quality of the clinical trial.
- The investigator and sponsors shall negotiate and provide for the expenses of the clinical trial in a written contract. The investigator may not charge the subjects the investigational products expenses during the clinical trial.

- After the clinical trial is completed, the investigator must prepare the final report with his signature and date, then forward it to the sponsor.
- For a clinical trial which is terminated, the investigator must inform the subjects, the sponsor, the EC (EC) and State Drug Administration and explain the reason.

7.3.3 Protection of a Subject's Interests and Ethics Committee (EC, SFDA 2010a)

In a clinical trial, the subject's interests must be fully protected and the trial shall be scientific and reliable. The subject's interests, safety and health are the top priority. The use of an EC and informed consent form are important methods to protect the subject.

To protect the interests of subjects, an independent EC shall be formed and such information filed with the CFDA. The EC shall consist of at least five members with diverse background.

The protocol of the trial must be reviewed and approved by the EC. Any amendment of the protocol may not be implemented without approval from the EC. Any SAEs that occur during the trial shall be reported to the EC.

The decisions regarding review and approval of the protocol by the EC shall be decided through discussion and voting. Ethnics Committee members shall avoid participating in the clinical trial. Experts who are not members of the committee may be invited to attend the meeting when necessary, but may not vote. The EC shall establish its working procedures. Written records for all meetings and the resolutions adopted during meetings shall be kept for 5 years after the completion of a clinical trial.

The EC shall strictly examine the following aspects of the protocol in order to protect the interests of subjects:

- the qualifications and experience of investigators and whether they will have enough time to participate in the clinical trial, and whether the staff and equipment conform with the requirements of the trial;
- whether the ethical principles are fully considered in the protocol, including the purpose of the investigation, the anticipated risks and benefits to the subject and other people, and whether the trial is scientifically designed;
- whether the method of subject admission and the information about the trial provided to the subject, or their families or legal guardians or legal representatives, is complete and easy to understand, and whether the method used to obtain informed consent form is proper;
- the treatment or insurance provided to a subject who is harmed or even dies due to his participation in the clinical trial.
- whether the recommendations to modify the protocol are acceptable; and,
- periodic examination of the degree of risks to subjects participating in the trial.

After receiving the application, the EC shall hold a meeting as soon as possible to review and discuss it. The recommendation shall be issued in writing, including listing the attendance of committee members, their specialties and their signatures. The recommendation may:

- approve;
- approve after necessary modifications;
- disapprove;
- terminate or suspend an already approved trial;
- The investigator or its designated representative must explain to the subject the following clinical trial matters in detail:
- Participation by the subject is voluntary. The subject has the right to withdraw from the trial at any time during any phase and shall not be subject to discrimination or retaliation. The subject's medical treatment and interests shall not be affected.
- The subject shall be informed that his participation and personal trial data are confidential. The EC, drug administration authorities and the sponsor, when necessary, may check the subject's data according to regulations.
- The subject shall be informed of the purpose of the trial, the procedures and duration of the trial, examination and operational procedures, the predicted possible benefits and risks that the subject may suffer, and different groups in the trial in which the subject may be placed.
- Enough time must be given to the subject to consider whether to participate in the trial or not. For a subject who is unable to express his approval, his legal representative shall be informed of the above introduction and explanations. The explanation regarding the process of obtaining informed consent shall be made to the subject or his legal representative orally or, in a written language he can understand. During the trial, a subject has the right to know the trial information concerning himself or herself at any time.
- If any harm results because of the trial, the subject may receive medical treatment and appropriate insurance compensation.

The signature on the informed consent form shall be obtained only after the clinical trial has been explained in detail.

- The subject or his legal representative as well as the investigator responsible for the informed consent process shall sign and date the informed consent form.
- A subject who is incompetent may participate in a trial on the condition that the EC approves such participation in principle and the investigator considers that the trial will be beneficial for the subject. The informed consent form must be signed and dated by the legal guardian of the subject.
- If the subject is a child, the informed consent form must be signed by the legal guardian of the child. If the child can decide whether he is willing to participate, the informed consent form shall also be approved by the child.
- If in emergency, the informed consent form has not been obtained from the subject or legal representative, if an effective treatment is lacking but the investigational product could save life, recover health, or alleviate pain, the clinical trial may be conducted. However, the method used on the subject shall be explained clearly in the protocol of the trial as well as the relevant file, and approved by the EC in advance.
- If new information regarding the drug used in the trial is discovered, a written amendment of the informed consent form must be submitted to the EC for approval, after which the subject agreement must be obtained.

7.3.4 CRO's Responsibilities

- A sponsor may transfer any or all of the sponsor's trial-related duties and functions to a CRO, but the ultimate responsibility for the quality and integrity of the trial data always resides with the sponsor. The CRO should implement quality assurance and quality control.
- Any trial-related duty and function that is transferred to and assumed by a CRO should be specified in writing.
- Any trial-related duties and functions not specifically transferred to and assumed by a CRO are retained by the sponsor.
- All references to a sponsor in the CFDA guideline also apply to a CRO to the extent that a CRO has assumed the trial related duties and functions of a sponsor.
- In addition to the aforementioned responsibilities, global companies should carefully consider the following capabilities during the CRO selection process:
- An ideal CRO can efficiently target appropriate investigators and certified clinical sites (hospital/medical center) to participate in the trials
- An idea CRO should have strong local capabilities and possess all the functional staff including clinical operation, pharmacovigilance, drug handling, data management, statistics etc. the CFDA registration and regulatory knowledge are especially valuable.
- An idea CRO should also have the global and especially the regional countries registration and clinical trial experience with good credential and experience in the target therapeutic field.
- An accountable and reputable multinational or established local CRO with hands-on in-country experience and strong operating practices is the base to ensure the timeline and quality execution of the clinical trial.
- A qualified CRO should possess established SOPs for the overall clinical development process with rigorous training, monitoring, and auditing experience for investigators and site staff to ensure compliance with GCP, ethics and quality requirements.
- A capable CRO should have good communication skill, overall and contingency planning capabilities to meet various clinical trial challenges and unpredicted situations.

7.3.5 The Monitor's Responsibilities

The monitor's responsibility is to protect the subject's rights and interests in the clinical trial, ensure the record and data of the trial are correct and complete, make certain that the trial is conducted according to the approved protocol, and relevant rules and regulations.

The monitor is the major intermediary between the sponsor and the investigator. The number of monitors depends on the complexity of the clinical trial and the number of medical institutions participating in the trial. The monitor shall be qualified in medicine, pharmacy or relevant specialties and properly trained for the trial.

He/she shall be familiar with the relevant drug administration rules and regulations, familiar with the pre-clinical information of investigational product, information concerning the clinical trial, the protocol of the trial and relevant documents.

The monitor shall supervise and urge that the clinical trial be conducted according to the standard operating procedures (SOP), in order that the clinical trial comply with the protocol, including:

- Before the trial starts, confirm that the institution undertaking the trial already meets the appropriate requirements, including recruitment and training of the staff, the equipment of the laboratory is completed, the working conditions are good, all checks related to the trial have been made, estimate whether the number of subjects is adequate, study and become familiar with the requirements stipulated in the protocol together with the investigator.
- Monitor the institution and investigator undertaking the trial before, during and after the trial. Confirm that the informed consent form is obtained from all subjects before the trial. Learn of the recruitment rate of the subjects and the progress of the trial. Confirm that the records and report of all data are correct and complete.
- Confirm that all case reports are correctly filled out and in compliance with the source documents. Make certain that all errors or omission have been rectified or marked with the investigator's signature and date. The change of dosage, alternative treatment, concomitant medicine, intercurrent diseases, missed monitoring and checking of every subject shall be confirmed and written down. The verification of the selected subject's withdrawal and missed monitoring shall be stated in the case report form.
- Confirm that all adverse events have been recorded and SAEs have been reported within the required time period and filed.
- Verify whether the investigational product is supplied, stored, distributed and returned in accordance with relevant regulations, and correspondingly recorded.
- Assist the investigator in providing necessary notices and applications, and report the data and results of the trial to the sponsor.
- Should record clearly and exactly failures by the investigator during an on-site visit, trial, examination, and whether errors, omissions have been rectified.
- After every visit, a written report shall be submitted to the sponsor with the date of monitoring, time, monitor's name, the findings of the monitoring.

7.4 Clinical Trial Management and Quality Assurance

7.4.1 Records and Reports

The case report form shall be kept completely as original material of the clinical trial. The data of the case report form is from the original material and in compliance with the original material. All observations and results of the trial shall be recorded on the case report immediately, accurately, completely, standardized, truthfully, and be written in the case report form correctly. The case report and case report form may not be changed. In making any modification due to the written mistake, the original record shall be kept easy to recognize and the modification shall be signed and dated by the investigator.

The laboratory data of the clinical trial shall be recorded or the copy of the original report shall be pasted onto the case report form. Data within normal ranges must also be recorded. For data that noticeably deviates or data beyond the acceptable range, the investigator must verify it. Each type of test must clearly state the units of measurement.

The subject names should not be on the case report form in order to protect the subject privacy. The investigator should identify the subject in accordance with his code and keep record.

The final report of the clinical trial shall conform to the protocol and contain the following:

- The actual number of subjects/cases that randomly participated in each treatment group, and subject dropouts or removed during the trial and the reason.
- Compare the baseline characteristics among different medical treatment groups in order to determine their comparability.
- Conduct statistical and clinical analysis for all the indexes of the therapeutic effects evaluation. The explanation of statistical results shall focus on the significance of the clinical trial.
- The reasonable statistical analysis for adverse events and the laboratory indexes shall be included in the safety evaluation. The adverse events shall be described and evaluated in detail.
- In assessing therapeutic effects in a multicenter trial, the differences and their effects among each center must be taken into account.
- Relationship between the therapeutic effects and safety as well as risks and benefits for the investigational products shall be briefly summarized and discussed.

All data of the clinical trial shall be kept and managed in accordance with regulations (Appendix 2). The investigator shall keep the documents of the clinical trial for 5 years after the completion of the trial. The sponsor shall keep the clinical trial data for 5 years after the investigational product has been approved for marketing.

7.4.2 *Administration of Investigational Product*

Investigational product for a clinical trial may not be sold.

The sponsor is responsible for properly packing and labeling the investigational product and marking that the drug is specially to be used in a clinical trial. In a double blind clinical trial, the drug to be investigated and comparator or placebo shall be uniform in shape, smell, packaging, labeling and other features.

The use record of the investigational product shall include the information of quantity, loading, shipment, receipt, dispensing/handling, and the reclaim and destruction of unused drug.

The investigator is responsible for the administration of the investigational product. He must make certain all investigational products are only administered to the subjects of the clinical trial, and the dosage and method of use conform to the protocol. The surplus products shall be returned to the sponsor. The above procedures shall be handled and recorded by a specified individual. The investigational product should be managed by a specified individual. The investigator may not transfer the investigational product to any non-participant in the clinical trial.

The supply, usage, storage, return of unused investigational product should accept checking from relevant person.

7.4.3 Quality Assurance

The sponsor and investigator shall fulfill respective duty, comply with protocol strictly and adopt Standard Operating Procedure (SOP) to ensure the implementation of the quality control and quality assurance system of the clinical trial.

To assure the completeness, accurateness, truthfulness and reliableness of data, all observation results and findings in the clinical trial must be verified and each phase for data processing must involve quality assurance.

Drug administration authorities and the sponsor may authorize an auditor to execute systematic checks for operation and document file of clinical trial in order to evaluate whether the trial is conducted in compliance with the protocol, SOP and relevant regulations, whether the data is recorded timely, factually, accurately and completely. The audit shall be conducted by personnel not directly involved in the clinical trial.

Drug administration authorities shall inspect the investigator and sponsor regarding their respective tasks and implementation of such tasks in the trial. All medical institutions participating in the clinical trial and all documents and files (including medical records) shall accept inspection from drug administration authorities.

7.4.4 Record Keeping for a Clinical Trial

Good Clinical Practice (GCP) of Pharmaceutical Products [SFDA order No. 3] has been becoming effective since September 1, 2003. This GCP is promulgated in accordance with the Drug Administration Law of PRC and Implementing Regulation of Drug Administration Law of PRC, making reference to internationally recognized principles to ensure the standardization of clinical trials of drugs which will result in scientific reliability, and the protection of the interests and safety of the subject.

This GCP is required and will be observed in all phases of a clinical trial, the bioavailability trial or biological equivalence trial on the body and in the whole process of a clinical trial, including protocol design, organizing implementation, monitoring, auditing, recording, analysis, summarization and reporting.

The following record keeping for a clinical trial is required (Tables 7.1, 7.2, and 7.3):

Table 7.1 For preparation phase of the clinical trial

Documents to be kept		Investigator	Sponsor
1	Investigator's brochure	Keep	Keep
2	Protocol and its amendment (signed)	Keep original	Keep
3	Case report form (sample form)	Keep	Keep
4	Informed consent form	Keep original	Keep
5	Financial rules	Keep	Keep
6	Multi-party agreement (signed) (Investigator, sponsor, contract research organization)	Keep	Keep
7	Written approval from EC	Keep original	Keep
8	List of EC members	Keep original	Keep
9	Application for the clinical trial		Keep original
10	Laboratory information prior to the clinical trial		Keep original
11	Written approval from State Food and Drug Administration		Keep original
12	Investigator's resume and relevant documents	Keep	Keep original
13	Normal value range of laboratory testing related to clinical trial	Keep	Keep
14	Quality control certificate for medical or laboratory operation	Keep original	Keep
15	Label of drug to be investigated		Keep original
16	Shipping order for drug to be investigated and relevant materials of the trial	Keep	Keep
17	Testing certificate of investigational product		Keep original
18	Procedures of breaking blind of trial		Keep original
19	General randomization list		Keep original
20	Monitoring report		Keep original

7.4.5 Multicenter Trial

A multicenter trial consists of several clinical trials conducted by several investigators in different places and institutions in accordance with the same protocol. Each center starts and completes the clinical trial simultaneously. There is a principal investigator who is also the coordinating investigator of every center in the trial with overall responsibility of the multicenter trial.

The planning and implementation of a multicenter trial should consider the following:

- The protocol shall be jointly discussed and made by the principal investigators of each center and sponsor. Before it is implemented, approval from the EC must be obtained.
- Investigators meetings shall be held during the initial and middle stages of a clinical trial.
- The clinical trial shall be simultaneously conducted in each center.

Table 7.2 During the conducting phase of the clinical trial

Documents to be kept		Investigator	Sponsor
21	Updated investigator's brochure	Keep	Keep
22	Updated version of other documents (protocol, case report form, informed consent form, written situation notice)	Keep	Keep
23	Curriculum vitae of new investigator	Keep	Keep original
24	Updated normal value range of medical and laboratory tests	Keep	Keep
25	Shipping order for investigational products and relevant materials for clinical trial	Keep	Keep
26	Testing certificate of investigational product with new commission number		Keep original
27	Monitor's visiting report		Keep original
28	Signed informed consent form	Keep original	
29	Original documents of medical treatment	Keep original	
30	Case report form (filled out, signed and dated)	Keep original	Keep the copy
31	Investigator's report of serious adverse event submitted to the sponsor	Keep original	Keep
32	Investigator's report of unexpected serious adverse event submitted to State Drug Administration and EC	Keep	Keep original
33	Mid-term or annual report	Keep	Keep
34	List of codes confirmed by subject	Keep original	
35	Form of subject screening and inclusion	Keep	Keep
36	Registration form of investigational product	Keep	Keep
37	Signature sample of investigator	Keep	Keep

Table 7.3 After completion of the clinical trial

Documents to be kept		Investigator	Sponsor
38	Certificate for destruction of investigational product	Keep	Keep
39	Category of codes of the subject who completed the trial	Keep	Keep
40	Audit certificate		Keep original
41	Final monitoring report		Keep original
42	Certificate of treatment group and accessing the code		Keep original
43	Report of the completion of the trial submitted to the EC and State Food and Drug Administration		Keep original
44	Final report	Keep	Keep original

- The sample size and case allocation in each center must meet statistical requirements.
- The investigational product shall be administered, dispensed and stored, with the same procedures in different centers.
- The investigators participating in the trial shall be trained in accordance with the same protocol.

- A standardized assessment method shall be established. The laboratory and clinical methods of assessment applied in the trial shall be of the same quality control system. Laboratory inspection may be conducted by the central laboratory.
- The data shall be centrally managed and analyzed. A program for data transmission, management, inspection and inquiry shall be established.
- Ensure that investigators of each trial center observe the protocol and that an investigator's participation is terminated if he violates the protocol.

A multicenter trial shall establish a management system based on the number of centers participating in the trial, the requirements of the trial and the familiarity of the drug to be investigated. A coordinating investigator shall be responsible for implementing the whole trial.

7.5 Investigator Meeting

In China, all clinical trials are required to follow GCP by the CFDA regulations. Similar to ICH GCP section 5.23 requirements, the sponsors regardless are local or overseas should ensure their responsibilities. For global or multi regional or multicenter trials, investigator meetings are the important approach to meet the regulatory requirements. In addition, such investigator meetings will greatly benefit the overseas pharmaceutical companies to ensure their study timeline, the international standard and data quality.

Meeting sponsors often have certain mandates that require principal investigators and coordinators to participate in these programs. Discussions surrounding protocol, regulatory issues, enrollment criteria, procedures and safety issues are very critical to the success of a trial. Therefore, it is important for sponsors to have a clear objective when recruiting for these programs. Investigator meetings that have a clear focus on the science and are interactive tend to be better received by participating investigators.

Prior to the Investigator Meeting Activities

It is important to provide investigators and their study coordinators with as much information as possible prior to arriving at the meeting so they can be prepared.

The sponsor and the CRO should make sure that their internal team is well prepared, rehearsed and able to keep the discussion on point of each topic. The meeting arrangement should provide the environment that the participants can be able to interactive while staying on topic and to network with each other after each of the general session.

The Goals of the Investigator Meeting

- To ensures that all the site investigators and study coordinators involved in the study get the same information.

- To ensure that all investigators conduct the trial in compliance with the study requirements through the protocol and document training. The review in the corresponding therapeutic area, the protocol and associated documents, such as CRFs are essential elements.
- To document the responsibilities of all participating investigators prior to the start of the trial.
- To Instruct all investigators and study coordinators on following the protocol and completing CRFs; it is important to solicit feedback from the principal investigator at a pre-investigator meeting before finalization of the protocol and CRFs.
- To allows all those involved in the study to meet in one place, to share their best practice and have an open discussion with peers regarding the key challenges in the study. Regarding protocol and CRF questions or suggestions that the sponsor could not answer during the meeting, the sponsor should address them in a follow-up letter or further integrate/modify the corresponding CRF pages.
- To provide Investigators and their study coordinators the opportunity to discuss study logistics and to meet key sponsor/CRO personnel, including clinical directors or managers, CRAs, Project Managers, Medical Officers, etc.
- To facilitate communication among investigators. Sponsor and CRO personnel during the study.

In addition to the CRO or sponsor's capability for such meeting, the use of an event organizer should also be considered.

For multi-regional or large studies, multiple regional meetings should be considered to ensure the aforementioned goals to be met.

The Proper Timing and Place of the Investigator Meeting

Due to the busy schedule of the clinicians in China, weekend or partially weekend meeting should be considered. Whilst the Investigator will not have to arrange cover for their clinical duties, they have to use their personal times. The investigator meeting should be held 3–5 weeks prior to investigational drug shipment to their hospital sites.

Based on the distribution of the certified clinical sites by the CFDA, most of the sites are in the major cities, such as Shanghai, Beijing, Guangzhou, Nanjing, Xian and Wuhan etc. Therefore, the meeting should be held in a central and accessible location. Some sponsors also prefer to have such investigator meetings held in the cities with scenic spots and historical sites. The costs could be eventually be similar. The local CROs or the local event organizers usually have very good ideas (Table 7.4).

Post Investigator Meeting Activities

The CRO should send a thank you letter to all meeting participants and the pending answers for the questions that required follow up and clarification. For those Investigators or their research associates that were unable to attend the meeting, CRO should send them the presentation copies. Provide a Certificate of Attendance to all participants who attended the meeting as documentation of the train-

Table 7.4 Typical investigator meeting section content and timing

Time	Topic		Speaker
8:00 a.m.	Welcome and opening remarks		Sponsor leader
8:15 a.m.	Study background and rationale (preclinical overview)		Sponsor or CRO pre-clinical leader
9: 00a.m.	Clinical background (Phase 1 and 2 outcome)		Sponsor or CRO medical/clinical leader
9:30 a.m.	Global/Multi-regional Project Timelines		Sponsor or CRO project manager
9:45 a.m.	Coffee break		
10:00 a.m.	Protocol overview		Sponsor or CRO medical/clinical leader
	Study design		
	Inclusion/exclusion criteria		
	Concomitant medication		
	Treatments		
10: 45 a.m.	AE/SAE and pregnancy reporting		Sponsor drug safety director or medical director or medical monitor
11: 15 a.m.	Good clinical practice		Sponsor or CRO QA/QC leader
11.45 a.m.	*Lunch*		
1.00 p.m.	Study procedures or assessments		Sponsor or CRO trial manager
1.45 p.m.	Session A: Coordinators: CRF/source document completions, drug accountability	Session B: Investigators: Financial Sponsor representative disclosure, marketing impacts, protocol Q&A	Sponsor or CRO medical/clinical leader or trial manager/CRA leader
3.00 p.m.	*Coffee break*		
3.15 p.m.	Study monitoring, drug accountability, Q&A		Sponsor or CRO trial manager or CRA
3: 45 p.m.	Central Laboratory		CRO or hospital laboratory representative.
4:15 p.m.	Adjourn		Sponsor leader

ing they have received. For those sites unable to participate in the meeting due to various reasons, training is preferred to be provided to them during the site initiation visit.

7.6 Explanation of Terms of this GCP

Clinical Trial: A Clinical Trial is a systematical investigation of drugs conducted on anybody (patient or healthy volunteer) in order to prove or reveal the function, adverse reaction and/or absorption, distribution, metabolism and excretion of the drug being investigated. The purpose of a clinical trial is to define the therapeutic efficacy and safety of the drug.

Protocol: A document that describes the background, rational, objectives design, method and organization of the trial, including statistical considerations and requirements for conducting and completing the trial. The protocol must be signed and dated by sponsor, principal investigator and the institution in which the investigation is conducted.

Investigator's Brochure: A compilation of the clinical and non-clinical data on the investigational product already obtained before the clinical trial that will be conducted in subjects.

Informed Consent: A process by which a subject voluntarily confirms his or her willingness to participate in a particular trial, after having been informed of all aspects of the trial that are relevant to the subject's decision to participate. Informed consent is documented by means of a written, signed, and dated informed consent form.

Informed Consent Form: An Informed Consent Form is a certification to prove that each subject is voluntarily participating in a certain trial. The investigator must explain to the subject about the nature and purpose of the trial, the anticipated risks and benefits, the alternative medical treatments, and the subject's rights and obligations stipulated in the Declaration of Helsinki, in order that the agreement to participate is based on a good understanding of the trial.

EC: The EC is an independent organization consisting of people specialized in the medical field, legal experts and other people from non-medical fields whose responsibility it is to ensure the protocol and its appendix are ethical and to provide a public guarantee to ensure the protection of the rights, safety and well-being of subjects. Organizations and persons who conduct the clinical trial shall not interfere or affect the structure and activities of the committee.

Investigator: The Investigator is responsible for conducting the clinical trial and for the quality of the trial and the subject's safety and interests. The investigator must be qualified for conducting the trial by his specialty, qualifications, and capability. In a multicenter clinical trial, a chief investigator is appointed to take charge of the overall implementation of the clinical trial and act as the coordinator among each center.

Coordinating Investigator: An investigator assigned the responsibility for the coordination of investigators at different centers participating in a multicenter trial.

Sponsor: The Sponsor is a company, institution or organization who initiates a clinical trial and is responsible for initiating, managing, financing and monitoring the trial.

Monitor: Person appointed by and responsible to the sponsor who is responsible for monitoring and reporting the situation of the trial which is being conducted and verifying the data.

Audit: Audit is a type of systematic check conducted by persons who are not directly involved in the trial. The purpose of an audit is to determine whether the implementation of the trial, the recording and analysis of data comply with the protocol, SOP and relevant regulations.

Inspection: The act by drug administration authorities in conducting an official review of documents, facilities, records and other aspects of a clinical trial. Inspection can be done in the institution where the trial is conducted, or in the locality of the sponsor or the contract research organization.

Case Report Form (CRF): The Case Report Form is a kind of document designed according to the protocol to record data of each subject during the conducting of the trial.

Investigational Product: Study drug, comparator and placebo used in a clinical trial.

Adverse Event: An untoward medical event in a patient or clinical investigation subject administered a drug and which does not necessarily have a causal relationship with this treatment.

Serious Adverse Event: A Serious Adverse Event includes inpatient hospitalization, prolongation of hospitalization, disability/incapacity, effect on work capability, life threatening, death, congenital anomaly etc., which occur during a clinical trial.

SOP: Standard and detailed written instructions made to ensure every function in a certain clinical trial is conducted and completed effectively.

Blinding/Masking: A procedure in which one or more parties to the trial are kept unaware of the treatment assignments. Single blinding refers to the subjects being unaware, and double-blinding refers to the subjects, investigators, monitor or data analyst being unaware of the treatment assignments.

Contract Research Organization (CRO): Contract Research Organization is technical or commercial institution. The sponsor may authorize the CRO to conduct some work and tasks in a clinical trial. This authorization must be stipulated in writing.

Article 69: The SFDA shall be responsible for interpretation of this GCP.

Article 70: This GCP shall be effective from September 1, 2003; simultaneously, the former GCP issued on September 1, 1999 is annulled.

7.7 Guidance for Ethical Review of Investigational Drug Clinical Trials

State Food and Drug Administration No. 436, November 2, 2010

Chapter I General Provisions

Article 1 For the purpose of strengthening the guidance and administration of ethical review of investigational drug clinical trials, and standardizing the activities of the ethical review of ethics committee (EC) so as to ensure that investigational drug clinical trials meet the requirements of science and ethics, the guidelines are formulated in accordance with the Good Clinical Practice (GCP) for Pharmaceutical Products, the Declaration of Helsinki of the World Medical Association, and the International Ethical Guidelines for Biomedical Research Involving Human Subjects of the Council for International Organizations of Medical Sciences.

Article 2 An ECEC reviews the scientific merits and ethical rationality of investigational drug clinical trials to protect study participants' dignity, safety, rights and interests, to promote the development of investigational drug clinical trials in a healthy and scientific way, and to gain the public trust and support in investigational drug clinical trials.

Article 3 It must be under the premise of abiding by the State constitution, law, regulations and relevant stipulations that ECs conduct ethical review of investigational drug clinical trials independently and shall accept the supervision and administration by drug regulatory agencies.

Article 4 The drug regulatory agencies shall establish the procedures for inspecting and assessing the activities of EC review of investigational drug clinical trials, and shall instruct and administer the activities of ethical review.

Chapter II Organization and Management of the EC

Article 5 The establishment of an EC should comply with the applicable administrative stipulations of the State. An EC should constitute the members with backgrounds in multiple disciplines, including professionals related to medicine, professionals not related to medicine, legal, expert and the persons independent from the clinical research or trial institution, at least five people and in the even ratio of gender. It should ensure that the EC members have the experience and qualifications to jointly review and assess a trial's scientific merits and ethical rationality. The constitution and activities of an EC should be free from the influence of any participants involved in trials.

Article 6 There should be documents in writing, which define an EC's

organizational structure, competent department, responsibilities, member qualification requirements, conditions and terms for serving, work responsibilities of its office, establishment of procedures for selection and appointment of the members and office secretary etc.

Article 7 The institution/that establishes an EC should provide EC with essential support, set up an independent office with necessary facilities for office work to ensure the communication with sponsors and the confidentiality of relevant documents.

Article 8 The members of an EC may be created through recruitment, or recommendation, etc. The committee has a director and several deputy-directors who are elected by the committee members.

Article 9 Any committee members should consent to make public for their names, occupations and affiliations, and sign a confidentiality agreement on review subject, study participants information and relevant matters of participants, and sign a declaration of conflict of interest.

Article 10 The EC may engage an independent consultant or appoint an executive one. By request of the committee, the independent consultant contributes consultancy to certain issues of a trial protocol, but the consultant has no right to vote on the ethical review. The consultant may be an expert in ethics, law, special diseases or methodology, or a representative of a population of a special disease, a special region population/ethnic group or other bodies with special interests.

Article 11 The EC should establish a training mechanism of continuing education targeting new committee members, and organize the training of GCP of relevant law and regulations, the skills required by the ethical review of investigational drug clinical trials, and SOPs of the EC.

Article 12 The EC should formulate SOPs and system to ensure the criteria and consistency in ethical review. At minimum, the content should include the following aspects:

1. the formulation of SOPs and guide for ethical review application;
2. the EC's organization and management: the establishment of the EC, the means to maintain the confidentiality of ethical review, the management of conflict of interest, the training of committee members and its office staff, the engagement of independent consultants;
3. the methods of ethical review: scheduled meeting review and ad hoc meeting review, fast review;
4. the ethical review flow procedure: accepting and processing an ethical review application, preliminary review, follow-up review and passing on review decision;
5. meeting management: meeting preparation, meeting procedure, meeting minutes;
6. document and file management: making up files, archiving, retrieval and photocopying.

Chapter III Responsibilities of the EC

Article 13 The EC should continuously improve its organizational management and system construction according to the need of ethical review, and perform its responsibility of protecting study participants' safety, rights and interests.

Article 14 The EC should independently, fairly, justly and timely conduct the review of ethical issues in the investigational drug clinical trials submitted by applicants. Apart from review and supervision of the investigational drug clinical trials undertaken by its institution, the EC may conduct the ethical review of investigational drug clinical trials entrusted by other institutions.

Article 15 When the EC, conducts review and supervision of drug clinical trials, it may exercise the following power:

1. approve/not approve a drug clinical trial;
2. conduct follow-up review of an approved clinical trial; or
3. terminate or suspend an approved clinical trial.

Article 16 After an EC is established, it should timely submit relevant documents to the SFDA and its provincial level SFDA for the record. The documents submitted for the record are as follows: list of the names of EC director and members (their resumes attached), the constitution of the EC, and its relevant working procedures and system.

Article 17 The EC should report its annual situations of ethical review to the SFDA and its provincial food and drug regulatory department.

Chapter IV Application for Ethical Review and Its Acceptance

Article 18 The EC should provide the applicants of ethical review with consultant services for the matters involved in the ethical review, and with application form, informed consent form and formats of other documents needed by application for ethical review; it should formulate clear stipulations for matters related to accepting an application for ethical review.

1. should specify the document list that must be submitted and the number of copies of document needed for review;
2. should define primary requirements, form, criteria, timeline and procedure for accepting an application for review;
3. should define primary requirements for submission and acceptance of an amendment application and a supplementary application, timeline, procedure, conditions and requirements of a dossier, etc.

Article 19 After receiving an application from an applicant of ethical review, for the documents submitted for review that are incomplete or fail to meet the requirements, the EC should give the applicant one-off notice of all content to be supplemented and corrected. After accepting an ethical review application, the EC should inform the applicant of the scheduled time that the ethical review meeting is to be held.

Article 20 An applicant of ethical review must submit the application for ethical review to the EC according to its stipulations and requirements. The application documents submitted for ethical review include (but not limited to the followings):

1. an application form of ethical review (it should be signed and dated);
2. a protocol of clinical trial (version no. and date should be noted);
3. an informed consent form (version no. and date should be noted);
4. relevant materials for recruitment of study participants;
5. the case report form;
6. the investigator's brochure;
7. the resumes of principle investigators;
8. the Approval Letter of Drug Clinical Trial of the State Food and Drug Administration;
9. other EC's statements of their crucial decisions on the application for the clinical trial, the justification for previous negative conclusion should be presented; and
10. the testing report for passing of the investigational drug.

Article 21 The EC should decide the review methods for the accepted application, and choose its principle review member. An independent consultant may be engaged when necessary.

Chapter V Ethical Review of the EC

Article 22 The EC should stipulate the quorum required for convening an ethical review meeting. The committee members attending a meeting should at least exceed half of the total and be no less than five. The attending members should include professionals related and not related to medicine, the person independent from the research/trial institution and, of both genders.

Article 23 The director (or an authorized person) will chair the ethical review meeting. An independent consultant may be invited to attend the meeting to provide advices when necessary; the principle investigator/sponsor may participate in the meeting to present the protocol or explicate special issues. The secretary of the EC should summarize the meeting's discussion and review decision to form the meeting records. The meeting records should have a procedure to get it approved.

Article 24 The EC may establish a "principal review system". The committee may designate one to two principal members for a trial review according to the principle of specialty related and ethical issue related.

Article 25 The EC takes the scheduled meeting review as the major method of review. A fast review may be conducted for any one of the following circumstances: (1) the clinical trial protocol that has been approved by the EC with minor modification, which does not impact on the risk-benefit ratio of the trial; (2) the trial that has not yet enrolled any study participants or the annul/periodical follow-up review of a trial that has completed its intervention measures; or (3) the review of the anticipated SAEs.

Article 26 The fast review is handled by one to two members. A trial approved by a fast review should be reported at the next meeting of the ethical committee members. A fast review should be transformed to a meeting review if there exists any one of the following circumstances:

1. negation is the review opinion;
2. the two handling members do not have an agreeable conclusion; or
3. the members propose a meeting review.

Article 27 When the study participants' safety is threatened by a severe or serious problem that occurs during a trial, the EC should convene an ad hoc meeting to review the circumstance and take response measures to protect the study participants' safety, rights and interests when necessary.

Article 28 The main content of an ethical review (Annex 1):

1. the design and implementation of the trial protocol;
2. risks and benefits of the trial;
3. the recruitment of study participants;
4. the details given by the informed consent form;

5. the process of informed consent;
6. the medical treatment and protection of the study participants;
7. privacy and confidentiality; and
8. the trials involving vulnerable persons.

Article 29 For the purpose of ensuring the quality of ethical review and its review meeting, the EC should manage and control the quality of ethical review. The meeting of ethical review should be conducted following the stipulated procedure and agenda. Sufficient deliberation should be given for reviewed documents so as to ensure that the committee members are able to sufficiently present different opinions on their own.

Article 30 The EC should specifically pay attention to such issues as trial's scientific merits, safety, fairness, the protection of study participants, the informed consent form and the process of informed consent, conflict of interest, etc.

Article 31 For a multi-center clinical trial, the ethical review should take the consistent and timely completion as the primary principle. A multi-center clinical trial may establish a work procedure for the coordination of conducting reviews:

1. the EC of the head institution in conducting the multi-center trial is responsible for reviewing the scientific merits and ethical rationality of the trail protocol;
2. under the premise that all ECs of the participating institutions accept the review opinion of the EC of the head institution, they are responsible for reviewing the feasibility of the trial to be conducted in their institutions including the qualifications and experience of the investigators, and whether they have enough time to take part in the clinical trial, study members staffed and conditions of facilities. The EC of each participating institution is entitled to approve or disapprove the trial proposed to be conducted in its institution;
3. once an EC of a participating institution makes a proposal that a trial protocol must be amended, a document in writing should be compiled and reported to the sponsor or the trial institution responsible for the whole plan of trial for its consideration and forming a consistent opinion for the amendment so as to ensure that all trial institutions have the same trial protocol to follow;
4. the EC of every institution should conduct follow-up review of the trial undertaken by its institution. If any serious adverse event occurs, the ECs of all institutions should be responsible for reviewing them in time and inform the sponsor of the review opinion. Based on the consideration of study participants' safety, the EC of every institution should be entitled to terminate the trial undertaken by its institution;
5. the institution heading the trial should give follow-up review opinion of the clinical trial timely to every participating institution for the record.

Chapter VI Resolution and its Delivery of Ethical Review

Article 32 The ethical review meeting takes a vote on resolution and votes by over half number of attending members is deemed as review resolution of the EC.

Article 33 When the EC passes a review resolution, the following conditions should be met:

1. the application dossier is complete;
2. the number of attending members reaches the quorum required;
3. the review procedure is followed; the key review points are comprehensively examined and sufficiently discussed.
4. While discussing and voting, the sponsor and the committee members with conflict of interest are cleared off the meeting; and 5. absent member is not permitted to vote by proxy of other members.

Article 34 Any clinical trial to be approved must at least meet the following criteria:

1. the risk-control response measures have been prepared for the anticipated risks in the course of the trial;
2. the risks to the study participants are relatively reasonable against their benefits;
3. the selection of the study participants is fair and just;
4. the information in the informed consent form are sufficient and the process of getting informed consent meets the stipulations;
5. when necessary, the trial protocol should possess adequate data and safety supervision plan to ensure the safety of the study participants;
6. protect privacy of study participants and secure confidentiality of data; and
7. there are relevant special protective measures for the trials involving vulnerable persons.

Article 35 There are several outcomes for the review opinion of an EC:

1. agree;
2. agree after necessary amendments are made;
3. re-review after necessary amendments are made;
4. disagree; or
5. termination or suspension of an approved clinical trial.

Article 36 The secretary of the EC should timely summarize the meeting minutes after the meeting and compile the opinion/approval letter of ethical review based on the meeting minutes and review conclusion. The opinion/approval letter of ethical review should be signed by the director (or the authorized person) and stamped with the seal of the EC. The details of the opinion/approval letter of the EC include:

1. primary information
    1. the information of a trial: name of the trial, sponsor, review opinion/ serial no. of approval letter;
    2. the clinical trial institution and investigators;
    3. meeting details: meeting time, location, the form of review, and documents reviewed, of which version number and date of both clinical trial protocol and informed consent form, should be noted.

4. the dates for issuing the approval letter/opinion of ethical review; and
5. the contact person and contact method of the EC;

2. Review opinion and resolution;

1. when the review resolution is "agree", the EC's requirements for conducting follow-up review is notified at the same time as the review resolution is informed;
2. when the review decision is "agree after necessary amendments are made" or "re-review after necessary amendments are made" the detailed opinion for amendments is explicated, and the requirements and re-submission flow for the protocol are informed;
3. when the ethical decision is "disagree" or "termination or suspension of an approved clinical trial", sufficient justification must be given and the sponsor is informed that it may either clarify the matters concerned or lodge an appeal against the resolution.

Article 37 After the ethical review opinion/approval letter verified and signed by the director (or the authorized person) of the EC, it should be timely delivered to the applicant.

Chapter VII Follow-up Review after Ethical Review
Article 38 The EC should conduct follow-up review for all approved clinical trials until they are accomplished;

Article 39 The review of protocol amendment refers to the review of any amendment made to an ongoing trial protocol in the course of the trial. Any amendment made to the trial protocol being implemented should be submitted to the EC to be reviewed for approval before it can be carried out. The EC should request the sponsor and/or investigator to submit the details regarding to the amendment including (but not limited to) the followings:

1. the amended content and the justification of the amendment;
2. impact of amended protocol on anticipated risks and benefits; and
3. impact of amended protocol on the rights and benefits, and safety of study participants.

The EC conducts a review of the protocol amendment with the focus mainly on trial risks and benefits and provides a review opinion. For the protocol amended to avoid an urgent harm to the study participants, the investigator may carry out the amendment prior to the review for approval by the EC, and the amendment should be then reported to the EC in writing timely.

Article 40 Annual/periodical follow-up review. When conducting preliminary review, the EC should decide the frequency of the annual/periodical follow-up review, at least once a year, depending on the degree of the trial risks. The EC should request the investigator to timely submit the report. The details of the annual/periodical follow-up review report include (but not limited to) the followings:

1. the progress of the trial;
2. the number of cases enrolled, completed and withdrawal
3. confirmed SAEs reported in time and properly treated; and
4. any event or new information that might impact on the trial's risks and benefits.

After reviewing the research progress, the EC shall reassess the trial's risks and benefits.

Article 41 The review of serious adverse events (SAEs) refers to the review of the SAEs reported by the sponsor/or investigator including their degree and range, the impact on the trial's risks and benefits, and study participants' medical protective measures.

Article 42 The review of non-compliance/violation of protocol refers to the review of the event, occurring in a clinical trial, that the protocol is not followed or violated. The EC should request the sponsor/or investigator to explain the cause of the event, its impact and handling measures, and investigate whether the event impacts on the safety, rights and benefits of the study participants and on the trial's risks and benefits.

Article 43 The review of the early termination of a clinical trial refers to the review of a trial that is prematurely terminated by the sponsor or investigator. The EC should request the sponsor or investigator to report the justification for the early termination and the subsequent treatment of the study participants, and check whether their safety, rights and benefits are ensured.

Article 44 The review of trial completion refers to the review of the completion of the clinical study report. The EC should request the sponsor and/or investigator to report the situation of the trial accomplishment and review the protection of the study participants' safety, rights and benefits.

Article 45 The applicant should be informed in time for the resolution and justification of follow-up review.

Chapter VIII Management of the EC Documents

Article 46 The EC should possess an independent file management system. The EC's documents for making up files and archiving include documents in management and in trials for review.

Article 47 The management documents of the EC include (but not limited to) the followings:

1. its working procedures, post responsibilities, SOPs and the guide for ethical review application;
2. the appointment documents of the committee members, their resumes and training records, and signed confidentiality agreement and the declaration of conflict of interest; and
3. its annual work plan and summary.

Article 48 The EC's documents for the review of clinical trials include the followings:

1. all dossiers submitted by the investigators or sponsors for review;
2. working form of ethical review, meeting attendance sheet, vote sheet, meeting minutes, the committee's approval letter/opinions and related letters of correspondence;

The ethical review documents should be kept appropriately for 5 years after the clinical trial is completed, or to further extend according to relevant requirements. The archiving document list is seen in annex 2.

Article 49 The EC should formulate relevant stipulations for retrieval and photocopying of the documents to ensure security and confidentiality of documents.

Chapter IX Supplementary Provisions

Article 50 The mechanism of information exchange and work cooperation may be established between and by ECs so as to facilitate capability of ethical review.

Article 51 ECs established prior to implementation of the guidance should, within 1 year from the date of implementation of the guidance, improve their organizational management and system construction according to relevant requirements of the guidance, and report to the SFDA and their provincial level regulatory agencies for the record.

Article 52 This guidance shall be implemented from date of its promulgation.

Annex 1 Main Content of Ethical Review

1. **The design and implementation of a trial protocol**

   1.1 The trial meets the scientific principle commonly-recognized, and based on literatures, sufficient laboratory study and animal experiments.
   1.2 The rationality of trial design and establishment of control group related to trial aims.
   1.3 The criteria of study participants' early withdrawal from a trial and the criteria of suspension or termination of a trial.
   1.4 The inspection and audit plan of an ongoing trial including the establishment of an independent data and safety monitoring board when necessary.
   1.5 The investigators' qualifications and experience, and sufficient time available for conducing the clinical trial, study members staffed and the conditions of the facilities etc. meet the trial's requirements.
   1.6 Clinical trial result report and the way to publish it.

2. **The risks and benefits of the trial**

   2.1 The assessment of the nature of the trial's risks, magnitude and occurring likelihood.
   2.2 The minimization of the risks within the possible range.
   2.3 The anticipated benefit assessment: the study participants' benefits and social benefits.

2.4 The rationality of the trial's risks and benefits:

2.4.1 For the trial with the prospect of direct benefits to the study participants, the anticipated benefits and risks should at least be equivalent to those of the current alternative treatment available. In terms of the anticipated benefits of the study participants, the trial's risks must be rational.

2.4.2 For the trial without the prospect of direct benefits to the study participants, the risks must be rational in terms of anticipated social benefits.

3. **The recruitment of study participants**

3.1 The characteristics of the study participants (including gender, age, and race etc.).

3.2 The fair and just distribution of the trial's benefits and risks among the targeted disease population.

3.3 The mode and method of recruitment to be used.

3.4 The way used to inform the study participants or their representatives of the information related to the trial.

3.5 The criteria of inclusion or exclusion of a research participant.

4. **The details notified by the informed consent form**

4.1 The objectives of the trial, the procedures that the trial should follow (including all invasive operations), trial period.

4.2 The anticipated risks and inconvenience of the study participants.

4.3 The anticipated benefits. The study participants should be informed when they do not directly benefit from the trial. 4.4 The alternative treatment available for the study participants and its important potential risks and benefits.

4.5 Whether the study participants receive any compensation.

4.6 Whether study participants participating in the trial need bear any expense.

4.7 The degree of confidentiality of the relevant records by which study participants can be identified and the explanation statement that the sponsor of the trial study, the members of EC, and governmental regulatory agencies, when necessary, may access the information of the study participants according to the stipulations.

4.8 The treatment and corresponding compensation that study participants may obtain if harm related to the trial has done to them.

4.9 It has been stated that the participation of the trial is voluntary or that the participants may reject the participation of the trial or be entitled to withdraw from the trial at any phase without being discriminated or avenged and without affecting their medical treatment, rights and benefits.

4.10 When the issue of the rights of the study or study participants is raised or the injury occurs related to the trial, there are the contact person and contact number available for dealing with the circumstance.

5. **The process of informed consent**

5.1 The informed consent should meet the principle that the participant is fully informed, sufficiently understand and at liberty choose participation in the trial.

5.2 The statement for informed consent should be popular and easy to be understood and suitable for the understanding level of the research participant population.
5.3 There is a detailed description stating that how the informed consent is obtained, including who is in charge of obtaining it, and the stipulations for the signature of the informed consent form.
5.4 When planning to enroll the study participants who are unable to give their consent, justifications for that should be sufficient, and there must be a detailed statement indicating how to obtain their consent or the consent from their authorized representatives.
5.5 There are the stipulations for hearing the opinions or replying to the questions raised by the study participants or their representatives in the course of the trial.

6. **The medical treatment and protection of the study participants**

6.1 The qualifications and experience of the investigators should be relevant to the trial's requirements.
6.2 The justification for not giving the conventional treatment due to the trial's aims.
6.3 The medical care security provided for the study participants during and after the trial.
6.4 Appropriate medical care monitoring, psychological and social supports provided for the study participants.
6.5 The means to be taken to deal with the circumstance that a research participant voluntarily withdraws from the trial. 6.6 The criteria for providing the investigational product for extending use, emergency use or for sympathetic reason. 6.7 The statement of whether the investigational product is continuously provided for the study participants after the trial is completed.
6.8 The statement explaining the expenses that the study participants need to pay.
6.9 The compensation provided for the study participants (including cash, services and/or presents).
6.10 The compensation and medical treatment provided for the study participants due to the trial-related injuries/disability/death.
6.11 Insurance and compensation for injuries.

7. **Privacy and confidentiality**

7.1 The stipulations for persons who may consult the personal information of the study participants (including medical records, biological samples).
7.2 The measures to ensure the confidentiality and security of personal information of the study participants.

8. **The trial involving**

8.1 Only vulnerable persons are used as study participants, can the trial be well conducted.
8.2 The trial targets on the disease or health problem that is unique to vulnerable persons.

8.3 As the trial does not provide the possibility of direct benefits for study participants of vulnerable persons, the trial's risks generally are not allowed to be larger than the minimal risks, unless the EC consents to the marginal increase in degree of the risks.
8.4 When a study participant is unable to give sufficient informed consent, the informed consent from his or her legal representative should be obtained and, at the same time, consent should still be obtained from the study participant if possible.

9. **The trial involving a special disease population, a special region population/ethnic group**

a) 9.1 The trial's impact on a special disease population, a special region population/ethnic group.
b) 9.2 The external factors that influence an individual's informed consent.
c) 9.3 The plan for the consultation of the said population/group during the trial.
d) 9.4 The trial is beneficial to the local development, for instance, the enhancement of the local medical and health services and the improvement of research capability and the capability to cope with the demand of the public health.

Annex 2 The List of Archiving Documents of the EC

1. **The type of management documents**

1.1 The work procedures and persons' responsibilities of the EC.
1.2 The professional resumes and appointment documents of the EC's members.
1.3 The training documents of the EC's members.
1.4 The guidance for the application for ethical review.
1.5 The SOPs of the EC.
1.6 The technical guidance for the major ethical issues pertaining to clinical trials.
1.7 The documents and records of expenditure management.
1.8 Annual work plan and summation.

2. **The type of trial review documents.**

2.1 The dossiers submitted by the applicants.
2.2 The acceptance notice of application.
2.3 The review work forms of the EC.
2.4 The agendas of the EC's meetings.
2.5 The meeting attendance forms of the EC.
2.6 The vote sheets of the EC.
2.7 The meeting minutes of the EC meetings.
2.8 The opinion/approval letters of ethical review.
2.9 The liability declaration of the ethical review applicants.
2.10 The correspondence between the EC and applicants or other relevant persons regarding to the issues of application, review or follow-up review.
2.11 The relevant documents of the follow-up review.

Annex 3 List of Terms

- A special disease population or a special region population/ethnic group: the population or group that possesses similar a characteristic and the characteristic can be the same/similar region, the same value, the common interest or the same disease suffered from.
- Confidentiality: to prevent all the ownership information or individual identification information from being leaked to the unauthorized.
- Conflict of interest: it is because that the EC member has a related interest with the trial for review, which would undermine his or her impartiality and independency to conduct the review from the perspective of protecting the study participants. A conflict of interest usually happens when the EC member has an interest relation with the trial for review in the aspect of economy, material, institution, and social relations.
- Data and Safety Monitoring Board: an independent data and safety monitoring board that sponsor is responsible for setting up. Its responsibility is to regularly assess trial progress, analyze safety data and important indexes of effects, and make proposal to the sponsor of the trial's continuation, modification, or early termination.
- EC: an independent organization consisting of medical professionals, legal expert and non-medical persons. Its responsibility is to review the clinical trial protocol and the annexes if they are conformed to morals, and to provide public assurance for ensuring protection of study participants' safety, health, rights and interests. The composition of the committee and its all activities are free from the intervention or influences of the clinical trial organization and implementers in the trial.
- The informed consent: refers to the process that, after informed of every aspect of a trail, a prospect research participant voluntarily confirms to content participation in the clinical trial, and the participant shall sign and date an informed consent form as a proof document.
- The informed consent form: a proof document that a research participant voluntarily participates in a trial. The investigator shall tell the research participant the nature, aims, possible benefits and potential risks of the trial, alternative treatments available, and the research participant's rights and obligations which are conformed to the Declaration of Helsinki so as to enable the research participant to fully understand the trial before confirming his or her willingness.
- Minimal risk: refers to that an anticipated risks' possibility and degree are not greater than those in daily life, a regular physical examination, or psychological test.
- Multicenter trial: refers to a clinical trial that follows the same protocol, is conduced in multiple trial sites and taken charge by several investigators who implement and accomplish the trial respectively.
- Non-compliance/violation: refers to the circumstances of the deviation of the trial protocol approved by the EC, and the deviation not approved by the committee in advance or non-compliance/violation of the stipulations for human subjects protection and the requirements of the EC.

- Protocol amendment: refers to a written revision of or clarification to the protocol, and other documents and information that related trial organizations implement.
- Quorum: refers to the stipulated number and qualifications of the committee members attend a meeting to review a trial and make a resolution, i.e. for an effective meeting, the number and qualifications of the committee members should be required.
- Research participant: an individual who participates in biomedical research may be in treatment group, control group or observation group, including a healthy volunteer or a volunteer no direct correlation with the population targeted by the trial, or a patient from the disease population targeted by the trial.
- Standard Operating Procedure (SOP): detailed operating instructions in writing formulated to ensure the consistence of implementation so as to achieve the special aims.
- Serious adverse event: the event occurs in the course of a clinical trial, and causes inpatient hospitalization for treatment, or the prolongation of existing hospitalization, injuries, disability or incapacity for work, life-threatening, or death or a congenital anomaly defect and so on.
- Unanticipated adverse event: the nature, degree of seriousness or frequency of the adverse event, different from those of the anticipated risks depicted by the set protocol or other relevant documents (such as investigator's brochure and investigational drug insert sheet).
- Vulnerable persons: the population relatively (or absolutely) have no ability to maintain their own interests, usually referring to the people whose ability or freedom is restricted and are unable to give their consent or dissent, such as minors, the psychotic etc. of the persons who are unable to give their informed consent.

References

SFDA (2003) Administrative measures for the import of drugs. Order No. 4. Issued by the State Food and Drug Administration on August 18, 2003

SFDA (2007a) Provisions for drug registration, No. 28. Issued by the State Food and Drug Administration on June 18, 2007 http://eng.sfda.gov.cn/WS03/CL0768/61647.html

SFDA (2007b) Provisions for drug registration, No. 28.; Annex 2: Registration categories and application information requirements of chemical drugs. Issued by the State Food and Drug Administration on June 18, 2007

SFDA (2007c) Provisions for drug registration, No. 28; Annex 3: Registration Categories and Application Information Items Requirements of Biological Products. Issued by the State Food and Drug Administration on June 18, 2007

SFDA (2010a) Guidance of ethical review for drug clinical trials. Issued by the State Food and Drug Administration on November 2010

SFDA (2010b) Good manufacturing practice for pharmaceutical products, Order No. 79, Order by Ministry of Health of the People's Republic of China. Issued by the State Food and Drug Administration, February 2011, http://www.doc88.com/p-991218878276.html

SFDA (2011a) Guiding principle of phase I clinical trial management (interim). Issued by the State Food and Drug Administration on December 2011

SFDA (2011b) Management guide of laboratories serving to bio-sample analyses in clinical trials (interim). Issued by the State Food and Drug Administration on December, 2011

Chapter 8
Strategic Drug Development in China and Surrounding Countries

Ming Q. Lu, Yanbin Xie, Qinping Liao and Yuyuan Tan

8.1 Introduction

China's pharmaceutical market was ranked the third largest in the world and its pharmaceutical sales reached $ 66.7 billion in 2011. It is estimated that China will sustain a 15–18 % growth rate for the next few years and become the second largest in the world with sales exceeding $ 155 billion by 2016 (IMS 2012). China's pharmaceutical market will be the main competitor of the US by 2020.

Since China joined the World Trade Organization (WTO) on Dec. 11, 2001, more and more overseas pharmaceutical companies have entered China's drug market. From the hospital pharmaceutical market to market share aspects, the multinational and joint venture pharmaceutical companies showed a clear advantage in profit. Based on market penetration and share data, the top five companies were all overseas pharmaceutical companies in 2011. By 2012, the sales of imported drugs already shared one-fourth of the Chinese drug market.

Since the major pharmaceutical regulation "Provisions for Drug Registration" became effective in 2007 (SFDA 2007), many new policies and guidelines have been issued and become effective, such as the "Green Channel" (SFDA 2009) and "Transfer Rules" in 2009, and the recent Amendment to the Drug Registration

M. Q. Lu (✉)
Helsinn Therapeutics (U.S.), Inc., 1140 US Highway 22, Suite 101, Bridgewater, NJ 08807, USA
e-mail: Mingqilu@verizon.net

Y. Xie
China ICON PLC., Room 1502-1506, Tower B Global Trade Center, No.36, North Ring East Road, Dongcheng District, 100013 Beijing, P. R. China

Q. Liao
Division of Gynecology/Obstetrics and Pediatrics, Beijing Tsinghua Chang Gung Hospital, Changping Tiantongyuan, No. 168 Litang Road, 102218 Beijing, P. R. China

Y. Tan
Beijing PRI BioScience Development Co, Ltd., C-505 Building 102, Zhu Jiang Di Jing No.28, Guangqu Road, Chao Yang District, 100022 Beijing, P. R. China

M. Q. Lu (ed.), *Approaching China's Pharmaceutical Market*,
DOI 10.1007/978-3-319-15576-0_8

Regulation in December 13, 2013. These changes may also have significant impact on the multinational pharmaceutical companies' new drug registration pathways and strategic planning. For multinational pharmaceutical companies, new drug categories mainly involve in two classes:

- Investigational drugs never marketed in any country are defined as Class I new drugs.
- Drugs marketed in other countries but not yet in China belong to Class III new drugs.

For multinational pharmaceutical companies in the current regulatory environment, drug registrations can be practically divided into two strategies:

- Integrate Chinese clinical study into international, multi-center clinical trials (IMCT). This pathway enables the synchronization of the clinical study with the global clinical development program for market approval. In the recent CFDA issued draft Guidance for IMCT (CFDA 2014), IMCT includes two forms of clinical trials:

    a. The first type of Multi-regional Clinical Trials (MRCT), also known as cross-regional (such as Asia and Europe) clinical trials, refers to the trials using the same clinical trial protocol, trials that are conducted simultaneously at multiple centers in different regions. Such trials are truly global MRCTs, here we use MRCT for convenience;
    b. In the cases that greater safety risks may be incurred in clinical trials under the same protocol, or sometimes due to other timing factors, the sponsor may conduct regional multi-center clinical (RMCT) trials in different countries within a region, such as in Asian countries only (here we name it RMCT for convenience). Please note that in the past, many different terms have been used, which have caused significant confusion on the part of multinational companies.
    c. For those who have taken the MRCT pathway, it is common that a Chinese clinical trial cannot fit the global clinical study timeline due to various reasons. In such a case, multinational pharmaceutical companies may still use the RMCT pathway to initiate an Asian regional clinical program including a few surrounding countries with the main focus on Chinese population (Kang 2012). In the draft IMCT guidelines, it is stated that if the IMCT data is used for drug registration in China, it shall be derived from at least two countries including China (CFDA 2014).

- An alternative way is to wait for the new investigational drug approval in overseas' markets. The clinical trials in China can be initiated thereafter to follow the imported drug registration pathway. Based on the current CFDA regulation, such a trial needs a comparatively small sample size of 100 pairs as defined under Class III new drugs. However, this pathway is less and less frequently used due the lengthy time frame it requires.

Based on the CFDA's annual report on new drug reviews and approvals, IMCT applications have increased steadily since 2008. Among those applications, obviously,

Table 8.1 Comparison of IND, CTA and NDA timeframe for chemical drugs. (Source: CDE, Annual Drug Approval Report 2013)

Approval timeframe for chemical drugs in China			
	January 2012	December 2012	December 2013
	Waiting period (months)	Waiting period (months)	Waiting period (months)
IND	6	4	6
CTA	12	15	19
NDA	11	12	14

some of the applicants didn't realize that such applications also have to follow the requirements of Provisions for Drug Registration (Li 2008). The number of global trial applications in the first half of 2013 basically matched the total numbers for 2012 and 2011 combined IMCT applications as reported in China Pharmaceutical News.

Among the global clinical trials, the largest proportion of applications is concentrated in drugs for cancer treatment (CFDA 2014). The main driving force is its fast approval nature compared to the traditional lengthy drug import license application (IDL) pathway. In past years, many multinational pharmaceutical companies have taken the MRCT or RMCT pathways for CTA applications. Due to the trade-off of this pathway, which we'll discuss in the following sections, the CFDA is in the process of reviewing the overall IMCT practice with a potential adjustment to slow down or add more review time (CFDA 2014).

Based on the CDE annual drug approval report in 2013, the average approval timeframe for investigative new drugs (IND) of category I drugs and clinical trial authorization (CTA) of category III drugs has been delayed from 2 months in 2012 to 4 months. From the industry survey results, the delay is much more compared to the CDE annual report ("China Regulatory Update: NPC, Medical Device Regulation Overhaul, Annual Drug Approvals"—*PharmAsia News,* Apr. 8, 2014 8:51 AM GMT).

Registration of these two classes of new drugs also depends on whether the investigational new drugs are manufactured in China or overseas. Generally, multinational pharmaceutical companies in China could be divided into two categories based on their manufacturing status, including:

- Companies with local manufacturing facilities including fully owned or partially owned by joint venture or partnership;
- Companies without local manufacturing facilities.

As clarified in Provisions for Drug Registration (SFDA Order No. 28) issued on July 10, 2007, the classifications of the new drug for both local and import drug are consistent. For multinational pharmaceutical companies with local manufacturing facilities, there are more options. They may follow the new drug application pathway for local manufacturers and also may apply through import drug registration pathway by its branch in China. The pathways highly depend on their internal global strategies. The following graph provides rough ideas for the potential registration pathways in China (Fig. 8.1):

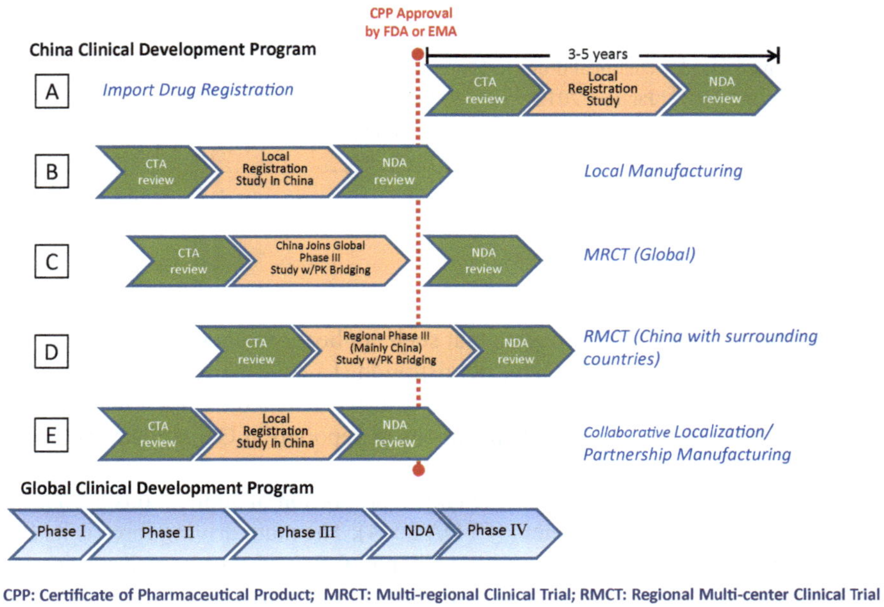

Fig. 8.1 Potential registration pathways in China

The strategic new drug development pathways of multinational pharmaceutical companies for locally and overseas manufactured drugs will be discussed separately in this chapter.

8.2 Global Companies with Manufacturing Facilities in China

For global companies with manufacturing facilities in China, their new drug development pathways are more flexible. They may act as a local pharmaceutical company to initiate the CTA application with locally manufactured clinical supplies. The CTA package preparation should follow the classifications of the drug categories (Fig. 8.2). The clinical development plan and protocols should follow the minimum requirements for sample size, etc. After the completion of the clinical trials, NDA package for marketing approval should be filed. As a locally manufactured new drug, the monitoring period will protect the drug, i.e. during this period, no any manufacturing or import application of the same chemical entity or its formulations will be approved by regulatory the CDE.

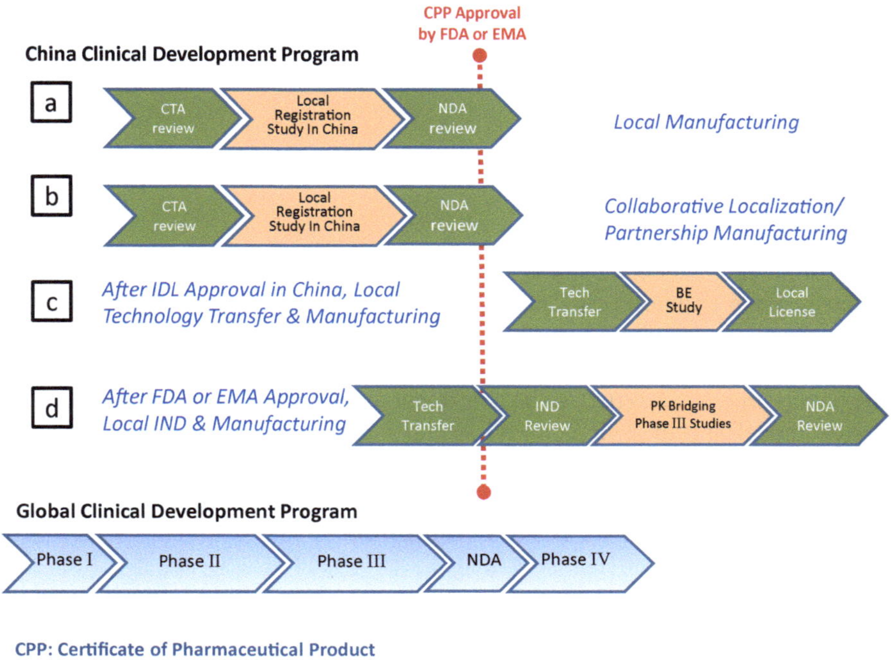

Fig. 8.2 Global company registration pathways for drugs manufactured or to be manufactured in China

In this approach, the drug approval in China is totally is independent. It offers a great potential advantage for early launch of a drug in China ahead of other countries (Fig. 8.2a).

In consideration of the down-side of import drug license pathway for Class III drug: more and more global companies with local manufacturing facilities are actively exploring the Class I NDA pathway to design a full development program in China based on the CFDA annual reports for drug registration. One of the commonly accepted strategies is to initiate the clinical activities early in China following Class I category drug development strategy (Kang 2012) . Using this method, they can catch up to global development speed, and will be able to join the IMCT and to synchronize the global development speed in the western world. The success of this path could give global companies a very early entry into the Chinese market compared to the traditional import drug pathway or aforementioned IMCT pathways being implemented by the multinational pharmaceutical companies without local manufacturing capabilities. Global Company Registration Pathways for Drugs Manufactured or to be manufactured in China have different advantages and disadvantages with different timeframes as well. In comparison to Model a or b as indicated in Fig. 8.2, Model c and d don't show any advantages in terms of timeframe. However, they may also provide benefit for a long run for the global companies due to the comparatively cheaper labor cost in China (Thoelke 2013; Su 2013) . Regarding Model b in Fig. 8.2, it will be discussed in the following sections.

8.3 Global Companies Without Manufacturing Facilities in China

Both of the more common strategies, MRCT or RMCT pathway and import drug pathway, have trade-offs, advantages, and disadvantages. Multinational pharmaceutical companies should base their decisions on their individual situations. For global companies without manufacturing facilities in China, they need to apply for the import drug license (IDL) to be able to put their drugs in the China market. The current models include four pathways as illustrated in the Fig. 8.3.

8.3.1 MRCT Pathway (Cross-Regional)

MRCT pathway has become more accepted by multinational pharmaceutical companies in recent years compared to the traditional pathway of import drug registration as the Class III drug application (Fig. 8.3c, d). The main reasons for the gradual rejection of the traditional pathway are its lengthy process and comparatively shorter product life under patent protection.

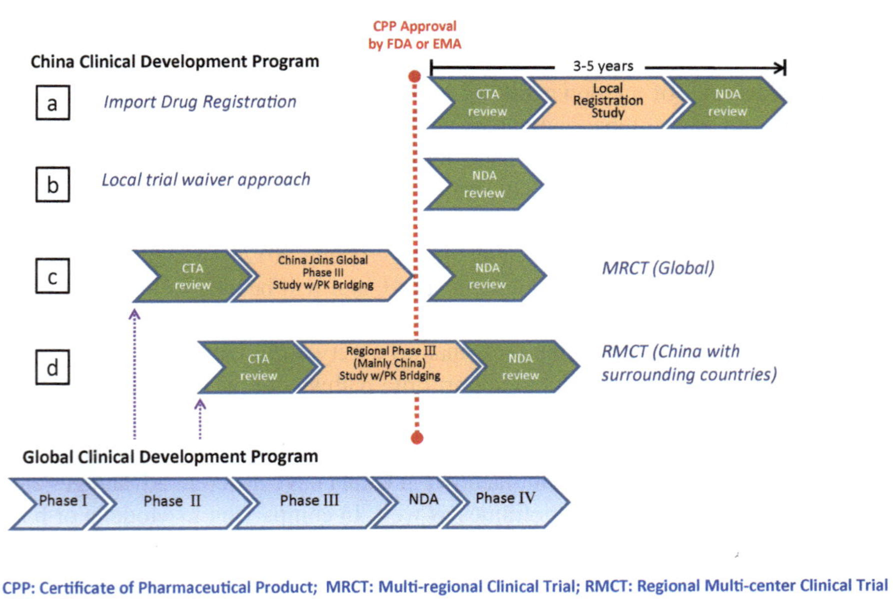

Fig. 8.3 Pathways to get import drug license

The CFDA accept the IMCT data with appropriate Chinese population if the IMCT complies with the regulatory requirements, follows GCP, and has prior CTA approval. Upon the completion of the IMCT, the companies have to submit the IMCT study report for evaluation. This pathway is suitable for the new chemical drug application, but not the therapeutic biological products. For biologics, the multinational pharmaceutical companies usually have to register their through the import drug application pathway.

To accelerate the new drug registration process, shorten launch timelines, and synchronize the global market approval, conduction of the MRCT trials with the integration of the Chinese population in China was considered the most common, practical pathway (Fig. 8.3c). Using this strategy, multinational pharmaceutical companies may take the advantage of MRCT for China registration. Since this path allows the clinical program to start earlier and before the overseas market approval, submission of NDA to the CFDA for approval could happen right after the overseas' approval. An estimated timeframe reduction in China is roughly 1.5 years. For selection of this path, the companies should always keep the following conditions for their global protocol design and reports (SFDA 2007) in mind:

- To meet the China registration requirement, a sufficient number of patients from China, >100 pairs of patients in the MRCT study are needed;
- A local bridging pharmacokinetic study with 20–30 subjects is also needed. Theoretically, there is a China-Japan-Korea Working Group on ethnic factors in clinical trials, which aims to enhance clinical trial cooperation and reduce the unnecessary effort in drug development among three countries. Based on the past experience, the CFDA does not officially accept bridging study outcomes conduced outside mainland China. However, phase I results Conducted in Hong Kong, Taiwan with same ethnical group or Japan or Korea populations could facilitate the regulatory review process for CTA application.
- In addition to the MRCT study report, an independent country study report for China with appropriate statistical evaluation is required. The multinational pharmaceutical companies should always keep in mind if the study outcomes in the country report could show the significance in both statistical and clinical aspects as required in the western world.
- In the case that market approval is delayed in the western world, the drug registration will be delayed as well since this regulatory path is highly depends on the overseas approval.

For the drugs in oncology, HIV or the fields with extremely unmet medical needs, in other words, in the Green Channel, the opportunities are high to enroll China in the global clinical program through this MRCT path. Overall, to be successful using this pathway, multinational pharmaceutical companies have to make their decision far ahead of the MRCT to overcome the above potential hurdles.

8.3.2 RMCT (China with Surrounding Countries) Pathway

When multinational pharmaceutical companies decide to pursue the RMCT strategy for their new drug registration, they may be met with some common practical problems, e.g. the differences caused by ethnic factors or healthcare system. Such differences could be directly related to the patient pharmacokinetic, pharmacodynamics profile or the patient sensitivities and tolerability. In addition, the comparatively long and unpredictable CTA approval time in China may significantly decrease the opportunities for China to join the global clinical program or cause an overall global timeline delay due to the limited recruitment window for patients.

In such situations, the localized RMCT (Fig. 8.3d), i.e. including China with surrounding countries, pathway should be considered. The localized RMCT shares a common feature as the global MRCT that the China development program could start before the drug is approved overseas. In this pathway, the China with the surrounding countries' clinical program could be initiated ahead of the NDA approval in the western world. In addition, localized RMCT could make it comparatively easy to handle issues, such the difference in sensitivity, tolerability or healthcare, or long time for CTA approval, which could preclude China participating global MRCT.

One of the big advantages of this pathway is that because the number of patients assigned to China in a global MRCT is very often not enough to meet the regulatory requirement for approval, the localized RMCT could use the China focused nature to meet this requirement.

In summary, multinational pharmaceutical companies should take advantages of this localized RMCT pathway, especially in the following situations:

- Differences due to ethnic factors were found in pharmacokinetic, pharmacodynamics profile, patient sensitivities or tolerability;
- Differences were found for healthcare systems, which prevent or make the global MRCT hard to be in practice in China;
- Long or unpredictable CTA approval time may impact the global MRCT or the overall timeline for NDA approval in the western countries;
- The global MRCT could not meet the CFDA regulatory requirement for minimum patient number recruited in China, or the statistical and medical significance;
- Logistic and ethical issues could include the key medical device or equipment, or positive drugs in the global MRCT are not available in China, or certain treatment or diagnostic methods or placebo are not accepted from ethical aspect.

Facing the above situations, the multinational companies should rigorously initiate consultation with the local key opinion leaders (KOLs) in the corresponding field and also the regulatory experts for the RMCT. In China, those top KOLs are not only the experts in the medical field, but also the experts in drug development. More importantly, many of them are the reviewers or senior reviewers of the CFDA for the corresponding medical fields. One of the other critical factors for success in this pathway is that the multinational pharmaceutical companies should pay extreme attention to the CRO selection. Striking a balance between global and local CRO, the ideal CRO should possess the global knowledge for clinical trial conductance with strong local clinical trial experience in the corresponding fields.

In both scenarios (MRCT and RMCT), the companies could take advantage of the shorter timeline for China registration.

8.3.3 Advantages of IMCT (MRCT and RMCT)

Both the MRCT and RMCT strategies possess the following distinct advantages:

- Compared to the traditional import drug registration, IMCT approach could be initiated before the drug market approval overseas. Due to the parallel nature with the overseas clinical program, the registration approval in China can be shortened 3–4 years.
- Basically, MRCT adopts the same clinical design, endpoint measurements, inclusion or exclusion criterial, treatment or dosing strategy, statistic evaluation and quality management. Therefore, it provides a good comparison between the safety and efficacy profile in different ethnic groups.
- MRCT outcomes provide a more integrated picture for patient responses to the investigational new drug in various geographic regions, healthcare systems, nutritional and living habits, and health-economic conditions.

8.3.4 Disadvantages of IMCT (MRCT and RMCT)

The downsides of MRCT could be summarized below:

- Due to the limited sample size of Chinese patients in the MRCT, the independent report about clinical research data in Chinese is often limited. It is difficult to show a statistic and clinical significance. Based on the limited data in Chinese population in MRCT, it is hard for the regulatory agency (CDE) to make a clear judgment about whether a new drug can be used in China's vast patient populations. They often need to rely on the global clinical findings arising security concerns;
- To compare China subgroups and the consistency of the results with global MRCT data, there is a lack of authority recognized statistical method. In most cases, the agency reviewers could only judge it by their experiences, the level of understanding of the data and risk control measures to judge new drugs;
- For the MRCT, different countries may urge the modifications of the clinical trial protocols; therefore, the overseas drug evaluation agencies in other countries may face the same approval or decision-making hesitations. Comparatively, the CDE usually has much less clinical data in Chinese than the United States

and Europe for their populations. As such, there could be a review issue and a decision-making risk.

8.3.5 Special Consideration

For IMCT trials, the multinational pharmaceutical companies should take advantage of the "Regulation of New Drug Registration Special Review Procedure" or sometimes called "Green Channel" issued on January 9th, 2009 (No.17) by the CFDA. If the drug meets the criteria and gets approval for special review procedure from the CFDA, it could be a significant advantage for the applicant company, including a fast review and approval timeframe. There are four types of new drug registrations eligible for Green Channel.

- Class I and 2 of Chinese traditional medicines
- Chemical drugs, active pharmaceutical ingredients, or biological products that have never been marketed in the world (Class 1)
- New pharmaceuticals for AIDS, cancer or other serious diseases, which have been proven with significant clinical benefit
- New pharmaceuticals targeting diseases that have no effective therapeutic drugs

Among the four types of candidates, the last three types could be useful for CTA and NDA applications. Once the investigational new drug is granted as a "Green Channel" candidate, multinational pharmaceutical companies could:

- get additional opportunities to communicate with the CDE to enhance information exchange and discussion on technical issues with signed meeting minutes available to the company;
- get permission to submit a new document for panel meeting, communication meeting or critical safety information.
- obtain priority in review and approval process to shorten the review cycle time;

8.3.6 Import Drug Pathway

For import drug pathway, the Certificate of Pharmaceutical Product (CPP) is needed for filing. In other words, the application for marketing approval in China can only start after the companies have obtained the approval overseas in some major countries. Once the companies obtain approval, they may start the process to apply for a clinical trial authorization (CTA) to conduct a registration study. The clinical trial for such registration path is comparatively small, which is typically in the size of >100 pairs of patients for chemical drugs and >300 patients for biologics. A pharmacokinetic study in Chinese subjects is often required as well. Once the registration study is completed, multinational companies may submit the clinical data package along with NDA package for marketing approval and an Import Drug

License (IDL). This is the most traditional and straightforward approach to register a drug in China (Fig. 8.3a).

8.3.6.1 Advantages of Import Drug Registration

Compared to the IMCT strategy, the advantages of this approach include the following:

- The probability of success is high since the drug has been approved overseas with the entire set of dossier available. The new drug has been used in a fairly big study population overseas and has passed the beginning years of high-risk stage.
- The import drug registration study can be a miniature of the pivotal Phase III trials and simply mimic the pivotal Phase III trials conducted overseas with a limited scope only in China. Therefore, the investment is relatively small.

8.3.6.2 Disadvantages of Import Drug Registration

The disadvantage of this pathway is that there is a delayed time gap between the market approval in China and the first market approval overseas. Since a CPP is required for filing the import drug CTA application, the earliest time point to initiate the process is at least 6 months following the market approval overseas. The regulatory review time for CTA is estimated about 10–18 months and for NDA is about 12–15 months. In considering the clinical trial and overall time needed, the drug lag could be easily 5 years or more after the overseas approval. Due to the limited patient sample size in local registration study, the China clinical data package is very often considered less comprehensive.

Most of the clinical trials for import drug registration use the bridging study. In some therapeutic fields, it is a big challenge to find surrogate endpoints with high academic value. Regarding the evaluation of surrogate endpoints, it is often difficult to reach a consensus between the CDE reviewers and medical experts of multinational companies. In most of the cases in which there is even existence of the acceptable surrogate endpoints, it is also impossible to obtain the clinical endpoint data simultaneously for comparison with the surrogate endpoint data.

8.3.7 Perspectives from CDE Reviewers Regarding IMCT Pathways

In general, CDE reviewers also measure the advantages and disadvantages of the IMCT strategy from their viewpoint. For the diseases or medical conditions without effective treatment medication or need urgent treatment drugs, the two prominent advantages, speed and global development synchronization, are more likely to be fully taken. The CDE may speed up the drug registration processes, as well as encourage the global synchronization of the drug development and cooperation of the global large-scale clinical trials. Especially in recent years, the CDE has been actively involved in joint development opportunities. They fully acknowledge that in today's increasing convergence of the global disease spectrum, the research and development of new drugs for some of the major diseases highly rely on the strength of global cooperation. To meet such goals and solve unmet medical needs, no single country can accomplish it alone. From the regulatory viewpoint of the CDE, opportunities are more important than the time and global cooperation is more important than the time of registration.

Based on China's current "Drug Registration Regulation," IMCT is allowed for the investigational drug in China only if the company has accomplished phase II clinical trials overseas. Usually, a pharmacokinetic study is required to bridge the population difference ahead of the IMCT. This regulation is based on the concerns that IMCT protocol from multinational pharmaceutical companies comes to China applying for a synchronous implementation in Chinese patients. In this case, the CDE faces a brand new chemical entity. They understand neither the pharmacokinetic behavior of this investigational drug in Chinese population, nor the suitability of the doses in the protocol for the Chinese patients. Therefore, it is not easy for the CDE to make the decision to allow the Chinese to participate in the synchronous IMCT due to the lack of the firm basis of the scientific background (Kang 2012). To address these concerns, suggestion from the CDE is to actively promote the launching of the early clinical trials in China including the first dose in Chinese people, and proof of concept studies.

In recent years, early clinical research has become a hot topic in the current global synchronization developed among the regulatory reviewers and multinational pharmaceutical companies. It is considered feasible that multinational pharmaceutical companies may simply select the appropriate projects and research units with risk control capabilities in China. The following requirements are mandatory to be complied with:

- The investigators should have the GCP training and certification by the CFDA with corresponding filed experience, risk control and handling capability for the clinical program;
- The review of the ethics committee has to be thorough to meet the purpose of protecting the safety and interests of the subjects, rather than a simple form of review and administrative review;
- Pharmaceutical companies have the capability and mechanism for serious adverse events handling and reporting;
- Clinical trials program open to the public, implement registration and accept the supervision of the society and public opinion;
- Clinical risk control plans and procedures in the clinical protocol, and having a strong enforceability;
- Clear data management and monitoring procedures.

The CED believes that with the early results of clinical trials in China, they can make the operation of IMCT more scientifically sound. The current practice is that multinational pharmaceutical companies bring the clinical trial protocol design to China to enroll a certain number of Chinese patients. In such cases, the clinical protocol design takes limited consideration and measure for the patient pharmacokinetics, safety and healthcare situations of the Chinese patients. By contrast, with the results of early clinical studies in China, pharmaceutical companies could take these results into the global development consideration, which will enhance the late stage protocol design. The suitability of the Chinese patients for the protocols will be greatly improved.

In summary, the CDE encourages companies to develop the drugs tor diseases without effective treatment or diseases that need urgent treatment in China through IMCT (CFDA 2014).

The CDE is favorable to use IMCT for (1) the new drugs aiming to treat the urgent medial disorders or diseases, and (2) the new drugs that have to be developed through the global cooperation in large-scale clinical trials carried out simultaneously in China.

In addition, the CDE encourages simultaneous, early clinical trials in China to promote new drugs approval in China and global market.

Very recently, the reported consensus is that the CFDA hopes to have more local trials and intends to narrow IMCTs to orphan drugs and diseases with high or large unmet medical needs. To speed up the review and approval process for new drugs, the CFDA has recently released several measures. The priorities are to further improve a special review mechanism, and to enhance clinical study review. The special review mechanism issued in February 2013, was intended to accelerate review and approval for drugs with high efficacy for major diseases and domestically developed novel compounds ("SFDA Proposes New Review Channel for Innovative Drugs"—PharmAsia News, Jan. 15, 2013 10:04). Such changes may favor the companies with local manufacturing facilities and slow down some of the IMCT approval process. Currently, nearly half of IMCT applications are for oncology trials in China. Facing the recent regulatory changes in IMCT pathway, multinational pharmaceutical companies should also adjust their regulatory strategies correspondingly, e.g. they may put the investigational drugs in orphan drug category, or drugs with urgent or high unmet medical needs in IMCT for China new drug development. Alternatively, they may consider local Class I development pathway if they possess the capability or through the following collaborative localization strategy.

8.3.8 Future Directions for -IMCT Pathways

To further standardize and the IMCTs, the CFDA issued a draft Guidance for International Multicenter Clinical Trials, No. 698 on Nov. 21, 2014 for public comment. It is stated in the guidance that as a development model, IMCT allows sharing of global drug development resources, global synchronization of drug research and development can reduce unnecessary repetition of clinical trials and shorten the time gaps in drug marketing among countries. This draft Guidance has clarified many concepts and requirements which are consistent with previous regulations (SFDA Order No. 28, 2007; SFDA Order No. 17, 2009). For example, if the IMCT data is used for drug registration in China, it shall be derived from at least two countries (one of which shall be China) and shall be in line with the requirements.

8.3.8.1 The Guidance Consists of Eight Sections

1. Background
2. Objectives and Significance
3. General Requirements
4. Considerations on Trial Standardization
5. Considerations on Scientificity
6. Requirements on the Report of Registration Application
7. Requirements on Changes to Study Protocol
8. Requirements on On-Site Inspection

In this guidance, a majority of the contents are consistent with global trial standards. Such requirements to multinational pharmaceutical companies belong to the common clinical practice. However, there are some new requirements to which specific attention should be paid. Those requirements will be briefly discussed in this section.

8.3.8.2 MRCT and Regulations

In recent years, the IMCT for registration has expanded from the International Conference on Harmonization (ICH) region to non-ICH regions including China. IMCT allows sharing of global drug development resources and global synchronization of drug research and development. IMCT can reduce unnecessary repetition of clinical trials and shorten the time gaps in drug marketing between countries or regions.

Multi-regional Clinical Trial (MRCT), also known as inter-regional (such as Asia and Europe) clinical trials, refers to the trials which are conducted simultaneously at multiple centers in different regions according to the same clinical trial protocol. Where greater safety risks may be incurred in clinical trials under the same protocol, the sponsor may conduct regional multi-center clinical trials (RMCT) in different countries within a region. Those two forms of clinical trials are both regarded as the IMCT. According to the *Drug Registration Regulation*, where the IMCT data is used for drug registration in China, it shall be subject to the provisions of such Regulation with respect to clinical trials.

8.3.8.3 Encouragement for IMCT with Focused Disease Conditions

Sponsors are encouraged to conduct IMCT in China in the fields of severe diseases or those with unmet clinical needs, to study in the early stage the feasibility of global pivotal studies and regional studies in China, and to conduct pivotal studies in China as well as regional clinical trials targeted for Chinese patient populations. In the same aspect, China's pharmaceutical research and development pharmaceutical companies are also encouraged to conduct IMCTs to accelerate the internationalization process of drug clinical development in China.

General Requirements
Before carrying out the IMCTs, sponsors shall consider the following issues:

- Basic conditions for the IMCT application: The same study protocol shall be used for all the centers around the world for the same IMCT. The consistency among investigators with respect to understanding of trial protocol and relevant evaluation indicators is important to reduce evaluation discrepancies among different centers and among different investigators.
- For large-scale IMCTs, it is usually required that companies set up the endpoint evaluation committee and the data and safety monitoring committee for key indicators to ensure the reliability of study findings and avoid deviation from the study's designed objectives.
- Selection of IMCT strategies: Prior to the development of the global research and development plan, research is conducted based on the disease epidemiology and medical practices in each region and country to identify the differences in the indicators closely associated with the evaluation of drug efficacy among different regions or countries. The sponsor shall determine the clinical strategy for the later stages, i.e. either conducting global synchronized development or regional synchronized development or carrying out developments specific to different countries.
- With regard to IMCT data for drug registration application in China, (a) first the overall evaluation of the global study data and then further trend analysis of the study data for patients in Asia or China are required; (b) second, attention is to be paid to whether the sample size of Chinese patients in the total number of subjects in the study is big enough to evaluate and demonstrate the safety and efficacy of the product for patients in China.
- All research centers participating in the drug clinical trials shall be subject to on-site inspections organized by the relevant drug regulatory authorities in China.

8.3.8.4 Considerations on Trial Scientificity

The design of the clinical trial protocol as a whole must meet both scientific and ethical requirements. For the IMCTs, in addition to the considerations on disease epidemiology, differences in medical practice, differences in drug metabolism, and dose selection the following should also be considered:

- Selection of control products

In the IMCTs, companies are required to conduct full argumentation with respect to the proposed reference drug, and consider their indications approved, availability and usage in the relevant countries. In cases of different therapeutic guidelines and when different therapeutic drugs are used as the gold standard in different countries, it is crucial to expound and prove the basis of determination of the reference drug. Regarding the selection of the placebo, it is mandatory to fully consider the differences in the approval procedures and standards of the ethics committees or other relevant organizations in different countries and regions.

- Efficacy evaluation indicators

For pivotal IMCT, it is recommended to establish the unified endpoint evaluation committee for independent evaluation of the primary efficacy endpoints, and to set up clinical trial center laboratories to conduct the unified testing of the important laboratory parameters to ensure the objectivity and consistency of the study findings.

- Sample size considerations

Different countries or regions may have different regulation systems and different requirements on the sample size of the patients for registration application. Without violating the regulations of any country or region, the sample size shall be reasonably distributed among different countries and centers, and corresponding scientific and legal basis for determination of such distribution shall be provided. In addition to satisfaction of the scientific principles required in statistics, it is also obligatory to fully consider the epidemiological characteristics of disease, the representativeness of sample selection and other relevant factors so as to determine the number of cases to be distributed among different regions and countries.

- Other statistical considerations

For the IMCTs, it is required to first develop the statistical methods to evaluate if there is trend consistency between the subgroup outcomes and the overall outcomes. It is required to conduct subgroup comparison for those important endpoints, i.e. primary efficacy and important secondary efficacy endpoints to analyze the trend of differences.

- Collection and evaluation of adverse events/reactions

It is recommended that companies establish independent data and safety monitoring committee to ensure the study quality and standardization. The sponsor shall follow the ICH guidelines and the country regulations to establish sound communication mechanism, submit safety-related information to all the research centers and their competent regulatory authorities on a regular basis, and keep all the communication records. For significant safety events or efficacy issues, including the decisions made by the data and safety monitoring committee, ethics committee and regulatory authorities, the sponsor shall inform the Chinese regulatory authorities and relevant agencies and personnel within 3 days.

- Other considerations

a. It is necessary to establish the independent data and safety monitoring committee and develop specific work mechanisms and procedures for the pivotal studies which have relatively large sample size and relatively long study duration, especially for those which are driven by clinical events. With regard to the studies where Chinese patients account for more than 20 % of the total number of patients, experts from China shall be included in the global independent data monitoring committee.

b. In the event that human factors may have impact on the determination of study outcomes, such as the pivotal IMCTs with radiographic evaluation results as the primary evaluation endpoint, it is necessary to establish the unified endpoint evaluation committee to conduct the unified independent evaluation for the primary efficacy endpoints. With regard to the trials that Chinese patients account for more than 20 % of the total patient number, experts from China should be included into the independent endpoint evaluation committee.
c. Center laboratory, transport and testing of blood and tissue samples: In the event of using the laboratory evaluation parameters as the primary efficacy and/or the important safety evaluation parameters, it is recommended to establish the center laboratory to conduct testing in a unified manner. In the event of establishing regional center laboratory, it is required to verify the quality control consistency among different laboratories to ensure the consistency and reliability of the experimental results. If it is necessary to send blood or tissue samples overseas for testing, such acts shall be subject to the requirements under relevant regulations.

8.3.8.5 Requirements on the Report of Registration Application

Wherever the sponsor intends to use the IMCT data to support its registration application in China, it shall submit the global study report, statistical analysis reports and databases of the accomplished IMCT as well as related supporting data, and shall summarize the subgroup study findings and conduct comparative analysis thereof.

The study report shall first summarize and analyze the overall global study data and then compare the efficacy and safety data of Asian populations with that of non-Asian populations and conduct trend analysis thereof. It shall also compare the efficacy and safety data of Chinese population with that of populations of other countries and conduct trend analysis thereof.

In the event of termination or failure of the IMCT, the sponsor shall submit the summary of study findings and the reasons for failure/termination to the regulatory authorities.

8.3.8.6 Requirements on Changes to Protocol

In the event of protocol changes during the course of the clinical trial, the sponsor needs to file the change with relevant authorities and go through the ethical review for changes which in principle do not increase the risk of subjects, such as mere modification of typos in the protocol.

In the event of changes that seriously jeopardize the safety of subjects or the purpose or quality of the clinical trial, the sponsor shall promptly inform the drug regulatory authorities and the ethics committees of the contents and grounds of such changes, including:

1. Dose or time of administration increase, or significant increase in subject number;
2. Increasing or reducing safety monitoring or diagnostic parameters which may have important impact on the safety and scientificity of the clinical trial;
3. Changes of the principal investigators;
4. Increasing or reducing clinical trial groups;
5. Changes of the main objectives of the clinical trial;
6. Changes of the primary endpoints which may significantly impact on the safety and scientificity of the clinical trial;
7. Changes of the measurement method of the primary endpoints;
8. New toxicological or pharmacological test data change the risk-benefit ratio of the clinical trial;
9. Endpoint Changes of the clinical trial;
10. Inclusion and exclusion criterion changes which may have important impact on the safety and scientificity of the clinical trial;
11. Reducing the monitoring frequency;
12. Revocation of the data and safety monitoring committee;
13. Changes of the investigational drug or changes of the administration route.

8.4 Collaborative Localization Strategy

In recent years, in addition to the well-known examples of partnership established in China, such as a clinical pharmacology unit of AstraZeneca and Peking University Third Hospital, an infusion center of Johnson and Johnson and PLA General Hospital for its biologic clinical trials, more and more of such partnerships have been established to collaborate on new drug development. Regarding this trend, a few models are commonly accepted, including:

- partnership through licensing or a co-development approach;
- establishment of a joint venture company.

The establishment of those partnerships could greatly benefit the development of new drugs in China for the multinational pharmaceutical companies. One of the prominent benefits is they will be treated similarly to local manufacturing companies through this collaborative localization strategy (Fig. 8.1e).

By such strategy, the new drug development projects may also meet various incentive policies issued by Chinese government for encouraging new drug development, such as the "green channel" or fast track for investigational new drugs. Those policies or guidance will greatly accelerate the drug development processes through their faster regulatory review, more available meetings and communications with regulatory agencies.

It is also very important for multinational pharmaceutical companies to consider this strategy if the expected patent lives of their investigational drugs are not long enough or near or already expired upon approval. Based on the current guidance, local companies may develop their generic versions in line with the brand new drug. Similar to Bolar exemptions in the western world, local companies could put their generic versions soon after the patent expiration. By this collaborative localization strategy, multinational companies may gain up to a 5 year monitoring period protection as a Class I category drug in China.

Upon approval of the new drug in China, they may also qualify for the government supportive funding for their research and development activities. They may also possibly gain the support in market access. It is obvious that this pathway offers a great potential alternative benefit for the companies to develop their investigational drugs in China.

In addition to the aforementioned advantages of this pathway, companies should always use integrated thinking about their potential development strategies and take the following factors into consideration, such as their corporate overall goals, priorities, research pipeline, country expertise, and global human resource allocations, China market needs, fitness of local healthcare environment and competitors' status as well.

To target the best development scenario, one of the major factors for success is employee localization. Without local expertise, it is impossible to get the local regulatory insight, to fit the CFDA's regulatory requirements, to understand healthcare system and the standard treatment, and the unmet medical needs. One of the other very common hurdles for many multinational pharmaceutical companies is that they usually feel it is hard to find a suitable partner in China. Overall, strong local medical key opinion leaders and drug development experts are critically important for success.

In summary, all the regulatory strategies have their own pros and cons. Therefore, the pharmaceutical companies should evaluate their own situations to measure the development strategies and decide which is the most appropriate one for their investigational drug development in China.

8.5 IMCT Process in China

In general, multinational pharmaceutical companies should consider the overall processes for IMCT (MRCT and RMCT) application and conduction logistics to efficiently meet their registration goals. Since the RMCT is designed with a focus on the Chinese market, the CFDA approval is the critical milestone regardless the company possesses the local manufacturing facilities or not. Once they get CFDA approval, they should immediately initiate the surrounding country regulatory actions

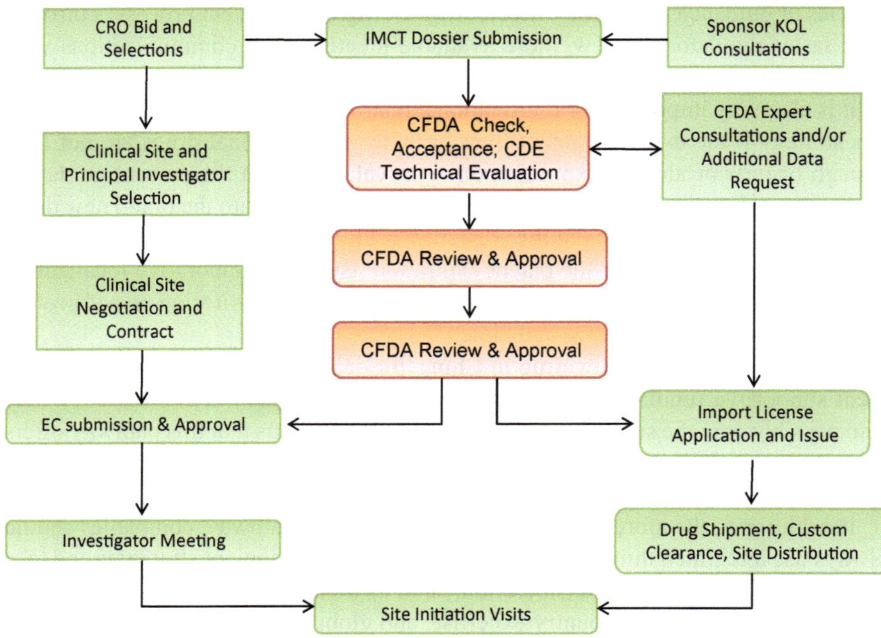

Fig. 8.4 IMCT application process in China

as well. Regarding the strategy for surrounding countries, we'll discuss it separately in the following sections. The dossier format in CTD is acceptable in simplified Chinese. The regulatory timeframe is still much longer than that of other countries. Technically, it is different from other Asian countries in that the companies have to get the CFDA approval to move to the next step for EC approval.

While the companies or their CROs are in the process of applying for clinical trial authorizations (CTA), they should also initiate the clinical CRO selection. It is important that the CRO has the local IMCT experience and the knowledge in the corresponding therapeutic field, key opinion leaders (KOLs), clinical sites, EC approval, import drug license application and drug handling. The following Fig. 8.4 provides a basic flow chart for the overall process.

8.6 Involvement of Other Asian Countries in RMCT

For MRCT trial application in China, most of international pharmaceutical companies include a minimum of three countries in their trial with the focus of China. Generally, the most commonly involved countries or special regions in the local RMCT of China include South Korea, Thailand, Indonesia, Singapore, Taiwan, Hong Kong, Malaysia, Vietnam and Japan. In consideration of the other Asian countries' involvement and selection strategies, we'll introduce some basic factors for consideration in this section.

8.6.1 Clinical Trial Regulations in Other Asian Countries

8.6.1.1 Regulatory Approval Processes for Clinical Trials—Thailand

In Thailand, the approval of clinical trial is operated by a non-profit organization, named Clinical Research Collaboration Network (CRCN), CRCN is an organization under the Medical Research Foundation. In 2012, CRCN changed its name to the Medical Research Network.

To get clinical trial approval, many country regulatory agencies have judicial authorities, including (a) Thai FDA; (b) Ministry of Public Health (MOPH), such as Department of Medical Services (DMS), Department of Communicable Disease Control (DCDC), Ethical Review Committee for Research in Human Subjects (ERC), National Sub-Committee of HIV Vaccine (NSCHIV); (c) Specific regulations of medical schools and hospitals (IDAT).

The clinical trial approval includes the following processes:

- Submission of the clinical trial application package to DMS
- Review of the application package by ERC
- Approval for clinical trial of the import drug by the new drug division
- The FDA grants permission.

Multinational pharmaceutical companies have to get approval from an authorized ethics committee, together with the following essential documents and preparations, including: details CMC description of the investigational drug; pre-clinical research data and outcomes; standard clinical trial protocol; the amount of drugs needed for the trial; a power of attorney. The approval process usually takes 14 weeks and approval is only valid for 1 year.

8.6.1.2 Regulatory Approval Processes for Clinical Trials—Indonesia

The National Agency of Drug and Food Control (NA-DFC) is responsible for clinical trial approval. Basically, all clinical trials have to comply with guidelines published in 2001 on Good Clinical Practices (GCP). The procedure comprises the following steps:

- Submission of the study proposal to the Institutional Review Board (IRB),
- Submission of the application package to NA-DFC including the essential documents including: research proposal; informed consent form (ICF); investigator's brochure; details of drug description to be used in clinical trial; approval letter of the IRB.
- Similar to the US FDA process for IND, the NA-DFC reviews the application and authorizes the clinical trials. In certain cases, it may ask for additional information. The NA-DFC's review will not exceed 10 days from the date of receipt. In the absence of a response above 10 days, the authorization is considered to be granted.

- Before the clinical trial initiation, an adequate compensation to the subjects for all damages or injuries incurred as a result of the trial have to be ensured by the companies.
- In the case that the clinical site intended for use is not usually used for healthcare purposes, the site has to be authorized by the NA-DFC.
- For serious adverse drug reactions, they have to be reported to the IRB and NA-DFC.
- At the end of the trial, multinational pharmaceutical companies have to report the termination date to the NA-DFC and IRB.

8.6.1.3 Regulatory Approval Processes for Clinical Trials—Singapore

The Singapore Guideline for Good Clinical Practice (SGGCP) was adapted from the ICH Guideline for GCP. Ethical and scientific standards to conduct clinical trials were set by SGGCP thus providing assurance for the credibility of the results obtained from the clinical trials. In Singapore, the Medical Clinical Research Committee (MCRC) is responsible for the authorization of clinical trials. All the clinical trials on investigational new drug require Clinical Trial Certificates (CTC) from the Singapore's Health Sciences Authority (HSA) and health products regulation group (HPRG).

The clinical site investigator must apply and obtain both ethics and regulatory approvals before initiating any clinical. The EC's responsibilities are similar to that of the western world, including reviewing all the trial documents including protocol, the consent form, the investigators brochure, recruitment procedure, advertising material etc.

Application procedure for CTC:

- Submission of the application form and the required supporting documents as specified in the application form by clinical investigator.
- The original set of application with its supporting documents must be submitted in five duplicated sets. Electronic applications for CTC are acceptable online via prism@hsa.
- The HSA issues regulatory approval and CTC is specific for each institution or site involved in the clinical study.
- A CTC is valid for 2 years. If a trial is not completed within 2 years, the multinational pharmaceutical company must apply for extension of the CTC and also submit interim clinical trial reports in support of the extension.

8.6.1.4 Regulatory Approval Processes for Clinical Trials—South Korea

The Korea Food and Drug Administration (KFDA) under the Ministry for Health, Welfare and Family Affairs (MIHWFA), is responsible for ensuring the safety and efficacy of foods, pharmaceuticals, medical devices and cosmetics, and supporting the development of the food and pharmaceutical industries.

The responsibilities of National Institute of Food and Drug Safety Evaluation (NIFDS), under the KFDA, include scientific investigation, research and evaluation to secure food and drug safety. The key functions of NIFDS include conducting risk assessments, monitoring food and drugs, developing guidelines and testing assays to support the policy for protection and promotion of public health.

In South Korea, the KFDA grants approval to new drugs. The KFDA also investigates basic research, efficacy, preclinical, and clinical data. The KFDA aims to make its decisions for approval within 95 days, with 70 days allocated to screen the safety and efficacy through data, and 25 days for the license review. The application documents can be submitted through its online system. During the review process, the task force team checks the documents submitted by the companies for completeness. In case of incompleteness, the task force team will ask the applicant to provide it within 5 days. The preliminary reviews of the results, technology, safety, efficacy, data quality, and social impacts are carried out by the pharmaceutical safety policy division and the drug evaluation department. Based on satisfactory review, the KFDA provides a certificate of approval to the companies or request supplemental information from the companies.

8.6.1.5 Clinical Trial Regulations—Taiwan

For MRCT application, the multinational pharmaceutical companies should consult the Center for Drug Evaluation (CDE) for their advice. The revised application will be further reviewed by the International Review Board and CDE and the Bureau of Pharmaceutical Affairs (BOPA). The above regulatory agencies will decide to grant or refuse the clinical trial application in Taiwan.

8.6.1.6 Regulatory Approval Processes for Clinical Trials—Philippines

The Philippines FDA (PFDA) is in charge of the clinical trial protocol approval for investigational new drugs or biological products. All relevant documentation and information regarding the investigational drug are required. GMP, GLP and GCP are mandatory.

IMCT Application procedure:

The company files a letter of application with proper documents support.

The PFDA evaluates the completeness of submitted documents, the clinical trial protocols with their KOLs, and clinical pharmacologists.

The main points to be considered in the evaluation include: previous clinical trials from Phase I-III; the target indication; compliance of GLP, GMP and GCP; the medical need and value of the investigational drug; qualification of the investigators, sites, monitors and companies; clinical endpoints and content of the protocol; EC or IRB in place.

If necessary, the PFDA may request the company, monitor, or principal investigator to address more questions or ask for advice from external experts. The clinical trial protocol will be approved by the PFDA if the application meets all of the requirements.

8.6.1.7 Regulatory Approval Processes for Clinical Trials—Malaysia

The application of a clinical trial is reviewed by two committees. The Research Review Committee (RRC) reviews the scientific value of research proposal. The Medical Research Ethics Committee (MREC) reviews the ethical aspects of the research study.

IMCT Application procedure:

- The company should fill out the application form and submit it to the secretariat, Standing Committee for Medical Research (SSCMR).
- The RRC and MERC review the documents, comment on it and then pass it on to the SSCMR for review. SSCMR forwards it to investigator for corrections and amendments. The investigator corrects the application and re-submits it to SSCMR.
- The SSCMR forwards all results and comments given by RRC and MERC to the Director-General of Health, Malaysia. The Director General of Health issues the final decision on application and informs the SSCMR. The SSCMR then informs the company for its decision of the approval or rejection.
- The total time period of clinical trial approval from submission to RRC and MERC to the final approval by the Director General of Health in Malaysia is 12–16 weeks.

8.6.2 Regulatory and Clinical Trial Start-up Timelines

When a multinational pharmaceutical company intends to launch an IMCT, the timeframe related to each procedures and the overall timeline have to be taken into consideration. While many CROs may have a slightly different timeline based on their own experience or the nature of the clinical programs, it is very much agreed that China takes the longest time for regulatory approval for the IMCT compared to other Asian countries. The following table provides a very rough idea about the timeframe needed to launch an Asian regional trial in different countries or regions for consideration.

In addition to the listed factors in the above table, the investigational drug import license, shipment, and custom clearance timeframe should also be considered. Generally, the time needed could range from 1 to 2 weeks. However, for some countries, it could require a much longer time, e.g. it needs 2–4 weeks in Indonesia, and 8–12 weeks for Philippines to accomplish such logistic procedures.

8.6.3 Other Factors to be Considered—Regulatory Requirement for Patient Numbers

When a multinational pharmaceutical company is planning to run a global MRCT or local RMCT, they may also consider the Asian pacific strategies regarding the

Table 8.2 Regulatory and clinical trial start-up timelines

Country	Dossier format	Acceptable language	Regulatory approval	EC approval	Site Contract negotiation	Post-approval to first SIV
China	Local or CTD	Simplified Chinese	8–10 months	6–8 weeks	10 weeks	1–2 weeks
Note: Regulatory approval first, then EC approval						
Thailand	ICH or ASEAN CTD	English & Thai	4 weeks	6–8 weeks	8–10 weeks	1–2 weeks
Note: EC approval first, then regulatory approval						
Indonesia	ASEAN CTD	Bahasa & English	6–8 weeks	4–8 weeks	8–10 weeks	1–2 weeks
Note: EC approval first, then regulatory approval. Regulatory and scientific committee (EC) approval may run parallel with EC approval						
Malaysia	ICH or ASEAN CTD	English	6–8 weeks	6–8 weeks	8–10 weeks	1–2 weeks
Note: Regulatory and EC approval may run parallel						
Philippines	ICH or ASEAN CTD	English	8–12 weeks	8–12 weeks	8–12 weeks	1–2 weeks
Note: Regulatory and EC approval may run parallel						
Singapore	ICH or ASEAN CTD	English	6–8 weeks	4–8 weeks	8–10 weeks	2–4 weeks
Note: Regulatory and EC approval may run parallel						
S Korea	ICH or ASEAN CTD	Korean & English	12–16 weeks	6–8 weeks	4 weeks	4 weeks
Note: Regulatory and EC approval may run parallel						
Taiwan	ICH or ASEAN CTD	Chinese	8–16 weeks	12 weeks	8–10 weeks	2 weeks
Note: Regulatory and EC approval may run parallel						

EC ethics committee, *SIV* site initiation visit, *ASEAN* The Association of Southeast Asian Nations, *CTD* Common technical document

surrounding country import drug license (IDL) application. However, the regulatory requirements for IDL are very different and it highly depends on the corresponding country's policies.

In general, the requirement of the original country's approval is a must to get the IDL.

The minimum local patient number is critical for the utilization of IMCT data for application of marketing access authorization in China and other Asian countries.

For China IDL approval following the Class III drug regulatory pathway, the minimum local patient count should be at least 100 patients in active treatment arm.

For Korea IDL approval, local PK study can be waived if local data available. There is no defined patient number by regulations. Generally, 50 patients in active treatment arm may be considered acceptable for oncology drug IDL while for other category drugs, 100 patients in the active treatment arm should be considered.

For Taiwan IDL approval, local PK study can be waived if local or global clinical trials include Taiwanese. By principle, the number of valid Taiwanese patients in an IMCT should be at least 80 or more than 10% of the total patients.

For the rest of the countries, such as Singapore, there is no requirement for specific patient numbers or local PK bridging studies.

References

CFDA (2014) Guidance for International Multicenter Clinical Trials (IMCT) (Trial), Draft for Public Comment, No. 698; by the CFDA; Issued on Nov. 21, 2014

Kang CL (6 June 2012) International multi-center clinical trials and early studies of the Chinese attitude. Medicine Economic News

Li YJ et al (14 January 2008) Consideration for the requirements of an international multi-center clinical trial application dossier. Guangzhou Biomedical Net. http://old.newstar-chem.com/display.asp?id=2462. Accessed 26 Dec 2012

SFDA (18 June 2007) Provisions for drug registration, No. 28. http://eng.sfda.gov.cn/WS03/CL0768/61647.html. Accessed 12 Dec 2013

SFDA (2009a) Administrative regulations for technology transfer registration of drugs http://wenku.baidu.com/link?url=SJvYCdADZ5oKa_sJi5HznUyXwS1flViCg_M6gjIc_fcuWHVnkjDb9ugPMrbrr3bzO7fJLgtXQIso. Accessed 10 Nov 2013

SFDA (2009b) Regulations of special examination and approval in new drug registration. Issued by the SFDA on January 7, 2009

Su L (2013) Drug development models in China and the impact on multinational pharmaceutical companies. FDLI, Update, pp 19–23; Sept/Oct 2013

Thoelke KR (2013) Including China in your global clinical development strategy why, when and how. The 5th China Clinical Trials Outsourcing Congress, March 4–5, 2013

Yang, B (15 January 2013) SFDA proposes new review channel for innovative drugs. PharmAsia News

Chapter 9
Drug Safety Monitoring and Reporting Systems in China

Ming Q. Lu, Qinping Liao, Jianpeng Wang and Tao Lv

9.1 Introduction

It is estimated that the total value of drugs on the Chinese healthcare market reached RMB 1114 billion in 2013. In this market, imported drugs accounted for roughly one fourth. The Chinese healthcare market will undoubtedly attract more and more multinational pharmaceutical companies in the coming decades.

China has its own regulations, policies, and management system, all of which differ greatly from those of the western world. While such regulations are constantly changing and improving to harmonize with international standards, some disparities remain to fit the local healthcare environment and culture specificities (Xu and Wang 2009) . For example, there are stark differences in the following aspects:

1. Regulatory system and structure: China's operates at the national level, province level and even city level. There are safety monitoring centers or authorities, while there are only national-level regulatory agencies in most of the western world;
2. Reporting forms: China doesn't accept CIOMS I or MedWatch forms, and they have their own form and requirements;
3. Investigators have more responsibilities: they are required to report to ethics committee (EC), Sponsor and multiple regulatory agencies at different levels;

M. Q. Lu (✉)
Helsinn Therapeutics (U.S.), Inc., 1140 US Highway 22, Suite 101, Bridgewater, NJ 08807, USA
e-mail: Mingqilu@verizon.net

Q. Liao · T. Lv
Division of Gynecology/Obstetrics and Pediatrics, Beijing Tsinghua Chang Gung Hospital, Changping Tiantongyuan, No. 168 Litang Road, 102218 Beijing, P. R. China

J. Wang
Echocardiography, Cardiovascular Institute and Fuwai Hospital, Chinese Academy of Medical Sciences, 100037 Beijing, P. R. China

M. Q. Lu (ed.), *Approaching China's Pharmaceutical Market*,
DOI 10.1007/978-3-319-15576-0_9

4. Reporting content: all serious adverse event (SAEs) are required to report regardless of causalities in their clinical trials; Suspected Unexpected Serious Adverse Reaction (SUSAR), Adverse Drug Reactions (ADRs) and cluster Adverse Events (AEs) are required to report for their marketed drugs;
5. Reporting time frames: the time frames required by the CFDA corresponding regulations are very different from the western world; it is highly dependent on the drug's status, e.g. drugs in the clinical trials stages or in the market already; it also depends on the nature of the events;
6. Drug categories: chemical drugs, traditional Chinese Medicine (TCM), and vaccines have different safety monitoring and reporting requirements. See details in the corresponding sections (CFDA 2014; Zhang 2012) .

In addition to these aspects, the cultural differences between China and overseas countries as well as the language barriers will add more challenges to multinational pharmaceutical companies.

In the following sections, we'll analyze the differences between China and the western world regarding safety monitoring and reporting systems. Key regulations will be discussed. Considering the disparities regarding the drugs under clinical development and those with marketed status, we'll discuss the corresponding regulatory requirements, monitoring and reporting procedures in different sections. The reporting items, forms, procedures and time limits as required by the corresponding regulations will be introduced.

9.2 Historic Development of Regulations for Safety Management

Since the launch of China's Adverse Drug Reaction Monitoring System in 1988, ADR Monitoring has become an important approach and measure to detect drug safety information, strengthen drug safety supervision, promote the safe and rational use of clinical drugs, and control drug risks. It has thus played an important role in the assurance of drug safety for the public.

Before 1989, the Chinese Ministry of Health (MOH) had already established about ten preliminary safety Monitoring Units in China. However, the data was mainly collected through literature review and case reports from hospitals and patients. The ADR monitoring system in China was established for western chemical drugs in 1989 as a voluntary reporting system with a National Center collecting and compiling reports. The regulations for safety management have been enhanced significantly after year 2000 as marked by the promulgations of "Pharmaceutical Administration Law of the People's Republic of China" in 2001, "Good Clinical Practice of Pharmaceutical Products" in 2003, "Provisions for Drug Registration" in 2007 (SFDA 2007), and "Adverse Drug Reaction Reporting and Monitoring Provisions" in 2011 (MOH and SFDA 2011) etc. Very recently, from the issued "Regulations for Management of Reporting Serious Adverse Events from Vaccine

Clinical Trials (Trial)" in 2014 (CFDA 2014), we can clearly see that significant effort has been made by the CFDA, which brings the Chinese regulations closer to international standards.

9.3 The Adverse Drug Reaction Monitoring System in China

The ADR Monitoring Center of the Chinese Ministry of Health (MOH) was established in 1989 with responsibilities for both chemical drugs and traditional Chinese medicine drugs (TCMs). In 1998, the National ADR Monitoring Center in China became a member of the WHO International drug monitoring program. In 1999, the National ADR Monitoring Center improved its regulation, organization and network infrastructure across China. The ADR monitoring system plays an essential role in identifying, reporting and managing drug safety events.

In addition to the CFDA National ADR Monitoring Center affiliated to the Chinese Ministry of Health, China has also established 34 provincial level monitoring branches by 2011. In recent years, the number of electronic submission users is steadily increasing. The pharmaceutical manufacturers and health care providers file ADR case reports directly via electronic submission system. In 2010, there were 40,826 registered users on the network, of which 21,785 (53.4 %) are medical institutions, 15,919 (39.0 %) are enterprises, and 3122 (7.6 %) are individuals and other users. In addition, general public can also file case report(s) through phone call, fax to city level, provincial monitoring center Based on the received information, the staff in the monitoring center will fill out a report form (SFDA 2012).

In 2011, the national ADR Monitoring System made a significant enhancement of the countrywide network, 333 provinces, autonomous regions and cities established the ADR Monitoring institutions or designated specialized agencies and personnel responsible for ADR Monitoring. Such progresses set up a solid foundation for the implementation of ADR Monitoring and reporting.

Another significant improvement is the re-constructed The ADR Monitoring Information Network System. The nationwide computerized ADR surveillance information system was initiated in 2003, aiming for the real-time online reporting. This system included the following major contents for ADR revaluations:

- data collection procedures
- case definitions, follow-up and assessment
- diagnostic criteria for ADRs
- procedures for communication with pharmaceutical manufacturers on safety issues
- focused surveillance of essential medicines

This computational platform provides basic capability for data storage and processing, identification of risk signals and overall evaluation. Based on the system evaluation outcome, the agencies are able to make their measurements and decisions, including package insert/instruction revision, suspension or withdrawal from market etc. Through this network, the National ADR Monitoring Center identified a series of drug safety problems in the clinical practice. The drug safety/risks were efficiently controlled after timely and appropriate assessment. This computerized system for coverage of direct reporting was expanding along with increasing online reporting units in 2011. The ADR monitoring system and network provided an effective warranty for the safe use of drugs throughout the country. The ADR surveillance in China has grown rapidly, made remarkable achievements, and continued its improvement.

9.4 Safety Management Related Regulations

9.4.1 Pharmaceutical Administration Law of the People's Republic of China, 2001

A series of regulations between 1999 and 2011 by MOH and SFDA have advanced the performance of the Centre. Especially in 2011, a further revision of the "Adverse Drug Reaction Reporting and Monitoring Provision" (MOH and SFDA 2011) was issued. This publication clarified the responsibilities of the ADR monitoring bodies of the local and provincial level (municipal, provincial or county), further standardized the procedures of ADR reporting and management, including the procedures for investigation and verification on serious ADR or mass ADR. It also strengthened the roles of pharmaceutical manufacturers, raised the technical standard of ADR assessment to advocate ADR research, and notably introduced concepts of focus monitoring and ADR information management. In addition, other regulations provide articles related to ADR monitoring. For example, in Chap. 10 of the "Good Manufacturing Practice For Drugs (2010 Revision)" (MOH and SFDA 2010), the section "Complaints and adverse reaction reports" was specially set up to strengthen the responsibility of pharmaceutical manufacturers with requirements for a dedicated ADR monitoring team to collect, investigate and manage ADR reports, take control of drug risk management and report ADRs to the Pharmaceutical Supervisory and Administrative Department. The assessment procedures of safety issues have been improved through the promotion of ADR research, focused monitoring, and ADR information management.

Pharmaceutical Administration Law of People's Republic of China, Article 71 issue in 2001 already clearly stated that a reporting system over any adverse reactions of pharmaceuticals shall be practiced by State. Pharmaceutical producing enterprises, pharmaceutical trading enterprises, and medical institutions shall conduct regular surveys on the quality, curative effects and adverse reactions of the pharmaceuticals they have produced, traded or used. When serious adverse reactions possibly related to the use of the pharmaceuticals are discovered, they must be promptly reported to the pharmaceutical supervisory and administrative departments and the administrative departments of health of the provinces, autonomous regions and municipalities directly under the central government. Detailed measures shall be formulated jointly by the pharmaceutical supervisory and administrative department under the State Council and the administrative department of health under the State Council.

Regarding the pharmaceuticals which have been confirmed to cause serious adverse reactions, the pharmaceutical supervisory and administrative department under the State Council and of the provinces, autonomous regions and municipalities directly under the central government, shall take urgent control measures including the cessation of the production, sale, and use of the pharmaceuticals, shall organize appraisals within 5 days, and shall make decisions on their administrative handling within 15 days from the conclusion date of the appraisals.

The first paragraph specifies the ADR monitoring and reporting system. ADR are classified as type A (Quantitative exceptions), and type B (quality). Type A is caused by pharmacological enhancement, and it can be predicted. It has high incidence in the population but its mortality is low. Type B is independent of the normal pharmacological effects. It has low incidence in the population but its mortality is high. Briefly, ADRs in China may mainly include side effects, toxicity, allergic reactions, drug addiction, mutagenic, teratogenic, carcinogenic effects and other adverse reactions. In accordance with the provisions of this article, when a serious ADR is identified, it has to be reported to the local province, autonomous region, or municipality directly under the central government and drug supervision and management departments and the public health administrative department in a timely manner. The second paragraph of the article confirmed the handling procedure for drug serious adverse reactions. The drug regulatory department under the State Council or of the provinces, autonomous regions, municipalities directly under the Central People's government could take the action to stop drug production, sale, or use in emergency control measures. They may use the emergency control measures once the ADRs are confirmed based on the integrated information of ADRs in domestic and overseas regions.

In addition to stop the production, sale, use of emergency control measures for the serious adverse reactions, the regulatory agencies are required to organize the authentication within 5 days, provide the technical basis for the administrative process. Relevant, administrative supervision departments shall make administrative decisions within 15 days after the authentication conclusion is drawn. The administrative decisions generally include two types: i.e. (1) to revoke the drug approval number or the drug import registration certificate, or, (2) continue the use of the drug under controlled condition through amending the specification, adjusting the dosage, adding attention and given special warning measures.

9.4.1.1 Good Clinical Practice of Pharmaceutical Products, the SFDA Order No. 3, 2003

There are four articles related to the safety management, i.e. Article 10, 26, 40 and 47 (SFDA 2003). Article 10 clarified that the protocol of the trial must be reviewed and approved by the Ethics Committee. When conducting a clinical trial, any amendment of the protocol may not be implemented without approval from the Ethics Committee. Any SAEs that occur during the trial shall be reported to the Ethics Committee. Article 47 defined the monitors responsibilities, i.e. the monitor shall supervise and urge that the clinical trial be conducted according to the standard operating procedures (SOP), and in compliance with the protocol, as well as confirm that all AEs have been recorded and SAEs have been reported within the required time period and filed.

Importantly, Article 26 defined the investigator's responsibilities for handling SAEs. i. e., the investigator has an obligation to adopt and make a record of necessary measures to protect the safety of the human subjects. If an SAE occurs during a clinical trial, the investigator shall immediately provide appropriate medical treatment to the human subject and report to drug administration authorities, the sponsor and the Ethics Committee. The investigator shall sign and date this report. In Article 40, it is clearly stated that the sponsor and the investigator shall study the SAEs immediately after occurrence and take necessary measures to ensure the human subject's safety and interests. Adverse events shall be reported to drug administration authorities, health administrative authorities and the other investigators conducting clinical trials on the same drug.

9.4.1.2 Provisions for Drug Registration, the SFDA Order No. 28, 2007

This is one of the most important regulations for pharmaceutical companies. There are four articles related to the safety management, i.e. Article 41, 42, 43 and 44 (SFDA 2007).

Article 41 defined the timeframe for reporting of SAEs and to whom the report should be sent. It is stated that if any SAE occurs during the clinical trial, the investigators shall report to the drug regulatory departments of the relevant provinces, autonomous regions or municipalities directly under the Central Government and the State Food and Drug Administration (now named CFDA) and notify the applicant within 24 h, and report to the ethic committee in time.

Article 42 stated their potential actions in case of violations. In any of the following circumstances during a clinical trial, the State Food and Drug Administration may order the applicant to modify the protocol, suspend or terminate the clinical trial:

1. The ethic committee fails to perform its duty;
2. Safety of the subjects cannot be adequately ensured;
3. A serious adverse event is not reported within the specified timeline;
4. There is evidence to prove that the drug used for the clinical trial is not effective;
5. A quality problem of the drug used for the clinical trial occurs;
6. There is fraud in the clinical trial; or
7. There is any other case violating Good Clinical Practice.

Article 43 clarified more potential actions that may be taken under certain conditions. Where there is any large-scale and unexpected adverse reaction or SAE, or

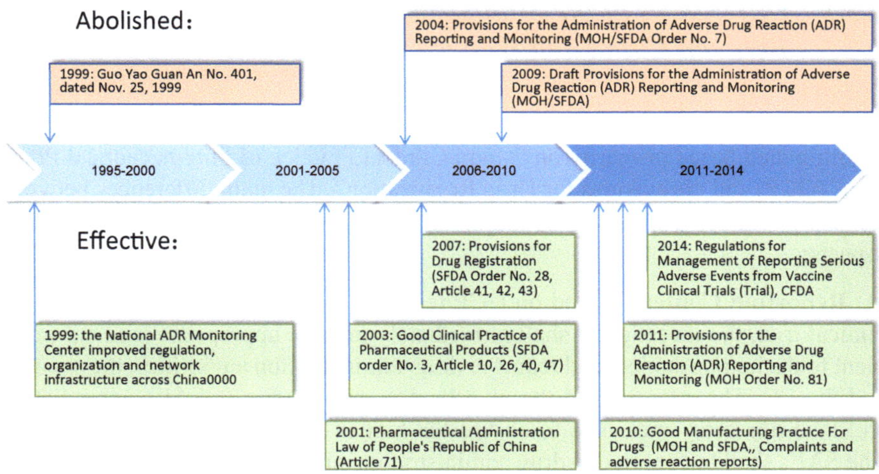

Fig. 9.1 Historic development outline of safety regulations in China

there is evidence to prove any serious quality problem of the drug used for a clinical trial, the State Food and Drug Administration or the drug regulatory department of the province, autonomous region or municipality directly under the Central Government may take emergency control measures and order to suspend or terminate the clinical trial. The applicant and clinical trial institution must stop the clinical trial immediately.

Article 44 is about reporting of SUSAR cases that occur overseas for multinational pharmaceutical companies when they conduct the international clinical trial in China. An overseas applicant intending to conduct an international multi-center clinical trial in China shall submit an application to the State Food and Drug Administration in accordance with the Provisions, and fulfill all the corresponding requirements. When conducting an international multi-center clinical trial in China, if there are any observed SUSAR cases in any country, the applicant shall, in accordance with relevant regulations, report to the State Food and Drug Administration in time; articles 41 and 44 set up the basis for clinical trial SAE case reporting that the whole country follow currently (Fig. 9.1).

9.5 Safety Management in Clinical Trials

It is important to understand the local safety monitoring and reporting requirements when multinational companies conduct their clinical trials in China. In the following sections, the differences of regulatory requirements for monitoring and reporting will be discussed. Since the requirements for clinical sites and investigators are set strictly by the CFDA, many clinical institutes have their own standard operational procedures for handling safety issues occurred in clinical trials. The common procedures and requirements from the clinical sites will be introduced as well.

9.5.1 Differences of the Monitoring Reporting Requirements Between China and Western Counties

Safety monitoring practice during the clinical trials of new investigational drugs is formulated based primarily on "Good Clinical Practice of Pharmaceutical Products" (GCP) and "Provisions for Drug Registration". The main differences between reporting requirements in China and those in ICH countries include the following aspects:

(1) Reporting Content Based on GCP requirements, if an SAE occurs during a clinical trial, the investigator shall immediately provide appropriate medical treatment to the human subject and report to drug administration authorities, the sponsor and the EC. The sponsor and the investigator shall study the SAEs immediately and take necessary measures to ensure the human subject's safety and interests. The SAEs shall be reported to drug administration authorities, health administrative authorities and the other investigators conducting clinical trials on the same drug. Based on Provisions for Drug Registration, if any SAE occurs during the clinical trial, the investigators shall report to the drug regulatory departments of the relevant provinces, autonomous regions or municipalities directly under the Central Government SFDA and notify the applicant within 24 h, and report to the EC in time (SFDA 2003).

Therefore, it is clear that SAEs occurring during clinical trials should be reported in accordance with regulatory requirements and the timeframe is within 24 h.

Based on ICH E2A "Guidelines of clinical safety data management-definitions and standards for expedited reporting", the required expedited reporting standard is suspected, unexpected, serious adverse reactions (SUSAR) cases only (ICH E2A 1994). For expected ADR, regardless it is serious or none serious, there is no requirement for expedited reporting.

For the definition of the adverse event, adverse reaction, serious adverse events, unexpectedness and causality evaluation criteria, there are no much differences globally (see the following for the corresponding definitions):

Adverse Event: An untoward medical event in a patient or clinical investigation subject administered a drug and which does not necessarily have a causal relationship with this treatment.

Serious Adverse Event: A serious adverse event includes inpatient hospitalization, prolongation of hospitalization, disability/incapacity, effect on work capability, life threatening, death, congenital anomaly etc., which occur during a clinical trial.

Unexpected adverse reactions: The nature, extent or frequency of the consequences is inconsistent with previously expected risk profile or other relevant information (e. g investigator's brochure) described for adverse reactions. Investigator's brochure is the main reference document for determining the expected or unexpected adverse reactions.

Causality evaluations: Based on the GCP, the relationship between adverse events and study drugs are divided into five levels, i.e. definitely related, probably related, possibly unrelated, irrelevant, unable to determination. However, similar to the western world, there is no standard nationwide nomenclature for causality assessment.

(2) Reporting Timeframes Based on "Provisions for Drug Registration", investigators should report serious adverse events occurred during a clinical trial within 24 h (SFDA 2007). Based on ICHE2A, fatal or life-threatening, unexpected ADR should be notified as soon as possible but no later than 7 calendar days after first knowledge by the sponsor and the complete report as possible within 8 additional calendar days. All other serious, unexpected ADRs should be reported no later than 15 calendar days after first knowledge by the sponsor (ICH E2A 1994).

(3) Reporting Requirements and Forms There is no special description about the content requirements. In Regulations for Management of Reporting Serious Adverse Events from Vaccine Clinical Trials (Trial), issued by the CFDA on January 17, 2014 (CFDA 2014), Article 6 provided some corresponding requirements. Briefly, (a) The content of the first report should comprise at least an SAE name, or a preliminary diagnosis, basic information about a subject, a test vaccine information. (b) If it is an unexpected event, severity, causality, the treatments and reporting sources, etc. should be provided. (c) For the follow-up report, it should be comprised of newly acquired SAE information, the modified information on the previous report and the necessary explanations, analysis and evaluation of SAE and their possible hints, and the outcomes of risk assessment for the subjects. Even though the requirements are for vaccine, it provides helpful reference for the SAE report of other medications.

Based on ICHE2A requirements, a serious ADR should meet the minimum reporting standards, namely: a subject's details, suspected test drug, the report source, the event name and the consequences of the event as indicated in the CIOMS-I form. In addition, the report form adopted in most countries, i.e. CIOMS-I form is acceptable, while in China, different companies may use different forms for SAE records and reporting. Compared with the CIOMS-I form, GCP SAE report form includes extra items, i.e. the medical institutions, medical field name and the name of the reporting unit; however, this does not include concomitant medication use and sponsor's information.

(4) Evaluation and Causalities Based on the attached form for SAE reporting in the annex of GCP, the relationship between adverse events and study drugs are divided into 5 levels, i.e. definitely related, probably related, possibly unrelated, irrelevant, unable to determination (SFDA 2003).

Assessments of adverse reactions associated with the marketed drugs are different from the investigational drugs in clinical trials. They are divided into six categories: i.e., definitely, probably, possibly, probably unrelated, pending evaluation, cannot be evaluated. For causality assessments between the adverse reactions and investigational drugs, the commonly used terms include: certain, probable/likely, possible, unlikely etc.

Based on ICH Guideline E2A for clinical safety data management, there is currently no standard international nomenclature for causality assessment. For expedited reporting of SUSAR, many terms and scales are used to describe the degree of causality e.g., certainly, definitely, probably, possibly or likely related, remotely related or not related.

It is similar to the western world in that there is no universal grading or fixed terminology for causality assessments. In general, China's causality assessments for marketed drugs are consistent with the WHO grading standards (five-scale grading system).

(5) Reporting Parties According to GCP (Article 26), if an SAE occurs during a clinical trial, the investigator shall immediately report to drug administration authorities, the sponsor, and the EC. The sponsor and the investigator shall study the SAEs immediately and take necessary measures to ensure the human subject's safety and interests. The SAEs shall be reported to drug administration authorities, health administrative authorities and the other investigators conducting clinical trials on the same drug. Based on Provisions for Drug Registration (Article 41), if any SAE occurs during the clinical trial, the investigators shall report to the drug regulatory departments of the relevant provinces, autonomous regions or municipalities directly under the Central Government SFDA and notify the applicant within 24 h, and report to the EC in time (SFDA 2007).

Thus, both investigators and sponsors are responsible for reporting SAEs. In accordance with the ICH requirements, sponsor is responsible for Suspected Unexpected Serious Adverse Reaction (SUSAR) to the regulatory authorities (Table 9.1).

9.5.2 General Safety Monitoring and Reporting Requirement and Processes

Due to the differences in monitoring and reporting systems for drug adverse event between China and western countries in clinical trials, the investigators are responsible for reporting an SAE within 24 h. The report will be submitted to not only EC, sponsor, but also various levels of the CFDA agencies. The investigators usually use the 5-level grading scales for causality assessment and report the SAE in simple Chinese using the format of an SAE form. Due to the complicated responsibilities of the investigators, many medical institutes/hospitals with the CFDA qualified sites have their own standard practices for adverse events and SAE processing procedures.

Those standard operating procedures were developed for AEs and SAEs management to ensure timely processing of AEs and SAEs occurring in clinical trials, and maximize the protection of the interests of the subject. The corresponding requirements and procedures usually include the following aspects.

Table 9.1 Comparison of differences of the monitoring and reporting requirements between China and western counties

Items	CFDA	ICH Countries
Regulatory agencies	CFDA at country level; CFDA at province level and even city level has safety monitoring centers	FDA or EMA: there are only country level regulatory agencies existing in most of the western world to accept safety reports
Reporting forms	China has their own form and requirements	MedWatch or CIOMS I
Overall reporting responsibilities	Both investigators and sponsors have the responsibilities for reporting SAEs to regulatory authorities	Sponsors have responsibilities for SUSAR report to the regulatory authorities
Investigator reporting responsibilities	To report to local ethics committee, sponsor and multiple regulatory agencies at different levels, i.e. CFDA at province and state levels	Report to ethics committee, CRO/sponsor
Sponsor reporting responsibilities	To report all SAEs in clinical trials to regulatory agencies and other investigators; To report overseas SUSAR to CFDA	To report to central ethics committee, other investigators and country regulatory agencies, e.g. FDA and EMA
Reporting content	1) All SAEs are required to report regardless of causalities in their clinical trials; 2) Suspected Unexpected Serious Adverse Reaction (SUSAR), Adverse Drug Reactions (ADRs) and cluster Adverse Events (AEs) are required to report for marketed drugs	Suspected Unexpected Serious Adverse Reaction (SUSAR)
Reporting time frames	The time frames are different for drugs in the clinical development stages and in the market. SAE in Clinical trial <24 h	The time frames are the same for drugs in the clinical development stages and in the market. Fatal or Life-Threatening SUSAR ≤ 7 calendar days and the complete report as possible within 8 additional calendar days. All other SUSARs ≤ 15 calendar days after first knowledge by the sponsor
Drug categories	Chemical drug, traditional Chinese Medicine (TCM) and vaccine have different safety monitoring and reporting requirements, e.g. for vaccine, SAE ≤ 24 h by investigator; fatal or life-threatening SUSAR ≤ 7; other SUSARs ≤ 15 calendar days by sponsor, which is closer to the western standards. While for chemical drugs, they all follow the rule of SAE ≤ 24 h	The same for various drug categories
Causalities	No standard nomenclature. Usually, (1) 5-level system: definitely related, probably related, possibly unrelated, irrelevant, unable to determination for clinical events; (2) 6-level system: definitely, probably, possibly, probably unrelated, pending evaluation, cannot be evaluated	No standard international nomenclature; Binary system (Yes, No) gets popular in recent years

9.5.2.1 Requirements Prior to the Clinical Trail

Medical institutes/hospitals and EC have common requirements for study material, the contents of the protocol, and the plan for handling medical emergencies, as listed below:

- Sponsor should provide pre-clinical safety research data and other safety related data, and includes such information in the investigator's brochure.
- To clearly state the AE definition, the severity criteria and causality evaluation criteria between AEs and investigational drug, e. g., certainly related, probably related, possibly unrelated, unrelated and unable to be determined).
- The protocol should clarify that investigators should fill out an AE form, record the onset time, severity, duration, treatment and outcome.
- Before the initiation of the clinical trial, the trial members must get familiar with the contents of the plan about how to prevent and treat medical emergencies for the patients.
- The patients should be informed about the contact information of the investigators, nurses or the EC.

9.5.2.2 Processing and Recording of Adverse Events

Inpatients

- If the adverse events occurred during hospitalization, the following procedures should be followed:
- Once the adverse events are found, the doctor on duty shall promptly inform the investigator. If necessary, symptomatic treatment could be started first. The investigator should conduct a preliminary assessment of the adverse events, including severity and causality assessment, and then provide further treatment advice.
- General adverse events: carefully observe the progress, or provide corresponding treatment for the symptoms based on protocol;
- Important adverse events: Investigator should promptly inform the principal investigator (PI), and in accordance with protocol requirements suspend the investigational drug, adjust drug doses and provide corresponding treatment. If necessary, PI can decide whether to take emergency unblinding;
- Serious adverse events: In accordance with the standard procedures, initiate the treatment and report the events promptly per SOP requirement.
- Investigators provide the proper treatment. If the patient's damages are beyond the treatment capacity of the department, the investigator should notify emergency response teams and initiate the contingency plan for handling such cases.

Outpatients

- After the awareness of adverse events, investigators need to get details about the symptoms, signs and location, etc.; provide necessary explanations and guidance to the patients; conduct a preliminary assessment of the AE severity and causality.

- If the patient is in a local medical facility, the investigator should get in touch by phone with the admission doctor to verify the severity of adverse events again and provide treatment advice;
- General adverse events: Patient can go to a local hospital for treatment initially, and inform the investigator about the event outcome;
- Important adverse events: Recommend patient to go back to the hospital for treatment or go to a local hospital for treatment, and promptly inform the PI. If the local hospital has limited or poor conditions, the hospital conducting the clinical trial should send medical doctors to treat the patient. The doctor may carry emergency envelopes to prepare for an emergency unblinding. In accordance with the protocol, the investigator may take the following procedures, including discontinuation of the drug, adjustment of drug doses and treatment of the symptoms or disease conditions.
- Hospital or institutional clinical trial organization staff may assist the clinical trial research team to track the adverse events, until they are properly resolved or reach a stable condition.

9.5.2.3 Processing and Reporting of Serious Adverse Events (SAEs)

General Procedures

- When an SAE is suspected, the doctor should inform the PI or other responsible doctors on site. If the illness is serious or judged as necessary, the doctor should immediately stop the investigational drug, start the treatment or rescue procedures and simultaneously inform the PI.
- When an SAE is identified, the doctors should administer the appropriate treatment or immediate rescue measures for the clinical manifestations in accordance with clinical standard treatment guidance. If an SAE is serious with toxic outcome caused by overdose, the investigator should decide the action to accelerate the excretion of drugs and take other rescue measures to stabilize the patient's vital signs. When necessary, ECG monitoring or relevant department consultations should be taken, and the plan for the prevention and treatment of medical emergencies and patient damage should be initiated.
- For outpatients, if an SAE is identified, it is suggested that the patients should come back to the hospital immediately. If the patient is unable to come to the clinic, the patient should go to a local hospital. The PI should be informed simultaneously for further treatment advice. If the patient is admitted in a local hospital, the local doctor should be contacted for details and be given treatment suggestions. When necessary, unblinding envelopes should be brought to the local or original hospital to assist the medical treatment.
- When an SAE is identified, the responsible investigator must report it within 24 h in writing to the PI, the ethics committee of drug clinical research organizations, sponsors, SAE commissioner in GCP center; GCP central office shall report the SAE to the State Food and Drug Administration (SFDA), the Provincial Food and drug Authority. For SAE report, the form provided by the sponsor or

the standard form provided by the SFDA could be used. For a sponsor-provided report form, it has to be in compliance with all legal and regulatory requirements of reporting procedures.

Emergency Unblinding

- If an important adverse event occurs, it is required to identify the drug category immediately during the rescue process. The PI should decide if emergency unblinding is needed. Once the code is unblinded, the patient will be discontinued. The CRA should be informed for the treatment outcome. The investigator should document the reasons for unblinding in the CRF, and provide the date and signature.

Recording

- Investigators should make a record of adverse events. The recording should include minimum the following information: description of adverse events, the onset time, end time, severity and frequency, the need for treatment, and the treatment.
- Record the SAE onset, development and treatment processes as detailed as possible in the source documents and record them in the CRFs. Follow up the SAE until a proper solution or stable condition is reached or the cause is clear. In this situation, the investigator should provide the final report to the PI, GCP center, EC, sponsor, and the CFDA (if necessary, a written report should be provided to certain agencies).

Note (Table 9.2 and 9.3):

Follow up report should be submitted within 24 h of notification (Fig. 9.2).

Follow up report should be submitted within 24 h of notification.

Table 9.2 The SFDA recommended analytical methods for adverse reaction

Items/Causality	Definitely related	Probably related	Possibly	Suspicious	Impossible
Occurs in a plausible time relationship to drug administration	+	+	+	+	–
Known types of drug response	+	+	+	+	–
Reduce or disappear after stopping the drug	+	+	±	±	–
After repeating the drug administration, the reaction appears again	+	?	?	?	–
Unable explain by the disease, or concomitant medication use	+	+	-	±	–

Table 9.3 Serious adverse event report form (sample)

Report Type	□ Initial □ Follow-up □ Summary			Report Time： DD MM YY	
Medical Institute & Medical Specialty				Phone:	
Report Unit Name				Phone:	
Investigational Drug Name	Chinese：				
	English：				
Drug Registration Category, Classification & Dosage Form	Category：□ TCM □ Chemical □ Therapeutic Biological Product □ Preventive Biological Product □ Other___________ Registration Classification： Dosage Form:				
Clinical Study Phase & Classification	□ I □ II □III □IV □ Bioequivalent □ Clinical Verifications			Clinical Trial Indication：	
Subject Basic Status	Name Initial (Pinyin):	Birthday:	Gender: □ Male □ Female	Height (cm)：	Weight (Kg)：
	Complicating disease and treatment：□ Yes □ No 1.Disease：_________Treatment Drug：________Usage & Dosage：_____________ 2.Disease：_________Treatment Drug: __________ Usage & Dosage：_____________ 3.Disease：_________Treatment Drug: __________ Usage & Dosage：_____________				
SAE Medical Term (Diagnosis)					
SAE Status	□ Death _____DD___MM____YY □ Hospitalization ☒ Prolonged Hospitalization □ Disability □ Dysfunction □ Cause birth defects □ Life Threatening □ Other				
SAE Onset Time： _____DD___MM____YY		The Time of Investigators learned SAE: ___________DD___MM____YY			
Measures Taken for Test Drug Administration	□ Continue Dosing ☒ Decrease Dose □ Drug Suspended and Resumed □ Drug Stopped				
SAE Outcome	□ Symptom Disappeared (Saquela ☒ Yes ☒ No) ☒ Symptom Continue				
Relationship of SAE and Test Drug	□ Definitely Related □ Probably □ Possibly Unrelated				
	□ Definitely Unrelated ☒ Unable to Determine				
SAE Report Status	Domestic： □ Yes □ No □ Unknown Overseas： □ Yes □ No □ Unknown				
Details of SAE Onset Status and Treatment Process:					

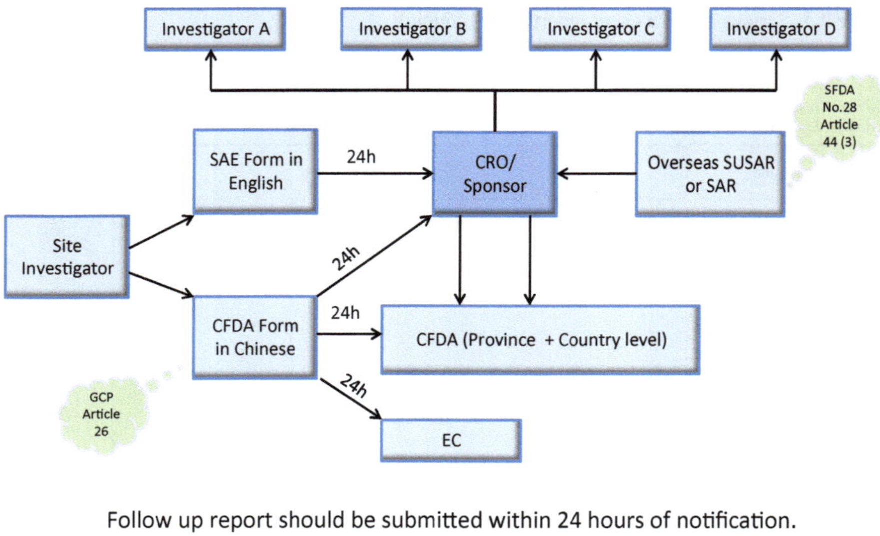

Fig. 9.2 The current flow-chart for investigational drug SAE reporting in china

9.5.3 The CFDA Issued "Notice on the issuance of Regulations for Management of Reporting Serious Adverse Events from Vaccine Clinical Trials (Trial)"

Issued on January 17, 2014 by the China Food and Drug Administration (CFDA 2014)

For the Food and Drug Administration of provinces, autonomous regions and municipalities, the Xinjiang Production and Construction Corps, and Drug Administration of the Health Department of General Logistics:

To further enhance the safety/risk management in vaccine clinical trials, reinforce the assurance for the safety of subjects, according to China's "Provisions for Drug Registration" and "Good Clinical Practice", with reference to international general principles, the CFDA organized the development of "Regulations for Management of Reporting Serious Adverse Events from Vaccine Clinical Trials (Trial)" (hereinafter referred to as the "Regulations"), which was issued on January 17, 2014. The "Regulations" comprise 16 Articles, requiring the vaccine clinical trial sponsors, institutions and investigators to follow the "Regulations" and report serious adverse events (CFDA 2014).

The CFDA requires Food and Drug Administration departments of all provinces, autonomous regions and municipalities directly under the central government to perform the following duties: First, to urge the parties involved in vaccine clinical trials to actively perform the duties of safety monitoring and reporting of serious adverse events in accordance with the requirements of the "Regulations", among which Suspected Unexpected Serious Adverse Reactions (SUSAR) and Periodic Safety Update Reports (PSUR) shall be submitted to the CFDA Center for Drug Evaluation by the sponsor in accordance with the "Regulations".

Second, to strengthen the supervision and inspection on the reporting of serious adverse events (SAEs) from vaccine clinical trial in daily administration, all departments shall take the serious adverse events as an important clue and perform targeted supervision and inspection of the vaccine clinical trial sponsors, institutions, investigators and other parties. (2014-01-17)

9.5.3.1 Regulations for Management of Reporting Serious Adverse Events from Vaccine Clinical Trials (Trial)

Issued on January 17, 2014 by the China Food and Drug Administration (CFDA 2014)

Article 1 The provision is prepared according to the "Drug Administration Law of the People's Republic of China", "Drug Registration", "Good Clinical Practice", laws and regulations etc., with reference to the international standard rules, to standardize the vaccine serious adverse events reporting in its clinical trials, to enhance vaccine safety information monitoring and ensure subject safety.

Article 2 The vaccine clinical trials in this provision refer to the vaccine clinical trials approved by the drug administration department of the State Council. All parties involved in the vaccine clinical trials should report serious adverse events to the drug regulatory authorities in compliance with this provision.

Article 3 The sponsor is responsible for safety information monitoring and serious adverse event reporting of the vaccine clinical trials. The sponsor shall designate a full-time staff responsible for clinical trial safety information monitoring and management of serious adverse event reports; should develop a clinical trial safety information monitoring and serious adverse event reporting standard operating procedures, and training of all relevant personnel; should master the latest clinical trial process safety information, safety risk assessment in a timely manner, and to notify investigators and the relevant regulatory authorities for the relevant information.

Article 4 The institutions for vaccine clinical trials should establish a clinical trial safety information reporting system, to create conditions for serious adverse event reporting. Investigators should collect safety information of serious adverse events in a timely manner, record serious adverse events truthfully and report it promptly to the sponsor, the Ethics Committee, and the relevant provincial regulatory agencies.

Article 5 Serious adverse event reports are divided into individual case reports and periodic safety reports.

Article 6 Individual case reports of serious adverse events include initial and follow-up reports.

a. The content of the first report should comprise at least a serious adverse event name, or a preliminary diagnosis, basic information about a subject, and test vaccine information. If it is a unexpected event, severity, and relevance to the test vaccine, the treatments, reporting sources, etc.
b. The content of the follow-up report should include newly acquired serious adverse event information, the modified information on the previous report and the necessary explanations, analysis and evaluation of serious adverse events and their possible hints, and the outcomes of risk assessment for the subjects.

Article 7 The content of the periodic safety reports should at least include subject risk analysis of the same vaccines in the clinical trials, all emerging safety information during the reporting period, a summary table of all serious adverse events, a summary table of all suspected unexpected serious adverse reactions (SUSAR).

Article 8 Investigators made aware of serious adverse events should immediately initiate the first report, in any case not later than 24 h after informed.

Article 9 After the sponsor is informed of serious adverse events, the sponsor should immediately conduct a comprehensive analysis of the serious adverse event to assess its severity, its relevance to the experimental vaccine, and whether it is an expected event. According to the nature of serious adverse events (category) and the following time limits, the sponsor should submit the first report to Center for Drug Evaluation of the State Food and Drug Administration (the "Administration"), the local provincial regulatory authorities and informed the relevant principal investigators in the clinical trial institutions:

a. For death or life-threatening suspicious and unexpected serious adverse reactions, the sponsor should report as soon as possible after the first informed, but no more than 7 calendar days, and report relevant follow-up information in the subsequent 8 calendar days.
b. For non-fatal or non-life-threatening suspicious and unexpected serious adverse reactions, the sponsor should report as soon as possible after the first learned, but no more than 15 calendar days.
c. For information about other potentially serious risks, the sponsor should report as soon as possible after being initially informed, but no more than 15 calendar days.

Article 10 Investigators and sponsors after the first reports should continue to monitor and follow up on the serious adverse events, and submit reports to promptly deliver new information or modified information corresponding to the previous reports, etc.

Article 11 The Ethics Committee should accept reports of serious adverse events and safety information etc., and, in a timely manner, control what happened, act correspondingly to the situation, track and review the treatments, reporting, and risks of the serious adverse events of the clinical trials.

Article 12 Either the sponsor, clinical trials institutions and investigators, the relevant ethics committees or provincial regulatory authorities, may suspend or terminate the clinical trials based on clinical trial safety/risk assessment that is needed to stop clinical trials. They should provide justification, inform other relevant parties, and provide report to the relevant regulatory authorities.

Article 13 Investigator and sponsor shall provide the relevant information of the serious adverse events and safety/risk assessment reports in a timely manner based on the requirements of the regulatory administration and ethics committee. Investigators should promptly forward the safety information of the clinical trials from the sponsor to the Ethics Committee.

Article 14 The sponsor shall submit periodic safety reports to Center for Drug Evaluation of the CFDA, the local provincial regulatory authorities and principal investigators of the clinical trials in all participating institutes. Periodic safety reports mainly mean annual reports; or in some situations, the periodic safety reports should be submitted periodically in writing by higher requirements of regulatory agencies and ethics committees.

Article 15 The CFDA accepts serious adverse events reported in the vaccine clinical trials in paper and electronic ways. According to the report, the proposed suspension, termination of vaccine clinical trials or other advice may be given when necessary.

Article 16 The CFDA shall make a decision based on technical advice. For those sponsors, clinical institutes and investigators who failed to report serious adverse events in accordance with the provision and caused the detriment of subjects, cases shall be handled according to the law.

Accessories: suspicious and unexpected serious adverse reaction case report forms

9.6 Safety Management for Post-Marketing Drugs

9.6.1 Introduction

The Ministry of Health of the People's Republic of China revised its Provisions for the Administration of Adverse Drug Reaction (ADR) Reporting and Monitoring (MOH and SFDA 2012), Order No. 81 on May 4, 2011. The provisions became effective on July 1, 2011, which aimed to establish a new safety administration paradigm for post-marketing drugs, to enhance the protection of human subjects and to improve pharmacovigilance (PVG) and risk management standards in China. At the same time, the previous version (Order No. 7, March 4, 2004) was annulled. The new version based on its draft issued on June 30, 2009 (trial) integrated many feedback inputs to harmonize local requirements with ICH-GCP global standards, including privacy in case reporting and aggregative report format as well as reporting timeline.

The key elements of Order No. 81 are highlighted as follows:

- The roles and responsibilities of the SFDA, the National Center for ADR Monitoring, the Provincial Center for ADR Monitoring, manufacturers, suppliers, hospitals and individuals;
- Requirement for independent PVG organizations, systems and staff at each manufacturer, including more proactive safety monitoring standards;
- Definitions of the Local Individual Case Safety Report (ICSR), the Multi-Case Report, the Overseas Case Report for import products (CIOMS II Line Listing) [3] and the Periodic Safety Update Report (PSUR);
- Mandatary archiving and documentation in PVG systems;
- Description of PVG activities in association with drug re-registration;
- Outline of the compensation conditions.

Based on the provisions of the Administration of ADR Reporting and Monitoring, multinational pharmaceutical companies are required to adjust their operations in order to be in compliance with the regulations in post-marketing drug safety. In addition, based on the concepts defined in the provisions, they may also need to adjust their practices related to safety reporting and monitoring processes in clinical trial or pre-clinical researches.

While the global clinical trials keep increasing and more overseas-marketed drugs are available in China, the Chinese regulatory authorities continue their effort to improve their management systems and regulations to coincide with international standards. International pharmaceutical companies should strictly follow Chinese regulation requirements and their concepts, e.g. they should use the Provisions attached corresponding forms to report their adverse events or ADRs, instead of the globally accepted CIOMS I form, including: Adverse Drug Reaction/Event Report Form; Cluster of Adverse Drug Events Information Form; and Overseas Adverse Drug Reaction/Event Report Form (Fig. 9.3).

9.6.2 Provisions for Adverse Drug Reaction Reporting and Monitoring

No. 81 of the Ministry of Health, the People's Republic of China, Issued on 4 May 2011

Chapter I General Provisions (MOH and SFDA 2011)

Article 1 The Provisions are formulated in accordance with the Drug Administration Law, other relevant laws and regulations of the People's Republic of China for the purpose of strengthening supervision over drugs in the market, standardizing adverse drug reaction (ADR) reporting and monitoring, and controlling drug risks in a timely and effectively manner to ensure the public safety of drug use.

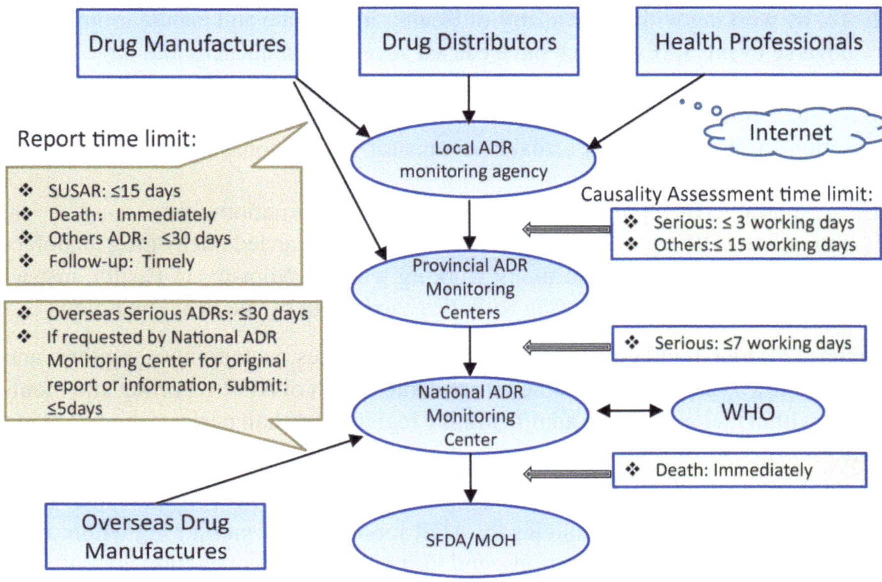

Fig. 9.3 ADR Reporting procedure for marketed drugs

Article 2 The Provisions are applicable to ADR reporting, monitoring and supervision within the territory of the People's Republic of China.

Article 3 The State puts the ADR reporting system into practice. Drug manufacturers including overseas manufacturers of imported drugs, drug distributors and medical institutions shall report their identified ADRs in accordance with the provisions.

Article 4 The State Food and Drug Administration (SFDA) shall be responsible for implementation of ADR reporting and monitoring across the nation. Local drug regulatory departments shall be responsible for implementation of ADR reporting and monitoring within their respective administrative regions. Health administrative departments at various levels shall be responsible for the implementation of the ADR reporting system by medical institutions within their respective administrative regions.

Local health administrative departments at various levels shall establish and maintain an ADR monitoring agency to be responsible for the technical aspect of ADR reporting and monitoring within their respective administrative regions.

Article 5 The State encourages all citizens, legal persons and other organizations to report ADRs

Chapter II Responsibilities

Article 6 The SFDA shall be responsible for the implementation of ADR reporting and monitoring across the nation and shall perform the following duties:

1. To, by working with the Ministry of Health, prepare regulations and policies for ADR reporting and monitoring, and to supervise implementation thereof;

2. To, by working with the Ministry of Health, investigate and handle group ADR/adverse events (AEs) which have caused severe consequences and have significant impact nationwide, and to release relevant information;
3. To take emergency control measures over drugs which have caused identified serious ADR or cluster AEs, make administrative decisions, and make announcement to the public;
4. To bulletin ADR reporting and monitoring outcomes nationwide;
5. To inspect ADR reporting and monitoring activities carried out by drug manufacturers and distributors, and to, by working with the Ministry of Health, inspect ADR reporting and monitoring activities carried out by medical institutions.

Article 7 Drug regulatory departments of provinces, autonomous regions and municipalities shall be responsible for implementation of ADR reporting and monitoring within their respective administrative regions and shall perform the following duties:

1. To, by working with the health administrative department at the same level, prepare regulations and policies for ADR reporting and monitoring within their respective administrative regions, and to supervise implementation thereof;
2. To, by working with the health administrative department at the same level, investigate and handle cluster AEs which have caused severe consequences and have great impact within their respective administrative regions, and to release relevant information;
3. To take emergency control measures over drugs which have caused identified severe ADR or cluster AEs, make administrative punishment decisions, and make announcement to the public;
4. To issue bulletin on ADR reporting and monitoring within their respective administrative regions;
5. To inspect ADR reporting and monitoring activities carried out by drug manufacturers and drug distributors within their respective administrative regions, and to, by working with the health administrative department at the same level, inspect ADR reporting and monitoring activities carried out by medical institutions within their respective administrative regions; and
6. To organize propaganda and training on ADR reporting and monitoring within their respective administrative regions.

Article 8 Drug regulatory departments at municipal/county level under their competent provincial department shall be responsible for implementation of ADR reporting and monitoring within their respective administrative regions. They shall, by working with the health administrative department the same level, investigate cluster AEs within their respective administrative regions and take necessary control measures, and shall execute propaganda and training on ADR reporting and monitoring within their respective administrative regions.

Article 9 Health administrative departments above county level shall strengthen regulatory management of clinical use of drugs by medical institutions, and shall take emergency control measures against identified serious ADR or cluster AEs within their scope of power according to law.

Article 10 The National ADR Monitoring Center shall be responsible for the technical aspect of ADR reporting and monitoring and shall perform the following duties:

1. To collect, evaluate, feedback and report ADR reporting and monitoring data across the nation, and to construct and maintain the National ADR Monitoring Information Network;
2. To prepare the technical standards and norms for ADR reporting and monitoring, and to provide technical guidance to local ADR monitoring bodies;
3. To organize the investigation and evaluation of serious ADRs, and to assist relevant departments to execute investigation on cluster AEs;
4. To release ADR alerts; and
5. To organize propaganda, training, research and international exchange regarding ADR reporting and monitoring.

Article 11 ADR monitoring bodies at provincial level shall be responsible for the technical aspect of ADR reporting and monitoring within their respective administrative regions and shall perform the following duties:

1. To collect, evaluate, feedback and report ADR reporting and monitoring data within their respective administrative regions, and to maintain and manage the ADR monitoring information network;
2. To provide technical guidance to ADR monitoring bodies at municipal/county level (which municipality or county is divided by districts);
3. To organize the investigation and evaluation of serious ADRs within their respective administrative regions, and to assist relevant departments to execute investigation on cluster AEs;
4. To organize propaganda and training on ADR reporting and monitoring within their respective administrative regions.

Article 12 ADR monitoring bodies at municipal/county level under their competent provincial department shall collect, verify, evaluate, feedback and report ADR reporting and monitoring data within their respective administrative regions, organize the investigation and evaluation of serious ADRs within their respective administrative regions, assist relevant departments to execute investigation on group ADRs/AEs, and organize propaganda and training on ADR reporting and monitoring.

Article 13 Drug manufacturers, drug distributors and medical institutions shall establish an ADR reporting and monitoring system. Drug manufacturers shall set up an independent unit and designate full-time staff to be responsible for the ADR reporting and monitoring. Drug distributors and medical institutions shall set up or designate full-time or part-time staff(s) from an independent unit to be responsible for the ADR reporting and monitoring

Article 14 Personnel engaged in ADR reporting and monitoring shall have medical, pharmaceutical, epidemiological, statistical or other relevant background, and be capable of making scientific analysis and evaluation of ADR.

Chapter III Reporting and Processing

Section I Basic Requirements

Article 15 Drug manufacturers, drug distributors and medical institutions shall, when becomes aware of any suspected ADR, report through the ADR monitoring information network. If online reporting is not available, paper report shall be submitted to the local ADR monitoring agency instead, and the local ADR monitoring agency shall make online reporting accordingly.

The reported information shall be true, complete and accurate.

Article 16 ADR monitoring agencies at various levels shall evaluate and manage the ADR reporting and monitoring information within their respective administrative regions.

Article 17 Drug manufacturers, drug distributors and medical institutions shall support the investigation on ADRs or cluster AEs carried out by drug regulatory authorities, health administrative departments and ADR monitoring agencies, and shall provide necessary materials to facilitate the investigation.

Article 18 Drug manufacturers, drug distributors and medical institutions shall set up and maintain an ADR reporting and monitoring documentations.

Section II Individual Adverse Drug Reactions

Article 19 Drug manufacturers, drug distributors and medical institutions shall collect ADR actively, and shall, when becomes aware of an ADR, make detailed recording, analyze and process, fill the "ADR/Event Report Form" (see Exhibit 1) and then submit.

Article 20 For domestic drugs within the new drug monitoring period, all the ADRs shall be reported. For other domestic drugs, new and/or serious ADRs shall be reported.

For imported drugs, all the ADRs occurred within 5 years from the date of initial importation permission shall be reported; and new and/or serious ADRs occurred after such 5-year period shall be reported.

Article 21 Drug manufacturers, drug distributors and medical institutions shall report any new and/or serious ADR within 15 days after awareness. Death cases shall be reported immediately, and other ADRs shall be reported within 30 days. Follow-up information, if applicable, shall be reported in a timely manner.

Article 22 Drug manufacturers shall investigate death cases known to them via collecting all basic information, the usage of all drugs, the onset and treatment of ADR, etc. They shall prepare an investigation report within 15 days, and submit it to provincial ADR monitoring agency where it is located.

Article 23 Upon discovering a new and/or serious ADR, individuals may report to the treating physician, or to the manufacturer or distributor of the drug or the local ADR monitoring agency. If necessary, personal medical notes shall be provided.

Article 24 ADR monitoring agencies at municipal/county level shall review the authenticity, integrity and accuracy of the ADR reports received by them. The review and evaluation of serious ADR reports shall be completed within 3 working days upon receipt thereof and that of other reports shall be completed within 15 working days upon receipt thereof.

ADR monitoring agencies at municipal/county level t shall investigate the death cases known to them via collecting all basic information, the usage of drugs, the onset and treatment of ADR, etc. They shall accomplish an investigation report within 15 days, and submit it to the drug regulatory agency and the health administrative department at the same level as well as higher level ADR monitoring agency.

Article 25 ADR monitoring agencies at provincial level shall complete the evaluation within 7 working days after receiving the comments on serious ADR from the lower level ADR monitoring agency.

For death cases, both the ADR monitoring agency at provincial level where the event occurs and the ADR monitoring agency at provincial level where the drug manufacturer is located shall promptly execute investigation and evaluation based on the investigation report. If necessary, site investigation shall be executed. The evaluation results shall be submitted to the drug regulatory department and the health administrative department at provincial level as well as the National ADR Monitoring Center.

Article 26 The National ADR Monitoring Center shall promptly make analysis and evaluation of death cases, and submit the evaluation results to the SFDA and the Ministry of Health.

Section III Cluster Adverse Events

Article 27 Drug manufacturers, drug distributors and medical institutions shall, immediately upon awareness of any cluster AE, report to the drug regulatory department, the health administrative department and the ADR monitoring agency where it is located by telephone or fax. If necessary, bypassing reporting may be made. Meanwhile, they shall fill out the "Group AE Basic Information Form" (see Exhibit 2) and the "ADR/AE Report Form" for every case, and submit it through the ADR monitoring information network.

Article 28 Drug regulatory authorities at municipal/county level shall, immediately upon knowledge of any group ADR/AE, execute site investigations together with the health administrative department at the same level. The investigation results shall be promptly submitted level by level to food and drug administration department and the health administrative department at provincial level.

The Food and Drug administration department and the health administrative department at provincial level shall jointly supervise and guide the investigation executed by the drug regulatory department at municipal/county level. They shall make analysis and evaluation of cluster AEs, and execute site investigation on cluster AEs which have great impact within their respective administrative regions. The evaluation and investigation results shall be promptly submitted to the SFDA and the Ministry of Health.

The SFDA and the Ministry of Health shall jointly execute investigations on cluster AEs which have caused serious consequences and have great impact across the nation.

Article 29 Drug manufacturers shall, immediately upon awareness of any cluster AEs, investigate onset of the cluster AEs, the usage of all drugs, the diagnosis and treatment of the patient as well as the manufacture, storage, distribution of the drug and any similar AEs in the past. They shall prepare an investigation report within 7 days and submit the same to the food and drug administration department and the ADR monitoring agency at provincial level where it is located. Meanwhile, the drug manufacturer shall promptly carry out self-examination to find out the cause of the event. If necessary, the drug shall be suspended for manufacturing, marketing and usage and be recalled. Such actions shall be reported to food and drug administration department at provincial level.

Article 30 Drug distributors shall, upon awareness of any cluster AEs, immediately notify the drug manufacturer and carry out self-examination. If necessary, drug sale shall be suspended. The drug distributor shall also assist the drug manufacturer to take relevant control measures.

Article 31 Medical institutions shall, upon awareness of any cluster AEs, treat the patient actively and execute clinical investigation to find out the cause of the event. If necessary, usage of the drug may be suspended and other emergency measures may be taken.

Article 32 The drug administration department may take measures such as suspending the production, sale, drug usage or recalling the drug. The health administrative department shall actively organize treatment for the patient.

Section IV Oversea Serious Adverse Drug Reactions

Article 33 In case of oversea serious ADRs relating to an imported drug or a domestic drug including cases collected through the spontaneous reporting system, cases discovered in post-market clinical research, and cases reported in the literature, the drug manufacturer shall fill out the "Overseas ADR/AE Report Form" (see Exhibit 3), and submit to the National ADR Monitoring Center within 30 days upon awareness. Drug manufacturer shall submit original reports and relevant information within 5 days if requested by National ADR Monitoring Center.

Article 34 The National ADR Monitoring Center shall make analysis and evaluation of the ADR reports received by them, and report to the SFDA and the Ministry of Health every 6 months. Potential safety concerns identified shall be timely reported.

Article 35 In case an imported drug or a domestic drug is suspended from marketing or using or is withdrawn from an overseas market due to ADR, the drug manufacturer shall submit a written report to the SFDA and the National ADR Monitoring Center within 24 h.

Section V Periodic Safety Update Reports

Article 36 Drug manufacturers shall make periodic review and analysis of adverse reaction reports and monitoring data by them. They shall summarize safety information collected from both domestic and abroad, perform risk and benefit assessment, and prepare periodic safety update reports (PSURs). The National ADR Monitoring Center will prepare specific guideline for such PSURs.

Article 37 Manufacturers of domestic drugs within the new drug monitoring period shall submit a PSUR every year after they obtain the new drug manufacturing license until the first re-registration date. Thereafter, they shall submit a PSUR every 5 years. For other domestic drugs, a periodic safety updating report shall be submitted every 5 years.

Manufacturers of imported drugs shall submit a PSUR every year from initial import permission until the first re-registration date. Thereafter, they shall submit a periodic safety updating report every 5 years.

The date when the drug approval document is obtained shall be the starting point of information to be summarized. Each periodic safety updating report shall be submitted within 60 days following data lock date.

Article 38 The periodic drug safety update reports of domestic drugs shall be submitted to the ADR monitoring agency at provincial level where the drug manufacturer is located. The periodic drug safety update reports of imported drugs (including imported sub-package drugs) shall be submitted to the National ADR Monitoring Center.

Article 39 ADR monitoring agencies at provincial level shall summarize, analyze and evaluate the periodic safety updating reports received by them, and submit the analysis and evaluation results of the previous year to the drug regulatory department at provincial level and the National ADR Monitoring Center on or before 1 April of each year.

Article 40 The National ADR Monitoring Center shall summarize, analyze and evaluate the periodic safety updating reports received by them, and submit the analysis and evaluation results of the previous year to the State Food and Drug Administration and the Ministry of Health on or before 1 July of each year.

Chapter IV Drug Intensive Monitoring

Article 41 Drug manufacturers should periodically review the safety profiles of their own products, and carry out the intensive monitoring for the drugs within the New Drug Monitoring Period as well as imported drugs within the first 5 years of import. The monitoring data should be integrated, analyzed, evaluated and reported as required. Drug manufactures should also take the initiative to carry out drug intensive monitoring for their other drugs.

Article 42 Drug regulatory departments above the provincial level may, require drug manufacturers to perform intensive monitoring for specific drugs based on their clinical use and adverse reaction monitoring results. If necessary, they may also organize the ADR monitoring agencies, medical institutions and research institutes directly to carry out drug intensive monitoring.

Article 43 ADR monitoring agencies above the provincial level are responsible for supervising and inspecting the intensive monitoring activities carried out by drug manufacturers, and evaluating the intensive monitoring reports technically.

Article 44 Drug regulatory departments above the provincial level and health administrative departments at the same level may jointly designate a medical institution as the monitoring site to undertake the drug intensive monitoring.

Chapter V Evaluation and Control

Article 45 Drug manufacturers shall make analysis and evaluation of the ADR reports and monitoring data collected by them, and take the initiative to carry out drug safety researches.

For drugs with identified serious adverse reaction, the manufacturer should notify healthcare professionals, patients and the public of such ADRs as well as instructions for rational drug use through effective channels in a timely manner. The drug manufacturer shall take measures such as modifying the labels and package inserts, suspending production, sale and use of the drug, and recalling the drug to reduce and/or prevent from repeated re-occurrence of ADRs. For drugs with risks overweighing benefits, the manufacturer shall take the initiative to apply for revocation of the drug's approved license.

Drug manufacturers should report the drug safety information and measures taken to their provincial drug regulatory department and the SFDA.

Article 46 Drug distributors and medical institutions should make analysis and evaluation of the ADR reports and monitoring data collected by them, and take effective measures to reduce and/or prevent from re-occurrence of ADRs.

Article 47 The provincial ADR monitoring agencies at the provincial level should make comprehensive analysis on the ADR reports received by them on a quarterly basis. They shall, extract and evaluate the concerned safety information, propose risk management recommendations, and report to the provincial drug regulatory department, provincial health administrative department and the National ADR Monitoring Center in a timely manner. The provincial drug regulatory departments shall, depending on the evaluation results, take the measure such as suspending production, sale and use of the concerned drugs or recalling the drugs. They shall also supervise, inspect and report such measures to the health administrative department at the same level.

Article 48 The National ADR Monitoring Center shall make comprehensive analysis on the ADR reports received by them on a quarterly basis. They shall extract and evaluate the concerned safety information, propose risk management recommendations, and report to the SFDA and the Ministry of Health in a timely manner.

Article 49 The SFDA may, based on the drug analysis and evaluation results, require the drug manufacturer to execute the safety or efficacy study. If necessary, the SFDA should take measures such as ordering the drug manufacturer to modify the product package insert, suspending production, sale and use of the drug, recalling the drug. For drugs with significant ADRs, the approval documents should be revoked and the measures taken shall promptly be reported to the Ministry of Health.

Article 50 ADR monitoring agencies above provincial level may, if necessary, require drug manufacturers, drug distributors and medical institutions to provide relevant information to assist in the analysis and evaluation. Drug manufacturers, drug distributors and medical institutions shall actively cooperate in this regard.

Chapter VI Information Management

Article 51 ADR monitoring agencies at various levels should make statistical analysis on the ADR reports and monitoring data received by them, and provide feedback in an appropriate form.

Article 52 The National ADR Monitoring Center should release ADR alerts in a timely manner based on the results of comprehensive analysis and evaluation on the ADR reports and monitoring data.

Article 53 Drug regulatory departments above the provincial level should regularly release the ADR reporting and monitoring information.

Article 54 The following information should be centrally released by the State Food and Drug

1. Fail to establish and maintain the ADR monitoring files;
2. Fail to report, investigate, evaluate and handle ADRs or cluster AEs as required;
3. Fail to submit PSURs as required;
4. Failure to carry out drug intensive monitoring as required;
5. Fail to cooperate in the investigations on serious ADR or cluster of AEs;
6. Other violations of the Provisions.

Where a drug manufacturer falls under the above circumstance (4) or (5), the license renewal of the relevant drug shall not be approved as per the Drug Registration Regulation.

Article 59 Where a drug distributor falls under any of the following circumstances, the local drug regulatory department shall give a warning and order to make correction within a set time limit. If no correction is made within the set time limit, a fine less than RMB 30,000 Yuan may be imposed:

1. Fail to designate the full-time or part-time staff to be responsible for the ADR reporting and monitoring work within the enterprise;
2. Fail to report, investigate, evaluate and handle ADR or cluster of AEs as required;
3. Fail to cooperate in the investigation on serious ADR or cluster of AEs.

Article 60 Where a medical institution falls under any of the following circumstances, the local health administrative department shall give a warning and order to make correction within a set time limit. If no correction is made within the set time limit, a fine less than RMB 30,000 Yuan shall be imposed. In serious cases with severe consequences, the local health administrative department shall give the relevant responsible person an administrative sanction:

1. Fail to designate the full-time or part-time staff to be responsible for the ADR reporting and monitoring work with the institution;
2. Fail to report, investigate, evaluate and handle ADRs or cluster of AEs as required;
3. Fail to cooperate in the investigation on serious ADRs or cluster of AEs.

The drug regulatory department should transfer cases to the health administrative department at the same level to deal with when finding any of aforementioned violations.

The health administrative department shall inform the drug regulatory department at the same level of its administrative penalty decisions against any medical institution in a timely manner.

Article 61 Where the drug regulatory departments, health administrative departments or ADR monitoring agencies at any level, and any of their staff as well, violate the Provisions with serious consequences in the course of doing ADR reporting and monitoring work, the violator(s) shall be subject to administrative sanction according to the relevant provisions.

Article 62 Where any drug manufacturer, drug distributor or medical institution violate the relevant provisions, causing damage to drug users, the violator shall bear the compensation liability according to the provisions.

Chapter VIII Supplementary Provisions

Article 63 Definition of terms in the Provisions:

A. Adverse drug reaction (ADR): a response to a qualified drug that is noxious and unintended, and which occurs at normal dose under normal use.
B. ADR reporting and monitoring: the process of finding, reporting, evaluating and controlling ADRs.
C. Serious ADR: any of the following harmful reactions caused by use of the drug:
    1. Results in death;
    2. Is life-threatening;
    3. Results in carcinogenesis, teratogenesis or birth defects;
    4. Results in persistent or significant disability or capability
    5. Requires inpatient hospitalization or prolongation of existing hospitalization;
    6. Any untoward medical occurrence considered medically significant, one of outcomes listed above will occur if no actions are taken.
D. New ADR: an ADR which is not listed in the product labeling. Where an ADR is described in the product labeling but the nature, severity, consequence or frequency is inconsistent with or worse than those described in the product labeling, such ADR shall be treated as a new ADR.

E. Cluster of AEs: an event which occurs in a relatively concentrated period of time and area, damaging or threatening the health or life of a certain number of people during or after use of the same drug, and which requires emergency treatment.

"The same drug": a drug which is produced by the same manufacturer with the same drug name, and is in the same formulation and strength.

a. Drug intensive monitoring: drug safety monitoring activities carried out to investigate the characteristics, severity frequency and the like of ADRs to further understand the clinical use and the occurrence of ADRs of one drug.

Article 64 Overseas manufacturers of imported drugs may entrust their offices or agencies in China to fulfill ADR reporting and monitoring obligations on behalf of them in compliance with the requirements for drug manufacturers as defined in the Provisions.

Article 65 Regarding the adverse reaction reporting and monitoring of vaccines, the Ministry of Health and the SFDA stipulate otherwise provisions, such stipulations shall prevail.

Article 66 Drug regulatory departments at the provincial level, or at autonomous regions or municipalities shall be in conjunction with the health administrative department at the same level to constitute provisions for the adverse reaction reporting and monitoring of preparations made by medical institutions.

Article 67 The Provisions shall come into force as of July 1, 2011. The Provisions for Adverse Drug Reaction Reporting and Monitoring, Order No.7 of the State Food and Drug Administration published by the State Food and Drug Administration and the Ministry of Health on March 4, 2004 shall be repealed simultaneously.

Appendixes:

1. Adverse Drug Reaction/Event Report Form
2. Cluster of Adverse Drug Events Information Form
3. Overseas Adverse Drug Reaction/Event Report Form

9.6.2.1 Appendix 1—Adverse Drug Reaction/Event Report Form (Table 9.4)

The following are the notes related to the terms in the form:

- **Serious adverse drug reaction means one of the following circumstances by drug use that caused damage:**

1. death;
2. was life-threatening;
3. was carcinogenic, teratogenic, birth defects;

Table 9.4 Adverse drug reaction/event report form

Patient Name:	Gender: Male ☐ Female ☐	Birth: DD MM YY Or A Age:	Nationality:	Weight (kg):	Contact Information:

The Original Disease:	Hospital: The Case No.:	Prior ADR/Event: Yes ☐______No ☐ Unknown ☐ Family ADR/Event: Yes ☐______________No ☐ Unknown ☐

Relevant Important Information: Smoking History ☐ Drinking History ☐ Pregnancy Period ☐ Liver Disease History ☐ Renal Disease History ☐ Allergic History ☐______ Other ☐

Medication	Approval No.	Trade Name	Generic Name (Dosage Form)	Manufacturer	Batch No.	Dosage and Administration(Single dose, pathway, times/day)	Starting and ending times for medication	Reasons for Drug Use
Suspected								
Concomitant								

ADR Term:	ADR Onset Time: DD MM YY

Description of the ADR Process including symptoms, signs and clinical tests as well as treatments etc. (Attachment if needed):
ADR/Event Outcome: Cure ☐ Improved ☐ No Improvement ☐ Unknown ☐ With Sequela ☐ Manifestation: __________Death ☐ Direct Cause of Death: __________ Death Time: DD MM YY
After the withdrawal or reduction of drug, is the reaction / event reduced or disappeared? Yes ☐ No ☐ Unknown ☐ No withdrawal or reduction of drug ☐ Whether the same reaction / event again appeared, after the suspected drug was use again? Yes ☐ No ☐ Unknown ☐ No Repeated Use ☐
Influence to the original disease: Not obvious ☐ Disease process prolonged ☐ Condition worsened ☐ Caused sequela ☐ Led death ☐

Causality Assessment	Evaluation from Reporter: Definitely ☐ Probably ☐ Possible ☐ Possibly Unrelated ☐ To be evaluated ☐ Unassessed ☐ Signature: Evaluation from Report Unit: Definitely ☐ Probably ☐ Possible ☐ Possibly Unrelated ☐ To be evaluated ☐ Unassessed ☐ Signature:

Reporter Information	Telephone:	Occupation: Doctor ☐ Pharmacist ☐ Nurse ☐ Other ☐
	E-mail:	Signature:

Report Unit Information	Unit Name:	Contact:	Telephone:	Report Date: DD MM YY

Manufacture enterprises: Please fill in the information source where it came from	Medical Institute ☐ Distributor ☐ Individual ☐ Literature ☐ Post-Market Research ☐ Other ☐
Note	

4. resulted in significant and permanent disability or organ damage;
5. led to hospitalization or prolonged hospitalization;
6. led to other important medical events, such as the potential cases listed above without treatment.

- **New ADR:**

Refers to adverse drug reaction not listed in the instructions. Or, it has been described, but the nature, the extent, the consequence or frequency of the adverse reactions occurred are insistent with the specification describes in the instructions, or more serious. Such cases should be treated in accordance with the new ADR processes.

- **Reporting timeframe:**

The new serious ADRs should be reported within 15 days after informed of the date of discovery; deaths must be reported immediately; other ADRs should be reported within 30 days. For follow-up information, it shall be reported promptly.

- **Other notes:**

1. Suspected medication: used in patients with suspected adverse reactions associated with the medication.
2. Concomitant medications: When the ADR happens, in addition to the suspected medication, other medications that the patients take including patients got by themselves or herbal medicines.
3. Dosage: including dose/time, route of administration, the daily frequency of administration, e.g., 5 mg, orally, twice daily.

- **Report processing:**

All reports will be entered into the database. Professionals will analyze the relationship between drugs and adverse reactions/events. According to the universality or the severity of the risks of drugs, the decision shall be made whether you need to take relevant measures, such as adding a warning message in the package insert, update information on the safe use of medicines and so on. In rare cases, when the risk is deemed greater than the drug benefits, the drug shall be removed from the market.

9.6.2.2 Appendix 2—Cluster of Adverse Drug Events Information Form (Table 9.5)

9.6.2.3 Appendix 3– Overseas Adverse Drug Reaction/Event Report Form (Table 9.6)

Table 9.5 Table of cluster adverse drug events

Occurrence area:			Application units:		No of people used the drug:	
No. of People with AEs:			No. of people with SAEs:		No. of Death:	
Date of the first dose: DD MM YY				Date of the first case: DD MM YY		
Suspected Drug	Trade Name	Generic Name	Manufacturer	Drug Specification	Batch No.	Approval No.
Device	Product Name		Manufacturer	Batch No.	Registration No.	
	This column refers to the instrument used simultaneously with suspected drug use. The instrument related to adverse events may be associated with the use of groups of syringes, infusion sets and other medical equipment.					
The manifestation of adverse events:						
The description and treatment status of the cluster adverse events (attachment if needed):						
Reporting units comments						
Information of the reporter	Telephone:		E-mail:	Signature:		
Information of report Unit	Report Unit:		Contact:	Telephone:		

Report date: DD MM YY

Table 9.6 Overseas adverse drug reaction/event report form

Trade Name (Chinese: English:)

Generic Name (Chinese: English:) Dosage Form ( )

Code	AER/Event Name	ADR/Event Onset Time	ADR Outcome	Dosing Start	Dosing End	Usage & Dosage	Reason of Drug Use	Gender	Age	Initial/ Follow-up Report	Source of Report	Country of Origin	Domestic Receipt Date	Note

Note: Please fill in the number of your unit number; For adverse results, please fill in: cured, improved, not improved, sequelae, death, or unknown; For report source, please fill: spontaneous reports, studies, literature and so on.

Report Unit: Contact: Telephone: Report Date:

9.7 The roles of the CFDA in management of drug safety information

Since the initiation of Adverse Drug Reaction Monitoring System in1988, ADR Monitoring has become more and more important for collecting drug safety information, strengthening drug safety supervision, promoting safety guidelines for clinical drug administration, and risk-controlling. The CFDA plays a key role in the management of this system to ensure drug safety for the public. The annual report for "national adverse drug reaction monitoring and supervision" reflects the roles of the CFDA in organizing and analyzing the safety information.

On May 31, 2012, the SFDA released the 2011 Annual Report for National Adverse Drug Reaction Monitoring, which elaborates on national Adverse Drug Reaction (ADR) reporting of 2011 (SFDA 2012), including three aspects of the general situation of ADR reporting, the statistical analysis of adverse drug reactions/events, and a summary of risk control measures.

9.7.1 Collection and Summary of Drug Safety Information

Based on China's annual report of 2011, there were a total of 852,799 case reports of adverse drug reactions/events (ADR/ADE); 637 ADR cases, on average, were reported per million people; the ADR cases included 145,769 new and serious adverse reactions/events, accounting for 17.1 % of the total case reports over the same period. A total of 83.1 % of the ADR reactions/events reports were from medical institutions, 13.7 % were from the pharmaceutical manufacturer and sale enterprises, and 3.2 % were from individuals' reports. Most of the ADR reports still came from medical institutions, even though the reports from drug manufacturers and distributors witnessed a slight increase (CFDA 2012).

In 2013, the National Adverse Drug Reaction Monitoring Network received 1317 million ADR/ADE reports, up by 9.0 % year from the previous year. Approximately 291,000 new and serious ADR/ADE cases were reported in 2013, accounting for 22.1 % of the total number of the reports over the same period. ADR reporting coverage rate reached 93.8 % at the county level; and 983 ADR cases, on average, were reported per million people (CFDA 2014). From 1999 to 2013, the Network cumulatively received nearly 6.6 million ADR/ADE reports.

In 2013, with the participation and joint efforts of medical institutions, pharmaceutical manufacturers, distributors and other parties, the national ADR/ADE reports saw a steady growth in number (Fig. 9.4). The majority of 2013 ADR/ADE reports were still from medical institutions (Fig. 9.5), while those from pharmaceutical manufacturers increased when juxtaposed with the data from 2012. The number of serious case reports rose by 22.5 % year on year, and its proportion (4.3 %) increased by 0.5 % year on year. Since the Serious ADR/ADEs constitute one of the most important indicators to assess the quality of reports, it is evident that the safety monitoring system is constantly improving.

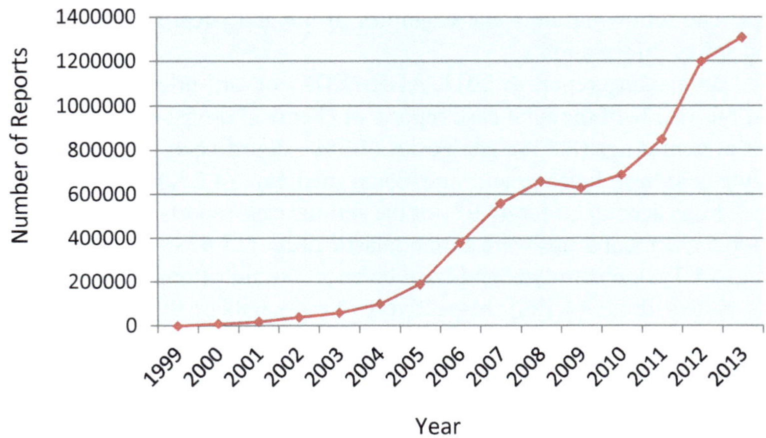

Fig. 9.4 1999–2013 Growth trend of ADR/ADE reports in China. (Source: The Annual Report for National ADR Monitoring with modification)

Fig. 9.5 Source distribution of 2013 ADR/ADE reports. (Source: The Annual Report for National ADR Monitoring with modification)

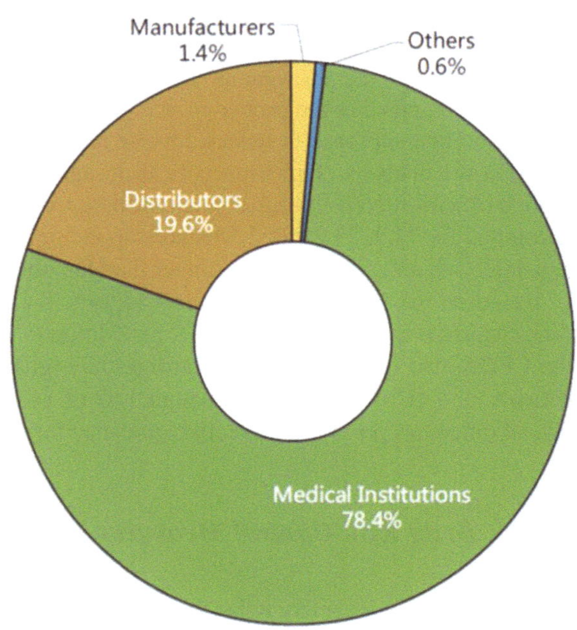

9.7.2 Analysis of the Safety Information and Advice for Drug Safe Use

By analyzing safety information reports, one can see that the CFDA constantly releases their statistical outcomes and provides precautions to healthcare societies and the public. Such information helps the healthcare personnel with ensuring safe use of the corresponding drugs, especially in special populations or in special categories of drugs. The following are some examples of the analytical results based on the reported safety information.

Based on a safety report in 2011, ADRs/ADEs of anti-infective chemicals accounted for 51.2 % of the total case reports of chemical drugs; followed by cardiovascular system drugs (8.5 %); analgesics (7.2 %); digestive system drugs, (5.6 %); electrolyte/acid-base balance and nutritional medicine (4.2 %). The anti-infective chemical drugs accounted for 44.9 % of the serious case reports, the other 4 categories of top 5 chemical drugs were antineoplastic drugs (15.9 %), cardiovascular system drugs (4.7 %), electrolyte/acid-base balance and nutritional medicine (4.3 %), nervous system drugs (4.1 %), respectively. Nearly half of the reports of serious cases related to anti-infective drugs.

The anti-infective chemical drugs were 3.6 % lower than those in 2010. This may be the outcome of the enhancement of the regulatory use of anti-infective drugs by medical institutions.

The routes of administration of 2011 ADR/ADE Reports were mainly intravenous injection, accounting for 55.8 %; followed by oral administration (39.3 %). As to the distribution of chemical drugs, the reported routes of administration of 2011 serious ADRs/ADEs were mainly intravenous injection, accounting for 73.4 %; followed by oral administration (20.0 %); other routes of administration (6.6 %.). The data indicates that the intravenous route of administration implies higher risk, therefore, it is obvious that the proper choice of administration routes and formulations is an important approach to reduce adverse reactions.

From the analysis of pharmaceutical dosage forms in 2013: of all ADR/ADE reports of anti-infective drugs, injections, oral preparations and other dosage forms accounted for 74.3, 23.2 and 2.5 %, correspondingly. The injection-related cases in anti-infective drugs were 14.5 % higher than that the overall reports.

Based on the CFDA's annual safety reports, the rank of specific anti-infective drugs was also analyzed and reported. In addition to the above analytical outcomes, the CFDA also issued cautions regarding the vigilance for drug safety in elderly patients, and TCM injection as the main risk of TCM preparations, etc. Those statistical outcomes provide an effective guidance for the public's safe use of drugs.

9.7.3 Drug Risk Control Measures

For drugs found with safety risks, the CFDA has taken a series of risk control measures in a timely manner. The risk control measures may include, but not limited to the following aspects (SFDA 2012; CFDA 2014):

1. Releasing drug safety warning information in a timely manner:
   In 2011, a total of nine volumes of "Adverse Drug Reaction Information Bulletin" were released to notify the safety information of nine categories of drug varieties, and 11 volumes of "Pharmacovigilance Express" were released to report the safety information of more than 60 drugs. While in 2013, a total of 7 issues of Adverse Drug Reactions Information Bulletin were released, to notify

safety information of 8 categories of drugs; and 12 issues of Pharmacovigilance News were released to notify safety information of more than 70 drugs.

2. Revising the product packaging inserts:
   In May 2011, the SFDA issued a notice to strengthen the usage management of nimesulide oral preparations, including the prohibiting use for children under 12, the restricted indications, dose, treatment phases, and other specific measures.
   In 2013, a total of 22 drugs revised the package inserts with supplement of the safety warning information.
3. Revoking relevant drug approval documents or drug standards:
   In January 2011, the SFDA decided to gradually withdraw pharmaceutical preparations containing dextropropoxyphene from China's market. The monitoring and research data of that drug indicated that the pharmaceutical preparation containing dextropropoxyphene has serious cardiac toxic and side effects, and the overdose of these drugs can be life threatening. Therefore, its risks outweighed its benefits in China. The production, sale and use of pharmaceutical preparations containing dextropropoxyphene should cease as of July 31, 2011, the approval documents of which were also revoked.
   In 2013, the CFDA evoked the drug approval evidential documents for buflomedil and meprobamate preparations.
4. Organizing the investigation and handling of serious ADR events.
5. Interviewing or notifying individual enterprises found with risk hazards in the monitoring process.

9.8 Progress and Perspectives in Global Drug Safety Monitoring, Reporting, Evaluation and Management in Clinical Trials

In the previous sections, the major differences between China and the western world for current regulations regarding safety monitoring and reporting requirements were discussed. As the major differences are for investigational drug monitoring and reporting in the clinical development stages, rather than the market ones, we'll further explore the recent year of progress in safety management fields and how to handle the safety reporting requirements globally in order to be in compliance with these steps of progress.

The safety monitoring and reporting system in China is complicated. The major differences include, (a) The investigators are responsible to report SAE within 24 h to regulatory agencies at various levels; (b) The causality assessment is graded at 5 levels, and, (c) SAEs should be reported in the format of a severe adverse event form; (d) both investigators and sponsors need to report the SAEs to the regulatory agencies.

Very recently, the CFDA issued "Regulations for Management of Reporting Serious Adverse Events from Vaccine Clinical Trials (Trial)" on January 17, 2014, which indicated the requirements for vaccine, SAE $\leq$24 h by investigators. However, the requirements for sponsor are that fatal or life-threatening SUSAR $\leq$7; other SUSARs $\leq$15 calendar days by sponsor, which is closer to the western standards (CFDA 2014).

Due to the enforcement of the FDA Final Rule for IND Safety Reporting in recent years, the SUSAR reporting requirements are consistent in some ways, but also different in some aspects from other countries (FDA 2011). Under 21 CFR 312.64, investigators are required to provide a causality assessment for SAE reported to the sponsor. For serious and unexpected events, the sponsor considers the investigator's causality assessment but submits an IND safety report only for those events for which the sponsor determines there is a reasonable possibility that the drug caused the event, regardless of the investigator's causality assessment. While in the other European countries, both causality assessment from investigators and sponsors will be counted. Therefore, for multinational pharmaceutical companies, integrated knowledge of safety reporting requirements from various countries should be considered to meet global drug development needs.

9.8.1 Impact of the FDA Issued Final Rule for IND Safety Reporting

The FDA issued a final rule entitled "Investigational New Drug Safety Reporting Requirements for Human Drug and Biological Products and Safety Reporting Requirements for Bioavailability and Bioequivalence Studies in Humans" which became effective on March 28, 2011 (FDA 2011).

The revised FDA regulations pertaining to safety reporting for drug and biologic products under an IND application aim to decrease the number of IND safety reports that are uninterpretable or do not contribute to a better understanding of the developing safety profile of the drug or biologic. The changes in 21 CFR 312 will impact IND safety reporting, protocols and study plans as well. In past practices, both sponsors and investigators had "over-reporting" safety events. In addition, the term "adverse drug experience" often caused confusion that led to the sponsors over-reporting all SAEs, even when there was little reason to believe they were associated with the investigational drug. The new regulations removed the old term "adverse drug experience" and replaced it with two terms: "adverse event" and "adverse reaction". These new terms are more consistent with worldwide safety reporting terminologies.

9.8.1.1 Qualification Criteria for IND Safety Report to the FDA

- For suspected serious adverse events that are unexpected, the sponsor submits an IND safety report only for those events of which the sponsor determines there is a "reasonable possibility" i.e., there must be evidence to suggest a causal relationship, regardless of the investigator's causality assessment.

- The FDA expects such information to be based on unblinded analysis of the events;
- Findings from other studies: findings "suggest a significant risk in humans exposed to the drug" in other studies, including epidemiological studies, analyses of multiple studies, and clinical studies other than those conducted under the present IND. In other words, information that could lead to safety-related changes in the protocol, informed consent document, investigator brochure or other aspects of the clinical investigation should be reported.
- Findings from animal or in-vitro testing: If animal or in-vitro testing suggests a significant risk to humans exposed to the drug, including reports of mutagenicity, teratogenicity, carcinogenicity or organ toxicity, then an IND safety report is needed.
- An increased rate of occurrence of serious suspected adverse reactions: If "any clinically important increase in the rate of a serious suspected adverse reaction over that listed in the protocol or investigator brochure" is discovered, IND safety report is needed. This added requirement is consistent with ICH corresponding guidance that the sponsor track and identify changes in rates of adverse events during the conduct of a clinical trial.
- If a serious suspected adverse reaction is anticipated for the drug class, but not specifically mentioned for the particular investigational drug, it would be considered "unexpected," and is reportable the first time it occurs.

9.8.1.2 Requirements for the Report from Investigators

Under the FDA's revised reporting requirements in 21 CFR § 312.64 (b), investigators are required to immediately report any SAEs to the sponsor, regardless of whether there is a relationship between the event and the investigational drug, including expected events listed in the protocol or the investigator's brochure. The investigators are required to provide an assessment as to whether there is a "reasonable possibility." (Table 9.7)

Note:

Reporting Responsibilities of Investigators under 21 CFR 312.64(b) and Sponsors under 21 CFR 312.32 (c) (1) (i) for Serious and Unexpected Suspected Adverse Reactions

Source: modified based on the FDA "Guidance for Industry and Investigators Safety Reporting Requirements for INDs and BA/BE Studies", December 2012.

The sponsor reports serious and unexpected suspected adverse reactions to the FDA and all participating investigators.

In summary, the new safety reporting requirements clarified that before submitting an IND safety report, the sponsor needs to ensure that the event meets all three of the definitions including: suspected adverse reaction, serious, and unexpected.

Table 9.7 Investigator and sponsor reporting responsibilities

Term	Investigator Responsibility	Sponsor responsibility	Final determination responsibility
Serious (or life-threatening)	Yes (Investigator must report all SAEs to the sponsor immediately)	Yes	An event is considered serious or life-threatening, based on either the investigator's or sponsor's opinion
Unexpected	No (No requirement to assess "expectedness")	Yes	The sponsor is responsible for determining whether event meets the definition of "unexpected," based on whether the event is listed in the investigator brochure (IB); or if an IB is not available, is not consistent with the risk information described elsewhere in the general investigational plan or elsewhere in the current application
Suspected Adverse Reaction (reasonable possibility)	Yes (Investigator must provide sponsor with an assessment of causality)	Yes (Sponsor determines reportability, regardless of investigator's assessment)	The sponsor is responsible for determining whether there is a reasonable possibility that the drug caused the adverse event, taking into consideration the investigator's assessment

For the follow-up reports, sponsors need to evaluate information and decide the significance of information to be submitted, i.e. the information does significantly affect the care of the subjects or conduct of the study. For minor refinements that do not significantly affect care of subjects, there is no need to submit a report. Any relevant additional information that the sponsor obtains that pertains to a previously submitted IND safety report must be submitted to the FDA as a Follow-up IND Safety Report without delay, as soon as the information is available.

9.8.2 Trend and Changes for Causality Assessment in the Western World

Binary System for Causality Assessment In the past decades, more and more new drugs have been put on the market and there has been a dramatic increase in investigational drugs under development. The corresponding adverse drug reaction reporting has also significantly increased. Causality assessment has become a greater challenge for medical institutes and multinational pharmaceutical companies (Naidu 2013). The CIOMS VI Working Group recommends that the investigator be asked to use a simple binary decision for drug causality (related or not related) for serious adverse events (CIOMS Working Group VI 2005). The rationale of this recommendation by CIOMS Working Group VI includes: (a) various gradients of relatedness offer little or no advantage in data analysis or regulatory reporting; (b) binary was favored by a majority of the CIOMS VI Working Group members. The causality assessment has no standard international nomenclature. The definitions for AE causalities vary among different sponsors and countries.

The Commonly used Terminologies for AE Causalities Include *Definite*: Occurs in a plausible time relationship to drug administration; cannot be explained by concurrent disease or other drugs or chemicals; follows a clinically reasonable response upon withdrawal (dechallenge); and is confirmed by reappearance of the reaction on repeat exposure (rechallenge).

Probable: Follows a reasonable time sequence to administration of the drug; is unlikely to be attributed to concurrent disease or other drugs or chemicals; and follows a clinically reasonable response upon withdrawal (dechallenge);

Possible: Follows a reasonable temporal sequence from drug administration and could also be explained by concurrent disease or other drugs or chemicals.

Not related/remote: Follows a temporal relationship to drug administration, which makes a causal relationship improbable and in which other drugs, chemicals or underlying disease provide plausible explanations.

In recent years, the binary system (Yes, No) has gotten popular and has become increasingly accepted by many multinational pharmaceutical companies in their clinical trials. The main reasons include (a) The traditional grades of causality as mentioned above, i.e. definite, probable, possible etc. provide little practical advantage or meanings. For regulatory reporting requirements, only "related" or "unrelated" is needed. (b) There is a poor inter-rater agreement using terms defined in traditional grading systems. Therefore, binary yes/no system for causality (i.e., related/not related) assessment is highly recommended by many pharmacovigilance professionals.

Use of Binary for Causality Assessment—Relationship to Study Drug *Related*: Any AE for which there is a reasonable possibility that the drug caused the AE. A "reasonable possibility" means there are facts (evidence) or arguments to suggest a causal relationship, regardless of whether there are less or more degrees of certainty between the drug and the AE.

Not Related: Any AE for which there is not a reasonable possibility that the drug caused the AE.

The commonly accepted conversion between the traditional and binary grading system is listed below (Fig. 9.6).

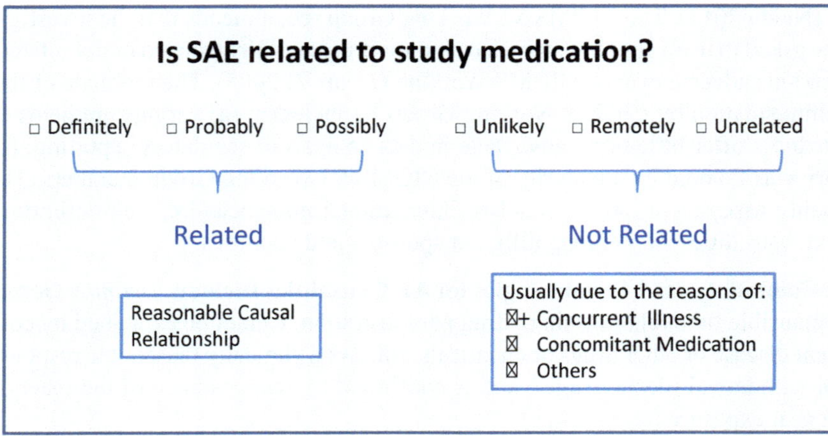

Fig. 9.6 Investigator's causality judgment—conversion between traditional and binary grading systems

9.8.3 Global Clinical Trial Drug Safety Reporting Considerations

When multinational pharmaceutical companies conduct a local or MRCT trial in China, they need to consider if all the regulatory requirements by the CFDA have been fully met. Therefore, a thorough understanding of the regulations is essential to avoid any incompliance issues. For example, the SFDA No. 28 Article 44 requests that multinational pharmaceutical companies report any SUSAR cases that have occurred overseas to the CFDA when conducting an MRCT in China in time. SAE's may not fit the FDA expedited reporting criteria for SUSAR based on the sponsor's judgment; however, they may meet the SUSAR reporting criteria for the EMA, Canada or Japan regulatory agencies since both investigator's or sponsor's judgments are counted. In such cases, the sponsor should report the SUSAR to the CFDA.

Since all SAEs must be reported to the CFDA, sponsors need to follow this regulation to report SAEs to the CFDA. Multinational pharmaceutical companies should use a valid conversion method to identify SAE causalities from their MRCT in China to determine the event reportabilities for western countries. Based on the new the FDA final rule for IND safety reporting, certain SAEs may not meet the SUSAR reporting criteria for the FDA, but they may need to be reported to the EMA, Canada or Japan etc. Therefore, as a multinational pharmaceutical company, an integrated and comprehensive understanding of the regulatory requirements in major geographic regions is an important factor for global success (Fig. 9.7).

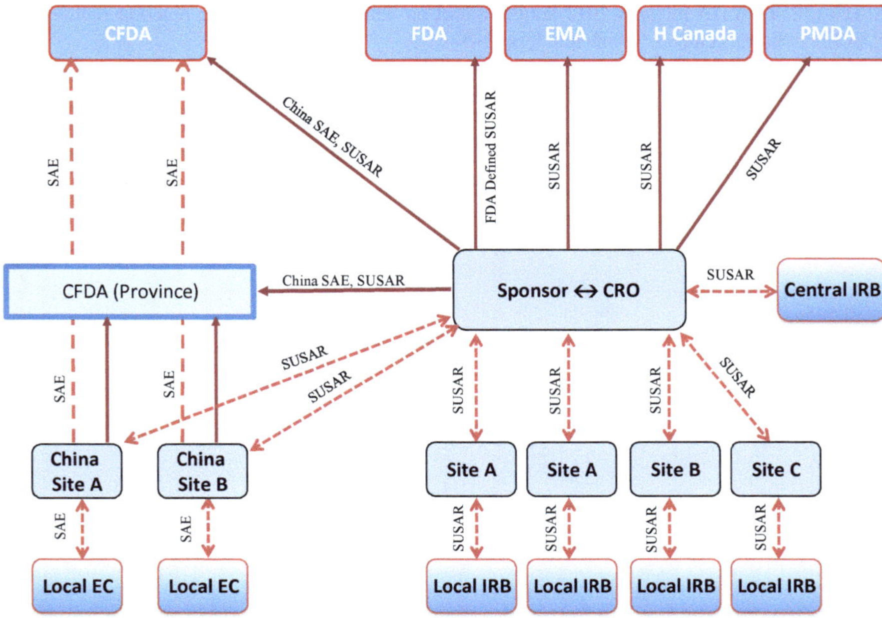

Fig. 9.7 SAE/SUSAR reporting procedure

References

CFDA (2014) Regulations for management of reporting serious adverse events from vaccine clinical trials (Trial)

CIOMS Working Group VI, Geneva (2005) Management of safety information from clinical trials: report of CIOMS working group VI

FDA (2011) Investigational new drug safety reporting requirements for human drug and biological products and safety reporting requirements for bioavailability and bioequivalence studies in humans. 75 Fed Reg. 59935, Sept 29, 2010

ICH E2A Guideline (1994) Clinical safety data management: definitions and standards for expedited reporting

MOH, SFDA (2010) Good manufacturing practice for drugs (2010 Revision). http://eng.sfda.gov.cn/WS03/CL0768/65113.html. Accessed 17 Oct 2014

MOH, SFDA (2011) Adverse drug reaction reporting and monitoring provision. http://www.sfda.gov.cn/WS01/CL0053/62621.html. Accessed 26 Oct 2014

Naidu RP (2013) Causality assessment: a brief insight into practices in pharmaceutical industry. Perspect Clin Res 4(4):233–236

SFDA (2003) Order No 3, Good clinical practice of pharmaceutical products

SFDA (2007) Order No 28, Provisions for drug registration; 2007 http://eng.sfda.gov.cn/WS03/CL0768/61647.html. Accessed 12 Dec 2013

SFDA (2012) SFDA releases 2010 annual report on national adverse drug reaction monitoring. China Pharmaceutical Newsletter 4, pp 5–6

SFDA (2014) SFDA releases 2013 annual report on national adverse drug reaction monitoring. China Pharmaceutical Newsletter 5, pp 2–5

Xu B, Wang Y (2009) International comparison of the monitoring systems of drug safety in clinical trials. Chinese J New Drugs 18:1291–1293

Zhang L et al (2012) Pharmacovigilance practice and risk control of traditional chinese medicine drugs in China: current status and future perspective. J Ethnopharmacol 140(2012):519–525

Chapter 10
In Vitro Diagnostic Product Development

Cheng Xu, Edbert D. Lu and Jianpeng Wang

10.1 Introduction

In 2007, the diagnostics market in China was valued at approximately \$ 3.3 billion, which increased steadily at a CAGR (Compound Annual Growth Rate) of 12%, reaching \$ 5.8 billion in 2012. It is projected to reach \$ 17.5 billion by 2020 at a CAGR of 15% from 2013, driven by increased awareness of early diagnosis of medical conditions, promotion of the concept of personalized medicine and technological advances in diagnosis techniques (Country Focus 2013).

In China, in vitro diagnostic (IVD) reagents refer to the reagents that can be used alone or in combination with instruments, apparatuses, equipment, or a combination of systems used in disease prevention, diagnosis, and treatment.

Using different classification methods, IVD reagents can be divided into various categories. For instance, based on clinical needs, the IVD reagents can be classified into six categories: hematological, biochemical, immunological, molecular, microbiological, or point-of-care testing (POCT) reagents.

While using a technical platform or testing methods as the classification criteria, the IVD reagents can be categorized as: immunochemistry, biochemistry, genomic, proteomic or metabolomics reagents (Fig. 10.1). Depending on the product risk level or registration pathway, IVD reagents in turn can be divided into: class I, class II, and class III products. The classification in the following figure is considered as the most common classifications of IVD reagents.

C. Xu (✉)
Shanghai Zhangjiang Center for Translational Medicine, Shanghai Biotecan Co., Ltd., Building 3, 899 Zuchongzhi Road, 201203 Shanghai, P. R. China
e-mail: chengx@biotecan.com

E. D. Lu
Molecular and Cellular Biology, University of California, Berkeley, CA 94720, USA

J. Wang
Echocardiography, Cardiovascular Institute and Fuwai Hospital, Chinese Academy of Medical Sciences, 100037 Beijing, P. R. China

M. Q. Lu (ed.), *Approaching China's Pharmaceutical Market*,
DOI 10.1007/978-3-319-15576-0_10

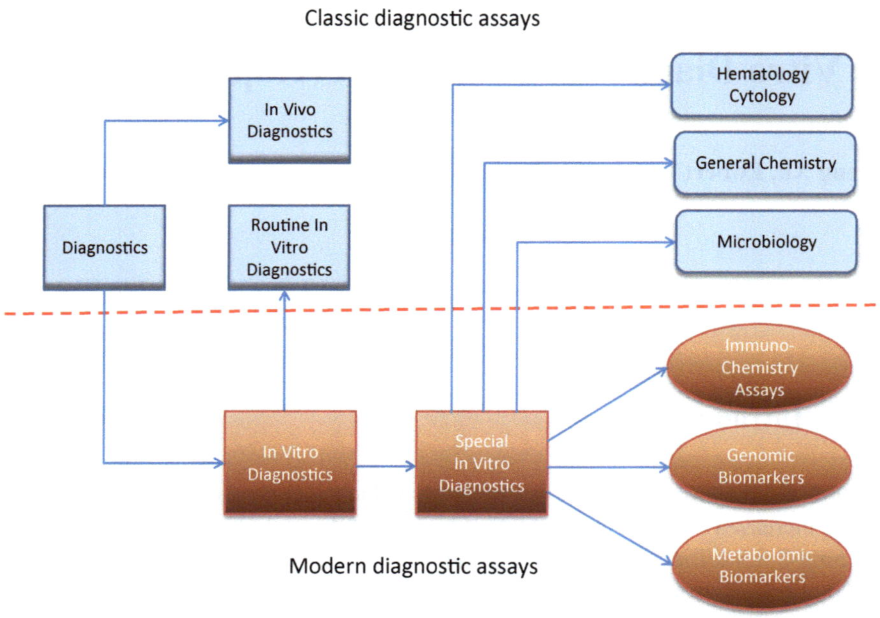

Fig. 10.1 Classification scheme of medical diagnosis

With breakthroughs in bioscience and biotechnology, undoubtedly many opportunities to survive longer and live healthily have been brought to patients who suffer from various diseases. In the Organization for Economic Co-operation and Development (OECD) countries, the largest market for IVD reagents is in North America, and the second largest is in Western Europe. In the past 20 years, the IVD industry has gone through four technological revolutions, involving the chemical diagnostic reagents, enzymes, immunoassays and probe technology. Every revolution has pushed clinical diagnostic reagents technology to a new level with greatly increased commercial value and investment value. Two-thirds of the world's medical decisions are made based on diagnostic information, while diagnosis expense only accounts for less than 10 % of total healthcare expenditure; therefore the diagnostic industry has broad development space (Insight 2012).

Since 2005, the in vitro diagnostics industry has been one of the key sectors supported by the central government. The State Development and Reform Commission, the Ministry of Science, and the Ministry of Health have introduced a number of policies for the promotion of IVD reagents as well as diagnostic instruments to enhance the competitiveness of domestic diagnostic reagents enterprises. Data show that since 2006, the domestic IVD reagent industry has an annual growth rate of about 15–20 %. In 2008, the Chinese IVD market reached 9.5 billion RMB (Chinese currency), and in 2010, the market has increased to 12.2 billion RMB (~2 billion USD). By 2015, China's IVD market size is expected to exceed 30 billion RMB and become the world's third largest market while the average annual growth rate will still remain at 15–20 %. With China's new healthcare reform, more attention has been put on the people's quality of life. Hence, a potentially huge incremental market for the in vitro diagnostics industry will come after the healthcare reform. Data show that national investment to basic health systems has increased to 1000 billion RMB. The biochemical diagnostic products for common diseases are the main segment benefited from these investments. Several sub-sectors of the diagnostic reagent industry have investment opportunities, and the market for home diagnostic reagents will be the focus of attention (ASKCI 2014).

China accounts for one-fifth of the world's population, but the in vitro diagnostics industry only accounts for about 7.8 % of the global IVD market. The diagnostic product per capita amount in China is $ 2.75, well below the US $ 25–30 per capita and other developed countries. From a more practical point of view, in clinical practice abroad, the inspection (diagnosis) costs typically account for 20–30 % of hospital revenue; while the inspection (diagnosis) fee in a typical Chinese hospital accounts for about 11 % of total hospital revenue, much lower than the proportion in hospitals in developed countries. While the government is adjusting the drug price to cancel the additional cost for patients, more and more hospitals have focused their attention on diagnostic, pathology laboratories to generate the revenues (Datamonitor 2008).

Due to the fast-growing market of the IVD market, the Chinese central government started to establish more and more regulatory policies to manage and supervise the development of this industry. The China State Food and Drug Administration (SFDA) issued "Measures for the Administration of In vitro Diagnostic (IVD) Reagents (Interim)," No. 229 on April 19, 2007 and became effective on June 1, 2007 (SFDA 2007). In the same year, the SFDA issued "Guidance for clinical research technology of in vitro diagnostic reagents" (SFDA 2007a) and "Guidance for writing instructions of in vitro diagnostic reagents" (SFDA 2007b). The appropriate food and drug administration responsible for implementation of this guidance are the agencies at the level of provinces, autonomous regions and municipalities directly under the central government. In recent years, the central government has recognized that the regulations for supervision and administration of in vitro diagnostic reagents are far behind the rapid population growth and thriving economy increase over the past 30 years. The Chinese state council issued the latest "Regulations for the Supervision and Administration of Medical Devices" on February 12, 2014, and it came into effect as of June 1, 2014 (CFDA 2014). Before long, the China Food and Drug Administration issued a series of the latest regulations on in vitro diagnostic reagents on July 30, 2014, and they have come into force as of October 1, 2014. The overseas in vitro diagnostic reagents exported into the Chinese market have been subject to administration of overall new regulations on in-vitro diagnostic reagent registration since October 1, 2014.

10.2 In Vitro Diagnostic Market and Environment in China

A complete IVD industry includes the upstream sector, raw material supply chain, and the downstream sector known as the demand industries. The upstream raw material sector provides raw biochemical materials, including diagnostic enzymes, antigens, antibodies and other biological products. The downstream demands come mainly from medical testing, blood screening, research laboratories etc. The medical testing is currently the most important consumption whereabouts of IVD reagent.

Currently, there are nearly 60,000 IVD reagent products users in China, including 20,291 hospitals, 38,475 township hospitals, more than 300 blood banks, as well as emerging medical centers and independent clinical testing laboratories. Molecular diagnostics is a fast-growing segment of the IVD market. Up to the end of 2013, the growth rate was almost double compared to that of 5 years ago (Beijing Huayan Zhongshang Economic Information Center 2010).

The major driving force for China's fast-growing IVD market is the need for targeted therapies or in other words, the need for personalized medicine. In this aspect, IVDs are mainly used to identify suitable patients for targeted therapy, especially in the field of oncology. In addition, it can be used to determine the effective dosing of certain drug treatments such as Warfarin dosing and Plavix dosing etc. Due to the significant improvement of the patient treatment efficacies and survival benefit through targeted therapies or personalized medicine as determined by in vitro molecular diagnostics, the fast market growth will be maintained in the next decade.

Another impelling force for the growth of the IVD market is the emerging technology to replace the traditional technology to perform mandatory tests. The novel technology usually has several obvious advantages, such as higher accuracy, non-invasiveness, less painful, lower risk, earlier diagnosis (detection) etc. A recent event in the field of prenatal testing, non-invasive prenatal testing (NIPT) to be exact, is an excellent example to show the effect of new technology on the IVD market size and capital market. A single NIPT test can potentially expanded the total IVD market by 50 % (details in Chap. 8.2.2).

The third reason linked to the increase of the total IVD market is the apparent rise of the prevalence of major severe diseases, such as cancer, cardiovascular diseases, diabetes etc. Obviously, the increase of the disease prevalence has a direct link to the deteriorating environmental condition and the subtle change in dietary habits. Mass media and healthcare organizations have started to divert more attention of general public to health related topics and people in the general population are now more willing to pay for health management expenses, such as physical examinations and even molecular diagnostic tests, to lower the risk of severe diseases. To meet the need for a safer and healthier life plan, molecular diagnostic tests such as hereditary cancer screening, i.e. tests equivalent to BRC Analysis (Myriad Genetics Products), cancer early detection tests, i.e. tests equivalent to Cologuard (Exact Science Products), and even service as cutting-edge as whole genome or whole exome sequencing and analysis, start to gain recognition and promotion among health management organizations in China. The fact that in 2014 three companies in China separately bought from Illumina Inc. the Hiseq X Ten sequencers, of which the sequencing capacity greatly exceeded the needs of the current market (for research purpose, clinical testing and health management service altogether) is a perfect example that shows that high-end molecular testing service has started to gain momentum in China's emerging market.

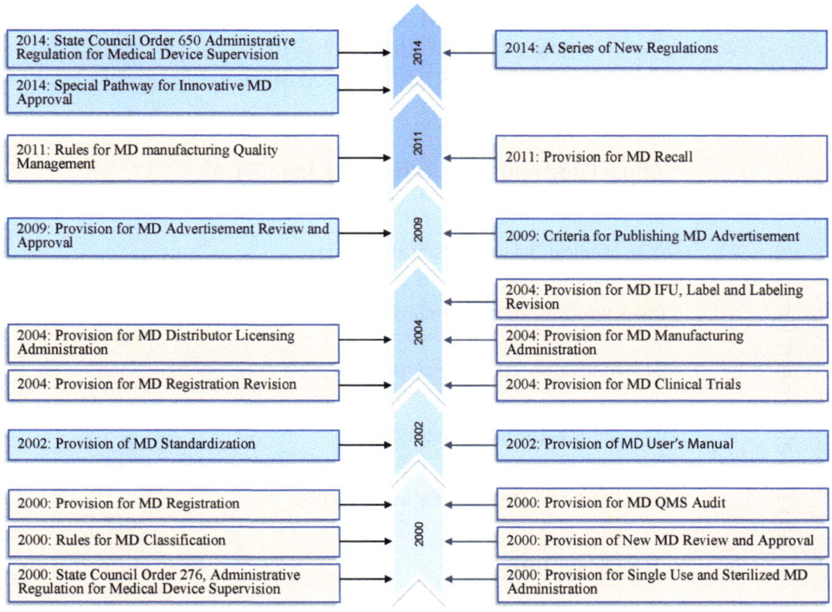

Fig. 10.2 The CFDA regulations relevant to in-vitro diagnostic reagents in China

The rest of the driving force comes from the recent change in birth control regulation in China, as second children are allowed in many areas in China now.

10.2.1 Important Regulations Relevant to in-Vitro Diagnostic Reagents in China

In China, the regulations issued by the central government have a great impact on the IVD industry. Since 2006, the regulatory framework in China for in-vitro diagnostic reagents has undergone significant changes, yet the current existing regulations and guidance for in-vitro diagnostic reagents are still much behind of international standards. In 2014, "Regulations for the Supervision and Administration of Medical Devices" was issued on February 12 by the Chinese state council and became effective on June 1, 2014. Very recently, China Food and Drug Administration (CFDA) promulgated a series of the regulations on in-vitro diagnostic reagents on July 30, 2014, effective as of October 1, 2014. The multinational in-vitro diagnostic reagents imported into China's market need to follow these new regulations on in-vitro diagnostic reagent registration. A brief outline of the relevant regulations for in-vitro diagnostic reagents is listed chronologically in Fig. 10.2.

From Fig. 10.2, overseas companies can easily see that many regulations have been issued since 2000. In 2014, a series of new regulations were issued by CFDA. The most influential key regulations for in-vitro diagnostic reagents are indicated in Fig. 10.3, which will be discussed in the chapter.

Fig. 10.3 Key regulations for in-vitro diagnostic reagents in China

The revised regulations become more scientifically sound and sophisticated (Table 10.1). Based on the regulations in Table 10.2, it is evident that the government encourages the local companies for their research and development activities. Comparatively, it is getting stricter and adds more requirements for the reagents from overseas companies.

Since the new regulations are developed on the basis of previous ones, there are still many similarities. In the following Table 10.2, we listed the major differences and changes for readers to be easily understandable.

In China, the policy issued by the central government has had a great impact on IVD industry. In 2007, the SFDA issued "Measures for the Administration of IVD Reagents (Interim) "(SFDA 2007) and "Guidelines for Writing the Instruction of In vitro Diagnosis Reagent" (SFDA 2007a). These regulations and guidelines have laid the groundwork for the development of IVD reagents. The medical department in the government of each province has subsequently established guidelines to standardize the application and review process of new IVD reagents from biotech companies and institutions.

In 2013, the state council issued "Bio-industry development plan." The plan specifically aimed to promote the development of IVD reagents that focus on early screening, diagnosis, efficacy evaluation, prognosis evaluation, diagnosis of birth defects and other needs, the development of high-throughput, high-precision testing instrument and reagents. The plan also pointed out that the government of each level should pay close attention to the following aspects:

Table 10.1 In-vitro diagnostic reagent registration related regulation revisions

Year	State Council and the CFDA Regulations
1996	SPAC offering for medical device registration
1997	Registration of all medical devices was required before placing on market
2000	First state council regulation of medical devices enacted
2000	SPAC enacted provisions for MD registration
2004	SPAC enacted provisions for MD registration revised
2014	State Council regulation for MD revised
2014	The CFDA releases revised provisions for MD registration (CFDA Order No.4, 2014)

Table 10.2 Comparison of requirements in new regulations for IVD approval vs. those in old regulations

No.	New regulation key points	Previous regulation
1	More class II and class III devices are required to do clinical trials in China, and the rest of the them may be exempted from clinical trials through pre-determined exemption list or application case by case	Import devices are usually exempted for clinical trials
2	More information is required for submission, including product risk management, product research and development, production information, and clinical literature even if trials in China are exempted	These are generally not required for import device
3	A check list of essential requirement for safety and effectiveness must be provided in submission	Not required
4	The developer of an innovative device may apply for registration and hold the certificate of registration before massive production	Applicant who submit for registration must have got manufacturing license
5	When the CFDA many use provincial FDA or technical organization outside of food and drug administration to carry out some practical tasks related to product registration	The SFDA does all tasks for registration of all import and class III device
6	Time line of technical evaluation (assessment) for class III device is prolonged to 90 working days, while 60 working days for class II	Sixty working days for class II and III
7	The CFDA technical evaluation will focus on change or modification when reviewing submission for change. Changes are defined in two categories: (1) change which needs evaluation and approval; (2) change which just needs filing and recording	The SFDA reviews all aspects of device even if submission just for change
8	Validity period of registration is prolonged to 5 years, when expired, application for extension, rather than re-registration must be submitted, and simpler than initial	Four years, and reregistration almost like new/initial registration
9	Registration Certificate is reformed, the initial registration number will be kept with device in life time, and attached with new change approval(s) if any	Registration number changes when device re-registered.
10	Fees for application of registration and filing are required to be paid by applicant, but the amount of fee has not been decided	No fee since 2004

1. Accelerate the development of molecular diagnostics, biochips and other emerging technologies;
2. Accelerate the industrialization of immune biomarkers, personalized medicine, pathogens and other IVD products;
3. Promote the development of rapid field detection of pathogens in blood and other sample, immunological assay, and other IVD instruments, and;
4. Promote large-scale production of the instrument and reagent mentioned above.

It was mentioned in the plan that constructions of IVD reagents development and industrialization platforms are recommended. These platforms serve as incubators to strengthen the raw material production, such as enzymatic reagent, diagnostic antibodies, etc., to build traceability system and its reference laboratory networks.

In October 2014, the state council issued “Several Suggestions to Accelerate the Development of Technology Services” (State Council 2014). The suggestions indicate that the central government and the provincial government would accelerate the development of third-party inspection and certification services, and encourage equal participation and competition of inspection and certification units of different forms of ownership in the market, would improve the inspection and certification units. The state would construct industrial measuring and testing service centers to strengthen national metrology testing network and build a science and technology innovation alliance. The state would also build a unified regulatory system for inspection and certification to promote the international mutual recognition of testing certification.

10.2.2 Market Analysis of in Vitro Diagnostic Industry in China

In 2010, the China IVD market size was $ 2.07 billion (about 13.68 billion RMB), including the IVD instrument market of $ 570 million (about 3.78 billion RMB) and IVD reagent market of $ 1.5 billion (about $ 99 billion RMB). Three years later, in 2013, the China IVD market size was valued at $ 3.47 billion and the number is expected to reach $ 4.3 billion in 2014 (Zhiyan Consulting Group 2013a, b). In addition, McEvoy and Farmer believes that China’s population accounts for one-fifth of the world’s population, but the IVD market share accounts for only 3 % of the world market, and the Chinese per capita annual use of IVD products is only $ 1.5, while the per capita use of IVD products in developed countries has reached $ 25 ~ 30. So, a vast IVD market growth is expected in the next few years, and the growth rate will maintain at 15–20 % (Zhiyan Consulting Group 2013a, b).

10.3 Registration and Development Pathway

10.3.1 Notice on Domestic in Vitro Diagnostics Registration

Issued by the State Food and Drug Administration on November 5, 2012

For those overseas companies that have local/domestic manufacturing facilities, they may follow the domestic IVD reagents registration pathway if they are qualified.

10.3.1.1 General Provisions (Table 10.3)

10.3.1.2 Principle for Product Classification and Name

IVD reagents are classified into Class III, II and I products in accordance with their risks.

A. Class III (The Third Class) Products

1. Reagents in relation to the determination of pathogenic antigen, antibody and nucleic acid;
2. Reagents in relation to the match of blood type and tissues;
3. Reagents in relation to the determination of human genes;
4. Reagents in relation to the determination of hereditary diseases;
5. Reagents in relation to the determination of anesthetic, psychiatric drug and toxic medicine for medical purpose;
6. Reagents in relation to the determination of target of curative medicines;
7. Reagents in relation to the determination of indicator of tumor;
8. Reagents in relation to allergic reaction (sensitinogen).

B. Class II (The Second Class) Products
Apart from Class III and Class I products, others fall into Class II products, which mainly include the followings

1. Reagent for the determination of proteins;
2. Reagent for the determination of sugar;
3. Reagent for the determination of hormones;
4. Reagent for the determination of enzymes;
5. Reagent for the determination of esters;
6. Reagent for the determination of vitamins;
7. Reagent for the determination of inorganic ions;
8. Reagent for the determination of drug and its metabolic substances;
9. Reagent for the determination of autologous antibody;
10. Reagent for the determination of microbes or allergic test;
11. Reagent for the determination of other physiological, biochemical or immune function indicators.

Table 10.3 Document categories and the requirements

Document category	Details and requirements of the document	Department to prepare the information
(1) Application form of registration of domestic IVD	1. All entries of the form shall be filled in accordance with the requirements described in the instructions	
	2. Application for remission or exemption of clinical trials (For remission or exemption of clinical trials for rare disease, special diseases and other conditions, the applicant shall submit such an application along with the registration application documents, stating the reasons therein and provide relevant documentation)	Regulatory affairs (RA) (the reasons of remission or exemption of clinical trials shall be provided with the assistant of clinical department)
(2) Certifications	1. Copy of enterprise's production license and business license	RA (original copy shall be provided)
	1) The applied product shall be within the scope of the production license	
	2) They are All the above certification shall be within the validity period	
	2. A statement of authenticity of the documents submitted	RA
	1) The list of the submitted documents shall be accompanied by a promise of the consistency between the "research data of major production processes and reaction system" with the QMS assessment data	
	2) The applicant's commitment for legal liabilities	
3) Description documents	1. Product Expected Use	Clinical departments,
	1) Expected use of the product	market departments,
	2) Background of the clinical indications in relation to the expected use	quality control department,
	3) Relevant clinical or lab diagnosis methods	RA
	2. Product Description	Production research and development department, quality control department, RA
	1) Technical mechanism of the products	
	2) Source and preparation method of main raw materials	
	3) Major production process	
	4) Preparation methods and sources of quality control substance and reference (standard) substances	

Table 10.3 (continued)

Document category	Details and requirements of the document	Department to prepare the information
	3. biological safety explanations	Production research and development department, Quality control department, RA
	1) Certifications and explanations are required for the human-derived material about infectious diseases (HBV, HCV, HIV etc.)	
	2) Cattle, sheep-derived materials should be explained according to "About contain cattle, sheep -derived material matters related to Medical Device Registration Notice" (CFDA No. [2006] 407)	
	3) Materials of other animal and microbial sources should offer Appropriate documentation approving the safety of product transportation, process and the environment of the users	
	4) Instructions and related documents for the above and other specific viral inactivation taken to ensure the safety of the test method	
	4. Summary and evaluation on major research findings	RA
	1) Summary on major research findings	
	2) Evaluation on relevant products	
	5. Others	Marketing department, clinical department, and RA
	1) The approval of same kind of product for in the domestic market and international market	
	2) The adopted technical method and clinical applications of relevant products	
	3) Identity and difference of the product in registration application compared with same type products at home and abroad	
	4) For new diagnosis reagent products, the applicant shall provide literature information about the relations between the subject substance and the anticipated applicable clinical indications	
(4) Product instructions	1. The format of the package inserts shall be in line with the "Guidelines for Compiling the Package Inserts of IVD"	Marketing department, clinical department, and RA
	2. Package inserts shall be in duplicate with a statement of mutual consistency	

Table 10.3 (continued)

Document category	Details and requirements of the document	Department to prepare the information
(5) Intended product standards and its preparation explanations	1. The intended product standards and the preparation explanations shall be in duplicate with a statement of mutual consistency	Quality control department, and RA
	2. The format of intended product standards shall be in line with GB/T1.1	
	3. If national standards or industry standards is adopted as product applicable standards, the applicant shall submit	
	1) A statement of the applied product's compliance with national standards and industry standards	
	2) A statement of commitment for post-marketed product quality	
	3) Explanations of the classification of product packaging specifications	
(6) Registration testing report	1. Originals of registration testing reports issued by competent testing institutions accredited by the CFDA	Production research and development department, quality control department, RA
	2. The packaging specifications of the testing product shall be within the range of the registration application	
	3. Testing type shall be registration testing	
	4. For Class III products, registration testing of three consecutive production sample batches shall be conducted	
(7) Information about the study on major raw materials	1. Major raw materials include antigen, antibody, selection and preparation of quality control substance	Production research and development department, quality control department, RA
	2. Reference substance (calibration substance) and information about the study on their quality standards	
	3. Trial information about the specific data of quality control substance, reference substance (calibration substance)	
(8) Information about the study on main production technology and reaction system	1. Main process includes solid phase carrier, coloration systems and indicating system, etc.	Production research and development department, quality control department, RA
	2. Composition of the reaction system	
	3. Requirement of sample	
	4. Reagent use amount	
	5. Reaction conditions	
	6. Calibration method	
	7. Quality control method	

Table 10.3 (continued)

Document category	Details and requirements of the document	Department to prepare the information
(9) Information about the evaluation on analytical Performance	1. Analytical sensitivity, analytical specificity, test range, accuracy, inaccuracy within the same batch samples and inaccuracy among different batches	Quality control department, RA
	2. In case the product in registration application includes different packing specification, then sample of each packing specification is needed for test information of the above evaluation items	
	3. In case the product in registration application is applicable to different type of instrument, then sample is needed for test information of the above evaluation items or on different type of instrument	
	4. Evaluation on analytical performance of multiple batches of product will effectively ensure the stability of production process and product quality	
	5. If the products are finished by committing the relevant agencies according to the 21th item of IVD Registration Regulation (Trial), Data in the report commissioned by the project shall indicate the name, provide both agreement and to ensure the authenticity of all test data and information	
(10) Determination of reference value (range)	1. Sample source used to determine the reference value (range)	
	2. Determination method for the reference value (range)	
	3. Detailed trial information about the determination of the reference value (range)	Quality control department, RA
	4. If the program is completed by commissioning organizations according to the 21th item of IVD Registration Regulation (Trial), Application materials must state the name of commissioned projects, provide both agreement and guarantee the authenticity of all test data and information	
(11) Stability data	1. Basis for determining the stability of the research methods	Quality control department, RA
	2. Specific methods and process of the stability study	
	3. At least three batches of samples that are stored under real storage conditions till they reach the expiry date	
	4. Accelerated damage trial information shall be provided if necessary	

Table 10.3 (continued)

Document category	Details and requirements of the document	Department to prepare the information
(12) Clinical trial data	1. Class III products: the applicant shall carry out clinical trials in no less than three (including three) provincial health care institutions	Clinical department, RA
	2. Class II products: the applicant shall carry out clinical trials in no less than two (including two) provincial health care institutions	
	3. For special-purpose products, the applicant can conduct clinical trials in qualified municipal-level and above centers for disease control, specialized hospitals or inspection and quarantine institutions, detoxification center and other institutions	
	4. Clinical trial agreement: signed by clinical trial institutions and the applicant	
	5. Clinical trial protocol: signed and sealed by the primary leaders (signature), clinical trial organizations (seal), person and institution in charge of statistics, the applicant, and the ethics committee (leading unit)	
	If the clinical trials aren't subject to the consent of the Ethics Committee, the leading unit shall still provide a description of the ethical issues with signature	
	6. Clinical trial reports issued by the institutions, the cover of which shall include	
	1) Name of the product used in the clinical trial	
	2) Start and finish dates of clinical trials	
	3) Signatures of all main person responsible for the clinical trials, the signature of clinical trials institution, the signature and seal of Statistics head and the stamp of the applicant	
	4) The contact and contact information of the product registration applicant, the reporting date and the locations for archiving of original data	
	7. Summary report of the results of all clinical trials	
	1) The reports shall be completed by the leading unit or the applicant	
	2) The contents of the cover shall be the same as those of the clinical trial reports of various clinical trial institutions	

Table 10.3 (continued)

Document category	Details and requirements of the document	Department to prepare the information
	8. Detailed information of clinical trials, including the results of all clinical trials, other testing methods or other basic information of diagnostic reagent products, such as testing methods, sources of diagnostic reagent products, package inserts and registration approvals and so on	
	9. The batch numbers of clinical trial samples must match with those used by the applicant for intended product standards testing, and the pre-clinical testing reports can be either the applicant's self-test report, or testing report issued by other competent testing institutions entrusted by the applicant	
	10. For calibration products, quality control products, and reference solution etc., clinical trial data need not to be provided	
	11. The "seals" of clinical trial institutions mentioned in this section refers to the official seals of clinical trial institutions and/or competent departments responsible for the trials in clinical trial institutions	
(13) Production and self-test records	Provide copies of three consecutive batches of production and self-test records	Production research and development department , quality control department, RA
(14) Sample package and labeling		Product packaging department, quality control department, RA
(15) Quality management system and evaluation report	1. For application of initial registration of Class II and III IVD, the following documents shall be submitted	Quality control department
	1) Application form for IVD production QMS assessment	
	2) IVD production QMS assessment report	
	3) IVD development verification report form	
	2. For initial registration of products under existing QMS assessment report, the following documents shall be submitted	
	1) Application form for IVD production QMS assessment	
	2) Original IVD production QMS assessment report	
	3) IVD development verification report form	

Table 10.3 (continued)

Document category	Details and requirements of the document	Department to prepare the information
	3. The QMS assessment report of the following three categories of IVD shall be issued by CFDA Center for Food and Drug Control	
	1) Reagents related to pathogenic antigens, antibodies, nucleic acid and other testing	
	2) Reagents associated with blood and tissue typing	
	3) Reagents associated with allergic reaction (allergen)	
	The QMS assessment report of other Class II and III IVD shall be issued by drug administration departments of the provinces, autonomous regions and municipalities that the enterprises locate	

This table lists the registered document items of domestic IVD reagents, detailed information on the content, and the requests of these items. It should be pointed out that during the preparation of registration, the technological data could be provided by associated departments, including research and development, quality control, clinical and market departments, besides RA which is responsible for communication and data compilation and writing. Once the data is ready, including clear information for each state department data transfer, the item should be marked and signed by relevant responsible individual

C. Class I (The First Class) Products

1. Microbe culture medium (not for microbe identification and allergy test);
2. Products for sample treatment such as hemolytic reagent, dilution solution and stain solution.

10.3.1.3 Information Requirements for the First Registration Application and Explanations

Issued by the State Food and Drug Administration on November 5, 2012 (SFDA 2012) (Table 10.4)

Table 10.4 Information requirements for the first registration application

Application Items	Class III	Class II	Class I
1. Application Form	V	V	
2. Certificate documents	V	V	V
3. General information	V	V	V
4. Product Instructions	V	V	V
5. Draft product standard and compilation explanations	V	V	V
6. Registration test report	V	V	×
7. Information about the study on main raw materials	V	△	△
8. Information about the study on technology and reaction system	V	△	△
9. Information about assessment of analytical performance	V	V	△
10. Information about reference value (range)	V	V	△
11. Information on stability study	V	V	△
12. Clinical trial information	V	V	×
13. Production and self -test records	V	V	V
14. Sample of package and label	V	V	V
15. Check report on quality control system	V	V	△

Explanations for Application Materials

1. Registration Application Form The applicant shall fill out the registration application form in accordance with the requirements.
2. Certificate Documents
   1. A copy of the business license of the applicant and a copy of manufacturing enterprise permit (the product in registration application shall fall into the production range of specified in manufacturing enterprise permit).
   2. Statement of the applicant on the authenticity of the submitted materials.
3. General Information
   1. Product Expected Use: Expected use of the product, background of the clinical indications in relation to the expected use, for example, the incidence of clinical indications, susceptible population; relevant clinical or lab diagnosis methods, etc.
   2. Product Description: It includes the technical mechanism of the product; source and preparation method of main raw materials; major production

process; preparation methods and sources of quality control substance and reference (standard) substances.
3. Explanations about biological safety: Explanations of the researcher about the test methods including inactivation on the above raw materials to ensure the safety of the use and the environment during the transportation and utilization of the products because major raw materials of IVD reagents may be prepared be biological materials such as various animal tissues, pathogens, human tissue or body liquid after treatment or the addition of certain substances.
4. Summary and evaluation on major research findings of relevant products.
5. Others: It includes the approval of same kind of product for going on the market at home and abroad. The adopted technical method and clinical applications of relevant products; identity and difference of the product in registration application compared with same type products at home and abroad. For new diagnosis reagent products, the applicant shall provide literature information about the relations between the subject substance and the anticipated applicable clinical indications.

4. Product Instructions: It shall comply with relevant requirements of the Regulations on the Instructions, Label and Package Mark of Medical Devices and be compiled with reference to relevant technical guidance. Product name in the instructions may include at the same time the general name, commodity name and English name. The general name shall comply with relevant naming principle specified in the Measures on the Management of the Registration of IVD Reagents.
5. Drafting Product Standard and Developing Explanations: The text and compilation explanations of the draft product standard shall comply with relevant provisions of Measures on the Management of Medical Device Standards. For Class III products, the contents of draft product standard shall be developed according to the Specifications on Biological Products (2000).
6. Registration Test Report Registration Test Report given by a testing institution recognized by China Food and Drug Administration.
7. Information About the Study on Major Raw Materials Major raw materials include antigen, antibody, selection and preparation of quality control substance, reference substance (calibration substance) and information about the study on their quality standards; trial information about the specific data of quality control substance, reference substance (calibration substance).
8. Information About the Study on Main Production Technology and Reaction System: The main production process includes solid phase carrier and coloration systems, etc.. Reaction system includes sample collection and treatment, sample use amount, reagent use amount, reaction conditions, calibration method (if necessary), quality control method, etc.
9. Information about the Evaluation on Analytical Performance

Generally speaking, evaluation on analytical performance includes such items as analytical sensitivity, analytical specificity, test range, accuracy, inaccuracy within the same batch samples and inaccuracy among different batches. The outcomes of the evaluation on analytical performance are important bases for the development of product standard. Researchers shall employ multiple batches of product to carry out the above performance evaluation. The draft product standard based on statistical analysis of the outcomes of the evaluation on analytical performance of multiple batches of product will effectively ensure the stability of production process and product quality. In the case that the product in the registration application includes different packing specification or is applicable to different type of instrument, then a sample of each packing specification is needed for test information of the above evaluation items or on different type of instrument.

10. Determination of Reference Value (Range): The sample source used to determine the reference value (range) shall be explained in detail. Explain the determination method for the reference value (range) and provide detailed trial information about the determination of the reference value (range).
11. Information about Stability Study: It includes the stability study information of at least three batches of samples that are stored under real storage conditions till they reach the expiry date. Accelerated damage trial information shall be provided if necessary.
12. Information about Clinical Trial: Clinical trial shall be carried out in accordance with relevant technical guidance with the provision of clinical trial information.
    1. Clinical trial agreement and clinical trial program.
    2. Clinical trial reports of each clinical trial institution and the summary report on all clinical trial results. The clinical trial reports of each clinical trial institution shall be printed with the official seal of the competent administrative department on clinical trial.
    3. Attachments: detailed information about clinical trial, including all clinical trial results; basic information about the adoption at the same time of other trial method or diagnosis reagent products such as trial method, source of diagnosis reagent product, product instructions and approval of the registration, etc.

Note: In case of calibration and quality control materials and reference solution etc., there is no need for clinical trial information.

13. Production and Self Check Records: Provide with a copy of the production and self-check records of three consecutive batches of products.
14. Sample Package and Label: It shall comply with the requirements of the Regulations on the Management of the Instructions, Label and Package Mark of Medical Devices. The label of product external package must include the general name, name of the manufacturing enterprise, product batch number and points for attention. It may at the same time be printed with the general name, commodity name and English name of the product. The general name shall comply with the naming principle of the Measures on the Management of Registration of IVD Reagents. For various components of IVD reagent product such as calibration and quality control materials and cleaning solution, the package and label must be printed with the Chinese name and batch number of

this component. In case that various components with different batch number but with same product batch number cannot be replaced, both the product batch number and that of each component shall be indicated.

15. Check Report on Quality Control System: When the applicant applies for the first time for the registration of Class III and II products, the applicant shall provide a check report on quality control system produced by relevant drug administrative department. When the applicant applies for the registration of Class I products, the applicant shall provide a self-check report on the quality control system if necessary.

Note:

1. The above application materials shall be signed and sealed by the manufacturing enterprise. "Sign and seal" refers to the printing of the seal of the enterprise or the signature by legal representative or head together the printing of the seal of the enterprise.
2. In the case that some trial information of the registration application of a domestic product is provided by an overseas research institution, it shall be attached with an explanation document on the items and pages of relevant information produced by the overseas research institution and a certificate testifying that such institution has legal registration and been notarized in foreign country or region. However, information required under items 9, 11, 12 and 13 must be the trial information obtained from the test of the products by a manufacturing enterprise within the mainland of China.

10.3.1.4 Notice on Initial Registration for Domestic in Vitro Diagnostic Reagent

Issued by the State Food and Drug Administration on April 17, 2014 (CFDA 2014a)

A. Project Name Domestic Medical Device Registration

B. Content of Licensing Initial registration for domestic IVD

C. Basis for Implementation "Regulations for Supervision and Administration of Medical Devices", "Provisions for Medical Device Registration", "Provisions for Registration of IVD (Interim)"

D. Fees No charge

E. Quantity Restrictions No quantity limit for the licensing

F. List of Application Documents

- Item 1: Application form of domestic IVD registration;
- Item 2: Copy of enterprise's production license and business license;
- Item 3: A statement of authenticity of the documents submitted;
- Item 4: Summary data

- Item 5: Package inserts;
- Item 6: Intended product standards and its preparation explanations;
- Item 7: Registration testing report;
- Item 8: Research data for major raw materials;
- Item 9: The research data for main production technology and reaction system;
- Item 10: Analysis of performance evaluation data;
- Item 11: Determination of reference value (reference range);
- Item 12: Stability research data;
- Item 13: Clinical trials data
- Item 14: Production and self-test records;
- Item 15: Sample of packaging and labeling;
- Item 16: Quality management system evaluation report.

G. Requirements for Application Dossier A) General requirements for the dossier:

1. The dossier shall be bound into books.
2. The first page of the dossier is a list of application documents, which shall be arranged in order as per "General requirements". Each document shall be separated by labeled slip sheets and marked with data item number.
3. The dossier shall be in one full copy (product standards and product package insert shall be in duplicate).
4. All documents in the dossier compiled by the applicant or agent shall be printed in A4 size paper, the contents are complete, clear, without alteration; documents issued by the Government and other agencies shall be provided at the original size, where the bound volumes shall not be split without authorization.
5. The copies of the document shall be clear and consistent with the originals.
6. The contents of application document (application form, approvals for marketing, product standards, testing reports, and package insert) shall be consistent. The trade name and English name, if any, shall be marked.
7. The application documents shall be in Chinese, and translated documents shall be accompanied with the originals.
8. Product name shall meet the nomenclature rules stipulated by the "Provisions for Registration of IVD (Interim)".
9. The electronic versions of the following registration document shall also be submitted:

    1. Application form
    2. Abstracts of the literature review, wherein: the intended use of the product (500 words or less), product description (200 words or less), biological safety explanations (100 words or less), summarizes and evaluation of the main findings (200 words or less) and others (200 words or less);
    3. Intended product standards and its preparation explanations;
    4. Package inserts

The above electronic documents, except for the application forms, shall be WORD document without exception, which can be edited and modified.

B) Specific requirements for application documents:

1. Application form of registration of domestic IVD;
    1. The "electronic application software 2010 for the registration of medical devices (IVD)" can be downloaded from www.cfda.gov.cn;
    2. All entries of the form shall be filled in accordance with the requirements described in the instructions;
    3. For remission or exemption of clinical trials for rare disease, special diseases and other conditions, the applicant shall submit such an application along with the application documents, stating the reasons therein and provide relevant documentation.
2. Copy of enterprise's production license and business license;
    1. The applied product shall be within the scope of the production license;
    2. All the above certification shall be within the validity period.
3. A statement of authenticity of the documents submitted;
    1. The list of the submitted documents shall be accompanied by a promise of the consistency between the "research data of major production processes and reaction system" with the QMS assessment data;
    2. The applicant's commitment for legal liabilities.
4. Package inserts
    1. The format of the package inserts shall be in line with the "Guidelines for Compiling the Package Inserts of IVD ";
    2. Package inserts shall be in duplicate with a statement of mutual consistency.
5. Intended product standards and its preparation explanations;
    1. The intended product standards and the preparation explanations shall be in duplicate with a statement of mutual consistency;
    2. The format of intended product standards shall be in line with GB/T1.1;
    3. If national standards or industry standards are adopted as product applicable standards, the applicant shall submit:
        i. A statement of the applied product's compliance with national standards and industry standards;
        ii. A statement of commitment for post-marketed product quality;
        iii. Explanations of the classification of product packaging specifications.
6. Registration testing report;
    1. Originals of registration testing reports issued by competent testing institutions accredited by the CFDA;
    2. The packaging specifications of the testing product shall be within the range of the registration application;
    3. Testing type shall be registration testing;
    4. For Class III products, registration testing of three consecutive production sample batches shall be conducted.

7. Clinical trials data

    1. Class III products: the applicant shall carry out clinical trials in no less than three (including three) provincial health care institutions.
    2. Class II products: the applicant shall carry out clinical trials in no less than two (including two) provincial health care institutions.
    3. For special-purpose products, the applicant can conduct clinical trials in qualified municipal-level and above centers for disease control, specialized hospitals or inspection and quarantine institutions, detoxification center and other institutions.
    4. Clinical trial agreement: signed by clinical trial institutions and the applicant.
    5. Clinical trial protocol: signed and sealed by the primary leaders (signature), clinical trial organizations (seal), person and institution in charge of statistics, the applicant, and the ethics committee (leading unit).

If the clinical trials aren't subject to the consent of the Ethics Committee, the leading unit shall still provide a description of the ethical issues with signature.

6. Clinical trial reports issued by the institutions, the cover of which shall include:

    i. Name of the product used in the clinical trial;
    ii. Start and finish dates of clinical trials;
    iii. Signatures of all main person responsible for the clinical trials, the signature of clinical trials institution, the signature and seal of Statistics head and the stamp of the applicant;
    iv. The contact and contact information of the product registration applicant, the reporting date and the locations for archiving of original data.

7. Summary report of the results of all clinical trials:

    i. The reports shall be completed by the leading unit or the applicant;
    ii. The contents of the cover shall be the same as those of the clinical trial reports of various clinical trial institutions.

8. Detailed information of clinical trials, including the results of all clinical trials, other testing methods or other basic information of diagnostic reagent products, such as testing methods, sources of diagnostic reagent products, package inserts and registration approvals and so on.
9. The batch numbers of clinical trial samples must match with those used by the applicant for intended product standards testing, and the pre-clinical testing reports can be either the applicant's self-test report, or testing report issued by other competent testing institutions entrusted by the applicant.
10. For calibration products, quality control products, and reference solution etc., clinical trial data need not to be provided.
11. The "seals" of clinical trial institutions mentioned in this section refers to the official seals of clinical trial institutions and/or competent departments responsible for the trials in clinical trial institutions.

8. Production and self-test records;

Provide copies of three consecutive batches production and self-test records.

9. Quality management system evaluation report.

    1. For application of initial registration of Class II and III IVD, the following documents shall be submitted:

        i. Application form for IVD production QMS assessment;
        ii. IVD production QMS assessment report;
        iii. IVD development verification report form.

    2. For initial registration of products under existing QMS assessment report, the following documents shall be submitted:

        i. Application form for IVD production QMS assessment;
        ii. Original IVD production QMS assessment report;
        iii. IVD development verification report form.

    3. The QMS assessment report of the following three categories of IVD shall be issued by the CFDA Center for Food and Drug Control:

        i. Reagents related to pathogenic antigens, antibodies, nucleic acid and other testing;
        ii. Reagents associated with blood and tissue typing;
        iii. Reagents associated with allergic reaction (allergen).

    4. The QMS assessment report of other Class II and III IVD shall be issued by drug administration departments of the provinces, autonomous regions and municipalities that the enterprises locate.

10. The application documents shall be signed and sealed by the applicant, unless otherwise instructed. "Signed and sealed" means sealed by manufacturer, or signed by its legal representative, responsible person, plus corporate seal. The seal must be the manufacturer's official seal, and registration stamp shall not be used.
11. If some testing data in the application documents are provided by overseas study institutions, explanations about the data items, page numbers etc., and certifying documents proving that the institution has been legally registered overseas and notarized shall be provided. However, performance evaluation analysis data, stability studies, clinical trial data, production and self-test records must be generated by using products domestically produced by Chinese manufacturers.

H. Application Process Diagram

For the IVD market approval, the overall processes include five essential steps as indicated in the following flowchart, see Fig. 10.4.

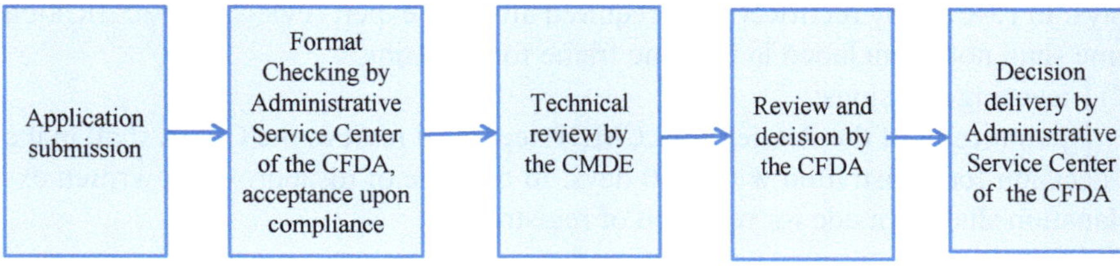

Fig. 10.4 Application process flowchart

I. Approval Procedures

A) Acceptance:

After the application is filed to the Administrative Acceptance Service Center, if the application dossier submitted is in accordance with the list in section VI of this Notice, the format examination shall be conducted by the staff of the Center in accordance with the "Notice on the issuance of the formats and requirements for IVD registration application dossier" (SFDA 2007c). These potential scenarios may include:

- Where the application item is not subject to administrative approval according to the regulation, a decision of non-acceptance shall be notified to the applicant immediately.
- Where the application item is not within the functions of the administrative authority, a decision of non-acceptance shall be made immediately, and the applicant shall be informed to launch the application to relevant administrative authority.
- Where in the application dossier, there are errors that can be corrected on the site, the applicant shall be allowed to make the corrections on the site.
- Where the application dossier is incomplete or does not meet the statutory format, the applicant shall be informed of all the supplements and amendments to be made once and for all on the spot or within 5 days.
- If the applicant is not informed within the above-mentioned period, the application shall be deemed as accepted from date of receipt of application materials.
- Where the application dossier is within the functions of the administrative authority, the application materials are complete and comply with the statutory format, or
- Where the applicant has submitted all supplements and amendments in accordance with the requirements of the administrative authority, the application for administrative approval shall be accepted.

B) Review:

Once the application is accepted, Administrative Service Center shall deliver the application dossier to the Center for Medical Device Evaluation (CMDE) for technical review, which includes product testing and expert review, and not exceed 60 days. In case of any rectification is required after the expert review, the rectification time shall not be included in the time frame for licensing.

C) Licensing decisions:

Upon receipt of the dossier after CMDE technical review, the CFDA shall make a decision for registration within 30 days. In the case of disapproval, a written explanation shall be made for rejection of registration.

D) Delivery:

Within 10 days from the date of decision making of administrative approval, the CFDA Administrative Service Center shall deliver the decision to the applicants.

J. Commitment Time Frame

The administrative licensing decision shall be made within 90 days from the date of acceptance.

K. Authority of Implementation

Implemented by the CFDA

Accepted at the CFDA Administrative Service Center

L. Changes

For alterations of registration and licensing items after the approval of IVD registration, the applicants shall apply for alterations to relevant drug administration departments. For alterations of registration items, the applicant shall apply for the changes within 30 days from the date of the change. For alterations of licensing items, the applicant shall apply for the changes and implement them after approval, if alterations of licensing items occur within 6 months before the expiry of the registration certificate, application for change can be made along with renewal of registration. If marketed products change the basic reaction principle or analytical sensitivity index with a new clinical diagnostic significance, they shall be handled in accordance with the initial application for registration.

M. License Validity and Renewal

A medical device registration certificate is valid for 4 years. The applicant shall apply for the renewal of registration to relevant drug administration departments within 6 months before the expiry of the registration certificate. If the production and sales of a product are still necessary after renewal of registration before the expiry of the registration certificate, the applicant shall apply in accordance with the procedures and requirements for initial registration.

N. Annual Inspection or Annual Review of the License None

O. Institutions for Inquiries and Complaints

Inquiries: the CFDA

Complaints: the CFDA Bureau of Investigation and Enforcement, Department of Legal Affairs

Note: The time frame of this Notice counts on working days, excluding legal holidays

10.3.2 Notice on Overseas In Vitro Diagnostic Reagent Registration

Issued by the State Food and Drug Administration on April 17, 2014; (CFDA 2014b).

For the overseas companies without local/domestic manufacturing facilities, they may follow the domestic IVD reagents registration pathway if they are qualified. Otherwise, the overseas companies should follow the following listed document requirement to submit their applications. See Items under F for details.

A. Project Name Initial registration of import medical devices

B. Content of Licensing Overseas IVD registration

C. Basis for Implementation "Regulations for Supervision and Administration of Medical Devices", "Provisions for Medical Device Registration", "Provisions for Registration of IVD (Interim)".

D. Fees No charge

E. Quantity Restrictions No quantity limit for the licensing

F. List of Application Documents Please note that in comparison to the required application documents for domestic IVD reagent, there are 20 required items for overseas application instead of 16 items for that of domestic application. Item 1–6 are unique for overseas in IVD reagent registration The rest Items from 7 to 20 are the same to the domestic IVD reagent applications, but with different requirements for Items 8, 12, 13, 14, 15, 16 and 18. See details under "G. Requirements for application dossier".

- Item 1: Overseas IVD registration application form;
- Item 2: Certification of overseas manufacturers;
- Item 3: Certifying documents of foreign government authorities' approval for the product to be marketed in the country (region) of origin;
- Item 4: Certifying documents of overseas manufacturer's compliance of "GMP" in countries or regions of origin, or other QMS certification documents;
- Item 5: Copies of designated agent's letter of entrustment/commitment, business license or institutional registration certificate (photocopy);
- Item 6: Copies of letter of entrustment/commitment of designated registration agent, business license or institutional registration certificate (photocopy);
- Item 7: A statement of authenticity of the documents submitted;
- Item 8: Summary data
- Item 9: Package insert
- Item 10: Intended product standards and its preparation explanations;
- Item 11: Registration testing report;
- Item 12: Research data for major raw materials;
- Item 13: The research data for main production technology and reaction system;
- Item 14: Analysis of performance evaluation data;

- Item 15: Determination of reference value (reference range);
- Item 16: Stability research data;
- Item 17: Clinical trials data
- Item 18: Production and self-test records;
- Item 19: Sample of packaging and labeling;
- Item 20: Quality management system evaluation report.

G. Requirements for application dossier:

A) General requirements for the dossier:

1. The dossier shall be bound into books.
2. The first page of the dossier is a list of application documents, which shall be arranged in order as per "General requirements". Each document shall be separated by labeled slip sheets and marked with data item number.
3. The dossier shall be in one full copy (product standards and product package inserts shall be in duplicate).
4. All documents in the dossier compiled by the applicant or agent shall be printed in A4 size paper, the contents shall be complete, clear, without alteration. Documents issued by the Government and other agencies shall be provided at the original size, where the bound volumes shall not be split without authorization.
5. The copies of dossier shall be clear and consistent with the originals.
6. The contents of application document (application form, approvals for marketing, product standards, testing reports, and Package inserts) shall be consistent. The trade name and English name, if any, shall be marked.
7. The application documents shall be in Chinese, and translated documents shall be accompanied with the originals.
8. Product name shall meet the nomenclature rules stipulated by the "Provisions for Registration of IVD (Interim)".
9. The electronic versions of the following registration document shall also be submitted:

    1. Application form
    2. Abstracts of the literature review, wherein: the intended use of the product (500words or less), product description (200 words or less), biological safety explanations (100 words or less), summarizes and evaluation of the main findings (200 words or less) and others (200 words or less);
    3. Intended product standards and its preparation explanations;
    4. Package inserts

The above electronic documents, except for the application forms, shall be WORD document without exception, which can be edited and modified.

B) Specific requirements for application documents:

1. Overseas IVD registration application form;

    1. The "electronic application software 2010 for medical devices (IVD) registration" can be downloaded from www.cfda.gov.cn;

   2. All entries of the form shall be filled in accordance with the requirements described in the instructions;
   3. The "applicant" item shall be filled in English;
   4. For remission or exemption of clinical trials for rare disease, special diseases and other conditions, the applicant shall submit such an application along with the registration application documents, stating the reasons therein and provide relevant documentation.

2. Certification of overseas manufacturers;

   1. Qualifications for legal production of medical devices: if the documents have product category description, the category shall cover the applied product;
   2. The name of the manufacturer shall be consistent with that in the application form;
   3. Copies shall be signed and sealed by the original certificate issuers or notarized by the local notary organizations;
   4. All the above certification shall be within the validity period.

3. Overseas governmental authorities' approval documents for marketing of the product in the country (region) refer to the documents issued by the government authorities of the country (region) of the applicant

   1. If the marketing-approval documents are copies, they shall be sealed by the original authorities who issue the documents, or notarized (completely) by corresponding notary organizations.
   2. For overseas products not subject to medical device market approvals, the applicant shall provide:

      i. Documents proving that the products are not managed as medical devices in registration;
      ii. Documents proving that the products are legally marketed in the country of origin.

   3. Certifying Documents (if any) for approvals of change issued by the country (region) of origin.
   4. All the above certification shall be within the validity period (if any).
   5. The name of the product and packaging specifications (if any) in the Documents shall be consistent with the applied product.
   6. The name of the manufacturer shall be consistent with that in the application form;
   7. If the manufacturer name is inconsistent with the name of the applicant in the registration application form, such as in mergers, acquisitions, and other cases, the applicant must provide the corresponding certifying documents.

4. Certifying documents of overseas manufacturer's compliance of "GMP" in countries or regions of origin, or other QMS certification documents;

   1. Copies shall be signed and sealed by the original certificate issuers or notarized by the local notary organizations;

   2. All the above certification shall be within the validity period (if any).
   3. QMS documentation shall include the applied product;
   4. The name of the manufacturer shall be consistent with that in the application form;
   5. If the manufacturer name is inconsistent with the name of the applicant in the registration application form, such as in mergers, acquisitions, and other cases, the applicant must provide the corresponding certifying documents.

5. Copies of designated agent's letter of entrustment/commitment, business license or institutional registration certificate (photocopy);

   1. Designated agent's certificate of entrustment;
   2. Certificate of the applicant's registered office in China or copy of the business license of its domestic agency (photocopy);
   3. Agent's certificate of entrustment.

6. Copies of letter of entrustment/commitment of designated registration agent, business license or institutional registration certificate (photocopy);

   1. Copies of letter of entrustment;
   2. Certificate of the applicant's registered office in China or copy of the business license of its domestic agency (photocopy);
   3. Registration agency's letter of commitment.

7. A statement of authenticity of the documents submitted;

   1. The Statement shall the list of all application documents;
   2. Original statement shall be issued by the applicant;
   3. Chinese statement shall be issued by an agent;
   4. The Statement shall express commitment of legal responsibility.

8. Package insert

   1. Product's original package inserts and complete translation;
   2. The format of the package inserts used in China shall be in line with the "Guidelines for Compiling IVD Package Inserts";
   3. If the original packages have no inserts in original language, the applicant shall provide explanatory documents and compile Chinese package inserts for products used in China in accordance with the "Guidelines for Compiling IVD Package Inserts";
   4. The package inserts for products used in China shall be in duplicate, and attached with a statement of consistency of the two.

9. Intended product standards and its preparation explanations;

   1. The intended product standards and preparation explanations shall include both English and Chinese version, the Chinese version shall be in duplicate, and attached with a statement of consistency of the two;
   2. The Chinese version of the intended product standards shall be in line with the requirements of GB/T1.1;

3. The English version of the intended product standards shall be signed by the applicant, the Chinese version shall be signed by the applicant or its agent;
4. If the product adopts national standards and industry standards as applicable standards, the applicant shall submit:

   i. A statement of the applied product's compliance with national standards and industry standards;
   ii. A statement of commitment for post-marketed product quality;
   iii. And explanations of the classification of product packaging specifications.

10. Registration testing report;

    1. Originals of registration testing reports issued by competent testing institutions accredited by the CFDA;
    2. The packaging specifications of the testing product shall be within the range of the registration application;
    3. The testing type shall be import registration testing;
    4. For Class III products, registration testing of three consecutive production sample batches shall be conducted.

11. Clinical trial data

    1. Overseas clinical trial data.
    2. Specific requirements for domestic clinical trial data:

       i. Class III products: the applicant shall carry out clinical trials in no less than three (including three) provincial health care institutions.
       ii. Class II products: the applicant shall carry out clinical trials in no less than two (including two) provincial health care institutions.
       iii. For special-purpose products, the applicant can conduct clinical trials in qualified municipal-level and above centers for disease control, specialized hospitals or inspection and quarantine institutions, detoxification center and other institutions.
       iv. Clinical trial agreement: signed by clinical trial institutions and the agent or the applicant.
       v. Clinical trial protocol: signed and sealed by the primary leaders (signature), clinical trial organizations (seal), person and institution in charge of statistics, the applicant, and the ethics committee (leading unit).
          If the clinical trials aren't subject to the consent of the Ethics Committee, the leading unit shall still provide a description of the ethical issues with signature.
       vi. Clinical trial reports issued by the institutions, the cover of which shall include:
          Product name used in the clinical trial;
          Clinical trials start and finish dates;
       vii. Signatures of all main person responsible for the clinical trials, the signature of clinical trials institution, the signature and seal of Statistics head and the stamp of the applicant;

viii. The contact and contact information of the product registration applicant, the reporting date, the locations for archiving of original data.
ix. Summary report of the results of all clinical trials:
The reports shall be completed by the leading unit or the applicant;
The contents of the cover shall be the same as those of the clinical trial reports of various clinical trial institutions.
x. Detailed information of clinical trials, including the results of all clinical trials, other testing methods or other basic information of diagnostic reagent products, such as testing methods, sources of diagnostic reagent products, package inserts and registration approvals and so on.
The batch numbers of clinical trial samples must match with those used by the applicant for intended product standards testing, and the preclinical testing reports can be either the applicant's self-test report, or testing report issued by other competent testing institutions entrusted by the applicant.
xi. For calibration products, quality control products, and reference solution etc., clinical trial data need not to be provided.
xii. The "seals" of clinical trial institutions mentioned in this section refers to the official seals of clinical trial institutions and/or competent departments responsible for the trials in clinical trial institutions.

12. Production and self-test records;

Provide copies of three consecutive batches production and self-test records.

13. Quality management system evaluation report (if any).

Overseas QMS assessment report shall be completed within valid registration period and issued by the CFDA. For Class I products, the manufacturer's QMS self-test report shall be provided if necessary.

14. Dossier Items 8, 12, 13, 14, 15, 16 and 18 shall be completed overseas by the applicant.
15. Application dossier shall be original, unless otherwise noted, and signed by the applicant; the Chinese version shall be signed and sealed by the agent. "signature and seal" of the dossier in original language: signature of the applicant's legal representative, responsible person, or signature plus stamp of the organization, notarized document issued by notary institution in jurisdiction of the applicant; "signature and seal" of the dossier in Chinese: Agents' organization seals, or seals of their legal representative, responsible person and organizations.

H. Application Process Diagram
For the IVD market approval, the overall processes include five essential steps as indicated in the following flowchart, see Fig. 10.5. From this figure, you may see the processes are the same to the domestic IVD reagent applications.

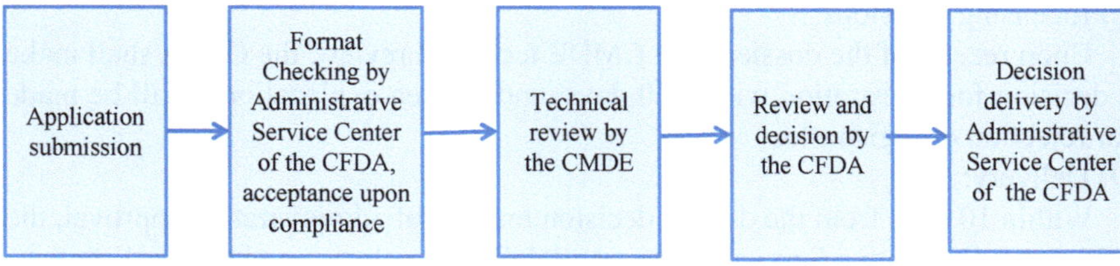

Fig. 10.5 Application process flowchart

I. Approval Procedures

A) Acceptance:

After the application is filed to the Administrative Acceptance Service Center, and the application dossier submitted is in accordance with the list in VI of this Notice, the format examination shall be conducted by the work staff of the Center in accordance with the "Notice on the issuance of the formats and requirements for IVD registration application dossier" (SFDA 2007c). The potential scenarios may include:

- Where the application item is not subject to administrative approval according to law, a decision of non-acceptance shall be notified to the applicant immediately.
- Where the application item is not within the functions of the administrative authority, a decision of non-acceptance shall be made immediately, and the applicant shall be informed to launch the application to relevant administrative authority.
- Where in the application dossier, there are errors that can be corrected on the site, the applicant shall be allowed to make the corrections on the spot.
- Where the application dossier is incomplete or does not meet the statutory format, the applicant shall be informed of all the supplements and amendments to be made once and for all on the spot or within 5 days.
- If the applicant is not informed within the above-mentioned period, the application shall be deemed as accepted from date of receipt of application materials.
- Where the application dossier is within the functions of the administrative authority, the application materials are complete and comply with the statutory format, or
- Where the applicant has submitted all supplements and amendments in accordance with the requirements of the administrative authority, the application for administrative approval shall be accepted.

B) Review:

Once the application is accepted, Administrative Service Center shall deliver the application dossier to the Center for Medical Device Evaluation (CMDE) for technical review, which includes product testing and expert review, and not exceed 60 days. In case any rectification is required after the expert review, the rectification time shall not be included in the time frame for licensing.

C) Licensing decisions:

Upon receipt of the dossier after CMDE technical review, the CFDA shall make a decision for registration within 30 days, and written explanations shall be made for rejection of registration.

D) Delivery:

Within 10 days from the date of decision making of administrative approval, the CFDA Administrative Service Center shall deliver the decision to the applicants.

J. Commitment Time Frame

The administrative licensing decision shall be made within 90 days from the date of acceptance.

K. Authority of Implementation

Implemented by the CFDA

Accepted at the CFDA Administrative Service Center

L. Changes

For alterations of registration and licensing items after the approval of IVD registration, the applicants shall apply for alterations to relevant drug administration departments. For alterations of registration items, the applicant shall apply for the changes within 30 days from the date of the changes. For alterations of licensing items, the applicant shall apply for the changes and implement them after approval.

If alterations of licensing items occur within six months before the expiry of the registration certificate, application for change can be made along with renewal of registration. If marketed products changed the basic reaction principle or analytical sensitivity index with a new clinical diagnostic significance, they shall be handled in accordance with the initial application for registration.

M. License Validity and Renewal

Medical device registration certificate is valid for 4 years. The applicant shall apply for the renewal of registration to relevant drug administration departments within six months before the expiry of the registration certificate. If the production and sales of a product are still necessary after renewal of registration before the expiry of the registration certificate, the applicant shall apply in accordance with the procedures and requirements for initial registration.

N. Annual Inspection or Annual Review of the License None

O. Institutions for Inquiries and Complaints

Inquiries: the CFDA

Complaints: the CFDA Bureau of Investigation and Enforcement, Department of Legal Affairs

Note: The time frame of this Notice counts on working days, excluding legal holidays

10.4 Measures for the Administration of in Vitro Diagnostic Reagents (Interim)

No.229; Issued by the State Food and Drug Administration on April 19, 2007 (SFDA 2007)

Chapter 1 General Provisions

Article 1 The Measures for the Administration of In vitro Diagnostic (IVD) Reagents (Interim) is formulated in accordance with the Regulations on the Supervision and Administration of Medical Devices and the Measures for the Administration of Medical Device Registration, with a view to regulating the administration of IVD reagents.

Article 2 The Measures applies to the research and development, clinical trials, registration inspection, product registration and supervision and administration of IVD reagents.

Article 3 The IVD reagents mentioned in these Measures refer to the IVD reagents administered as medical devices, including the reagents, reagent cartridges, calibrators, quality controls, etc. for in vitro inspection of human body specimen (various body fluids, cells, tissue specimen, etc.) in the course of disease prevention, diagnosis, treatment monitoring, prognosis observation, health status evaluation and inherited disease prediction, which can be used independently or in combination with instruments, devices, equipment or systems.

The IVD reagents legitimately stipulated by the state for use in blood screening and radionuclide-labeled IVD reagents do not belong to the administration scope of the Measures.

Article 4 Registration of IVD reagents refers to the approving process in which the authorities of drug supervision and administrations implement a systematic evaluation on the research conducted by the registration applicant as regards the safety, effectiveness and quality controllability of the products to be put on market and its results, and determine whether to approve such application, in accordance with legal procedures and the application of the registration applicant.

Article 5 The State implements classified registration administration of IVD reagents.

Class I IVD reagents made within territory shall be examined by drug supervision and administration authorities having districts established therein where such authorities reside, and medical device registration certificates shall be issued after approval.

Class II IVD reagents made within territory shall be examined by authorities of drug supervision and administrations in provinces, autonomous regions and municipalities directly under the central government, and medical device registration certificates shall be issued after approval.

Class III IVD reagents made within territory shall be examined by the State Food and Drug Administration, and medical device registration certificates shall be issued after approval.

IVD reagents made abroad shall be examined by the State Food and Drug Administration, and medical device registration certificates shall be issued after approval.

The registration of IVD reagents manufactured in Taiwan, Hong Kong or Macao shall be carried out with reference to the relevant provisions in connection with foreign medical devices.

Article 6 The authorities of drug supervision and administrations in provinces, autonomous regions and municipalities directly under the central government are responsible for verification of the RESEARCH AND DEVELOPMENT status and production conditions of the applied products in their own administrative areas, assessment of the quality management system of the manufacturing enterprise, and implementation of supervision and administration for the products put on the market.

Article 7 The applicant for the registration of IVD reagents (hereinafter referred to as the "applicant") refers to any manufacturing enterprise that puts forward the application for the registration of IVD reagents, assumes corresponding legal responsibilities, and holds the registration certificate after such application is approved.

Domestic applicants refer to manufacturing enterprises legitimately registered within Chinese territory.

Foreign applicants refer to manufacturing enterprises legitimately registered outside Chinese territory.

Foreign applicants shall carry out the registration of IVD reagents through their offices located within Chinese territory or by entrusting agencies within Chinese territory.

Personnel who handle the issues concerning the application for the registration of IVD reagents shall have corresponding professional knowledge, and are familiar with the laws, regulations, rules and technical requirements as regards the registration administration of IVD reagents.

Article 8 Foreign applicants shall entrust legitimate organizations within Chinese territory as their agencies, and if the foreign applicants have set up offices within Chinese territory, their agents shall be such offices; if the foreign applicants have no office within Chinese territory, they shall entrust other independent legal entities as their agents. The agents shall perform the following duties:

(I) Liaison with competent authorities and foreign applicants for application;
(II) Faithful and accurate conveying of relevant regulations and technical requirements to the applicant;
(III) Gathering of information about unfavorable incidents related to medical devices after being put on the market and feedback to foreign applicants, and in the meantime reporting to China's corresponding medical device supervision and administration departments.

Article 9 In case the applicant entrusts a registration agency to handle issues concerning the registration of IVD reagents, except for the application for changing the agent or registration agency, other issues of application shall be concretely handled by such registration agency.

Article 10 The quality management system of the manufacturing enterprise of IVD reagents shall comply with the requirements of Detailed Rules for the Implementation of the Production of IVD Reagents, and foreign manufacturing enterprise shall also conform to the requirements of quality management system in the country or region of production.

Article 11 The manufacturing enterprise of IVD reagents shall have after-sale service ability in technical training, consultancy, etc. that matches its products applying for registration.

Foreign manufacturing enterprises can carry out after-sale service in technical training, consultancy, etc. through their offices that reside within Chinese territory or by entrusting agencies within Chinese territory.

Chapter 2 Product Classification and Naming Principles

Article 12 According to the product risk degree, IVD reagents are successively classified into Class III, Class II and Class I products.

(I) Class III products:

1. Reagents related to the inspection of antigen, antibody and nucleic acid, etc. for pathogen;
2. Reagents related to blood group and tissue typing;
3. Reagents related to the inspection of human gene;
4. Reagents related to inherited diseases;
5. Reagents related to the inspection of narcotic drugs, psychotropic drugs and toxic drugs for medical use;
6. Reagents related to the inspection of targets sites of curative drugs;
7. Reagents related to the inspection of tumor markers;
8. Reagents related to allergy (allergen).

(II) Class II products: products not clearly defined as Class III and Class I products are Class II products, mainly including:

1. Reagents used for protein inspection;
2. Reagents used for carbohydrate inspection;
3. Reagents used for hormone inspection;
4. Reagents used for enzymes inspection;
5. Reagents used for esters inspection;
6. Reagents used for vitamin inspection;
7. Reagents used for inorganic ion inspection;
8. Reagents used for the inspection of drugs and drug metabolites;
9. Reagents used for auto-antibody inspection;

10. Reagents used for microorganism identification and medicine sensitivity experiments;
11. Reagents used for the inspection of indexes for other physiological, biochemical and immune functions.

(III) Class I products:

1. Microorganism culture medium (not used for microorganism identification and medicine sensitivity experiments);
2. Products for specimen treatment, e.g. hemolytic agents, diluents, staining solutions, etc.

Article 13 If the inspection of some Class II products, e.g. protein, carbohydrate, hormone, enzymes, etc. is used for the monitoring of tumor diagnosis, auxiliary diagnosis and treatment process, or used for diagnosis and auxiliary diagnosis, etc. of inherited diseases, these products are registered and administered as Class III products. Among the reagents for inspection drugs and drug metabolites, if the drugs belong to the scope of narcotic drugs, psychotropic drugs and toxic drugs for medical use, they are registered and administered as Class III products.

Article 14 For IVD reagents such as calibrators and quality controls, if not sold independently, the registration needn't be applied for independently; if sold independently, the registration needs to be applied for independently, and their class is the same as those IVD reagents in clinical use in the meantime. As for multiple calibrators and quality controls, their class is the same as higher-class IVD reagents used in the meantime.

Article 15 For products only used for research, not used for clinical diagnosis, the registration needn't be applied for, but their instruction manuals and package labels must indicate the words "For research only, not for clinical diagnosis".

For special substances that do not have diagnosis functions without any modification, and can become compositions of IVD reagents only after marking or optimization, the registration needn't be applied for. When put on the market for sales, such substances shall be furnished with information about their origins, compositions, titers or active units, etc. and indicated with the words "For research only, not for clinical diagnosis" in the meantime.

Article 16 The State Food and Drug Administration is responsible for defining the classification of IVD reagents, and making adjustment according to such circumstances as product risk.

As for IVD reagents that cannot be defined according to the above classification principles, the registration applicant shall put forward the application for classification definition with the State Food and Drug Administration. The application for classification definition shall be submitted together with the general summary materials, product instructions, and information about the classification of similar products in domestic and foreign registration and administration.

Article 17 IVD reagents applying for registration shall adopt general names in compliance with the naming principles.

Naming principles for IVD reagents: product names of IVD reagents are generally composed of three parts:

First part: name of the substance tested.

Second part: usage, e.g. diagnosis serum, diagnostic reagent cartridge, quality control, etc.

Third part: method or principle, e.g. enzyme linked immunity method, colloidal gold method, etc., this part shall be listed in parentheses.

If the substance for inspection have too many components or under special circumstances, the substance can adopt the indication name related to the product or other substitute names.

Chapter 3 Product Research and Development

Article 18 Organizations engaged in the research and development of IVD reagents shall have the personnel, site, equipment, instruments and management system that match the project of experiments and research, use laboratory animals, reagents and raw materials, etc. that comply with relevant requirements and provisions, and guarantee the authenticity of all the experimental data and materials.

Article 19 The product research and development work done for applying for the registration of IVD reagents shall include: selection and preparation of main raw materials; determination of the product manufacturing process; formulation of registered product standards; product stability research, reference value (reference scope) determination, product performance evaluation, etc. The applicant can either carry out product research and development by referring to relevant technical guidance principles, or adopt different experimental methods or technical means, but shall explain their reasonableness.

Article 20 Product performance evaluation refers to the evaluation on the analytical performance and clinical performance of the IVD reagents.

Analytical performance mainly includes analytical sensitiveness, analytical specificity, diagnostic scope, diagnostic accuracy, within-run imprecision, between-run imprecision, etc.

Analytical performance mainly includes clinical sensitiveness, clinical specificity, etc.

Article 21 The registration applicant can either independently accomplish or entrust relevant research organizations to accomplish the research and development of IVD reagents, and the evaluation of analytical performance. The registration applicant shall provide application materials indicating the name list of entrusted items, attached with agreement of both parties, and guarantee the authenticity of all the experimental data and materials.

Article 22 The clinical performance evaluation of IVD reagents shall be accomplished through clinical experiments. The clinical experiments of IVD reagents shall be accomplished by the applicant before putting forward the application. The relevant provisions in Chap. 4 of the Measures apply to the requirements on clinical experiments.

Article 23 The State Food and Drug Administration and authorities of drug supervision and administrations in provinces, autonomous regions and municipalities directly under the central department carry out verification on the product research and development situation in their administrative areas when necessary, require the applicants or research organizations undertaking the experiments to conduct experiments repeatedly according to the material items, methods and data for the application, and assign personnel to verify the experiment process on the site, or entrust relevant research organizations to conduct the experiments repeatedly.

Chapter 4 Clinical Experiment

Article 24 The clinical experiments of IVD reagents (clinical validation including comparative research with the products already put on the market) refers to the systematic research on the clinical performance of IVD reagents in corresponding clinical environment.

Article 25 The specimens for clinical experiments shall be prepared at the workshops that conform to the requirements of the Detailed Rules for the Implementation of the Production of IVD Reagents, and the production process shall be in strict compliance with the requirements of the Detailed Rules for the Implementation of the Production of IVD Reagents.

Article 26 The applicant can either independently conduct the inspection of specimens for clinical experiments according to the product standards formulated, or entrust other competent inspection organizations to conduct the inspection, and only after qualifying for the inspection can the specimens be used for clinical experiments.

Article 27 When the same registration application includes different packaging specifications, the specimens of one packaging specification can be adopted to conduct the clinical experiments.

Article 28 The applicants for Class III products shall choose no less than 3 (including 3) provincial-level health and medical institutions, and the applicants for Class II products shall choose no less than 2 (including 2) provincial-level health and medical institutions to carry out the clinical experiments.

For special-purpose products, the clinical experiments can be conducted at such organizations as disease control centers, specialized hospitals or inspection and quarantine institutes and detoxification centers above the municipal level that meet the requirements.

Article 29 The organizations of clinical experiments shall have the personnel, site, equipment, instruments and management system that match the research project, and guarantee the authenticity of all the research data and materials.

The organizations and personnel participating in the clinical experiments shall understand the responsibilities and obligations of the personnel of clinical experiments, and make records of clinical experiments in a timely manner, accurately and faithfully.

Article 30 The applicant shall sign a clinical experiment agreement with the clinical experiment organization, formulate and perfect the clinical experiment scheme by referring to relevant technical guidance principles, provide specimens for clinical experiments free of charge, and pay the expenses for clinical experiments.

Article 31 The number of cases for clinical experiments shall be determined according to the purpose of clinical experiments, statistical requirements, and by referring to relevant technical guidance principles. Technical guidance principles for clinical experiments are issued separately.

For rare diseases, special diseases and other circumstances, if the applicant requests to decrease the number of cases for clinical experiments or not to perform clinical experiments, the applicant shall submit the materials for registration application together with the application for decreasing the number of cases for clinical experiments or exempting the clinical experiments, and explain the reasons in a detailed way. The technical review organization of authorities of drug supervision and administration shall make the decision after all-round technical review of the materials for registration application, and if clinical experiment needs to be supplemented, shall inform the applicant in the form of supplementary materials.

Article 32 When applying for foreign product registration, foreign clinical experiment materials are required. The applicant shall consider at the same time many factors such as the epidemiological background, characteristics of pathogenic microorganisms in different countries or regions, and normal reference values (or reference scope) applicable to crowds of different species, and carry out corresponding clinical experiments within Chinese territory in accordance with the requirements of clinical experiments.

Article 33 After accomplishing the clinical experiments, the organizations of clinical experiments shall respectively issue the reports of clinical experiments. The applicant or the unit leading the clinical experiments shall summarize the results of clinical experiments and complete the summary report of clinical experiments in accordance with relevant technical guidance principles.

Article 34 If the organization of clinical experiments is found to have breached relevant provisions or fail to execute the scheme of clinical experiments, the applicant shall urge the organization to correct; if the circumstances are serious, the applicant can require the organization to suspend or terminate the clinical experiments, and report to the provincial-level authorities of drug supervision and administration in the locality and the State Food and Drug Administration.

Article 35 If the applicant breaches relevant provisions or requests to change the data, conclusions of the experiments, the organizations and personnel participating in the clinical experiments shall report to the provincial-level authorities of drug supervision and administration in the locality and the State Food and Drug Administration.

Article 36 The State Food and Drug Administration and authorities of drug supervision and administrations in provinces, autonomous regions and municipalities directly under the central government need to carry out supervision and inspection on the implementation status of the clinical experiments.

Chapter 5 Assessment on Quality Management System of Manufacturing enterprise

Article 37 The manufacturing enterprise of IVD reagents shall establish corresponding quality management system, form files and records, implement them and maintain effective operation.

Article 38 The assessment on quality management system of manufacturing enterprise refers to the process of all-round assessment conducted by the authorities of drug supervision and administration on the circumstances of establishment and fundamental operation of the quality management system of the manufacturing enterprise.

Article 39 Before applying for the registration of Class II and Class III products and re-registration, the applicant shall pass the assessment on quality management system by the authorities of drug supervision and administration. For the first registration application, the assessment on quality management system also includes onsite verification of the research and development situation of the products applying for the registration. In case of applying for the registration of Class I products, the applicant shall independently organize the verification of the quality management system.

Article 40 The concrete requirements for the assessment on the quality management system of the manufacturing enterprise shall be separately stipulated by the State Food and Drug Administration.

Chapter 6 Product Standards and Registration Inspection

Article 41 The product standards for IVD reagents refer to technical requirements on standard substances, quality indexes and production process, etc., stipulated for ensuring the product quality of IVD reagents, including national standards, industrial standards and registered product standards.

The standard substances of IVD reagents refer to the substances for the inspection of IVD reagents, which have determined characteristic quantity values and are used for evaluating diagnostic methods, including standards and references.

Article 42 The applicant shall formulate the standards for the applicant products under the precondition of stable quality of raw materials and stable production process, in accordance with the results of product research and development, clinical experiments, etc., and by referring to relevant documents, national standards and industrial standards, etc. The product standards formulated by the applicant shall not be lower than national standards or industrial standards.

Article 43 The product standards formulated by the applicant will become registered product standards after being approved by the authorities of drug supervision and administration and being registered, and the manufacturing enterprises must execute such registered product standards.

Article 44 The registration inspection refers the process in which the medical device inspection organization (hereinafter referred to as "inspection organization"), recognized by the State Food and Drug Administration and having corresponding inspection scope, puts forward suggestions on the science and reasonableness of the standards or references adopted for the product standards submitted by the applicant, in terms of the items and indexes, in accordance with relevant research data, standards of domestic and foreign similar products and relevant national requirements, and carry out the inspection of specimens submitted for inspection, and issue test reports.

Article 45 As for the application for the first registration of IVD reagents, registration inspection is generally not required for Class I products; registration inspection shall be carried out for Class II and Class III products; registration inspection with specimens of 3 consecutive production batches shall be carried out for Class III products.

The specimens for registration inspection of domestic manufacturing enterprises are drawn out on site after being qualified for the assessment on the quality management system of the manufacturing enterprise by the authorities of drug supervision and administration. The specimens for registration inspection of domestic manufacturing enterprises are drawn out by the applicant independently.

Article 46 When carrying out the registration inspection, the applicant shall submit written application to the inspection organization, and provide the necessary relevant technical materials, specimens and standards or references.

When the same registration application involves different packaging specifications, the registration inspection can be carried out for products of one packaging specification only.

Article 47 The medical device inspection organizations shall carry out the work of registration inspection within the authorized inspection scope, and shall issue test report within specified working time period.

For products not listed in the authorized inspection scope of the inspection organization, the State Food and Drug Administration shall designate the inspection organization with the ability to undertake the inspection to carry out the inspection.

Chapter 7 Registration Application and Approval

Article 48 The registration application mentioned in this chapter refers to the registration application put forward by the applicant for its manufactured IVD reagents not put on the market within Chinese territory, i.e. the first registration application.

Article 49 According to the classification principles of IVD reagents, in case the domestic applicant plans to apply for the registration of Class III and Class II products, the applicant shall put forward the application to the corresponding authorities of drug supervision and administration after accomplishing the product research and development, clinical experiments, registration inspection and passing the assessment on the quality management system, and submit materials for registration application according to the requirements in Appendix I of these Measures.

In case of applying for the registration of Class I products, the applicant shall put forward the application to the corresponding authorities of drug supervision and administration after accomplishing the research and development work, and submit the materials for registration application according to the requirements in Appendix 1 of these Measures.

Article 50 According to the classification principles of IVD reagents, in case the foreign applicant plans to apply for the registration of Class III and Class II products, the applicant can put forward the application for product registration to the State Food and Drug Administration according to these Measures after accomplishing the clinical experiments and registration inspection for the products. In case of applying for the registration of Class I products, the applicant shall put forward the application for product registration to the State Food and Drug Administration according to these Measures.

In case of applying for the registration of overseas products, such products shall be granted overseas medical device marketing approval; for overseas products not required to be granted medical device marketing approval, relevant documents proving that such products are not registered and administered as medical devices and that such products are legally marketed in the country of origin shall be provided.

Article 51 The registration units of IVD reagents shall be single reagents or single reagent cartridges, and one registration unit can include different packaging specifications.

Article 52 The materials for registration application shall be written in Chinese. The application materials translated according to materials in foreign languages shall be provided with original text in the meantime. The materials for registration application shall be complete, standardized, and the data must be authentic and reliable. When the documents not publicly published are cited, the documents proving that the owner of materials allows the usage shall be provided.

The applicant shall take full responsibility for the authenticity of the materials for registration application.

Article 53 The administrative acceptance organization of the authorities of drug supervision and administration shall carry out the form examination for materials for registration application. If the materials meet the acceptance requirements, the organization shall accept the materials and issue the acceptance notice; if the materials fail to meet the requirements, the organization shall not accept the materials, and inform the applicant in writing.

Article 54 The technical review organization of the authorities of drug supervision and administration shall carry out all-round technical review on the materials for registration application, and can recall the original research materials when necessary. In case expert consultancy or hearing is required during the review, the technical review organization shall inform the applicant in writing. The time required for consulting with experts or conducting the hearing is not calculated into the time period of the review.

Article 55 When the technical review organization conducts technical review on the materials for registration application, if the applicant is required to supplement the materials, the technical review organization shall issue the written notice of supplementing materials only one time. The applicant shall submit supplementary materials only one time within 60 working days according to the requirements of the notice of supplementing materials. The time required for the applicant to supplement the materials is not calculated into the time period of review.

Article 56 If the applicant has objection to the content of the notice of supplementing the materials, the applicant can put forward the written suggestions to corresponding technical review organization, explain the reasons and provide corresponding materials of technical support.

Article 57 For the products examined as conforming to provisions and approved for registration, the corresponding authorities of drug supervision and administration shall issue the Medical Device Registration Certificate within specified time period. The registered product standards and product instructions shall be approved by corresponding authorities of drug supervision and administration according to the application materials of the applicant, and sent to the applicant in the form of appendix.

The Medical Device Registration Certificate remains effective for 4 years.

Article 58 If the products are deemed as not conforming to the provisions after examination, the authorities of drug supervision and administration shall make the decision not to register and explain the reasons, notify the applicant in writing within stipulated time period, and in the meantime inform the applicant that the applicant enjoys the right of reexamination and applying for administrative reconsideration or lodging administrative litigation.

Article 59 According to the provisions of Article 23 in these Measures, if repeated experiment is required but the applicant refuses, and the authorities of drug supervision and administration orders the applicant to correct but the applicant refuses to correct, the registration application for this product will not be accepted any longer; for products already accepted, the authorities of drug supervision and administration will make the decision not to register.

Article 60 The authorities of drug supervision and administration shall publicize the approving process and results, and shall declare to the society and conduct the hearing as regards important issues of permission involving public interests.

Article 61 After IVD reagents are put on the market, their product standards and instructions must be consistent with the contents approved by the authorities of drug supervision and administration.

The applicant shall trace the safety and effectiveness of the products put on the market, and shall put forward timely application for modifying the product standards or instructions when necessary. The applicant shall take full responsibility for the correctness and accuracy of the product standards and instructions.

Chapter 8 Change Application and Approval

Article 62 After the registration application of IVD reagents is approved, in case of change of the issues concerning registration and permission; the applicant shall put forward the change application to corresponding authorities of drug supervision and administration according to the provisions in Article 5 of these Measures. In case of change of registration issues, the applicant shall put forward the change application within 30 days since the change takes place; in case of change of permission issues, the applicant shall put forward the change application and implement the change after the change application is approved. When handling the issues concerning change applications, the applicant shall submit the application materials according to corresponding requirements in Article 2 of these Measures.

Article 63 The change of registration issues includes the following circumstances:
(I) Change of the name of manufacturing enterprise;
(II) Change of the registered address of manufacturing enterprise;
(III) Change of registration agency;
(IV) Change of agent.

Article 64 The change of permission issues includes the following circumstances:
(I) Change of main materials such as antigen and antibody in the course of production;
(II) Change of inspection conditions and reference values (or reference scope), etc.;
(III) Change of the items, indexes, experimental methods, etc. set in the registered product standards;
(IV) Change of the contents in product instructions, e.g. change or addition of packaging specifications, addition of applicable models, etc.;
(V) Change of product storage conditions and/or product warranty period;
(VI) Increase of the clinical application scope, e.g. increase of clinical indications, increase of the types of specimens for clinical diagnosis, etc.;
(VII) Change of production address (material change of production site);
(VIII) Other changes that could influence the safety and effectiveness of products.

Article 65 In case of applying for the change of production address (material change of production site), the applicant shall apply for assessment on the quality management system of the new production site. When the quality management system meets the requirements after assessment, the applicant shall submit the application materials according to corresponding requirements in Article 2 of these Measures.

Article 66 The following circumstances do not belong to the issues of change application as stipulated in this chapter, and shall be handled as the first registration application:

(I) Change of basic reaction principles of the products already put on the market;
(II) Change of analytical sensitiveness of the products already put on the market, which also has new significance of clinical diagnosis.

Article 67 If the change of permission issues takes place within 6 months before the registration certificate expires; the applicant can put forward the application together with the re-registration.

Article 68 The authorities of drug supervision and administration shall carry out the examination of the issues of change application, and approve the change application in the form of Approval of Change Application for IVD Reagents. The effective period of the Approval of Change Application for IVD Reagents is the same as the original registration certificate, and the applicant shall apply for re-registration when the effective period expires.

Article 69 The relevant provisions in Chap. 7 of these Measures apply to the accepting and approving procedures for the change application.

Chapter 9 Application and Approval of Re-registration

Article 70 The re-registration of IVD reagents refers to the approving process implemented for continuing the production and sales of the products after the product registration certificate expires.

Article 71 The applicant shall put forward the re-registration application to the corresponding authorities of drug supervision and administration according to the provisions in Article 5 of these Measures within 6 months before the product registration certificate expires, and submit the application materials according to corresponding requirements in Appendix 3 of these Measures.

In case the applicant puts forward the re-registration application and issues of change application at the same time, the applicant shall make explanation and submit the application materials according to the provisions concerning re-registration application and change application.

Article 72 For the product re-registration, if the product has no change whatsoever compared to the approved contents of the original registration, the registration inspection is generally not required.

Article 73 If the applicant fails to put forward the re-registration application before the registration certificate expires but needs to continue the production and sales of the products, the product registration shall be handled according to the procedures and requirements for the first registration application.

Article 74 The re-registration will not be accepted under any one of the following circumstances:

(I) Failure to comply with the requirements put forward by the authorities of drug supervision and administration when approving the marketing of the products;
(II) Failure to fulfill the responsibilities for product quality, failure to report serious adverse events, or failure to effectively deal with the serious consequences caused by the products;
(III) The quality management system of manufacturing enterprise fails to comply with the requirements;
(IV) It is deemed that the safety and effectiveness of the products cannot be guaranteed after re-evaluation of the authorities of drug supervision and administration;
(V) Other circumstances not complying with the provisions of the authorities of drug supervision and administration.

Article 75 The relevant provisions in Chap. 7 of these Measures apply to the accepting and approving procedures for the re-registration application.

Chapter 10 Withdrawal, Return and Review of Registration Application

Article 76 For the accepted registration application, the applicant can apply for the withdrawal of the registration application with the corresponding authorities of drug supervision and administration at any stage of the approving procedure. In case the registration application is actively withdrawn, the registration can be applied for again.

Article 77 If the accepted registration application comes under any one of the following circumstances, the authorities of drug supervision and administration shall return the application, explain the reasons in writing and inform that the applicant enjoys the right of review and administrative reconsideration.

(I) The applicant fails to submit the supplementary materials within the specified time period;
(II) The products applying for registration do not belong to the scope stipulated by these Measures;
(III) Other circumstances requiring the return of application.

Article 78 If the applicant has any objection to the decision made by the authorities of drug supervision and administration to return the application or not to approve the registration, the applicant can put forward the review application with the corresponding authorities of drug supervision and administration within 10 working days since the day of receiving the notice that the application is returned or the registration is not approved.

The contents of review application are limited to the original application issues and the original application materials.

Article 79 After receiving the review application, the authorities of drug supervision and administration shall make the review decision within the specified time period, and notify the applicant in writing. If the original decision is maintained, the authorities of drug supervision and administration will not accept the review application put forward again by the applicant.

Article 80 If the applicant has any objection to the decision made by the authorities of drug supervision and administration to return the application or not to approve the registration, and has applied for administrative reconsideration or lodged administrative litigation, the authorities of drug supervision and administration will not accept the review application put forward by the applicant.

Chapter 11 Supervision and Administration

Article 81 Any dispute of patent right, which arises during the examination of the registration application for IVD reagents or after the application is approved, can either be resolved by the parties concerned through friendly consultation, or resolved by departments managing the patent work or people's court in accordance with the provisions of relevant laws and regulations.

Article 82 In case of circumstances stipulated in Article 69 of the Administrative License Law of the People's Republic of China, the authorities of drug supervision and administration can withdraw the approving documents for relevant products according to the request of interested person or according to its duties.

Article 83 After the registration of IVD reagents is approved, if the quality management system of the manufacturing enterprise for IVD reagents is not effectively operating, the provincial-level authorities of drug supervision and administration of the region where the enterprise resides shall order the enterprise to correct or rectify within specified period according to the seriousness degree of the case.

Article 84 If the agent entrusted by the overseas applicant fails to perform corresponding responsibilities, refuses to report serious adverse events of the products, or fails to effectively deal with the serious consequences caused by the products, the authorities of drug supervision and administration shall punish the agent according to relevant laws and regulations, and release the product risk information to the society.

Article 85 Under any one of the following circumstances, the authorities of drug supervision and administration will cancel the documents approving the product registration.

(I) The documents approving the product registration expired but not renewed;
(II) Termination by legal entity or other organizations in accordance with the law;
(III) The documents approving the product registration are cancelled, withdrawn, or revoked according to the law;
(IV) Other circumstances under which the administrative license shall be canceled according to relevant laws and regulations.

Article 86 If the Medical Device Manufacturing enterprise License of the manufacturing enterprise is cancelled, the product registration certificate held by the enterprise will be annulled automatically, and the authorities of drug supervision and administration will cancel its documents approving the product registration, and make public.

Article 87 Any breach of other relevant provisions in these Measures will be punished by the authorities of drug supervision and administration in accordance with the Regulations for the Supervision and Administration of Medical Devices and the Provision on Medical Device Registration.

Chapter 12 Supplementary Provisions A

Article 88 The product registration No. in the registration certificate is arranged as follows:

x(x)1(Food)YJX(x2)xxxx3 No.x4xx5xxxx6. Among them:

x1 is the abbreviation for the location of the authority in charge of registration examination and approval:

The word of"Guo" is the abbreviation for a Class III medical device manufactured domestically or abroad, as well as those from Taiwan, Hong Kong and Macao;

The abbreviations of provinces, autonomous regions or municipalities directly under the central government where authorities in charge of registration examination and approval reside for Class II medical device made within the territory;

And the combination of abbreviations for provinces, autonomous regions, municipalities directly under the central government where authorities responsible for the registration and approval of a Class I medical device and abbreviations for city-level administrative areas having districts established therein where such authorities reside shall be expressed as xx1 (In cases where there is no corresponding city-level administrative areas without districts divided therein, the abbreviation shall only be used for provinces, autonomous regions or municipalities directly under the central government);

x2 is the type of registration (Zhun, Jin and Xu): The word of "Zhun" shall apply to a domestic medical device. The word of "Jin" shall apply to a foreign medical device; The word of "Xu" shall be applicable to medical devices from Taiwan, Hong Kong or Macao;

xxxx3 is the year in which the registration is approved;

x4 is the product class classified for administration convenience;

xx5 is the code for a specific variety of product (that for IVD reagents is: 40);

xxxx6 is the serial number of registration.

Article 89 The time period for examination of IVD reagents by the authorities of drug supervision and administration shall be specified according to the provisions concerning the time period of examination in Provision on Medical Device Registration.

Article 90 The variety scope of the IVD reagents legitimately stipulated by the state for use in blood screening, and the reagents related to the inspection of narcotic drugs, psychotropic drugs and toxic drugs for medical use, both of which are mentioned in these Measures, shall comply with relevant provisions of the state.

Article 91 The right of interpretation of these Measures shall be vested with the State Food and Drug Administration of the People's Republic of China.

Article 92 These Measures shall become effective as of June 1, 2007.

10.5 Guidance for Writing Instructions of in Vitro Diagnostic Reagents

No. 240, issued by the China Food and Drug Administration, on April 28, 2014 (CFDA 2014c)

10.5.1 Overview

Clinical study of IVD reagents (including clinical validation which carries a comparative study with marketed products) refer to the systematic study of the reagents' clinical performance in the appropriate clinical settings.

On the basis of clinical units meeting requirements, meeting the minimum sample size requirements for clinical studies, the applicant should develop a clinical research program, the performance of which proves to be in accordance with the purpose of the product, related disease prevalence, and statistical requirements. The research should also divulge controlling trial errors to the utmost extent, improve the quality of research, and carry out scientific and rational analysis of research results. The clinical study report is a summary of the clinical research process and results, and is an important basis for the evaluation of the product's effectiveness and safety, which is also to be listed. This report is one of the important documents needed for product registration.

The guiding principle only gives general requirements for the clinical studies of IVD reagents. Because IVD reagent products can be developed relatively fast and can meet many clinical purposes, the clinical research methods and contents of various products are not the same all the time. For the registration process, the applicant should develop a reasonable clinical research program based on product characteristics and clinical use purposes. The SFDA will also revise the guidelines in a timely manner, based on the need of development of IVD reagents.

The development of IVD reagent products which are used for blood screening and the radionuclide-labeled products, also refer to this guideline for clinical research.

10.5.2 The Basic Principles of Clinical Research

A. Basic Requirements

1. Ethical considerations: Researchers should consider the subjects' risk suffered from the obtainment of samples, including blood, amniotic fluid, pleural effusion, ascites, tissue fluid, thoracic fluid, tissue biopsy, and bone marrow, etc., or clinical study results. Researchers should submit the ethical review comments and the informed consent of subjects to the ethics committee. As to exceptions: if it is objectively impossible to obtain informed consent from subjects, or if the clinical research has almost no risk for the subjects, researchers do not need to submit the ethics committee review comments and the informed consent of subjects, but should provide instructions on ethics matters.
2. Must comply with the ethical guidelines of Helsinki Declaration. The rights, safety and willingness of research subjects are more important than the need of research.
3. Keep the secrets of research subjects, and respect for individual privacy. Prevent research subjects from being discriminated or harmed due to the test results.
4. The results of pre-clinical studies should fully support the necessity of carrying out clinical research.

B. Requirement of Clinical Research Unit and Personnel

1. Clinical research unit of diagnostic reagents should be legal entities that engaged in human health or disease prevention, diagnosis, treatment and epidemiological investigations, etc. The products under research should be within the scope of their expertise.
2. Clinical research unit must have the appropriate professionals and technical personnel, must have equipment suitable for the research, and must be able to ensure the implementation of the study.
3. In general, the clinical research of diagnostic reagents should be completed in at least two (including two) provincial healthcare units. For products with special clinical purpose, clinical studies can be carried out in the centers for disease control at city level, special hospital, inspection and quarantine institute, or drug treatment centers, etc.
4. The applicant should select its research unit based on product characteristics and clinical use purposes, and a combination of factors that include races of different areas, epidemiological background, and characteristics of pathogenic microorganisms, etc.
5. Before the start of clinical studies, the registered applicant and clinical research staff should carry out pre-trials of clinical research, which can help to carry out training on clinical research staffs, making them familiar with and master the instruments applicable to the product, methods of operation, technical performance, etc., so as to minimize the experimental error.

6. During the whole process of clinical studies, the applicant should consider recruiting professionals of epidemiology, statistics, clinical medicine, laboratory medicine (or knowledge), so as to ensure the research methods are scientifically reasonable.

10.5.3 Design Principles of Clinical Studies

A. Study Methods

1. Clinical studies of new diagnostic reagent products

1.1 For new diagnostic reagent products, select the appropriate subjects for the study and make synchronous blind comparison of the clinical research products with the diagnostic gold standard.

As for the diagnostic reagent products used for the early diagnosis, treatment monitoring, and prognosis, etc.: while conducting comparative studies with the gold standard, you must also keep track of research subjects. Prior to the study, researchers should be clear of the inclusion criteria, follow-up criteria, and follow-up time.

1.2 Determine the gold standard

The gold standard refers to the diagnostic method currently recognized as the most reliable, accurate, and the best method, also known as the standard diagnostic method. The gold standard commonly used in clinical application includes: histopathological examination (biopsy, autopsy), surgery findings, diagnostic imaging (CT, MRI, Color Doppler Ultrasound), isolation and culture of pathogens, and the conclusion of long-term follow-ups. The gold standard is a specific diagnostic method that can correctly distinguish between "sick" and "disease-free" statuses.

1.3 Selection of the subjects of study

The subjects in a study should be divided into two groups: one is the group of patients with a special disease determined by the gold standard and the other is the control group (or normal group) of subjects, defined by those without the disease confirmed by the gold standard. The patient group should include different kinds of cases of the disease, such as typical and atypical symptoms, the stage from early to late, the condition from mild to severe, and patients of different ages, etc., so as to reflect all the characteristics of the disease. The control group should include subjects without the disease identified, and with no symptoms that can be confused with cases of this disease.

1.4 Parallel test

Both the sample group and the control group should undergo a blind parallel test using the new test method and gold standard. Compare the test results determined by the gold standard and the new method, calculate the statistical parameters. Then, evaluate the new product based on these indicators.

During the whole process of trial operation and when judging the test results, blind procedure (using double blind method as much as possible) is the key to ensure true and reliable diagnostic test results.

2. Clinical research of the products when there are similar products already approved for the market

After selecting the marketed products, carry out comparative experimental study of these marketed products and the new product using clinical samples, in order to prove that the new product under clinical research is equivalent to the marketed products.

2.1 Selection of the control products

Under the premise of using the marketed products as control products, these marketed products should be generally considered to have good quality to meet current clinical application. At the same time, the technical information of the selected products should be fully understood, including methodology, purpose and scope of clinical use, key performance indicators, traceability of standards or calibrators, recommended reference values (reference range), etc., in order to can carry out scientific analysis of the test results.

2.2 Principle of the selection of study subjects, refer to section 1.3.

2.3 Inconsistent results obtained in comparative study

When the results from the new product are inconsistent with the results obtained from the gold standard, additional parallel tests should be performed again by using the gold standard or other methods, so as to analyze the results of clinical study.

3. About the application of changing clinical research method

Estimate the impact on the product performance that the changes may bring, use comparison test methods for the product before and after change, proving that the product after change meets the quality level of the product before change.

4. About the clinical research methods of imported products

For imported products, changes due to the target population species and regions may affect some of the major technical indicators and effectiveness of the product. Applicant and/ or clinical investigators should consider the epidemiological background in different countries or regions, the characteristics of pathogenic microorganisms, applicable reference values (or reference range) for different species populations and many other factors, and carry out targeted clinical studies.

B. Sample Size of Clinical Research

The registered applicant (referred to as the applicant) and/ or clinical investigators should determine the clinical research samples size based on the clinical purpose of the product, clinical incidence of diseases associated with the product. Under the premise of complying with the guidelines for the minimum sample requirements, must also meet the statistical requirements.

For rare diseases, special diseases, and special circumstances, the sample size can be reasonably reduced, but the applicant should explain the reason to meet the requirements of assessment.

1. General requirements
   1.1 For the third category products: the minimum number of samples in clinical studies should be at least 1000 cases.
   1.2 For the second category products: the minimum number of samples in clinical studies should be at least 00 cases.
   1.3 For the first category products: under normal circumstances, there is no need to conduct clinical research.
2. Special requirements
   2.1 For the statutory project of blood screening, and the diagnostic reagents intended to use for blood screening: the minimum number of samples in clinical studies should be at least 10,000 cases.
   2.2 For the diagnostic reagents of pathogen detection using in vitro nucleic acid amplification (PCR) method: the minimum number of samples in clinical studies should be at least 500 cases.
   2.3 For the diagnostic reagents related to the detection of narcotic drugs, psychotropic substances, toxic drugs for medical use: the minimum number of samples in clinical studies should be at least 500 cases.
   2.4 For the IVD reagents of radionuclide-labeled: the minimum number of samples in clinical studies should be at least 500 cases.
   2.5 For the new diagnostic reagent products (products whose registration has not been approved in the country, products whose analytes are the same but the analysis sensitivity indicators are out of the registered product scope, and products that have new clinical diagnostic significance), the sample size requirements for clinical research should be the same as the third category products.

10.5.4 The Writing of Clinical Study Report

The clinical study report should clearly and completely explain the overall design and key points of the test, should orderly describe the implementation process of test, and should include the necessary basic data and statistical analysis methods.

The applicant or institutions responsible for clinical research should summarize the reports of all clinical research units, and complete clinical research summary report. The format and content of the clinical study report are as follows.

A. Cover Paper

Cover paper is the first part of each clinical study report. All of the individual clinical study report should include this part.

1. Cover title

Include the common name of clinical research products, research starting time, research completion time, the principal investigator (signature), research units (stamped), principle statistician signature and his unit stamp, product registration applicant (stamped), contact information of registered applicant, the reporting date, the original data storage location.

2. Table of Contents

List the contents directory of the clinical trials report and the corresponding page numbers.

3. Clinical study abstract

Briefly introduce the clinical study.

4. Research staff

List the information of principal investigators in clinical trials, including the name, the organization, research responsibilities in the study and resume (listed in attachment). The list of major investigators should include the leading researchers, the major participants of various units, the principle statistician, the authors (in charge of the writing) of the clinical study report.

5. Abbreviations

List the full names of the abbreviations used in clinical study report.

B. Text Content and Reporting Formats

1. The basic content

1.1 Introduction

Introduce the background related to the clinical study products, including:

1) the source, biological and physicochemical properties of the measured object;
2) intended clinical purpose, the indication of the targeted population, clinical or laboratory methods currently used for this indication;
3) the method used, the principles of the method, technical requirements, etc.;
4) the application status of domestic and foreign marketed products.

Describe the relationship between the applicant and the clinical research unit.

1.2 Purpose of study

Describe the purpose of clinical research.

1.3 Management of the clinical study

Describe the clinical trial management structure. Management structure includes the principal investigator, the main participants, laboratory quality control, statistics/data management, and the problems occurring in the study and treatment measures.

1.4 Trial design

1.4.1 Description of the overall trial design and solutions

Description of the overall trial design and solutions should be clear and concise, using charts and other visual presentation when necessary. Modifications of the program carried out during the test, sources of information outside the program should also be described in details.

1.4.2 Trial design and research methods selection should include the following:

i. Sample size and the most accurate evidences for sample selection.
ii. Sample selection basics, inclusion criteria, and exclusion criteria.
iii. Sample collection, preservation, and transportation methods, etc.
iv. Establishment of gold standard or comparative tests products.
v. The names, specifications, source, batch number, validity and storage conditions of all products used in clinical studies and the registration status of comparative test products.
vi. Quality control methods. Quality control methods should be briefly described.
vii. Statistical analysis methods of clinical research data.
viii. Modifications of the program during the course of the trial.
ix. Under normal circumstances, the clinical trial design should not be changed. Any modification of the study should be recorded. Elaborate the change time, reason, process and the presence of record, and demonstrate its impact on the evaluation of the entire study.

1.5 Clinical findings and analysis
1.6 Discussions and Conclusions

2. A description of the particular circumstances of clinical studies
3. Accessories

3.1 The product manual of all diagnostic reagents used in clinical studies.
3.2 All test data of clinical studies.
3.3 Main references

10.6 Clinical Research of In Vitro Diagnostic Reagents Class II

Since the in vitro diagnostic (IVD) reagents have features such as short development time and broad span of clinical usage, the applicant should use different clinical research methods and content. Before applying for the evaluation of the IVD reagents, the assessment of products' performance and generation of products' standards should be performed. Before the start of clinical evaluation, according to the products' features and usage, the applicant should determine the method of evaluation, formulate reasonable clinical evaluation scheme, reasonably and systematically evaluate clinical performance of the products. This section only presents the general requirements for the selection of the clinical trial units, samples, preparation, and clinical trial data analysis to serve as a guide for clinical research of IVD reagents' consistency trials.

The applicant should establish a reliable and reproducible clinical evaluation scheme, according to the national laws, regulations, standards and technical guidelines in their request to reasonably evaluate the product's safety and effectiveness.

A. Selection of Clinical Trial Unit

Before the start of clinical evaluation, the applicant should select the clinical trial unit according to the features of product. The clinical trial unit should have an appropriate facility and personnel to meet the needs for the trial, the selection of trial unit shall meet the following requirements:

In this section, the trial system refers to the system that perform the clinical testing on the sample using the new method, the control system refers to the system that perform the testing using the control sample and control method.

1. applicant should select at least 2 (including) health institutions of provincial level, for products of special use, applicant can also choose institutions above city level, including centers for disease control, specialized hospitals or inspection, quarantine bureau and detoxification center. Trial labs shall comply with the requirements of the "measures for the management of clinical laboratory of medical institution"; priority should be given to laboratories approved by the CNAS—CL02 "medical laboratory guidelines for recognition (ISO 15189:15189) or GB17025 standards approved laboratories".
2. The trial system used by the laboratories should be complete and effective, detecting system should include the detection system and the control detection system. Reagents, calibration, instruments used by control detection system should be approved and registered; the main performance indexes of analysis (such as accuracy, precision, linear range, reference range, measurement range, etc.) should meet clinical requirements. Trial system and control system should have the same type of detection methods (such as both of enzyme-linked immunosorbent assay, ELISA, or both of chemiluminescence immune response), if they couldn't be compared using the same method, select the control method as close to the trial system as possible.
3. Lab should have thorough intralab quality control program; preferred lab should have "satisfaction" level interlab quality control evaluation for two-consecutive-years.
4. The person in charge of the trial project should have corresponding qualifications (at least intermediate class for project director), and have certain experience with the control system.
5. Lab should have access to all the types of samples for the clinical trial.

B. Selection of Testing Samples

1. Sample requirements should be determined: serum/plasma with clear anticoagulant, storage condition, frozen (or not) and samples to be avoided.

Note: If possible, try to collect fresh samples. If only frozen samples are available, storage condition and the lifetime of the samples should be recorded, which need to be considered in data analysis.

Avoid using samples that have been contaminated or damaged, such as hemolysis, blood lipid, or turbidity should be avoided.

Selection of sample trial system and control system and its requirements should be consistent.

2. The distribution of the samples' number should be taken into account. Samples' number should be chosen according to the requirement of statistics and related guidelines.

For quantitative type products, the scope of the detection system should cover the full range of the sample concentration, should include the level for medical decision-making, and should have uniform distribution. If possible, try to allow 50% of the sample concentration to distribute out of the reference range, but within the measurement range. As to qualitative trial products, positive and negative samples, as well as samples that are close to the critical value range should be included, and the samples' numbers should be evenly distributed.

C. Preparation Before Trial

1. Principle investigator in charge of the trial must be familiar with the evaluation of clinical trials. Also, the principle investigator should be familiar with the features, such as the detection and maintenance of detection system and the control system. Preliminary experiments should be performed.
   The intralab quality control
2. Appropriate quality control procedures should be established for detection system and control system to guarantee the reliability of trial results.

D. Management of Trial Process and Data Analysis

For this section, we'll use a marketed product to evaluate the consistency of the trial system and control system, and to evaluate the sensitivity, specificity and other parameters that should be considered in clinical trials. For quantitative detection, analyzing biased estimation could be used for evaluation; for qualitative detection, consistency of trial result could be used for evaluation.

1. Management of trial process

The trial should be completed on a separate day (5 days, for example). The number of samples to be tested on each day should be specified. The trial time for each day should be determined by stability and trial duration, and the principle to determine the trial time is that the trial time shall not be longer than stable time of the content in the sample under trial. Daily trial must ensure that the same sample in the trial system and control system can be completed in time.

The order of sample testing should be stipulated in the process of detection, control system first, and trial system next; or trial system first, then control system. During the trial, observe the outliers. The number of outliers must not exceed 2.5 % of the samples; namely in 100 samples of clinical trials, there should be no more than three outliers. If there are 3 or more than 3 outliers, the investigator should look for the reason. If it's just a problem of one sample, replace the sample; if no reason can be found and the result affects the "equivalent" analysis, stop experiments and notify the applicant.

2. Data analysis for bias estimation

2.1 Plotting

i. Draw scatter plot of each measured value for trial system and the corresponding control system; Y axis for trial system, X axis for control system.
ii. Draw plot for difference between trial system and control system each time and corresponding control. Draw plot of system average value (center horizontal line is zero).

2.2 Visually select the linear range to calculate the corresponding coefficient

Visually select the data in the linear range, the nonlinear segments can be discarded; if the linear range is too short, then stop the evaluation. To make better correlation analysis, linear segment requires $r > 0.975$, if $r < 0.975$, the sample number should be increased to expand the scope of the data.

2.3 Establish the regression equation and perform analysis

Calculate the value of "a" and "b", list the linear regression equation.

$$Y = a + bX$$

Calculate average bias B and standard division (SD) between trial system and control system.

$$B = \sum \frac{Yi - Xi}{N}$$

$$SD = \sqrt{\frac{\sum_{1}^{N} [(Yi - Xi) - B]^2}{(N - 1)}}$$

B is the average bias estimation of appropriate concentration range; X is the value for control system; Y is the value for trial system; SD is the standard division between two systems. Calculate Xc, B^c and the 95 % level range.

$$\mathrm{B}^\wedge\mathrm{c} = \mathrm{a} + (\mathrm{b} - 1)\mathrm{Xc}$$

$$\mathrm{B}^\wedge\mathrm{c}\ 95\% = \mathrm{B}^\wedge\mathrm{c} \pm 2\mathrm{SD}/\sqrt{N}$$

2.4 Interpretation of the results

Compare the expectation bias with the limit of allowed error (the limit value of allowed error should be less than or equal half of CLIA88 or external quality assessment range). If the expectation bias is less than the limit of the allowed error, then the trial system can be accepted; otherwise, the trial system cannot be accepted.

2.5 Statistical analysis

Perform a paired t test for trial and control systems. If the error turns out to be significant, there is systematic error between the systems, and further analysis will be needed. Redesign of trial scheme is needed if necessary.

3. Consistency of the data analysis for qualitative detection products

Clinical trials should also focus on diagnostic sensitivity, degree of specificity, positive coincidence rate, and negative coincidence rate. The diagnostic gold standard should be used to select the positive and negative sample for the trial. This article only introduces the method to use the marketed (approved) product for control system to evaluate the consistency of the trial system and control system. Most qualitative detection products only give counting statistics as the result. The statistical analysis can be performed using the following table (Table 10.5):

Table 10.5 Summary of paired counts

		Control system		Together
		Positive	Negative	
Trial system	Positive	a	b	a+b
	Negative	c	d	c+d
Together		a+c	b+d	a+b+c+d

Perform Kappa consistency analysis: if the Kappa coefficient is larger than 0.8, the two systems are highly consistent; if 0.4< Kappa coefficient <0.8, the two systems are consistent, and comparison between positive coincidence rate and negative coincidence rate is needed; if Kappa coefficient is less than 0.4, the two systems are not consistent.

Comparison between positive coincidence rate and negative coincidence rate is needed. In general, equations are as follows:

$$\text{Positive coincidence rate} = \frac{a}{a+c} \times 100\%$$

$$\text{Negative coincidence rate} = \frac{d}{b+d} \times 100\%$$

If both coincidence rates meet the clinical requirements, then two methods or products are equivalent. If there is a big gap between the two coincidence rates, redesign of clinical trial scheme is needed.

10.7 In Vitro Diagnostics Reagents Instructions

In vitro diagnostic (IVD) reagents instructions include important information such as the intended use of the product, test methods, interpretation of test results, precautions, etc. They are important technical documents that can guide users to operate the product correctly, and guide clinicians to accurately understand and rationally make use of the test results.

This guidance details the formats and contents of the IVD reagents instructions. It is based on the relevant requirements of "Provisions for Drug Insert Sheets and Labels" and "Provisions for the Instructions, Labels and Package of Medical Devices" issued by the State Food and Drug Administration (CFDA), refers to IVD reagents preparation documents published by EMEA, FDA and 1FCC etc., and has been shaped by work experiences on the registration management of drugs, in order to offer principle-based guidance to the preparation of IVD reagents instructions. It also provides technical references for the review of them by the registration management department.

The contents of the IVD reagents instructions on different clinical purposes vary because of the rapid development, the wide field span, and the largely differing clinical purposes of the products. Registration applicants shall prepare the instructions based on product characteristics and clinical purposes, so that the followers can get accurate information from them.

Requirements for the format and contents of the IVD reagents instructions

Product Name

1. General name:

The general name shall conform to nomenclature principles stated in "IVD Reagent Registration Management (For Trial Implementation)". The general name and the English name of products included in "China biological products procedures" shall be consistent with those appeared in "China biological products procedures".

2. Trade name:

The trade name of a product shall not be placed in the same line with the general name and its font area per character shall be no bigger than twice of that of the general name. Do not use absolutized expressions to exaggerate or assert the effects of the product and do not break other rules and regulations.

Packing Specification
Indicate the number of samples tested, such as xx tests/kit, xx servings/kit, xx ml.

Intended Application

Detail the intended use of the product, such as qualitative or quantitative determination, screening, self-test, confirmation, etc. Describe the background of clinical indications associated with the intended use and relevant clinical or laboratory diagnostic methods.

Testing Principles

Detail the testing principles and methods. Use diagrams when necessary.

Major Components

1. For reagents included in the kit:
   1. Describe the name, number and ratio or concentration of each reagent in the reaction system, and provide its biological sources, activity and other characteristics if it is important for correct operations.
   2. Specify whether the reagent from kits of different lot numbers can be interchanged.
2. For reagents not included in the kit but required for testing: Manufacturers should list the names and purity of such agents, and provide diluted or mixed methods and other relevant information.
3. For standards (calibrator) and quality control samples:
   1. Describe their main ingredients and their biological sources.
   2. Indicate the valuation and traceability of the standard (calibrator).
   3. Illustrate the allowable range of the quality control samples.

Storage Conditions and Period of Validity

1. Indicate the storage conditions of the products, for example, 2~8 °C, below −18 °C, avoiding frozen and other factors affecting the product stability, including the light, humidity, etc. If the stability of the kit or reagents differs from that of the original packaging when opened, then the storage conditions of the kit or reagents after being opened shall also be noted.
2. Period of validity: Illustrate the Expiry Date under storage conditions. If the stability of the kit or reagents differs from that of the original packaging when opened, then the Expiry Date of the kit or reagents after being opened shall also be noted.

Applicable Equipment

Indicate the proper instruments, and provide all information about the instruments in order to make the best choice for the users.

Requirements for Samples

Illustrate the followings:

1. Precautions when collect the samples.
2. Anticoagulants or protecting agents necessary for the stability of each component of the samples.

3. Known interferences.
4. Storage, handling and transportation methods for the stability of the samples.

Test Methods

For the correct operation, specify each step of the test as follows:

1. Reagents preparation: dilution, mixing and other necessary procedures of the reagent components.
2. Test conditions required: pH, temperature, time required for each step of the test, the wavelength, the stability of the reaction products. Take precautions during the test.
3. Calibration procedures (if required): the preparation and use of the standard (calibrator), and drawing methods of the standard curve.
4. Quality control procedures: use of the quality control materials and the quality control methods.
5. Calculation of the test results, including the explanation of each coefficient and each calculation step. If possible, illustrate them.

Reference Value (Reference Range)

Illustrate the reference value (reference range), and briefly describe the methods determining the reference value (reference range).

Explanations for Test Results

Illustrate factors which may affect the test results; describe the circumstances in which validation tests are needed.

Limitations of Test Methods

Illustrate the limitations of the test methods.

Products Performance Index

Illustrate the main performance indices of the products.

Precautions

Indicate the necessary precautions, such as the product is used only for IVDs.

If the product contains substances of human or animal origin, a warning of potential infectivity should be given.

References

Annotate references cited.

Manufacturers

- Illustrate the manufacturer of the product from the following aspects:
- Company name:
- Address:
- Indicate the address in detail; The registered address and production address should be listed separately if they are not the same.
- Postcode:
- Phone and Fax Numbers:

- Websites:
- Illustrate the name, address and contact details of the after-sales service company for the imported products.

License Number of Medical Devices Manufacturing Enterprises
Indicate the license number for the domestic medical devices manufacturing enterprises.

Medical Devices Registration Certificate Number
Indicate the registration certificate number of the product.

Product Standard Code
Indicate the product standard code of the product.

Approval and Modification Date of the Instruction
Indicate the date of approval of the instructions, and also specify the modification date of them if a change request was made before.

Reference

ASKCI Consulting Co., Ltd. (2014) 2013–2018 China IVD industry analysis and investment strategy report, September, 2014
Beijing Huayan Zhongshang Economic Information Center (2010) 2010–2014 Chinese clinical IVD market Investment advice and industry analysis report, 2010
Business intelligence network "2011–2015 Chinese IVD industry market research and investment opportunity analysis report", October, 2010, Report R54557
CFDA (2014) Regulations for the Supervision and Administration of Medical Devices, February 12, 2014
CFDA (2014a) Notice on initial registration for domestic IVD registration issued by China Food and Drug Administration on April 17, 2014
CFDA (2014b) Notice on overseas IVD registration issued by China Food and Drug Administration on April 17, 2014
CFDA (2014c) Guidance for writing instructions of in vitro diagnostic reagents; issued by China Food and Drug Administration on April 28, 2014
Country Focus (2013) Healthcare, Regulatory and Remboursement Landscape—China Reference Code: GDHC0052CHR. Publication Date: July 2013
Datamonitor (2008) Molecular Diagnostics: a primer on an emerging sector, 2008
Insight (2012) 2011–2015 China IVD market research and investment forecast report, Report 121939, 2012
SFDA (2007) Measures for the Administration of In vitro Diagnostic Reagents (Interim); Issued by the State Food and Drug Administration, No. 229, April 19, 2007
SFDA (2007a) Guidance for clinical research technology of in vitro diagnostic reagents; Issued by the State Food and Drug Administration, No. 240; April 28, 2007
SFDA (2007b) Guidance for writing instructions of in vitro diagnostic reagents; Issued by the State Food and Drug Administration, No. 240; April 28, 2007
SFDA (2007c) Requirements for the format of application documents in IVD reagent registration; Issued by the State Food and Drug Administration, No. 609, Sept. 30, 2007
SFDA (2012) Information Requirements for the First Registration Application and Explanations; Issued by the State Food and Drug Administration on November 5, 2012

State Council (2014) Several Suggestions to Accelerate the Development of Technology Services; issued by the state council in October 2014

Zhiyan Consulting Group (2013a) 2013–2018 China IVD industry research and investment strategy consultation report, August, 2013

Zhiyan Consulting Group (2013b) 2014–2019 China medical device in depth market research and investment strategy report, December, 2013

Index

A

Acute/single dose toxicity, 295, 332, 359, 432
Adjustment, 152, 153, 185
Advantages of IMCT, 515
Advantages of import drug registration, 517
Adverse drug reaction (ADR), 562
Adverse event, 194, 341, 395, 427, 478, 538
Alarm limit, 186
Ampoule, 207
Application dossier writing requirements in CTD format, 3
Audit, 144, 200, 206, 487, 491

B

Batch, 139, 141, 155, 162, 163, 186, 349, 431
Batch production record, 162, 186
Bian, Y.W., 7, 8
Bioequivalence study, 72, 281, 472
Biologics registration classification and application material requirements, 97, 218
Bulk product, 184

C

Callback, 185
Carcinogenicity test, 379
Case report form, 205, 206, 400, 407, 486, 487
Certified documents, 304, 334, 430
CFDA Structure and Function, 245
Chen, X., 225
China Food and Drug Administration (CFDA), 239, 280, 507, 583
Chinese medicine, natural medicine registration classification and application material requirements, 97
Clean room, 207, 209
Clinical development plan, 468
Clinical research of in vitro diagnostic reagents class II, 635
Clinical study information, 444
Clinical study plan and study protocols, 400
Clinical study report, 296, 332, 333, 403
Clinical trial, 55, 72, 281, 317, 333, 335, 341, 392, 393, 396, 397, 400, 407, 416, 457, 468–470, 475, 483, 501, 518, 527, 543, 592, 597, 599, 601, 606, 609, 639
Clinical trial management, 483
Clinical trial protocols, 469
Collaborative localization strategy, 524
Comparison of differences of the monitoring and reporting requirements, 543
Compliant, 213, 214, 216
Compliant after rectification, 213, 214, 216
Compulsory Licensing for Patent Exploitation, 230
Conducting phase of the clinical trial, 487
Confidentiality, 505
Confirmation, 7, 139, 157–159, 164, 186
Confirmation and validation, 158, 164
Conflict of interest, 505
Contract research organization,
Correction limit, 186
Cross pollution, 185

D

Delivering, 139, 182, 185
Deng, R., 225
Design of packaging and labeling, 295, 331, 333, 342, 430
Disadvantages of IMCT, 515
Disadvantages of import drug registration, 517
Discharging, 173, 185
Draft of quality specification and notes, and providing reference standard, 295, 332, 333, 349, 431
Drug clinical trials, 110, 451

M. Q. Lu (ed.), *Approaching China's Pharmaceutical Market*,
DOI 10.1007/978-3-319-15576-0

Drug dependence, 380, 382
Drug insert sheet, 120, 122, 408, 409
Drug intensive monitoring, 563
Drug labels, 125, 410
Drug monitoring term table, 97
Drug name, 334, 348
Drug re-registration application material requirements, 97
Drug supplementary application—registration matters and application material requirements, 97

E
Emergency unblinding, 546
Enterprise, 41, 46, 99, 101, 160, 175–177, 179, 182, 183, 186, 304, 317, 326, 443, 464
Equipment, 133, 139, 150, 641
Ethical review, 400
Extending, 184

F
Fast track mechanism, 463

G
General pharmacology, 295, 356, 357
General requirements for clinical phases, 470
General safety monitoring and reporting requirement and processes, 542
Global companies with manufacturing facilities in China, 510
Global companies without manufacturing facilities in China, 512
Gong, S., 463
Good laboratory practice,
Guidance, 1, 3, 4, 218, 219, 330, 331, 338–340, 343, 344, 346–349, 351, 356, 359, 361, 368, 372, 385, 390, 391, 400, 403, 492, 508, 519, 520, 573, 581, 629
Guidance for writing instructions of in vitro diagnostic reagents, 581, 629

H
Huang, Y., 3, 334

I
Import drug pathway, 516
Import drug repackaging, 446
Import drug repackaging application and approval, 446
Import record keeping, 100
In vitro diagnostic, 581, 640
In vitro diagnostic market and environment, 581
Informed consent, 199, 205, 400, 402, 486, 491
Informed consent form, 205, 486
Infusion bottles, 207
Initial registration for domestic IVD, 598
Inspection, 48, 60, 97, 99–102, 104, 105, 107, 108, 138, 139, 164, 168–170, 175, 180, 186, 200, 211, 213, 214, 216, 405, 407, 448, 492, 520, 620
Inspection result exceeding standard, 186
Investigational product, 197, 484
Investigator, 188, 192, 199, 200, 205, 206, 280, 296, 298, 310, 332, 333, 400, 430, 478, 486–489, 491, 543, 544, 551, 574, 576
Investigator meeting, 488
Investigator's brochure, 205, 400, 486
Involvement of other Asian countries in RMCT, 526

J
Jin, S., 463

K
Kaitin, K, 225
Kang, C.L., 508, 511, 518

L
Law, 2, 5–9, 11, 12, 14, 17, 18, 22, 24, 26–28, 31–38, 42, 48–52, 55–59, 62–67, 70, 84, 88, 90, 93–95, 97, 101, 105–107, 120, 128, 130, 139, 187, 188, 207, 214, 221–225, 229, 231, 239, 285, 408, 412, 413, 446, 448, 464, 485, 534, 536, 549, 552, 627
Li, Y.J., 509
Liu, C., 221

M
Material, 139, 142, 153–156, 160, 172–174, 177, 184, 187, 296, 309, 311, 321, 331, 421
Material and product, 153
McKenna, C., 240
Medicinal aluminum foil, 207
Medicinal desiccant, 207
Medicinal ointment tube, 207
Medicinal prefilled syringes, 207
Medicinal rigid plate, 207
Medicinal stopper, 207
Meng, L., 242, 243
Middle control, 166, 187
Minimal risk, 505
Ministry of Health, 139, 239–242, 245, 276, 534, 535, 551–554, 557–561, 563, 580

Monitor, 145, 188, 195, 200, 206, 482, 483, 487, 491
Multicenter trial, 505
Mutagenicity tests, 355, 371

N
Naidu, R., 575
Narcotic drugs, 19, 42, 43, 45, 46
New drug application, 288, 467, 470
Non-compliance/violation, 505
Non-compliant, 213, 214, 216

O
Objectives and basis for research and development, 336
On-site verification, 212
Operation procedures, 143, 150, 164, 165, 175, 184
Organization and Management of the EC, 493
Organization and Personnel, 130, 139, 142
Overseas IVD registration, 605, 606

P
Package, 162, 163, 167, 171, 184, 251, 407, 589, 596, 597, 599, 600, 605, 606, 608, 640
Patent Lawsuits in China, 235
Patent Protection in China, 222
Period of double examination, 184
Pharmaceutical information, 130, 295, 332, 333, 422
Pharmacodynamics, toxicity and pharmacokinetics change, 295, 332, 432
Pharmacology and toxicology study information, 130, 295, 299, 332, 422, 444
Phase 1 clinical trials, 470
Phase 2 clinical trials, 471
Phase 3 clinical trials, 471, 472
Phase 4 clinical trials, 472
Pollution, 166, 185, 187
Primary pharmacodynamics, 295, 332, 355, 432
Principle for Product Classification and Name, 587
Printing wrapper, 156, 187
Processing and recording of adverse events, 544
Processing and reporting of serious adverse events, 545
Product, 2, 57, 58, 70, 71, 83, 84, 87, 96, 99–101, 105, 139, 155, 156, 161, 170, 179, 182–184, 187, 188, 200, 207, 213, 214, 217, 226, 233, 285, 290, 300, 308, 313, 319, 343, 351, 414, 418, 424, 435, 443, 445, 446, 484, 492, 516, 588, 589, 593, 595, 596, 599, 606, 608, 609, 615, 617, 620, 640, 643
Product's lifecycle, 184
Production technology, 185
Protocol, 188, 191, 199, 205, 423, 486, 490, 491, 506, 520, 523
Protocol amendment, 506
Psychotropic drugs, 20, 38–40

Q
Qu, M., 221
Quality assurance, 138
Quality control, 141, 150, 168, 169, 171, 192, 205, 362, 406, 470, 478, 486, 589–591, 593, 635, 642
Quality specification, 297
Quarantine, 184
Quorum, 506

R
Raw material, 38, 39, 154, 187, 345
Reconciliation, 187
Regulation, 2, 6, 112, 113, 115, 116, 130, 139–143, 145, 158, 159, 170, 173, 181, 183, 184, 186–188, 211, 222, 285, 302, 303, 413, 418, 423, 424, 455, 456, 463, 473, 474, 485, 508, 509, 516, 518, 520, 561, 591
Regulations of special examination and approval in new drug registration, 3
Regulatory requirement for patient numbers, 530
Renew process, 185
Repeated dose toxicity, 295, 332, 361, 432
Reporting parties, 542
Reprocessing, 184
Requirement for the clinical study, 305
Re-registration application, 69, 288
Responsibilities of the EC, 494
Roth, R.I., 128, 421

S
Safety management in clinical trials, 539
Salako, Q., 251, 253, 254, 463
Selection basis and quality specification of immediate packing material and container, 295, 332, 352, 431
Semifinished product, 155, 166, 187
Senior administrator, 140, 185
Serious adverse event, 395, 506, 544, 547, 549

Sponsor, 139, 188, 193, 200, 477, 486, 487, 489–491, 533, 543, 544, 574
Stability, 174, 295, 320, 321, 323, 325, 332, 333, 344, 351, 431, 591, 597, 599, 606
Stage manufacturing method, 185
Su, L., 512
Summary of global clinical study information, 296, 298, 332, 333, 391
Summary of main study work, 292, 331, 333, 337, 430
Summary of Pharmaceutical Study, 295, 297, 309, 332
Summary of pharmacology and toxicology study, 295, 297, 332, 353
Supplementary application, 69, 86, 287, 443, 453
Supplementary application and approval procedure, 443
Supplier, 177, 178, 185

T
Technical review, 210
Test report of drug sample, 295, 332, 333, 350, 431
Testing for drug registration, 88
The source, test report and quality specification of drug substance and excipient, 295, 300, 332, 351, 431
The State Drug Administration (SDA), 240
The state pharmaceutical clinical cancer research base, 273
The state pharmaceutical clinical research base, 255
Thoelke, K.R., 254, 512
Timeline, 67, 90, 453
Trade secret, 231

U
Unanticipated adverse event, 506

V
Validation, 139, 157, 158, 173, 187, 346, 431
Ventilator, 186
Vulnerable persons, 506

W
Wei, J., 254
Withdraw of goods, 186
Wrapper, 155, 184

X
Xu, B., 533

Y
Ye, B., 221

Z
Zhang, L., 534
Zhang, Q., 224
Zhang, S.S., 3, 334
Zhao, Y., 234

MIX
Papier aus verantwortungsvollen Quellen
Paper from responsible sources
FSC® C105338

If you have any concerns about our products,
you can contact us on
ProductSafety@springernature.com

In case Publisher is established outside the EU,
the EU authorized representative is:
Springer Nature Customer Service Center GmbH
Europaplatz 3, 69115 Heidelberg, Germany

Printed by Libri Plureos GmbH
in Hamburg, Germany